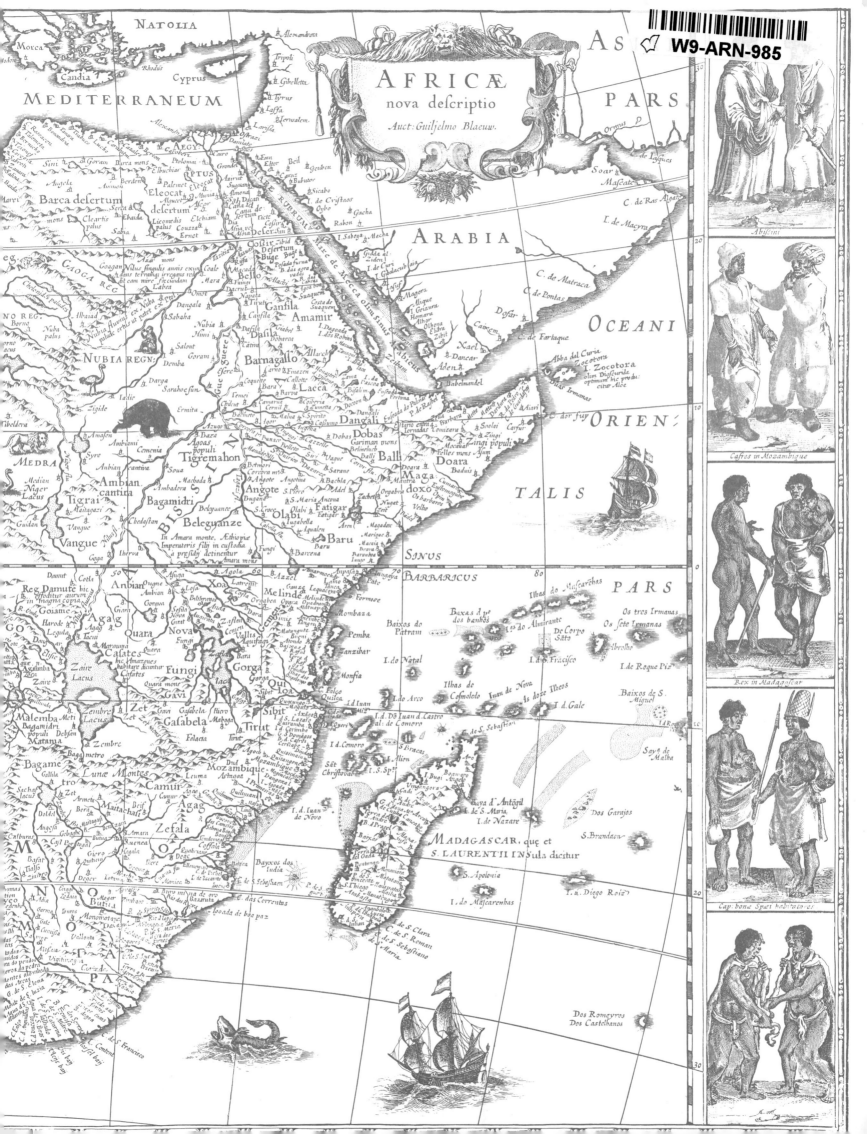

AFRICÆ
nova descriptio
Auct: Guiljelmo Blaeuw.

NATOLIA

AS PARS

MEDITERRANEUM

ARABIA

OCEANI

ORIEN:

TALIS

PARS

Candia

Cyprus

MEDRA

CAOGA REG

Barca desertum

Eleocat desertum

NUBIA REGN:

BISSINA

Tigremahon

Ambian cantira

Tigrai

Bagamidri

Beleguanze

Vangue

Dangali

Dobas

Balli

Doara

Maga doxo

Baru

Barnagallo

Amamir

Ganfila

Lacca

Aden

Zocotora

SINUS BARBARICUS PARS

Reg Damute

Anbian

Xoa

Melinde

Mombaza

Pemba

Zanzibar

Monfia

Quiloa

Sibit

Tirut

Mozambique

MADAGASCAR, quæ et
S. LAURENTII INSula dicitur

Goiame

Agag

Quara

Nova

Fungi

Gorga

Qui loa

Zet

Galabela

Camir

Agag

Zefala

MONO MOTAPA

Luna Montes

Abissini

Cafres in Mozambique

Rex in Madagascar

Cap: bonæ Spei habitatores

Cultural Atlas of
AFRICA

Editor Graham Speake
Art Editor Andrew Lawson
Map Editor Liz Orrock
Text Editor Jennifer
Drake-Brokman
Design Adrian Hodgkins
Production Clive Sparling
Index Barbara James

For revised edition
Project Managers Graham Bateman,
Richard Watts
Editors Lauren Bourque, Asgard
Publishing Services
Map Editor Tim Williams
Picture Research Claire Turner
Design Christopher Howson

AN ANDROMEDA BOOK

Planned and produced by
Andromeda Oxford Limited
11–13 The Vineyard, Abingdon
Oxford OX14 3PX

Published by Checkmark Books, an
imprint of Facts On File

Copyright © 1981 by Andromeda
Oxford Limited
Copyright © 1998 by Andromeda
Oxford Limited for revised edition

Checkmark Books, an imprint of
Facts On File, Inc.
11 Penn Plaza
New York NY 10001

Library of Congress Cataloging-
in-Publication Data available from
Facts On File.

Facts On File books are available at
special discounts when purchased in
bulk quantities for businesses,
associations, institutions or sales
promotions. Please call our Special Sales
Department in New York at
(212) 967-8800 or (800) 322-8755.

You can find Facts On File on
the World Wide Web at
http://www.factsonfile.com

ISBN 0-8160-3813-9

Origination by Chapman Brothers,
Oxford; M.B.A. Ltd, Chalfont St Peters,
Bucks

Maps drawn and originated by
Lovell John, Oxford; Cosmographics,
Watford

Printed in Spain by
Fournier A. Gráficas SA, Vitoria

This book is printed on acid-free paper

10 9 8 7 6 5 4 3 2 1

Frontispiece A miscellany of
African masks. Left to right:
Biombo, Congo (DRO); Bedu,
Ghana; Ngi, Congo (DRO);
Chokwe, Congo (DRO);
N'tomo, Mali. Overleaf, left to
right: Kota reliquary head,
Gabon; Dan, Liberia; Bwani,
Congo (DRO); Pende,
Congo (RO).

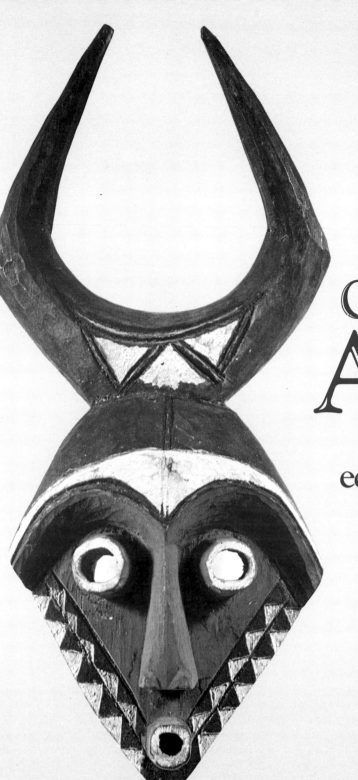

Cultural Atlas of
AFRICA

edited by Jocelyn Murray

Revised Edition

Checkmark Books™
An imprint of Facts On File, Inc.

CONTENTS

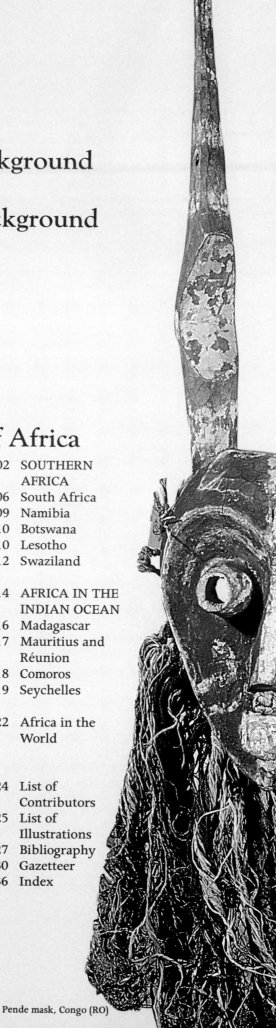

Pende mask, Congo (RO)

Special Features

List of Maps

INTRODUCTION

The continent of Africa is so vast and so rich in contrasts that a lifetime's travelling in it could scarcely skim the surface of its diversity. For hundreds of years fabulous tales of the dark continent fired the imagination of Europe. Where was the land of punt where the ancient Egyptians traded for spices? Was there really a great Christian emperor, Prester John, ruling the in the African heartland? Where did the Nile rise, and what was the secret of its annual flooding? The early Portuguese sails, edging their way along inhospitable coasts, were far from answering any of these questions, and the mapmakers who largely relied on their accounts could draw only the outline of the shores and had to fill the unknown interior with pictures of monstrous men and beasts. Thus Africa became known through myths, rather than by facts, and new myths still spring up to replace the old: the l9th-century picture of "the African jungle" is now supplanted by another fallacious image – Africa as vast safari park.

Myths about physical geography are in the end less damaging than the African people and their "primitiveness", but both varieties must be fought. For misconceptions persist at every level and even within Africa itself there is lack of knowledge in one area or region about the basic historical and geographical facts of another region. Ignorance has been compounded by the presence of differing colonial regimes, knowledge of different European languages, and consequent restriction of access to information for linguistic reasons. Moreover, the story of man in Africa can be traced over millions of years, and the tall pastoralist Maasai of East Africa and the forest-dwelling pygmies demonstrate mankind's physical ability to adapt to different environments and ways of life. Africa gave birth to one of mankind's first essays in civilization in the astonishing flowering of arts and sciences in the third millennium BC; at the other end of the scale Kalahari hunter-gatherers still lead the precarious life of their Stone Age forebears. The 19th-century Zulu king Chaka organized his armies into one of the most efficient fighting machines the world has ever seen. The serene artistry of the Benin bronze heads suggests a totally different spiritual dimension. Faced with these contrasts, we are forced to asked if there is, indeed, something "African" to discover – *négritude*, the "authenticity" of Zaire/Congo, the *ujamaa* of Tanzania – which links and binds together the people of vastly separated countries and cultures. If we over-emphasize the variety that Africa encompasses we are in danger of not even looking for, let alone finding, the unity.

Africans themselves are still wrestling with the question of identity since their emergence from sixty, seventy or eighty (seldom longer) years of colonial rule. A vast continent was divided up by lines ruled on maps in European offices. Kingdoms, clans, families, were split up. Assorted educational systems, alien languages, new religions, and varying versions of all these have resulted in modern African nations which owe as much, or nearly as much, to the colonial regime under which their borders were defined as to preexisting ethnic and cultural boundaries.

To understand the context and significance of events and processes in Africa today – more than thirty years, for most nations, since the colonial period ended – facts are needed to replace the myths. Both within and outside Africa there is need for a book that will provide an introduction to the continent as a whole. The *Cultural Atlas of Africa* aims to do just this, by a combination of text, illustrations and maps. The maps are perhaps the key contribution: whatever is said about Africa needs to be grounded in the physical realities of the continent. The book is first of all an atlas, but it is an atlas set with the historical context. It has drawn upon the knowledge of many experts in its endeavor to be true to the diversity, while seeking to present the unity, of the continent.

And since those first exciting days when colony after colony gained its independent identity, changes have continued. Names have changed, of lakes and rivers, of towns and cities, even of the nations themselves – and sometimes been changed again. The first leaders of new nations have been replaced – whether peacefully or after violence. The former Portuguese colony of Angola and the once German colony of South West Africa remained as such until 1992 and 1990. The nation-state of South Africa has emerged, but only in 1994. A few territories – like Mayotte in the Indian Ocean – are still dependencies by choice. The tragic inter-ethnic wars of Rwanda and Burundi have brought exile and death to tens of thousands. In the south of Sudan a civil war continues.

Africa's plains have been surveyed, its mountains climbed, its rivers harnessed for hydroelectricity, its minerals exploited, and its inhabitants drawn into the mainstream of 20th-century life and towards the dawn of the 21st-century. But its future presents a formidable challenge, not only for the peoples of Africa themselves, but for all the world's inhabitants. This atlas presents – as an interim report – the present situation, the nature of the challenge, and the response to it.

Acknowledgments
I should like to thank a number of people whose advice and support have been of great help to me in the preparation of this book. Kent and Nancy Rasmussen in Los Angeles gave me hospitality at an early stage. In Aberdeen Roy Bridges and Jeffrey Stone were constant critics and friends. Many others could be named, but behind everything else lie the continuing work and wisdom of Graham Speake, who with his wife Jennifer also gave hospitality.   J.M.

PART ONE
THE PHYSICAL BACKGROUND

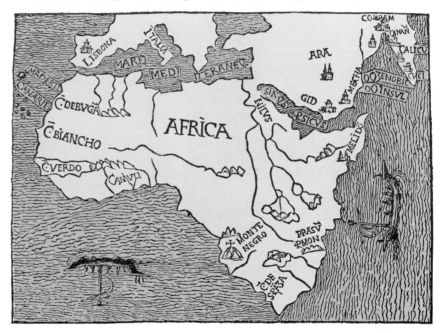

THE GEOGRAPHY OF AFRICA

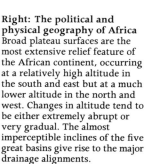

The continent of Africa is exceeded in area by Asia alone. With an area of 30 420 000 square kilometers, it is three times the size of Europe and four times the size of the USA. Moreover, it is a remarkably compact continent. The islands have a total area of only some 624 000 square kilometers and 95 per cent of that figure is accounted for by the fourth largest island in the world, Madagascar. The mainland is regular in outline, with no great gulfs or other deep embayments, so that the coastline is shorter in total length than that of any other continent.

Africa lies astride the equator; three-quarters of its surface area is within the tropics. Despite the fact that the total latitudinal extent of over 61° is approximately bisected by the equator, some two-thirds of the area of Africa lies in the northern hemisphere. The maximum longitudinal extent, from Senegal to Somalia, is some 69°. At the equator, the longitudinal distance between coasts is less than half that figure, and the distance diminishes with distance southward. The continent is all but an island. The boundary between Africa and Asia lies not at the northwest part of the isthmus north of the Gulf of Suez, but stretches the 240 kilometers or so between the Gulf of Aqaba and the Mediterranean Sea.

The shape of the African continent is the product of its evolution through geological time. About 180 million years ago, proto-Africa lay at the heart of a super-continent consisting of several of the great mobile plates that comprise the earth's crust. During the Cretaceous period the plates began to drift apart, leaving the African plate isolated, except for a few offshore remnants of continental rock such as Madagascar. With the passage of time, the African plate was increasingly isolated, except in the northwest where collision with the Eurasian plate gave rise to great earth movements and to mountain ranges. Elsewhere, isolation produced its own stresses in the African plate. Rift systems, whose origin may date to the breakup of the super-continent, remained active; extensive basins were the product of gentle upwarping of the intervening surfaces. In addition, the attritional action of wind and water, which had shaped the surface of the super-continent, continued to act on its isolated remnant, redistributing material and creating stress by sheer weight of sediments or by relieving the underlying strata. The relative altitude of land and sea has changed on an unknown number of occasions. A range of interconnected processes are therefore responsible for the primary component of African landscapes: the extensive plateau surfaces. These are sometimes separately discernible at different altitudes, often merging, but higher in the south and east and lower in the north and west.

Gradual change of altitude over distance characterizes much of Africa. Where depression and upwarping of the surface are relatively recent, then great shallow basins remain discernible at the continental scale. These are not necessarily totally enclosed basins nor are they features that can be demarcated by lines on maps. At their margins they merge imperceptibly into the adjacent higher plateau surfaces, but by means of contours and drainage lines, they can easily be identified. Lake Chad and the Okavango Delta are local inland drainage basins within two of the great shallow depressions that cover much of the surface of Africa.

Movement in the earth's crust also gives rise to more dramatic relief features. Where crustal movements, either vertical or horizontal, have induced tension exceeding the strength of the subsurface strata, then faults occur, either singly or in pairs or clusters. These sometimes cause slopes whose steepness is in sharp contrast to the adjacent plateau surfaces and the slopes occur as individual escarpments or as great trenches or uplifted blocks of varying width. One of the earth's longest rift systems passes from the Red Sea, through the Ethiopian highlands and through East Africa where it bifurcates before reappearing in southern Africa. The Great Rift Valley is best known in East Africa, where its location is emphasized by the alignment of some of the East African lakes, but it is equally well seen in the Luangwa valley of Zambia or in the Ethiopian highlands east of Addis Ababa.

Steep slopes are not solely the product of faulting. At quite different periods of geological time, violent crustal movements on the continent's periphery, associated with the drift of the African tectonic plate, have led to folding and uplift of strata in the Cape ranges and the Atlas Mountains. Subsequent

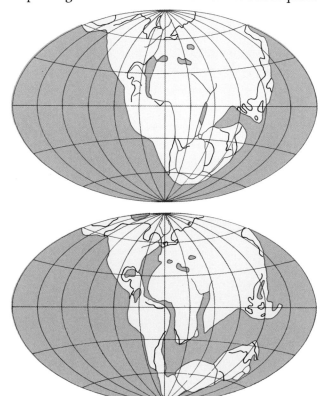

Right: The political and physical geography of Africa Broad plateau surfaces are the most extensive relief feature of the African continent, occurring at a relatively high altitude in the south and east but at a much lower altitude in the north and west. Changes in altitude tend to be either extremely abrupt or very gradual. The almost imperceptible inclines of the five great basins give rise to the major drainage alignments.

Left In the early Mesozoic era (above) the African continental plate lay at the center of the proto-continent named Pangaea (all land). During the Cretaceous era (below) South America and Africa began to drift apart and the Indian Ocean opened up between the African and Asian land masses. Fossils provide evidence of former land connections between the southern continents. For example, a fossil plant (Glossopteris) occurs in late Paleozoic deposits in South America, South Africa, Madagascar, India and Australia.

erosion has sharpened the relief. The stability of the African continent was tested in what were major phases of mountain building in Eurasia and America, when little lasting impact was made on the interior of the continent. The Benue trough, with its dissected scarp topography, is one of the few examples of disruption of the inexorable leveling of the interior.

Landforms characteristic of erosion by water and wind also disrupt the extensive flat surfaces, although it is their intermittent occurrence as much as their outward forms that makes them so noticeable. One such form is the tabular landform epitomized in Table Mountain near Cape Town and occurring across southern Africa in association with hardened sediments and lavas. Further types include the dome-shaped inselbergs with widespread occurrences across Africa, also steep-sided ridges associated with veins of especially resistant rock, well seen in Zimbabwe, and the dune forms and blow-outs of the sand deserts. Lavas and dolerites give rise to level surfaces and adjacent very steep slopes; for instance, in Nigeria, Libya, and in Africa south of the equator where they underlie the Victoria Falls and its gorges. Perhaps the most striking single erosional feature is the Great Escarpment – an almost continuous feature around southern Africa, from Zimbabwe to Angola – cutting through rocks of varying resistance and in places more than 2000 meters high, forming a formidable barrier to movement. Depositional features are as significant as eroded forms. These vary from the great spreads of ancient sandstones that underlie the Sahara and much of southern Africa, to unconsolidated sediments that are still being laid down in the great river basins, such as the Barotse Plain and the Kafue Flats of the Zambezi basin, and in the Kalahari. These features extend the nearly level surfaces produced elsewhere by erosion, accentuating already widespread plantation.

One further process which has created some of Africa's best-known landscapes is volcanism. Volcanic forms include such well-known cones as Kilimanjaro and Mount Cameroon. Volcanism is often associated with the tensions and stresses of the rift system, which allow molten material or ash to penetrate the earth's crust and sometimes to reach the surface, as is still occurring, for example, in Congo (DRO), Cameroon and Kenya. Volcanic explosions in the past have left vast steep-sided depressions or calderas, such as Ngorongoro in Tanzania, or clusters of much smaller lake-filled depressions, as in southwest Uganda. The remnants of dikes, sills and ancient volcanic necks add to the array of volcanic forms which in parts diversify the flat surface of the continent.

The main drainage alignments of Africa are remarkable in that the great rivers appear to take the most indirect route to the sea. The upper Niger aims for the center of the Sahara before it eventually turns seaward. The upper Zambezi heads south towards the arid Kalahari before turning eastward to the Indian Ocean. The controlling factor is the great sequence of down-warped basins which draw excess surface water from their flanks towards the center before allowing an outlet to be explored. The marginal escarpments of the central plateaus mean that the lower courses of rivers are characterized by waterfalls and cataracts. The great natural lakes of Africa, like most of its physical attributes, are very unevenly distributed and are almost exclusive to the trenches and basins of the east.

Africa's coastline has been presented in a historical context as forbidding. In fact there is a diversity of coastal forms. One consistent feature is that indentations of any size or economic significance are few. Sand bars maintained by longshore drift and mangroves shield much of West Africa, as do coral reefs in East Africa. Heavy swell is continuous on many coasts facing great expanses of open ocean, and river mouths are marked by great sedimentary deltas rather than estuaries. Shingle is not a common tropical beach material and the extent of sand beaches from the Mediterranean to the extreme south of the continent far exceeds any conceivable tourist market.

Climate

The availability of water is a powerful determinant to man's activities in Africa, and African climatology is dominated by the study of rainfall. Average rainfall is a familiar concept, particularly in temperate climates, but in Africa the pattern of mean annual rainfall is a statistical abstraction that hides the most significant characteristics of the rainfall regime. Certainly, the map of mean annual rainfall locates the great deserts and the limited extent of areas with high annual rainfall totals. It also emphasizes north–south gradients in rainfall amounts along the southern margins of the Sahara, but elsewhere it obscures the marked zonal (east–west) alignment of the isohyets.

The really significant features of African rainfall regimes are to be seen by examining the sequence of monthly charts. Only then is it apparent that, in the depths of the northern hemisphere winter, almost the entire continent north of the equator, except the Mediterranean shoreline, is arid. Six months later, the situation is reversed, but between these two extremes, the zonal belt of rainfall appears to have marched from one hemisphere to the other, although this requires qualification. The underlying causes in the southern hemisphere atmosphere of January rainfall maxima from Mozambique to Angola have ceased to exist, and circumstances conducive to rainfall in July occur independently in the northern hemisphere from Ethiopia to Gambia. In the intervening periods, conditions giving rise to cloud formation in depth, and therefore the possibility of rainfall, occur erratically in the equatorial belt but with particular uncertainty in the east, thus giving characteristic variability to low-latitude rainfall in April and October.

The great deserts of Africa are not the products of purely African circumstances. They result from atmospheric processes on a global scale. The Sahara, including arid Somalia, is a part of an immense desert stretching from Morocco to Baluchistan. This is the result of subtropical subsidence of air which prevents cloud formation in depth and is a major feature of the general atmospheric circulation of the globe. The Namib Desert is a product of the same processes in mirror image in the southern hemisphere, aided by the local factor of a cold offshore current. The fact that southeast Africa is seasonally rather than permanently arid points to the fact that where the altitude of the surface is great enough to raise the land surface above the intensely persistent

Top In eastern Mpumalangma and Northern Province of South Africa, horizontally bedded rocks have been uplifted to heights in excess of 2000 meters and have then been deeply dissected to form the rugged landscape of the northern Drakensberg. The Blyde river, a tributary of the Olifants river, has cut a gorge 1000 meters deep to create scenery in spectacular contrast to the great expanse of almost level plateau surface to the west.

Above Most African deserts are flat and featureless expanses of gravel and sand, but the Namib Desert of southwestern Angola and western Namibia has extensive occurrences of sand dunes. The dune forms are constantly changing and are the product of the direction and strength of the wind and the supply of sand.

high pressure of subtropical sea level conditions, then rain is possible at the time of year when atmospheric pressure is, in any case, not so high. This is confirmed in the northern hemisphere by the wetter Ethiopian highlands which are in a latitude otherwise associated with aridity.

Rainfall in Africa usually originates in one of several types of quite severe atmospheric disturbances. These include thunderstorms, but also assemblages of many individual thunderstorms in, for example, the cloud clusters now recognized through satellite observations as a major feature of the global circulation. In south central Africa, summer rain occurs in outbreaks of several days in duration with intervening clearer spells. Occasional tropical cyclones bring intense rainfall to southeast Africa. Elsewhere, atmospheric pressure conditions which encourage rainfall are brought about irregularly throughout the wetter season, so that an important characteristic of African rainfall is its intensity and short duration within the so-called wet seasons. This is clearly seen in the relative small number of rain days and the high thunderstorm incidence over much of the continent.

Temperature is less of a variable factor in African climates. In a compact continent, altitude is as important as latitude in understanding temperature regimes. Mean monthly maxima in excess of 32°C are found over most of Africa, with a tendency for an increase with distance from the sea. There is not a great range of variations in maximum temperature. Similarly, there is only a small range of minimum temperatures and indeed of annual temperature regimes. By contrast, much of the continent experiences diurnal temperature ranges in excess of 15°, so that the differences between night and day are more pronounced than between seasons.

Scarcity of recording stations means that atmospheric observations other than rainfall and temperature are available only in a few local situations. It is, however, possible to consider factors such as sunshine and wind speed by use of observed distributions of vegetation, the plant being taken as a barometer not only of commonly recorded meteorological elements but also of those not readily available. This has the advantage of presenting climate as it really is, as an interrelated set of phenomena forming a single complex, rather than as individual elements, separated as an artificial device of convenience. The best-known scheme of this kind for the classification of climate into types is that of Köppen. This scheme applied to Africa provides a useful synopsis at the continental scale, if not for local areas. The system uses rainfall and temperature values to locate the limits of occurrence of certain groups of plants, which are themselves in part a reflection of all of the elements that comprise a climate. The resultant distribution demonstrates the extent of seasonality as a primary factor in African climates. Most of the continent beyond the deserts or semideserts (B category) experiences a pronounced dry season (w or s subcategory). The continuously watered parts of this continent (f subcategory) are confined to the extreme southeast and to a restricted equatorial occurrence in low Africa. The seasonal wet-and-dry regimes dominate Africa, an environmental fact of great economic significance.

The disastrous sahel drought in the 1970s means that Africa looms large in current concern about climatic change. The drought has been ascribed solely to environmental mismanagement by man because the years of low rainfall are within the bounds of expectation on the basis of existing statistics of sub-Saharan rainfall. However, major fluctuations in rainfall amounts from year to year, or over short periods of several years, are a feature of the climates of the arid margins. Although no long-term cyclic change is evidenced by recent droughts in the sahel, as well as in East and southern Africa, they highlight the fact that in the desert margins long-term averages have little meaning. Much more important is variation from the average, especially where the averages are in themselves so low as to make many agricultural practices marginal.

Soils

African soils are the consequence of four interacting factors. First, the form of the land determines whether an area experiences net loss or net accumulation of loose material, or whether it is an area of transference. Areas of overall removal have steep slopes where loose material is raw and the soils imperfectly developed. Accumulation occurs in valley bottoms, the centers of the great basins, and along coastal margins. In between, the character of the soil is in part controlled by the local rate of accumulation as opposed to removal, that is, the local nature of transference.

Climate is the second factor influencing soil development. Non biological reactions increase in speed in proportion to the increase in temperature while biological reactions are facilitated within limits by warmth. This is seen in Africa in the exceptional depth achieved by soil-forming processes and the extensive transformations that take place in the material, although both of these attributes are only achieved where rainwater is adequate.

The close correlation between the distribution of soil and vegetation is an indication of the importance of plant cover in soil formation. A plant cover regulates the supply and removal of loose material, adds organic matter throughout the soil, facilitates the movement of minerals and the subsequent creation of horizons within the soil and assists in the breakdown of solid particles through the production of acids and other compounds. The complexity of the interaction between soils and vegetation means that very different processes are initiated under such differing vegetative associations as rain forest or savanna.

The fourth factor is the nature of the parent material. In areas of overall removal, underlying basalt, for instance, will yield a very different spectrum of minerals from, say, schist or granite, though the mineral composition of any one rock type is far from constant. In areas of transference or accumulation the situation is greatly complicated by the likelihood of mixed origins, and in both of these areas soils are frequently residues of prolonged and active weathering and leaching of the minerals, much reducing the potential utility of the soil to man. With some notable exceptions in areas of volcanic ash and recent alluvia, African soils are poor in the minerals valuable in agriculture.

The single most extensive soil type is the raw

mineral soil of the deserts where biological activity is at a minimum. These cover some 28 per cent of the continent. A further 20 per cent of the continent is covered by soils that are weakly developed due to lack of either moisture, movement or, in situations of relatively rapid accumulation or removal, time. Such shallow soils cover large areas of southern, eastern and northern Africa. Almost as extensive are the ferrallitic soils which have suffered extensive leaching. These acid clay soils, extensive in wetter zones, frequently exhibit the tendency towards horizontal accumulation of certain oxides, which in its fully developed form is known as laterite. Between the mineral soils of the deserts and the ferrallitic soils lie the ferruginous soils, and the brown-red soils of the desert margins. Together they cover about the same area as the ferrallitic soils, but they are the soils of the seasonally wet and dry climatic regimes of Africa. Under short but intense periods of leaching, the movements of minerals vary according to their particular properties, producing a soil with a characteristic profile and often of low fertility. On the desert margins the increasing deficit in soil moisture is in part counteracted by and leads to the development of deep root systems which have the effect of distributing organic matter through the profile.

At the continental scale, there is clear correlation between vegetation and climate, particularly the seasonal distribution and amount of rainfall. Starting from parts of the continent with highest annual rainfall totals and very short dry seasons, there are tall rain forests characterized by great variety of species, grouped by height, but with a lower density than is sometimes suggested. Several subtypes of rain forest are recognized. As the length of the dry season increases on the rain forest margins, these give way to mosaics of woodland and grassland. Deciduous tree species replace the evergreens of the rain forest and canopies are characteristically lower and less dense. Variety is provided in the form of denser tree cover along watercourses but the moist woodland savanna, typified by the *miombo* woodland of East Africa, is extensive. On its drier margins, tussocky grasses are increasingly predominant and the forested margins of water courses are even more apparent. As the length of the dry season further increases, short grasses predominate and widely dispersed tree species capable of withstanding long dry periods, such as *acacia*, occur. On the desert margins, savanna gives way to desert steppe characterized by sparsely distributed succulents and species with deep root systems. True desert vegetation varies according to location. In the Sahara vast areas exhibit only very few shrubs or grasses, according to the nature of the underlying surface. In the western Namib Desert dew provides a water source to the benefit of the abundant succulents. The temperate margins of the continent, north and south of the desert, have their own characteristic vegetative associations, as do the upper slopes of mountains in tropical Africa. On Mount Kenya, for example, above the cultivation level, montane forest gives way to bamboo, heather, alpines and finally to lichens at the summit. The tree ferns and giant groundsel of the upper slopes of Ruwenzori are particularly spectacular.

The above generalizations are perhaps valid at the continental scale, but these zonations are now so disrupted on the ground that they are fast becoming conceptual rather than real. There has long been debate about the role of deliberate burning in producing the vegetative characteristics of much of seasonally wet and dry Africa. Fire is used to induce new growth of grass for cattle or to prepare for cultivation. Man has probably been a major influence on African vegetation for a very long time, but the substantial increase in the area under domesticated livestock with uniform grazing habits or under cultivation means that the vegetation over much of Africa is becoming as man-made as it is in Europe. To map vegetation on the ground is to map land use and, in areas of dense population, climax vegetation is not to be found. For example, in southern Nigeria, patches of secondary forest are almost the only visible reminder of formerly extensive rain forest.

The vegetation cover of Africa is therefore increasingly the product of human activity, primarily of agricultural systems. All systems may be categorized as either fallow or permanent, depending on whether or not land is allowed to lie fallow. Two common subtypes of fallow systems are shifting cultivation and bush fallow. The first is a long fallow system in which the farmer may not return to land he has cultivated, whereas bush fallow is a form of rotation within a finite area of land and may not involve the movement of the homestead. Permanent farming may be further subdivided into small- and large-scale systems. Small-scale systems include: specialized horticulture adjacent to urban areas; mixed livestock and land husbandry with the cattle aiding the maintenance of fertility of permanently utilized land; a mixture of bush fallow and permanent cultivation incorporating particular crop sequences and the application of refuse to aid maintenance of fertility in permanently cultivated areas; and commercial tree crop farming. Permanent large-scale systems include the long-standing plantation agriculture characterized by high yields from large areas by means of sophisticated technology and management, often expatriate in origin. A similar system has recently been introduced under state control in many African countries to meet rapidly increased demand for food from urban dwellers. Farm settlements with a degree of cooperative control and centralized decision-making are a third subtype of permanent large-scale farming.

A major determinant upon agricultural practices is the incidence of trypanosomiasis; that is, the infection of many of the vertebrates of Africa, including man, by trypanosomes or parasites of the blood and sometimes of other tissues. The consequent disease takes a variety of forms, including sleeping sickness in man and nagana in cattle. Absence of cattle due to prevalence of the disease is a major control on the type of agriculture that can be practiced, since cattle are beasts of burden. The ecology of trypanosomes is extremely complex. More than 50 species of wild animals, together with some birds and reptiles, are known to host the parasites. Transmission from one animal to another may be carried out by any one of 34 species, subspecies and races of tsetse fly (*Glossina*) and the distribution of these vectors is the only clear determining factor on the incidence of the diseases.

Top Fishing festival at Argungu, northwest Nigeria. Every stream or pond is a potential source of fish for protein-deficient diets and communally organized netting and trapping in Africa are common, often by people who have traditionally established rights to particular waters. Some large lakes and rivers have considerable commercial fisheries based on urban markets. However, in the seasonally wet and dry tropics, fishing may not be possible all the year around. It is particularly prone to disruption at times of high water.

Above The scenery of much of southern Africa is epitomized in the nearly level sufaces of the upper Zambezi basin, which is in part inundated seasonally by the Zambezi river. However, at the Victoria Falls, the character of the river changes. The river is eroding intersecting fractures in successive horizontal beds of basalt and plunges into the Batoka gorge, spanned by the combined road and rail bridge linking Zambia to Zimbabwe. The gorge tightly confines the river to a narrow course for some 100 kilometers before opening out into the fault-controlled Zambezi valley now occupied by the man-made Lake Kariba. The falls are an escape route for the Zambezi river from the great down-warped inland basin of southern Africa which successfully retains the drainage of much of southern Angola in the Okavango Swamps of northeast Botswana.

Game parks and fisheries

While some wild animals do suffer from trypano-somiasis and deaths occur in endemic areas, survivors probably acquire a natural immunity. The fact that wild animals are able to maintain their populations in infected areas has to some degree shielded them from competition by man. It is in these areas not usually coveted for agriculture that many of the game conservation projects were originally established. The other pronounced feature of the parks of Africa is their preponderance in the seasonal wet and dry climates of Africa. The open savannas are the home of most of the spectacular fauna of Africa. Almost every African country has designated one or more national parks. These represent a significant part of the total land use, but outright protection is no longer the prime objective. Increasingly, national parks are considered to be a special kind of land utilization, affording not only tourist and recreational facilities, but also acting as sources of meat to be culled on a sustained yield basis. They are also locations for other controlled usages, such as timber extraction, afforestation, pastoralism and fishing. In some parks illegal hunting for meat, ivory and skins has severely reduced the large fauna although there are also instances of population explosions in the protected environments of the parks, beyond the carrying capacity of the park area.

While the sea fisheries of West Africa, Angola, Namibia and South Africa have attracted increasing international attention, the freshwater fisheries of Africa are valuable sources of protein for a great many people. The great lakes and swamps of Africa, including man-made lakes such as Kariba, in most cases have fisheries, often operated by a great many small producers and served by many private vehicle owners who transport the fish to urban markets. The great rivers have commercial fisheries, where adequate transport is accessible to take the fresh or dried fish to market. But elsewhere in rural Africa, almost any stream or pond is a potential source of fish to supplement starch-based diets.

Population

The population distribution of Africa is the product of economic, social and political factors, variously operating in the past as well as at present, but always within the constraints and conducive features of the diverse physical environment. The climatic factor undeniably explains the extremely low population densities in the great Sahara and Namib/Kalahari deserts of Africa, and, to a lesser extent, in the Horn of Africa. Mountain ranges such as the Drakensberg, Ruwenzori and the Atlas also occasion low population densities. On the other hand, the lower slopes of Kilimanjaro and Mount Cameroon provide conditions attracting high densities. In other areas population densities are extremely variable. High densities may change to low densities quite suddenly, as they do in parts of Nigeria or Kenya, and often more abruptly than can be explained by any corresponding physical environmental changes. In such circumstances the past is probably the clue to the present.

The quality of census data in Africa varies greatly from country to country. Costs of enumeration, unskilled enumerators, illiteracy, census evasion and the impermanence of people's homes are among the problems of taking a census in Africa. International comparison is therefore difficult. Nevertheless, there is an extraordinary diversity of population totals and densities in Africa. Totals range from not many more than 70 000 people to more than 90 million, though a great many countries have fewer than 10 million. On the mainland densities range from 1 per square kilometer to more than 280. There is no typical population size in African countries and high density does not imply pressure upon resources any more than low density implies an absence of population pressure.

Mineral resources and energy

The diverse but unequally distributed mineral resources of Africa are a product of its geological history. Underlying almost the entire continent and outcropping over about half of its surface area is the complex basement group of rocks over 500 million years old. These Precambrian rocks vary greatly in type, but the metamorphic rocks of the upper Precambrian contain many valuable minerals such as copper, chrome and gold. Four main series of younger sedimentary rocks rest upon the basement. The oldest are Paleozoic and occur extensively in North Africa and the Cape ranges, but are not heavily mineralized. The Karoo series of Carboniferous and later date is extensive and largely undeformed in southern Africa, and includes enormous reserves of coal. In the Mesozoic era, continental and marine sediments were deposited widely in northern Africa and have been found to contain not only valuable mineral and oil deposits, but also water-bearing strata. Tertiary and Quaternary strata are found in the great basins and along coasts. They contain the oil deposits of West Africa.

Africa's mineral resources are exceeded only by those of North America, and what the North American continent lacks, Africa can provide. In base metals Africa's resources are unbalanced; copper resources far exceed those of lead, zinc or tin. In light metals the position is similar, with high-grade bauxite reserves far in excess of magnesite or titanium. Proven resources of strategic metals are not always readily divulged, but substantial reserves of uranium, lithium, columbium and tantalum are known. Data on precious minerals are also not always available, but the continent's gold and platinum reserves are renowned, as are the reserves of gem and industrial diamonds. Many semiprecious stones and abrasives are known in significant quantities. Reserves of industrial metals such as mercury, sulfur, antimony and arsenic are small, but there are large known reserves of minerals used in agriculture, such as phosphate, potash and salt. There are abundant supplies of the raw materials of the cement industry and also of other building materials such as gypsum, asbestos and vermiculite. Overall, the continent is well endowed, but the resource bases of individual nations vary from great extent and diversity to almost total paucity. Known reserves of iron ore have increased recently, but where an energy source is available production of iron and steel may gradually assume a more widespread distribution. The potential for growth in the steel industry is emphasized by the very large proportion of world reserves of other steel industry metals such as ferrochromium, manganese, cobalt and vanadium.

Africa has a number of extensive coal deposits. Seams are often thick and undisturbed by comparison with Europe but quality is often low. In the past, immediate access was often not available and large resources remained uneconomic. The quickening pace of development, including the utilization of available resources, has increased the number of mines in operation. The extreme imbalance in the distribution of coal reserves, which are largely confined to southern Africa, is mirrored by the distribution of oil and natural gas, located in the coastal states of North and West Africa. Petroleum is even more valuable than coal to a developing country and hence the major discoveries since 1956 have been particularly opportune. Once a field has been brought into production, a refinery is an attractive proposition to reduce foreign exchange expenditure, despite small local markets for refined products. Even countries without their own oil reserves have built refineries to process imported crude oil in order to reduce the cost of the finished product. The result is that some refineries operate at less than their optimum economic level.

The great river systems of Africa are developed in shallow basins in the extensive plateau surfaces so that the run-off from vast catchment areas, channeled into single great streams, descends to sea level in short distances by means of falls and rapids. This provides enormous potential for the generation of power, a potential which has already been in part tapped in such spectacular schemes as Kariba, Aswan, Kainji, Akosombo, Cabora Bassa and the Orange River scheme. in a continent with approximately 10 per cent of the world's population, it has been estimated that the potential for hydroelectric power generation is more than a third of the global potential. In relation to the size of its population, the continent has slightly more than its share of coal and oil reserves and substantially more of its share of natural gas reserves; yet annual per capita energy consumption is substantially lower than any other continent. The development potential is therefore great. Consumption of energy varies greatly from country to country. South Africa is by far the greatest consumer of energy; elsewhere the countries with high rates of energy consumption tend to be those with large extraction industries such as Libya, Gabon, Zambia and Zimbabwe.

Transportation and communications
The transportation network of Africa is more rudimentary and less integrated than in any other continent. Since an efficient transportation system is a prerequisite, if not a catalyst, for economic development, Africa's transportation map is changing more rapidly than elsewhere. In particular, the network of railroads is increasing. There are, however, five different gauges of track in operation, even after the abandonment of some very small gauges; hence problems of interrupted flow remain even after separate systems are linked. Also, existing lines were sometimes constructed to meet needs that no longer exist, such as an exhausted mineral deposit, so that there are problems of wrong location as well as inadequate density. The rate at which further lines will be constructed depends on the rate of development of processing industries which reduce the need for long-distance haulage of bulky and heavy raw materials.

Inland waters are relatively insignificant in Africa's transportation network. Distances are too great for canal construction and the large rivers are frequently unsuitable for navigation because of rapids, large seasonal variation in flow and impeded mouths, so that they are used as transportation arteries only locally. The East African lakes have regular services operating over distances similar to the limited riverine transportation. The great rivers are impediments, particularly to road transportation, which must use time-consuming ferries in the absence of costly bridges (costly either because of the width of the rivers or the low density of the traffic).

In a continent where distances are great and economic activity concentrated, air transportation would seem to have great potential. However, the products of Africa are frequently bulky and would-be travelers live at income levels at which saving of time is less important than savings in cost. Nevertheless, a proliferation of internal airlinks and a great increase in the numbers of airports of international standards have come about due to the formation of national airlines. Internal flights are often by small passenger craft, and the transcontinental components of national airline fleets are often very small and maintained on a contract basis by Western airlines.

Increasing international air traffic has not posed any significant threat to the traditional surface routing of trade through the major seaports of Africa. Sophisticated port facilities are recognized as imperative even to severely undeveloped economies, since the cost of delay in handling both imports and exports is high. Transshipment by boats standing off shore is no longer acceptable, and a modern African port must provide deepwater berthing for rapid handling of general cargo, in part containerized, and it may also have to provide specialized terminals for the handling of specific commodities such as petroleum, phosphate, iron ore and timber. Occasionally, such commodities are moved to and from the port by pipeline or conveyor, adding a new component to the transportation network.

Road transportation is the major component of the network because of flexibility. Both vehicles and services can be readily adapted to local needs, reaching areas inaccessible by any other means. Cost of road construction and maintenance is high. Long distances and low traffic densities make the high costs of bridges, culverts, drains and hard surfacing uneconomic, particularly in high-rainfall areas. Tarred routes have been disparately constructed with national needs in mind – usually the main arteries connecting the capital to regional centers – but international roads are often of a lower standard. International programs of upgrading are under way, including the Trans-Sahara and Trans-Africa (east-west) highways.

International comparison of road vehicles in use is a reflection of relative personal prosperity and economic activity. A car is an economic and social asset and road haulage is so important that many state road transportation corporations have been formed. South Africa and the North African countries are high on the list. In this respect, as in so many others, the distribution of material well-being across the continent is very uneven.　　　　J.C.S.

Geology and (inset) rift systems and volcanoes
The ancient Precambrain basement complex of extremely resistant rocks underlies much of the continent and outcrops extensively. It is widely overlain by Tertiary or even more recent sediments, although the earlier sedimentary strata of the Karoo system are widespread in southern Africa, and North Africa has its own pre-Tertiary sedimentary series. Chronological gaps in the form of unconformities are frequent in such an ancient landmass.

The rift valleys of East Africa form the largest rift valley system in the world. It has evolved over millions of years, resulting in many different valley forms; including single faults, stepped faults and secondary faulting. It has been partly infilled by great flat spreads of volcanic rocks but the many volcanic cones in East Africa are also associated with the rift system. By contrast, the great basins are scarcely discernible to the observer on the ground but their vast expanse implies significant relief amplitude.

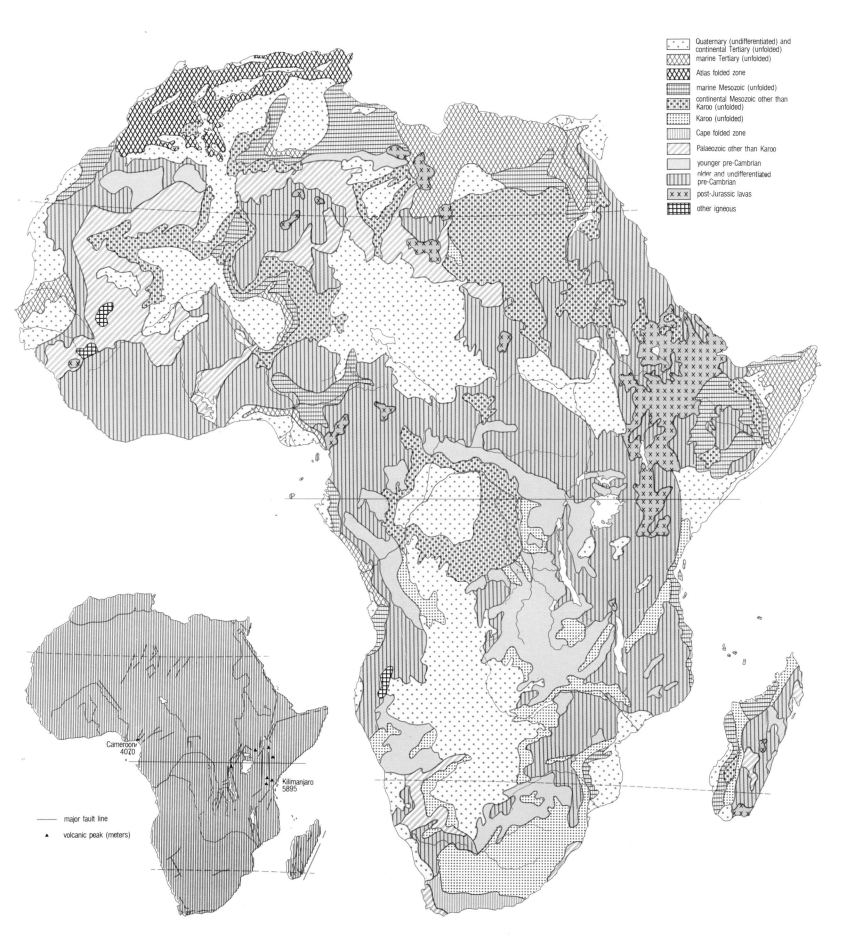

Quaternary (undifferentiated) and continental Tertiary (unfolded)
marine Tertiary (unfolded)
Atlas folded zone
marine Mesozoic (unfolded)
continental Mesozoic other than Karoo (unfolded)
Karoo (unfolded)
Cape folded zone
Palaeozoic other than Karoo
younger pre-Cambrian
older and undifferentiated pre-Cambrian
post-Jurassic lavas
other igneous

Cameroon 4070

Kilimanjaro 5895

major fault line
volcanic peak (meters)

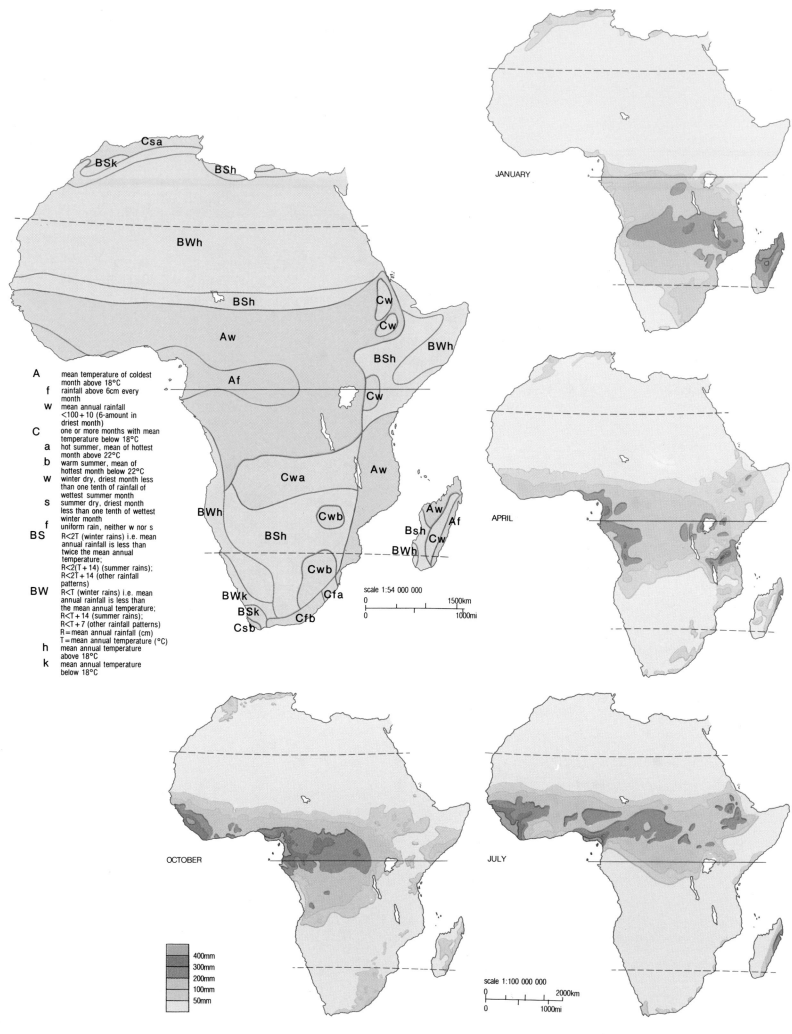

Csa

BSk

BSh

BWh

BSh

Cw

Cw

BWh

BSh

Aw

Af

Cw

A   mean temperature of coldest
     month above 18°C
  f rainfall above 6cm every
     month
  w mean annual rainfall
     <100+10 (6-amount in
     driest month)
C   one or more months with mean
     temperature below 18°C
  a hot summer, mean of hottest
     month above 22°C
  b warm summer, mean of
     hottest month below 22°C
  w winter dry, driest month less
     than one tenth of rainfall of
     wettest summer month
  s summer dry, driest month
     less than one tenth of wettest
     winter month
  f uniform rain, neither w nor s
BS   R<2T (winter rains) i.e. mean
     annual rainfall is less than
     twice the mean annual
     temperature;
     R<2(T+14) (summer rains);
     R<2T+14 (other rainfall
     patterns)
BW   R<T (winter rains) i.e. mean
     annual rainfall is less than
     the mean annual temperature;
     R<T+14 (summer rains);
     R<T+7 (other rainfall patterns)
     R=mean annual rainfall (cm)
     T=mean annual temperature (°C)
  h mean annual temperature
     above 18°C
  k mean annual temperature
     below 18°C

Cwa

Aw

BWh

Cwb

Aw

Af

BWh

Bsh

Cw

BSh

Cwb

Cfa

BWk

BSk

Cfb

Csb

scale 1:54 000 000

0   1500km

0   1000mi

JANUARY

APRIL

OCTOBER

400mm
300mm
200mm
100mm
50mm

JULY

scale 1:100 000 000

0   2000km

0   1000mi

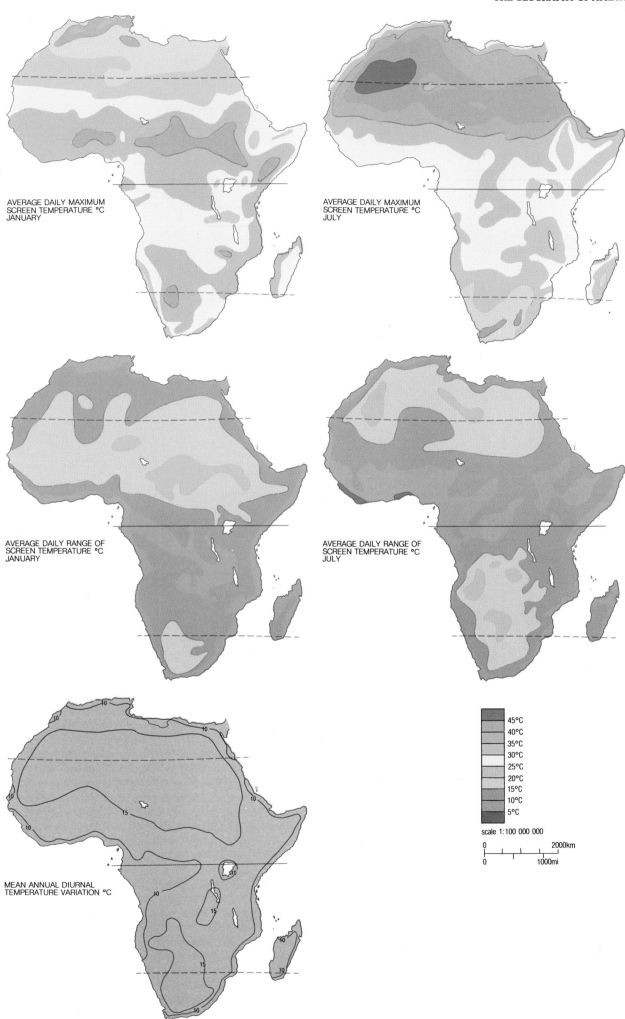

Far left: Climatic types (after Köppen)
Apart from the extensive hot deserts (BW), African climates are predominantly seasonally wet and dry (BS, Aw, Cw, Cs). The extent of rain forest climatic regimes (Af) is much more confined than is frequently supposed. Temperate regimes with rain all year (Cf) are even more restricted.

Left: Rainfall: monthly mean for January, April, July and October
The marked seasonality of African rainfall regimes is apparent in the almost total aridity of the continent north of the equator (except for the Mediterranean littoral) in January, by comparison with the absence of rainfall south of the equator (except at the Cape) in July. The midseason months of April and October are times of particularly great uncertainty in occurrence and amount of rainfall.

Right: Temperature: average daily maximum, January and July; average daily range, January and July; mean annual diurnal temperature variation
The principal characteristic of African temperature regimes is high diurnal range, so much so that mean daily temperature (usually obtained from the mean of the maximum and minimum temperatures) has very little significance. Temperature maxima vary markedly from one half of the year to the next in all but the lowest latitudes, so that most of Africa has a winter. Also the average daily range tends to be more marked in winter, but the compact shape of the continent and the lack of maritime influence on temperatures are stressed by the sharp increase in daily range away from coasts.

AVERAGE DAILY MAXIMUM
SCREEN TEMPERATURE °C
JANUARY

AVERAGE DAILY MAXIMUM
SCREEN TEMPERATURE °C
JULY

AVERAGE DAILY RANGE OF
SCREEN TEMPERATURE °C
JANUARY

AVERAGE DAILY RANGE OF
SCREEN TEMPERATURE °C
JULY

MEAN ANNUAL DIURNAL
TEMPERATURE VARIATION °C

45°C
40°C
35°C
30°C
25°C
20°C
15°C
10°C
5°C

scale 1:100 000 000

0   2000km
0   1000mi

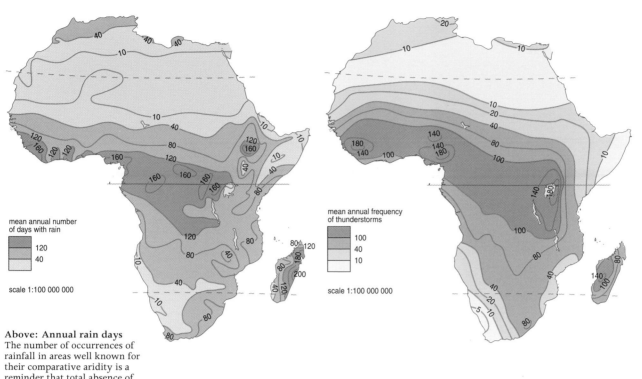

**mean annual number
of days with rain**

120
40

scale 1:100 000 000

**mean annual frequency
of thunderstorms**

100
40
10

scale 1:100 000 000

Above: Annual rain days
The number of occurrences of
rainfall in areas well known for
their comparative aridity is a
reminder that total absence of
rainfall is confined to the
northeastern Sahara. On the
other hand, for almost all of the
continent, the majority of days in
the year are rainless.

**Above right; Thunderstorm
frequency**
Areas of high thunderstorm
frequency during seasons of
rainfall incidence have an
additional element of uncertainty
in their rainfall regimes, in that
thunderstorms may sometimes be
very localized in occurrence.
Marked variations in annual
totals may therefore be
experienced over very short
distances, particularly in
strongly seasonal ranfall
regimes.

Right: AIDS in Africa
First recognized in the early
1980s, Acquired Immune
Deficiency Syndrome (AIDS) is
pandemic in Africa. Eastern
Africa was one of the earliest
regions affected and continues to
have the highest rates of
infection. In Africa the disease is
primarily heterosexual and is
found in rural as well as urban
locations. It is also transmitted
by breastfeeding. The impact of
the disease is enormous: patients
become too ill to work or attend
school; families lose their
incomes, or, in rural areas, their
immediate food supply, which
means that children in school
usually leave to work the land.
Orphaned children are given to
the care of grandparents who no
longer have adult children to
care for them as they age; both
groups become dependent on the
state (which is far from wealthy)
if there is no family left to help
them or if the family is too poor
to support any more relatives.
Employers in cities routinely
lose employees. Preventive
education is having some
success, but the burden on each
country's resources remains
overwhelming.

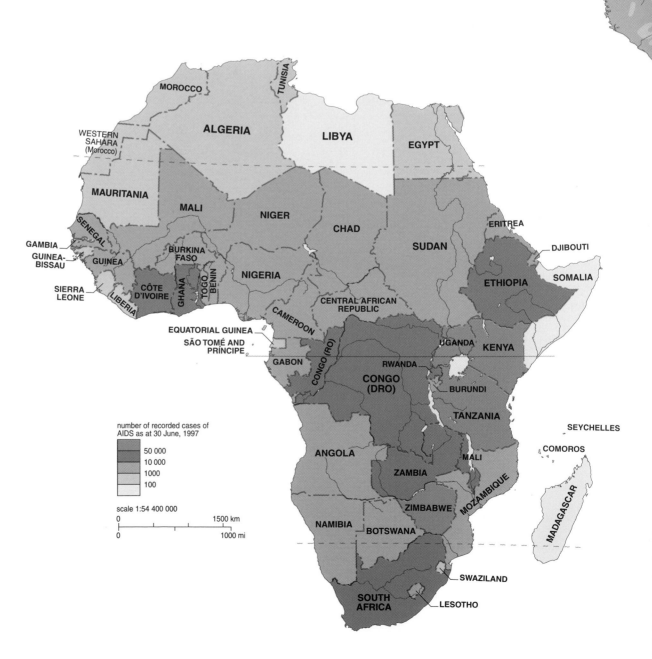

**number of recorded cases of
AIDS as at 30 June, 1997**

50 000
10 000
1000
100

scale 1:54 400 000

0   1500 km
0   1000 mi

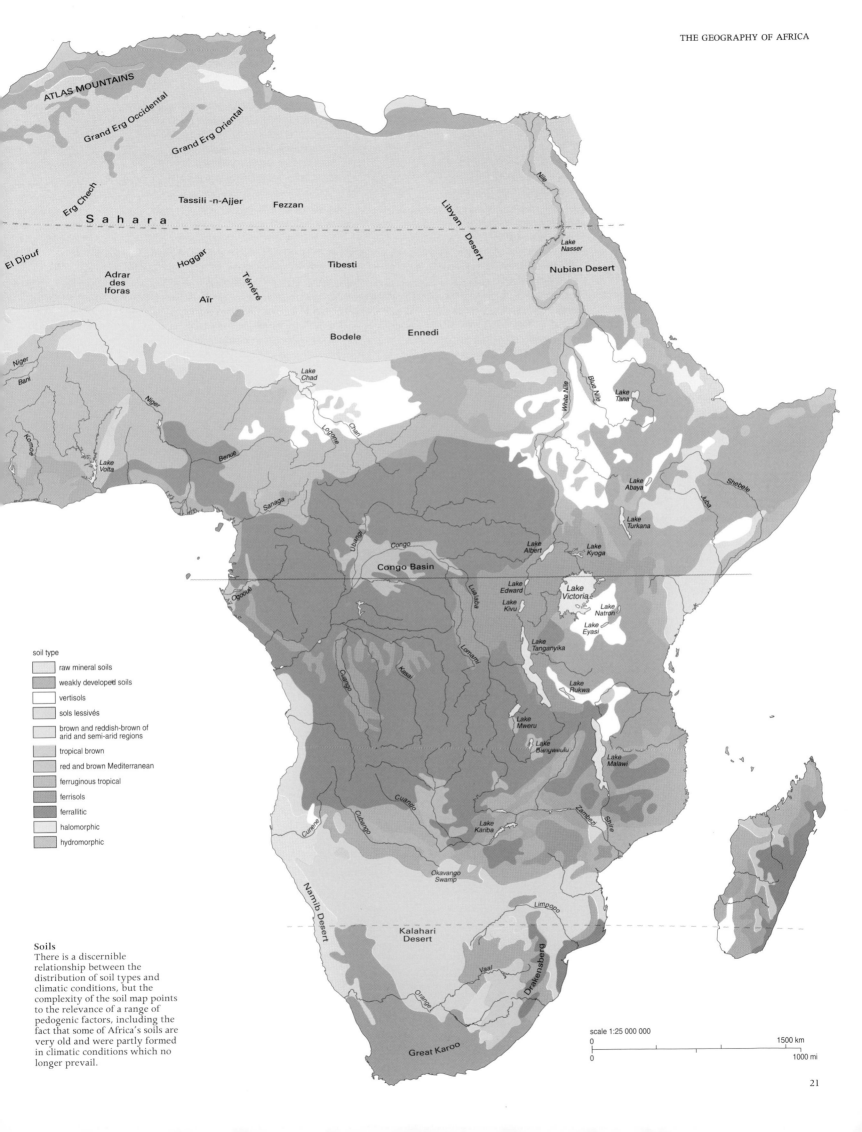

ATLAS MOUNTAINS

Grand Erg Occidental

Grand Erg Oriental

Erg Chech

Tassili -n-Ajjer

Fezzan

S a h a r a

Nile

Libyan Desert

Lake Nasser

El Djouf

Hoggar

Tibesti

Nubian Desert

Adrar
des
Iforas

Aïr

Ténéré

Bodele

Ennedi

Niger

Bani

Niger

Lake Chad

Logone

Chari

White Nile

Blue Nile

Lake Tana

Komoé

Lake Volta

Benue

Sanaga

Lake Abaya

Shebele

Juba

Lake Turkana

Ubangi

Congo

Lake Albert

Lake Kyoga

Congo Basin

Ogooué

Lualaba

Lake Edward

Lake Kivu

Lake Victoria

Lake Natron

Lake Eyasi

Lomami

Lake Tanganyika

Cuango

Kasai

Lake Rukwa

soil type

Lake Mweru

Lake Bangweulu

Lake Malawi

Cuango

Zambezi

Shire

Cubango

Cunene

Lake Kariba

Okavango Swamp

Namib Desert

Limpopo

Kalahari Desert

Vaal

Drakensberg

Orange

Great Karoo

	soil type
	raw mineral soils
	weakly developed soils
	vertisols
	sols lessivés
	brown and reddish-brown of arid and semi-arid regions
	tropical brown
	red and brown Mediterranean
	ferruginous tropical
	ferrisols
	ferrallitic
	halomorphic
	hydromorphic

Soils
There is a discernible relationship between the distribution of soil types and climatic conditions, but the complexity of the soil map points to the relevance of a range of pedogenic factors, including the fact that some of Africa's soils are very old and were partly formed in climatic conditions which no longer prevail.

scale 1:25 000 000

0   1500 km

0   1000 mi

21

Population and (inset) rate of change

Beyond the deserts of Africa, rural population densities are extremely variable, reflecting not only environmental and current economic conditions but clearly showing the impact of historical movements of people. High concentrations may occur in and around large towns as a result of recent migration, but they also occur in some of the more remote rural areas where they are frequently the product of precolonial events.

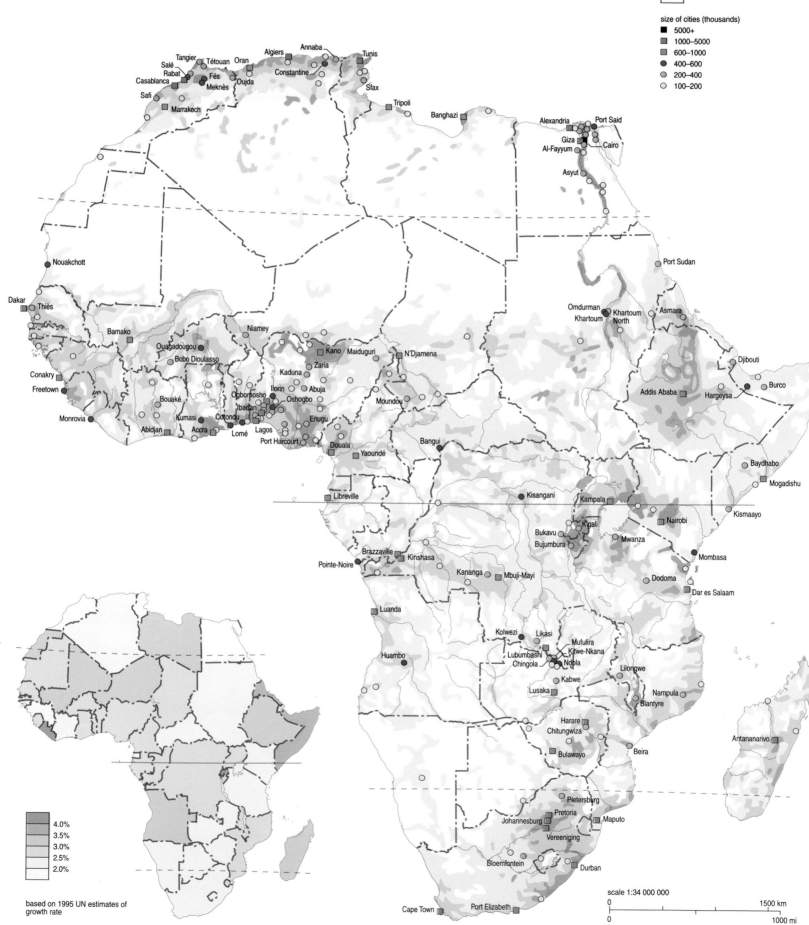

persons per square km

200
100
50
10
1

size of cities (thousands)

■ 5000+
■ 1000–5000
■ 600–1000
● 400–600
● 200–400
○ 100–200

4.0%
3.5%
3.0%
2.5%
2.0%

based on 1995 UN estimates of growth rate

scale 1:34 000 000

0   1500 km

0   1000 mi

PART TWO
THE CULTURAL BACKGROUND

LANGUAGES AND PEOPLES

In precolonial times the peoples of Africa were divided into hundreds of different nationalities and ethnic groups, of greatly varying size and with great differences in culture and values. In some cases multi-ethnic states – such as Ethiopia in the late 19th century or the empire of Mali in the 14th century – encompassed many peoples under a single central political authority. In other cases, ethnicity was coterminous with the political unit – as in the 19th-century kingdom of the Zulu of southern Africa – while at the other extreme there were ethnic groups – such as the Chaga of Kilimanjaro – divided into many tiny independent political units, some no larger than a village. The European conquests lumped different peoples together in new ways in the colonial territories of the early 20th century. The modern independent states of Africa, as inheritors of the colonial boundaries, today seek to blend their various peoples together into single nations, but it is safe to say that the older ethnic ties remain potent forces in African life down to the present.

Europeans have generally called African ethnic groups "tribes," but there is no need to continue to use such an ill-defined and in many cases prejudicial term. In the 19th century the Zulu nation-state – ruled by a king – was no more a tribe than England was under Henry VIII. The Igbo of Nigeria (17 million strong) are called a tribe, while many a much smaller ethnic group in Europe has been dignified as a "nationality." Yet at the same time "tribe" could be applied to a tiny African village community of no more than a few hundred people.

The one consistently valid way of classifying African societies is by the languages they speak. People in Africa, as elsewhere, tend to identify themselves by their home language (and indeed this identification seems generally to coincide with what the Europeans thought of as "tribes"). Over 1000 languages are spoken in Africa. Some – like Mandinke, Igbo, Yoruba and Hausa in West Africa; Swahili in East Africa; Amharic and Oromo (erroneously called Galla) in the Horn of Africa; Zulu and Sotho in southern Africa; and Arabic in northern Africa – have millions of speakers. Most languages have between a few hundred and a million speakers, while a few, like Kw'adza of Tanzania, are known by only a very few old people and are close to extinction.

With the exception of a few languages of relatively recent introduction to the continent, the home languages of Africa all belong to just four language families. The exceptions include: English, used by communities of settler descent in Liberia and southern Africa, and in a creole form (Krio) especially in Sierra Leone; Afrikaans, a form of Dutch used in southern Africa by people of European settler descent; Spanish, in the Canary Islands; Portuguese, by the Cape Verdians; several languages of Indian communities settled in East and South Africa, notably Urdu, Hindi and Gujarati;

and Malagasy, the language of Madagascar. Malagasy belongs to the Malayo-Polynesian family, all the others to Indo-European. Five Indo-European languages (English, French, Portuguese, Spanish and Italian) are used as second languages in various African countries, the first three being by far the most important.

The four recognized African language families, to which the rest of the continent's languages belong, are Niger–Kordofanian, Khoisan, Afroasiatic (Hamito–Semitic) and Nilo-Saharan. There remain disputes among scholars about the specific details of internal classification of each family, and also some legitimate doubts about the membership of a few particular languages in one or another of those families. A few scholars hold out against this scheme of language classification, established only during the 1950s. But the accumulation of new evidence over the subsequent four decades has progressively strengthened the case for the overall classification, so far as to put its general (though not specific) correctness beyond doubt.

Niger–Kordofanian languages fall into two primary divisions. The Kordofanian subfamily consists of about 20 languages spoken by relatively small communities in the Nuba mountains of the Republic of Sudan. In contrast, the Niger–Congo subfamily spreads across half of Africa and its several hundred languages are spoken by well over 150 million people. The ancient homeland of Niger–Congo was West Africa, where today a great diversity of Niger–Congo languages are spoken. At the far west along the Atlantic coast can be found peoples speaking such languages of the West Atlantic branch of Niger–Congo as Wolof in Senegal and Temne in Sierra Leone. The Fulani cattle-herders of the sahel zone of West Africa also speak a West Atlantic tongue. All across the vast interior watershed of the Niger river live speakers of languages of another branch, Mande, the best-known of these being the Mandinke or Mandingo. South of the great bend of the Niger, especially in Burkina Faso, are located the poorly known languages of the Gur branch of Niger–Congo, while through southern Ghana, Togo, Benin and southern Nigeria are found the Kwa languages. The language of the Asante empire of the 18th and 19th centuries and those of the Yoruba and Igbo peoples of Nigeria all belong to the Kwa branch of the family. Still further east, in parts of eastern Nigeria and in Cameroon, southern Chad and the Central African Republic, are languages of the Adamawa–Ubangian branch. The most important language of this branch, Zande, is in fact spoken across several hundred kilometers stretching from the Central African Republic and Congo (DRO) in the east into the far southwestern portions of Sudan.

The most widespread and best-known subgroup of Niger–Congo is the Bantu languages, which cover most of the vast southern third of Africa, from the equatorial rain forest of Gabon and southern

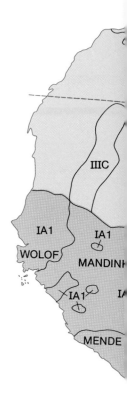

Language families today (after Greenberg)
The enormous linguistic diversity of Africa poses peculiar problems for the cartographer. With very few exceptions (such as Arabic used as a lingua franca by non-Arab populations in North Africa) language and ethnic identity are the same. Most educated people are bilingual, particularly in areas where one of the colonial languages – usually French or English – still enjoys official status. The fragmented geographical distribution of some language families reflects historical upheavals and migrations which have complicated the picture presented by the language distribution of earlier periods (see maps on page 26).

IA
ABIC

IIIC

IIIC   IIIC

IIIC   IIIC

IIIC

IIIC

IIIC

IC

IIIC   IIIC

ARABIC

IIIB

IIIA

TUAREG

IIE

NUBIAN

IIIC

IIB

IIID1

BEJA

IIA

IIA

IIE   IIE

IIID2

HAUSA

IIIE

IIIA

IIE   IIE

KANURI

IIC

IIE

IIH

IA3

IIIE

IID

IIE

IB

IIID2

DOGON

ARABIC

AMHARIC

IIIE

IIIE

IIE

III

IA4

IIC

IIG

IIIE

IIF

DINKA

IIIA

SOMALI

AKAN EWE YORUBA

ZANDE NUER

III

IIIF

OROMO

IIID3

IGBO

IA4

IA6

IIF

IIIE

IIF

IIE

GANDA

FANG

LUO

KIKUYU

MAASAI

CHAGA

KONGO

IIID4

IVC

IA5

IVB

SWAHILI

IIID4

YAO

LELE   LUBA

MBUNDU

BEMBA

IVA1

CHEWA

IVA2

SHONA

IVA1

MALAGASY

IVA2

IVA2

THONGA

V

IVA2

IVA3

IVA2

NAMA

SOTHO

TSWANA

ZULU

VI

I	Niger-Kordofanian
	IA Niger-Congo
	IA1 West Atlantic
	IA2 Mande
	IA3 Voltaic
	IA4 Kwa
	IA5 Benue-Congo
	IA6 Adamawa-Eastern
	IB Kordofanian
	IB1 Koalib
	IB2 Tegali
	IB3 Talodi
	IB4 Tumtum
	IB5 Katla

II	Nilo-Saharan
	IIA Songhai
	IIB Saharan
	IIC Maban
	IID Fur
	IIE Eastern Sudanic
	IIF Central Sudanic
	IIG Berta
	IIH Kunama
	III Koman

III	Afroasiatic
	IIIA Semitic
	IIIB Egyptian
	IIIC Berber
	IIID Cushitic
	IIID1 Beja
	IIID2 Agaw
	IIID3 E Cushitic
	IIID4 S Cushitic
	IIIE Chadic
	IIIF Omotic

IV	Khoisan
	IVA South African Khoisan
	IVA1 N South African Khoisan
	IVA2 C South African Khoisan
	IVA3 S South African Khoisan
	IVB Sandawe
	IVC Hatsa

V	Austronesian Malagasy

VI	English, Afrikaans and indigenous Bantu languages

scale 1:25 000 000

0 _____ 1500km

0 _____ 1000mi

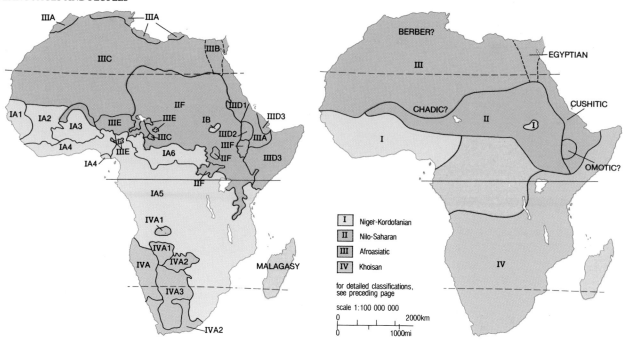

I	Niger-Kordofanian
II	Nilo-Saharan
III	Afroasiatic
IV	Khoisan

for detailed classifications,
see preceding page

scale 1:100 000 000

0 ————————— 2000km

0 ————————— 1000mi

Far Left: Language families c. 1000 AD (after Greenberg) In the north a major difference from the present is the wider extent of the Nilo–Saharan language family. Afroasiatic languages were confined to the shores of the Red Sea and the Horn of Africa in the east and had not penetrated far into the interior. In the south the distribution of Khoisan speakers was considerably more extensive.

Left: Language families c. 2500 BC (after Greenberg) These locations are only approximate. The comparatively confined range of the Niger–Congo languages is noticeable. Khoisan speakers are shown as ranging over the whole southern and eastern third of the continent. They were later to be pushed back by incoming Bantu speakers of the Niger–Congo language family.

Right The Nuba live in the hills of Kordofan, southwest of Khartoum, Sudan. They spoke an Eastern Sudanic language which is now being replaced by Arabic. The men are famous as wrestlers

Cameroon to the highlands of Kenya and from the Ubangi river in the Central African Republic nearly to the Cape of Good Hope in South Africa. Swahili is a Bantu language originally spoken by people living in city-states along the Indian Ocean coasts of Africa between the 9th and 18th centuries. During the 19th century Swahili traders, opening up overland routes into the East African interior, established their tongue as the market language of a region reaching from the east coast as far west as eastern Congo (DRO). Now spoken by hundreds of thousands of people as a first language, Swahili has millions more who speak it as a second language, and has become the national tongue of several East African countries. Other well-known Bantu languages include: Zulu; Kongo, the language of the important 15th- and 16th-century kingdom of Kongo; Lingala, a lingua franca of modern Congo (DRO); Shona, spoken by the majority of people in Zimbabwe; Bemba, spoken by several million in Zambia; Ganda, the language of precolonial Buganda – the kingdom from which modern Uganda takes its name; and Gikuyu (Kikuyu) of the eastern Kenya highlands, the home language of the late president of Kenya, Jomo Kenyatta.

Despite their vast extent today, Bantu languages belong to just one subgroup of the Benue-Congo branch of Niger–Congo, the other languages of which are limited to parts of central and southeastern Nigeria. They only spread over the regions they now occupy during approximately the last 4000 years. The ancestral Bantu language, which we call proto-Bantu, was spoken somewhere probably in eastern Nigeria; that is, in West Africa, like the rest of Niger–Congo at that time. Then for reasons we do not yet understand, early Bantu communities began expanding into new territories, first through the equatorial rain forest belt and along its margins and then, between about 500 BC and 300 AD, eastward and southward into eastern and southern Africa. We do not know what languages preceded the Bantu in the equatorial forest and the adjoining savannas, but in eastern and southern Africa the earlier languages often belonged to the Khoisan family and, in parts of East Africa, to the Afroasiatic and Nilo-Saharan families.

Several millennia ago the Khoisan languages apparently predominated all across the lands from Somalia and Kenya clear to the Cape of Good Hope. Only relics remain today of that former distribution. Nama, a Khoikhoi language spoken by 50 000 or more people in Namibia, accounts for perhaps 40 per cent of the remaining Khoisan populations. In the 17th century there were still perhaps 200 000 speakers of the related Cape Khoikhoi (the so-called Hottentot) dialects between the Cape and the Transkei, but disease and expropriation of grazing land by European settlers destroyed the Khoikhoi economic base and with it the Cape Khoikhoi language and ethnic identity. A large number of Khoisan languages with usually a few hundred speakers each are scattered across the Kalahari region of southern Africa. These are spoken by the Bushmen or San, some of the few remaining hunter-gatherer societies of the continent. Two Khoisan languages also persist in East Africa: Sandawe, with more than 25 000 speakers; and Hatsa, with a few hundred. The Hatsa are hunter–gatherers like the San, whereas the Sandawe are mixed agriculturists and the Khoikhoi, herders of sheep and cattle.

The Afroasiatic family, under the older name Hamito–Semitic, has long been recognized as a linguistic unit. Its best-known branch is Semitic, which includes among its languages Hebrew, Arabic, Aramaic (the language of Jesus) and ancient Akkadian. All are languages of Asia, except for Arabic which spread across North Africa during the Muslim Arab conquests of the 7th and 8th centuries, continuing during the past 1000 years into parts of the eastern and central Sudan belt as well. One small subgroup of Semitic, the Ethiopic languages, is spoken entirely in Africa, but it was brought into Ethiopia and the Horn by south Arabian immigrants during the first millennium BC. Amharic, the national language of Ethiopia, belongs to the Ethiopic subgroup. The other five accepted branches of Afroasiatic are all purely African in their distributions, and it is now generally agreed by scholars of Africa that the Afroasiatic family had its distant origins in Africa, probably as much as 15 000 years ago, in or near Ethiopia.

The Chadic branch consists of about 100 languages spoken in Niger, northern Nigeria, Cameroon and Chad. The most important of these by far is Hausa, which with upwards of 23 million speakers is one of the world's most important languages.

The Berber branch is more widespread geographically but has far fewer speakers and languages than Chadic. Expanding about 2000 years ago all across North Africa and through large parts of the Sahara, the Berber languages persist today only in enclaves in the now Arabic-speaking North Africa and in the central Sahara. Most famous but not most numerous of the Berbers are the camel-owning Tuareg of the desert. The extinct Guanche language of the Canary Islands was probably related fairly closely to Berber.

The Egyptian branch of Afroasiatic, represented by ancient Egyptian and its descendant form Coptic, has now become wholly extinct, having gradually been replaced by Arabic between the 7th and 18th centuries. But the Cushitic and Omotic branches, on the other hand, each consist of large numbers of extant languages, some very important indeed. Cushitic languages extend in the north from Beja, along the Red Sea hills of the Republic of Sudan, southward more than 1500 kilometers to north central Tanzania, where the Southern Cushitic languages, are found. The most prominent of these is Iraqw. The two most important Cushitic languages today, both with several million speakers, are Somali, the national language of Somalia, and Oromo (Galla) of Ethiopia. Both belong to the Eastern sub-branch of Cushitic. The Agaw (Central Cushitic) languages of central and northern Ethiopia have largely been eclipsed by intrusive Ethiopic languages such as Amharic, even as the Southern Cushitic languages (once widespread in Kenya and Tanzania) have retreated before Bantu expansion. However the Eastern Cushitic peoples remain numerous and prominent in the affairs of Ethiopia and the Horn of Africa. The Omotic languages predominate through the southwestern portions of Ethiopia and apparently have done so for many millennia. The most notable Omotic tongue is Kafa, the language of an important kingdom from the 14th to the 19th centuries.

The languages of the fourth African family, Nilo-Saharan, are scattered across 6000 kilometers in an east–west direction, from Songhay at the bend of the Niger to the Koman languages of the western Ethiopian foothills and the Nilotic languages of East Africa. Songhay was the language of the huge Songhay empire of the late 15th and early 16th centuries, while Kanuri was the dominant tongue of the Kanem and Bornu kingdoms of Lake Chad between the 9th and 19th centuries. Important Nilo–Saharan languages in the eastern Sudan included Nile Nubian: the spoken and written language of the medieval Christian kingdoms of Nobatia and Alwa, and possibly the extinct language of ancient Meroë. A variety of Nilo–Saharan languages continue to be spoken in the Republic of Sudan and in Chad today. The best-known of these are Dinka, Shilluk and Nuer, all belonging to the Nilotic subgroup of the Eastern Sudanic branch of Nilo-Saharan. Other Nilotic peoples, the most famous of which are the Maasai, live in parts of Uganda, Kenya and Tanzania, into

which regions their ancestors spread during the past 2000 years. Along the southern edges of the Republic of Sudan, into portions of northeastern Congo (DRO) and westward as far as central and southern Chad can be found peoples speaking languages of the Central Sudanic branch of Nilo–Saharan, among them the Mangbetu of Congo (DRO) and the Bagirmi of Chad. Other major divisions of Nilo–Saharan are formed by the Maban languages of eastern Chad and the Fur language of Darfur in western Republic of Sudan.

The Nilo–Saharan languages apparently once extended across nearly the whole Sudan belt of Africa. In the west, between Lake Chad and the Songhay-speaking areas along the Niger, the once continuous Nilo-Saharan territories were broken by the intrusion several thousand years ago of the Chadic peoples. In the eastern and central Sudan, Bedouin Arabs have made deep inroads into formerly Nilo-Saharan speech areas during the past 1000 years.

Africa is the home of an equally diverse array of human cultures. Hardly anything can be said to be typically or universally African. Africa has patrilineal and matrilineal societies and even some in which descent is traced bilaterally. Its precolonial political systems ran the gamut from empires and sacral kingships, to age-based republics, to village democracies, and its social systems ranged from highly stratified slave-holding societies to completely classless communities. Yet there are a few sets of associated culture traits that recur very widely through the continent and what is interesting is that in a number of cases these traits seem characteristic of particular linguistic groupings of peoples.

Polyrhythmic music, and dance, for which the principal accompaniment is the drum, is often thought of as quintessentially African. In fact it appears to be a feature of culture particularly associated with Niger-Congo peoples. It has spread so widely because Niger–Congo societies, especially the Bantu, have covered so much of the continent and it has come to have an enormous impact on modern Western popular music and dance because so many of the African slaves transported by Europeans were of Niger–Congo background. Outside of Niger–Congo-speaking regions in Africa other music styles, frequently based on stringed instruments, tend to prevail, along with quite different styles of dance.

Another widespread culture feature is religion based on veneration of ancestors. Again this belief system shows up among Niger-Congo speakers and those peoples influenced by them. In some cases, as among the Yoruba of Nigeria, the elevation of some royal or heroic ancestors to a special high status has added the dimension of a sort of polytheism to the basic ancestor religion. In the eastern Sudan, on the other hand, peoples such as the Nilotic Nuer and the Maasai attribute no particular role to the ancestors at all and instead focus religious observance on one God or Divinity, symbolically linked with the sky and rain. This religion seems to have spread at an early date to the adjoining Ethiopian regions, for it reappears among Omotic peoples, like the Kafa, and Cushites, like the Oromo. Still another pattern of belief occurs among some of the Omotic and Cushitic peoples of southern Ethiopia; there the focal rites of

African physical types
What do the peoples of Africa look like? Basically, people of three different physical types have lived in Africa for thousands of years. In the extreme north were brown-skinned people of similar stock to others living around the Mediterranean; in West and central Africa were people of the type we call Negroid – dark brown to black skin, tightly spiraled hair. Over much of the rest of Africa were the hunter-gatherers who have for long been known as Bushmen: smaller than the West African Negroes, and with yellowish skin, but with spiralled hair.

Over the centuries these different stocks have moved and mingled. There are certain physical types which may be thought of as typical of a given area, but there are no really abrupt divisions between one people and another. Broadly speaking, lighter people are found in the extreme north and the extreme south of Africa, and darker people in the hotter equatorial regions. In Africa may be found both the tallest people (on average) in the world – the Dinka of the southern Sudan – and the shortest – the pygmies of Congo (DRO). As well as the peoples of indigenous stock, there are also in Africa Arabs, whose ancestors have lived in Africa for many generations; Europeans, as in South Africa; and peoples of established mixed race, especially in the old Portuguese colonies but also in South Africa. Here we present a selection of portraits of African peoples.

Kabyle man, Algeria.

Coptic girl, Egypt.

Bobo elder, Burkina Faso.

Woman from Omdurman, Sudan.

Tutsi man, Rwanda.

Shilluk man, Sudan.

Turkana man, Kenya.

Karamoja woman, Uganda.

Maasai girl,
Tanzania.

Baulé woman, Côte d'Ivoire.

Mbuti pygmy, Congo (DRO).

San (Bushman) girl, Botswana.

Shangaan man, Mozambique.

Swazi man, Swaziland.

Left Supporters of the African National Congress (ANC) celebrate at a rally during South Africa's first multi-racial election campaign in 1994. The ANC draws much of its mass support from the Xhosa people, while the rival Inkatha Freedom Party is Zulu-dominated.

the community were directed toward the god of the particular community. A fourth distinctive African religion turns up among Khoisan peoples, who saw the vicissitudes of life as reflecting a dualism in the supernatural realm between a good god and an evil one, or between a good god and a variety of harmful spirits.

If there is one nearly pan-African culture feature it is the circumcision of young people, especially as a sign of their graduation into adulthood. By no means universal, it is still found in one form or another in half or more of the societies of Africa and turns up in cultures as widely separated as those of the Bantu-speaking Xhosa of South Africa, the Igbo of West Africa and the Cushitic Iraqw of Tanzania. It is a very widespread feature of Niger-Congo cultures and is nearly universal among Afroasiatic peoples. It is probably because of its ancient Afroasiatic roots that the custom passed as a normative practice into the Jewish and Muslim religions. Circumcision is rarer among Nilo-Saharan speakers, except where they become Muslim, and is generally lacking in Khoisan cultures.

African peoples have also frequently been classified by physical appearance; that is, according to supposed racial types. It remains a popular approach in talking about distant peoples, both because of the 20th-century preoccupation with "race" and because, more legitimately, we all want to be able to visualize what the subjects of our interest "really" look like. It is indeed interesting, for example, that Africa contains some of both the shortest and the tallest people in the world. The pygmies of the equatorial rain forest (rarely reaching even 125 centimeters in height) appear to be distinctive in some features other than just stature, yet on the whole they fit within the broad range of African physical variation and today speak only the Bantu or Central Sudanic languages of their neighbors. In contrast, adult males among the Nuer and Dinka (Nilotes of the southern Republic of Sudan) average close to 180 centimeters in height; taller even than Americans, northwestern Euro-

peans and Polynesians. In other features of their outward appearance Africans also vary considerably across the span of the continent.

Classifications of people by physical appearance, however, turn out to be fraught with grave difficulties. The older textbooks on Africa speak of Negroid, Bushmanoid ("old yellow-skinned" or "yellow-brown-skinned") and Hamitic ("brown" or "Afro-Mediterranean") races, dividing the peoples of the continent up according to such characteristics as darkness of skin and width of nose, and even current books still use such terms. But modern physical anthropology has shown "race" in this sense to be a scientifically untenable concept. There are indeed variations in human appearance across Africa. But, leaving aside distinctively European settler populations, the variation tends to be gradual and cumulative, with the frequency of occurrence of one feature of human appearance increasing, another decreasing, as one moves progressively across the continent.

For instance, the frequency of occurrence of lighter skin tones tends to increase in Africa as one goes either northward or southward from the areas of most direct sunlight. There are undoubtedly parts of southern Africa where expansion of Bantu-speaking peoples from the equatorial regions has increased the rate of occurrence of quite dark skin, but that is not at all the same as saying — as many books on Africa do — that one "race" of people has supplanted another.

The frequency of broad noses, as another example, increases as one goes south and southwestward in Africa. But because again a gradual change in frequency of occurrence is involved, there is no basis for postulating, as earlier writers did, that the presence of narrow noses meant some sort of quasi-European or Arab-like people had once settled in a place. We may well wish to know what physical characteristics are common among this or that African people, but we will have to be specific in our description and do without the comfortable oversimplification of race.　　C. E.

RELIGIONS

The diverse religious situation in today's Africa reflects a series of historical developments. The inhabitants of Africa north of the Sudan belt are almost all Muslims, with the exception of the minority Coptic Church in Egypt. Similarly, the Horn region and the East African coast as far south as northern Mozambique are Islamic, although in central Ethiopia there is again an ancient church which has strong links with the Egyptian Church. South and east of these almost totally Islamic zones there are regions where Muslims are a majority or a very strong minority. In western Nigeria and in Tanzania there are large Islamized rural populations, and in cities and large towns all over the continent Muslims are an important minority.

Outside the Muslim areas Africans observe traditional ethnic religious practices to a greater or lesser degree, with Christian minorities of varying sizes. Statistics are hard to come by and unreliable, but Christians are almost certainly in a majority in a number of areas, such as eastern Nigeria, Uganda, Lesotho and parts of South Africa. Some Christians may be first-generation converts, but others come from families which have been Christian for several generations, even as far back as the early 19th century.

However the religious situation is still very fluid. In one household, say in western Nigeria or the southern Sudan, may be found brothers who follow, respectively, traditional beliefs, Islam and Christianity. In very many cases the parents are still followers of traditional religion while all their children have become Christians or Muslims. Again, men and women move from one set of beliefs and practices to another and back again as life crises occur which appear to be helped by one faith or another. There is a great deal of pragmatism in the African approach to religion.

As a generalization it may be said that Christianity and Islam are the religions of the cities, but there are many exceptions. Nevertheless, it is difficult for men and women to carry the traditional religion – so linked to a locality, to local shrines and the local community – to a distant place. One of the strengths of the two world religions has been the way in which they have been able to unite people of different cultural backgrounds. On the other hand, there are places where Christianity or Islam has become within a few generations the folk religion of a rural area.

It is only fair to say that in Africa, as in other parts of the world, there are to be found an increasing number of men and women who reject all religious answers and would call themselves agnostics or atheists. Increasingly Western-educated young people fall into this category. But Africans have been, and still are, religious people and the atheists are fewer than one might expect.

Although it is true that Christianity and Islam are "traditional religions" for many Africans, it is convenient to reserve the term for the religious beliefs and practices of ethnic groups in Africa, for which no other convenient term exists. There may often be no word to translate "religion" in an African language, but religious beliefs are extremely important. Religion is linked to every part of life, not hived off as has become the case in the West, and every event in the life of an individual or a society is thought to have a supernatural cause. One acquires one's religion as a birthright; there is no conversion to it in Western terms, though there are ceremonies marking the life stages which are also connected with one's religious role in society. However, where men or women changed their social and political allegiance by accident of war, by purchase or by marriage, they would also change their religion.

It is difficult to discuss African religions historically. This is not to say that they have been totally static or that beliefs of one group may not have influenced and changed the beliefs of other groups. There is evidence to show that this has happened in some cases and it must have happened in many more. But without internal written documents, and with few shrines and temples built in long-lasting materials, it is difficult to record change over a long period. In most cases we can only discuss traditional religion from accounts written in the comparatively recent past.

Since each society differs in details of belief and practice, scholars have looked for a unifying concept that would enable them to speak of African religion rather than of African religions. For many 19th-century Europeans this concept was animism: the belief in myriad spirits inhabiting the material world. Ancestor worship was another such unifying concept. Scholars today prefer not to use either term, but both express some understanding of aspects of African belief. Some other terms – black magic, juju, fetish worship – are misleading and show no understanding of what they purport to describe.

A more recent student of African religion has written of the *force vitale* (living force) that links the animate and material worlds. This, like the rejected term animism, expresses the strong belief in a world where material objects possess, or are associated with, a living soul or spirit. This may be thought to be the spirit of a r   y dead ancestor, a nature spirit, or the spirit of a long-dead ancestor who has become a deity. All have power to bring good or evil consequences to the living.

This belief widely held across Africa, is associated with what has been called ancestor worship but which is better termed reverence for the living dead. Those of the clan who have died are still close at hand and are remembered by name for two or three generations. Gifts are offered to them at the household shrine, which may contain their bones. A little beer is spilled for them when men are drinking together and the news of the clan is reported to them. When illnesses or misfortunes occur a

African religions

Islam is the religion of the north, including the northern section of many of the West African nations. It is the religion also of the northeast, especially Somalia and the northern Sudan. In Muslim areas neither Christianity nor traditional religions have much following. Over the rest of Africa Christians of different denominations are found in greater or smaller numbers alongside adherents of traditional practices. Roman Catholics are strongly represented everywhere, and especially in the former Belgian territories of Congo (DRO), Rwanda and Burundi. Anglicans are almost completely confined to the former British territories. In South Africa the Dutch Reformed Church is part of the Afrikaner tradition, and Presbyterians of reformed theology are strong in Malawi, Kenya and Ghana. Lutheran churches are strongest in the former German colonies.

Methodists, Baptists and Congregationalists, Jehovah's Witnesses and Seventh Day Adventists are all to be found, following traditions taught by Western missionaries. The so-called independent churches are strongest in Ghana and Nigeria, Congo (DRO), Kenya, Zimbabwe and South Africa.

Right From the Kongo people in lower Congo (DRO) come figures usually known as nail fetishes. Nails and scraps of cloth are stuck into the figure, as need arises, to deflect evil influences from the individual. A "medicine" for the same purpose may be kept in a receptacle within the figure.

modern international boundary

area of Muslim majority today

area of significant Muslim minority today

southern extent of Muslim religion in 19th century

area where Christianity existed 1792

advance of Christian missionaries

missionary frontier and date

● Protestant mission

○ Catholic mission

Protestant mission

ABC	American Board of Commissioners for Foreign Missions
BM	Basel Mission
BpMS	Baptist Missionary Society
CMS	Church Missionary Society (C of E)
CSM	Church of Scotland Mission
DRC	Dutch Reformed Church
FCS	Free Church of Scotland
FFMA	Friends Foreign Mission Association
HAM	Heart of Africa Mission
LIM	Livingstone Interior Mission
LMS	London Missionary Society
MB	Moravian Brethren
MEC	Methodist Episcopal Church (USA)
NAM	North African Mission
NMS	Norwegian Missionary Society
PB	Plymouth Brethren
PCUS	Presbyterian Church of USA
PEC	Protestant Episcopal Church (USA)
RMS	Rhenish Missionary Society
SPG	Society for the Propagation of the Gospel (C of E)
UMCA	Universities Mission to Central Africa
WMS	Wesleyan Methodist Missionary Society

Catholic mission

F	Franciscans
HGF	Holy Ghost Fathers
SJ	Jesuits
WF	White Fathers

scale 1:34 000 000

0 ——— 1500 km

0 ——— 1000 mi

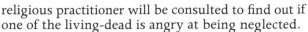

Top An Asante priest from southern Ghana. Such a personage is usually a man of prestige and influence in the local community.

Above Ancestor figures often mark burial places, where offerings are left for the departed ancestors. This remembrance pole is to appease the spirit of a young boy in southeast Angola.

Below A sacrificial ceremony in southern Ghana. Sacrifices of living animals are made to appease the living-dead or to show respect and worship to the High God. The celebrant may be the clan head or, in the ceremonies of popular cults, a professional priest who is keeper of a shrine.

religious practitioner will be consulted to find out if one of the living-dead is angry at being neglected.

The head of the family or clan usually acts as priest when offerings are made, though when there is a shrine with wider associations there may be full-time professional priests. But in almost every society there is a religious specialist often termed a witch doctor. His function is not to bewitch, but to discover the source of any form of evil and to advise how it might be got rid of. He may also be a herbalist and healer. Evil may come from neglected ancestors, from malevolent spirits or from witches. Witches are ordinary members of the community who may inherit their power or who may become witches involuntarily, through jealousy, hatred or greed. The elimination of witchcraft is important, for the witch may not know that he or she has bewitched another person. Magic and witchcraft cannot, in the African context, be entirely separated from religion. Charms are used to protect the wearers from evil spirits and it is such charms which in parts of West Africa were called fetish or juju. These names were also given to representations of gods and spirits placed in shrines. But to call the religion fetish worship or juju worship is wrong; the African does not believe that the representation is the spirit, any more than a Roman Catholic Christian believes that the image is the saint.

Belief in a high god, creator of the universe, is almost universal in Africa. But in many traditions he is not prayed to, being seen as remote and no longer concerned with human affairs, and the spirits are the important supernatural phenomena. In a few traditions intermediary spirits are almost absent and sacrifice is made to the one high god. Are Africans then monotheists? The question is hard to answer. Are the spirits gods? But there are few societies which might be called polytheistic in the Western sense, having a pantheon of named gods. One such is the Yoruba of western Nigeria, with gods like Shango, deity of lightning and thunder.

African religion is life-affirming, and contains little of asceticism. Its paramount values are harmony and unity within the family and clan, and with the living-dead and the spirits. It is essentially communal, not individual, and Africans who become Christians or Muslims carry these values into their new faith.

Arising out of Judaism, Christianity's essential message was that Jesus of Nazareth was the Messiah or Christ and the Son of God. His followers preached his resurrection and ascension and forgiveness of sins to those who believed this gospel, throughout the Greco-Roman world of their day. This included Egypt and North Africa as part of the Mediterranean complex, so there have been Christians in the African continent since shortly after the death of Christ. There have been, broadly, three phases of Christian penetration into Africa. The first was limited to North Africa and northeast Africa, and came to an end with the rise of Islam. The second phase was from the end of the 15th century when European sailors began to travel around the coast of Africa. A new phase began at the end of the 18th century which continues to the present day.

The origins of Christianity in Egypt are lost in legend, but a strong church existed there by the 2nd century AD. It established itself also across North

Africa, and Alexandria and Carthage (near modern Tunis) became centers of Christian learning. The Church produced scholars and martyrs. Christianity also traveled south along the Nile and into the highlands of Ethiopia. Christian churches flourished in the kingdoms of Nubia and survived into the 12th century. In Egypt the Arab-Muslim invasions of the 7th century reduced the number of Christians, but the Coptic Church has continued up to the present day. In the rest of North Africa, the ancient churches have disappeared completely. The Church has also survived in Ethiopia, keeping its links with the Egyptian and Syrian Churches. It has evolved distinctive styles of art and architecture and a unique liturgy that includes dancing and drumming – sure signs of African cultural adaptation. Another feature of the Ethiopian Church is its strong tradition of monasticism; it is from the monks that its bishops are chosen.

The second phase began when Europeans began to sail around Africa, from the end of the 15th century. The first were the Portuguese, who carried priests with them, and missionary work was begun in some areas. Greatest success was in the kingdom of Kongo (present-day Congo (DRO)) where the king and many of his court were baptized. A son of the king, educated in Portugal, was consecrated bishop. Yet this church never took deep root. The economic and territorial ambitions of the Portuguese were one handicap. Little has remained of the Christianity of the 16th and 17th centuries.

But from this time onwards there were many European coastal settlements, originally founded to provision ships. Later they developed into trading bases, forts and, tragically, depots for slave trading. At the Cape of Good Hope, a considerable number of the Dutch garrison became permanent settlers and as they flourished so did their Calvinist faith. At almost all the forts there were European chaplains who conducted schools for the settlement's children, including those of mixed race. A small number of local African children also attended the schools and received Christian teaching. But African Christians were not to be found far from the coastal settlements until the end of the 18th century.

At this time a new spirit of evangelization emerged in Europe and North America, coinciding with a reaction against the slave trade. Some former slaves were returned to form the basis of new settlements in Sierra Leone, Liberia, Libreville (Senegal) and, to a more limited extent, at Mombasa, and they came back as Christians. Such black Christians, whether returned former slaves or converts from the old coastal settlements, became the partners of the white missionaries in the pioneering ventures of the 19th century. But it was not until the partition of Africa among the Western powers, at the end of the century, that most Christian missions could really establish themselves in the interior. Now they were under the protection of colonial governments and able to use the new roads and railroads.

As the first phase of Christianity in Africa bequeathed churches linked to the eastern section of Christianity, so the second and third phases were linked to the western Church. The second phase began with Roman Catholics, with Protestants coming later to the forts; the third phase began with Protestant initiatives. But Roman Catholics soon followed, and today they outnumber Protestants in Africa. There is today a third grouping in black Africa, not linked to either Roman Catholic or Protestant, except where they have joined local councils of churches. They are sometimes termed independent or separatist churches. Some arose as schisms from mission-founded churches; others were established by leaders who had been under Christian influences of one kind or another. Since they have been less directly under the influence of western Christianity, these churches afford us valuable insights into the most Africanized forms of Christianity.

In worship they are vigorous and exuberant, using African musical instruments, dancing and drumming. Processions with banners are often seen, and many have uniforms for their members - usually white with symbolic badges and headgear. In many churches the person of the Holy Spirit is given a particularly high place, so much so that they are termed Pentecostal churches, though there is no direct connection with western Pentecostalism. A large grouping of these churches in West Africa are called *aladura* churches, and the term, meaning one who prays, indicates their particular emphasis on prayer for physical and spiritual healing. In other parts of Africa the same emphasis is found. In some churches Western and traditional medicines are totally proscribed. Whether or not this is the case, these churches place a high value on the harmony and unity of the fellowship and of the individual within himself.

Islam, like Christianity, entered Africa within a short time after its inception. Like Christianity, Islam owes much to the ancient religion of the Hebrews. Jesus is recognized as a prophet in the line of the prophet Moses, but the last and greatest prophet is Muhammad, who taught submission to the one god, Allah. As early as 640 AD, within eight years of Muhammad's death, some of his Arabic followers had begun their conquest of Egypt. These first Muslims came not as missionaries but as soldiers and settlers, and were often welcomed as saviors from the oppressive rule of Byzantium. They did not (as is sometimes believed) force their religion on the local people and were particularly tolerant of Jews and Christians, "people of the Book," who were not idolators. But over the years, as the result of intermarriage and to gain relief from taxation, many Christians became Muslims. Apostasy for Muslims was punishable by death.

The central tenet of Islam is belief in the one God, and confession of this belief is the first of the five "pillars of Islam." The others are daily prayer; giving of alms; pilgrimage to Mecca if possible; and the keeping of the fast in the month of Ramadan. The teachings of Muhammad, communicated to him by Allah, have been written down in the sacred Koran. Where Christians have stressed the necessity for the Bible to be translated into local languages so that it may be read by all believers, Muslims on the other hand emphasize the necessity for learning Arabic, so that the Koran may be read in the original. Its translation is not approved of by the most orthodox Muslims. So, as the religion spread, literacy in Arabic spread also.

Following the Arab conquest of Egypt, Islam slowly spread among the coastal and inland peoples of North Africa. Eventually, except for the Coptic

Top A Roman Catholic village church in Cameroon. Such small churches may be found over most of Africa, often built simply of local materials and identified only by their cross. The services are often led by a catechist or lay reader, for priests and ministers are too few, and consequently the sacraments are confined to special and infrequent occasions.

Above In lower Congo (DRO) the Christian tradition goes back to the coming of Portuguese explorers and missionaries in the 15th century. This cross with an African Christ speaks of the localization of Christianity which has taken place over the centuries.

Top In All Saints Cathedral in Nairobi, Kenya, African and European Christians kneel together to take communion from African and European priests. For many years this church was attended only by Europeans; now it is a parish church for all.

Above Processions and open-air celebrations are a feature of Christian churches of all traditions, reflecting the old customs whereby ceremonies were not confined to a special building. The procession here is of a Roman Catholic sorority in Cameroon.

Overleaf The Friday Mosque at Mopti, Mali. Wherever Muslims are found, mosques are built, for though the faithful may pray anywhere, there is an obligation to pray together where possible, and especially on the holy day, Friday. The mosque has a minaret from which the prayer call goes out, and here local materials have been used and local traditions followed to create a truly African mosque.

remnant in Egypt, North Africa became and has remained deeply Muslim in religion, culture and legal systems, with Islam as the state religion.

In a second phase Islam spread across the Sahara into West Africa, and up the Nile into the Sudan. The agents of Islam at this stage were traders and clerics, who often settled on the outskirts of West African cities, establishing their own mosques and schools and remaining somewhat separate from the local population. The ruling classes tended to adopt the new religion while the people of the countryside remained wholly outside it. By the 13th century the ruler of Mali and the ruler of Kanem were Muslims, and the great Mansa Musa of Mali astounded the Muslims of Egypt with his wealth and power when he went on the pilgrimage to Mecca in the 14th century. Islam also traveled down the east coast of Africa, taken by seafaring Arabs, some of whom settled and built up coastal cities. Here also some urbanized local people became Muslims. But at this time, in both West and East Africa, Islam continued as a parallel rather than as a replacement religion for traditional beliefs.

From the mid-18th century a new phase began. One development, continuing to the present day, has been the growth of adherence to *tariqa*, religious orders or brotherhoods, founded by charismatic religious reformers. Members of *tariqa* have their own special forms of devotion which they perform in addition to the required prayers. The two most influential and largest tariqa are the Tijaniyya and the Qadiriyya. Another development, not unconnected to the first, was a new exclusiveness and aggressiveness. African traditions and customs were no longer to be tolerated. The leaders were in many cases clerics, who had studied and traveled widely in the Islamic world. They set out to cleanse and purify the religion of fellow Muslims and to bring others into the faith, by force if necessary, using the concept of the *jihad* (holy war). These men, starting as religious reformers, often ended as rulers of great states. Such were Usuman dan Fodio of Sokoto (northern Nigeria) and 'Umar ibn Sa'id Tall of Tukolor (western Sudan). In areas where such movements occurred the structure of society became deeply Islamized, although large numbers of people remained outside the faith, and Islam became the state religion.

The fourth phase came with the expansion of Western influence and the imposition of new colonial regimes. In cities and towns all over Africa adherence to Islam became one mode of adaptation for the migrant entering an urban trans-ethnic community. Unlike Christianity, Islam did not have the advantage of proselytization through mission schools, but again it did not usually have the disadvantage of Christianity's link with the conqueror. Some rural communities also adopted Islam in the closing years of the 19th century. In areas where Islam had spread in this fourth phase, however, it is usually in competition with Christianity and traditional religion (in the countryside) and with modern secular society, and is strictly a religion rather than a total way of life.

Islam, which appears so monolithic to the outsider, has its own internal divisions: the main one, going back to the conflict over Muhammad's successors, resulted in the Sunni and Shi'i schools. Virtually all the Muslims of Africa are Sunni; the only Shi'i Muslims are Asian migrants in East Africa. Also to be found in a number of places are missionaries of the unorthodox Ahmaddiyya sect (with headquarters in Pakistan) whose influence is perhaps greater than their number. They have been active in controversy with Christians, and have pioneered in translating the Koran into African vernaculars.

Both Islam and Christianity are vital and growing religions in Africa today. In the worldwide gatherings of both faiths, African representatives are an increasingly important section. At the same time the observance of traditional religious rituals is probably decreasing, although some young university-educated people are advocating a deliberate return to traditional culture, including its religious aspects. It is doubtful whether the majority of Africans will ever take this seriously. Even where a head of state has sought to impose such a return (as with the call for "authenticity" in former Zaïre) it has not succeeded. African traditional values will certainly continue but in combination with many aspects of the modern industrialized West.

It is easy to cite political and sociological reasons for the moves to Islam and Christianity. But these are religions, and there are deep religious reasons too. Perhaps the strongest appeal of the two world religions is their emphasis on the power of God. There is a great deal of fear in traditional beliefs - fear of spirits and ancestors whose power to do evil seems to be exercised arbitrarily. This calls for a continued watch over one's actions, so that no unintended offense is committed. The high god was very remote, beyond the reach of man, for good or evil. But in Christianity and Islam the creator-god is preached as powerful and concerned with men and women: "Allah the compassionate"; "God is love." Both religions (despite sad failures) do unite their followers in a super-ethnic fellowship that seems to offer a better future for nations often torn by internal divisions.   J.M.

Yoruba Traditional Religion

Though the majority of the Yoruba in Nigeria and Benin (formerly Dahomey) are either Christian or Muslim, Yoruba traditional religion is by no means extinct. Moreover not only does it flourish among a minority of the estimated 13 million Yoruba in West Africa but it also survives in a very pure form in the West Indies and Brazil, having been implanted there during the era of the trans-Atlantic slave trade.

Yoruba traditional religion has a four-tiered system of spiritual or quasi-spiritual beings. The Supreme Being, Olodumare, also known as Olorun (owner of heaven), occupies the top tier. His ministers, the subordinate gods (*orisha*) are ranged along the second tier in some form of hierarchical order. Obatala is the most important of these lesser gods. Following on the subordinate gods, on the third tier are the deified ancestors such as Shango. Then there are the spirits associated with natural phenomena such as the earth (Ile), the rivers, mountains and trees.

The Supreme Being, Olodumare, is regarded as immortal, unique, omniscient, omnipotent and completely impartial in his judgments. The Yoruba, though they do not erect temples and shrines in his honor, do invoke, petition and praise Olodumare. By way of contrast, the subordinate gods and other spiritual beings have their own priests, temples, sanctuaries and shrines.

In addition to the more personal and private forms of worship given to Olodumare and the public cults associated with the lesser gods, respect and reverence for ancestors and divination constitute integral parts of Yoruba traditional religion. The Ifa oracle is the most widespread of the divination systems. Throughout Yorubaland there are dances and masquerades connected with the veneration of the dead and the health and general well-being of the community as a whole. The Oro and Egungun masquerades are two of the more widespread of the cults associated with the dead and the health of the community.   P.C.

Left A shrine of Obatala, who is widely acknowledged by the Yoruba to be the most important of the lesser gods. According to a number of Yoruba creation myths he played the major role as Olodumare's chief executive in the creation of the world. After Obatala himself had been taught how to mold the human form by Olodumare, he began to fashion men and women who were then infused with the principle of life by the Supreme Being.

Right The trickster god, Eshu, the harbinger of both good and evil, is the principal intermediary between heaven and earth. Eshu informs Olodumare of the activities both of the subordinate gods and of men. He has a place in every traditional household and no one fails to propitiate him.

Below There are different kinds of priests and sacred persons in Yorubaland. There are, for instance, priests attached to temples who offer sacrifices of various kinds, propitiatory, votive, thanksgiving and preventative among others. Then the different gods and deified ancestors have their own priests.

The priests of Shango are called Magba, those of Orunmila, Babalawo. After long and arduous training the priests are consecrated and invested with the power to offer sacrifice. In addition to the priests there are the sacred people, the mediums and devotees who look after the temples and shrines. Then there are the diviners. A priest may also divine, but a diviner may not offer sacrifice.

Below Some of the Yoruba divinities are worshiped on a more or less local basis, but others like Ogun are reverenced and worshiped throughout Yorubaland. Ogun, according to tradition, used his machete to clear a pathway for the gods when they first came to inhabit the earth. And on account of his skill with the machete and his strength he came to be regarded as the god of hunters, blacksmiths, butchers, barbers, soldiers and today truck and taxi drivers and all those who work with iron and steel.

It is Ogun too who witnesses pacts and convenants. When an adherent of the Yoruba traditional religion goes to a law court today he swears not on the Koran or Bible but on a piece of iron which is taken to represent and symbolize Ogun.

Above Great heroes or very gifted individuals are on occasions deified by the Yoruba. Shango, the power of the thunderstorm, the wrath of Olodumare, was, according to legend, king of Oyo. He was an autocrat and on discovering that attempts were being made to assassinate him, he fled Oyo and punished his former subjects by destroying their homes and villages by means of thunderstorms. The inhabitants of Oyo, believing that Shango had committed suicide and could not be responsible for their misfortune, consulted the oracle only to be told that Shango was in fact the author of their calamities.

The process of appeasement and propitiation began, ending in the deification of Shango. Today shrines of Shango abound everywhere in Yorubaland, and he is widely known also in North and South America and the West Indies. Only the Magba, the priests of Shango, are allowed to arrange for the burial of those killed in a thunderstorm.

Left The Yoruba use several different systems of divination. The most important objects in the Ifa system are the specially selected palm nuts, the tray which must be of a rectangular, circular or semicircular shape, the bell made of ivory or wood and used to invoke the oracular spirit, and the lots which may be animal teeth, cowrie shells or bits of broken pottery.

The Ifa priest (the Babalawo), perhaps the most highly trained of all the Yoruba priests, works from a group of 16 poems (*odus*) which are believed to contain all the experiences a human being is capable of undergoing.

Orunmila, one of the most important of the subordinate deities, is the power behind the oracle. He is imbued with Olodumare's wisdom and it is his favor that people seek.

Above left The Egungun masquerade was and still is today for some a social and religious function of great importance. The Egungun himself is regarded as the embodiment of the spirit of a deceased person believed to have returned from the spirit world to visit his "children." No part of the Egungun's body can be exposed to view for in seeing it one would cast eyes on the spirit enshrined therein and thereby break the spell and die.

Egunguns are thus robed from top to toe in costumes of cloth and fitted with a mask which is often a caricature of an animal such as a python or leopard, or a European or some other "foreigner." After a town or village has been purified with holy water and medicines, the masqueraders appear and the dancing and acrobatics begin.

Above left Some of the divinities associated with natural phenomena, the earth, rivers, mountains and trees, are male, some female, some good, some evil. Yemoja, a female deity and beneficent, is the goddess of rivers, streams, lakes and water in general: all water flows out from her body. Olokun, a male divinity, resides in the sea, controls its anger and distributes its benefits. Oya, goddess of the river Niger, is the author of heavy gales and strong winds. Oshun is the tutelary divinity of Oshogbo, and associated with a river bearing the same name. Oshun is a fertility goddess, who by means of her medicinal waters, gives the joy of childbirth to barren women.

The Ethiopian Church

The Ethiopian Church, monophysite in theology, goes back at least to the 4th century. It was once the most southern of a series of Christian churches along the Nile valley, but the Christian kingdoms of Nubia were gradually overwhelmed by Muslims from the north, and by the 15th century their Christianity had completely disappeared.

The Ethiopian Church survived. Its patriarch was an Egyptian appointed by the patriarch of Alexandria. At the capital of the kingdom, Aksum, the liturgical and literary language Geʿez developed. As well as the connections with Egypt, there were links with Jewish religion. King Solomon was believed to have fathered the child of the Queen of Sheba, and this child, Menelik, the Lion of Judah, was the founder of the Solomonid dynasty.

Most spectacular of the monuments of the Ethiopian Church are the monolithic churches of Lalibela, a remote mountain village in Welo Province, north of Addis Ababa, but once Ethiopia's capital. King Lalibela was founder of a new dynasty which took power from the Solomonid dynasty early in the 12th century. His immense church-building project, in which he used up his wealth, probably began as an effort to legitimize his rule and enhance his capital. But according to Ethiopian legend the task conferred sainthood on the king himself, who after the work was completed abdicated his throne and became a contemplative.

J.M.

The Ethiopian Church retains many features of other Eastern churches, such as a dual clergy of village priests, who must be married, and monks, from whom alone the bishops are chosen. It has preserved also some ancient Jewish customs such as circumcision and observance of the Sabbath (as well as Sunday). But its liturgies and ceremonies, though showing borrowings, have developed a distinct indigenous flavor.

Bottom Christmas at Lalibela. White-robed monks (blowing trumpets) line the rim of one of the trenches, while priests below join in dancing the liturgy to celebrate the birth of Christ.

Below Ecclesiastical education, including the reading of Geʿez, has traditionally taken place in monastery schools; here a deacon learns from older clergy in a monastery in Aksum, Tigre.

Left From above the stone church of St George at Lalibela shows as an immense cross. A square ditch was dug into the living rock, and the cruciform church was hewed out and hollowed inside. Entrance is by the sloping trench showing to the left of the church. Its roof is almost exactly level with the surrounding ground surface.

Top St George's Church rises 12 meters from a platform base which follows the cruciform shape of the church. It is only one of several similar churches at Lalibela; among others are the churches of St Mary, St Mascal and St Merkurios.

Above Murals depicting biblical scenes and incidents in the lives of saints are a feature of Ethiopian churches and monasteries. St George, slaying the dragon, with a frieze of typically Ethiopian cherubs, is shown in this mural from a church at Lake Tana, to the west of Lalibela.

EARLY MAN IN AFRICA

In his work on evolution in the 19th century, Darwin intimated that humans are probably of African origin because our closest living relatives, the gorilla and the chimpanzee, are entirely African and it seems reasonable to suppose that a common ancestor of humans and apes would have lived in Africa. This intuition of Darwin's has been vindicated by palaeontological and anthropological research. Olduvai Gorge in northern Tanzania and other sites in Kenya, Ethiopia, and South Africa have yielded a large collection of fossil specimens from which a meaningful pattern is becoming clear. We can now trace our ancestry back almost to the point at which two evolutionary lines diverged, one leading to modern apes, the other to humans. The available fossil evidence, with dates spaced from 4.5 million years ago to the present day, demonstrates that it was in Africa that this divergence occurred.

Our evolution was both biological and cultural. We are closely related to the African apes but not descended from them; together, we and the great apes are placed in the zoological family Hominidae. We should imagine a common ancestral group, living in the African woodland savannas several million years ago. One division of this group (ancestors of the gorillas) began specializing in forest living, mainly on the forest floor, and feeding on ground vegetation; a second (ancestors of the chimpanzees), lived in both forest and woodland, sometimes climbing, sometimes walking on the ground, and feeding on fruit and some meat, often using simple tools to obtain food. The third division kept its options open with one of its variants, possibly a forest-dweller, developing bipedalism (walking on two feet). Bipedalism left the hands free for holding, carrying, throwing, and manipulating. Dr Mary Leakey's recognition of bipedal footprints in

Olduvai Gorge cuts across the middle of the Serengeti Plain, Tanzania. A hundred meters deep and several kilometers long, the eroded sides of the gorge reveal two million years of human evolution in successive geological strata. From the 1930s onwards excavations here have uncovered a unique sequence of stone tools and fossil remains.

Early Stone Age sites

Early *Homo* fossils along with pebble tools, have been found at Olduvai Gorge, Lake Turkana, and elsewhere. *Homo erectus*, associated with the Acheulian (handax) culture, spread through most of the continent and beyond, between about 1.4 million and 100 000 years ago.

Middle and Late Stone Age cultures

Coinciding with the emergence of *Homo sapiens* around 100 000 years ago, the Middle Stone Age saw the beginnings of regional specializations in human culture. The map shows the three main traditions that can be discerned from the archaeological record.

The development of African agricultural systems (after Shaw, Harlan and others)

Agriculture in Africa began around 5000 BC. It was partly an indigenous development and partly due to the importation of food crops (wheat, barley) and domestic livestock from the Near East. African cereals (millet, sorghum) began to be cultivated in the area associated with the aquatic lifestyle of the Late Stone Age. Old Guinea crops (yam, oil palm, okra) were forest plants, the cultivation of which is of indeterminate antiquity. Southeast Asian crops (bananas, coconuts, etc.) were introduced from about 500 AD.

The spread of ironworking

Ironworking techniques appeared in North Africa in the middle of the last millennium BC. The general tendency of its spread from north to south supports those scholars who believe that iron technology was imported from the Near East.

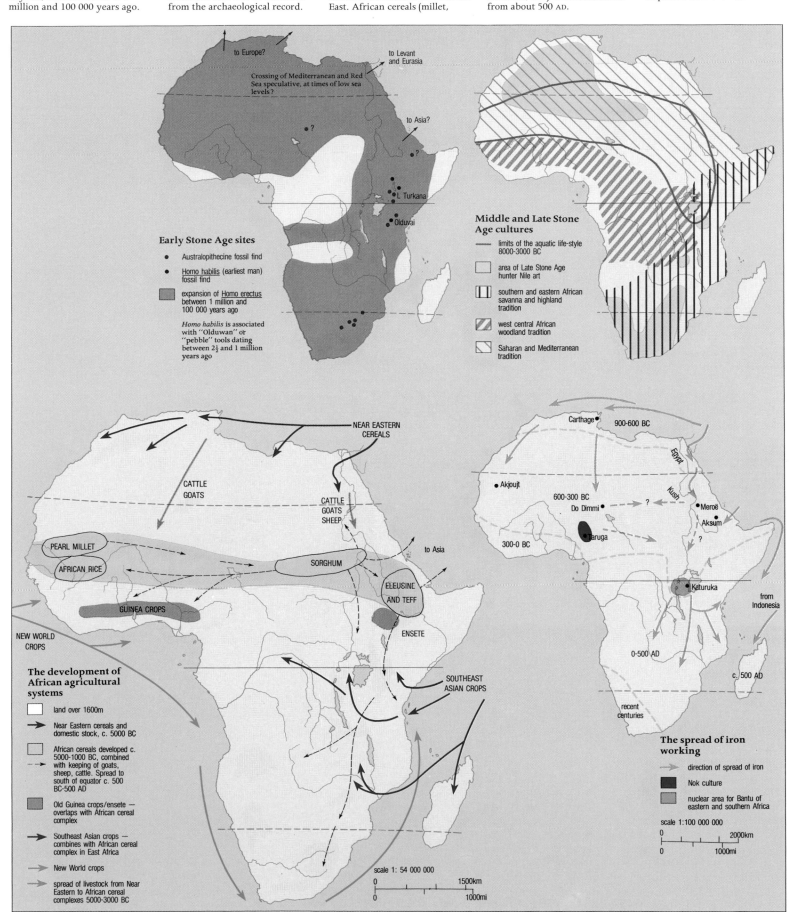

Early Stone Age sites
- ● Australopithecine fossil find
- ● *Homo habilis* (earliest man) fossil find
- expansion of *Homo erectus* between 1 million and 100 000 years ago

Homo habilis is associated with "Olduwan" or "pebble" tools dating between 2½ and 1 million years ago

Middle and Late Stone Age cultures
- limits of the aquatic life-style 8000-3000 BC
- area of Late Stone Age hunter Nile art
- southern and eastern African savanna and highland tradition
- west central African woodland tradition
- Saharan and Mediterranean tradition

The development of African agricultural systems
- land over 1600m
- Near Eastern cereals and domestic stock, c. 5000 BC
- African cereals developed c. 5000-1000 BC, combined with keeping of goats, sheep, cattle. Spread to south of equator c. 500 BC-500 AD
- Old Guinea crops/ensete — overlaps with African cereal complex
- Southeast Asian crops — combines with African cereal complex in East Africa
- New World crops
- spread of livestock from Near Eastern to African cereal complexes 5000-3000 BC

scale 1: 54 000 000
0 — 1500km
0 — 1000mi

The spread of iron working
- direction of spread of iron
- Nok culture
- nuclear area for Bantu of eastern and southern Africa

scale 1:100 000 000
0 — 2000km
0 — 1000mi

43

cemented mud at Laetoli, in northern Tanzania, shows that it was achieved at least 3.5 million years ago. *Ardipithecus ramidus*, the earliest known member of the human line, lived about 4.4 million years ago and may also have been bipedal.

The early members of the human line are known generally as australopithecines. They were small, standing about 1 to 1.5 meters tall, and had virtually no forehead, for their brain (measuring 500 cubic centimeters or less) was ape-sized, only about one-third of the capacity of that of a modern person. There were two types of australopithecines. The "robust" type, *Paranthropus* (sometimes called "nutcracker man"), had massive jaws, powerful molar teeth, and thick skulls to which huge jaw muscles were attached. They lived from about 2.6 to one million years ago.

It was probably from the other, lighter line, known as "gracile australopithecines", that modern humans arose. *Australopithecus anamensis*, living in Kenya about 4 million years ago, was bipedal but otherwise distinctly ape-like. *Australopithecus afarensis*, about 3.9 to 3.0 million years ago, and *A. africanus*, from 3 to 2 million years ago, had jaws, teeth and skeletons more like those of modern humans. Despite their name "gracile" australopithecines, their skulls were thicker than ours and their teeth bigger, but they had a smaller jaw and rounder foreheads than the "robust" ones.

The genus *Homo* emerged from australopithecine stock. There were several species, all much more primitive than modern humans; the best known is *Homo habilis*. Averaging 650 cubic centimeters, its brain was bigger than that of any australopithecine, and it may have been capable of some form of speech, but in many ways it still resembled the australopithecines.

The geographical extent of the australopithecines and early *Homo* species is imperfectly established. Plotting the finds merely records those places within the distribution area where unusually favorable conditions promoted fossilization, and where erosion, followed up by diligent scientific exploration, has revealed the bones. An alternative distribution test of earliest man may be attempted from stone tools, which preserve more readily than bones. The oldest known have been called "pebble tools" since frequently they were river pebbles from which a few flakes were struck to leave a crude cutting edge. Assemblages of such tools, associated with remains dated to 2.5–1.0 million years ago, are known from northern Tanzania, Uganda, Kenya, and Ethiopia. There are some examples in southern Africa and at the western and northwestern extremities of the continent.

Homo ergaster, which emerged two million or so years ago, was as tall as modern humans. Its brain size was about 800 cubic centimeters and it had a slender build with long legs, quite unlike *Homo habilis* and the australopithecines. About 1.4 million years ago the evolutionary line split into two; for the first time members of the human group (the species *Homo erectus*) spread out of Africa. Associated with the proto-human group that stayed in Africa was the development of more advanced and distinctive stone toolkits known as Acheulian, in which so-called handaxes are the most celebrated tool. Assemblages of Acheulian tools have been found in most countries in Africa.

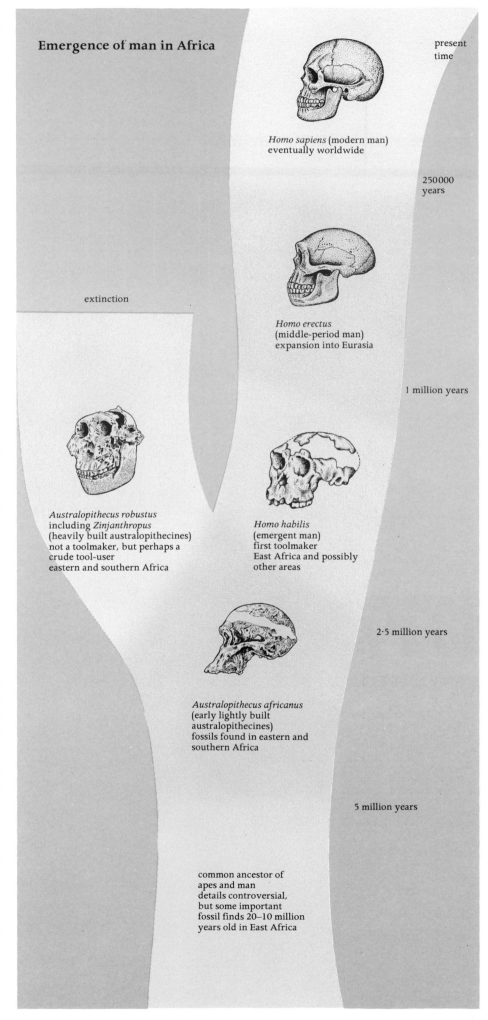

Emergence of man in Africa

present time

Homo sapiens (modern man) eventually worldwide

250000 years

Homo erectus (middle-period man) expansion into Eurasia

1 million years

extinction

Australopithecus robustus including *Zinjanthropus* (heavily built australopithecines) not a toolmaker, but perhaps a crude tool-user eastern and southern Africa

Homo habilis (emergent man) first toolmaker East Africa and possibly other areas

2·5 million years

Australopithecus africanus (early lightly built australopithecines) fossils found in eastern and southern Africa

5 million years

common ancestor of apes and man details controversial, but some important fossil finds 20–10 million years old in East Africa

The African archaeological sequence

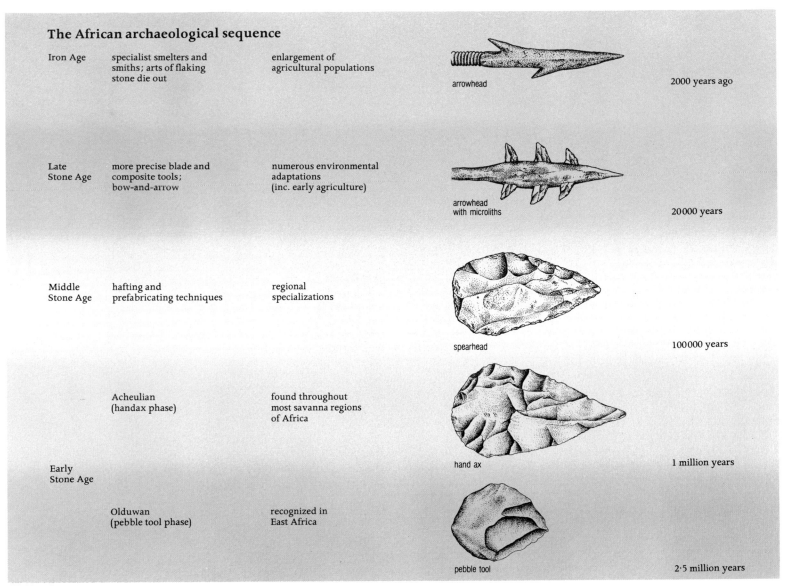

Iron Age	specialist smelters and smiths; arts of flaking stone die out	enlargement of agricultural populations	arrowhead	2000 years ago
Late Stone Age	more precise blade and composite tools; bow-and-arrow	numerous environmental adaptations (inc. early agriculture)	arrowhead with microliths	20000 years
Middle Stone Age	hafting and prefabricating techniques	regional specializations	spearhead	100000 years
Early Stone Age	Acheulian (handax phase)	found throughout most savanna regions of Africa	hand ax	1 million years
	Olduwan (pebble tool phase)	recognized in East Africa	pebble tool	2·5 million years

Above: The African archaeological sequence
The three-age system (Stone, Bronze, Iron Ages) does not apply in Africa, as, with the exception of Egypt, African cultures bypassed the Bronze Age. The dates of the different periods are very approximate and cannot be applied to the continent as a whole; for example, a Late Stone Age culture survived into the 20th century among the Bushmen of the Kalahari.

Left: The emergence of man in Africa
Available evidence suggests that the divergence of the evolutionary lines leading to humans and apes took place in Africa. *Australopithecus africanus* is known from skulls found at Taungs and Sterkfontein in South Africa. The "nutcracker man", *Paranthropus* species, found at Olduvai in 1959 by Dr Louis Leakey, was heavily built. That line became extinct about one million years ago.

It seems, however, that early people continued to shun the true forests of the Guinea coast and Congo basin and remained hunter–gatherers of the savanna. The many Saharan sites do not imply permanent occupation of the region, but periodic penetration and exploitation of the game at times when the climate was wetter, as the irregular succession of Pleistocene ice ages and interglacials brought alternately dry and wet conditions. Gradually Acheulian tools became more refined, and in total this technological tradition spanned a million years in Africa, eventually ending about 100 000 years ago, and from time to time Acheulian-using peoples spread into Europe, the Middle East, and Asia. In Europe, these Acheulian-users evolved into a sideshoot of the evolutionary bush, *H. neanderthalensis*, or "Neanderthal man", a contemporary of our direct ancestors, but not one of them.

Archaic humans appeared about one-quarter of a million years ago. They were similar to modern humans in many ways, but retained some primitive physical features from earlier species. Studies of the DNA carried in mitochondria, which are inherited only through the female line, led researchers to conclude some years ago that all modern humans carry mitochondrial DNA inherited from one female, who lived in Africa between 140 000 and 280 000 years ago (although it should not be thought that she was the only female alive at that time!). More recently, studies of the Y chromosome, inherited only through the male line, have found that apart from some Africans, all human males now carry genetic changes in that chromosome inherited from a male who lived in Africa between 100 000 and 200 000 years ago – but, once again, remember that he was not the only male. Genetic evidence therefore indicates that our direct ancestors lived in Africa.

Around 100 000 years ago – a time broadly coincidental with the emergence of the modern human type – real diversity in human ecology and behavior becomes apparent. The handaxes and other heavy equipment of the Early Stone Age were phased out. In their place were manufactured smaller, more precise and more efficient tools, the result of revolutionary techniques in working stone. These advances heralded greater ecological specialization, including penetration of the forests, and at the same time modern *Homo sapiens* spread out of Africa to replace Neanderthals and *Homo erectus* and occupy the whole world. Exquisite lanceheads for fishing have been found along forest rivers. In the eastern and southern grasslands there occur beautiful leaf-shaped points, doubtless used as spearheads for hunting savanna game. In the Sahara and the north, hafting was sometimes assisted by preparing a tang to the stone point. This tripartite division probably reflects reasonably

45

fairly the three main human-ecological regions of the continent, whose distinctive cultures evolved during the Middle Stone Age and continued in a way into the Late Stone Age, which dates from about 20 000 years ago.

The transition to Late Stone Age is marked by further technological innovations. Small fine blades were used in combination, several being inserted and glued into a groove prepared in a wooden handle or shaft, to produce knives, saws, spears and barbed arrows. The invention of the bow and arrow about this time marks an important advance in hunting technique.

As the Late Stone Age proceeded towards recent times, the archaeological evidence, helped by radiocarbon dates, reveals not only marked regional diversities but also cultural developments, some of them clearly reacting to environmental changes. These traditions and differences relate (though not always simply) to the cultural and population patterns of recent and present times. The first part of the Late Stone Age corresponded with a dry period in the tropics. But around 9000 BC a marked wet trend set in and lasted, with some oscillations, till 3000 BC. This promoted an extension of the savanna grasslands (and savanna animals, including ones that early man relied on for food) into the southern Sahara and its central highlands. It also meant longer and more permanent rivers, and the enlargement of lakes and the creation of new ones. Various fishes were thus able to extend impressively their ranges; hippos and crocodiles moved into the central Sahara.

Human populations likewise adapted to these new conditions and increased their numbers and their range. From around 7000 BC there radiated across the continent (from the western Sahara to the Nile and upriver to the East African rift valleys) a distinctive water-oriented way of life. These communities hunted aquatic animals and fished intensively, using nets, bone-pointed spears and harpoons, later supplemented by hook and line. With a reliable and concentrated food supply (even, it seems, without any formal cultivation) some communities became relatively settled and developed new crafts. Boating is an obvious one; but there is also evidence of matting, basketry and, most interesting of all, pottery.

This aquatic lifestyle began to break up regionally after 5000 BC, once the wet peak had passed. By 2000 BC it survived in only a few, rather secluded localities by shrunken lakes and rivers. This retreat coincided approximately with the advance of pastoralism and cultivation. Maybe some of the waterside people were assimilated piecemeal into the new food-producing communities: indeed much of the process of ennobling certain nutritious wild plants and grasses of the African savanna may have been pioneered by these settled and skilled waterfolk.

Although this last point remains speculative, what is now clear is that African agriculture was historically an indigenous development, and not something introduced from outside. This is especially true of West Africa where almost all the food crops of historical significance, in the forest and savanna zones alike, have been developed from wild African plants. In the savanna belt south of the Sahara several grasses were transformed into important and productive grain crops in the last five millennia BC.

Most important of these cereals is sorghum (guinea-corn), whose region of origin is between Lake Chad and the upper Nile. Of the true millets, eleusine (or finger) millet is native to the eastern African highlands, pearl (or bullrush) millet to the West African savanna and Sahel. And around the swamps of the upper Niger an indigenous rice was exploited and developed. While cereals are not naturally suited to wet forest regions, there is archaeological evidence for the early use of oil palm, and it is likely that this was accompanied by suitable tuberous starches. The yam which is now and has for a long time been the staple of southern Nigeria and Ghana is a seedless crop and as such leaves no obvious archaeological trace, so its real antiquity remains unknown. By about 2500–2300 BC (radiocarbon dates), eleusine millet, native to and domesticated in Africa, was being grown in South Asia.

Some crops have been introduced to sub-Saharan Africa in later times. Especially important for the wetter regions of eastern and equatorial Africa is the banana, which was carried around the Indian Ocean in the first millennium AD. Once adopted in Africa it has been enormously diversified to suit a variety of soils, climates, purposes and tastes. In very recent centuries several New World crops have been added, notably maize and cassava. The temperate cereals of Near Eastern origin, wheat and barley, have of course been very important for North Africa, and were cultivated in Egypt from about 5000 BC. Further south their relevance has been extremely marginal.

Cattle, goats and sheep penetrated from northern Africa to become the important domestic animals of the African savannas (with goats being kept by cultivators in the forest clearings too). They were kept in North Africa as early as 5000 BC and in the favorable conditions then prevailing their range was soon extended up the Nile and into the central Saharan highlands. This brought pastoralists into contact with the earlier established aquatic people. Drier conditions affected both economies; they forced Saharan cattle southward no later than 3000 BC. By 1000 BC cattle and goats were being kept by the forest edge in West Africa and also over much of the East African highlands.

Thus, from about 7000 BC, productive economies based on fishing, livestock and various types of agriculture were pioneered, with success leading to cultural and population expansion. We are not yet able to assign these various developments to particular ethnic or language groups, but the combined efforts of linguists, anthropologists and archaeologists are making some progress here. What is clear is that these various economic and cultural developments were formative in the dominance of the modern Negroid type in sub-Saharan Africa.

From much earlier, probably Middle Stone Age times, a general distinction was emerging between the African peoples south of the Sahara and the Caucasoid type of the Mediterranean, including North Africa. For in its more arid periods the Sahara constituted a barrier, at least relatively. Within the African stock subdivisions naturally developed. The pygmy subtype adapted to a specialized hunting-gathering life in the thick forests of the Congo basin; in southern Africa and in east-

Top Tuareg relax in front of prehistoric paintings in a rock shelter at Sefar in the Tassili-n-Ajjer, southern Algeria. The monstrous human figure, 3·25 meters tall, forms the centerpiece of a scene with supliant women. Several distinct styles appear in Saharan rock art but they are difficult to date precisely.

Above Masked hunters attack an eland in this scene from the Kamberg rock shelter in the Drakensberg mountains of eastern South Africa. Eland, often depicted with meticulous realism, were a favorite subject of Bushman art.

ously. Archaeologically this Early Iron Age settlement across the savannas of eastern and southern Africa is documented by numerous sites of agricultural homesteads with distinctive related pottery styles. By contrast, in most regions north of the equator, agriculture and pastoralism were considerably older, so that iron when it first appeared did not promote such spectacular population movements. It did however improve agricultural efficiency. There were, moreover, all sorts of minor adjustments within an already very complicated situation — as the linguistic map for the whole region between the Sahara and the equator shows.

Recent archaeological research indicates that as early as 600 to 300 BC iron was being mined, smelted and forged by a number of widely separated communities in the savannas and woodlands as far south as Lake Victoria. Three regions in particular stand out: central Nigeria, the interlacustrine region (notably northwestern Tanzania) and the middle Nile. It is now clear that there was a rapid radiation of the knowledge of iron between the Sahara and the equator (and even beyond) around the middle of the first millennium BC.

Some scholars argue that ironworking may have been invented south of the Sahara, independent of outside stimulus. However, as new discoveries push the dates back closer to those for the Mediterranean, it becomes more likely that developments in the two regions were connected, especially in view of the basic similarity of techniques. A central Saharan link looks likely from comparison of early smelting furnaces in Nigeria with those of northwestern Africa. From the beginning, however, iron technology south of the Sahara and the toolkits produced for domestic, agricultural and military purposes began developing along lines distinct from those of the Mediterranean.

In this period it is possible to discern some of the broader ethnic, linguistic and cultural groupings of African peoples that still persist — the Bantu, for instance. But the individual peoples of recent centuries had not then emerged, nor on the whole had the famous kingdoms of later Africa. A few examples belong to this Early Iron Age period; especially celebrated is the kingdom of Cush (or Kush) along the middle Nile which flourished during the last centuries BC and the earliest AD.

Despite instances of contact with the wider world in Early Iron Age times, either across the Sahara or through the Red Sea and Indian Ocean sailing routes, the fuller development of such commercial and cultural contact has happened during the last millennium. But it should not be inferred from this that trade was previously unknown in Africa: local and regional trade in essential commodities was definitely ancient (and was a prerequisite for the evolution of long-distance traffic in precious goods). Grains and other cultivated foods, livestock and skins would have been traded within African communities and between neighboring ones, especially along the borders of contrasting ecological zones. Crafts, moreover, imply specialization and trade; of these, pottery and more particularly ironworking tended to be concentrated in suitable localities. Sources of salt are rare in the interior and were therefore prized, influencing the siting of markets, and the directions of trade.

J.E.G.S.

ern Africa as far north as Tanzania, the type known as "Bushmanoid" was dominant until the early centuries AD. In these southerly savanna regions agriculture and domestic livestock penetrated late, only during the Iron Age. Here a hunting and gathering culture persisted and is well attested at numerous campsites. Many of these are natural rock-shelters, where the hunters frequently painted the animals they loved to chase: eland, giraffe, elephant and others, often realistically and beautifully executed. Thousands of such paintings are known in southern Africa; there is a smaller group, probably related, in central Tanzania. (But the hunter rock art of the Sahara, generally older than the cattle paintings there, is probably unrelated to that of the south.) The tradition is clearly many thousands of years old. The so-called Bushmen, now confined to semidesert areas of the Kalahari, are essentially descendants of this once widespread hunting population in eastern and southern Africa. Studies of surviving Bushmen communities and of their Khoisan languages are therefore important in assisting an understanding of the Late Stone Age way of life and in particular of the beliefs behind the rock art. But the comparison is not a perfect one, for the present Bushmen are confined to semi-desert areas, having over 2000 years lost the best savanna lands to the southward-expanding agricultural and iron-using Bantu.

The expansion of people with early Bantu languages through the southern third of Africa during the first five centuries AD showed agricultural economy and iron technology extending their ranges together where neither had been known previ-

KINGDOMS AND EMPIRES

In Africa as everywhere else in the world, people organized themselves for countless millennia into small, more or less self-sufficient political communities. From about the fourth millennium BC they began forming more centralized units, owing allegiance to a king. By the middle of the 19th century the majority of Africans were under some kind of monarchical rule. But one must beware of seeing the establishment of royal government as inevitable progress or an inner teleological necessity. Many rejected it. Well into the 20th century millions remained for choice within loosely organized political structures, without kings or apparatus of continuous government, including large populations like the Igbo and Tiv of modern Nigeria.

If people reorganize themselves politically with a new form of government there must first be some organizing stimulus. The earliest African kingdom, Egypt, grew up through control of the flood waters of the Nile delta. Predicting and controlling annual floods demanded rigorous organization of land and people – under control of one ruler. From towards the end of the fourth millennium BC Egypt was united under a succession of kings who ruled, with interregna, until the conquest by the Greeks in 332 BC, leaving for posterity a wonderful legacy of building, painting and sculpture, much of it designed to glorify the monarchy.

Higher up the Nile arose the kingdom of Cush (or Kush). A province of Egypt at some periods, it developed as a separate entity with its own distinctive culture. During the 8th century BC Cushite kings conquered Egypt and ruled it for about 80 years. Subsequently it survived as a separate kingdom, wealthy from trade in tropical produce, and exploiting its iron resources, with its capital eventually at Meroe. Temples, burial pyramids and palaces were built, deriving stylistically from Egypt but executed in a distinctively Meroitic style. A Meroitic script evolved, quite different from the Egyptian hieroglyphs. In the 4th century AD it was destroyed, probably by neighboring Nubian peoples who founded their own kingdoms which were converted to Christianity by missionaries from Constantinople.

In the rest of Mediterranean Africa the organizing stimulus came from outside. Phoenicians founded the Carthaginian republic, stimulating their African neighbors to form rival inland kingdoms: Numidia (roughly modern Algeria) and Mauretania (roughly modern Morocco). The Numidians allied with the Romans to destroy Carthage, but ultimately both kingdoms were annexed to the Roman empire. The Romans also annexed coastal Tripolitania and Cyrenaica which were Greek settlements, but not their hinterland where, in country now desert, the African kingdom of Garama maintained its independence.

During the 7th century the whole of Mediterranean Africa was conquered by Muslim Arabs. The Berbers, lineage-based desert peoples like the Arabs, adopted Islam, but grew restive under Arab rule. In the 9th century the Berber Fatimid family asserted political independence and conquered a state which extended over Egypt to Syria and Arabia. During this period of African empire, Cairo (the Fatimid capital) was built up with beautiful palaces and mosques, including the great center of higher Muslim learning, the Al-Azhar mosque, founded about 970. In the 12th century Turkish rulers drove the Fatimids from Egypt. Thenceforth Turkish governments (after 1453 centered on Constantinople) held sovereignty over Egypt until the 20th century.

In the Maghreb, Berber rule continued. Two successive Muslim reform movements (known to Europeans as Almoravid and Almohad) extended it north over Spain. But by the 13th century the empire had broken down into small rival states. During the 16th century most of the Mediterranean shore became part of the Turkish empire. Morocco however remained independent under its own Muslim rulers.

Trade sometimes provided the stimulus towards the institution of monarchical government. The kingdom of Aksum, on the northeastern edge of the Ethiopian plateau, grew wealthy through control of the neighboring Red Sea port of Adulis, trading

African kingdoms
At successive periods kingdoms and empires covered much of Africa, though there were always peoples who for choice retained loosely structured political organizations. Almost all were of African origin. Only along the Mediterranean shore, where Romans and then Arabs invaded, and in the east African city-states were outside political influences significant. Elsewhere indigenous political systems developed, reflecting the socioeconomic organization of the different peoples. The early 19th century in particular was a period of widespread state building, with powerful rulers creating nation-states all over the continent – a process thwarted in the last decades of the century by European conquest.

scale 1:54 000 000

0   1500km

0   1000mi

By the beginning of the 1st century AD Aksum, from which the kingdom of Ethiopia was to emerge, was a powerful trading state. Its kings caused tall, flat-sided monoliths (stelae) to be raised, some over 30 meters high. Originally there were more than a hundred at Aksum. Now only one remains standing.

with the Indian Ocean countries and dominating the peoples of southern Arabia. Its kings commemorated their glories with stone stelae, up to 30 meters high, surmounting subterranean royal tombs. In the mid-4th century King Ezana adopted Christianity. But with the rise of Islam, Aksum lost control of the seaboard to Muslim rulers. It developed inland as the mountain kingdom of Ethiopia, with its heartland in Amhara on the northwestern plateau. The Ethiopian Church followed the monophysite belief of the Coptic Church of Alexandria, but with its own liturgical language, Ge'ez, and distinctive rites. It was closely linked with the monarchy and used as an instrument of government, particularly after the accession of the Solomonian dynasty in the 13th century. The kings enriched it with landed estates. Churches and monasteries proliferated.

Trade also provided an organizing stimulus in West Africa: kingdoms grew out of markets. Trade across the Sahara was immensely stimulated when camels were introduced in about the 3rd century AD. Gold mined in the forest country around the sources of the Niger, Senegal and Volta was taken north to market centers on the grassland edge of the desert (the sahel) and thence by camel to North Africa. Much of it was ultimately exported to Europe, which relied on West African gold until American resources became available. Those who

gained control of an urban market center could levy customs duties and taxes on the traders and brokers, and extract the surplus product from the surrounding lineage-organized farmers and pastoralists, thus turning themselves into kings.

Some of the sahel kingdoms were founded by Berber or other desert peoples who moved south to dominate the trading cities, others by indigenous individuals or groups who gained power by force or persuasion. Ghana, the largest of the early kingdoms of the western Sudan, was already flourishing by the 8th century. Its Soninke king and his opulent court were supported by control of the export trade in gold, copper and salt, and of the subject rural population.

North African traders brought Islam to the western Sudan. Most traders adopted it, but the mass of the people retained their own religions. Indeed until the 20th century Muslims were a small minority in West Africa. Hence any king who adopted Islam had to go on performing indigenous rituals to keep his people's allegiance. The king of Takrur in the far west is believed to have been the first to adopt Islam, in the 11th century. In the kingdom of Mali, which succeeded Ghana during the 13th century as the predominant state in the western Sudan, the kings became Muslims. Some undertook the pilgrimage to Mecca, including

Great Zimbabwe

In the gold-mining country around the Zambezi, kingdoms grew up from about the 7th century AD, evidenced by the discovery of royal burial sites. In the eastern part (modern Zimbabwe and Mozambique) walled stone enclosures, *zimbabwes*, were built for the kings. The ruins of several hundred survive. The most spectacular is the palace known as Great Zimbabwe, built by the Shona people. Construction was spread over about 400 years. Work began in the early 11th century and reached its peak in the early 15th. Then the king moved away. It is not altogether clear why the site was abandoned, but it seems likely that the soil around it had become exhausted and could no longer maintain a royal court. Pastoralism was the dominant method of subsistence, and the land may have been overgrazed. Though no longer a royal residence, it remained an important religious shrine until the 19th century. Despite legends put about by Europeans prospecting for gold that Great Zimbabwe was built by mysterious Asian or European immigrants, archaeologists have conclusively shown that it and the other *zimbabwes* were of African construction. C.F.

Mansa Musa, whose spectacular munificence, lavishing presents of gold as he went, caused the price of gold in Egypt to fall. In the late 15th century the Mali hegemony was replaced by that of Songhay, which survived until 1591 when it was overthrown by invasion from Morocco.

Trade from the central Sudan went north-eastward to Tripoli and Egypt. South of Lake Chad the kingdom of Kanem (later Bornu) was founded in the 8th or 9th century by the Saifawa dynasty which ruled until 1846. Eastwards the Keira dynasty founded the kingdom of Darfur. Further east, in the Nile valley, Muslim rulers supplanted the Christian kings of Nubia during the 14th century. Later they were conquered by the Funj people who moved up the Nile, adopted Islam and established the kingdom of Sinnar. Thus right across the Sudan, from Nile to Atlantic, stretched a series of kingdoms in which Muslim rulers controlled non-Muslim, lineage-organized peoples.

In the grasslands and forests of the lower Niger too, kingdoms grew up from market centers. The Hausa kingdoms developed through trade, Katsina and Kano growing into large cities through industry (textile-weaving and leather-working for export) as well as commerce. Further south were the Yoruba kingdoms, of which Oyo in the northern grasslands grew to dominate the rest; near the coast was Benin. The forest kingdoms carried on the fine sculpture tradition already evolved among the so-called Nok people further north, and created new and rich styles of court art, particularly in Ife and Benin. Across the Niger a royal burial containing elaborate sculpture has been found at Igbo-Ukwu.

From about the end of the first millennium BC, iron-using peoples who spoke some kind of Bantu language began moving out from a homeland in the grasslands between Lake Chad and the Benue river. They moved gradually, in small communities, not as an invading horde, among the indigenous hunter–gatherer and pastoral peoples. Eventually they peopled most of subequatorial Africa. Those who settled in the mineral-rich country around the upper reaches of the Zaïre and Zambezi exploited the gold, copper and iron resources. Gold was exported overseas (as from West Africa), carried down the Zambezi to Sofala and thence to the Indian Ocean trading sphere. Chinese porcelain and other Oriental wares were imported in exchange. Here, too, kingdoms grew up, through control of trade and of natural resources, particularly cattle. In the kingdoms of the lower Zambezi the Shona people constructed large stone buildings for their kings, the most famous being Great Zimbabwe. Further inland the Lunda, Luba and Bemba also organized kingdoms.

Along the East African coast Arabs and other Asians came to trade with the Bantu population. Their market centers developed into 30 city-states, including Mogadisho, Malindi, Mombasa and Kilwa, each under its own ruler, competing for control of the gold trade from the south. Politically disunited, they shared a common religion, Islam, and the Swahili language and culture that grew up among the Afro–Arab inhabitants – a fusion of Bantu and Arabic elements. Handsome mosques and palaces were built in a distinctive style out of locally cut coral.

It is not clear what stimulated the organization of kingdoms around the great lakes. State building seems to have begun at a period when immigrant pastoralists combined with indigenous cultivators; mixed farming gave rise to a better diet, and hence larger populations. Some kingdoms were founded by immigrants from the upper Nile valley, like the Luo. An earlier generation of historians assumed that they all derived from conquest by pastoralist Nilotes. But though in all the kingdoms (which included Bunyoro, Buganda, Nkore, Rwanda and Burundi) ruling clans claiming alien origin maintained an ascendancy, sometimes based on control of cattle, over subordinate clans, there is no evidence that they had a common origin or formed a cohesive conquest group. East of the great lakes the peoples retained their loosely structured political organizations.

Forms of government varied greatly, but it seems safe to say that these African kingdoms, excepting ancient Egypt, were usually constitutional monarchies. Though in any society where sacred and secular are not strictly differentiated – which they were not in these kingdoms – a ruler will tend to claim divine authority, divinity was hedged. Royal power was limited by recognized political controls – often relics of the non-hierarchical forms they had superseded. Succession disputes, when a king died, prevented the accumulation of hereditary powers that automatic primogeniture may bring. Wealth was customarily redistributed, preventing capital formation by kings or subjects. Usually men ruled, but in some kingdoms queen mothers had recognized powers.

Direct European trading contacts, beginning in the 15th century, gradually drew coastal West Africa into the orbit of expanding European capitalism. Africa became a market for the growing manufactures of Europe and a supplier of raw materials and labor – the slaves shipped across the Atlantic. But in most places the political structures were unaffected. Europeans came as traders, not invaders, paying customs duties and rents to African rulers who retained sovereignty over the European trading posts. Some kingdoms grew more powerful through the slave trade, particularly Asante and Dahomey.

Only in southern Africa did the Portuguese establish a small colonial presence, in coastal Angola (where, after a century of warfare, they destroyed the Mbundu kingdom and seriously weakened the inland kingdom of Kongo) and to a much lesser extent in coastal Mozambique. They also dominated the East African Swahili city-states until supplanted there in the 17th century by the sultans of Oman.

In the extreme south, around the Cape of Good Hope, the rainfall pattern did not fit the Bantu-speaking peoples' agriculture. The land was inhabited by small, loosely organized chiefdoms of cattle-herding Khoikhoi (Hottentots). In 1652 the Dutch East India Company established a trading post among them. Eventually, by persuasion and then force, the European settlers (who came to call themselves Afrikaners) reduced the Khoikhoi to subjection.

The 18th and 19th centuries saw a political transformation of the western Sudan. Many strict Muslims resented having to obey nominally Muslim governments which tolerated and practiced non-Muslim rites. About 1725 a full-scale *jihad* started in

Above left The kingdom of Bunyoro, in what is today Uganda, was probably founded in the 15th century, one of the largest of the great lakes kingdoms. Here the Mukama (king of Bunyoro) appears with his royal retinue and regalia. The monarchy was abolished in 1966.

the upland kingdom of Fouta Djallon where a group of Muslim scholars and traders, supported by discontented non-Muslims with political grievances, overthrew the government and established a Muslim state. Their success set off a series of *jihads* throughout the western Sudan, the most famous being those of Usuman dan Fodio in Hausaland, which began in 1804, and of al-Haj 'Umar in Segu (Upper Niger) in the early 1860s. The old kingdoms were replaced by new Muslim states, governed ostensibly by the *shari'a* (Muslim law), though it could not always be strictly enforced.

Among the Yoruba, the kingdom of Oyo broke down, and from the early 1820s the Yoruba states began fighting one another, each trying to gain supremacy. *Jihad* leaders from Hausaland, called in to help, ended by taking over northern Yorubaland themselves. Their advance southwards, "to dip the Koran into the sea," as they put it, was checked at the edge of the forest country. Meanwhile the Yoruba civil wars continued intermittently, almost until the end of the century.

Some Muslim leaders used the rhetoric of *jihad* to create personal empires. Such were Samori Touré, who conquered a large area around the upper Niger in the 1870s and 1880s, and Rabih who, having established himself in the central Sudan, southwest of Darfur, advanced westwards and in 1893 conquered Bornu, where in 1846 a Muslim leader had supplanted the ancient Saifawa dynasty. In the eastern Sudan another Muslim leader, Muhammad Ahmad, proclaimed himself the *Mahdi* in 1881, and conquered a large state which was taken over at his death by his successor the *Khalifa* Abdallahi. So by the last decades of the 19th century nearly the whole Sudan, from Nile almost to Atlantic, was ruled by recently installed, dynamic Muslim governments.

In Egypt, nominally part of the Turkish empire, during the early 19th century an Albanian officer, Muhammad Ali, became hereditary ruler of what was virtually an independent state, modeled on the secular states of Europe, and expanding up the Nile. In Ethiopia, where feuds among the nobility during the 17th and 18th centuries almost dissipated central authority, the power of the monarchy was revived in the early 19th century by a usurping king, Tewodros. Under the rule of his successors, notably Menelik, Ethiopia became a powerful, aggressive state, whose boundaries by 1902 stretched far beyond the area of the historic kingdom over the whole plateau and down on to the coastal plains.

In southern Africa radical political changes were stimulated early in the 19th century by the transformation of the Nguni peoples of the southeast coast from a lineage-based society into a militarized nation-state, the Zulu kingdom. Under their ruthless king Chaka, the Zulu conquered their neighbors and set off a series of bitter wars (the *Mfecane*) which depopulated large parts of the interior, leaving them vulnerable to Afrikaner expansion. Sotho refugees from these wars were organized by a skillful leader, Moshoeshoe, into the mountain kingdom of Lesotho. Near the Indian Ocean coast others, under Sobhuza, founded the Swazi kingdom. To the west Tswana kingdoms developed. Thus the political pattern changed, states based on national allegiance replacing the former lineage-based systems.

Aggressive migrant armies from Chaka's kingdom moved north. The Ndebele, under Mzilikazi, established themselves among the Shona beyond the Limpopo. The Ngoni, under Zwangendaba, brought under their rule peoples in the modern Tanzania, Malawi and Zambia, over 1600 kilometers away from their homeland. Such large-scale militarized invasions were something new – very

Above A ceremonial procession in Niger. The military strength of the kingdoms of the western Sudan, which flourished from about the 8th to the 19th century, was based partly on cavalry. Horses had to be imported from North Africa across the Sahara to Bornu and the other kingdoms, as they do not breed easily in central Africa.

Above right Muhammad Ali (1769–1849), a Turkish officer of Albanian origin, seized power in Egypt in 1805 with the help of the Cairo population, and founded a dynasty that ruled until 1952. He sent military expeditions up the Nile and established Egyptian claims over what is today the Republic of the Sudan.

different from the small-scale movements hitherto usual.

The Omani Sultan Seyyid Said, who controlled the East African coastal cities, made Zanzibar his capital in 1840. Trading networks were established inland along routes already opened up by Nyamwezi ivory traders. As well as ivory, the Zanzibari traders obtained slaves which were in demand on Zanzibar Island, where a plantation economy developed, growing cloves for export. Small communities of Zanzibari traders settled themselves along the inland trade routes, trading with African suppliers.

Enterprising African traders took advantage of the expanding economy to gain political power – for example, Msiri, who won himself a kingdom in the Lunda country of the eastern Zaïre basin, ruling his subjects autocratically. A few Zanzibari traders, notably Tipu Tib, also turned themselves into rulers. The new trading networks opened up the lakes kingdoms, till then unconnected to the coast by trade, particularly Buganda, where the kings began seeking to break down existing constitutional checks and introduce absolute rule. The disturbances caused by the Ngoni invasions also stimulated political change. The Fipa and Hehe peoples of present-day southern Tanzania seem to have reorganized themselves into more centralized monarchies. Thus from the upper waters of the Zaïre, eastwards to the coast, political allegiances and structures were changing.

By the last decades of the 19th century the older kingdoms and clan-based communities were disappearing. States of new types, organized on their own indigenous lines, were dividing up the continent, an internally generated political process that owed little to European pressure. This already partially completed African partition of Africa was however forestalled by the European partition.　　　C.F.

Asante Ceremonial Regalia

The kingdom of Asante, in the modern state of Ghana, rose to power in the early 18th century under *Asantahene* (king) Osei Tutu. To strengthen the power of Asante he and his chief priest revised the constitution, deliberately using regalia as constitutional symbols. Until his time the royal throne (a stool) had symbolized the individual ruler. Osei Tutu substituted for it a special Golden Stool, said to have descended from heaven into his lap, symbolizing the Asante nation. Thus the ruler would die, but the nation live on in the stool. Every year the people assembled after the yam harvest for a national festival, the *Odwira* (misleadingly called by Europeans the Yam Custom), where the nation was glorified, and the national identity of its people reinforced, by purificatory ceremonies linking together the living and the dead. The Golden Stool,

hung with the golden death masks of generals defeated by Asante armies, was carried in procession and placed on a throne without ever touching the ground. Royal power was further manifested in the proliferation of regalia worn and used by the *Asantahene* and his subordinate chiefs, devised as symbols of their political status. Shielded from the sun by vast umbrellas, which were topped by gold-plated insignia with symbolic meanings, they were loaded with ornaments, usually of gold or gold-plated, since Asante lies in a gold-mining region. Their golden crowns, breastplates, bracelets, rings, even sandals, were worked with elaborate designs of symbolic significance, conveying an overwhelming sense of opulence, dignity and supernatural authority.

C.F.

Above A chief wears a distinctive *kente* cloth, woven on a narrow loom. The narrow strips are sewn together into a cloth, worn thrown over one shoulder. There are special types of patterned silk cloths worn only by royalty and chiefs.

Top right Asante thrones take the form of backless stools. Some chiefs also have *asipim* chairs with backs, as depicted here, probably copied from chairs used by early European traders. The wooden frame is studded with brass nails.

Right Elderly chiefs, holding gold-hilted state swords and protected by umbrellas, mourn the death of *Asantahene* Sir Agyeman Prempeh II in 1970. Installed in 1935, Prempeh II revived the monarchy, suppressed during the first decades of British rule, and restored its ceremonies to something of their former splendor.

Far right Musicians with drums and wooden gongs at the *Asantahene*'s funeral. The royal funeral ceremonies are spread out over a whole year after an *Asantahene*'s death and involve all the people.

Far left Chiefs with their retinue of wives and attendants waiting on the *Asantahene,* protected by ceremonial umbrellas and attended by a musician with a side-blown horn. The chief in the foreground wears a distinctive *kente* cloth, a gold-hilted state sword, a gold bracelet and an elaborate gold ring.

Left Chiefs attending on the *Asantahene* wearing ceremonial gold-plated headdresses.

Below Musicians blowing side-blown ivory horns at an Asante state ceremony. Each chief has his own horn-blower who carries out special duties. He sounds on his horn the distinctive notes which identify the chief and warn people of his presence. Each type of horn has its own name.

EUROPE IN AFRICA

In the last two decades of the 19th century almost the whole of Africa was rapidly taken under European political control; the colonies and protectorates which were then established are substantially the states of modern independent Africa. Yet the interaction between Europe and Africa has a history going back much further and modern Africa is as much the creation of this earlier series of contacts as of the colonial period itself. Of course, neither the story of European contacts nor that of the creation of states tells the whole story of modern Africa; even at the height of colonial rule, Africans maintained their own ways of organizing their social lives, worshiping God and expressing their cultural values. Nor were they wholly without the ability to take initiatives in the political and economic fields.

Certainly the voyages promoted by Prince Henry the Navigator in the 15th century resulted in contacts on a basis of equality with societies on the western side of Africa. Along the West African coast as far as the Bight of Benin, the Portuguese and other European traders accepted a role as tenants of African rulers. Further south and on the east, however, by about 1600, when the great military fortress of Fort Jesus had been built at Mombasa, the Portuguese were attempting to dominate – for several reasons. In the first place Islam had to be made to yield to Christianity. Hence the attempt to take the ancient Christian kingdom of Ethiopia into the Catholic fold involved a bitter war with the surrounding Muslims in the 1540s. The Muslims were defending not only Islam but also the Arab domination of the Indian Ocean network of trade. Military overlordship seemed to be the prerequisite for any economic benefits. The major prize was the gold trade of Sofala and Kilwa but the Portuguese soon found that control of the coastal outlets would not secure the supply; expeditions were therefore sent inland to gain control of the Zambezi valley and the gold-producing empire of Monomotapa.

In western Africa the principal economic prize was slaves. Portuguese demands soon outran what was offered by the Africans with whom they traded; this was the principal reason for the breakdown, for example, of the initially good relations between the Europeans and the Kongo kingdom. The Portuguese, though few in number and weak in real resources, had a margin of technological and organizational superiority over Africans, but this was outweighed by difficulties of disease and communications. Already by the mid-17th century their position along the Guinea coast had been overtaken by more active Dutch, French and British competitors who had built up a formidable collection of trading posts and castles along the coast. In East Africa a resurgence of Arab power, led by adventurous traders from Oman, resulted in the fall of Mombasa in 1699. Africans themselves in the Angola and Mozambique regions coped with the Portuguese as just one group who had to be

Above African artistic traditions were often adapted to provide comments on the new colonial situation. Here a carver from the Congo (Zaïre) has amusingly characterized the Belgian official of the 1920s in his chauffeur-driven car.

Left One item among grafitti by 17th-century Portuguese soldiers on the gun platform of the S. Mateus bastion of Fort Jesus. Perhaps the artist was hoping for relief from the sea during the long siege by the Omanis in 1698–99.

Right An example of the latest in European fortification science, Fort Jesus at Mombasa was built in 1593–96 to enable the Portuguese to dominate the East African coast. Though impregnable, it could be starved into submission, as in 1699.

managed in the ever-changing political struggle. Much as one might emphasize the independence and enterprise of rulers like Queen Nzinga of Matamba in dealing with the Europeans, perhaps a disturbing pattern had been set: one of the principal prizes of political success in tropical Africa was access to European goods. The prices were high but did not seem high, for all that was demanded were things that could be extracted from, rather than produced by, the African environment – slaves, ivory and some gold.

By 1800 the slave trade had become very big business indeed. The greater volume of all trade between Europe and Africa was now in the hands of much more resourceful and powerful groups than the Portuguese. The pattern, however, remained the same: Europeans stayed on the fringes of the continent and the political initiatives in the interior undoubtedly lay with Africans. Yet they and large numbers of their fellows, whether they realized it or not, were having their lives affected by the demands of the European capitalist-organized trade centered on an Atlantic region or the European/Oriental capitalist nexus of the Indian Ocean.

From about 1800, there were signs that Europeans would intervene more. These signs included geographical exploration, missionary endeavor, mercantile activity, mineral prospecting, European settlement and increasing governmental interference. In crude terms, these developments might be explained by alterations in the nature of world market demands on Africa which were themselves a product of Europe's industrial revolution and the political and ideological changes that accompanied it. Equally crudely, it might be said that the effects of the new developments were to be largely disruptive. The disruption was sufficient by the end of the century, in the judgment of some historians, to cause Africans to lose control of their environment as well as their political destiny. Europeans themselves saw Africa as disordered and needing firm government; this was more than just an excuse for their ambitions. Indeed the image of Africa in European eyes as backward and disorderly may be one of the most important legacies of the 19th century for it underlies 20th-century racial attitudes.

The most dramatic manifestation of new European activity in North Africa was Napoleon's invasion of Egypt in 1798. Although the French forces were ousted by Britain and Turkey, the invasion marks the beginning of attempts to modernize Egypt with the aid of European advisers and entrepreneurs who also took part in the campaigns to bring more of the Nile valley into the Egyptian orbit. The French also undertook the other major European initiative in North Africa when Algeria was invaded in 1830 after a minor trading dispute. As more of the territory was captured during the next 40 years, settlers moved in to become wheat and vine growers.

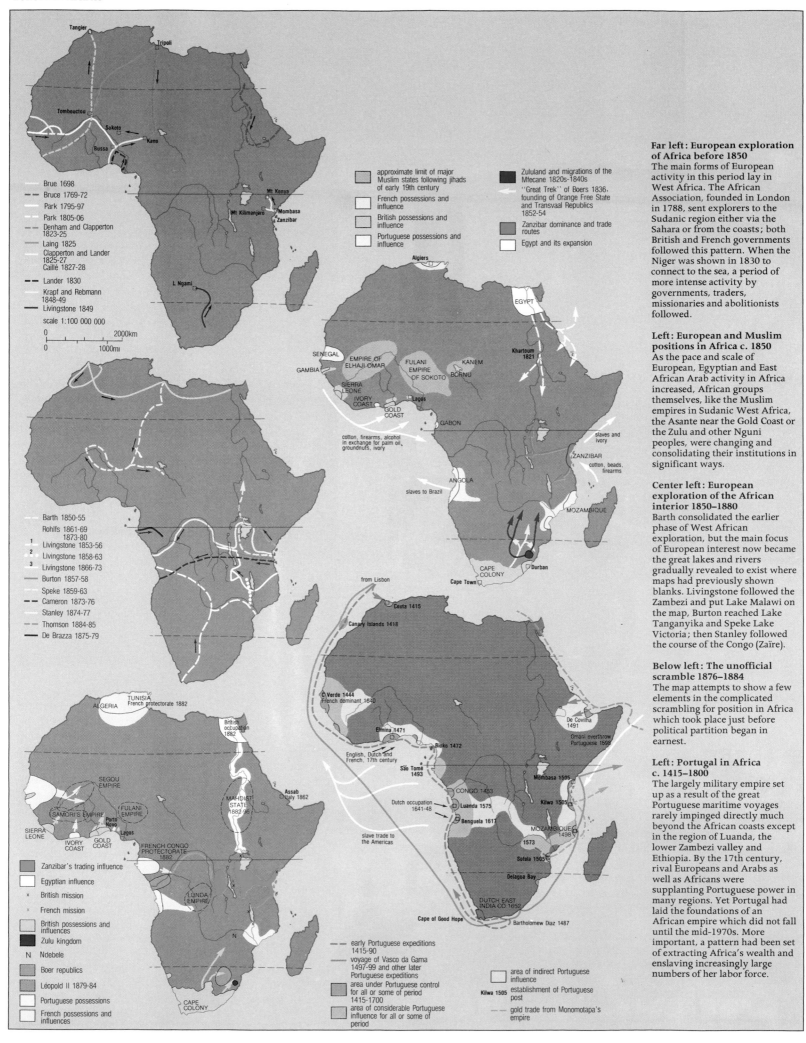

Far left: European exploration of Africa before 1850
The main forms of European activity in this period lay in West Africa. The African Association, founded in London in 1788, sent explorers to the Sudanic region either via the Sahara or from the coasts; both British and French governments followed this pattern. When the Niger was shown in 1830 to connect to the sea, a period of more intense activity by governments, traders, missionaries and abolitionists followed.

Left: European and Muslim positions in Africa c. 1850
As the pace and scale of European, Egyptian and East African Arab activity in Africa increased, African groups themselves, like the Muslim empires in Sudanic West Africa, the Asante near the Gold Coast or the Zulu and other Nguni peoples, were changing and consolidating their institutions in significant ways.

Center left: European exploration of the African interior 1850–1880
Barth consolidated the earlier phase of West African exploration, but the main focus of European interest now became the great lakes and rivers gradually revealed to exist where maps had previously shown blanks. Livingstone followed the Zambezi and put Lake Malawi on the map, Burton reached Lake Tanganyika and Speke Lake Victoria; then Stanley followed the course of the Congo (Zaïre).

Below left: The unofficial scramble 1876–1884
The map attempts to show a few elements in the complicated scrambling for position in Africa which took place just before political partition began in earnest.

Left: Portugal in Africa c. 1415–1800
The largely military empire set up as a result of the great Portuguese maritime voyages rarely impinged directly much beyond the African coasts except in the region of Luanda, the lower Zambezi valley and Ethiopia. By the 17th century, rival Europeans and Arabs as well as Africans were supplanting Portuguese power in many regions. Yet Portugal had laid the foundations of an African empire which did not fall until the mid-1970s. More important, a pattern had been set of extracting Africa's wealth and enslaving increasingly large numbers of her labor force.

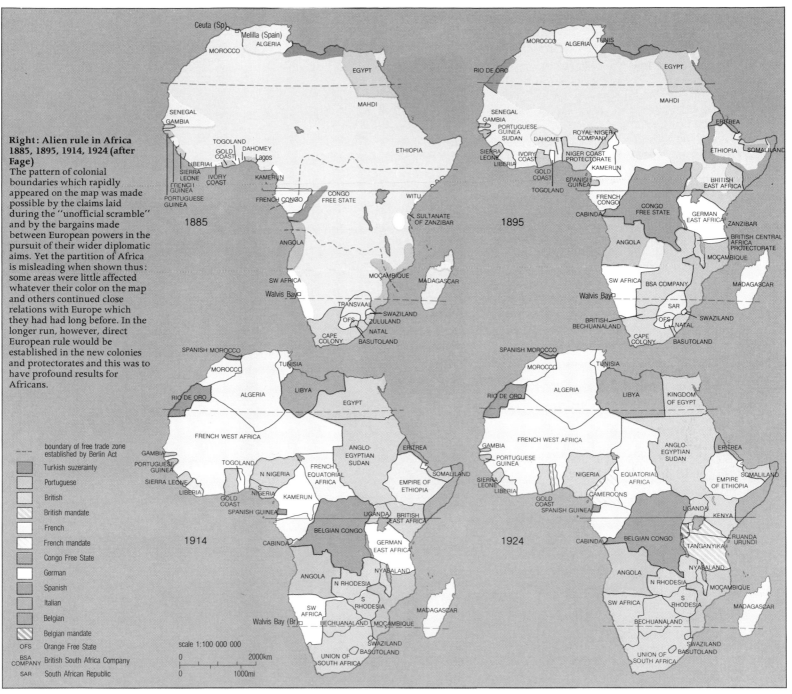

Right: Alien rule in Africa 1885, 1895, 1914, 1924 (after Fage)
The pattern of colonial boundaries which rapidly appeared on the map was made possible by the claims laid during the "unofficial scramble" and by the bargains made between European powers in the pursuit of their wider diplomatic aims. Yet the partition of Africa is misleading when shown thus: some areas were little affected whatever their color on the map and others continued close relations with Europe which they had had long before. In the longer run, however, direct European rule would be established in the new colonies and protectorates and this was to have profound results for Africans.

Map legend:
- – – – boundary of free trade zone established by Berlin Act
- Turkish suzerainty
- Portuguese
- British
- British mandate
- French
- French mandate
- Congo Free State
- German
- Spanish
- Italian
- Belgian
- Belgian mandate
- OFS — Orange Free State
- BSA COMPANY — British South Africa Company
- SAR — South African Republic

scale 1:100 000 000
0 — 2000km
0 — 1000mi

Less dramatic but in the long run more important were European moves in West Africa. Although James Bruce who explored Ethiopia in the 1760s may be an early example of the phenomenon, scientific exploration properly began with the foundation of the African Association in London in 1788. The Association believed that Europe's ignorance of Africa was "a reproach upon the present age." Later bodies like the Paris Geographical Society of 1821 and the Royal Geographical Society of 1830 were to continue to try to remove that reproach. Of course the desire to have accurate maps and accurate botanical and ethnographic information was itself a characteristic of the revolutionary and industrial age. At the more practical level, Europe's increasing wealth made it feasible to finance scientific expeditions which, in the long run, might lead to a pay-off of some kind. For example, the course and termination of the Niger became the great geographical question of the age and when Richard Lander demonstrated in 1830 that the river debouched into the Gulf of Guinea,

attempts to use it as a means of access to the far interior by steamboat soon followed.

If scientific inquiry was one sign of new European interests, determined attempts to promote the Gospel overseas were another. This characteristic of the evangelical revival was seen most clearly in West Africa in the work of the (Anglican) Church Missionary Society from 1806, the Methodists and the German Basel and Bremen societies. The story of these Protestant missions is part of the larger story of the revolution in moral attitudes which led to the growth of the anti-slave-trade movement. British abolitionists set up Sierra Leone in 1787 for freed slaves and, when the British government abolished the slave trade in 1807 and began to try to persuade other countries to do the same, a new era dawned. Missionary work was part of the larger philanthropic campaign to repair the ravages of the slave trade by introducing "legitimate commerce," education and Christian civilization. No doubt there was an element of hypocrisy here; if industrial Europe wanted palm oil rather than slaves it was as much a reflection of changing industrial needs as of changing morality. Nevertheless, the fervor of the Christian and humanitarian campaigns in West Africa was to help to change the face of the region.

Whatever the precise mixture of economic interest and humanitarian pressure which accomplished it, governments, especially the British and French, became increasingly involved in West African affairs. Officials on the spot gradually began to see the need to interfere in the interior and often did so even when the home governments maintained a cautious attitude. As the British took a firmer hold on the Gold Coast, for example, they found themselves in conflict with Asante power inland. French initiatives in the Senegal valley region led to the beginnings in the 1850s of a series of conflicts with Islamic kingdoms of the interior. In fact the early 19th century had seen the political transformation of the Islamic region as the result of a series of reforming *jihads*; empires such as that of al-Haj 'Umar or Muhammad Bello were certainly now strong enough to resist any European encroachments.

In eastern Africa there was a comparative dearth of European activity in this period. Although more European and American merchants arrived, the impact of Europe's economic revolution was mostly felt indirectly via India and Arabia. Thus Zanzibari traders began to wrest control of the slave and ivory trades between the interior and the coast from Africans. Yet the economic and strategic interests of France and Britain in the Indian Ocean made them take some note of what was going on and Zanzibar itself increasingly became a client state of the British.

In South Africa, British government involvement was much more direct. Although Cape Town was captured in 1795 and retained in 1815 for strategic reasons, the British soon found themselves beset with problems in the hinterland. The original Dutch settlers, reinforced later by French Huguenots, considered themselves as Afrikaners. Many of them, the so-called Boers, had become pastoralists, constantly seeking new areas outside the Cape Colony itself where the British provided some measure of protection for the Khoikhoi people whom Afrikaners had previously dominated or enslaved. The Great Trek of the late 1830s was partly a response to the abolition of slavery in the British empire in 1833. But by this period the trekkers had encountered Bantu peoples much more formidable than the Khoikhoi. The Bantu east of the Drakensberg range also needed more land, a desire seen most clearly in the rise of Chaka's Zulu state in the 1820s. Out of the consequent *Mfecane* (scattering of peoples), the Boer treks which eventually created the republics of the Orange Free State and Transvaal in the 1850s, the contests between the Africans and the Boers and the often unavailing attempts of the British to exert control were founded the roots of modern South Africa. The Boers, pious but narrow Calvinists, were determined to preserve their identity against British officials, soldiers and missionaries and even more against the black peoples around them.

The third quarter of the century was a classic age of scientific exploration in Africa with the focus now on the question of the Nile source and great lakes of East and central Africa. Although the

motives were broadly similar to those which had taken explorers into West Africa 50 years before, one great difference lay in the amount of public interest created in Europe. Indeed one of the most famous episodes, the meeting of Stanley and Livingstone, was a newspaper "scoop." Nor was interest confined to the adventure story element in the explorers' work: their verdicts on the condition of Africa nearly all suggested that increased European intervention was necessary. Great economic opportunities existed in the shape of mineral resources or supposedly fertile agricultural areas which Africans, either through inherent inabilities or restraints placed upon them by the slave trade, were incapable of developing. Great evangelical and educational opportunities existed for the missionary and both he and the trader could overcome problems of transport by using steamboats on the rivers and lakes discovered by the explorers. There were other signs of impending change. Diamonds were discovered at Kimberley in 1869 and gold was to be found in the Witwatersrand area of Transvaal in 1885; the Suez Canal was opened in 1869; Egypt established a claim to control of the upper Nile valley in the mid 1870s; in West Africa, the French began a project to develop rail and river traffic between their Senegal colony and the interior.

In 1876 Léopold II, King of the Belgians, called a conference of African explorers at Brussels which set up the International Association to continue the scientific exploration of Africa and begin the process of developing it. Under both the direct and

Above Many descendants of the 17th-century Dutch and French Huguenot settlers at the Cape moved northeastwards in the 1770–1870 period to become pastoral farmers, the "Boers." Their treks in search of the promised land free of British control led to serious clashes with the Bantu.

Below Human porterage was the only practicable transportation in most of interior tropical Africa. As international demand for ivory increased, long "caravans" of carriers marched hundreds of kilometers each with burdens of 35 kg or more. This porter's own meager supplies and possessions are tied to the tusk.

Below The *Ma Robert* on the Shire river, 1859. Livingstone experimented with river and lake steamboats as one means of replacing slave porterage in Africa during his Zambezi expedition of 1858–64.

Bottom A meeting of cultures. The Scottish explorer J. A. Grant's own sketch of his attempt to join in a dance in 1861 at Ukulima's village in what is now northern Tanzania.

Above If European and African interests clashed seriously enough, Europeans might bring the weight of their technological superiority to bear as Britain did in 1873 to subdue the Asante who threatened the political and economic interests of Britain and her African allies on the Gold Coast in West Africa.

Below Henry Morton Stanley (1841–1904), most effective – and ruthless – of explorers, "found"

Livingstone in 1871, solved the problems of the Nile and Congo in 1874–77, and helped create Léopold's Congo Free State and British possessions on the upper Nile in the 1880s. The ex-slave boy Kalulu, acquired in 1871, visited the US and Britain but was drowned on Stanley's next expedition.

Below right The German Dr Heinrich Barth (1821–65) led a British-sponsored expedition to

West Africa in the 1850s.

Bottom The greatest European explorer, David Livingstone (1813–73) worked almost continuously in Africa from 1841 to 1873. He evolved from conventional missionary to scientific explorer and advocate of "Christianity, Commerce and Civilization" to heal the "open sore of the world" – the African slave trade.

The Source of the Nile Debate

The quest for the source of the Nile excited 19th-century Europe because it involved adventurous exploration, intellectual controversy and individual rivalries. There was also interest in the political and economic implications of the discoveries. The Nile problem was only part of the larger task of delineating east central Africa's great lakes, rumored to exist on the basis of Classical sources like Herodotus and Ptolemy, 17th-century Portuguese accounts and confused reports by Arab ivory traders. As "armchair" scholarship and practical exploration revealed the existence of the lakes, the possibility of steamboats on them carrying commerce and the Gospel became attractive. In the 1880s this happened and the area of the source of the Nile itself in Uganda became a key strategic objective of rival imperialists.

R.C.B.

Right John Hanning Speke who reached the source of the White Nile in July 1862.

Below right James Bruce at the source of the Blue Nile drinking the health of George III, 1770. Although Pedro Paez and other Portuguese had visited the Blue Nile's source in Ethiopia, their reports remained little known. When therefore the eccentric Scottish laird James Bruce (1730–94) reached the spot on 4 November 1770, he claimed "a trophy in which I can have no competitor." This romanticized engraving well reflects his boast. Yet the major puzzle of the White Nile source remained.

Below left Grant's drawing of the source of the White Nile at the Ripon Falls, Uganda, shows the point where the river flows out of Lake Victoria. The falls are now submerged by the effects of a hydroelectric dam downstream.

Left and below right The White Nile and the great lakes, 1845–1873. The theoretical geographer Cooley argued that there was only one lake in East Africa even after explorers found more (map a). Erhardt heard on the coast of all three lakes but ran them into one (map b). The Royal Geographical Society then sent Burton and Speke to find the truth. They reached Lake Tanganyika, and Speke alone the southern end of Lake Victoria, immediately claiming it as the Nile source (map c). On a second expedition, now with Grant, Speke reached the Ripon Falls in July 1862 where the Nile flows out of Victoria. Baker came up the Nile to find Lake Albert as part of the Nile system, whereupon Burton and his allies, jealous of Speke, ingeniously showed that Lake Tanganyika could be the source of the Nile (map d). Speke accidentally shot himself dead and could not dispute this. The doubts encouraged Livingstone to believe the "fountains" even further south and he died trying to prove this (map e). In 1875–76 Stanley finally vindicated Speke and ended the vitriolic arguments about who deserved the palm Bruce had claimed in 1770.

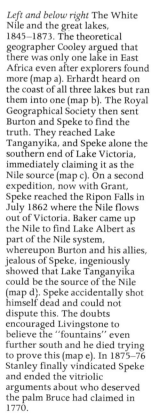

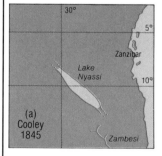

(a) Cooley 1845

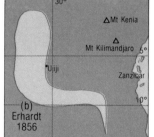

(b) Erhardt 1856

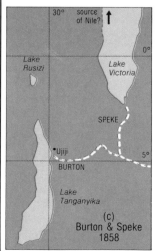

(c) Burton & Speke 1858

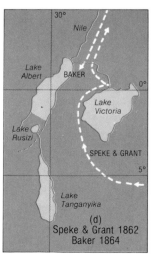

(d) Speke & Grant 1862 / Baker 1864

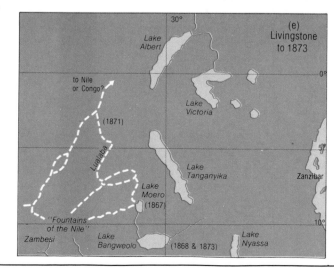

(e) Livingstone to 1873

Sir Richard Burton (1821–90). Arabist, linguist, explorer, not wholly respectable Victorian, Burton questioned Speke's 1858 and 1862 discoveries, refused to communicate with his ex-companion and generally injected controversy into the Nile source issue.

James A. Grant (1827–92). During their 1859–63 expedition, Speke denied Grant the chance to visit the actual source of the Nile. Yet Grant loyally supported Speke's geographical claims and was to become an acknowledged expert on African affairs.

Sir Samuel Baker (1821–93) traveled up the Nile valley to reach Lake Albert in March 1864, so supplementing yet complicating Speke's discovery. Baker later returned to the upper Nile to claim the area for the Khedive of Egypt – and to make a fortune for himself.

indirect influence of Léopold's initiative, a multitude of projects for Africa emerged. Few involved European governments which, for the most part, were still cautious about responsibilities in Africa. Yet this unofficial scramble of miners, merchants and missionaries was to create conditions which seemed to oblige official intervention.

When the major powers met at the Berlin Conference in 1884–85, their object was not to partition Africa but to try to limit the international friction beginning to be caused by the unofficial scramble. The ground rules of international conduct in Africa which they laid down did not, however, prevent the rapid assumption of European overlordship in the next ten years or so. Inevitably there were clashes of interest between unofficial agencies from different countries. Brazza, working for a French committee, and Stanley, working for the Belgian branch of the International Association, clashed over control of the access route to the interior via the lower Zaïre river. As thousands of British flocked into Transvaal in the wake of the mineral discoveries, bitter disputes broke out between these *Uitlanders* and the resident Boers. Europeans might also clash or cooperate uneasily with non-European agencies like Egypt or the Zanzibar sultanate as white men sought more direct influence on events. More significantly still, Africans were involved in a scramble for position and influence. Some might be detribalized Christian converts like the creoles of Sierra Leone, but most Africans remained subjects of African leaders who had modified old political structures or created new ones to meet 19th-century conditions. The states which men like Samori in West Africa or Mirambo in the east had built up now struggled to withstand the more determined initiatives from Europe. In some cases, Islam constituted a counterforce to the Europeans; such was the case with the Mahdists who took over the Sudan from Egypt in the 1880s or the Sokoto empire of the middle Niger.

If the situation in Africa itself seemed to cry out for the imposition of a European civil order, there were, too, European reasons for official anexations. First, in the conditions of the great depression of 1876–93 it seemed important to secure sources of raw materials and markets for the present or the future against possible rivals. Moreover, European traders in many regions no longer considered it possible to expand their activities within a context of African political control; they felt they needed a modern infrastructure of railroads, telegraphs and political control by European governments or, at least, chartered companies. Secondly, domestic difficulties in European states could to some extent be alleviated by expansionist policies. Thirdly, the general problems of international rivalries, particularly the rise of Germany after 1871, had implications for Africa.

The details of the process by which Africa was partitioned can be understood only by reference to the complex interweaving of all these African and European factors. Broadly speaking, however, it may be said that Léopold's ambition to create his own Congo Free State brought into question ill-defined rights of Britain, France and Portugal. Germany exploited the incipient rivalries in 1884–85 and annexations to establish claims rapidly

proceeded in West and East Africa. Most of the resulting conflicts were resolved in treaties of 1890–91. Meanwhile, in North Africa, local authorities found themselves unable to cope with the consequences of modernization; the classic case was Egypt where a proto-nationalist revolt in 1882 against the European-influenced Khedive's regime could be put down only by British occupation. This not only upset France but gave Britain a reason for wishing to protect the whole Nile valley. In South Africa, British attempts to impose some sort of overall control of both the Boers and the Bantu resulted in wars like the Zulu War of 1879 and the first Boer War of 1882. More successful were international arrangements with Germany and Portugal in 1890 and 1891 which kept them out of these southern African preserves of the British, which had by this time extended to the Zambezi and beyond with the energetic activities of the followers of Cecil Rhodes. The real crisis in South Africa, however, came in 1899–1901, when the British government, now fully associated with local British mining interests, fought the Boer War to bring the Afrikaners once more fully into the British empire. In 1910 a political compromise was reached and South Africa was given independence as a mixed Boer–British state. By the time the Boer War started, Britain had, fortunately for it, resolved most of its remaining difficulties with France over West Africa in 1898, though both powers were to find it difficult to overcome African resistance to overlordship. The sharpest clash came also in 1898 when, as Britain reconquered the Sudan from the Mahdists, a French expedition moved in to question Britain's right to control the whole of the Nile valley. A little earlier, in 1896, the only major and permanent repulse of an attempted European annexation occurred when Italy was defeated by Ethiopia at the battle of Adowa.

The rest of Africa was taken over and only relatively minor border readjustments occurred after 1900, although it was not until 1911 that Libya was taken over by Italy and Morocco by France. The bitter dispute with Germany on the latter occasion showed that African bargains could no longer be used as international safety valves. Indeed, Africa became heavily involved in World War I. Not only were campaigns fought on its soil as Germany's colonies were wrested from it, but thousands of Africans fought for their colonial overlords. The question of what to do with German territories provoked a new mini-scramble in 1919. The League of Nations B mandates given to Britain, France and Belgium in practice, if not theory, simply added to their possessions and South Africa with a C mandate over South West Africa began to incorporate the ex-German territory.

Colonial control for most Africans, then, began at the end of the 19th century. Obviously it brought tremendous changes, most notably by providing the basic political framework for the Africa of today. Yet in many ways what happened was only a speeding-up of processes of European–African interaction which had begun earlier. Perhaps the main effect was to set limits on the extent to which Africans could choose how far to allow their ways of life to be modified and on how far they could resist the peripherization of their economies. With political independence in the 1960s the process continues under slightly different rules.   R.C.B.

The Mapping of Africa

Very few maps were published in inter-tropical Africa prior to this century, so that it is tempting to suppose that the early printed maps of Africa are a chronicle of external penetration. This is not the case. External contact with sub-Saharan Africa by Arab travelers predates printing by many centuries, and the European map-publishing houses of the 15th century and later made use of Arab sources if they were available; but much was not available. Early maps of Africa printed in Europe are a very incomplete record of Arab knowledge. Furthermore, the content of early maps of Africa is not only a reflection of the number of accurate geographical facts known to the cartographer. It also reflects the demands of the readership which may have been happy to see maps used as frameworks for expressing myths, tradition or geographical speculation in what were otherwise blank areas. Such maps depict more of what was believed than what was known of Africa.

By the 19th century, a more scientific attitude prevailed. Great blank areas on maps of Africa suggest that the inclusion of unsubstantiated myth was no longer acceptable but it does not follow that what the cartographer shows is accurate. He was still dependent on travelers' reports of what they had seen and what they believed lay beyond their personal experience.

J.C.S.

Right John Senex's map of 1720 represents a transition in that an increasing amount of detailed information is now coming to hand but fables remain acceptable. Hence there is much detail along the coast and some firmly depicted features inland, although rivers tend to stop short through lack of knowledge, which is openly admitted in inscriptions. The state of Monomotapa had been contacted by the Portuguese and was known to exist, by contrast with other more ill-founded inscriptions in the interior and with the little tent symbols which are no more than embellishment. There are traits in this map of both a much earlier and a much later period.

Below The Catalan Atlas of 1375, a series of manuscript maps drawn on parchment. The radiating rhumb lines show that maritime charts were important sources of this document. The detail along the North African coast derives from charts and contrasts with the embellishment in the interior, although Moroccan merchants were the source of information about the Guinea coast.

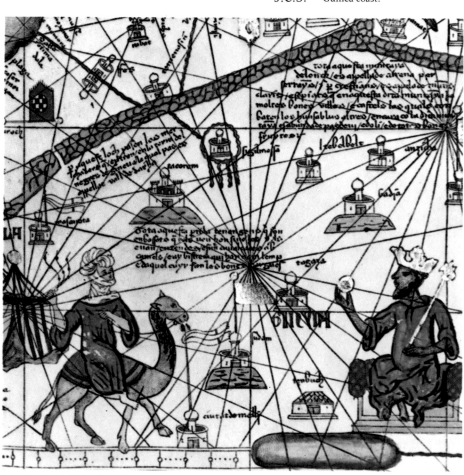

Left Münster's woodcut map of Africa, printed in 1540, derives in part from the work of Claudius Ptolemy, almost 1400 years earlier, but it also draws on Arab and Portuguese sources. The chain of mountains aligned east-west across North Africa was a Ptolemaic feature which also occurs on the Catalan Atlas. The Nile is shown rising in the Mountains of the Moon far to the south and the upper Niger is shown flowing in the wrong direction. These were features carried forward on maps for several centuries.

Above right A map published in London in 1822 contains less information about Africa south of the equator than the relatively accurate parts of the Senex map which was published 100 years previously. Little more had become known of the interior

but attitudes towards maps had changed. The cartographer was more reluctant to include uncertain information. This did not mean that what he included was correct. The Niger now becomes a possible tributary of the Nile and the Ptolemaic Mountains of the Moon remain one of the Nile sources.

Right During the early colonial period in British Africa, a great number of little-known but often very detailed manuscript maps were prepared by District Officers. The information on these maps was sometimes used in the first published large-scale maps of the territory. This section of a map of Magoye Subdistrict, Northern Rhodesia, was drawn in 1921 and shows both land alienated for commercial farming and adjacent African villages.

Communication by Rail

Africa's rail network is still in a very rudimentary stage of development, except in South Africa. Most lines run from the interior to the coast. There are few transcontinental links and existing lines are often not integrated with the growing network of all-weather highways. However, unlike elsewhere in the world, more lines are being built than are being taken up. The African network is expanding and there are a number of projected new lines undergoing feasibility studies. There is now an international body, the Union of African Railways, to foster pan-African integration, the main problem being the five different gauges which exist. Training programs have been established to overcome the shortage of skilled personnel and priorities worked out for the construction of international links and feeder lines.   J.C.S.

Right Two large 25NC 4–8–4 engines meet on the line from Bloemfontein to Bethlehem in South Africa, whose advanced rail network is being further expanded for strategic and economic reasons.

Below One of tropical Africa's earliest lines was constructed to run inland from the Kenya coast just before the turn of the century. It hastened the coming of the European settlers in Kenya, who proved it commercially viable.

Bottom The trans-Gabon railroad is one of Africa's new lines, although the incentive for its construction is the traditional reason of extraction of primary products, in this case timber and minerals.

Top The line from Mombasa was built largely by manual labor, not by Africans but by indentured laborers from India, most of whom returned home after completion of their contract.

Above Great distances and the low purchasing power of the potential passengers mean that most of the cheaper forms of public transport in Africa tend to be infrequent and overcrowded. Many lines are single track, necessitating stops for passing traffic, as here in Sudan.

Left A Sierra Leone station, a scene that is familiar elsewhere in Africa. Stations are simply constructed, without platforms, but may occur at short intervals along the line so that stops are frequent. There is usually ample time to purchase food and drink from numerous vendors.

THE AFRICAN DIASPORA

The word diaspora has traditionally been used to describe the experience of the Jews, scattered from their historical homeland in Israel. More recently, by analogy, the same word has been applied to the dispersal of peoples of African descent outside the African continent. The analogy is not entirely accurate: in contrast to the Jews, diaspora Africans came from a wide range of distinct cultures and they have been able to look back not only to a physical point of origin, but also to African societies which had not shared the experience of dispersal. Again, though the African diaspora communities, like the Jews, have succeeded in defining and maintaining their own cultures in foreign lands, they have been much more successful than the Jews in influencing the cultures of the societies in which they lived. In modern Brazil, for instance, the black presence has had a deep impact on the national culture and in most societies of the Caribbean the cultures of the diaspora communities have become the dominant ones. However, it is more important for African history that the diaspora has had an impact in the opposite direction. Here there is a striking parallel with the way Jewish communities throughout the world have affected the evolution of modern Israel. Pan-Africanism, and indeed modern African nationalism, would have developed along different lines without the interaction between African intellectuals and the diaspora communities of Britain, France and the Americas.

The African diaspora is still one of the most dramatic population movements in modern history, as emigration from the Caribbean continues to build new communities of African descent in France, Britain and the USA. Its origins go back at least to Classical antiquity, when small numbers of Africans were sold northwards down the Nile or across the Sahara. Throughout the European Middle Ages, and indeed until the late 19th century, these routes provided much greater numbers of black slaves for entrepôts on the Mediterranean, particularly Tripoli, Benghazi and Alexandria. Thence they were distributed throughout the Islamic world, from the Iberian peninsula to India. Though no scholar has gone beyond guessing at the numbers involved, it is clear that they were huge, perhaps as many as the victims of the Atlantic traffic. The mainland trade only began to slacken in the 19th century, when the European powers expanded their influence in the Mediterranean simultaneously with becoming committed to abolition.

It was easy to find alternative sources of supply. The Islamic world had always bought black slaves from fellow Muslims trading by sea south of the Horn of Africa. In the late 18th century the bulk of this trade fell into the hands of the Omani Arab sultans who conquered and settled Zanzibar. They developed new trade routes into the interior, to the great lakes and the Congo. Though they retained some slaves to staff their expanding clove plantations in Zanzibar and neighboring Pemba, they greatly increased the volume of the trade to the ports of the Red Sea and the Persian Gulf. From there African men and women continued to be dispersed throughout Islam. It is quite impossible to estimate the volume of the East African trade, which only slackened after the British–Zanzibari treaty of 1873 and was not fully eradicated until the present century. One educated guess is that by 1870 60 000 slaves were being exported from East Africa each year.

We know too little about the history of African expatriates in Islamic societies. Most of them were bought as domestic servants, some as concubines and many as eunuchs. At first they were also used extensively for military purposes. By the mid-11th century 30 000 out of the 100 000 troops in the Egyptian army were black, but this became much less acceptable after the "War of the Blacks" in 1169, when 50 000 African mutineers almost overthrew Saladin in Cairo. In North Africa many blacks became galley slaves, and in the city-states of the Persian Gulf they were used in date farming, as pearl divers, as port laborers and as sailors. A very few rose to political prominence, whether through domestic or military service: the 10th-century Nubian eunuch, Abu'l-Misk Kafur, became regent of Egypt; Sidi Badr briefly seized the throne of Bengal in the 1490s; Malik Ambar, the great 17th-century general, led the resistance of the Deccan against the Mughals. In Indian political history, groups of "Habshis" or "Siddis" have sometimes taken an important role. Those on Janjira Island, for instance, were in effect naval mercenaries whose friendship became crucial to the East India

Above The massive slave trade across the Sahara and the Indian Ocean had a less obvious demographic impact than the Atlantic traffic. But diaspora Africans played a range of roles in the societies of Islam and throughout Asia. Malik Ambar was an important figure in the history of 17th-century India.

Below Nothing about slavery horrified its critics more than the slave auction. The sentimental paternalism of American slaveholders could not get over the inconsistency of treating human beings as a form of real property. And it could not protect black children from being torn from their families under the auctioneer's hammer.

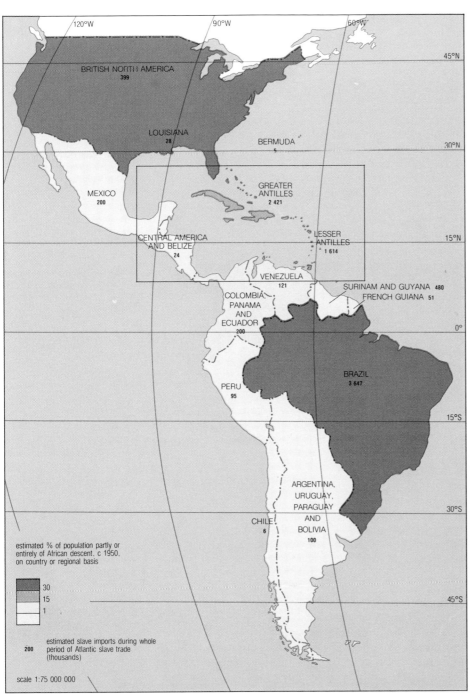

estimated % of population partly or
entirely of African descent. c 1950,
on country or regional basis

- 30
- 15
- 1

200 estimated slave imports during whole
period of Atlantic slave trade
(thousands)

scale 1:75 000 000

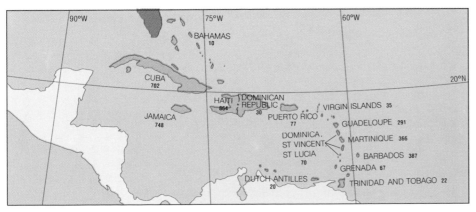

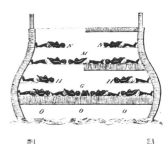

Left: The African diaspora in the New World (after Curtin).

Below Overcrowding on the Middle Passage is incomprehensible in terms of modern transportation. This diagram was used throughout the campaign against the slave trade. It shows an unusually large ship, carrying 500 or 600 slaves, in approximately the same cubic capacity as ten double cabins on the *QE 2*.

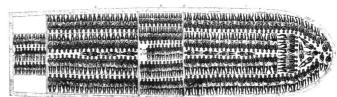

Company's 18th-century strategy for defending Bombay from the Dutch. The descendants of the Janjira Siddis, now politically weak, are still a recognizably distinct group. The same is true of the Nizam of Hyderabad's African Cavalry Guard, only disbanded in 1951. Siddi Risala, the neighborhood in which Hyderabadis of African descent live, still shows cultural survivals in music and dance and some local usage of Swahili words. In Iran, too, there is still a distinctive black community at Jiruft. In general, however, the descendants of diaspora Africans in Islam have tended to become absorbed into the wider culture. Except in special cases, the low proportion of blacks available for liaisons with other blacks, the relative cultural and racial receptivity of Islamic culture and the sheer lack of concentrated demographic mass have prevented the development of diaspora cultures similar to those of the Americas.

The diaspora entered a new phase in the 15th century, when the Portuguese broke the Islamic monopoly of trade with Africa and Asia by pushing down the Guinea coast and ultimately rounding the Cape to India. They quickly began to carry black people back to Europe and thence to the settlements in the New World. Before this, the few African slaves who reached Europe through capture, or through the Venetian and Genoan trade with the Levant and North Africa, had been mere exotics. Such individuals still appear in the modern period – like the Scottish "ladye with the meckle lippis" in Dunbar's poem, for whose favors James IV's knights jousted; like Ibrahim Hannibal, Peter the Great's black general, who provided the germ of the novelette by another figure of the diaspora, Alexander Pushkin; or like the black pages who remained fashionable among the European aristocracy until the 18th century. However, the new Portuguese trade, and the Dutch, British and French initiatives which followed, deposited Africans in Europe and its possessions in numbers which make it possible to speak of genuine diaspora communities. By 1551 a tenth of Lisbon's population of 100 000 was black, and by the 1590s it had its own annual African festival. However, Portuguese blacks were in the long run unable to remain culturally and racially distinct from the general population. The same was true of the smaller black groups in Spain and other European countries. The only real exception was Britain. After it acquired colonies in North America and the West Indies, and became heavily involved in the slave trade, it developed small but distinct communities of African descent in port towns like Bristol, Liverpool and London. Their total numbers may have been as high as 15 000 by the 1780s.

The African presence in Europe was never as significant as the great diaspora communities which emerged in the New World as a consequence of the Atlantic slave trade. The numbers carried to the Americas will never be known precisely. The most probable figure is between 10 and 11 million between Columbus's discovery of Hispaniola and the effective ending of the Cuban trade in 1868. Though lower than earlier estimates, this is still an enormous number, roughly equal to the whole population of the U S A in 1825. Although different national systems of ethnic classification make computation difficult, there are at least 60 million people of African descent in the Americas today. However, because different agricultural staples created different labor needs and because each produced its own demographic conditions, slave importations were unevenly distributed throughout the Americas. Moreover, they bear little relationship to modern population. The horrifying fact is that the slave population was able to maintain its numbers by natural reproduction only in the U S A. Under half a million Africans were brought to North America, but they had produced a population of four and a half million, four million enslaved, by the Civil War. Elsewhere, masters relied on the slave trade to replace the blacks who fell victim to the demands of the plantation. The British, French and Dutch West Indies had to carry close to four million into slavery. Almost as many went to Brazil alone – close to two million in the 18th century and over a million in the 19th. The Spanish possessions absorbed at least a million and a half new slaves, over a third of them going to Cuba during the 19th-century sugar boom.

It is difficult to be precise about the African origins of the slave trade's victims. Each of the trading nations relied on different parts of the continent in different political conditions and at different times. A majority of North American blacks came from the coastal societies of West Africa and the states of the western Sudan, although over a quarter probably originated in Angola and other parts of central Africa. The same areas provided the slaves for the British and French Caribbean. As the 18th century went on, they drew an increasing proportion of new blacks from Congo and Angola. These were a particularly strong element in the population of Saint Domingue at the time of the Haitian revolution. Brazil and the Spanish colonies also took slaves from the Guinea coast, but they relied more consistently than their neighbors on central African blacks shipped from ports like Luanda and Benguela. The trade from East Africa to the Americas was negligible until the mid-17th century, when the French began to carry slaves from Mozambique and other entrepôts. By the late 18th century these sources were being more energetically tapped by the Portuguese, particularly to provide slave labor for the Spanish settlements on the Plate. This trade was relatively unimportant for the British possessions, but it came to be even more significant to Brazil and Cuba in the 19th century, when the ports of West and central Africa came under increasing pressure from British naval patrols.

The black slaves of the Americas represented almost the whole range of African cultures. Even their masters were aware of the diversity of the civilizations from which they came. Though white perceptions were imprecise and inconsistent, they ascribed different values and characteristics to people of different origins – Asantes were quarrelsome, Congos stupid, Yorubas faithful, Bantus physically strong and so on. More important, different mixes of African nationalities meant that the complex diaspora cultures which developed during and after the slave period varied widely in different parts of the Americas.

Simpler demographic forces also had their impact. In areas like Chile, where black population was tiny, or like New England, where blacks were characteristically used side by side with servants of other races, the chances of maintaining a distinct culture during slavery or surviving as a viable community after it were slight. Even in Mexico, which absorbed an estimated 200 000 slaves, and where there are still over 300 000 citizens of identifiable African origin, diaspora Mexicans have tended ethnically and culturally to merge into the general population. Other environments were more favorable. Where large black populations lived close to an inaccessible hinterland, they usually produced communities of escapees who were quite independent of white society. Where the proportion of recent arrivals among escapees was high, which it commonly was, such groups evolved cultures which, though inevitably composite and adaptive, may be called genuinely African. The classic case is that of the Bush Negroes of French and Dutch Guiana, whose religious and political systems were almost wholly African. Today 25 000 of them maintain their distinctive ways in communities of their own. The most famous was the republic of Palmares, which used recognizably African forms of government and flourished for almost a century until it was crushed by Portuguese troops in 1695. The limitations of North American terrain prevented major communities of this sort developing, but stable maroon societies became a factor in most areas where slave population was dense enough.

No maroon community, however, became as threatening as the slaves of Haiti, the old colony of Saint Domingue, who rose en masse against their masters in the great revolution of 1791. The slaves in

Right The black religions of the New World are richly influenced by African traditions. Some forms, like those of the Bush Negroes, borrow minimally from Christianity. The black churches of the United States are among the most vigorous branches of modern protestantism. Haiti, the home of this priest, is the most complex religious melting pot in the Americas.

Below right In the 17th and 18th centuries runaway slaves of Angolan origin founded settlements in remote areas of the Brazilian forest, many of which survive today with a high degree of cultural and social independence. In this community near Diamantina a Negro woman perpetuates the African tradition of pounding foodstuffs with a pestle. However, the substance in the mortar is not millet or maize, but coffee beans.

Haiti heavily outnumbered the whites and they included an unusually high proportion of first-generation African arrivals. Voodoo was a major theme in resistance to the French. With the masters gone, Haitian culture retained an extraordinarily rich range of African adaptations in social structure, language, folklore, art, music and religion. However, only a minority of blacks in the Americas were able to evolve genuinely African cultures like that of the Bush Negroes; even Haiti absorbed much that was French or Christian. Other Caribbean islands are more Europeanized – but they too, particularly in Jamaica and Cuba, have drawn on their African background to mold their different varieties of creole language, their syncretistic forms of religion, their conceptions of magic and the supernatural, certain aspects of their kinship structure and their corpus of folklore.

Brazil is an entirely different case, where a predominantly European culture has been deeply influenced by the diaspora. Slavery was not abolished there until 1888. By then a richly diversified Afro–Brazilian culture had developed, both on rural plantations and among the urban slaves and free blacks of coast cities like Bahia. Its religious components are particularly interesting. Brazil, for instance, is the only American country with an Islamic tradition which is rooted in black Africa. However, the Brazilian slaves and their descendants also managed to preserve Africanisms in language, music and dance, and to inject them into the mainstream of their country's extraordinary polyglot culture.

Though it has not always been their own choice, North American blacks have also managed to survive as distinct communities. However, their distinctiveness has depended on a culture which has incorporated fewer African survivals than that of any other large group of African descent in the New World. Though the slave population of the South was colossal, the trade ended in 1807, and the vast majority of them were born into families already acculturated in America. This militated against extensive continuities with Africa. Even here, however, it is a myth that the black heritage was wiped out by the Middle Passage. Southern slaveholders were only too well aware of the connection between resistance and their slaves' alarmingly distinctive usages in religion, magic and music. Their Christianity took, and still takes, syncretistic forms, their folklore, games and humor have clear African antecedents, and their speech has developed along distinctive lines – not only in special cases like the Gullah dialect of the Sea Islands of South Carolina, but in the speech patterns and inflections which distinguish modern black English. Some black family structures and naming patterns may also be adaptations of African usages. Above all, the descendants of the slaves have adapted Africa's musical legacy to give America and the Western world the unique musical gift of jazz, one of the most powerful cultural forces in modern history. Even in the United States the diaspora carried a great deal of cultural baggage with it. Many younger American blacks have tended increasingly to try to fit their historical experience into a larger African framework – not only through adopting their own versions of African styles in dress and appearance, but through an intense

interest in their African origins. The furore over the television serial *Roots* in the late 1970s would have been unthinkable 20 years before.

Nevertheless, the tendency to look back to Africa is not new, and for modern African history it is the most important aspect of the diaspora. At the simplest level, it has brought many expatriates back to Africa. Some have traveled as individuals, like the missionaries from the Watchtower movement who deeply influenced the development of central African nationalism in the interwar years. Others have formed recognizable groups, like the Brazilians of Nigeria, Portuguese-speaking Fon, Ewe, and Yoruba who returned to Africa at the end of the slave-trade period and took a major role in the commercial life of Lagos. There were 3000 of them there by the 1880s, and they extended their operations throughout West Africa. Even in East Africa 150 Bombay Africans managed to return in 1875 to a settlement at Freretown, outside Mombasa. The most outstanding of all these group ventures was the colony of Sierra Leone, founded by British abolitionists in 1787. Although the bulk of its 19th-century immigrants were Africans of different cultures freed from captured slave ships, its first settlers were drawn successively from the diaspora community in England, from American blacks temporarily settled in Nova Scotia as a consequence of the American Revolution, and from the maroon Negroes of Jamaica.

Settlement in Africa has been particularly attractive to a series of groups from the USA. The most successful of such ventures is the black republic of Liberia. Though many blacks resented its white supporters' assumption that they had no place in America, it was founded by ex-slaves and governed by their descendants. Liberia's whole history has been strongly influenced by its economic and political ties with the USA. At the end of the 19th century, when Bishop Henry Turner of the African Methodist Episcopal Church revived the interest of poor American blacks in emigration, it was still Liberia which was the focus of their plans. In the 1920s the flamboyant nationalist leader Marcus Garvey was still interested in colonizing some of his American followers there.

For African history itself, however, the real importance of the diaspora is its influence on modern nationalism and pan-Africanism. A period of residence or study abroad has had an effect on almost every modern African leader by bringing him into contact with intellectuals from other black communities. The concept of *négritude*, which has been crucial to the ideologies of French-speaking Africa, would never have developed as it did if Paris had not provided a forum for interaction between men like Léopold Sédar Senghor of Senegal and Caribbean intellectuals like Aimé Césaire of Martinique and Jean Price-Mars of Haiti. The nationalism of anglophone Africa has also had its foreign debts. As early as 1915 the great revolt in the Shiré highlands of Nyasaland was led by John Chilembwe, who had been a student in Virginia. Hastings Banda and Kwame Nkrumah are better-known leaders who spent part of their student days in America. Other Africans were influenced by a period of military service outside their own country. Between the World Wars, another major factor was the influence of Marcus Garvey, the

Left The example of the new African nations overseas increased the cultural and political self-confidence of black communities in the United States, just as American society was entering a period of anxiety over pluralism and its own mainstream values. Alex Haley's *Roots,* which glued every black and many white Americans to the television, was itself part of a revolution in attitudes to Africa.

Below The 20th century has seen new bonds grow up between diaspora Africans throughout the world. One of the pioneers of the pan-African ideal was the Jamaican Marcus Garvey (1887–1940). His work in America had deep symbolic importance for several of the young men who became leaders in the new African nations.

Jamaican whose Universal Negro Improvement Association was the focus of American working-class black protest. Nkrumah once noted that he had been a more important influence than Lenin or Marx.

Modern African leaders have also been subtly influenced by the American and European contacts they have made through the pan-African movement. Its pioneers already worked in a web of influence stretching between Africa, Europe, the Caribbean and North America. Africanus Horton of Sierra Leone was educated in London and Edinburgh. Edward Wilmot Blyden lived in Liberia, but was born in St Thomas, and visited the USA 11 times between 1872 and 1888. In the 20th century a series of pan-African conferences gave young intellectuals a golden opportunity to make contacts in other diaspora communities. With the exception of Blaise Diagne, the deputy from French Senegal, the towering figures at the earlier conferences were all diaspora blacks: Duse Mohammed Effendi from Egypt, George Padmore from Trinidad, and above all W. E. B. Du Bois, the father of modern black consciousness in the USA. Duse Mohammed and Padmore, like the Guyanan leader Ras Makonnen, had prolonged spells of residence in Britain, where they had an incalculable influence on the way in which young Africans studying there perceived the common cause of colonial and particularly African peoples.

By the time of the Fifth Pan-African Congress, held in Manchester in 1945, the situation had changed. Du Bois was there as usual, Padmore was still joint secretary, but the main leaders were men from emerging Africa, like Nkrumah, Kenyatta, and I. T. A. Wallace-Johnson of Sierra Leone. Their future triumphs in forging nations would soon give a new source of pride to the tens of millions of diaspora Africans who had been born into alien societies far from the mother continent.   C.D.R.

THE GROWTH OF CITIES

The city is probably the last idea one would associate with Africa. Africa is certainly the least urbanized of all the continents and many of its cities are very new. But it also has a great diversity of regions: it can be claimed that one region, Egypt, gave birth to the oldest cities of all, and its northern fringe has for millennia shared in the urban civilization of the Mediterranean. We cannot generalize for the continent as a whole. But before looking at distinctive regions, different cultures and epochs, it is useful to examine the extent of urbanization today in purely arithmetic terms. This alone will indicate why Africa has experienced the sudden rise of urban problems on a massive scale.

In 1920 about 6·9 million (5 per cent of the population) lived in towns of more than 20 000; in 1930 the figure was 9·7 million (6 per cent); in 1940 13·8 million (7 per cent); in 1950 21·5 million (10 per cent); in 1960 36·4 million (13 per cent); and by the 1970s probably well over 50 million (16 per cent) would be urbanized.

Enclosed by the Sahel hills and a fortified city wall, the pirate stronghold of Algiers appears on a 17th-century map by the English cartographer John Speed. Despite the impression of compactness, Algiers at this period had a population of 100 000. From here Barbary pirates sailed out to prey on Mediterranean shipping.

Thus although the urban proportion of the population is still small, the ten-year increases have been progressively greater and the total number living in towns is now quite considerable. The jump between 1950 and 1960 was 69 per cent, the most rapid rate of increase in the world.

The percentage of town dwellers who live in cities of over 500 000 is also increasing: 13 per cent in 1920 and 30 per cent in 1960. The trend in Africa, as in many developing countries, is towards comparatively few very large cities rather than a great increase in the number of towns. Cities of over 100 000 flourish and attract the great majority of rural migrants.

Differences between African states are still very considerable. The most urbanized are South Africa, Egypt, Morocco and Algeria. On the other hand, populous states such as Ethiopia and Tanzania have little urbanization. Gabon and Namibia have small populations but a high degree of urbanization. Lastly, there are some very large cities: Cairo with five million people, Alexandria with two million, Lagos with one and a half, Addis Ababa, Johannesburg and Cape Town all with over a million and Algiers with just under a million.

Rapid growth and the attraction of the large metropolis are the two things that underlie the major problems of urbanization in Africa. In the smaller countries with very meager resources problems are no less acute because they are on a smaller scale. Before looking at these problems we should consider briefly the development of urbanization in the different regions of Africa as a necessary background to understanding their modern context.

Historically, three core areas of urbanization can be distinguished, separated greatly in space, time and in complexity of culture: the Mediterranean, Nigeria and South Africa. The Mediterranean fringe has shared in a series of urban periods. The great urban civilization of the Nile came and went; its impetus passed to Greece, but returned again to Egypt with Alexander. He built Alexandria, which by the beginning of the Christian era was a great trading center at the crossroads of Africa, Asia and Europe and may have had three-quarters of a million people. Here Greek, Jewish and Egyptian cultures blended and gave the city its renown as the scientific center of the world with one of the greatest libraries ever known. It declined with the 7th-century Muslim conquest, a decline which accelerated after the diversion of eastern trade routes via the Cape.

It was Muslim Arabs also who established a city just north of the ruins of Memphis in the year 641. In the 10th century it became a new capital, Al-Qahirah; by the 14th century Cairo was the biggest metropolis in Europe and the Middle East, with half a million people and a famous university. Although, like Alexandria, it lost its trade and declined in population after the 16th century, it remained a large city and grew dramatically in the 20th century, due to westernization. Meanwhile, Islam had spread throughout the whole of North Africa, and coastal cities flourished. Tunis was established in the late 17th century, near the site of Carthage. Further west a former Phoenician settlement gave way in the 10th century to the Muslim city of Algiers, dominated by the Turks in the 17th century, when it was a town of a 100 000 people. Muslim influence also extended up the Nile and beyond the Sahara. A great network of trade routes crossed the Sahara, linking east with west and the Mediterranean coast with the savanna forest lands bordering equatorial Africa.

This last domain was under Muslim control until the middle of the last century and its influence remains in the northern parts of the second core region of urbanization, in what we now know as Nigeria. Early 19th-century travelers have given us graphic accounts of the contemporary towns of Nigeria. In the northern grassland area, relatively rich in resources and well peopled, the towns were the centers of Saharan trade and owed much to Muslim influence. Now much declined, Tombouctou is a fabled example. Kano is no less famous. Many of these towns had populations of 20 000 or 30 000, and the chief city, Sokoto, may have had

100 000 when Europeans first reached the scene. They were mud-built walled towns, centering on market place, palace and mosque.

Between grassland and coast is a wide belt of forest land, and most of its towns reflect the Yoruba culture. The Yoruba, immigrants from the northeast, used towns, as did the Muslims, as a means of dominating and organizing the people they

conquered. They were bases of administration and power and formed a network within southern Nigeria. Each town center was dominated by the chief's compound set in a ceremonial space; trade was also important and the central market a major feature of the town. The first Europeans estimated their size; of the 34 they described, 24 probably had more than 10 000 people; 18 of these were over

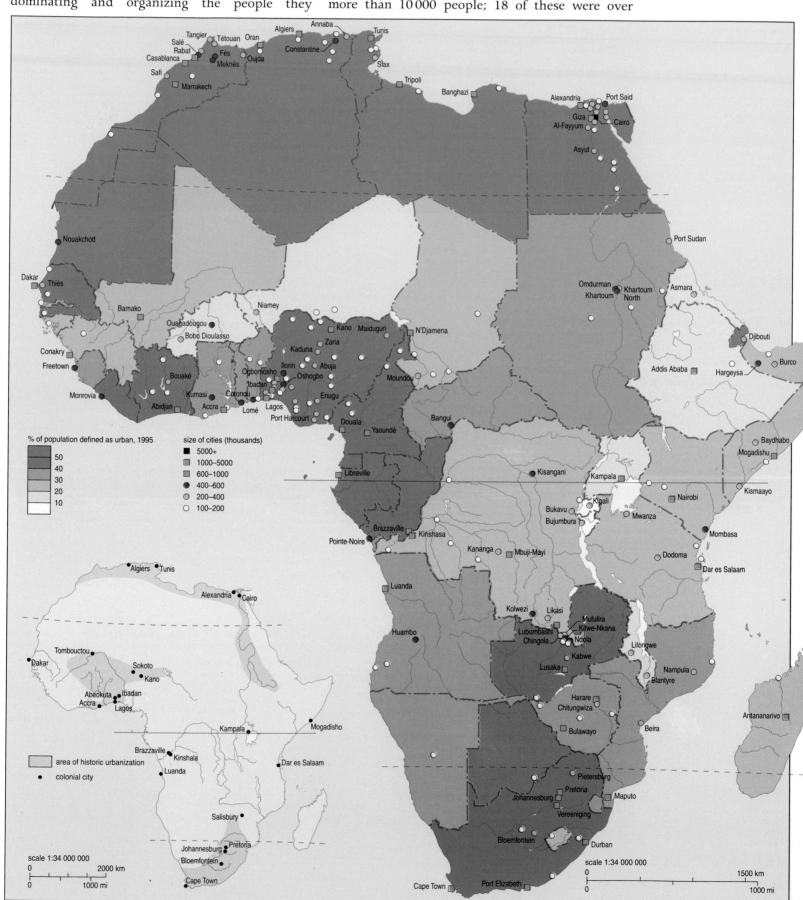

% of population defined as urban, 1995

- 50
- 40
- 30
- 20
- 10

size of cities (thousands)
- ■ 5000+
- ■ 1000–5000
- ■ 600–1000
- ● 400–600
- ● 200–400
- ○ 100–200

area of historic urbanization

• colonial city

scale 1:34 000 000

0   2000 km

0   1000 mi

scale 1:34 000 000

0   1500 km

0   1000 mi

The panoramic view of Ibadan in western Nigeria exhibits the contrast between old and new seen in many African cities. Modern skyscrapers in the city center tower above the corrugated iron roofs of a rundown residential suburb. A thriving Yoruba town in the 19th century, Ibadan maintained its economic importance under British colonial rule. Its significance as a market was enhanced by the construction of the Lagos–Kano railroad in the early 1900s.

The degree of urbanization of the African population
Rapid urbanization is a characteristic of many parts of Africa as the drive towards industrialization gathers momentum. Within the countries where such a process is taking place there is generally a pattern of explosive expansion of one or two urban centers into vast sprawling cities while the remainder of the country remains almost totally rural. Medium-sized industrial towns are rare. Clusters of places in this category often denote the presence of extractive industries based on mineral deposits. Most people still live in villages or in towns that have thrived by virtue of being traditional market or administrative centers.

20 000, 8 were over 40 000; Abeokuta may have been between 60 000 and 100 000 and Ibadan was probably more than 100 000. Although the majority of their people were farmers, these walled towns presented an impressive and distinctly urban scene and give this region of West Africa an important role in the urban story.

The third core region is southern Africa, where a transplantation of western European culture took place late in African history. Although the indigenous people now form the major part of this urban population, it has no local roots. The cultural gap between indigenous and European peoples was so great that the former have had no impact on either the system of cities or their form.

The earliest European city was Cape Town, which began as a supply station on the sea route between Europe and the East. It became a town under the Dutch, came under British rule in 1806, and became legislative capital of the Republic of South Africa in 1910. It is now a metropolis of 1·5 million; only a third of its population is white. Pretoria (500 000) and Bloemfontein (180 000), mid-19th-century Dutch foundations and formerly the capitals of independent states, are the administrative and judicial capitals respectively of the republic. Durban (one million), founded by the British in 1835, is one of the world's major commercial ports. Johannesburg (1·5 million) was an outcome of the gold rush of 1886 and Salisbury (500 000), the capital of Zimbabwe, was established in 1890 and grew rapidly after rail links were established with Beira. The urban populations of the South African cities, comprising whites, blacks, Asians and Coloreds, constitute a problem which is highlighted by racial segregation.

Outside the three major regions we can distinguish the colonial cities and recent administrative capitals, in which Europeans form a very small class of administrators and managers in an overwhelmingly indigenous urban population. For example, Dakar (500 000) has about 7 per cent white population; Accra (750 000) about 5 per cent; and Lagos (1·6 million) less than 1 per cent. The main characteristics of these cities are their newness, the size and Western appearance of the business and

administration centers and the contrasting shanty towns which extend for miles beyond. Some have long antecedents: Accra was established in 1482 and Luanda in 1576, both by the Portuguese; Dakar in 1670 by the Dutch. But many of them date from the 1880s when the continent was carved up between European powers; Dar-es-Salaam (German) in 1885, Mogadisho (Italian) in 1892, Kampala (Imperial British East African Company) in 1890. Kinshasa (1881) and Brazzaville (1883) grew up as river ports. All these cities owe their size to a great postwar boom.

The movement of tribal folk to the growing cities of Africa has had dramatic effects on their size and also on their nature. These cities have none of the resources which would enable them to absorb immigrants at the normal standard of housing and services. Outside the modern core of offices and administration buildings which most African cities have acquired, and the restricted areas which once housed colonial whites and which now house the native elite, most cities lack water, roads, sewerage and electricity, and the houses appear to be little better than crude shelters.

Shanty towns of this kind account for a very large proportion of the urban growth: 180 000 people in Casablanca live in *bidonvilles*, and a third of the population of Algiers and Oran. Hastily erected shelters of beaten tin cans, cardboard, odd bits of timber and corrugated iron, are typical of vast areas around the cities. Many squatters start life in slum property in the center of cities and their move to the periphery indicates their need to do something for themselves. Ramshackle though much of it appears, the resulting shanty town is often better than rural housing, and its nearness to possible work is a great advantage to the migrant.

In addition to such spontaneous or unauthorized squatters on land not legally acquired, many cities have sectors in which they try to regulate migrant housing. In South Africa the rigid segregation of black and white is reflected in the strict control of black settlements. One of the largest of these, Soweto, is on the outskirts of Johannesburg. Here some 35 000 sites were prepared before occupation, and the migrants were allowed to construct a temporary shack at the back of each site, to be replaced subsequently by a more permanent house at the front. The result is a mechanically organized and uniformly stereotyped city of half a million people, but one in which the physical standards of the houses are better than they would be in uncontrolled settlements.

Outside South Africa it is more usual to find a mixture of controlled and uncontrolled growth. For example, in Nairobi a valley to the east of the city has a settlement of more than 50 000; 20 000 of these are squatters and the remainder live on plots rented from landlords. Control, in private hands, means houses of slightly higher standards – timber with corrugated roofs, compared with mud and wattle – though amenities are minimal. About half the population of Lusaka lives in shanty towns and an increasing proportion are now engaged in a site-and-service scheme. Sites available for renting are prepared, provided with some amenities (such as water and sanitation, to be shared by several plots) and served by roads capable of taking buses. The occupier is helped to buy material to build his own house of brick and corrugated iron on a concrete floor. The minimal cost is still too great for most immigrants, who resort to illegal squatting. The Lusaka squatters, as in many cities, are not amorphous, haphazard groups, but are often highly organized, and able to look after communal needs, even sometimes trying to replicate their former village lives. This kind of settlement may well represent a traditional way of urban growth, but it is on a scale which is frightening. Experiments in providing infrastructure to encourage self-help are a way of ensuring some improvement.

Urbanization is very much more than a shift of population, the growth of cities and the proliferation of shanty towns. It implies radical change of life and conditions for those who have migrated there. Only in some of the older cities does the excess of births over deaths produce a natural growth: almost universally, a rapid rural population growth is sending its surplus to the cities. The attraction is almost wholly economic, but although work is the main lure of the city, we should not underestimate the non-economic motive. In some cultures the city confers status on those who live or have lived there. It also offers freedom from the restraints of the social group and the excitement of a more sophisticated way of life. Labor movements in Africa are of long standing and the attractions of the city are well publicized.

Severance from tribal life and commitment to the city may be neither complete nor final. Ties with villages are often maintained, for the insurance of the home agricultural plot sustains many, and a great number look upon the experience as transitory. Nevertheless, the social changes are permanent for many millions and this trend will accelerate as education and the media make information about cities more accessible and help to tie rural life to the city in a multitude of ways.

The migrant often pays dearly for his move. Attractive wages do not always compensate for exacting urban conditions and overcrowding. Density of population may be very high; in Accra in 1960 the density was 18·4 persons to the house; in Dar-es-Salaam, eight persons to a room of 30 square meters; and in many cities street sleepers are a

Above A township near Johannesburg houses African laborers who are prohibited by South Africa's apartheid laws from living in the predominantly white urban areas where they work. This housing is healthier than shantytown shacks but lack of medical, recreational and transportation facilities makes such townships unattractive places to live.

Left Kairouan in Tunisia is one of the holy cities of Islam and a pilgrimage center. Founded in 670, it served as a base for the Muslim subjugation of northwest Africa. Traditional courtyard houses cluster together along narrow streets. A minaret breaks the skyline.

reminder that some have no shelter at all. Because the majority of immigrants are young men (in Lagos 70 per cent are between the ages of 20 and 29), the population is unbalanced. Hopes for jobs are often illusory, for population growth far outstrips increase in employment. Malnutrition is rife, infant mortality is very high and life expectancy still hovers between 34 and 40. Although there are indications of some of the characteristics of Western cities – such as the substitution of impersonal relations for family networks and of secondary contacts for primary, the growth of anonymity and of antisocial behavior – this should not hide the degree to which traditional ways of life survive in the city. Tribal social relationships are maintained and links with rural life replenish older values; these factors make for stability and easier adaptation. Reasserting rural patterns cushions the impact of the city and makes the transition easier.

This also means that the influence of the city on the countryside may be less than one thinks. In any case it varies a great deal as the pattern of urban life varies in the many kinds of cities. The older native towns are much more homogeneous and socially balanced. Based on a traditional economy dependent on the land, they have always produced an entrepreneural class, and with education this has turned into an indigenous elite. Towns based on extractive industries, like Johannesburg, merely emphasize the cultural gap between exploiter and exploited. Between the tight administrative control of the latter and gradual emerging indigenous control of the former, are states like Zaïre, where the control is more theoretical than real. In between too are the older cities in the north, where multi-ethnic populations have for centuries played complementary roles in the economic and social life of the city.

In many ways cities are a link between tribal Africa and an emerging "political" continent. They are agents of change, but so far their effects have been modified by the weight of traditional culture, which is so often a feature of much of the life of the cities themselves.

E.J.

VERNACULAR ARCHITECTURE

The wealth and beauty of African architecture have for too long been sadly neglected and misunderstood. Despite its relatively low population density, much of the continent has a greater architectural complexity than any other continent. Over 1500 peoples live in Africa and it can be broadly stated that each one of these has a unique material culture, not in every detail but certainly in aggregate. To understand African houses it is important not just to look at the way they were built and what they were built of but to consider as well how they relate to the landscape around them and to the needs and beliefs of the people who built them. The enormous diversity of beliefs and practices in Africa, however, makes it very difficult to write about African architecture as a whole. Nevertheless, certain common characteristics do make it possible to offer a few generalizations about the attitudes that produced this architecture.

The ideal of perpetuating a lifestyle through the generations was fundamental to many African societies and total cultural heritages were handed down orally from one generation to the next. That is not to say that there was never any change, but that any change, social or economic, was subtly absorbed into a system that was fundamentally conservative in nature. Under such circumstances architecture became a group solution to habitation problems, communally worked out and reaffirmed by each generation. The houses fitted precisely the social and economic lifestyle of those who lived in them. They were purpose built and were built on the whole by those who lived in them.

House building was one of the main regular family tasks and a great deal of effort was devoted to the construction and finish. Indeed one can say without exaggeration that housing in traditional Africa was accorded a high political priority. Everyone had a house and no one went without and the people were proud to live in their houses because they were an outward symbol or manifestation of their community identity. In many African societies stress was laid on conformity rather than innovation, with unduly successful people being suspect. Often what was valued was congeniality and equality rather than aspirations to wealth in the form of cattle or crops. In many societies threats of witchcraft were used to safeguard these ideals. There was therefore no great incentive to use houses to absorb money or for a conspicuous display of wealth. As a result most houses were equal, or rather some were quantitatively rather than qualitatively grander than others. Villages became therefore a collection of similar houses which in themselves were a collection of similar buildings. It is very often difficult to tell where one house ends and another begins.

In Europe and North America it is common for a house to be under one roof. In Africa this was hardly ever the case. Houses were usually a collection of similar buildings linked together or surrounded by a wall or fence, each building becoming in effect one room of the homestead, with one specific purpose such as a kitchen, a bedroom, store etc. Physically, little distinction was made between one building and another in a homestead and the sleeping room and the storage hut would look identical from the outside. The buildings used by the head of the household were often not especially elaborate or larger than the rest, and sometimes the granary or the cattle house would be the largest building in the compound. In many parts of the Western world people believe in the idea of building for posterity and go to great length to preserve buildings for several generations. Most African villages eschewed this particular idea of permanence. There was no question of people adapting themselves to houses which may have been unsuitable or inadequate. There was always a quick response in buildings to changed family requirements, such as marriage, divorce or adoption of children. Buildings were put where people needed them and they were tailored to their needs.

Vernacular architecture generally is founded on an appreciation of environmental factors. Traditional communities have to take a long-term view of their habitat; the materials needed could not simply be plundered from the land but had to be utilized only in such quantities and at such times as to cause minimum harm to the surroundings. In Africa houses were often rebuilt at least every generation to reflect changed social groupings. This fact, taken together with the ideals of equality and universal housing already mentioned, had a profound influence on the sort of building that could be put up in any location. For there had to be sufficient materials for everybody all the time. It is perhaps not surprising that a significant proportion of African houses were built of vegetable materials which grow and are continually replaced and are therefore always ready when needed.

The temporary nature of many houses did not therefore reflect unstable or unsure societies. On the contrary the continual renewal of short-lived buildings bred feelings of permanence and security. Nor did it reflect a temporary solution to housing problems. House designs were very long-term solutions to the needs and constraints of any particular society and its environment. Indeed there is archaeological evidence from some areas to show that buildings built until recently were in a style that had remained basically unchanged for more than a millennium.

Pictures of traditional African villages taken over the last 50 years can give us a glimpse into the past, not because the buildings themselves are of any great age but because the way they are arranged and built has often persisted through many centuries. Actual family relationships vary from year to year as people are born, are married or die, yet the overall social structure and the physical manifestation of it – the houses and villages – remain unchanged. The traditional Dogon village is a good

Below The Mousgoum live on the flat flood plains between the Logon and Shari rivers in Cameroon. Their houses were built like pots of mud, sometimes using small stones. The striking relief decoration may have prevented rain eroding the buildings. This is an old photograph taken in about 1900.

Below Bamileke houses were built in dense clusters on the slopes of the lush grassland valleys of western Cameroon. Six to eight of these tall, square-plan buildings with conical roofs together formed a homestead.

Right This aerial view of Labbe Zanga village, Mali, expresses beautifully the relationship of individual buildings to homesteads and to the whole village. Many of the buildings shown are granaries. Here there is a short growing season and much food has to be stored.

example. The Dogon appear to have lived on the Bandiagara escarpment for at least 500 years and to be the direct descendants of the Tellem peoples whose buildings, carvings and textiles have been preserved, some from the 14th century, in the dry caves of the escarpment and show a remarkable continuity of material culture.

Although conservative in essence, African architecture did nevertheless have the capacity to adapt to ecological and social changes. But the changes facing it in the 20th century are probably more cataclysmic and irreversible than any before. In many areas tin roofs and cement blocks have all but swept away any traces of the local architecture. Paradoxically it survives best in the richer states of West Africa where mud was used as the building material and is relatively fireproof. Its continued survival will depend now not so much on the rate of economic growth as in a shift of attitude back towards a respect for and knowledge of local crafts and traditions. For the rest of the world, traditional African architecture shows signs of becoming the focus of much interest because of its human scale and elegant functional simplicity.

S.D.

Traditional House Types

Traditional African houses rarely consisted of one single building subdivided into rooms. The more usual arrangement was for each building of the homestead to be in effect a "room," the complete homestead being made up of a collection of buildings or "rooms," perhaps surrounded by a fence or wall.

The shape of these buildings varied enormously across the continent. At least 20 different major categories can be identified and each of these displayed numerous variations, not only in size and form but also in building materials.

The examples illustrated here have been chosen to represent some of the more common individual unit types as well as a few of the ways in which these were assembled to form homesteads.

S.D.

The Nuba peoples live in the hills of southern Kordofan. Many of their homesteads are built on the ring pattern with individual buildings linked by walls or fences. House walls are of red gravelly clay, sometimes mixed with stones and often built on a foundation of large boulders. Each house consisted usually of several bedrooms, a grinding room/store with grindstones set into a raised bench and sometimes a pig- or goat-house which had a bedroom above for young children.

Below Zulu homesteads, scattered across the undulating plains of the southeastern tip of Africa, were symmetrical arrangements of buildings within two concentric hedges or stockades. The inner circle surrounded the cattle kraal, underneath which storage pits were often dug, and the outer circle protected the homestead. Each homestead was usually made up of a room for each wife, arranged around the chief wife's room which normally faced the entrance gate, together with rooms for the unmarried sons and extra granaries.

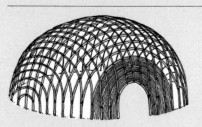

The framework of Zulu houses was an arrangement of two sets of semicircular hoops, arranged at right angles to one another and tied where they intersected. This framework was covered first with matting and then with thick layers of grass thatch.

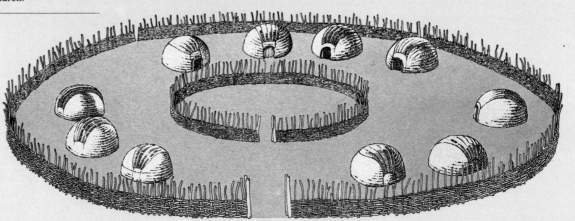

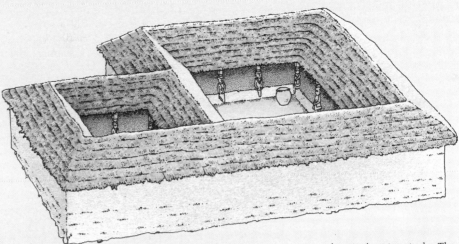

The Yoruba live in densely populated villages and towns in the forest areas of western Nigeria. Their houses were built around one large courtyard and sometimes also around subsidiary courtyards and impluvia – tiny courtyards often no more than 3 meters in diameter used not only to let in light and air to the surrounding rooms but also to collect rainwater in pots or tanks. The outside walls of the houses were built of puddled mud laid in courses, while the sides of the rooms facing the courtyards were often open between elaborately carved roof posts. Each house consisted of rooms for wives and children, a kitchen and a store as well as rooms for craftwork in the urban areas.

The Somolo live in southern Upper Volta. Their multistory houses, with walls of puddled mud and ceilings and roofs of palm fronds supported on posts, can be seen to be a coalescence of several circular buildings. In the center of each house there is a tiny courtyard. The thatched roof covers a granary. Houses sometimes consist of as many as 20 rooms, one for each wife, as well as kitchens, stores, children's rooms, granaries and grinding rooms.

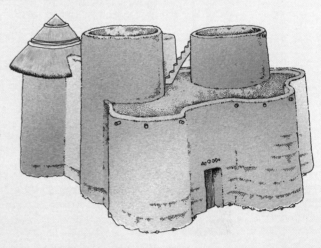

Above The Nupe live in densely populated settlements in central Nigeria along the fertile alluvial valleys of the river Niger and its tributaries. Their villages are scattered in irregular patterns over the flat plains, while their houses are collections of round-plan mud buildings within enclosing mud walls breached by a *kitamba* or entrance room. Inside the walls houses normally contained a room for each wife, a room for unmarried daughters, one for unmarried sons, an inner entrance room for visitors, a man's room, a stable and granaries – the small buildings raised up on staddle stones in the drawing.

Right The Asante live in the forest areas of southern Ghana. Their houses were traditionally built around one or more courtyards, and around each were four rooms joined at their corners with a short length of wall. Puddled mud was used for the walls, reinforced with a wooden framework. The sides of rooms facing the courtyard were often left open or partly enclosed with pillars of palm fronds covered with mud plaster. Many of the walls and pillars were ornamented with complex relief patterns. A detail from one such wall is shown here.

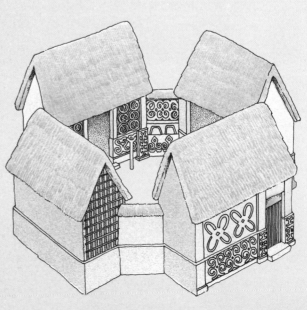

AFRICAN ARTS

Below This elongated Nok head was found at Katsina Ala in northern Nigeria. It takes its name from the village where tin-mining operations first brought to light similar naturalistic terracotta scultpures. The "Nok Culture" is now thought to date from around 200 BC.

Despite the numerous books on African art and the familiarity of many of its pieces, now prominently displayed in museums, much remains to be discovered about its creation and use. The only common characteristic of what is usually discussed under the term African sculpture is its non-abstract form. As well as wood, sculptures were made from iron, brass, terracotta, stone, basketry covered with clay or skin, ivory and even cloth and encompassed such varied forms as figures, dolls, masks, stools, headrests, staffs, bowls and so on.

The impulse behind the creation of traditional African art can only be understood with reference to the community that produced it. Indeed, African figurative sculpture can almost be thought of as the private face of the community in which it originated. Some of the sculpture was made to be seen only by the spirit world, some was never seen by women, and much, when not in use, was hidden away in rafters between ceremonial occasions or was housed in shrines to which noninitiates and strangers were not admitted. Many dancing masks were made to be seen in motion, swirling in semidarkness, lit up intermittently by the low flickering light of a fire, with deep recesses and strong contrasting planes catching the low light. Brightly lit and static in museums, wrenched from their contexts, they have lost half their power.

Since African art is essentially a community art, the form that sculptures took was on the whole very specific to the peoples who produced them. They used a language of shapes that was known and understood by both the artists and their patrons. The carver, for instance, was not an individual expressing his own personal feelings and taking inspiration at random; rather the art was produced to satisfy the needs of a community by someone who was closely integrated into that community. Nevertheless this did not mean that an artist's work was merely repetitive; on the contrary, an artist was free to evolve his own personal adaptations within a framework accepted by the community and his work might be either acclaimed or rejected.

This framework of forms often only had significance for the originating community and sometimes meant very little to even neighboring communities. Thus art was a unifying force within each community; it reasserted community identity by using a unique language. Misunderstandings, therefore, arise when norms from other cultures are used to assess African sculpture. Chokwe sculptures, for example, with half-open mouths and pointed teeth, are sometimes said by Western observers to look "fierce" or "cruel," although nicely pointed teeth are a mark of beauty among the Chokwe. Similarly vitality or movement is considered by many African carvers to exist only in works which are balanced, that is exactly symmetrical about a central axis, whereas Western observers consider those were the very sculptures which were most static.

In Africa all art is in some sense functional, although without adequate documentation it is often impossible to tell, just by looking at it, what a piece of sculpture was originally intended to be used for, whether to amuse the living or pacify the dead or botli. Among the Yoruba similar carvings found in shrines and in palaces had very different functions, the first to honor the spirits and the second to honor the Oba or king. In all cases the importance of a piece of sculpture lay not just within itself but depended on where it was, who owned it and how it was used. In some societies once a carver had finished a mask, it was then given its life-giving force through paint or continuous offerings of food or oil by its owner or guardian without which things it would have been worthless. Elsewhere the significance of a mask could be altered by it being bequeathed from one man to another.

Most of the vast amount of sculpture now housed in museums comes from western and central Africa with comparatively little from eastern and southern Africa. The exact reasons for this distribution are not yet quite clear. It is often stated that the settled agriculturalists of the rain forests and the savanna woodlands on the forest margins had the right materials (large enough pieces of wood) and the right political institutions to encourage the development and preservation of major works of sculpture, in contrast to the pastoralists and mixed farmers elsewhere. Nevertheless, in other parts of the world pastoralists have been very prolific producers of carvings. Another factor must be the high population density of parts of West and central Africa, which means that any carving tradition will produce many more pieces than in an area of low population density. A third important point is that eastern and southern African may not have produced as little as has been imagined. Recent research in Malawi has produced some interesting masks from an area formerly thought to be devoid of all figurative work.

In general, however, the finest works have come from areas where political institutions, settlement patterns and social organization made it possible for several carvers to thrive and to compete for patrons within a small area. The Yoruba kingdoms in western Nigeria, the Kuba of Congo (DRO) and the Bamoun in southern Cameroon are good examples. Each carver evolved his own personal adaptation of the accepted community style; the most successful ones gained more commissions and perfected their techniques still further. In several areas the names of the carvers from 50 years back are still known and their skills remembered. Carving was not in all instances a professional affair; among the Dogon and the Tiv, for example, carving was done by nonspecialists. In some instances a particular carver's success extended far beyond the boundaries of his own community, and masks, for example, would be bought from him to be used in ceremonies for which they were not specifically

Right Vivid white-faced masks such as this one were made by the Bapuna and neighboring peoples in Congo (DRO). Distinctive features are the tall three-lobed hairstyle, closed eyes, and scarification marks on the forehead and temple. The mask would have had striped cloth attached to it completely to enclose the dancer, who often performed on stilts. It seems to have represented the spirit of a young girl.

Below A Mangbetu pot from northeastern Congo (DRO). The Mangbetu are renowned for their body decoration, an art which is reflected on this fine anthropomorphic pot.

Above Much of Ivory Coast Baulé sculpture is gentle and humanistic, and was among the earliest African art to be admired by European collectors. This seated, bearded figure of an ancestor demonstrates the care typically taken by Baulé carvers to represent exact details of the hair and face.

Right This selection of baskets comes from Tanzania and Nigeria but is representative of baskets sold in markets all over Africa.
Center column, from the top
Large plaited basket, Adamawa, Nigeria. This basket was used for head carrying and its base is padded.
Wickerwork food basket, Kafanchan, Nigeria.
Coiled threshing basket, Nyamwezi, Tanzania.
Wickerwork sieve for straining grated coconut, Swahili, Tanzania.
Right hand column
Twined food cover, Bornu, Nigeria.
Twined basket, Pogoro, Tanzania.
Plaited and twined storage basket, Nyakusa, Tanzania.

designed. Trading of castings and carvings was certainly not unknown, too, and gifts of items of regalia were quite common from one ruler to another. Many of the African empires were organized around vassal chiefs who espoused the culture as well as the political institutions of the central rulers. The cultural influence of the Asante of Ghana over their hinterland is a good example; gold jewelry, silk *kente* cloth and gold-handled swords spread to the chiefs of surrounding peoples.

To give the study of African art a historical dimension is very difficult. Very little wood carving survives for more than 100 years. What historical

Below Decorated calabashes from Nigeria. Calabashes or gourds grow on creeping plants over fences and roofs or in between crops. When cut and dried they are used as rafts, food containers or as sound boxes for musical instruments and decorated in a variety of ways as illustrated here.

material we do have is of metal, terracotta, ivory and stone. Nevertheless the terracotta sculptures from Nigeria span two and a half millennia and so give a very good picture of stylistic development over a very long period of time. Much of the figurative sculpture is magnificent – the Nok and Ife terracotta heads and figures, the Benin, Ife and Igbo-Ukwu bronzes, the Benin and Afro–Portuguese ivories – but it is necessarily an arbitrary and unrepresentative part of the total production. The first Nok terracottas and some of the bronzes from Ife and Igbo-Ukwu were found by accident. Many pieces have been found above ground but obviously far from where they were made. Much of the early material is still unrelated to centers of production or to the societies that produced it and so its original purpose remains obscure.

Sculpture is only marginally important economically. By contrast pots, jewelry, textiles, baskets and ironwork are often very important and are traded in markets, either because they are surplus to requirements or because they have been produced for sale by specialist craftsmen. Pottery produced by specialist potters can sometimes be sold over very large areas. Kisi pots are famous all over southwest Tanzania: very thinly walled and a reddish color, they are carried by their makers in boats up and down Lake Malawi. The Bamessi women potters of the southern Cameroon have a virtual monopoly there, while the Degha of the Black Volta control the finest beds of clay and trade their wares to large areas of Ghana and the Ivory Coast.

Large bundles of calabashes on the backs of lorries or on boats on the Niger on the way to markets are a familiar sight; unfinished calabashes (dried but not decorated) are widely traded. Baskets for storage, carrying, threshing and straining are sold in markets all over Africa and all the various techniques of twining, plaiting, coiling and wickerwork are found. In West and central Africa cloth merchants crisscross the area carrying, for example, Yoruba narrow-strip cloths north and Hausa tie-dyed cloth south. Trans-Saharan trade may have atrophied, but elsewhere improved roads have speeded up the existing trade in locally produced craft goods. Handwoven and dyed cloths, for example, still manage to compete successfully with machine-made goods.

The individual artist is now becoming a part of the 20th-century African scene. In Nigeria the Oshogbo group of artists, who came to prominence in the 1960s, experiment with adaptations of traditional techniques, such as repoussé aluminum work with subjects often based on traditional folk tales. Elsewhere in Nigeria woodcarvers have been encouraged to produce plaques, doors and carvings for churches and secular buildings. In Tanzania the delicate lino prints of Francis Msangi contrast with the forceful sculptures now produced by Makonde artists to sell to visitors. Everywhere artists are emerging to supply patrons both in the urban areas of Africa and overseas with the kind of portable self-contained art they require. But this is very definitely an African art, linked with the sculpture of the traditional artist through shared techniques, background and motifs, the last often representations of folk tales now being written down by African writers. S.D.

Above White Hunter in the Pygmies' Jungle, painted in gouache on board, is by Twins Seven-Seven, one of the best-known Nigerian Oshogbo artists who came to prominence in the 1960s interpreting traditional legends with new techniques.

Left This font was carved by Bandele, one of several Yoruba carvers recently encouraged to use their skills to interpret Christian themes. He seems to have conceived it as a large drum.

Nigerian Bronzes

The history of Nigerian bronze casting cannot yet be written with completeness or certainty. Much of the corpus of works now known has been found accidentally – like the hoard dug up at Igbo-Ukwu in 1939, or the Ife bronzes excavated near the palace of Ife in 1937 – and so must represent only a fragment of the total production. At any time another chance find could completely alter the picture.

Most Nigerian bronzes were produced by the lost-wax process. A model of wax or latex was sandwiched between two layers of sun-baked clay held in place with iron pins. The wax or latex was melted out and replaced by molten bronze.

Bronze casting appears to have had many centers of production, the most prolific being the court of Benin where casting was a royal prerogative and persisted from the 16th to the 19th century. Further north, at Ife, the fine naturalistic bronze heads and figures were probably produced as early as the 12th century to commemorate Onis (chiefs) and, together with their terracotta counterparts, show a distinct feeling of continuity with the Nok terracotta sculptures of 1000 years earlier.

Elsewhere, centers of production probably existed in the lower Niger area around Ijebu, at Owo, as well as among the Tiv and Jukun and latterly around Adamawa.   S.D.

Below This bronze snufftaker was probably made earlier this century. It would have been worn on the little finger and snuff taken from the round top disk. The Tiv still have a lively casting industry but usually only produce small bronzes.

Below Ogboni Edan staffs were usually made in pairs representing the earth spirit in two forms, one male and one female, attached by a chain secured at the top of each head. They were used by the Oshugbo Ogboni cult which flourished around Ijebu.

Below Benin city was by the 15th century the center of a powerful state in the forest area west of the Niger delta. The 17th-century Dutch geographer Olfert Dapper described its palace as having "wooden pillars encased in copper, where their victories are depicted." Here is a plaque from

such a pillar showing hunters and leopards intertwined with stylized leaves and flowers.

Right Also from Benin is this superb bronze ram's head ornament worn on a belt by a chief, probably in the 17th century.

Right Bronze casting in Benin was the prerogative of the Oba and a court style evolved which over the centuries seems to have become almost stultified through lack of outside contact. This rather stiff horseman belongs to the middle period around the 17th century. The rider is shown wearing an elaborate headdress modeled to represent tiers of feathers.

Below About 27 bronzes are known from Ife – all found near the royal palace. It seems the art of Ife evolved in terracotta and was only later translated into bronze, perhaps in the 13th century. This figure probably represents an Oni bedecked in royal regalia. Ife sculpture in both bronze and terracotta is the most famous manifestation of naturalism in African art.

Above Small masks, such as this one, representing grotesque faces with snakes curling out of the nostrils, were used as hip pendants hanging from a girdle and worn with court dress in Benin.

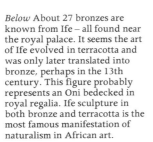

Above right This dwarf, one of the most naturalistic pieces to have been found at Benin, belongs to the earliest period, around the 16th century. It is close in style to the Ife tradition from which it is thought the technique of bronze casting may have been derived.

Right This is one of a group of bronzes in fluid style thought to have perhaps been made in the lower Niger area. It shows a hunter returning home with an antelope slung across his shoulders and a dog by his right foot.

Masterpieces of Wood Carving

Since African wood carving burst on the Western art scene in the early years of this century, "discovered" and patronized by Picasso, Matisse and their contemporaries, it has been collected avidly by museums and private collectors and much misunderstood. It has been valued for its so-called "brutalism," "cubism," "primitiveness" and so on without an understanding of the societies and attitudes that produced it. Over the last few decades, however, meticulous research into the names and styles of individual artists in many areas as well as into the uses and provenance of sculptures has done a lot to change this attitude. It is also beginning to show that African art is susceptible to the same techniques of analysis as Western art. It is hoped that over the next decade much more information will be collected which will lead to a better understanding of the historical perspective of African wood carving.   S.D.

Left These small figures made by an Ekoi carver are covered in skin. The practice of making skin-covered wooden masks, sometimes topped by small figures like these, was concentrated around the Cross river on the border of Nigeria and Cameroon. The masks belonged to associations which performed various rites and celebrations for members. Before use, a mask would usually be dressed up – polished with oil and decorated with feathers or quills.

Right Chokwe art has flourished in the large chiefdoms in the heart of Angola since they grew up in the 16th century. This statue, collected in 1878, was an effigy of the chief Chibinda. The large upturned hairstyle and exaggerated hands and feet, which apparently reflect their power and strength, are characteristic of much Chokwe sculpture.

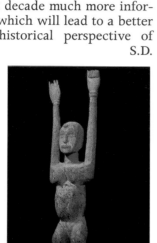

Above The Yoruba were among the most prolific producers of sculpture. Much was made for cults of major deities as furniture for shrines in the form of carved devotees, such as this piece.

Above Dogon wood carvings preserved in the dry caves on the Bandiagra escarpment in Mali are the oldest woodcarvings known to have survived in Africa. Some have been carbon dated to around 1400 AD.

Below The figures of the Bena Lulua of Congo (DRO) are very distinctive, with their heads and bodies covered in elaborate scarification marks and the navel always emphasized. All Bena Lulua carvings are thought to have been made before 1880 when religious pressures seem to have stopped production.

Left Headrests were used principally to preserve the elaborate, much-prized coiffure worn by Luba women of the Congo. They were also sometimes used in conjunction with small rectangular frames for divination. The hairstyles shown on this piece – a series of wavelike crests – are characteristic of the Luba Shankadi style.

Above This imposing couple from Côte d'Ivoire are Senufo ancestor figures – both male and female. Characteristic of the genre are their large size – up to 1 meter tall in some cases – and their rugged quality, accentuated in early examples by the weathering of the surface of the wood.

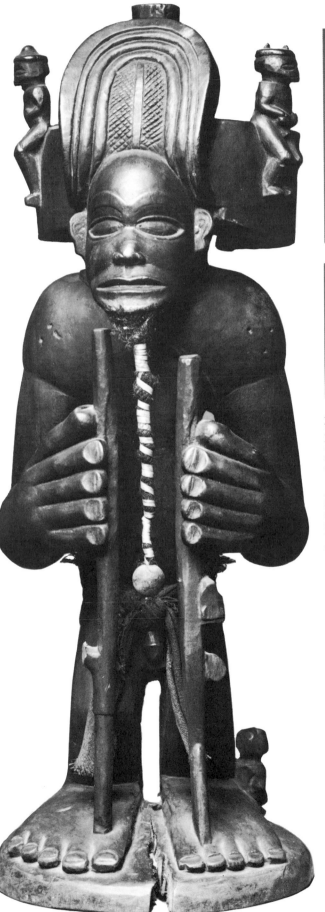

Left This Dan mask from Liberia may have been used for teaching initiates, although among the Dan the appearance of a mask is not always a reliable guide to its use, for masks were sometimes "promoted" from one activity to another. Masks such as these were sometimes used by members of the *Poro* men's society.

Right Compared with the wealth and volume of sculpture produced in West and central Africa, very little appears to have been made in southern Africa. This piece is one of the few examples of work by Sotho carvers and is the head of a staff.

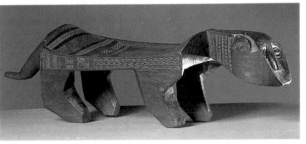

Above Headrests were designed to be used as pillows, thereby protecting elaborate hair decorations. This exmaple from southwest Tanzania has unusual carved decoration.

Below A detail of the face of a female caryatid on a Baluba chief's stool from Congo (DRO) said to have been carved by a "master of the long-faced style of the Buli." The female figures, whose hairstyles and cicatrization were carved with complete accuracy, seem to have been symbolic ancestor figures supporting the chiefs both physically and metaphorically, and may also have alluded to a Baluba practice of a member of the ruling family using a slave as a seat.

Above This Senufo equestrian figure from Côte d'Ivoire represents the *bandeguele*, a divinity used by divination experts as a messenger to the spirit world.

MUSIC AND DANCE

In a strict sense the term African music/dance applies today exclusively to the musical cultures of African peoples south of the Sahara, including the Khoisan peoples in the extreme southwest. In ancient time the black African cultural region extended much further north, as is evident, for instance, from rock paintings in the Sahara. The musical cultures of present-day North Africa are fundamentally different from those of black Africa, belonging to an Afro–Asian rather than an African stylistic area. Similarly the music and folk dances of European settler communities in southern Africa are not included under the term African music and dance.

Africa, so defined, contains the following song-style divisions according to Alan Lomax: Western Sudan, Equatorial Bantu, African Hunters, South African Bantu, Central Bantu, Northeast Bantu, Eastern Sudan, Guinea Coast, Afro–American, Muslim Sudan, Ethiopia, Upper Nile and Madagascar. The inclusion of an Afro–American region indicates that black Africa has been considered as culturally extending to include the African diaspora. The musical cultures of the Guinea coast (for instance, Yoruba and Fon), of the Congo/Angola region and to a lesser extent of southeast Africa have extensions in various parts of the New World. But only recently has it been possible to link precisely some stylistic elements in the various types of Afro–American music to local style areas in black Africa. Paul Oliver, for instance, has linked the roots of Blues with the large region of western Sudan, the hinterland of the West African coast.

In spite of the distinct musical traditions of North Africa and black Africa, there has been considerable historical interaction and cross-cultural contact between these two areas. Trade, slavery and Islamic colonization have resulted in the Islamization of African music in vast areas of black Africa, and also in the strong impact of black African musical traits in some areas of North Africa, as in southern Morocco. Muslim Sudan is one of the Islamized musical regions. In East Africa musical forms showing Arab or Islamic influence are found even far inland, for instance in southern Uganda, not only along the Indian Ocean coast. Several musical instruments of Arab introduction can be seen in these parts, the one-string fiddle being the most visible example. On the other hand, vast areas of black Africa are virtually free from Arab or Islamic influence. The traditional circumcision schools for boys found in west central Africa, with their associated dances and music, are an independent black African development and in no way to be related to Muslim practices.

It is now widely acknowledged that African music/dance in various parts of the continent has constantly undergone decisive changes in history. What is termed traditional music today is probably very different from what African music sounded like some centuries ago. Nor is African music always ethnic in the sense ethnomusicology would have it. Music forms and traits are not rigidly linked to ethnic groups; in addition the individual musician, with his individual style and creativity, is very important.

Ethnic groupings have themselves been in a state of continuous flux and musical traits and fashions have been exchanged across ethnic and linguistic boundaries. When the *likembe*, a small box-resonated lamellophone invented in the lower Zaïre region, began to spread upriver in the late 19th century, carried by Lingala-speaking porters and colonial servants, it was soon adopted by non-Bantu speakers such as the Ngbandi, Gbaya and Azande. The music of the *likembe*, which shows marked stylistic traits from western Bantu-speaking central Africa, was only gradually modified to suit local musical styles. At the beginning of the 20th century the *likembe* distribution area extended further northeast into Uganda, where it was adopted by the Nilotic Alur, Acholi and Langi. Later, workers from northern Uganda introduced the instrument to southern Uganda, where Bantu-speaking Soga and Gwere adopted it and have since produced outstanding composers and performers. In west central Africa the *likembe* gradually spread southwards from the Kasai (Zaïre) to eastern Angola and was adopted in the 1950s as far south as the Khoisan-speaking !Kung' of southeastern Angola. This example shows that distribution may change quite rapidly; distribution maps, therefore, are valid only if based on material collected within a relatively narrow time span and even so may present a fragmented and perplexing picture.

Extremely distant areas often show similar, even identical, traits, while adjacent areas may at the same time be set apart stylistically. The multi-part singing style in triads within an *equiheptatonic* tone system of the Baulé in the Ivory Coast is so close, if not identical, to the part-singing style of Ngangela-, Chokwe- and Luvale-speaking peoples in eastern Angola, that this is immediately recognized by informants from both cultures. Why this is so, is a riddle. The two areas are separated by several countries with different approaches to multi-part singing. Another historical riddle is the presence of practically identical xylophone playing styles and instruments in northern Mozambique (among Makonde- and Makua-speaking peoples) and certain peoples of the Ivory Coast and Liberia (especially the Baulé and Kru). The *jomolo* of the Baulé and *dimbila* of the Makonde are virtually identical instruments.

Diffusionist theories of different kinds have been offered to resolve such riddles. One explanation, by Arthur M. Jones, has been the suggested presence of Indonesian settlers in certain areas of East, central and West Africa during the early centuries AD, who would have been responsible for the introduction of xylophones and certain tonal-harmonic systems

Opposite Ensembles of composite gourd horns are a prominent feature of Nilotic musical cultures in the Sudan. In this picture, taken in the late 1950s, hunters are being called to assemble at a place known as Loitanit Rock in northern Karamoja, in the Uganda/Sudan border area.

Above African music is now becoming increasingly available to international audiences and to tourists in the form of public performances and concerts, outside its original social context. This performance by a Ghanaian player of the one-string fiddle demonstrates the presence of musical instruments of Arabic background in West Africa, as a result of the historical trans-Sahara trade routes. It is now found in many parts of the West African savanna belt, for instance among the Wolof of Senegal, the Hausa of Nigeria, the Songhay and Djerma of Niger and the Dagomba of Ghana.

Above At the climax of the *Nkili* dance a young man leaps high into the air, caught and steadied by a young woman. This little-known dance style is cultivated by the Humbi and Handa of southwestern Angola. It demands great precision from both dancers as well as strength on the woman's part.

(equipentatonic, equiheptatonic and Pelog scales). Ethnohistorians on the other hand have tended to stress the importance of coastal navigation, with Africans as hired or forced labor on European ships, as an agent of cultural contact.

Attempts at reconstructing African musical history are highly speculative without the evidence of historical sources. Such sources are, in fact, more abundant than might be expected, but should be distinguished as to whether they are internal or external, that is, whether they come from black Africans themselves or from outside observers. The most important ancient black African sources are archaeological (iron objects, such as bells or lamellophone notes), rock paintings (such as occur abundantly in the Sahara), and later art objects collected by contemporary observers. Equally important is the evidence from oral traditions.

Among the most important external sources are written and pictorial documents by visitors and travelers. Arab travelers visited the East African coast from the 10th century onwards. Early European records still await detailed evaluation by Afro-musicologists who are familiar with the musical areas concerned. A specific class of sources is musical notations from earlier centuries by Europeans. There are some 18th-century notations, but the 19th century is particularly rich. However, the notations by musically trained Westerners

rarely do justice to the intrinsic qualities of African music, and give a distorted picture depending on the specific musical background of each observer, and also because of the inherent cultural bias of the Western staff notation system itself. Nonetheless, these notations are not completely worthless. Though the music cannot be produced from them in a straightforward manner, it is possible after careful analysis to reconstruct at least approximately what the traveler may have heard. It has been possible, for instance, to interpret the notation by Carl Mauch (1872) of a *mbira dze midzimu* lamellophone tuning, which he observed in a village near the ruins of Great Zimbabwe, by comparison with present-day measurements of *mbira* tunings from the same area.

Sometimes historical data on African music/dance can be obtained indirectly from Latin American sources. Peoples deported from Africa to the New World most typically came from the hinterland and African trading groups acted as intermediaries for the European slave traders on the coast. The Ovimbundu of Angola, for example, filled such a role, selling war prisoners from eastern Angola to the Portuguese. As a result, music and dance of peoples from the interior of Mozambique and Angola became accessible indirectly from 18th- and 19th-century Brazil, at a time when European observers had not penetrated to such inland areas of Africa.

The shape of current African music and dance in sub-Saharan Africa results from a variety of historical changes: ecological, cultural, social, religious, political and so on. Change in the ecology was a long-term factor affecting population movement which in turn provoked changes in the expressive culture, including music and dance. Since the drying-out of the Sahara, populations have tended to shift southwards. In Tanzania within the last 20 years the Maasai have been grazing their cattle increasingly further south and in 1977 they were a common sight in Sangu country (east of Mbeya). When settled populations accepted the newcomers, they often adopted musical styles from them or new dance types. Thus, the choral singing style of the Maasai has had a fundamental influence on the vocal music of the Gogo of central Tanzania, as can be seen in their *nindo* and *msunyunho* chants.

If there is any trait in the black African music/dance cultures of nearly pan-African validity, it is the distinctive black African concepts about and attitudes towards motion. Movement style is what sets black Africa apart from the rest of the world. Unfortunately, this is an area where research is still in the initial stages. Dance research has been mostly descriptive and from a Western viewpoint as far as black Africa is concerned, and current systems of dance notation claiming universal applicability – Laban, Benesch and others – are even less adequate tools for capturing the structure and feel of African motional systems than is Western staff notation for African music.

One basic difference between European and black African dance cultures is that in the former the body tends to be used in a single block, while in black African dance movement it seems to be split into several seemingly independent body areas. Helmut Günther has characterized African and Afro–American dances with the term "polycentric" and has also pointed to a prevailing body attitude, the "collapse." Olly Wilson has pointed out that the most important trait which links black music in America with African music is motional behavior. Indeed, motional style, at least in its basic principles, has been among the most persistent traits in African cultures. In black Africa identical motional patterns and concepts embrace music and dance. An eminent guitarist from Malawi, Daniel Kachamba, once expressed it like this: "My fingers dance on the strings of my guitar."

As there is always more than one motional center in a given black African dance, so there is also in the playing of musical instruments. The musician does not only produce sounds but moves his hands, fingers, and even head, shoulders, or legs, in certain coordinated patterns during the process of musical production. The music is really the whole of the motional organization and this is one of the reasons why African music is not notated traditionally, in contrast to Western music. The lack of notation systems in black African music is not a deficiency; on the contrary, the idea of writing down music and "playing it from paper" (the expression of a traditional musician) would be utterly perverse in musical cultures where the motional aspect of musical production is so intimately linked with the auditory one.

Analysis of films has been crucial in the study of dance movement in black Africa, and many scholars are now using this method. Dauer proposed a geographical division of black Africa into several dance-style areas, for example Western Sudan, Sahara, West African Coast, Central African Bantu and Southern Bantu; these coincide to a great extent with the song-style regions of Lomax. Acknowledging that black African dances are "polycentric," these dance-style areas are based on the observation that in different areas different parts of the human body tend to be emphasized in dance practice. For instance, motional prominence of the pelvis is considered a diagnostic trait of the movement style of the southern Zaïre/Angola region. There is, however, a good deal of stylistic spill-over across the presumed dance-style areas. In masked dancing of the large Ngangela group of peoples in eastern Angola, for example, many different movement patterns are used by the same community, and each is identified with a local name. Which pattern is used depends on the type of masks.

In solo dancing, especially masked dancing, there are also movements aimed at communicating with the audience or submitting certain coded messages. A masked dancer is an actor who has to play out the character his mask represents. This includes not only dancing, but pantomimic action, gestures and certain styles of walking.

Masked dancing has an interesting distribution area in black Africa. It occurs in a variety of social contexts and often with different functions. It is widely found in West Africa and west central Africa, while it is rare in East Africa and absent in southern Africa. The Makonde, Makua, Ndonde and Chewa are the principal East African peoples with masked societies. One of the richest areas in masks is the culturally rather homogeneous territory comprising almost all of eastern Angola, northwestern Zambia and some southern parts of Zaïre. Among the Chokwe, Luvale, Luchazi, Mbunda, Nkangala, Lwimbi and others there is an abundance of mask types, each specific in appearance and meaning, with a well-defined place in a hierarchic order, specific movement reportories, gestures and pantomime. Most masks of these eastern Angolan peoples represent ancestral members of an ancient court hierarchy. Kings and members of the royal families, their officials and retinue, including servants and slaves, resurrect in the masked theater.

Movement organization in black African music/dance follows rigidly certain principles of timing. These cannot be compared with Western metrical systems. Black African systems of timing are based on at least four to five fundamental concepts:

1. The overall presence of a mental background pulsation consisting of equal-spaced pulse units elapsing ad infinitum and often at enormous speed. These so-called elementary pulses function as a basic orientation screen. They are two or three times faster than the beat or gross-pulse.

2. Musical form is organized so that patterns and themes cover recurring entities of a regular number of these elementary pulses, usually 8, 12, 16, 24 or their multiples, more rarely 9, 18 or 27 units. These are the so-called cycles; the numbers are referred to as form numbers.

3. Many of the form numbers can be divided and split in more than one way, thus allowing the

Top Nuba girls in Kordofan, Sudan, wearing decorative belts, perform a traditional dance with highly individualistic movements. Their bodies are smeared with sim-sim oil and ocher.

Center By striking the water surface, girls from southern Cameroon produce rhythmic combinations and sounds very close to those of a drum.

Above African music/dance is often linked stylistically with work movement. Here, three Chamba women ease their work of pounding grain by dropping their pestles in a rhythmic sequence.

Left This player of panpipes, accompanying himself with a rattle, is from Zimbabwe.

simultaneous combination of contradictory metrical units. For instance, the number 12, which is the most important one in African music, can be divided by 2, 3, 4 and 6.

4. Patterns of the same form number can be shifted against each other in combinations so that their starting points cross ("cross rhythms"). In certain instances they cross so completely that they fall between themselves (interlock) with no two notes sounding together ("interlocking combination").

In some areas there is a further principle of timing: the so-called time-line patterns. Broadly speaking, it is found in the areas covered by the Kwa and Benue–Congo subgroups of the Niger–Congo group of languages. Here we encounter time-line patterns in many (though not all) kinds of music to be danced to. These are short, usually single-note, rhythmic patterns, often of asymmetric structure, struck on a bell, a bottle, a high-pitched drum, the rim of a drum, or clapped with hands. A time-line pattern represents the *structural core* of a musical piece, something like a condensed and extremely concentrated representation of the rhythmic-motional possibilities open to the participants (musicians and dancers). Singers, drummers and dancers in the group find their bearings by listening to the strokes of the time-line pattern, which is repeated at a steady tempo throughout the performance. Time-line patterns are transmitted from teacher to learner by means of mnemonic syllables or mnemonic verbal patterns.

Musical patterns are often conceived as verbalized in black African cultures. The same applies to dance patterns. For example rattle playing is often taught with syllables such as *cha-cha-cha-cha* or *ka-cha-ka-cha-ka-cha*, depending on which pattern the student is expected to play. An important time-line pattern for the accompaniment of *likembe* music in eastern Angola is taught with the mnemonic formula *Mu chana cha Kapekula* (in the river grassland of Kapekula). The phonetic structure of such mnemonic patterns reflects the timbre, rhythmic and accental structure of the pattern to be played. G.K.

Musical Instruments

There is an abundant variety of musical instruments in Africa, some of which, such as lamellophones, are specific to this continent. Contrary to common Western belief, drums are not necessarily the "most typical" African musical instruments. Drums with a wooden body, for instance, are absent in areas lacking large trees; lamellophones with metal notes are traditionally found in places where a blacksmith is available; the hunting bow is used as a musical instrument (mouth bow) in Namibia and southern Angola, where the hunting-and-gathering background is strong. Some instruments may be in common use, others reserved for either men or women; some may belong to religious groups, others to traditional educational institutions; others may be associated with traditional political organizations, such as royal courts. G.K.

Right A rare type of musical bow called *sagaya* is found among the Humbi of southwestern Angola. Musician Pequenino uses an ordinary hunting bow with a brace added to transform it into a musical instrument. The brace divides the bow near the middle, giving two fundamental notes from the two unequal lengths of string; these are about a whole tone apart. For playing, the bow is held in the lips. The right hand holds a leather wand. The left hand supports the bow in the way shown in the photograph. The musician strikes one or other segment of the string, continually altering the shape and size of his mouth cavity. The melody formed implies a text, although the musician does not sing.

Right Some traditional African musical instruments are becoming increasingly rare. Madame Nke is one of the remaining players in southern Cameroon of the transversal flute called *oding*. This instrument is reserved for women. The playing style combines vocal sounds (often indistinguishable from those of the flute) with blown instrumental tones. Before playing, water is put into the flute. The plant, similar to a liana, from which this flute is made is not found in southern Cameroon which suggests that this flute was originally not indigenous to the area. Madame Nke's mother-in-law brought it from near Ngaoundere in the north.

Above The playing of so-called time-line patterns is a prominent feature in much music of the West African coast. The 12-pulse standard pattern, struck as 12 (x . x . xx . x . xx .), is the musical backbone of many performances in the area of the former kingdom of Dahomey. An eminent Fon singer, Soso Njako, uses a time-line pattern to accompany his songs. Holding a nail in his right hand he taps out the pattern on a bottle, while the left index finger silently taps a complementary pattern on the bottle's neck. Other instruments in this group include *ogo* (a large calabash struck with a leather flap) and *ogan* (a double bell on a stem grip). In the Fon language this kind of music is called *Toba*.

Above right A court musician of the Timi of Ede announces a visitor. He uses one of the most prominent musical instruments in Yorubaland: the *iya-ilu* (mother drum) of a *dundun* set of hourglass-shaped tension drums. The *iya-ilu* is a "talking drum" designed for performing recitals, announcements and praise poetry (*oriki*) for important persons. The principle of "talking" on a drum relies on the

fact that Yoruba is a tone language in which the meaning of a word depends partly on speech tones. The pitch-lines produced by the talking drum follow as closely as possible the tonal and rhythmic patterns of spoken texts. The drums of the *dundun* set have two membranes connected by leather thongs. By pressing the thongs with his left hand or arm the musician can change the pitch of the drum. A hooked stick is used for striking. Small bells, jingling during play, are attached to the drum.

Right Part of a percussion group from Togo. The *ogo* is a big calabash struck with a leather flap (*afafa*) made from antelope skin. The *Tochng* is a remarkable instrument consisting of two pails filled with water in which two calabashes of different size are floated. The player strikes them lightly with wooden sticks.

Below Court musicians of the emir of Zaria perform in front of his palace. Hausa music of northern Nigeria is characterized by strong Arabic, specifically Islamic, influences. Several instruments were imported from North Africa. The ensemble in this picture uses the following instruments: several double-skin cylinder drums with vibration string attached; double bells; and the *kakaki* metal horns. The court music ensemble of some 10 to 15 performers consists of men of a respectable age. Children of the large family of the emir and his retinue stand behind and watch the performance. One of the drummers sings praise songs and recitals in honor of the emir.

Below right A musician from northwestern Zambia plays the *likembe*. Of Congan (DRO) origin, the *likembe* (pl. *makambe*) is a distinctive kind of lamellophone, characterized by a box-resonator with a cut-out section on top projecting from one end of the hollowed-out box. Two sound-holes are burned into the body of the *likembe*, one in the end closest to the player's body, the other at the back of the instrument. The *likembe* is played with the thumbs, and by alternately opening and closing the back hole with the middle finger of his left hand the musician produces timbre modifications.

Above At a village near Atakpamé in Togo, two men play the *ogan*. The instrument comprises a double bell with a stem grip, one bell short and the other long, representing a mother with a child on her back. The bells are struck with sticks made of light wood. The *ogan* is one of the percussion instruments commonly used to accompany the *achya*, a very popular and highly acrobatic dance among the Fon people.

Above Xylophone player Jean Numbikamba represents an important central African instrumental tradition. This type of portable xylophone, with a rail to hold it away from the player's body and with gourd resonators equipped with mirliton buzzers, came to Cameroon from the south. Its most likely center of dispersal was the old kingdom of Kongo, where comparable instruments were seen by 17th-century missionaries. In Cameroon present-day oral tradition among the southern peoples confirms that when a chief intended to undertake a journey and visit neighboring areas, his xylophone band, which usually consisted of four musicians, went ahead walking and playing the processional music. This is why this particular variety of xylophone is designed to be portable. With the xylophone music spreading north into the interior of what is now Congo-Brazzaville and beyond, the possession of a band playing portable xylophones became a symbol of authority and status among many of the small chieftainships.

Above Uzavela walks with his *chihumba* through the plantation of a Portuguese farmer, where he was employed. The playing attitude is characteristic: the *chihumba* is carried on a string around the neck and held with the arcs pointing away from the player's body. The *chihumba* pluriarc or "bow lute" is an instrument very popular among the people of southwestern Angola. It is often played walking, during a long journey. Many songs refer to the long march with goods from the rural areas to the port of Benguela. Benguela was also an important center for the deportation of Angolans as slave workers to the New World, especially to Brazil. The pluriarc is one of the instruments which had already reached Brazil with the slave trade in the 18th century. The instrument seen in the present picture is practically identical in construction and playing technique with that reported from 18th-century Brazil.

Masks and the Dance

Traditionally in black Africa masks are an expressive aspect of exclusive associations (normally for men). Membership can only be achieved by submission to graded instruction and an often horrific initiation process. There are also in some societies women's associations with "masks." In local languages the same term is often used as for the masks of men, while Western observers would describe the women's "masks" as body paint.

Masked dancing provides a link between the secluded "masked society" and society at large. Access to the place where the masks are made and where the dancers dress is restricted, but the dance theater of the various masked characters takes place in public. A mask in black Africa is to be appreciated as a character in motion; it is the whole-face-cover and costume. Though "masked societies" have religious aspects, they should not be misconstrued as religious cult groups; masked dancers do not fall into "trance," nor are they possessed by spirits. Nor do the owners of masks practice "magic," though fanciful and misleading stories are often deliberately circulated.　　　G.K.

Above These masked dancers from southern Congo (DRO) belong to the Pende people. The Pende have much in common with the northeastern Angolan peoples in their traditional institutions and in the technology of making masked costumes in the form of an interlaced network.

Left Young girls of Bigene village, CAR, perform the *Akulavye* dance. During the dance the girls sit on chairs and move legs, arms, shoulders and breasts. They imitate the *siu*, an animal "with a white face, which often comes to the village to kill chickens.'

Below left The head of this bird mask from southeastern Angola is painted with white clay to resemble the white head of the fish eagle. The beak, in which a fish is grasped, is genuine. When dancing, the mask is made to imitate the yelping cries of the fish eagle.

Below This mask was photographed during the Ogun festival of the Yoruba in Nigeria. Ogun is the god of iron and war in Yoruba religion.

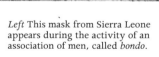

Left This mask from Sierra Leone appears during the activity of an association of men, called *bondo*.

Right Another mask from Sierra Leone demonstrates the great variety of theatrical characters, including modern ideas, which appear in the traditional dance dramas.

Below The masked society (*awa*) of the Dogon plays a vital role in preserving their elaborate mythology. Funeral rites are occasions for elaborate public dances, accompanied by chants in a secret language. Dancers wear vegetable fiber skirts stained red with a dye obtained from hibiscus leaves. Red costumes are particularly associated with the dancers who drive out the spirit of the dead person from its house. Another part of the rite recalls the Dogon myth of how death entered the world through the disobedience of young men. The dancers lash the ground around the corpse, seeking its forgiveness.

Below right Among the Luchazi, Mbwela and related peoples in eastern Angola and northwestern Zambia the local name referring to the masked characters is *makisi* (singular *likisi*). Among the Mbwela two categories of *makisi* are recognized. One is called *makisi avamala* (the ''masks'' of men), the other *makisi avampwevo* (the ''masks'' of women). A Western observer would not consider the latter to be ''masks'' at all, but rather women with body paint on. In the Mbwela conceptualization the ''masks'' of the women, as seen in this picture, are the equivalents of the masks in which men are hidden. The names of the individual ''masks'' of the women are exactly the same as those for the masks of the men, and the women also perform identical dance movements, as they are ascribed to the individual masked characters.

Above right and *right* One of the most spectacular masks of the Mbwela people in southeastern Angola is *ndzingi*. He is an anthropomorphic creature representing a giant living far away in the forest. He has a very large round head made from a scaffolding of twigs covered with barkcloth. The uninitiated are told that the impressive red mouth can swallow a dog. *Ndzingi* appears during the large masked festivals held to coincide with the *mukanda* circumcision school. In these festivals many individual masks appear in succession. Those performing well are usually rewarded with gifts, including money. Such earnings are used by the guardians of the boys' circumcision school to support the teaching activities. *Ndzingi* runs through the dancing square, threatening to beat anyone he meets with the twigs held in his hand. Then he begins to dance, stamping on the ground and shoveling up clouds of dust. But suddenly he staggers, the head wobbles as if it were dangerously loose, and finally he collapses, falling down ''dead'' on the ground, ''because the head is too heavy.'' Young boys, laughing and cheerful, run to ''help him up.'' This episode is repeated every few minutes until the dancer returns to the *mukanda*, to be replaced by another character.

EDUCATION AND LITERACY

The political changes that have altered the face of Africa have been accompanied by educational controversy. In all African countries the role of education is a debated subject, and discussion is sharpened by awareness that the education sector often consumes a quarter of governmental budgets and one-twentieth of gross national product. Education is widely hailed as a tool for liberation and a solution to economic problems, but it simultaneously causes many other difficulties.

Despite many changes in curriculum, goals and structure, there remains a discouraging, almost desperate continuity between much current debate and that which preoccupied colonial administrations. The links between education and the labor market, for example, and its effects on social stratification have been a focus of discussion for many decades.

A review of the role of education must begin with its classification. Educationists frequently remark that learning is a lifelong process extending far beyond the formal classroom and pervading every activity. Though the boundaries between each sector are not clear, it is common to describe education as formal, informal or nonformal. The formal sector refers to the highly structured, chronologically graded system running from primary school through university, and embraces the common conception of schools with desks and blackboards. Informal education is the truly lifelong process whereby every individual acquires attitudes, values, skills and knowledge from daily experience and the environment. Mother tongues, for example, are informally acquired, as is information gathered from the media and family. Nonformal education refers to organized activities outside the formal system intended to serve identifiable clienteles and learning objectives. It ranges from adult literacy classes to driving instruction and the Boy Scouts.

In part because of the cost of formal education, and in part because of its ineffective and sometimes counterproductive nature, attention in the mid-1970s focused on the potential of nonformal education. Programs in this sector also experienced drawbacks, however, so that towards the end of the decade attention was redirected towards basic formal learning. Strategies for eradication of illiteracy have also been reassessed, for in recent years governments have fought a losing battle. According to UNESCO, so fast has been the rate of population growth that, although the proportion of illiterates in Africa was reduced from 81 to 74 per cent between 1960 and 1970, the absolute number increased from 124 million to 143 million. Between 1974 and 1977 the estimated global number of illiterates increased by some 24 million, and in 1977 UNESCO decided not to award its two customary annual prizes for outstanding contributions to literacy.

A large number of African societies have specific traditional education systems. In many cases these include circumcision and other initiation ceremonies into adult life, and though their place is being usurped in the modern world, their continued existence remains important. Almost without exception, indigenous education has been non-literate, since only the Ge'ez speakers of Ethiopia, the Vai of Liberia and the Mum of Cameroon invented their own systems of writing. In some cases apprenticeship schemes are incorporated, and the system is structured according to age grades.

In the past, many Christian missionaries and other visitors to Africa classed indigenous education with the whole of traditional African life as primitive or barbaric, though the work of anthropologists has helped to rationalize views. Indigenous education must not be considered homogeneous throughout the continent; a child in a hunting band of Mbuti pygmies learns a different body of knowledge from one in the agricultural and politically centralized Hausa societies. Certain peoples, such as the Yoruba of Nigeria, also exhibit considerable internal social differentiation in education.

Formal systems have tended to take little account of traditional ones, though, while attempting to avoid a romantic view, the 1970s witnessed a growth of so-called community schools, which aimed to improve the relevance of education. Like every other aspect of African life, indigenous education responds to changing circumstances; instead of making hoes and cutlasses, apprentice blacksmiths increasingly weld burglar bars and repair motors. Yet modern skills are still widely acquired in the traditional way, through years of progressively more difficult work supervised by a master. And while the formal system remains limited in coverage, especially for girls, indigenous African education will continue an important role.

Particularly in North and West Africa, Islamic education systems also operated many centuries before the advent of colonial rule. The Al-Azhar University in Cairo was founded in the 10th century and is said to be the oldest in the world. Also prominent were the ancient universities of Fès and Tombouctou. In each case, learning took place in the mosque and was closely related to the Islamic religion.

In contrast to both indigenous and Western systems, Islamic education displays a remarkable homogeneity. At the lowest level is the *khalwa*, at which memorization of the Koran and accompanying rituals is taught, and at the secondary level is the *madrasa* at which a pupil deepens his Koranic knowledge and learns philosophy, jurisprudence and often some science. The time devoted to each unit varies widely, depending on the inclinations and abilities of both students and teachers, but an average pupil may spend four years at the basic level and a little longer in the *madrasa*. The highest level of learning often necessitates some travel in search of a particularly learned teacher for each subject.

There is no compulsion at a Koranic school, nor are there fixed periods of attendance. The schools operate from Saturdays to Wednesdays, and the year is divided into two terms separated by approximately three weeks' holiday after each major religious festival. Lessons are generally held twice or three times a day, in the early morning, the late afternoon and in the evening around a bonfire. This arrangement permits attendance at Western-type schools in the day and Koranic schools in the evening. The curricula of Islamic schools have been criticized for their inflexibility. In countries where Arabic is not the mother tongue, pupils are taught solely to recite the Koran, not to understand it. Similarly, at the secondary level, learning proceeds by listening to exposition rather than argument or discussion. However, the schools do provide valuable training in discipline and respect.

Attempts to integrate formal Western-type schools with Islamic institutions have met with varying degrees of success. Whereas in northern Nigeria, for example, the two systems broadly coexist side by side and attempts at integration have borne little fruit, in northern Sudan, partly because Arabic is a widespread mother tongue, integration is almost complete. This has the benefit of promoting the impact of schooling as well as maximizing use of resources. In parts of West Africa, members of the Ahmadiyya group have established formal schools. Many of them are staffed by missionaries from the Indian subcontinent and are thus parallel to the Christian missionary activities. However, more orthodox Muslims consider the Ahmadiyya heretics, and the latter's interest in Western-type schooling has become an additional reason why the orthodox often reject attempts at integration.

In the majority of African countries, the formal school systems were established by Christian

Below right; Adult literacy. Because of rapid population growth, in recent years most governments have been fighting a losing battle against illiteracy. Although the proportion of illiterates in most countries has been reduced, the absolute number has increased. One major problem, especially in rural areas, is that reading materials are in short supply, and because adults do not practice their skills, acquisition of literacy is not permanent. Nevertheless much has been achieved, and the proportion of literates will grow as primary schooling approaches universality and as many specific programs take effect.

Below National indicators on literacy. After U N E S C O 1995.

	Estimated adult (15+) illiteracy rate (%), 1995		Illiteracy rate among persons aged 25+ (%)		
	Male	Female	Year	Male	Female
Algeria	26.1	51.0	1987	50.2	79.5
Angola	—	—	—	—	—
Benin	51.3	74.2	1992	71.4 b	90.2b
Botswana	19.5	40.1	1991	58.8	59.8
Burkina Faso	70.5	90.8	1975	89.0	98.2
Cameroon	25.0	47.9	1987	43.0	68.0
Cape Verde	18.6	36.2	1990	34.9	62.5
Central African Republic	31.5	47.6	1988	60.0	87.0
Chad	37.9	65.2	—	—	—
Comoros	35.8	49.6	1980	50.0	66.8
Congo (DRO)	13.4	32.3	—	—	—
Congo (RO)	16.9	32.8	1984	41.4	69.9
Côte d'Ivoire	50.1	70.0	1988	63.4	85.3
Djibouti	39.7	67.3	1991	63.0	87.0
Egypt	36.4	61.2	1986	50.2	78.1
Equatorial Guinea	10.4	31.9	1983	28.7	64.5
Eritrea	—	—	—	—	—
Ethiopia	54.5	74.7	1984	73.6	89.2
Gabon	26.3	46.7	—	—	—
Gambia	47.2	75.1	—	—	—
Ghana	24.1	46.5	—	—	—
Guinea	50.1	78.1	—	—	—
Guinea-Bissau	32.0	57.5	1979	77.8	95.7
Kenya	13.7	30.0	1989	26.0	54.2
Lesotho	18.9	37.7	—	—	—
Liberia	46.1	77.6	1984	64.3	89.2
Libya	12.1	37.0	1984	37.3	83.2
Malawi	28.1	58.2	1987	37.2	74.6
Mali	60.6	76.9	1987	76.0	91.0
Mauritania	50.4	73.7	1988	61.0	80.0
Mauritius	12.9	21.2	1990	16.9	31.3
Morocco	43.4	69.0	1982	64.2	89.9
Mozambique	42.3	76.7	1980	65.8	93.8
Namibia	—	—	1991	26.8	35.0
Niger	79.1	93.4	1988	87.0	97.0
Nigeria	32.7	52.7	—	—	—
Réunion	—	—	1982	33.2	28.2
Rwanda	30.2	48.4	1978	55.6 c	84.6 c
São Tomé and Príncipe	—	—	1981	36.9	74.4
Senegal	57.0	76.8	1988	68.0	90.0
Seychelles	—	—	1987	23.0	21.0
Sierra Leone	54.6	81.8	—	—	—
South Africa	18.1	18.3	1980	26.4	30.1
Sudan	42.3	65.4	1993	42.6	74.1
Swaziland	22.0	24.4	1986	36.7	46.3
Tanzania	20.6	43.2	1978	46.2	80.0
Togo	33.0	63.0	1981	67.9 b	90.4 b
Tunisia	21.4	45.4	1989	42.2	67.7
Uganda	26.3	49.8	1991	37.1	66.7
Zambia	14.4	28.7	1980	44.3	74.3
Zimbabwe	9.6	20.1	1992	16.7 i	32.8 i

Key: — Not available; b Age 30+; c Those who completed less than four years of schooling; i Ages 25–64.

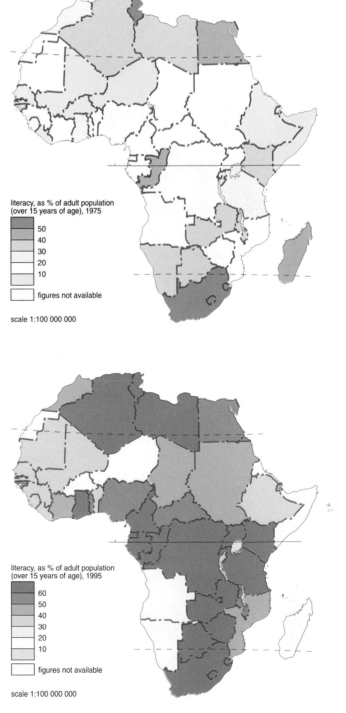

literacy, as % of adult population (over 15 years of age), 1975

- 50
- 40
- 30
- 20
- 10
- figures not available

scale 1:100 000 000

literacy, as % of adult population (over 15 years of age), 1995

- 60
- 50
- 40
- 30
- 20
- 10
- figures not available

scale 1:100 000 000

missionaries. Christianity was considered a religion of the book. It was not sufficient for a preacher merely to proclaim the Gospel; his congregation must literally see the Word as well as hear it. Missionaries therefore strongly emphasized the establishment of schools, sometimes according them precedence over more direct evangelism. "Where it is impossible for you to carry on both the immediate task of evangelism and your educational work," enjoined the Apostolic Visitor in Dar es Salaam in 1929, "neglect your churches in order to perfect your schools." Since work among the young was often more fruitful, and, it may be added, since the young had a greater life expectancy and were therefore a better investment, education of adults was often relegated to second place.

Several consequences arose from this pattern. The first was that territories frequently displayed as wide a range of systems and curricula as there were missionary groups in operation. This caused divisions in society, and some systems were barely relevant to their recipients' needs. For many years in Mozambique, for example, Anglican missionaries taught not in local languages, nor in Portuguese, but in English. Even where the missionaries employed more appropriate languages, they usually took limited account of the nature of the societies in which they worked, transplanting instead what they saw as the values of their own home countries. The practices of drinking and dancing, for example, were widely condemned, and the doctrine of celibacy of Roman Catholic priests often led to conflict because in almost all African societies the deliberate rejection of parenthood is anathema.

A second consequence was a tendency for the interests of missionaries, governments and various African groups to conflict. In the early years the governments role in education was usually restricted to provision of grants in return for fulfillment of certain minimum requirements. Their main concern was a supply of clerks for the administration and generally they were content to leave missionaries to their self-appointed tasks. The first government school in Lagos, for example, was opened only in 1896, 50 years after the first mission school, in response to an appeal from the Muslim community, which felt neglected. However, some colonial officers disliked the effect and type of education provided, and in northern Nigeria, for instance, missionary activities were tightly controlled to prevent interference with the existing social order and thus the institution of indirect rule.

In the period following World War II, it became clear to British, Belgian and French governments that the advent of independence was less distant than had hitherto been assumed and that increased educational provision at all levels was a necessity. Expansion of higher education was particularly notable. Between 1947 and 1950 institutes or university colleges were opened at Bukavu (Belgian Congo), Brazzaville (French Congo), Accra (Gold Coast), Ibadan (Nigeria), Makerere (Uganda) and Dakar (French West Africa). During the 1950s and 1960s this trend continued until almost every country had a university.

The rise of African nationalism owed much to the missionaries, for while the latter were often employed as a vanguard of imperialism, equally,

Above Children play outside a school in Tanzania. During the 1970s illiteracy was considerably reduced, but only a very small percentage of pupils progress beyond primary education.

Left Ugandan pupils assemble outside their primary school near Masaka in the south of the country. Secondary schools are few in Uganda, and enrollment in postprimary education is strictly limited.

Right A white-clad Muslim teacher instructs his class in a street in Kano, northern Nigeria. The pupils use wooden writing boards. Instruction in the Koran is the basic object of these Muslim schools which supplement more formal institutions run by government or missionary agencies.

through education, they helped lay nationalist foundations. It is perhaps ironic that in some ways missionaries played a greater role in the 1960s in newly independent countries, for in many cases they expanded their work and bridged the gap between the departing colonial and new indigenous administrations. The 20th century has witnessed increasing control of missionary educational activities, and in some territories all voluntary agency schools have been taken over by the government. The transition has not always been smooth: for example in Congo (DRO), financial and administrative difficulties forced the government in the mid-1970s to return proprietorship of many missionary institutions. This reflects the role that missionaries will continue to play for some time.

Frequently it is incorrectly asserted that colonial regimes provided only academic education and had no interest in technical training. On the contrary, several missions held in high regard what they called "the dignity of labor" and made considerable efforts to train artisans. Similarly, colonial reports continually stressed the dangers of an over-academic framework. The 1920s witnessed the establishment of Jeanes Training Colleges in East and central Africa, which introduced peripatetic teachers and emphasized agriculture and other practical subjects. Likewise, the Malangali School in Tanganyika sought relevance through use of traditional clothing instead of uniforms, twice weekly spear throwing and tribal dancing. These examples are by no means unique.

It is true, however, that school systems were based on those of the colonial powers. Pupils sat the baccalaureat, school certificate, or other metropolitan examinations, and studied the history, geography, flora and fauna of Britain, Frnce, Portugal, Spain and Belgium rather than their own regions. The worst excesses have no been rectified, though curricula are still influenced by European developments and by desires to adhere to external standards.

Similarly, although the need to provide agricultural and technical training is frequently restated, generally the same obstacles to its development remain. Missionary and colonial efforts were widely perceived by Africans as attempts to maintain European ascendancy by diverting scholars from "real" education into the more limited sphere of technical training. It was no coincidence that so large a proportion of nationalist leaders were lawyers, for it was through this type of training, not agricultural or technical, that they could attain an equal footing with the colonialists. In this sense, academic education was more vocational, because it led further. It may be added that the situation has not greatly changed today, and technical training will continue to be considered inferior so long as the economic structure awards preferable employment opportunities to those with academic backgrounds.

In the 1960s a large number of African nations attained independence. In these years of optimism, entitled "The First Development Decade" by UNO, education was widely seen as the means through which this development would be achieved and independence made real. The optimism was reflected in the targets set by the 1961 Conference of African Ministers of Education in Addis Ababa. By 1980 they aimed to have achieved universal, compulsory and free primary schooling; 30 per cent enrolment rates at the secondary level; and higher education for 20 per cent of those completing secondary. As many resources as possible were devoted to education, for it was considered an investment in human capital which would enable the new nations to catch up with the developed world. The 1960 Nigerian Ashby Report was not atypical with its suggestion that the people "will have to forgo other things they want so that every available penny is invested in education," continuing, "Even this will not be enough. . ."

As the decade progressed, however, increasing disparities in wealth made it clear that growth was not the same as development and that investments in education were not yielding their anticipated fruits. During the colonial era, policies had often deliberately aimed at creation of elites. These elites were widely applauded when the nations achieved independence, for they replaced the departing colonialists. But by the late 1960s the undesirable aspects of social stratification derived from education had become more serious. Unemployment, especially of primary leavers, but also of secondary and then university graduates, became an increasing problem. It added emphasis to charges that schooling was irrelevant and that educational expenditures were excessive. Since most school leavers sought employment in towns, debilitation of rural areas was added to the undesirable effects of the system.

The rapid educational expansion of the 1960s, and thus the rapid escalation of many problems as well as solutions, was brought not only by increased government and mission activity but also by a surge of self-help projects, of which Kenya's village polytechnics and Harambee schools provide good examples. Although the spirit of self-help was applauded, the uncontrolled nature of these projects accelerated qualitative decline and exacerbated the unemployment situation.

Though many countries have condemned the colonial mold, few have attempted fundamental reform. Tanzania stands out as the most ambitious. Its conscious change of direction was part of the 1967 Arusha Declaration in which the government recognized that for the majority of citizens, for some time to come, primary education would be a misnomer disguising its terminal nature. The Tanzanian government realizes that agriculture will remain the national mainstay for the foreseeable future, and is trying to implement an Education for Self Reliance policy which among other things hopes to reduce costs and promote relevance by requiring institutions to be self-sufficient. This is a brave experiment which is not being accomplished with ease and which, while other nations watch with interest, few have attempted to emulate. The majority have found it easier to retain the basic features of the existing model and make minor modifications to alleviate pressing crises.

As previously mentioned, the mid-1970s witnessed a major display of interest in nonformal education. This was partly because the international aid agencies were prepared to give it financial backing, and further illustrates the continued links between Africa and the developed world. The wide scope of nonformal education was seen as an advantage, for it hoped to promote both impact and cost effectiveness by avoiding compartmentalization. Whereas in the past many nonformal schemes had been designed to give a second chance to those who had missed or never been offered an earlier opportunity, educationists with renewed vigor asserted that nonformal learning could also complement the formal system. They further pointed out that too often literacy was seen as an end rather than a means, and that increased use of radios could fulfill some of the same functions.

Many nonformal programs, however, suffered the same fate as earlier technical schemes. They were sometimes implemented solely as a cosmetic, obscuring rather than removing the need for fundamental reform. The breadth of certain projects was also more of a problem than an advantage since the required cooperation of ministries and other agencies was not always forthcoming. The best avenues to advancement usually remained in the formal system and nonformal schemes therefore had limited appeal. This situation was linked to the structure of the economy and heavy emphasis on certification rather than possession of skills. Thus, while the nonformal fashion did much to widen perspectives and stimulate thinking, attention in the late 1970s reverted to the formal system and attempts to provide universal basic education.

At the beginning of the 1980s education remains a controversial subject. Even Nigeria with its petroleum revenues has found no easy answers to development issues, so that by contrast the prospects of poorer countries like Upper Volta and Mali appear all the bleaker. Yet the importance of education in development is undeniable. Perhaps the brightest and most promising aspect of the current picture is the ever-increasing body of research and the broader and more realistic perception of education that has evolved over the last two decades.

M.B.

Health and Healing

Health and wholeness – harmony of body and mind, and harmony within the community – are valued highly in Africa, perhaps the more because of the menace of tropical diseases. Illness and death, except in the very old, have been seen as evidence of ill will from humans or from the spirit world. Witchcraft, bringing misfortune, springs from envy and hatred. In every community specialist practitioners existed, to identify witches, to divine causes of illness and misfortune, and to prescribe treatment, sometimes magical, sometimes medicinal. Western forms of medical treatment have alleviated many diseases but Western physicians have sometimes neglected the spiritual causes of illness and disharmony. Some of the African independent churches refuse all medical treatment, traditional or Western, relying on healing through prayer and the laying on of hands. In some Christian and mission hospitals, doctors are acknowledging the need to treat the whole person – body and spirit as well.

HIV/AIDS

News of the HIV/AIDS global epidemic began to emerge in the late 1970s, although not until the 1980s did it begin to be recognized for what it was. It is clear that Africa – and specifically sub-Saharan Africa – was affected early. Under-reportage is still prevalent, but in 1998) it was estimated that over 30.6 million people worldwide are living with HIV/AIDS, and close to 21 million of these are in sub-Saharan Africa. Eastern and Southern Africa have the highest percentage of cases. Transmission is most commonly heterosexual, and as many as 50 per cent of those infected may be female.

New infections are believed to be very much greater than earlier estimates – probably close to 5.3 million in 1996, of whom at least 3.8 million are in Africa. Here a particular concern is the spread from mother to infant, at delivery or through breastfeeding. Breastfeeding is natural and cost-free, and bottle-feeding brings many other health risks. There are now effective antiviral drugs, but their cost greatly restricts their use in Africa.

Additionally, the number of children orphaned through the AIDS-related death of one or both parents presents a huge problem in many African countries. In Uganda, infection was early, and this is now estimated at more than 1.2 million children under the age of 18, increasing by 50,000 each year. These children, often taken in by elderly relations, are also likely to be denied education.

The first cases were reported in Uganda in 1982, and 8 per cent of the population is estimated to be currently affected. But there have also been striking advances in HIV/AlDS prevention and control. A Uganda AIDS Commission was set up in 1992. The proportion of Ugandan adults infected is continuing to drop, and there is evidence that preventive education aimed at young people is resulting in safer sexual practices, something which was questioned by many in the past.

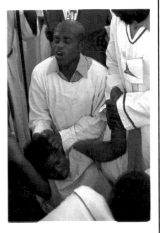

Above A prophet of the Vapostori – an independent Christian sect of Zimbabawe – lays hands on a young woman to cast out the evil spirit which possesses her and causes her illness.

Above left In northern Cameroon a sick woman lies on a mat in her compound with her family around her, as a traditional healer performs a ritual for her recovery.

Left Health workers in Senegal spray swampy ground to destroy the mosquito's which spread malaria and other diseases.

Below Vaccination of a child at a clinic in the city of Hargeysa in northwestern Somalia. Medical facilities in this poor country are confined to basic preventive measures such as this; drought and civil war have put Somalia's healthcare resources under further strain.

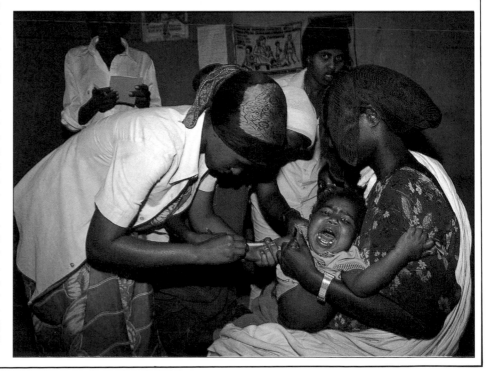

Game Parks and Conservation

The wildlife of Africa is now severely restricted by comparison with only a century ago, but Africa remains the last great home of much of the world's more spectacular wildlife. This is largely due to the great parks of Africa which have a history going back almost one hundred years, although their function has changed greatly in recent years. Initially, they were established to shelter and protect wildlife from the onslaught of man, although the removal of man the predator, far from restoring a balanced and natural state, sometimes meant a deleterious faunal population explosion. Increasingly, parks are seen not as sanctuaries and wilderness areas to be sealed off, but as areas to be utilized and managed like any other part of the country. It is now appreciated that a mixed faunal population more efficiently uses a much wider range of floral species and habitats than a corresponding cattle population. The conversion rate from vegetable to animal protein may therefore be much greater with a wildlife population, a very significant fact for a protein-deficient human population. This raises the possibility of game culling or game ranching for human consumption. Parks may serve other useful purposes, however. Not only do they form the bases of tourist industries. The well-being of the wildlife is not incompatible with controlled fishing, grazing and afforestation.   J.C.S.

Below Tourist lodges, particularly in parts of East Africa, combine luxurious accommodation with splendid opportunities for game viewing. However, it is debatable whether tourism does much to enhance the material well-being of the very low income earners, since much of the economic returns go to airlines, hoteals, car hire firms etc., and many of the tourists' needs may have to be imported.

Below Ngorongoro National Park in Tanzania, which occupies a huge volcanic crater, is one of several extensive areas designated for the country's abundant wildlife. Tourism, such as this photo safari, to such reserves is an increasingly important source of revenue.

Opposite above The professsional hunter of the turn of the century, who shot for the commercial value of the kill, was replaced by the safari hunter who was licenced, for a fee, to shoot a stipulated number and variety of species and hired the professional to guide him. The local inhabitants were often excluded, but professional guides had a vested interest in preventing extermination.

Opposite below Availability of modern firearms, the very high commercial value of wildlife products and the inability of parks authorities to patrol their extensive areas are severely reducing wildlife stocks in some parks, but the temptation of quick reward to people without employment or on very low incomes is great.

Right To combat the threat to wildlife in their national parks and game reserves, many African governments have formed anti-poaching squads. Here, a group of armed rangers is seen patrolling the Meru National Park in central Kenya.

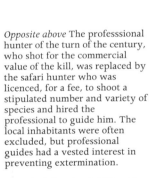

The Copper Industry

The discovery of copper deposits in Africa in the past was usually made by prospectors seeking more exotic minerals, but more recently they have been systematically sought in their own right. Copper is typical of many of the mineral deposits of Africa in that in total the continent is a major producer, but within the continent there is extreme maldistribution. Zambia and Congo (DRO) dominate the continent's league table of copper producers, since their common international boundary bisects the continent's largest deposit. South Africa, Namibia, Zimbabwe and Botswana are also major producers.

Great fluctuations in the price of copper on world markets have given rise to grave problems for the major producers who plan to finance development elsewhere in their country by means of copper revenues. The establishment of an international copper agreement by the world's producers has proved illusory, particularly by comparison with the success of the OPEC nations in the 1970s. Demand for copper is much more elastic than for oil. Economic recession among the industrialized consumers results in significant decline in demand, as do high prices which make substitute metals attractive. Political conditions or a mining disaster may lead to a sudden decline in output by a major producer, while profitable extraction is not solely the result of efficiency through economies of scale since some 40 per cent of world capacity is in the hands of a large number of small producer countries   JCS.

Above left Electrolytic processes are used to produce a highly refined product with a high value/bulk ratio. This is advantageous in view of the long haul to the seaports serving the Copperbelt.

Above The shallow oxide ores of Zambia are underlain by deeper sulfide deposits, extracted by underground mining. Both open-cast and underground methods are employed in Zambia and Congo (DRO).

Left Mufulira is a mining township making extensive use of low-value land, and one of a cluster of eight towns all in close proximity on the Zambian Copperbelt.

Above The ore is processed locally by the major producer countries, reducing costly haulage of bulky ores. The smelter at Mufulira, Zambia, is well served by the coal deposits and hydroelectricity production of the Zambezi basin.

PART THREE
THE NATIONS OF AFRICA

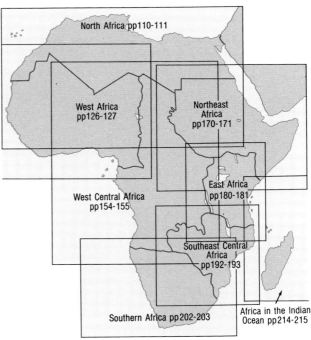

North Africa pp110-111

West Africa
pp126-127

Northeast
Africa
pp170-171

West Central Africa
pp154-155

East Africa
pp180-181

Southeast Central
Africa
pp192-193

Southern Africa pp202-203

Africa in the Indian
Ocean pp214-215

This section contains an account of each independent nation and territory in Africa, including the islands of the western Indian Ocean, with a map indicating mineral, agricultural and industrial resources for each country, and a regional map emphasizing physical features. The 55 nations have been divided into eight regions, and the basic category of division is purely physical propinquity. Some of the regions are generally accepted as such; this is especially true of North Africa. The physical description limits the region in cases like the islands; but in most other regions the allocation has of necessity to be arbitrary. Cameroon is here included in West Africa; many divisions would place that nation in West Central Africa. The totally arbitrary boundaries of the colonial period still prevail in Africa. In a matter of two or three generations new alignments and unions may have taken place, and an atlas of Africa in the year 2050 may show different and more rational regional and national divisions.

NORTH AFRICA

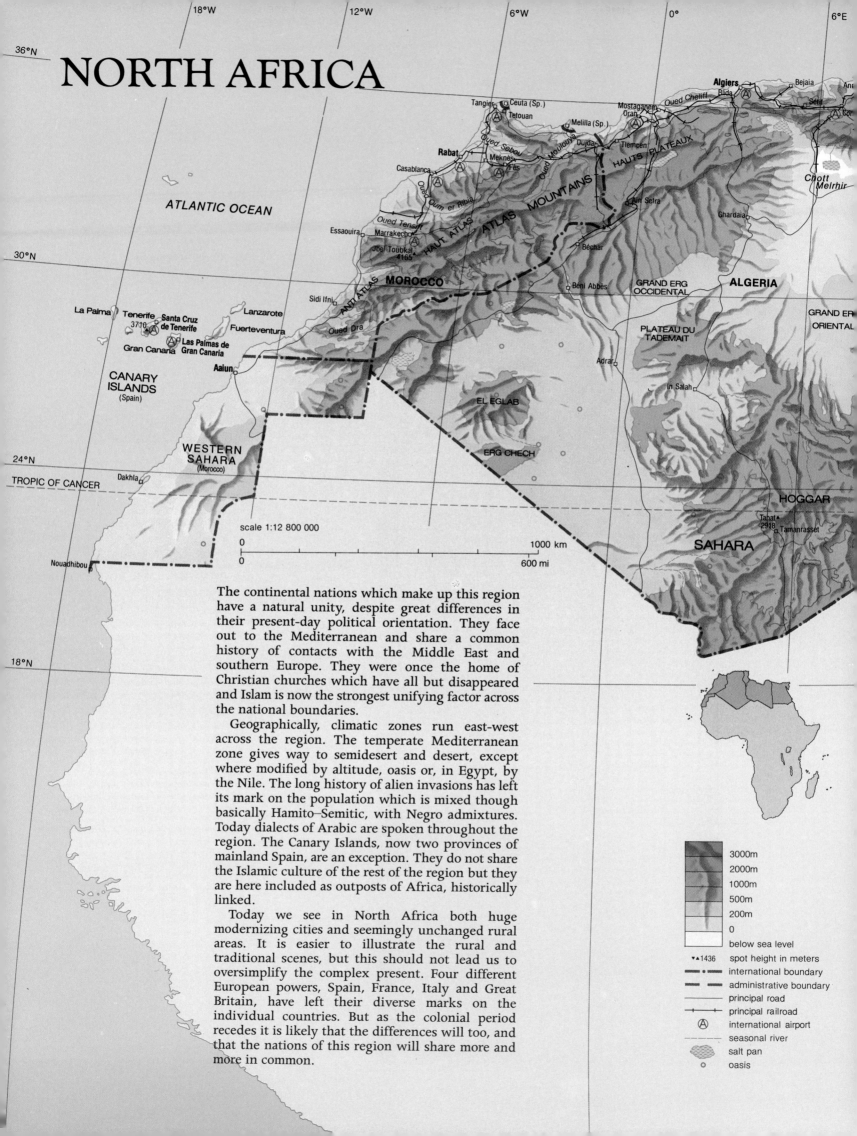

ATLANTIC OCEAN

18°W · 12°W · 6°W · 0° · 6°E

36°N
30°N
TROPIC OF CANCER
24°N
18°N

Algiers · Bejaia
Tangier · Ceuta (Sp.)
Tetouan · Mostaganem · Oued Cheliff · Blida
Melilla (Sp.) · Oran · Sétif
Oued Sebou · Oujda · Tiemcen · HAUTS PLATEAUX
Rabat · Meknès · Fes · Oued Moulouya
Casablanca · Oued Oum er Rbia · Aïn Sefra · Chott Melrhir
Essaouira · Oued Tensift · Marrakech · Ghardaia
Jbel Toubkal · HAUT ATLAS · ATLAS MOUNTAINS · Béchar
4165
MOROCCO · Béni Abbès · GRAND ERG OCCIDENTAL · ALGERIA
Sidi Ifni · ANTI ATLAS · GRAND ERG ORIENTAL
La Palma · Tenerife · Santa Cruz · Lanzarote · PLATEAU DU TADEMAIT
3710 · de Tenerife · Fuerteventura · Oued Dra
Las Palmas de · Adrar
Gran Canaria · Gran Canaria · In Salah
Aaiun
CANARY · EL EGLAB
ISLANDS · In Salah
(Spain)
WESTERN · ERG CHECH
SAHARA · HOGGAR
(Morocco) · Tahat
Dakhla · 2918 · Tamanrasset
SAHARA
scale 1:12 800 000
0   1000 km
0   600 mi
Nouadhibou

The continental nations which make up this region
have a natural unity, despite great differences in
their present-day political orientation. They face
out to the Mediterranean and share a common
history of contacts with the Middle East and
southern Europe. They were once the home of
Christian churches which have all but disappeared
and Islam is now the strongest unifying factor across
the national boundaries.

Geographically, climatic zones run east-west
across the region. The temperate Mediterranean
zone gives way to semidesert and desert, except
where modified by altitude, oasis or, in Egypt, by
the Nile. The long history of alien invasions has left
its mark on the population which is mixed though
basically Hamito–Semitic, with Negro admixtures.
Today dialects of Arabic are spoken throughout the
region. The Canary Islands, now two provinces of
mainland Spain, are an exception. They do not share
the Islamic culture of the rest of the region but they
are here included as outposts of Africa, historically
linked.

Today we see in North Africa both huge
modernizing cities and seemingly unchanged rural
areas. It is easier to illustrate the rural and
traditional scenes, but this should not lead us to
oversimplify the complex present. Four different
European powers, Spain, France, Italy and Great
Britain, have left their diverse marks on the
individual countries. But as the colonial period
recedes it is likely that the differences will too, and
that the nations of this region will share more and
more in common.

3000m	
2000m	
1000m	
500m	
200m	
0	
below sea level	
▼▲1436	spot height in meters
▬·▬·▬	international boundary
▬ ▬ ▬	administrative boundary
▬▬▬	principal road
▬+▬	principal railroad
Ⓐ	international airport
▬ ▬ ▬	seasonal river
	salt pan
○	oasis

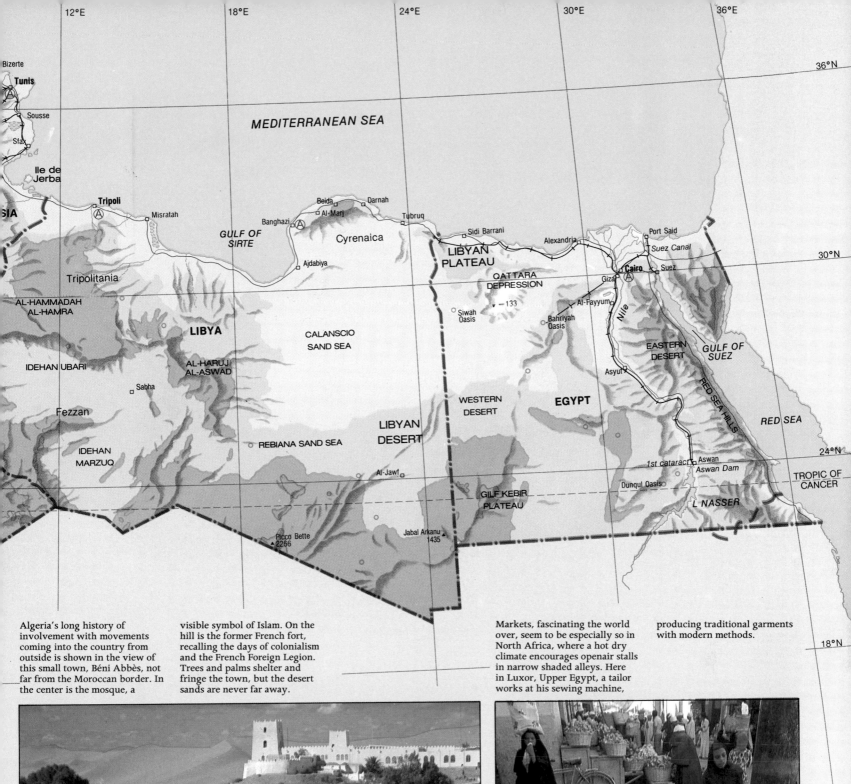

MEDITERRANEAN SEA

Bizerte
Tunis
Sousse
Sfax
Ile de Jerba

Tripoli
Misratah
GULF OF SIRTE
Banghazi
Beida
Al-Marj
Darnah
Tubruq
Cyrenaica
Sidi Barrani
Alexandria
Port Said
Suez Canal
LIBYAN PLATEAU
Cairo
Giza
Suez
Ajdabiya
Tripolitania
QATTARA DEPRESSION
−133
AL-HAMMADAH AL-HAMRA
Siwah Oasis
Al-Fayyum
Bahriyah Oasis
Nile
IDEHAN UBARI
LIBYA
CALANSCIO SAND SEA
EASTERN DESERT
GULF OF SUEZ
AL-HARUJ AL-ASWAD
Sabha
WESTERN DESERT
EGYPT
Asyut
RED SEA HILLS
RED SEA
Fezzan
LIBYAN DESERT
REBIANA SAND SEA
IDEHAN MARZUQ
Al-Jawf
1st cataract
Aswan
Aswan Dam
GILF KEBIR PLATEAU
Dunqul Oasis
L NASSER
TROPIC OF CANCER
Picco Bette ▲2266
Jabal Arkanu 1435

SIA

Algeria's long history of involvement with movements coming into the country from outside is shown in the view of this small town, Béni Abbès, not far from the Moroccan border. In the center is the mosque, a visible symbol of Islam. On the hill is the former French fort, recalling the days of colonialism and the French Foreign Legion. Trees and palms shelter and fringe the town, but the desert sands are never far away.

Markets, fascinating the world over, seem to be especially so in North Africa, where a hot dry climate encourages openair stalls in narrow shaded alleys. Here in Luxor, Upper Egypt, a tailor works at his sewing machine, producing traditional garments with modern methods.

111

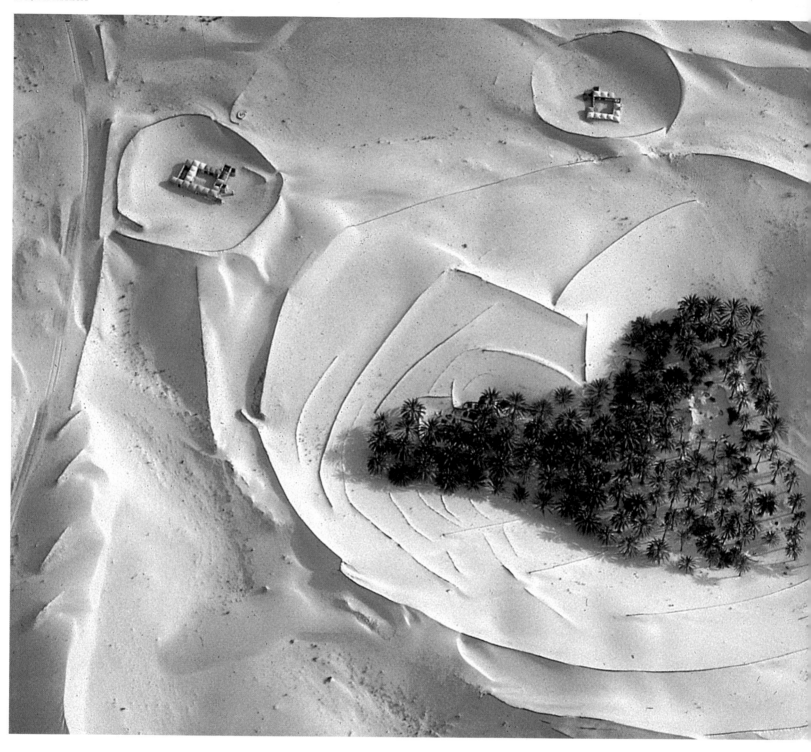

Above An aerial photograph of Souf, an oasis in the Algerian Sahara, shows clearly the tiny limit of cultivation and date palms, and the threat of the encroaching desert all around.

Right The discovery and utilization of oil in North Africa have brought great wealth, great power and attendant problems. Oil wealth is greatest in Libya, once an extremely poor country and now one of the richest; this illustration shows an oil installation in Algeria.

Far right A natural bay and artificial breakwaters combine to create a sheltered harbor at the Mediterranean port of Mers-el-Kebir, near the city of Oran in western Algeria.

Left At Hergla, on the east coast of Tunisia, a village woman carries water back from the well. Traditional dress is still often seen in the rural areas, and the village women are not veiled.

Overleaf In November 1975 about 350000 unarmed civilians, led by the king of Morocco, took part in the so-called "Green March" to assert Morocco's claims to the former Spanish Sahara, granted independence by Spain. It is still, as the Western Sahara, the scene of conflict between Morocco, Algeria, Mauritania and the internal Polisario movement.

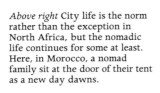

Above right City life is the norm rather than the exception in North Africa, but the nomadic life continues for some at least. Here, in Morocco, a nomad family sit at the door of their tent as a new day dawns.

Right In the villages of Egypt, pigeon houses are a universal feature with their nesting recesses and roosting perches. Pigeons form an important supplement to the simple vegetable diet of the farming population.

Egypt

Egypt lies on the northeastern limit of Africa, with its territory stretching to the Sinai region across the Gulf of Suez. The Nile, which flows from the south to the Mediterranean in the north, provides an irrigated agricultural area, but only 3.5 per cent of the whole country is cultivable. The Eastern Highlands and the Western Desert are barren regions. The climate is arid with an average rainfall of 80 millimeters per annum in the south. Near Alexandria rainfall rises to an average of 220 millimeters per annum. The population is a mixed one, though basically of Mediterranean stock.

The fertile valley of the Nile produced one of the earliest known civilizations. The dynasties of native Egyptian kings began in the third millennium BC and only ended with the conquest of Alexander the Great in the 4th century BC. The Ptolemaic Greek rulers were succeeded by the Romans, who in their turn were overthrown by the Muslim invaders of the 7th century. Medieval Egypt retained its own identity under a succession of Muslim dynasties, whose prosperity was ensured by the trade routes from the east which converged on the entrepôt port of Alexandria. In 1517 the Ottomans took Egypt and the country remained in Turkish hands until the 19th century.

The modern history of Egypt began with Napoleon's expedition to the country in 1798. The conquest was not successful, but it opened the way for an army officer, Muhammad Ali, to break with the Ottoman empire. He handed the state on to successors who attempted to develop the economy with cotton as the cash crop. Egypt's strategic importance grew with a project for a canal through the Suez peninsula. France and Britain invested in the Suez Canal Company, and in 1875 Britain gained a commanding control because of the financial difficulties of the Egyptian ruler, the Khedive Ismail. In the 1880s the country was torn by nationalist conflict which drew Britain more closely into its administration under the Consul General Evelyn Baring, later Lord Cromer. The British conquest of the Sudan at the end of the century, and France's growing involvement in North Africa, led to Britain's exclusive control of Egypt.

When World War I broke out, Britain declared a protectorate over Egypt, which played a notable part in the defense of the eastern Mediterranean and of the route to India. Egypt's role enabled it to demand some measure of independence in 1922. Its ruler was given the title of king and a constitution was granted. The interwar years saw a political struggle among the British, the king and the Wafd, or Constitutional Party. Political unrest and anxiety over the future of the canal made Britain reluctant to grant concessions to Egypt, but in 1936 the threat of Italy's ambitions in the Mediterranean forced her to grant a 20-year agreement which ended the British occupation of Egypt but secured Britain's right to bases in the Canal Zone.

Egypt also played an important part in World War II, and the Wafd party maintained loyalty to Allied interests although the king

115

favored the German cause. After the danger of invasion was over, political discontent increased. Communists and the radical Muslim Brotherhood vied to fill the vacuum created by the decline of the Wafd party, but it was the Free Officers of the Army who carried out a coup against the shaky regime of King Farouk in 1952. The monarchy was abolished and a program of land reform was begun. In 1954 Colonel Gamal Abdel Nasser became head of

Egypt

Official Name
Arab Republic of Egypt

Area
997 667 sq km

Date of Independence
1937 (Convention of Montreux)

Status and Name in Colonial Times
A long history of occupations and foreign-controlled monarchies: Egypt

Population
64 466 000 (UN est 1997)

Rate of Change
1.8%(UN est 1995–2000)

Capital City
Cairo (Al-Qahirah)

Population of Capital
6 663 000 (1990)

National Language(s)
Arabic; English, French

Gross National Product (US dollars)
660 per capita (1993)

Local Currency
1 Egyptian pound = 100 piastres = 1000 millèmes

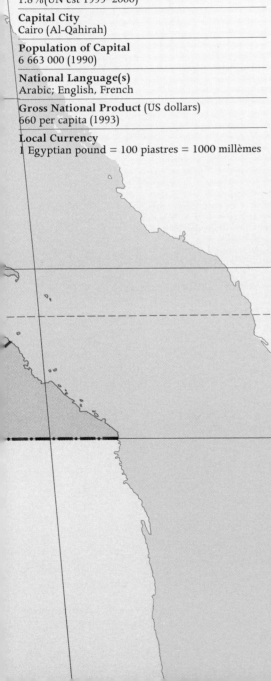

state. His position was firmly consolidated at home and abroad after the abortive Suez invasion by Britain, France and Israel in 1956. Egypt, in these years, was a leading advocate of Arab unity, forming a United Arab Republic with Syria between 1958-61. In May 1967 following Israeli/Syrian skirmishes on the Syrian frontier, Nasser ordered the removal of the United Nations peacekeeping force (in Sinai since 1956) and prepared for an attack on Israel. Israel however struck preemptively on 5 June, destroying the Egyptian air force and invading. After just six days of fighting, Egypt, defeated, accepted a ceasefire which left Israel in control of Gaza and a large area of Egypt including the whole Sinai peninsula. Nasser survived, but with his authority outside Egypt severely weakened, and still greater economic problems, not least loss of revenue from the closure of the Suez Canal.

The country possesses neither oil nor other natural mineral resources in any quantity, and a rapidly growing population has outpaced the supply of cultivable land. Attempts to remedy this by land redistribution met with little success, and ambitious economic plans, designed to diversify and industrialize the country, fared little better. Large-scale schemes were introduced with Russian technical and financial assistance, but the best known, the Aswan High Dam, has caused serious environmental problems.

Nasser died suddenly in 1970 and was succeeded by Colonel Anwar Sadat, who, increasingly impatient with Russian pressures, terminated Egypt's friendship treaty with the USSR. After an abortive merger with Libya and Syria, in 1973 Egypt launched a surprise attack on Israel, and was effectively defeated; under the US-brokered settlement, however, Egypt regained some territory and a UN buffer zone was introduced. Sadat lifted press censorship and released political prisoners as Egypt moved towards closer relations with the USA. In 1975 the Canal was reopened. However, poor economic performance led to increased living costs, which provoked food riots. In 1977 Sadat made a historic visit to Israel, addressing the Knesset, which led to the 1979 Camp David agreements. These strengthened his position with the USA and Europe, but weakened it with Egypt's Arab allies, which expelled the country from the Arab League. Sadat introduced further political reforms, but in 1981 he was assassinated by the extremist Islamic Jihad movement.

His successor, Hosni Mubarak, continued the rapprochement with Israel, siding with moderate states such as Jordan and the Gulf states. In 1982 Israel returned the Sinai. Egypt's active participation in the liberation of Kuwait during the 1990 Gulf War restored its Arab League standing, and it played an important role as honest broker in the diplomatic exchanges between Israel and the Palestine Liberation Organization that established Palestinian self-rule. However, Mubarak still faced serious domestic unrest, fueled by food shortages and the growth of Islamic fundamentalism. Mubarak accused Iran and Sudan of fomenting trouble, but the severely repressive measures he introduced were met by renewed violence.

Egypt has sought to steer a middle course between the West and Israel, and more extreme states such as Libya, often angering

both. Friction with the military regime in Sudan resulted in terrorist assassinations, including an attempt on Mubarak's life at the 1995 OAU conference in Addis Ababa. In the 1990s Islamic terrorists began the mass murder of tourists to disrupt this economically important trade. Egypt's failure to prevent this, evident in the 1997 Luxor massacre, attracted international criticism.

Libya

The state of Libya (the Socialist People's Libyan Arab Jamahariya) consists of three provinces linked by historical accident rather than geographical unity. These provinces are Tripolitania (now Western Province), Cyrenaica (Eastern Province) and Fezzan (Southern Province). The country stretches from the Mediterranean in the north to Chad and Niger in the south. The whole area is part of the North African plateau, varied slightly by hills behind the Mediterranean coastal region and high mountains in the south. The rest of the country is either desert or semi-desert with a rainfall of less than 200 millimeters per annum. The population is still less than the six million mark. Most Libyans live in Tripoli and its hinterland. Two ethnic groups predominate, the Mediterranean people in the north and the African Negroid people in the southern region of Fezzan.

Historically the three provinces developed differently: Cyrenaica under Greek influence and Tripolitania under Roman. Islam spread over the whole area in the 7th century, providing one unifying element. In the 19th century Ottoman rule linked the area in a loose political union. This was threatened by the strong Muslim revival movement in Cyrenaica led by a Muslim brotherhood under the leadership of the Sanusi family whose *zawiyas* (or settlements) spread throughout the province.

In the early 20th century Libya became the object of Italy's colonial ambitions. The Sanusi order united with the Ottomans against the Christian threat, but the defeat of the Ottoman empire in World War I and the exile of the Sanusi leader, Muhammad Idris, in 1922 opened the country to the Italians. The succeeding settlement was bitterly fought and costly to the Italian government. Libya became Italy's "Fourth Shore," and "demographic colonization" began in 1934 with Mussolini's accession to power. Landless peasants, particularly from Sicily and southern Italy, were settled on lands either taken from Muslim owners or hitherto unclaimed. By 1938, 10 per cent of the population of just over 880 000 were Italian settlers. Fascism took a strong hold on the colonial government.

World War II had a profound effect in Libya. The Italian, German and Allied armies fought backwards and forwards over the terrain for control of the strategically valuable points of Egypt and the Suez Canal. Italy's ultimate defeat meant that the area would not be returned to her direct rule, but France and Britain, still the most important powers in the region, disagreed about Libya's future. The USA had also developed strategic interests in the cold-war period and had built up the Wheelus Air Base near Tripoli. Finally the

NORTH AFRICA

Algeria

Official Name
Jumhyriya al-Jazairiya ab-Dimuqratiya ash-Shabiya

Area
2 381 741 sq km

Date of Independence
3 July 1962

Status and Name in Colonial Times
1871–1962 French *département*: Algeria (Algérie)

Population
29 473 000 (UN est 1997)

Rate of Change
2.3% (UN est 1995–2000)

Capital City
Algiers (Alger)

Population of Capital
2 168 000 (1995)

National Language(s)
Arabic; French, Berber

Gross National Product (US dollars)
1780 per capita (1993)

Local Currency
1 Algerian dinar = 100 centimes

MEDITERRANEAN SEA

ALGERIA

TROPIC OF CANCER

Legend:

- desert — scattered nomadic herding (camels, goats)
- seminomadic herding (goats, sheep) and cereal cultivation
- forest
- low-yield cultivation of wheat, barley, figs and olives
- intensive crop cultivation and cattle grazing
- fertile zone around oasis (palms, dates)
- oasis
- principal cash crops.
  - wheat/barley
  - vines
  - citrus fruits
  - olives
  - tobacco

- ⌾ mineral resource site
- ⌷ oil refinery
- ●—● oil/gas pipeline
- ⊠ oil field
- ▦ gas field
- ⊠ oil/gas prospecting
- Oran major industrial port
- Arzew major oil port
- Banghazi major fishing port
- ◯ tourist center

scale 1:8 000 000

0 ——— 400mi

118

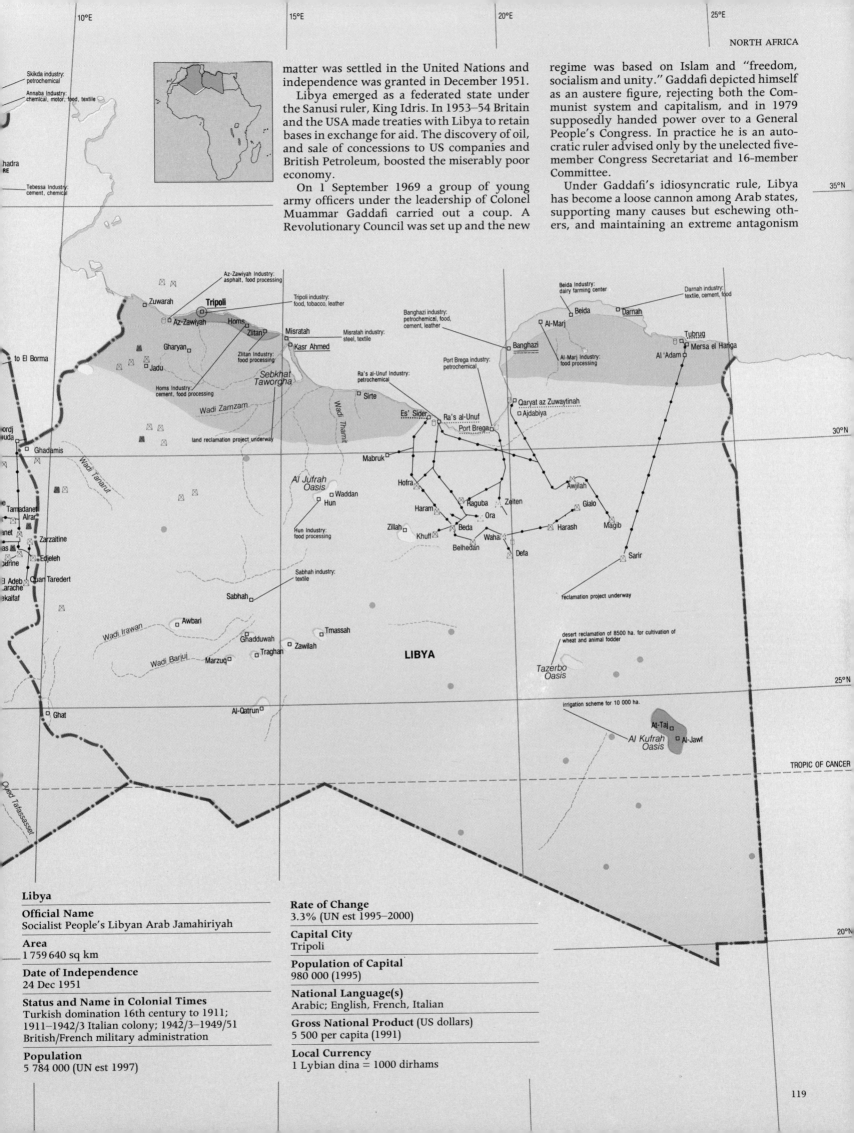

matter was settled in the United Nations and independence was granted in December 1951.

Libya emerged as a federated state under the Sanusi ruler, King Idris. In 1953–54 Britain and the USA made treaties with Libya to retain bases in exchange for aid. The discovery of oil, and sale of concessions to US companies and British Petroleum, boosted the miserably poor economy.

On 1 September 1969 a group of young army officers under the leadership of Colonel Muammar Gaddafi carried out a coup. A Revolutionary Council was set up and the new regime was based on Islam and "freedom, socialism and unity." Gaddafi depicted himself as an austere figure, rejecting both the Communist system and capitalism, and in 1979 supposedly handed power over to a General People's Congress. In practice he is an autocratic ruler advised only by the unelected five-member Congress Secretariat and 16-member Committee.

Under Gaddafi's idiosyncratic rule, Libya has become a loose cannon among Arab states, supporting many causes but eschewing others, and maintaining an extreme antagonism

Libya

Official Name
Socialist People's Libyan Arab Jamahiriyah

Area
1 759 640 sq km

Date of Independence
24 Dec 1951

Status and Name in Colonial Times
Turkish domination 16th century to 1911;
1911–1942/3 Italian colony; 1942/3–1949/51
British/French military administration

Population
5 784 000 (UN est 1997)

Rate of Change
3.3% (UN est 1995–2000)

Capital City
Tripoli

Population of Capital
980 000 (1995)

National Language(s)
Arabic; English, French, Italian

Gross National Product (US dollars)
5 500 per capita (1991)

Local Currency
1 Lybian dina = 1000 dirhams

towards the West and Israel. He has financed and armed terrorist movements, most notably the Palestine Liberation Organization, the Polisario in Western Sahara, and the Irish Republican Army. In the 1980s he began an aggressive campaign against the USA. Libyan planes and ships attacked US forces, but were swiftly destroyed. In 1986 he launched a terror campaign against US citizens in Europe. The USA responded by bombing a Tripoli army base. In the 1990 Gulf War, Libya confined itself to criticism of both sides. However, violent acts, such as the assassination of expatriate dissidents and the murder of a London policewoman by Libyan embassy staff, continued. Libya also intervened in the Chad civil war, and retains some Chadian territory in defiance of international arbitration. Gaddafi's refusal to extradite two Libyans accused of carrying out the 1988 plane bombing over Lockerbie, Scotland, led to the 1992 imposition of UN sanctions. Oil revenues remained high enough to render these ineffective.

Gaddafi's eccentricity and extravagant lifestyle – he was guarded by a battalion of picked female troops – provoked unease and apparently led to an abortive coup in 1993. After another murder attempt in 1995, Gaddafi expelled Palestinians and many other foreign workers. In 1996 UN sanctions were extended after it appeared that Libya was building chemical-warfare facilities. However, EU countries such as Italy, in whose major firms Libya has invested heavily, pressed to have them removed. In 1997 the Vatican exchanged ambassadors with Libya, and South African president Nelson Mandela made an official state visit.

Algeria

Algeria is the largest country of the Maghreb, stretching far into the Sahara in the south. The northern region comprises the mountainous area of the Atlas and the Mediterranean coastal strip on which the capital, Algiers, and the larger towns lie. The climate varies from Mediterranean (mild wet winters and hot summers) in the north to semi-arid steppe conditions in the south.

The modern territory of Algeria did not constitute a political entity in the Middle Ages. The region was converted to Islam and later came under the nominal overlordship of the Ottoman empire. The coastal towns under a bey provided shelter for the Barbary corsairs. In the early 19th century, western reaction against the slave trade and increasing strategic interests in the Mediterranean led to French interest in Algeria. On the specious excuse of an insult offered to the French consul the country was invaded by the French in 1830. The next 70 years were spent in bringing the country under French control by a harsh military policy. Land was confiscated and *colons* from France settled and took over political control. In 1871 the major part of Algeria became a French *département*, part of the mother country.

The indigenous Arab and Berber population had been reduced in numbers by the bitter wars and was left in economic and cultural poverty. Algerian troops fought for France in World War I and came into contact with nationalist ideas, but Algerian nationalism was slow in growing. In 1923 Messali Hadj started the first nationalist newspaper which a decade later was demanding complete independence for Algeria. More moderate nationalists like Ferhat Abbas were less sure that there was an Algerian nation to promote. The late 1930s and the World War II period, illustrating as they did the political and military weakness of France, encouraged more radical ideas among the Muslim population. Algeria, like Tunisia, had a Vichy government, but later in the war the Free French government set up its headquarters in Algiers. In 1943 Ferhat Abbas presented the "Manifesto of the Algerian people" asking for reforms and a constitution. This was rejected but it formed the basis of the nationalist movement in the immediate postwar years.

The period of violence began with the French suppression of riots at Sétif in May 1945 and the arrest of Ferhat Abbas. By 1947 numbers of Algerian Muslims were joining the Secret Organization (OS) and collecting arms and money. Attempts by the French to offer a limited constitution were no longer possible. In 1956 the various national groups joined with Abbas's National Liberation Front (FLN). The bitterly fought war of independence lasted until 1962. The success of the FLN caused a backlash from the French settlers in 1958. Supported by the army they caused the fall of the Fourth French Republic and the return to power of General de Gaulle. His cautious steps towards granting independence were countered in 1961 by the colonialist Secret Army Organization (OAS) which carried out terrorist attacks. In 1962 agreements were signed at Évian granting Algerian independence.

In 1963 Ahmed Ben Bella became president. His government was bedeviled by economic problems resulting from the war, the exodus of French professionals and skilled workers, and the strains of imposing a socialist system. In 1965 the increasingly autocratic Ben Bella was overthrown in a bloodless coup, and replaced by a largely military council headed by his Minister of Defense, Colonel Houari Boumédienne.

As president, Boumédienne continued the process of change, imposing a one-party state under the FLN with Islam as the official religion, and nationalizing foreign businesses, chiefly French oil interests. In 1977 a new constitution introduced an elected assembly, although Boumédienne remained president until his death in 1978. His successor, Colonel Chadli Ben Jedid, centralized presidential power, but in 1987, with the economy failing and oil prices falling, he relaxed some state controls. Amid growing social unrest he introduced increasing democratic reforms, resulting in a new constitution which ended one-party rule in 1989.

Much of this unrest was due to the rise of Islamic fundamentalism, represented by a new party, the Islamic Salvation Front (FIS). In 1990 they launched a campaign of strikes and confrontation intended to force presidential as well as parliamentary elections. This was eventually agreed, and in October 1991, under a new electoral law, the first round of multiparty elections were held. Amid charges of intimidation, the FIS won by far the largest number of seats. The government cancelled the second round of voting, outlawed the FIS and imposed a state of emergency. Chadli resigned and was replaced by a new ruling council.

Since then the country has been increasingly wracked by terrorism and repression. Muhammad Boudiaf, chairman of the ruling council, was the most prominent of many government figures assassinated. In 1993 Defense Minister Colonel Liamine Zeroual was appointed president, and in 1995 and 1997 Zeroual was endorsed in elections boycotted by the FIS. The possibility of negotiations with the FIS was thwarted by the appearance of more extreme Islamic splinter organizations, notably the Armed Islamic Group (GIA). The GIA has been blamed for a brutal terror campaign ranging from car-bombs to the systematic murder of foreigners and massacres of whole villages. However, many Islamists blame the security forces, who have also carried out indiscriminate killings. Algeria's economy, still largely oil-dependent, has been severely strained, and unemployment remains at over a third of the labor force. In 1998 attempts by the EU to mediate were not welcomed by either side.

Tunisia

Tunisia is the smallest state of the Maghreb, bounded on the north by the Mediterranean, on the west by Algeria and on the east by Libya. The country has a rich fertile area, comprising the Medjerda valley, the Mateur plain and the steppe from Hammamet to Gabès. There are some minerals, including phosphate, iron ore and lead. Petroleum and natural gas are now exported.

Tunisia was the center of the Carthaginian trading empire from the 6th century BC until its overthrow by the Romans in the 2nd century BC. Tunisia enjoyed prosperity under a succession of Muslim dynasties in the Middle Ages. Spanish and Ottoman ambitions in North Africa led to the overthrow of the last member of the Hafsid dynasty in 1574 and the establishment of Ottoman rule. In a few years Tunis regained independence under a bey who accepted the nominal overlordship of the Ottoman empire. The 19th century saw growing European interests in Tunisia as in Algeria. By the second half of the century the country was deeply in debt to foreigners and in 1869 France, Britain and Italy took over financial control. In 1881 France invaded the country and imposed the treaty of Kassar Said (or Bardo) on the bey, leaving him as nominal ruler with the French in charge of foreign, military and financial policy. Two years later a French protectorate was established and a French Resident General imposed. The office of bey was not abolished but he had little power.

Although Tunisia was deeply affected by French culture and education, it nevertheless kept its contacts with the Islamic world and its aspirations. In 1888 a Young Tunisian movement coupled demands for reform with a request for the restoration of the bey's authority. This achieved no success but one of its leaders launched the Destour or Constitu-

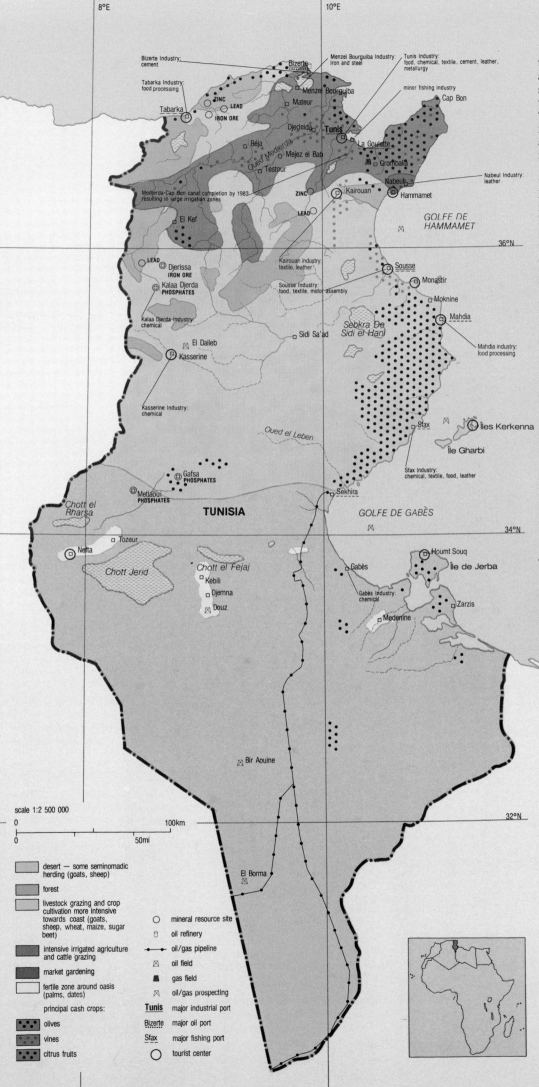

8°E 10°E

Bizerte Industry: cement
Tabarka Industry: food processing
Menzel Bourguiba Industry: iron and steel
Tunis Industry: food, chemical, textile, cement, leather, metallurgy
Bizerte
Menzel Bourguiba
Mateur
ZINC LEAD
Tabarka
IRON ORE
Djedeida Tunis
Béja
La Goulette
Oued Medjerda
Mejez el Bab
Grombalia
Testour
Medjerda-Cap Bon canal completion by 1983 resulting in large irrigation zones
minor fishing industry
Cap Bon
Nabeul Industry: leather
Nabeul
ZINC
Kairouan
Hammamet
LEAD
El Kef
GOLFE DE HAMMAMET
36°N
LEAD Djerissa
IRON ORE
Kalaa Djerda
PHOSPHATES
Kairouan industry: textile, leather
Sousse
Monastir
Sousse Industry: food, textile, motor assembly
Kalaa Djerda industry: chemical
Moknine
Sidi Sa'ad
Sebkra De Sidi el Hani
Mahdia
El Daileb
Kasserine
Mahdia industry: food processing
Kasserine industry: chemical
Oued el Leben
Sfax
Îles Kerkenna
Île Gharbi
Stax Industry: chemical, textile, food, leather
Gafsa
PHOSPHATES
Metlaoui
PHOSPHATES
Sekhira
Chott el Rharsa
TUNISIA
GOLFE DE GABÈS
34°N
Tozeur
Nefta
Chott el Fejaj
Houmt Souq
Chott Jerid
Kebili
Gabès
Île de Jerba
Djemna
Douz
Gabès Industry: chemical
Zarzis
Medenine
Bir Aouine
El Borma
32°N

scale 1:2 500 000
0 100km
0 50mi

desert — some seminomadic herding (goats, sheep)
forest
livestock grazing and crop cultivation more intensive towards coast (goats, sheep, wheat, maize, sugar beet)
intensive irrigated agriculture and cattle grazing
market gardening
fertile zone around oasis (palms, dates)

principal cash crops:
olives
vines
citrus fruits

○ mineral resource site
oil refinery
oil/gas pipeline
oil field
gas field
oil/gas prospecting
Tunis major industrial port
Bizerte major oil port
Sfax major fishing port
○ tourist center

tion Party in 1920. France conceded a few administrative reforms but no political representation. In 1934 a new generation of Destourians emerged under the leadership of a Tunisian lawyer, Habib Bourguiba. His organization of the party in the late 1930s built up a considerable opposition to the French administration.

During World War II Tunisia was placed under a Vichy government after the fall of France and became the supply base for Germany's campaigns in Libya. The nationalist leaders were imprisoned in France for the duration of the war. On his release Bourguiba traveled widely to explain the Tunisian point of view and in 1946 he spoke to the United Nations. Three years later he returned to Tunisia and began to work for the nonviolent achievement of political rights.

The early hope that France might accept his proposals was dashed by the reaction of the European settlers. Demonstrations against the regime began in 1952 and Bourguiba and the other nationalist leaders were imprisoned. Violence increased and in 1954 France agreed to grant internal self-rule to a country on the verge of civil war. Independence was eventually granted in 1956 and a year later Tunisia was declared a republic with Bourguiba as its head.

The new president steered a careful course between his need for Western aid and his desire to link Tunisia with the wider Arab world. In 1965 he opposed the Arab League's policy in Israel, but in 1967 Tunisia sent troops to support Egypt in the Six Days' War.

At home Bourguiba swiftly established a *de facto* one-party state, and with the Minister of Finance and Planning, Ahmed Ben Salah, he began a program of socializing the economy, collectivizing agriculture and appropriating French-owned land. Serious economic problems and social unrest resulted. In 1969 Ben Salah was imprisoned (he later fled into exile),

Tunisia

Official Name
Tunisia
Jumhuriya at-Tunisiya

Area
164 150 sq km

Date of Independence
20 Mar 1956

Status and Name in Colonial Times
1883–1956 French protectorate: Tunisia

Population
9 325 000 (UN est 1997)

Rate of Change
1.8% (UN est 1995–2000)

Capital City
Tunis

Population of Capital
1 395 000 (1994)

National Language(s)
Arabic; French

Gross National Product (Us dollars)
1 720 per capita (1993)

Local Currency
Tunisian dinar = 1000 millièmes

and some economic liberalization was allowed. However, in 1975 Bourguiba had himself elected president for life, and political unrest and repression increased. In 1979 relations with Egypt were severed over its peace deal with Israel.

Despite the introduction of a multiparty system in 1981, continuing economic failure led to conflict with trade unions and food riots throughout the 1980s. Meanwhile, rising Islamic fundamentalist groups began terrorist campaigns, resulting in mass imprisonments. The Palestine Liberation Organization set up its headquarters in Tunis at this time, and moves were made towards creating a union of the Maghreb states, including Algeria, Libya, Morocco and Mauritania, but this foundered on internecine disputes such as Libya's 1987 expulsion of Tunisian workers.

In 1987 Bourguiba was deposed on the grounds of mental incapacity and replaced by his prime minister, Zine al-Abidine Ben Ali, who introduced increasing political and economic reforms, including amnesty for political prisoners, and restored relations with Egypt. Ben Ali, sole candidate for all parties, was elected president in 1989. He began to improve relations with other neighboring states, especially Libya, creating the Maghreb Union. However, the government's equivocal stance during the 1990 Gulf War led to violent demonstrations by fundamentalist and pro-Iraqi groups, and an alleged coup plot led to further arrests of political activists.

In the mid-1990s relations with Algeria and Iran were restored, and Maghreb Union links with the EU established, resulting, in 1995, in an association agreement between Tunisia and the EU. The economy is now strong thanks to economic liberalization, but political repression continues.

Morocco

Morocco is a land of contrasts: geographical, historical and human. Within its borders are desert sands and thick forests; the rocky Atlas Mountains and fertile plains; sparsely populated desert and mountain areas and teeming cities like Casablanca, Rabat, Fès and Marrakech. It has known periods of chaotic

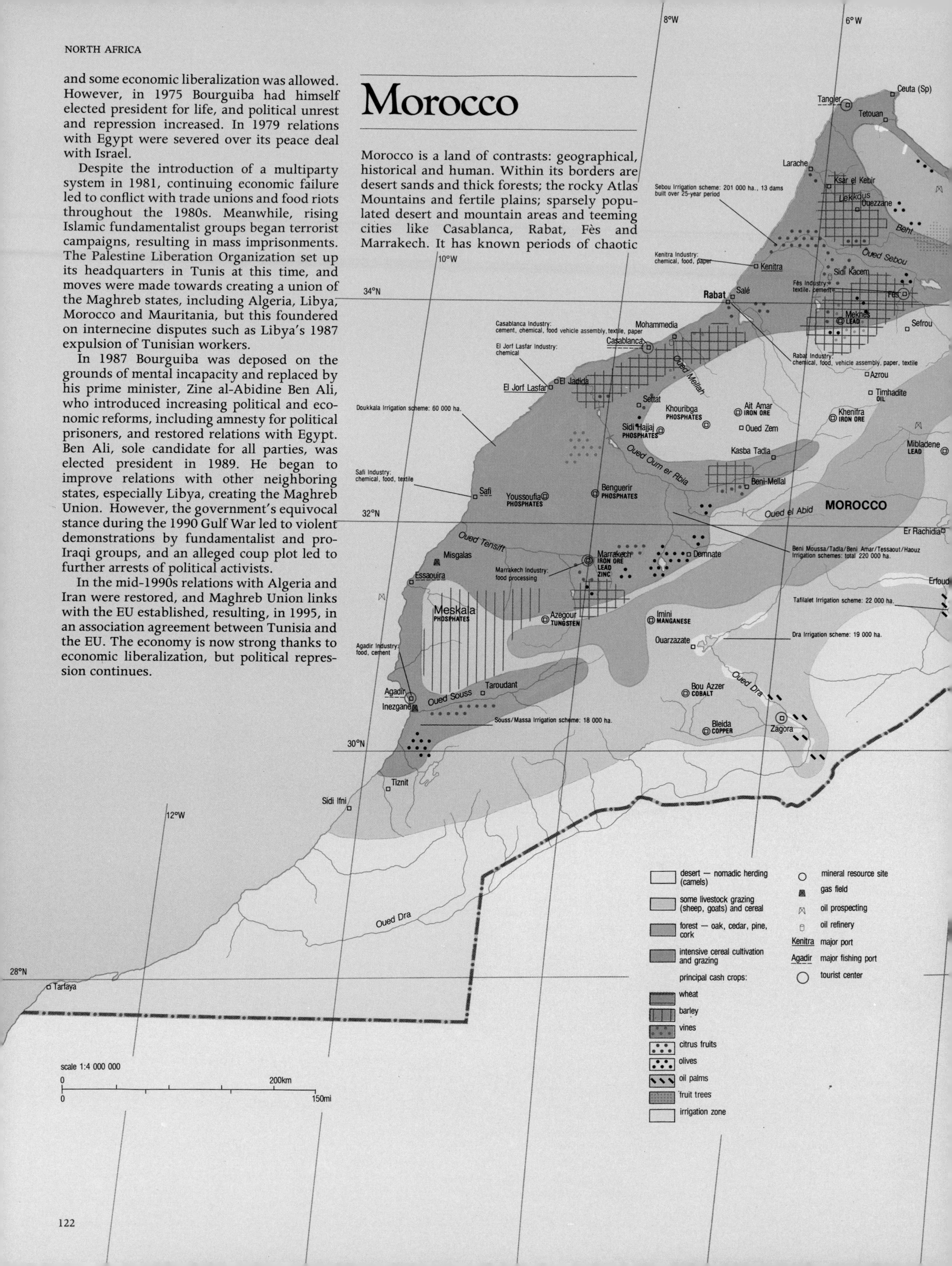

Map labels

Ceuta (Sp)
Tangier
Tetouan
Larache
Ksar el Kebir
Lekkous
Ouezzane
Beht
Sebou Irrigation scheme: 201 000 ha., 13 dams built over 25-year period
Oued Sebou
Kenitra Industry: chemical, food, paper
Kenitra
Sidi Kacem
Rabat
Salé
Fès Industry: textile, cement
Fès
Casablanca Industry: cement, chemical, food vehicle assembly, textile, paper
Mohammedia
Meknès
LEAD
Sefrou
Casablanca
El Jorf Lasfar Industry: chemical
El Jadida
Rabat Industry: chemical, food, vehicle assembly, paper, textile
Azrou
El Jorf Lasfar
Settat
Timhadite
OIL
Doukkala Irrigation scheme: 60 000 ha.
Khouribga PHOSPHATES
Ait Amar IRON ORE
Khenifra IRON ORE
Sidi Hajjaj PHOSPHATES
Oued Zem
Oued Mellah
Safi Industry: chemical, food, textile
Kasba Tadla
Mibladene LEAD
Safi
Youssoufia PHOSPHATES
Benguerir PHOSPHATES
Oued Oum er Rbia
Beni-Mellal
Oued el Abid
MOROCCO
Er Rachidia
Oued Tensift
Misgalas
Marrakech IRON ORE LEAD ZINC
Demnate
Beni Moussa/Tadla/Beni Amar/Tessaout/Haouz Irrigation schemes: total 220 000 ha.
Essaouira
Marrakech Industry: food processing
Erfoud
Meskala PHOSPHATES
Azegour TUNGSTEN
Imini MANGANESE
Tafilalet Irrigation scheme: 22 000 ha.
Ouarzazate
Dra Irrigation scheme: 19 000 ha.
Agadir Industry: food, cement
Bou Azzer COBALT
Oued Dra
Agadir
Inezgane
Oued Souss
Taroudant
Souss/Massa Irrigation scheme: 18 000 ha.
Bleida COPPER
Zagora
Tiznit
Sidi Ifni
Tarfaya
Oued Dra

Legend

- desert — nomadic herding (camels)
- some livestock grazing (sheep, goats) and cereal
- forest — oak, cedar, pine, cork
- intensive cereal cultivation and grazing
- principal cash crops:
- wheat
- barley
- vines
- citrus fruits
- olives
- oil palms
- fruit trees
- irrigation zone
- ○ mineral resource site
- gas field
- oil prospecting
- oil refinery
- Kenitra major port
- Agadir major fishing port
- ○ tourist center

scale 1:4 000 000
0 — 200km
0 — 150mi

122

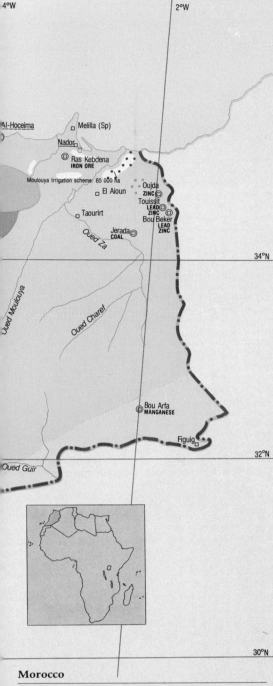

Morocco

Official Name
Kingdom of Morocco
Al-Mamlaka al-Maghrebia

Area
659 970 sq km (458 730 sq km excluding annexed portion of Western Sahara)

Date of Independence
18 Nov 1956

Status and Name in Colonial Times
1912–56 divided into French protectorate, Spanish protectorate and international zone of Tangier

Population
27 518 000 (UN est 1997)

Rate of Change
1.7% (UN est 1995–2000)

Capital City
Rabat

Population of Capital
1 220 000 (1993)

National Language(s)
Arabic, French, Spanish, English

Gross National Product (US dollars)
1 040 per capita (1993)

Local Currency
1 Moroccan dirham = 100 Moroccan francs

anarchy and internal strife and periods of highly centralized control; periods of intellectual and artistic glory and periods of decline; periods of conquest and empire and a period of foreign rule. Its people range from the traditional Berber-speaking mountain peasant tribesmen to the urbane, European-educated, French-speaking upper crust of Casablanca and Rabat. Even within the elite there are the traditional, old, wealthy families of Fès, many of whom cling to traditional Islamic values, the nouveaux riches who look to Europe and the USA, and the increasingly wealthy merchants from the Sous valley now established in Casablanca.

Morocco is a country demarcated by geographical features and molded by its people. Occupying the northwest corner of Africa, it has long Atlantic and Mediterranean coasts. The Rif and Atlas mountains form the backbone of the country and, together with its new and historic cities, give Morocco a unique character – a blend of the urbane life of the traditional Islamic city, the traditionalism of the mountain tribes and the hustle and bustle of growing modern urban centers.

As Mauretania Tingitana, Morocco made its first appearance in recorded history as a Roman province. Relics of the Roman presence can still be seen at Volubilis (near Meknès) and Lixus (near Larache). After the Romans left, local Berber tribes controlled the area until the Arab conquest in the 7th century. Morocco, or *al-Maghrib al-Aqsa* (the furthest west) as it is known to the Arabs, became the jumping-off point for the Muslim conquest of Spain in 711. However, Morocco soon reasserted its distinctive identity in the 8th century under Mulay Idris I and Mulay Idris II, who founded the first of a series of Moroccan dynasties. From the rise of the Idrissids until the Franco-Spanish partition into a dual protectorate in 1912, these dynasties ruled Morocco and surrounding areas from capitals in Fès, Marrakech, Meknès and occasionally Rabat. The Almoravids (11th–12th centuries) also ruled much of Islamic Spain, as did the Almohads (12th–13th centuries), who extended their control over present-day Algeria and Tunisia as well. The Merinid (13th–15th centuries) successors to the Almohads in Morocco were replaced by the Sa'adis (16th–17th centuries), who restored Moroccan control of extensive areas in the western Sudan and conquered Tombouctou in 1590. Following an extended period of political turmoil the 'Alawis replaced the Sa'adis in the 1660s and still rule Morocco today.

After the Franco-Spanish protectorate divided the country into two zones in 1912, a nationalist movement came into being. In the late 1940s and early 1950s King Muhammad V emerged as the spiritual leader of the independence struggle, and he and the 'Alawi dynasty retained control of the country once the French and Spanish restored Morocco's independence in 1956. Muhammad V (d. 1961) and his son, King Hasan II, have reigned and ruled ever since as constitutional monarchs presiding over a multiparty Chamber of Deputies, augmented in 1997 with an indirectly elected Chamber of Councillors. The king appoints the prime minister and cabinet. A loose royalist ruling coalition is opposed by various parties, of which the largest form the Bloc Démocratique. Despite episodes of unrest, chiefly over food prices, greater democracy has been introduced, especially in the 1992 constitution, amended in 1996. Similarly, press censorship is relatively relaxed.

Relations with neighboring states were bedeviled by the long-running dispute over the Spanish Sahara, now Western Sahara. Ceded under pressure by Spain in 1976 to Morocco and Mauritania equally, this territory was also claimed by the Polisario guerrilla movement. Morocco took over the Mauritanian zone in 1979. Terrorism, fighting and government repression in Western Sahara dragged on throughout the 1980s, leading to the acceptance of a UN peacekeeping mission in 1989. This produced no solution, however, and the dispute continued to smolder into the late 1990s.

The Maghreb Union, founded in 1989 with Algeria, Libya, Mauritania and Tunisia, has come to little. In the 1990 Gulf War Morocco supplied troops to defend Saudi Arabia but voiced support for Iraq, improving relations with both countries. King Hasan's support for the Middle East peace process restored diplomatic contacts with Israel in 1993–94, but these faltered over the West Bank settlement issue in 1997.

Recurrent droughts and a burgeoning population have forced Morocco to import large amounts of cereals and other foodstuffs, despite its vast fertile areas and extensive irrigation projects. However, it is now almost self-sufficient in meat production. Sale of fishing licenses, especially to EU countries, has become a significant revenue earner. Government-sponsored development has moved from agriculture to industry, particularly extraction of the country's immense phosphate reserves. These, nearly half the world's total, provide the main export, but the economy is more diversified than those of Morocco's oil-dependent neighbors. Manufacturing remains small-scale. Tourism, also economically important, was affected by isolated terrorist acts, but is recovering. EU countries, especially France, are major trading partners, and in 1996 a partnership agreement was signed. However, relations remain strained over Spain's North African enclaves and France's treatment of Moroccan guest workers.

Canary Islands

The Canary Islands are not a nation-state but comprise two provinces of the Spanish state on an equal basis with the mainland provinces. The islands were given the status of an autonomous community in 1982. Independence has some support, particularly among political parties of the left, but is an unlikely prospect in the near future owing to the high degree of cultural and political integration with the mainland.

The archipelago consists of seven islands: La Palma, Gomera, Hierro, Tenerife (which comprise the province of Santa Cruz de Tenerife), Lanzarote, Fuerteventura and Gran Canaria (province of Las Palmas). Geomorphologically the islands have been seen as an extension of the Saharan platform, but recent research considers only Lanzarote and Fuerteventura as extensions of the continental

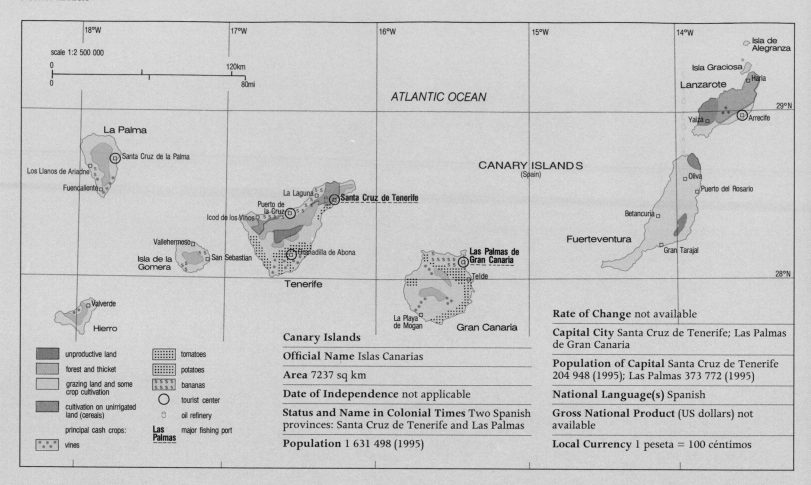

Canary Islands

Official Name Islas Canarias

Area 7237 sq km

Date of Independence not applicable

Status and Name in Colonial Times Two Spanish provinces: Santa Cruz de Tenerife and Las Palmas

Population 1 631 498 (1995)

Rate of Change not available

Capital City Santa Cruz de Tenerife; Las Palmas de Gran Canaria

Population of Capital Santa Cruz de Tenerife 204 948 (1995); Las Palmas 373 772 (1995)

National Language(s) Spanish

Gross National Product (US dollars) not available

Local Currency 1 peseta = 100 céntimos

crust, with a non-continental origin for Gran Canaria and the others.

The hydrology of the archipelago presents stark contrasts. Fuerteventura and Lanzarote are desert islands, with virtually no surface water and a maximum of 30 rain days per year. Gran Canaria, Tenerife and La Palma are miniature continents, each divisible into three climatic zones: a coastal zone (below 300 meters altitude) characterized by high mean temperature and low mean precipitation, where irrigation agriculture is practiced; a temperate zone, whose upper limit varies from 600 to 900 meters; and a subalpine region with low temperatures and high precipitation. At 3718 meters above sea level, Pico de Teide on Tenerife is the highest peak on Spanish territory.

Before the European conquest, the Canaries were inhabited by the Guanches, whose culture was related to that of the North African Berbers. In 1402 Norman French knights conquered Lanzarote, Fuerteventura, Hierro and Gomera in the name of the king of Castile. The islands with denser native populations were conquered directly by Castile: Gran Canaria in 1478–83; La Palma in 1491; and Tenerife in 1493–96. Unlike the Norman islands, which were ruled as feudal fiefs, the latter three were controlled directly by the crown, and their administration anticipated the organization of the future American colonies. The three islands were organized together with a common *audiencia*, or appeals court, in 1526, although each was considered a municipality, administered by a city council, or *cabildo*. The surviving natives were converted to Christianity and quickly assimilated into the Spanish population. The islands early

became a point of transit between Spain and her American colonies and have steadily provided migrants to Spanish America.

Development of irrigation in Gran Canaria, Tenerife and La Palma permitted the installation of sugar plantations in the 16th century. Sugar technicians were recruited from Madeira, and Canarians later manned the sugar mills of Mexico and the Caribbean. Unable to meet the competition of British West Indian sugar, agriculture shifted to grapevines. A dominant trade pattern of the 17th century was the exchange of wine with British New England in return for dried fish, and oak staves for wine pipes. Wine gave way between 1825 and 1885 to another monoculture, the *Opuntia* cactus on which the dye-yielding cochineal insect feeds.

The current economy of the Canaries is dominated by tourism and agriculture, with little industry. Bananas have been the monoculture of the 20th century, along with tomatoes, potatoes, and a wide variety of fruit including citrus fruits, figs and peaches. Vegetables are also grown, as are sugar cane, wine grapes and flowers. Most cereal grains have to be imported. In Lanzarote, a curious system of constructing microcatchments (*gavias*) of rocks and volcanic ash has accounted for the displacement of sheep and camel herding by agriculture over the past two centuries.

The mild winter climate makes the Canaries a favorite year-round destination with tourists from northern Europe, especially Germany and Britain. In recent years this, and their clear air and altitude, have also made them a favorite location for major astronomical installations, such as the 165-inch William Herschel reflector telescope.

Industrial development has been minimal, limited by lack of water and local energy sources. The establishment of free ports in 1852 failed to stimulate the economy, owing to the smallness of the local market. Until the 1950s the only large industry was a petroleum refinery established in 1927. The industrial sector is now dominated by food processing, the production of cigars and cigarettes from imported tobacco, chemicals and textiles.

Western Sahara

Western Sahara, formerly Spanish Sahara, lies between Morocco and Mauritania along Africa's Atlantic coast. The desert territory is divided into two regions: Saguia el Hamra in the north and Wadi adh-Dhahab (Rio de Oro) in the south. Both are sparsely populated. Nocturnal dew and infrequent rains allow some agriculture along a 10-kilometer-wide coastal strip, and there is a small fishing industry. However, the major economic resource is the huge phosphate deposit at Boukra, about 160 kilometers inland from the capital, Aaiun. Proven reserves total more than 2000 million tons, most of it accessible to open-pit mining.

The population is low, and many of the people are desert nomads. For the most part Saharans are members of major Arab tribal groups – Reguibat, Ould Delim, Tekna – or a number of smaller tribes. Even those who live in the principal towns – Aaiun, Smara and Dakhla – are, for the most part, only a few years, or at most a generation, away from the tribal encampment.

For centuries such tribesmen have lived a simple nomadic life in close communion with nature. In the latter years of Spanish rule some attempts were made to settle them. Migratory routes were cut off for some and jobs created for others by the opening in 1972 of the 158-kilometer-long conveyer belt from Boukra's phosphates to the port at Aaiun, although shortage of water now hinders its operation. During the 1970s more than 25 per cent of the populace was employed in the phosphates industry. With the upheavals of the war, however, little has been certain about the economy.

Western Sahara's legal status has been long unresolved and is at present in limbo. From the 1880s it was ruled by Spain, most recently as an overseas province. Years of Moroccan and Mauritanian pressure, citing historical and dynastic links dating back to the 11th century, culminated in King Hasan of Morocco's 1975 "Green Invasion", a peaceful mass march into the territory by some 350 000 Moroccans. In February 1976 Spain withdrew, leaving the territory equally to the two countries, who partitioned it, but their claims to sovereignty were not supported by the International Court of Justice.

The Popular Front for the Liberation of Saguia el Hamra and Rio de Oro (Polisario Front), sponsored by Algeria and later also by Libya, then began a guerrilla campaign to establish Western Sahara as an independent state, the Democratic Arab Republic of Sahara (RASD). In 1979, after serious defeats by Polisario troops, Mauritania withdrew and Morocco annexed the whole territory. It contained Polisario operations by creating a gigantic sand-wall, equipped with electronic sensors, around a large area. Lucrative coastal fishing rights were sold to other countries such as Spain. The Organization of African Unity recognized the RASD in 1980 and admitted it in 1984, causing Morocco's resignation, and in 1985 the UN recognized the region's right to self-determination. Neither side could conclusively defeat the other, and in 1990 they agreed to a UN peace plan based on a ceasefire and referendum. Morocco immediately began a program of mass settlement, and obstructed the UN peacekeeping force. Among charges of human-rights abuse, voter registration for the referendum was interminably spun out throughout the 1990s. The Polisario, disowned by Algeria and, despite the ceasefire, increasingly harassed by Moroccan forces, became defeated and demoralized. The referendum may be postponed until well into the 21st century.

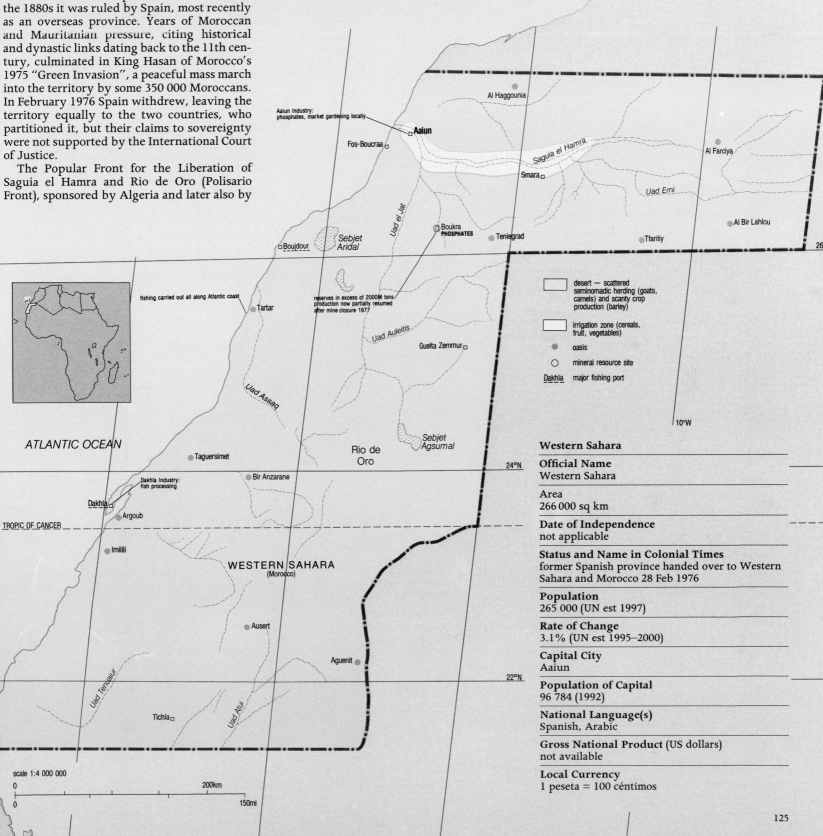

Western Sahara

Official Name
Western Sahara

Area
266 000 sq km

Date of Independence
not applicable

Status and Name in Colonial Times
former Spanish province handed over to Western Sahara and Morocco 28 Feb 1976

Population
265 000 (UN est 1997)

Rate of Change
3.1% (UN est 1995–2000)

Capital City
Aaiun

Population of Capital
96 784 (1992)

National Language(s)
Spanish, Arabic

Gross National Product (US dollars)
not available

Local Currency
1 peseta = 100 céntimos

WEST AFRICA

This region's greatest claim to unity may be the fact that much of it constituted the French West African Federation during the colonial period, from the late 19th century up to 1960. But there are also the former British colonies, from tiny Gambia to gigantic Nigeria, the Portuguese possessions of Guinea-Bissau and Cape Verde, and independent but deeply Americanized Liberia. There were also the German colonies of Togo and Cameroon.

Historically some peoples lived in very small-scale, simply organized communities. But many lived in highly structured and widely flung chiefdoms and kingdoms. Indeed, one of the distinctive marks of this region of Africa may be its kingdoms and empires – Ghana, Mali, Benin. The earliest and greatest kingdoms arose in the northern grasslands, but others later grew up among the agricultural and fishing people of the southern forests. Crafts and the arts flourished in these kingdoms – delicate metalwork, carvings in wood and stone, weaving and dyeing, elaborate palaces.

The various independent nations which now make up West Africa have not thrown off completely the traces of their colonial past. The English/French divide still separates. Islamic nations like Mauritania and Niger provide a bridge between north and south. The presence of oil and minerals, only recently exploited, is opening a door to new economic opportunities, while subsistence agriculture, herding and cash crops still provide a living for the majority of West Africa's peoples.

Below left The Atlantic and the Guinea coasts of West Africa have been visited by western sailors and merchants since the 15th century. Fortified trading posts such as Cape Coast Castle in Ghana, illustrated here, were established by European merchants under the protection of local rulers. In the absence of deep-water harbors, canoes were used to transport people and goods from shipping standing off shore.

Below Lagos harbor, Nigeria. There are few good natural harbors in West Africa, and construction of port installations has not kept pace with modern demands. In many cases, ships must still stand off shore to be unloaded.

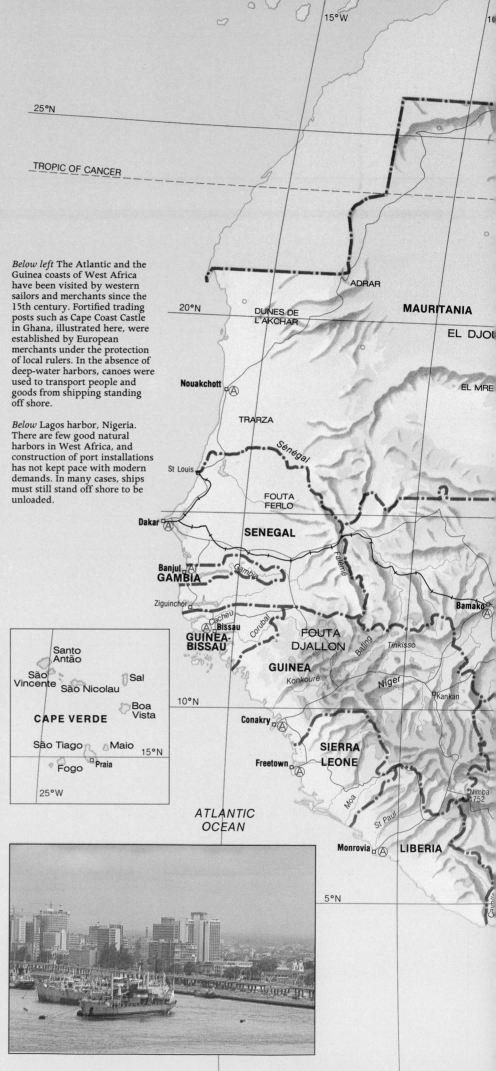

3000m
2000m
1000m
500m
200m
0

▲1752   spot height in meters
━·━·━   international boundary
━━━━   principal road
┼┼┼┼   principal railroad
Ⓐ   international airport
‑‑‑‑‑   seasonal river
         marsh
○   oasis

TROPIC OF CANCER

25°N

L HANK

PLATEAU DE
MANGUENI

SAHARA

TÉNÉRÉ DU
TAFASSASSET

SAHARA

20°N

ADRAR DES
IFORAS

AÏR
(AZBINE)

MALI

GRAND ERG
DE BILMA

Ténéré

Bagzane Mts
2022 ▲

Tombouctou   Niger

Agadez

Gao

NIGER

15°N

L Débo

Mopti

Birni Nkonni

Zinder

Komadougou Yobé

L CHAD

BURKINA FASO

Niamey

Bani

Ouagadougou

Sokoto

Zamfara

Kano

Hadejia

Maiduguri

Bobo Dioulasso

Red Volta

White Volta

Black Volta

Zaria

Komadougou Gana

Gongola

10°N

CHAÎNE DE
L'ATACORA

BENIN

Kainji
Reservoir

Kaduna

Kaduna

JOS
PLATEAU

Komoé

Tamale

Kainji Dam

Dimlang
2042 ▲

E D'IVOIRE

Bui
Dam

TOGO

Parakou

Abuja

NIGERIA

MASSIF
DE L'ADAMOUA

Bénoué

Bouaké

GHANA

L VOLTA

Ogbomosho

Oyo

Iwo
Oshogbo

Benue

Ngaoundéré

Yamoussoukro

Ibadan

Abeokuta

Kumasi

Akosombo Dam

Porto
Novo

Lagos

Benin City

Niger

Onitsha

Bandama

Abidjan

Lomé

Cotonou

CAMEROON

5°N

Accra

Bight of Benin

Port
Harcourt

GULF OF GUINEA

Cameroon
4070 ▲

Douala

Sanaga

Yaoundé

Nyong

scale 1:11 000 000

Bight of
Biafra

Dja

Ngoko

0   600 km

0   400 mi

Top In Burkina Faso a village elder stands by one of the grain stores which hold his family's provisions through the dry months between harvests.

Above left The Creoles of Sierra Leone and the Americo–Liberians of Liberia are descendants of freed slaves who migrated to or were returned to West Africa. They have tended to adopt Western styles of building and dress; this is an old corrugated-iron house at Lower Buchanan, Liberia.

Left At Ouâlata, in the dry semidesert of western Mauritania, mudbrick mud-plastered houses are painted and decorated with murals.

Above Oil extraction at Warri refinery in southern Nigeria. Petroleum production has made the Nigerian economy one of the strongest in Africa, despite concerns over damage caused.

Above right At markets all over Africa – this picture shows one in Dakar, Senegal – various types of baskets and woven goods for carriage, storage and furniture are made and sold.

Top right The Dogon people of Mali, from the area south of the Niger bend, live in villages, often built on steep hillsides, in rectangular walled compounds.

Right Groundnuts (peanuts) are an important cash crop, as well as a food, across the dry north of West Africa. At Kano, in northern Nigeria, pyramids made up of sacks of groundnuts are being demolished for export.

Far right Here in Kano, as in other parts of Nigeria, great earth vats are used for the indigo dyeing of locally woven cloth.

Cape Verde

Located in the Atlantic Ocean about 600 kilometers west of Senegal, between 14° 48′ and 17° 12′ N, and between 22° 40′ and 25° 22′ W, Cape Verde comprises ten islands and five islets in two groups. To the north are the Barlavento or Windward islands of Santo Antão, São Vicente, Santa Luzia, São Nicolau, Boa Vista and Sal, with the islets of Raso and Branco, and to the south the Sotavento or Leeward islands of Maio, São Tiago, Fogo and Brava, with the islets of Grande, Luís Carneiro and Cima. More than a third of the entire population lives on São Tiago, while Santa Luzia is uninhabited. Because many males have emigrated to Europe and North America in search of work, there are many more females than males in the population. Volcanic in origin (Pico do Cano on Fogo was active as recently as 1951), they present a jagged appearance with high coastal cliffs and are vulnerable to erosion. Only four of the islands, São Tiago, Santo Antão, São Nicolau and Brava, have year-round running streams, and aridity is characteristic despite the presence of an estimated two million hectares of as yet untapped water underground. The climate is warm, with the temperature varying from a mean high of 27° to a mean low of slightly above 21°.

Uninhabited at the time of their discovery in the 15th century, the islands became the possessions of Portugal, which sent among its settlers a high proportion of convicts. After the discovery of America, the islands achieved importance as an entrepôt for the slave trade, and blacks were imported to work the harbors and plantations. The breakdown of African tribal structures and widespread racial intermarriage in time evolved a multinational, nonracist culture leavened constantly by new arrivals from passing ships of many nations. Today the population mix is about 2 per cent white, 70 per cent mixed, the remainder black. This creole culture has a developed literature in Portuguese–African *crioulo*, and is strongly Roman Catholic. The decline of the slave trade in the 18th century meant declining prosperity. After 1747 cycles of drought and famine racked the islands, growing more devastating with the end of the slave trade in 1876.

In the decade following 1968 drought caused an almost complete cessation of agricultural production and required massive aid from other nations. Dissatisfaction with the Portuguese regime's failure to cope with the crisis contributed to the breakaway of the islands from the mother country in 1974, and in 1975 Cape Verde became an independent republic. The African Party for the Independence of Guinea-Bissau and Cape Verde (PAIGC), led by the first president, Aristides Pereira, set up a one-party state and aimed for union with Guinea-Bissau. After the coup there in 1980, the PAIGC was replaced by the Party for the Independence of Cape Verde (PAICV). Even so, Pereira remained in power until 1991, when multiparty elections gave the presidency to Antonio Mascarenhas Monteiro of the Movement for Democracy (MPD).

Despite attempts to build a market-oriented economy, Cape Verde is heavily dependent on external aid. It does export bananas, salt, physic nuts, coffee, fish, pozzolana, hides and potatoes, but the soil is poor, droughts are frequent, and much food has to be imported. Its chief economic importance is as a refueling station for ships and aircraft.

Cape Verde is a member of the Economic Community of West Africa (ECOWAS). The country cherishes its non-aligned status, and sat on the United Nations Security Council as a non-permanent member from 1992 to 1994.

Mauritania

The Islamic Republic of Mauritania came into existence in 1960, when France granted independence to most of its former African colonies. It had previously been a part of French West Africa. One of Africa's largest countries, with a population that is small in proportion, Mauritania lies with two-thirds of its area in the Saharan zone. Most of the country is a series of vast plateaus, consisting of sand over the western Saharan shield of crystalline rocks. Rainfall is minimal – always less than 100 millimeters annually. To the south the Saharan zone merges gradually into the sahel, with slightly higher rainfall and more abundant vegetation. While parts of the north cannot support even the camel, cattle as well as sheep and goats are grazed in the sahel. In the extreme south, along the Senegal river, is a narrow zone where fruit, vegetables and grains are grown. Along the Atlantic coast is a 30-kilometer strip where the hot dry climate is modified by oceanic trade winds.

Population densities and ways of life have been controlled by climatic factors. In the Saharan and sahelian zones, nomadism has been the only life possible outside towns and oases. Towards the Senegal border the people have been sedentary cultivators, and fishing was important along the Atlantic coast. Three-quarters of the population are Moors. Originally nomads and for centuries Muslim, they are of mixed Arab–Berber stock and speak dialects of Hassaniyya (Arabic modified by Berber vernaculars). A minority of Mauritanians, mainly in the extreme south, are black Africans – Fulani, Soninke, Bambara – speaking Nigritic languages.

Gradual contact with the West came through Portuguese, Dutch and French merchants venturing inland for trade, especially in gum arabic. It was not until 1899 that the French announced their intention of establishing rule over the territory "from the right bank of the Senegal" up to the borders of Algeria and Morocco, to which they gave the name of Western Mauritania. It became a protectorate in 1903–04 and a separate colony in 1920. Western education was accepted more readily by the Negro agriculturalists of the south, thus laying the grounds for future conflict. Political movements arose only in the late 1940s, and the first president, Moktar Ould Daddah, was a protégé of the French. Independence was granted in 1960 and an Islamic Republic proclaimed.

In 1968 Arabic became an official language, angering black Africans who did not speak it as a first language. Subsequent policies tended to suppress opposition from black Africans and from militant Islamic groups, often at the expense of human rights. Extensive mineral deposits (iron near Zouérate, and copper near Akjoujt) gave rise to increasing wealth. In 1975 Spain ceded the phosphate-

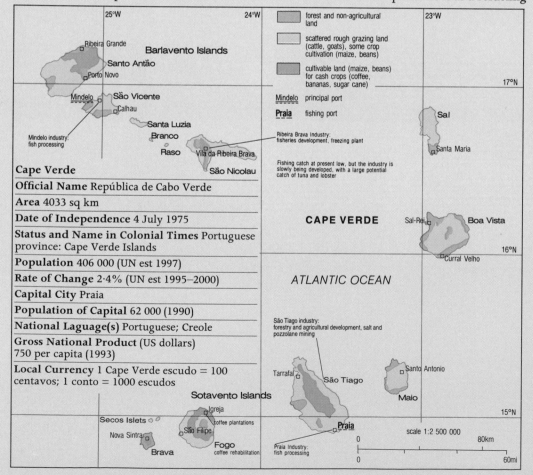

Cape Verde	
Official Name República de Cabo Verde	
Area 4033 sq km	
Date of Independence 4 July 1975	
Status and Name in Colonial Times Portuguese province: Cape Verde Islands	
Population 406 000 (UN est 1997)	
Rate of Change 2·4% (UN est 1995–2000)	
Capital City Praia	
Population of Capital 62 000 (1990)	
National Laguage(s) Portuguese; Creole	
Gross National Product (US dollars) 750 per capita (1993)	
Local Currency 1 Cape Verde escudo = 100 centavos; 1 conto = 1000 escudos	

Map legend:
- forest and non-agricultural land
- scattered rough grazing land (cattle, goats), some crop cultivation (maize, beans)
- cultivable land (maize, beans) for cash crops (coffee, bananas, sugar cane)

Mindelo — principal port
Praia — fishing port

Mindelo industry: fish processing
Ribeira Brava industry: fisheries development, freezing plant
Fishing catch at present low, but the industry is slowly being developed, with a large potential catch of tuna and lobster

Barlavento Islands: Ribeira Grande, Santo Antão, Porto Novo, Mindelo, São Vicente, Calhau, Santa Luzia, Branco, Raso, Vila da Ribeira Brava, São Nicolau, Sal, Santa Maria

CAPE VERDE
Sal-Rei, Boa Vista, Curral Velho

ATLANTIC OCEAN

São Tiago industry: forestry and agricultural development, salt and pozzolane mining

Tarrafal, São Tiago, Santo Antonio, Maio

Sotavento Islands
Igreja, Secos Islets, coffee plantations, Nova Sintra, São Filipe, Fogo coffee rehabilitation, Brava, Praia
Praia industry: fish processing

scale 1:2 500 000
0 — 80km
0 — 60mi

rich Spanish Sahara jointly to Mauritania and Morocco. The Algerian-backed Polisario movement within Western Sahara resisted this; the resulting guerrilla war soured relations with Morocco. It also weakened Daddah's government, which was overthrown by a military coup in 1978. After military setbacks, in 1979 Mauritania made peace with the Polisario and renounced its claim to Western Sahara.

In 1984 a bloodless coup brought Colonel Maaouya Ould Sidi Ahmed Taya the presidency; he also won the first multiparty presidential elections in 1992. 1994 saw controversial local elections, won by Taya's

Mauritania

Official Name
Republique Islamique de Mauritanie

Area 1 030 700 sq km

Date of Independence 28 Nov 1960

Status and Name in Colonial Times
French protectorate (part of French West Africa from 1903); 1920–60 French colony: Mauritania

Population
2 392 000 (UN est 1997)

Rate of Change 2.5% (UN est 1995–2000)

Capital City Nouakchott

Population of Capital 480 408 (1992)

National Language(s) French, Arabic

Gross National Product (US dollars)
500 per capita (1993)

Local Currency
1 ougiya = 5 khoums (= 5 francs CFA)
(CFA = Communaute financiere africaine)

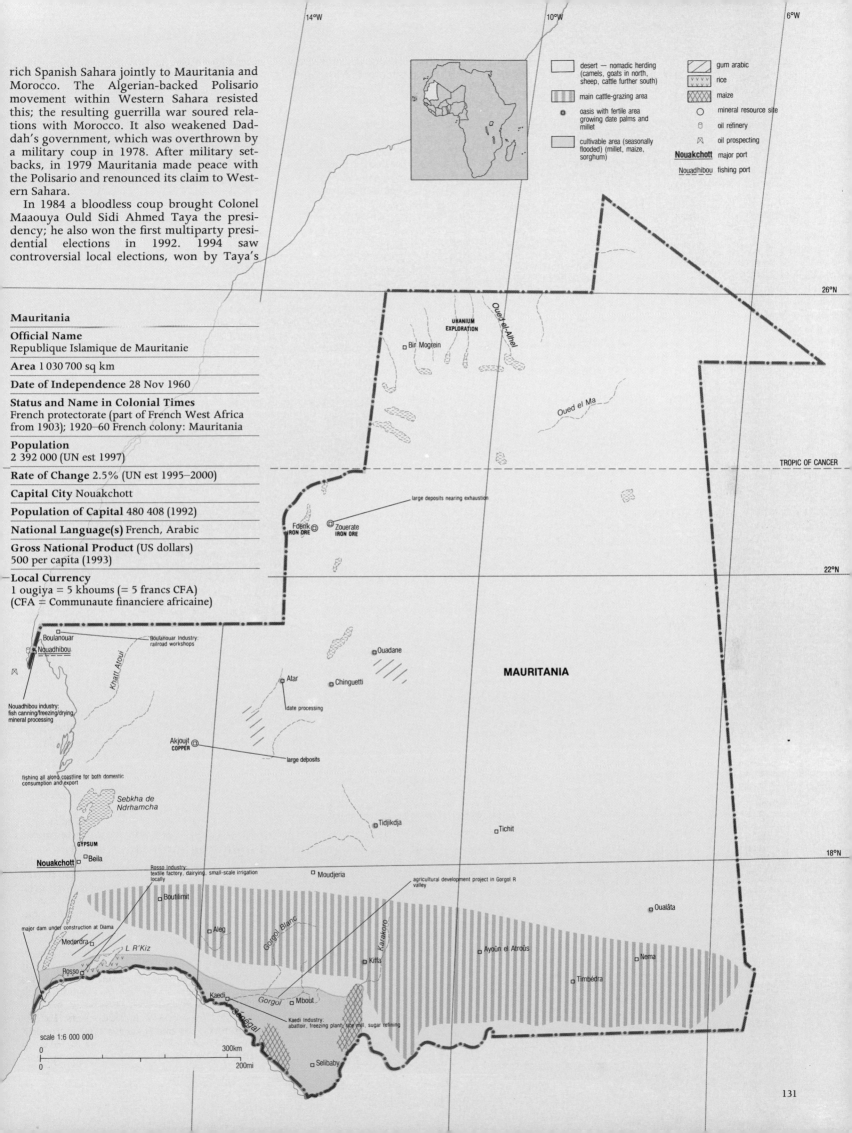

desert — nomadic herding (camels, goats in north, sheep, cattle further south)

main cattle-grazing area

oasis with fertile area growing date palms and millet

cultivable area (seasonally flooded) (millet, maize, sorghum)

gum arabic

rice

maize

mineral resource site

oil refinery

oil prospecting

Nouakchott major port

Nouadhibou fishing port

14°W 10°W 6°W

26°N

URANIUM EXPLORATION

Oued-el-Alhel

Bir Mogrein

Oued el Ma

TROPIC OF CANCER

large deposits nearing exhaustion

Fderik IRON ORE   Zouerate IRON ORE

22°N

Boulanouar   Boulanouar Industry: railroad workshops

Nouadhibou

Nouadhibou industry: fish canning/freezing/drying, mineral processing

Khatt Atoui

Ouadane

Atar   Chinguetti

MAURITANIA

date processing

Akjoujt COPPER   large deposits

fishing all along coastline for both domestic consumption and export

Sebkha de Ndrhamcha

Tidjikdja   Tichit

GYPSUM

Nouakchott   Beila   18°N

Rosso Industry: textile factory, dairying, small-scale irrigation locally

Moudjeria

agricultural development project in Gorgol R valley

Boutilimit

Oualâta

major dam under construction at Diama

Mederdra   Aleg

L R'Kiz   Gorgol Blanc   Karakoro   Ayoûn el Atroûs   Nema

Rosso   Kiffa   Timbédra

Kaedi   Gorgol   Mbout

Senegal

Kaedi Industry: abattoir, freezing plant, rice mill, sugar refining

scale 1:6 000 000

Selibaby

0   300km
0   200mi

131

Democratic and Social Republican Party (PRDS). The PRDS also dominated elections to the Senate in 1996, which were boycotted by opposition parties.

Much of the fast-growing population relies on agriculture and livestock for a living, though recurrent droughts have forced many nomads into the cities. The once-rich offshore fishing grounds have been badly depleted, and world demand for iron ore, which accounted for some 50 per cent of exports, has fallen. As a result, foreign debt has risen substantially and prospects for growth are poor.

Senegal

Senegal is situated at the western extreme of the African continent, bounded by Mauritania to the north and northeast, Mali to the east and Guinea and Guinea-Bissau to the south. To the west is the Atlantic Ocean. From the Atlantic the Republic of the Gambia protrudes into the Senegalese interior like a finger — the bizarre outcome of 19th-century European rivalries in the colonization of Africa. Senegal is drained by the Senegal, Gambia and Casamance rivers. The Senegal, the only navigable river, is no longer important as a waterway.

The transitional climate is reflected in the landscape: the north is semidesert, the middle belt is savanna and the south is given to rain forest. Rainfall varies from about 280 millimeters in the north to about 1650 millimeters in the south.

Senegal's principal ethno-linguistic groups include Wolof (about 25 per cent of the population), Serer, Fulani, Tukolor, Dyola and Malinke (Mandingo). Except for the largely nomadic Fulani, the rural populations are settled agriculturists. Senegal has five urban centers: Dakar (the capital), Saint-Louis, Rufisque, Thiès and Kaolack. The population is predominantly Muslim.

Early Arabic geographers refer to the 9th-century kingdom of Takrur on the Senegal river, one of the first Sudanese kingdoms to embrace Islam. From the 13th century, the Wolof empire dominated Senegal; in about 1488 a claimant to the empire visited Portugal. Senegal was an early participant in the Atlantic slave trade, but most slaves appear to have been transported from the Sudanic interior.

Senegal has strong historical ties with France. In 1638 French traders established a station, which later became the city of Saint-Louis, at the mouth of the Senegal river. The French were primarily interested in the gum arabic trade until the 1850s, after which the cultivation of peanuts began. The sale of peanut products to France has been the principal source of export revenue for Senegal ever since.

During the 19th century a series of Muslim *jihads* (wars of conversion) shook West Africa. The leader of one of the largest of these, al-Haj 'Umar, was born near Podor. 'Umar hoped to extend his conquests to the Senegalese coast, but was thwarted by the forces of the French general Faidherbe and forced to turn eastward. Faidherbe and his successors established military control over the Senegalese interior, putting down a number of resistance leaders.

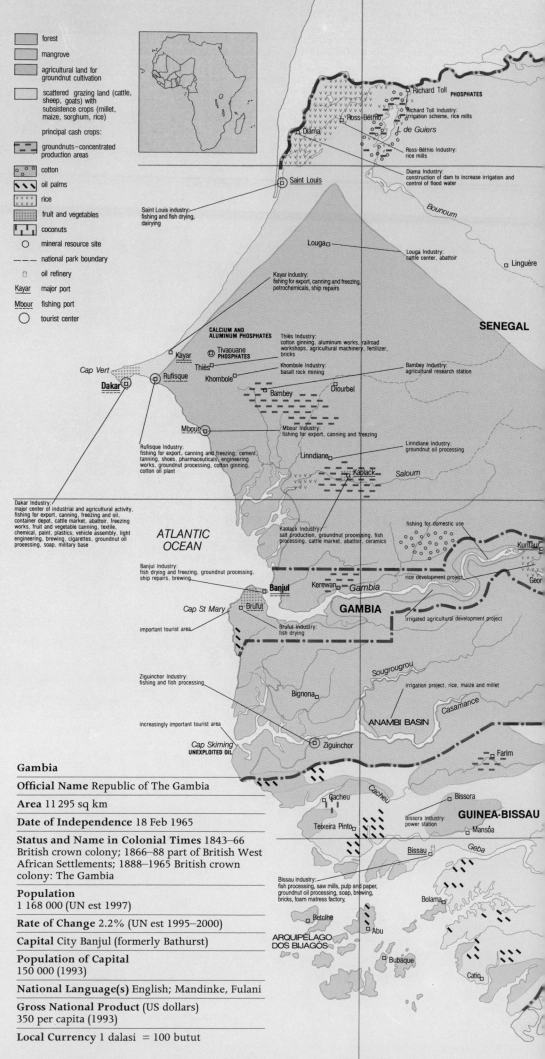

Gambia

Official Name Republic of The Gambia

Area 11 295 sq km

Date of Independence 18 Feb 1965

Status and Name in Colonial Times 1843–66 British crown colony; 1866–88 part of British West African Settlements; 1888–1965 British crown colony: The Gambia

Population
1 168 000 (UN est 1997)

Rate of Change 2.2% (UN est 1995–2000)

Capital City Banjul (formerly Bathurst)

Population of Capital
150 000 (1993)

National Language(s) English; Mandinke, Fulani

Gross National Product (US dollars)
350 per capita (1993)

Local Currency 1 dalasi = 100 butut

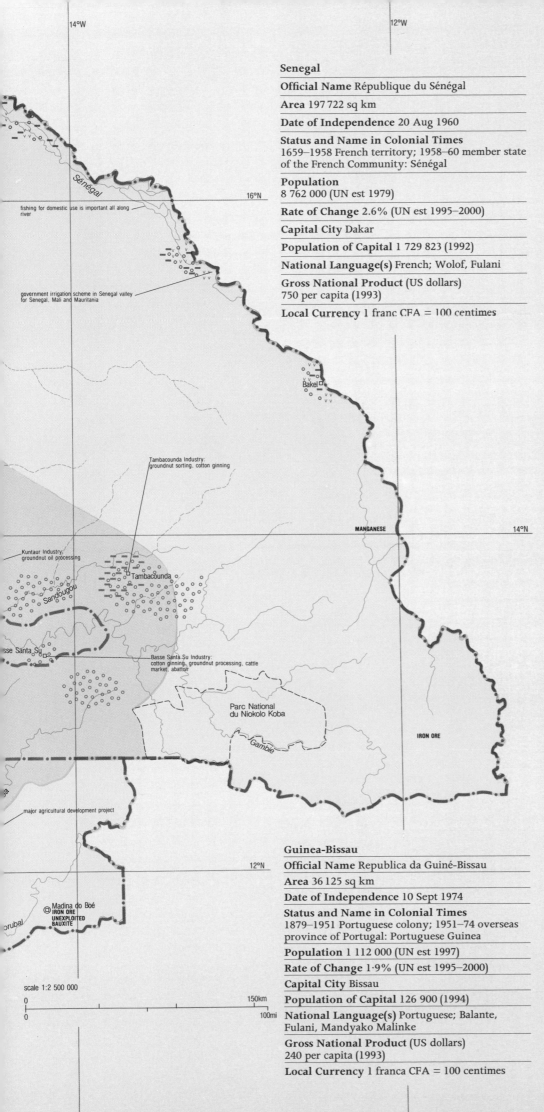

14°W

12°W

16°N

Sénégal

fishing for domestic use is important all along river

government irrigation scheme in Senegal valley for Senegal, Mali and Mauritania

Bakel

Tambacounda Industry: groundnut sorting, cotton ginning

MANGANESE   14°N

Kuntaur Industry: groundnut oil processing

Tambacounda

Sangougou

Basse Santa Su

Basse Santa Su Industry: cotton ginning, groundnut processing, cattle market, abattoir

Parc National du Niokolo Koba

Gambie

IRON ORE

major agricultural development project

12°N

Madina do Boé
IRON ORE
UNEXPLOITED
BAUXITE

orubal

scale 1:2 500 000

0   150km

0   100mi

Senegal

Official Name République du Sénégal

Area 197 722 sq km

Date of Independence 20 Aug 1960

Status and Name in Colonial Times
1659–1958 French territory; 1958–60 member state
of the French Community: Sénégal

Population
8 762 000 (UN est 1979)

Rate of Change 2.6% (UN est 1995–2000)

Capital City Dakar

Population of Capital 1 729 823 (1992)

National Language(s) French; Wolof, Fulani

Gross National Product (US dollars)
750 per capita (1993)

Local Currency 1 franc CFA = 100 centimes

Guinea-Bissau

Official Name Republica da Guiné-Bissau

Area 36 125 sq km

Date of Independence 10 Sept 1974

Status and Name in Colonial Times
1879–1951 Portuguese colony; 1951–74 overseas
province of Portugal: Portuguese Guinea

Population 1 112 000 (UN est 1997)

Rate of Change 1·9% (UN est 1995–2000)

Capital City Bissau

Population of Capital 126 900 (1994)

National Language(s) Portuguese; Balante,
Fulani, Mandyako Malinke

Gross National Product (US dollars)
240 per capita (1993)

Local Currency 1 franca CFA = 100 centimes

Senegal was to have been the showpiece for France's official policy of *assimilation*, the making of Africans into black Frenchmen. Senegalese in four cities had full French citizenship and considerable access to education. In the 20th century a number of Senegalese were elected to the French National Assembly, including the man who was to become Senegal's first president, Léopold Sédar Senghor. The assimilation policy could not work in the hinterland, however, and the French had to rule through local authorities.

During World War II France's African holdings became particularly important, supplying soldiers as well as a base of operations for de Gaulle. In 1946 French citizenship was extended to all Senegalese. In 1956 Senegal was granted internal self-government. Three years later it joined Mali in a short-lived federation, and in 1960 became an independent state with Senghor as president and Mamadou Dia as prime minister. Dia was imprisoned in 1962 after an alleged coup attempt, and Senghor assumed increased powers.

Senghor authorized two opposition parties in 1976, but under his successor, Abdou Diouf, the Socialist Party (PS) won over 80 per cent of the vote in the 1983 elections, prompting complaints of unfair practice. Similar charges, and violent protests, followed Diouf's victory in the 1988 and 1993 elections. There was another serious outburst of political violence after the devaluation of the CFA franc in 1994, which caused widespread hardship.

In 1989 a border dispute with Guinea-Bissau (resolved in 1995) stirred up discontent in Casamance, an area virtually cut off from the rest of the country by the Gambia. In 1990 the government sent in troops to deal with attacks by the Movement of Democratic Forces of Casamance (MFDC). Despite repeated efforts to negotiate a peaceful solution, 1998 saw renewed fighting. Another border dispute, with Mauritania, also began in 1989 and caused refugee movements in both directions.

At the time of Senegal's independence, it had one of the most developed economies in French West Africa. However, the loss of markets due to independence of its sister states, combined with France's decreased economic and physical presence and long periods of bad weather, has had disturbing effects on the economy.

Agriculture employs about 75 per cent of the labor force. Peanuts are still exported, but they are also grown for food along with millet, sorghum, rice and vegetables. Fish and fish products are now the principal exports, and make a significant contribution to the food supply. The sale of fishing licenses to EU countries is a welcome source of revenue.

Senegal's principal manufactured products are food, chemicals, textiles and refined (imported) petroleum, though offshore petroleum deposits are now being developed in cooperation with Guinea-Bissau. Phosphate mining contributes significantly to the economy, and there is potential for exploiting reserves of gold, salt, fuller's earth and natural gas. Tourism, a key element in the economy, has suffered from the unrest in Casamance, and the country continues to depend on foreign aid to offset a problematical balance of trade.

Legend

- forest
- agricultural land — crop cultivation (cassava, sorghum, rice, groundnuts, plantains in west, maize in southeast), cattle grazing in north
- major cattle grazing area — dwarf Ndama cattle

principal cash crops:
- bananas
- coffee
- pineapples, citrus fruits
- oil palms
- groundnuts
- rice (not a cash crop)
- ○ mineral resource site
- ⋈ oil prospecting
- Kamsar major port

scale 1:3 000 000

0 — 150km
0 — 100mi

Gambia

Gambia, one of Africa's smallest states, forms a finger-like protrusion jutting eastward from the Atlantic Ocean into the Republic of Senegal — perhaps the best example of the sometimes bizarre geographical and political ramifications of the European colonization of Africa. Its area is confined to the navigable valley of the Gambia river, extending 470 kilometers inland from the sea and measuring only about 24 kilometers across in most places. The land consists of mangrove swamps, marshes and woodland areas largely cleared for cultivation.

Keundara

Komba

Mali

Gaoual

Bafing

Kogon

Tinkisso

Labé Industry: orange essence distillery

Tougué BAUXITE

Ayé-Koyé BAUXITE

Labé

Dinguiraye

Boké Industry: aluminum smelting, oil palm processing

Boké BAUXITE large deposits

Fatala

Télimélé

FOUTA DJALLON

Dabola industry: groundnut oil plant, aluminum smelter

Bouka

Îles Tristao

GUINEA

Kankan Industry: regional marketing center, minor food processing, soya/rice commercial farms

Kamsar

Konkouré

Dalaba

Dabola BAUXITE IRON ORE reserves of 425 M tons

Niger

Kamsar industry: mineral port

Fria BAUXITE

Mamou industry: fruit canning, food processing, cold storage unit

Sanouya industry: textile mill

Kankan

Boffa Industry: oil palm processing

Kindia Industry: fruit canning, railroad workshops, food processing

Mamou

Boffa

Ouassou

Kindia BAUXITE

Sanouya

Faranah

Dubréka Industry: oil palm processing

Dubréka

Niandan

Conakry industry: timber, textiles, tobacco and cigarettes, oil palm processing, fruit canning, meat processing, cement, furniture, soap, plastics

IRON ORE

Conakry

Îles de Los BAUXITE mines exhausted

Forécariah

Kissidougou

Banankoro DIAMONDS

Forécariah Industry: banana processing

Bénty

Benty Industry: major port of export for bananas

Guékédou Industry: regional marketing center, coffee trading, minor food processing

DIAMONDS

Guékédou

Macenti

Guinea

Official Name
République de Guinée

Area
245 857 sq km

Date of Independence
2 Oct 1958

Status and Name in Colonial Times
French colony: Guinee Francaise (French Guinea)

Population
7 614 000 (UN est 1997)

Rate of Change
1.3% (UN est 1995–2000)

Capital City
Conakry

Population of Capital
950 000 (1991)

National Language(s)
French; Mandinke, Fulani, Soso, Kpele, Loma

Gross National Product (US dollars)
500 per capita (1993)

Local Currency
1 Guinean franc = 100 centimes

Annual rainfall is 1150 millimeters. Gambia's population is over 40 per cent Malinke (Mandingo); other major ethno-linguistic groups include Fulani, Wolof, Dyola, Serer and Soninke. About 90 per cent of the people are Muslims. Gambia's population is augmented by about 20 000 Senegalese nationals and, in addition, many Senegalese work there at harvest time.

Gambia's history is intertwined with that of Senegal. The region was a part of the Wolof empire, formed at the beginning of the 13th century. European contact dates from 1455 when the first Portuguese ship entered the Gambia river. In 1618 the British built a fort on a river island, and afterward the British and French fought intermittently for control of the river and its trade. Britain's supremacy became permanent after the establishment of Bathurst (now Banjul, the capital) at the mouth of the river in 1821, although the British later tried twice to trade their possession to the French, whose holdings in Senegal surrounded the tiny colony.

The people of the interior had for centuries resisted Islamic influences, but after 1850 a number of powerful Islamic leaders declared war on the local political leadership, and rapid conversion of the population ensued. In 1894 Britain declared a protectorate over the interior. The British governed through traditional rulers, giving little attention or money to Gambia until after World War II.

Gambia was slow to seek independence; political parties did not develop until the 1950s, and the earliest were based in the urban coastal area. However, David (later Sir Dawda) Jawara formed the People's Progressive Party to represent the interior, and was named prime minister after the elections of 1962, when internal self-government was achieved. Full independence came in 1965. In 1970 Gambia became a republic, with Jawara as president.

Jawara won every subsequent election, defeating an attempted coup in 1981 with the help of Senegalese troops. The resulting confederation of Gambia and Senegal, 'Senegambia', was dissolved in 1989 – and in 1994 a second, bloodless coup overthrew Jawara's regime and installed Lieutenant Yahya Jammeh as head of an Armed Forces Security Council. Jammeh survived another attempted coup in 1995, and announced elections in 1996 – though political parties active under Jawara, and anyone who had held ministerial posts in the previous 30 years, were barred from holding office. Jammeh himself stood as a civilian presidential candidate and was elected to office.

Before Jammeh's coup the Gambian economy had depended almost entirely on the peanut crop. His government set out to end that dependency and liberalize the economy. This proved difficult. The coup – coupled with a 50 per cent devaluation of the local currency, the CFA franc – damaged Gambia's entrepôt business and tourist trade, and led to loss of foreign aid. However, new funding partners emerged, overdue taxes were finally collected, and by the late 1990s the new regime was beginning to achieve the international recognition that it sought.

Guinea-Bissau

Bounded by Senegal on the north, the Republic of Guinea on the east and south and the Atlantic Ocean on the west, the Republic of Guinea-Bissau includes, in addition to its mainland territory, the Bijagós archipelago and a string of coastal islands. The country is low, rarely rising to more than a few hundred meters above sea level, and is crisscrossed by a large number of rivers which are used for transportation. From the coastal swamps and rain forests, which are gouged with numerous inlets, the land slopes upward to a heavily forested interior plain, then to characteristic African savanna. The climate is hot, ranging from a mean high of 29° to a mean low of 25°. The country receives all its annual rainfall between December and May, an average of 2413 millimeters along the coast and 1397 millimeters inland. Apart from about 3000 Portuguese and Lebanese and a relatively small percentage of mestizos, the population is black African and represents some 30 identifiable tribes speaking a variety of tribal languages and dialects, in addition to a Portuguese–African *crioulo* quite similar to that spoken in the Cape Verde Islands. About 60 per cent of the population, mainly coast dwellers, are animists and about 35 per cent are Muslims.

Prior to European exploration, the area was occupied by coastal farmers. The Portuguese first came to the Guinea coast in the middle of the 15th century and maintained settlements there for centuries because of the slave trade. The Colony of Portuguese Guinea was established in 1879, its borders finally demarcated in 1905. The Portuguese waged almost constant campaigns of pacification against the inhabitants from 1884 to 1917 and again in 1925 and 1936. In 1958 the massacre of 50 striking dockworkers at Pijiguiti inaugurated the liberation struggle which ended with the establishment of the Republic of Guinea-Bissau in 1974.

During the liberation struggle, the already precarious economy was all but destroyed, but the coming of independence found the African Party for the Independence of Guinea-Bissau and Cape Verde (PAIGC), led by Luiz Cabral, well prepared for power by reason of its prior administration of huge tracts of liberated territory. In 1980 a coup led by Commander João Vieira, president of the National People's Assembly, overthrew Cabral. Vieira survived another coup attempt in 1985, and in 1994, after many delays, was narrowly reelected in the first multiparty elections. 1995 saw the resolution of a long-running dispute with Senegal over maritime boundaries and over the petroleum resources exploited in these disputed areas.

These resources, and substantial, largely untapped deposits of phosphates and bauxite, could have a considerable effect on what is one of the world's poorest countries. They are, however, difficult to exploit because of poor infrastructure and high development costs. Guinea-Bissau is committed to economic reform, monetary stability, and growth in the private sector. The process has IMF support, but is being hampered by the government's failure to attain economic targets and by large-scale foreign debt. Meanwhile the economy remains almost entirely dependent on fishing and agriculture. Rice, maize, cotton and sugar cane are produced for domestic use, and cashew nuts, peanuts and palm kernels for export. Some rubber, livestock and lumber are also exported. What little industrialization Guinea-Bissau has is concentrated in processing agricultural products and in construction.

Guinea

The Republic of Guinea is bordered by the Atlantic Ocean to the west, by Guinea-Bissau, Senegal and Mali to the north and east, by Côte d'Ivoire to the southeast and by Liberia and Sierra Leone to the south. The country's four natural geographic regions are the mangrove swamps and marshy lands along the coast (Lower Guinea), the extensive Fouta Djallon highlands which rise sharply from the coastal plain (Middle Guinea), the highlands

Sankarani

12°N

10°N

8°N

Béyla
IRON ORE

Nzérékoré Industry:
timber, logging, saw mill

Mt Nimba
1752m
IRON ORE

135

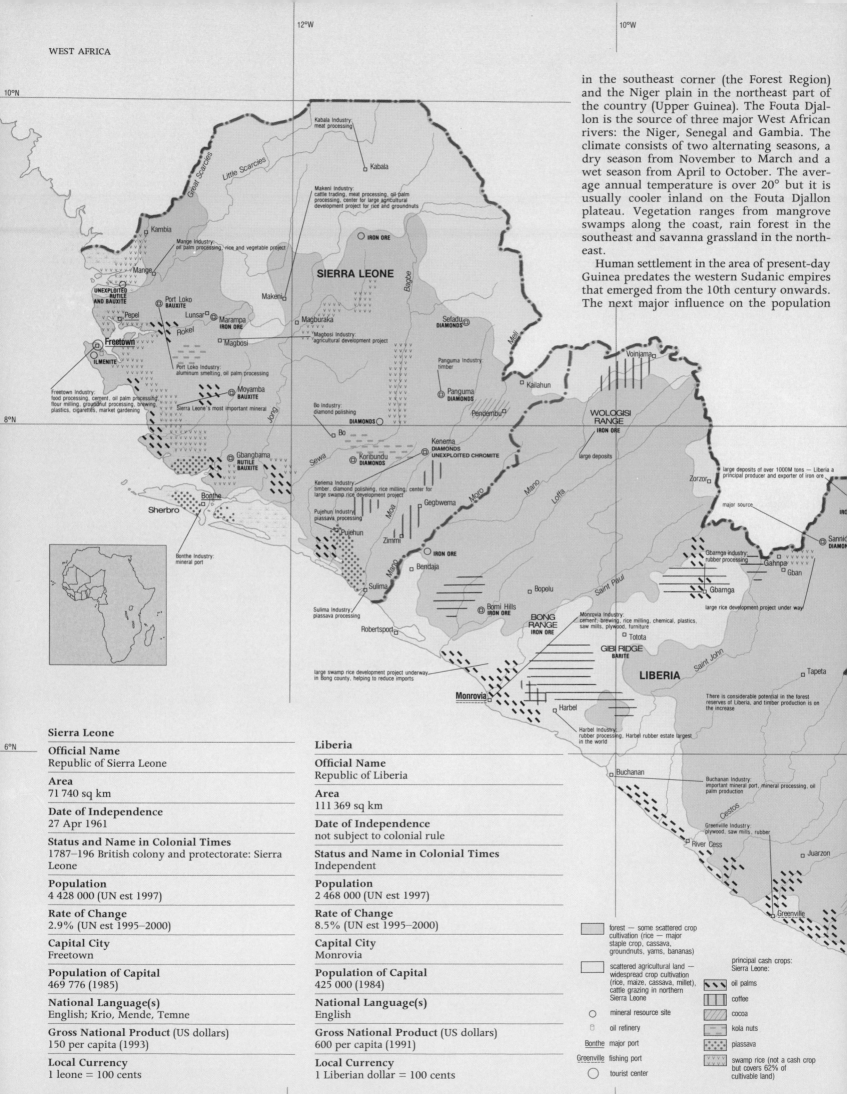

10°N

12°W

10°W

Kabala Industry: meat processing

□ Kabala

Makeni Industry: cattle trading, meat processing, oil-palm processing, center for large agricultural development project for rice and groundnuts

○ IRON ORE

Kambia

SIERRA LEONE

Mange Industry: oil palm processing, rice and vegetable project

□ Mange

Port Loko ◎ BAUXITE

Lunsar ◎ Marampa IRON ORE

Makeni □

Magburaka □

Sefadu ◎ DIAMONDS

UNEXPLOITED RUTILE AND BAUXITE

Pepel

Rokel

○ Freetown

ILMENITE

Magbosi □

Magbosi Industry: agricultural development project

Panguma Industry: timber

Panguma ◎ DIAMONDS

Port Loko Industry: aluminum smelting, oil palm processing

Freetown Industry: food processing, cement, oil palm processing, flour milling, groundnut processing, brewing, plastics, cigarettes, market gardening

Moyamba ◎ BAUXITE

Sierra Leone's most important mineral

Bo Industry: diamond polishing

□ Bo

DIAMONDS ○

Kailahun □

Pendembu

WOLOGISI RANGE IRON ORE

Voinjama

8°N

Gbangbama ◎ RUTILE BAUXITE

Sewa

Koribundu ◎ DIAMONDS

Kenema ◎ DIAMONDS UNEXPLOITED CHROMITE

large deposits

Zorzor □

large deposits of over 1000M tons — Liberia a principal producer and exporter of iron ore

Bonthe □

Sherbro

Jong

Kenema Industry: timber, diamond polishing, rice milling, center for large swamp rice development project

Gegbwema

Moro

Mano

Loffa

major source

IRO

Bonthe Industry: mineral port

Pujehun Industry: piassava processing

Pujehun □

Moa

Zimmi

Gbarnga industry: rubber processing

Gahnpa ◎

Sannie DIAMON

Gban □

Sulima Industry: piassava processing

Sulima □

Moa

○ IRON ORE

Bendaja

Bomi Hills ◎ IRON ORE

Bopolu □

Saint Paul

Gbarnga □

large rice development project under way

Robertsport □

BONG RANGE IRON ORE

Monrovia Industry: cement, brewing, rice milling, chemical, plastics, saw mills, plywood, furniture

Tapeta □

large swamp rice development project underway in Bong county, helping to reduce imports

○ Monrovia

Totota □

GIBI RIDGE BARITE

LIBERIA

Saint John

There is considerable potential in the forest reserves of Liberia, and timber production is on the increase

Harbel □

Harbel Industry: rubber processing, Harbel rubber estate largest in the world

in the southeast corner (the Forest Region) and the Niger plain in the northeast part of the country (Upper Guinea). The Fouta Djallon is the source of three major West African rivers: the Niger, Senegal and Gambia. The climate consists of two alternating seasons, a dry season from November to March and a wet season from April to October. The average annual temperature is over 20° but it is usually cooler inland on the Fouta Djallon plateau. Vegetation ranges from mangrove swamps along the coast, rain forest in the southeast and savanna grassland in the northeast.

Human settlement in the area of present-day Guinea predates the western Sudanic empires that emerged from the 10th century onwards. The next major influence on the population

Buchanan □

Buchanan Industry: important mineral port, mineral processing, oil palm production

Cestos

Greenville Industry: plywood, saw mills, rubber

River Cess □

Juarzon □

Greenville □

6°N

Sierra Leone

Official Name
Republic of Sierra Leone

Area
71 740 sq km

Date of Independence
27 Apr 1961

Status and Name in Colonial Times
1787–196 British colony and protectorate: Sierra Leone

Population
4 428 000 (UN est 1997)

Rate of Change
2.9% (UN est 1995–2000)

Capital City
Freetown

Population of Capital
469 776 (1985)

National Language(s)
English; Krio, Mende, Temne

Gross National Product (US dollars)
150 per capita (1993)

Local Currency
1 leone = 100 cents

Liberia

Official Name
Republic of Liberia

Area
111 369 sq km

Date of Independence
not subject to colonial rule

Status and Name in Colonial Times
Independent

Population
2 468 000 (UN est 1997)

Rate of Change
8.5% (UN est 1995–2000)

Capital City
Monrovia

Population of Capital
425 000 (1984)

National Language(s)
English

Gross National Product (US dollars)
600 per capita (1991)

Local Currency
1 Liberian dollar = 100 cents

forest — some scattered crop cultivation (rice — major staple crop, cassava, groundnuts, yams, bananas)

scattered agricultural land — widespread crop cultivation (rice, maize, cassava, millet), cattle grazing in northern Sierra Leone

principal cash crops: Sierra Leone:

○ mineral resource site

oil palms

oil refinery

coffee

Bonthe major port

cocoa

Greenville fishing port

kola nuts

○ tourist center

piassava

swamp rice (not a cash crop but covers 62% of cultivable land)

was the advent of Islam marked by the Muslim Fulani conquest of the Fouta Djallon during the second half of the 19th century. By the time of the French conquest in the 1890s Guinea's population consisted of the Susu along the coast, the Fulani on the Fouta Djallon, the Malinke in Upper Guinea and the Kissi, the Loma and the Kpelle, among others, in the forest region.

In September 1958, after about 60 years under French rule, Guinea became the first of the French colonies to declare independence. The French retaliated by blocking trade, while in Guinea all political power became vested in a single party, the Democratic Party of Guinea (PDG). Under President Ahmed Sékou Touré's regime, every Guinean was automatically a PDG member, and all opposition was ruthlessly suppressed. The regime was Marxist, and based on a centralized state-run economy, although cooler relations with the Soviet Union led to more openness in the early 1980s.

After Sékou Touré's death in 1984 the PDG government was overthrown by a bloodless military coup. The Military Committee for National Recovery (CMRN), led by Colonel Lansana Conté, dissolved the PDG and began to liberalize the economy. Following a referendum in 1990, a temporary council was set up to legalize political parties and arrange multiparty elections for the presidency and the legislature. In 1993, following mass protests, Conté set up a national electoral commission and presidential elections were held. They, too, were marred by violent protests – and they returned Conté, who had now resigned from the army, as president. Despite claims of electoral irregularities, the Supreme Court confirmed Conté's victory in 1994. Legislative elections were not held until 1995. Again there was widespread unrest, and again Conté's Unity and Progress Party (PUP) won a clear majority amid opposition claims of vote-rigging. After several months of protest the 37 elected members of the Coor-dination of the Democratic Opposition (CODEM) finally took their seats in the legislative assembly.

A mutiny by 2000 soldiers in 1996 escalated into a coup that almost overthrew the government. The presidential palace was shelled, and Conté himself taken prisoner. Some 50 people were killed, and hundreds more injured, before order was restored. The soldiers were promised an amnesty, but many were arrested, and 96 officers were put on trial in 1998 for their part in the mutiny.

The transition under Conté's regime from the former centralized Marxist system to a market-based economy has been slow and difficult. Guinea has more than one quarter of the world's reserves of bauxite, and mining accounts for the greater part of the country's exports. Yet despite its mineral, energy and agricultural resources it remains one of the world's poorest nations, with some 80 per cent of its work force employed on the land.

The economy has improved, but Guinea still finds it difficult to attract foreign investors. France is an important trading partner, but did not seem to oppose the attempted coup in 1996: it is therefore hardly surprising that Guinea, most of whose people are Muslim, has also forged significant links with Islamic states (most notably Iran) and with the People's Republic of China, who provided funds to build a new presidential palace after the coup attempt.

Relations with neighboring states have sometimes been difficult. Forces based in Guinea made several armed incursions into Liberia in 1993 and 1994, though the government always denied any responsibility for them. Soon afterwards Guinea received tens of thousands of refugees from the conflict in Liberia, and the following year, 1995, from the coup in Sierra Leone, causing severe food shortages. In 1995 there were also a number of incidents concerning the disputed border with Côte d'Ivoire.

Sierra Leone

Sierra Leone is bounded by Guinea to the north and east, Liberia to the southeast and the Atlantic Ocean to the west and southwest. From the ocean, mangrove swamps extend about 100 kilometers inland. An upland plateau covers the north and east, where there are also mountain ranges with some peaks exceeding 1800 meters. The country is mostly rain forest, although primary growth has been cleared for agriculture. Rainfall is heavy, particularly between June and September, and averages about 5000 millimeters in Freetown, the capital, and about 3500 millimeters in the north. None of the country's rivers are navigable.

The Mende people in the south and the Temne in the north together make up about three-fifths of the population. There are about nine smaller ethno-linguistic groups. The most prominent of these are the Creoles, citizens of Afro-European descent who live almost exclusively in the Freetown area and who comprise a western-educated elite. Krio, a language based on English but incorporating African and other European languages, is the tongue of the Creole people and is widely spoken throughout the country. About 30 per cent of the people are Muslims, Islam being most widely practiced in the north.

The origins of Sierra Leone's present ethnic composition are in the 15th and 16th centuries, when the "Manes" – probably refugees from the break-up of the great Sudanic empires – invaded the area and integrated with local peoples. The primary societal unit was the small chiefdom rather than the tribe.

The colony of Sierra Leone was founded in 1787 as part of a scheme to find a home for unwanted free blacks and whites living in England and North America. In 1808 it became a British Crown Colony, growing as the British captured slave ships and released their cargoes at Freetown. The descendants of these groups became the present-day Creoles. Western missionary education and religion were firmly rooted among Sierra Leonean Creoles, and throughout the 19th century they were prominent in politics and trade in all of England's West African colonies. The colony prospered from the second half of the 19th century, largely from the export of palm-kernel products.

The British annexed the interior in stages, and in 1896 declared a protectorate over what is present-day Sierra Leone. The Temne and Mende chiefdoms unsuccessfully resisted this loss of sovereignty in the 1898 Hut Tax War. The colony declined economically after the turn of the century. Creole merchants could not compete with expatriate traders and confined their activities to the Freetown area. At the same time, Creoles lost much of their influence in government.

The independence movement was initially dominated by the Creoles. However, the interior peoples became politicized after World War II, and in 1951, when the British granted a new constitution, an interior-based political party led by Sir Milton Margai won the national elections. He became prime minister when independence was achieved in 1961, but divided loyalties and uneven economic development led to continued instability.

Margai died in 1964 and was succeeded by his brother, Albert. The 1967 elections were won by Siaka Stevens; a series of military coups intervened, but in 1971 the country became a republic with Stevens as its president. In 1978 Sierra Leone became a one-party state. Stevens retired in 1985, but his corrupt regime continued under his successor, Major-General Joseph Momoh, who was overthrown in 1992.

In 1991 the Revolutionary United Front (RUF) launched an offensive against the government, which continued until 1996, when free elections were held and Ahmad Tejan Kabbah of the Sierra Leone People's Party (SLLP) was elected president. A few months later, in May 1997, he fell victim to another military coup which installed Major Johnny Paul Koroma as head of the Armed Forces Revolutionary Council (AFRC). Some RUF forces joined Koroma, but others did not, and conflict was renewed. A peace plan was agreed in October 1997, but the junta did little to implement it. Conflict and instability continued, and in February 1998 a Nigerian force invaded Sierra Leone with the stated objective of restoring democracy.

Economic imbalances account for much of Sierra Leone's political turmoil, but the eco-

8°W.

Tchien

Tchien Industry:
gold prospecting locally, timber

U RANGE
EXPLOITED
RON ORE

Douabe

Cavalla

principal cash crops:
Liberia:

rubber

coffee

cocoa

oil palms

sugar cane

rice

Harper Industry:
timber, plywood, brewing

Harper

scale 1:2 500 000

0 _____ 300km

0 _____ 200mi

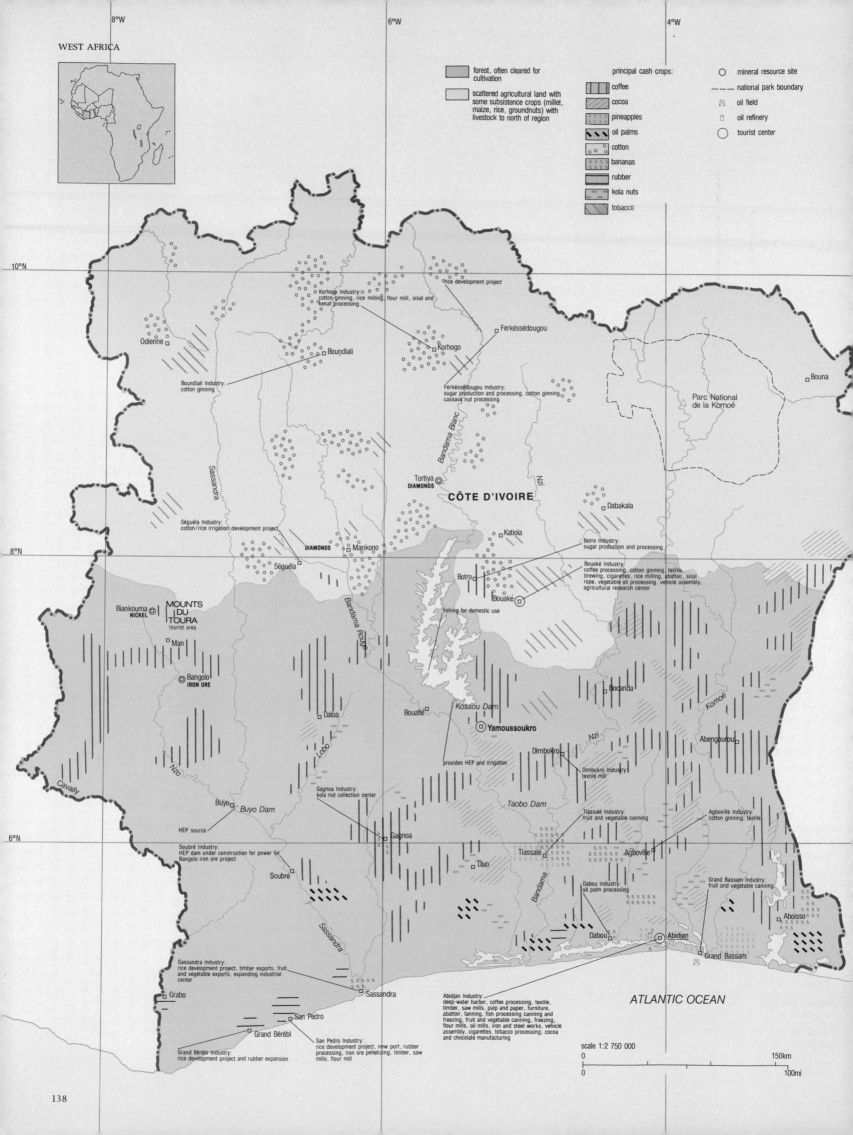

8°W | 6°W | 4°W

WEST AFRICA

10°N

principal cash crops:

forest, often cleared for cultivation

scattered agricultural land with some subsistence crops (millet, maize, rice, groundnuts) with livestock to north of region

coffee
cocoa
pineapples
oil palms
cotton
bananas
rubber
kola nuts
tobacco

○ mineral resource site
--- national park boundary
⊠ oil field
⊟ oil refinery
◎ tourist center

rice development project

Korhogo Industry: cotton ginning, rice milling, flour mill, sisal and kenaf processing

Odienne

Boundiali

Korhogo

Ferkéssédougou

Bouna

Parc National de la Komoé

Boundiali Industry: cotton ginning

Ferkéssédougou Industry: sugar production and processing, cotton ginning, cassava nut processing

Bandama Blanc

Sassandra

Tortiya
DIAMONDS

CÔTE D'IVOIRE

Dabakala

Séguéla Industry: cotton/rice irrigation development project

DIAMONDS Mankono

Katiola

Botro Industry: sugar production and processing

Séguéla

Bouaké Industry: coffee processing, cotton ginning, textile, brewing, cigarettes, rice milling, abattoir, sisal rope, vegetable oil processing, vehicle assembly, agricultural research center

8°N

Botro

Bouaké

Biankouma NICKEL

MOUNTS DU TOURA
tourist area

Man

fishing for domestic use

Bandama Rouge

Bocanda

Komoé

Bangolo IRON ORE

Daloa

Bouaflé

Kossou Dam

Yamoussoukro

Nzi

Abengourou

provides HEP and irrigation

Nzo

Lobo

Dimbokro

Nzi

Dimbokro Industry: textile mill

Buyo Buyo Dam

Gagnoa Industry: kola nut collection center

Taobo Dam

Tiassalé Industry: fruit and vegetable canning

Agboville Industry: cotton ginning, textile

Cavally

HEP source

6°N

Gagnoa

Tiassalé

Bandama

Agboville

Soubré Industry: HEP dam under construction for power for Bangolo iron ore project

Soubré

Divo

Dabou Industry: oil palm processing

Grand Bassam Industry: fruit and vegetable canning

Aboisso

Sassandra

Sassandra Industry: rice development project, timber exports, fruit and vegetable exports, expanding industrial center

Dabou

Abidjan

Grabo

Sassandra

Grand Bassam

ATLANTIC OCEAN

San Pedro

Grand Bérébi

San Pedro Industry: rice development project, new port, rubber processing, iron ore pelletizing, timber, saw mills, flour mill

Abidjan Industry: deep-water harbor, coffee processing, textile, timber, saw mills, pulp and paper, furniture, abattoir, tanning, fish processing canning and freezing, fruit and vegetable canning, freezing, flour mills, oil mills, iron and steel works, vehicle assembly, cigarettes, tobacco processing, cocoa and chocolate manufacturing

Grand Bérébi Industry: rice development project and rubber expansion

scale 1:2 750 000

0 150km
0 100mi

138

nomic effects of corruption and civil war have also been severe. Diamond deposits in the east have brought wealth to a few, but little to the country, since most of the diamonds have been smuggled out. Manufacturing is extremely limited. Around 71 per cent of the population are involved in agriculture – mostly subsistence farming – but after the 1997 coup basic food prices doubled or tripled. Crop production is in serious decline.

Liberia

Liberia's longest boundary is with the Atlantic Ocean to the southwest. It is bordered to the northwest by Sierra Leone, to the northeast by Guinea and to the east by Côte d'Ivoire. A coastal plain extends about 55 kilometers inland; beyond is a plateau covered by thick rain forest. The northern highlands feature mountains rising to over 1700 meters. Most of the country experiences the rainy season from May to October. Monrovia, the capital, receives 4650 millimeters of rain annually, and has an average temperature of 26°. The country is drained by 15 rivers, none of them navigable.

The Americo-Liberians, descendants of the founders of the republic, comprise about 5 per cent of the population, although they dominate the politics and economics of Liberia. They speak English, practice Christianity and adhere to Western patterns of social organization. The other Liberians comprise 16 ethnolinguistic groups, divided into 124 chiefdoms. The largest of these groups are the Kpelle, in the interior, and the Bassa, on the southern coast. The rural populations largely practice traditional religions; about 10 per cent of the population is Muslim. The country is considered underpopulated, with an average density of 145 per square kilometer.

Liberia's present-day settlement patterns began to emerge in the 15th and 16th centuries with the arrival of groups fleeing the break-up of the great Sudanic kingdoms. The first Americo–Liberians arrived from the USA in 1821 as the result of an American plan to finance the emigration and settlement of

Côte d'Ivoire

Official Name
République de la Côte d'Ivoire

Area 322 463 sq km

Date of Independence 7 Aug 1960

Status and Name in Colonial Times
1893–1960 French colony (part of French West Africa)

Population
14 299 000 (UN est 1997)

Rate of Change
2.0% (UN est 1995–2000)

Capital City Yamoussoukro

Population of Capital
120 000 (est 1988)

National Language(s)
French; Malinke

Gross National Product (US dollars)
630 per capita (1993)

Local Currency
1 franc CFA = 100 centimes

former slaves. They were joined by about 6000 Africans freed from slave ships by British and American patrols. In 1847 Liberia declared its independence. The nation in reality consisted of Monrovia and other centers of Americo-Liberian settlement, for there was no control over the interior until after 1915, when the last resistance movements were quashed.

American subsidies to Liberia decreased in the mid-19th century, and as exports also declined, Liberia looked to Europe for help, receiving loans on unfavorable terms. In 1927 the Firestone Company began its rubber plantation operations. Firestone became the dominant economic force in the country, and accordingly, Liberia's external orientation shifted back to the USA. In 1930 Liberia was internationally embarrassed when a League of Nations investigation implicated national leaders in forced labor schemes.

William Tubman, president from 1944 to 1971, was the first actively to advocate integration of the interior peoples into the political system. In 1945 they achieved representation in government, and in 1947 universal suffrage was declared. Liberia joined the Allies in World War II and became a strategic link in the supply route. Later it became a charter member of the UN. Since World War II Liberia has been able substantially to reduce its dependence on Firestone through diversification.

Tubman's successor, William Tolbert, was assassinated in a military coup led by Samuel K. Doe in 1980. In 1989 a savage civil war broke out, mainly between Doe's ethnic group, the Krahn, and the Gio and Mano peoples. The Economic Community of West African States (ECOWAS) tried to negotiate a ceasefire, and eventually sent in an armed monitoring group (ECOMOG). This was the first major peacekeeping operation not to be organized by the United Nations. In 1990 Doe was deposed and executed, but the war continued with unabated ferocity as rebel leaders Charles Taylor and Prince Johnson struggled for power. In 1995 the factions agreed a peace plan at Abuja, Nigeria, and a transitional government was set up under Wilton Sankawulo, but conflict resumed in 1996. After a series of ceasefires ECOMOG's efforts were finally rewarded later that year, when they began disarming the factions. 1997 saw free elections, which returned Charles Taylor as president, and in February 1998 ECOMOG announced, amid some skepticism, that its peacekeeping role was officially at an end. Some 115 000 people (6 per cent of the population) had been killed since the war began; perhaps half the population had been driven from their homes; 750 000 people had fled to neighboring countries; and a viable infrastructure had been destroyed.

The economic prospects for Liberia are unpromising, and reconstruction will depend on maintaining civil order. Before the war about three-quarters of the population had been engaged in agriculture, notably in production of the primary food crops. However, the conflict had a particularly severe effect on rural areas: as a result, emergency food aid was still required even after ECOMOG had begun to disarm the factions. Iron ore production, critical to Liberia's export trade, was suspended during the war, and rubber and forestry exports were reduced to nothing.

Côte d'Ivoire

Côte d'Ivoire (formerly Ivory Coast, but now known only by the French form) occupies about 1 per cent of the surface of the African continent. Approximately 46 per cent of Côte d'Ivoire is covered with rain forest, which is thickest in the southwest part of the country. The northern third of the country is wooded savanna land, which extends south between the Bandama and Nzi rivers to form the Baoulé savanna. The country is largely flat, rolling land except for the region of Man, which is noted for its beautiful mountains and waterfalls. Other hilly areas are near Boungouanou, the Baoulé chain and the granite domes and inselbergs of the Odienné-Boundiali region. The sea coast is of two very distinct types divided by the estuary of the Bandama river. West of the town of Fresco the coast is rocky with cliffs and small picturesque bays and beaches (San Pedro, Sassandra, Monogaga). East of Fresco a long sandy island separates the ocean from a series of lagoons stretching 300 kilometers to the Tano river and the border of Ghana.

The Côte d'Ivoire region is the meeting place of several major ethnic and linguistic groups. The original inhabitants are unknown but during the 16th to 18th centuries Mande speakers moved into the north as traders and settlers, brought by gold and kolanuts which they traded north to Mali. They founded Bornu (17th century) and such kingdoms as Kong (18th century) and Kabadougou (19th century). The Agni and Baoulé moved into the area east of the Bandama river as a result of the growth of the Asante empire in the 18th century and other Akan political developments.

The Ivory Coast (as it was known) was not hospitable to Europeans and, even though the French tried to establish themselves at Assinie in 1637 and again in 1838, they had only a nominal claim to a presence there until Arthur Verdier and his aide, Treich-Laplène, settled in eastern Ivory Coast during the 1870s and 1880s. The French explorer L. G. Binger who traveled down from the Sudan in 1887–88 was named the first governor of the colony in 1893 and such great colonialists as Maurice Delafosse and Jean Marie Clozel played a major role in the attempted "peaceful penetration" of the mostly unconquered interior of the Ivory Coast. The north of Ivory Coast was the scene of the last great struggles of the famous Malinke warrior Samori Touré, who set up his second empire in Dabakala (1893–98), destroyed Kong (1897) and finally was captured and exiled by the French in September 1898. In 1908 Gabriel Angoulvant was named military governor and he conquered by force of arms the many peoples of Ivory Coast. The conquest and wars of resistance lasted from 1908 to 1915.

In 1903 a railroad was begun from Abidjan, though it did not reach its present terminus, Ouagadougou, Upper Volta (now Burkina Faso), until 1954. It was not until 1950 that the Cânal of Vridi was opened and Abidjan became a seaport with ships able to enter the lagoon. The Ivoirian economy grew spectacularly, founded on its wealth of natural

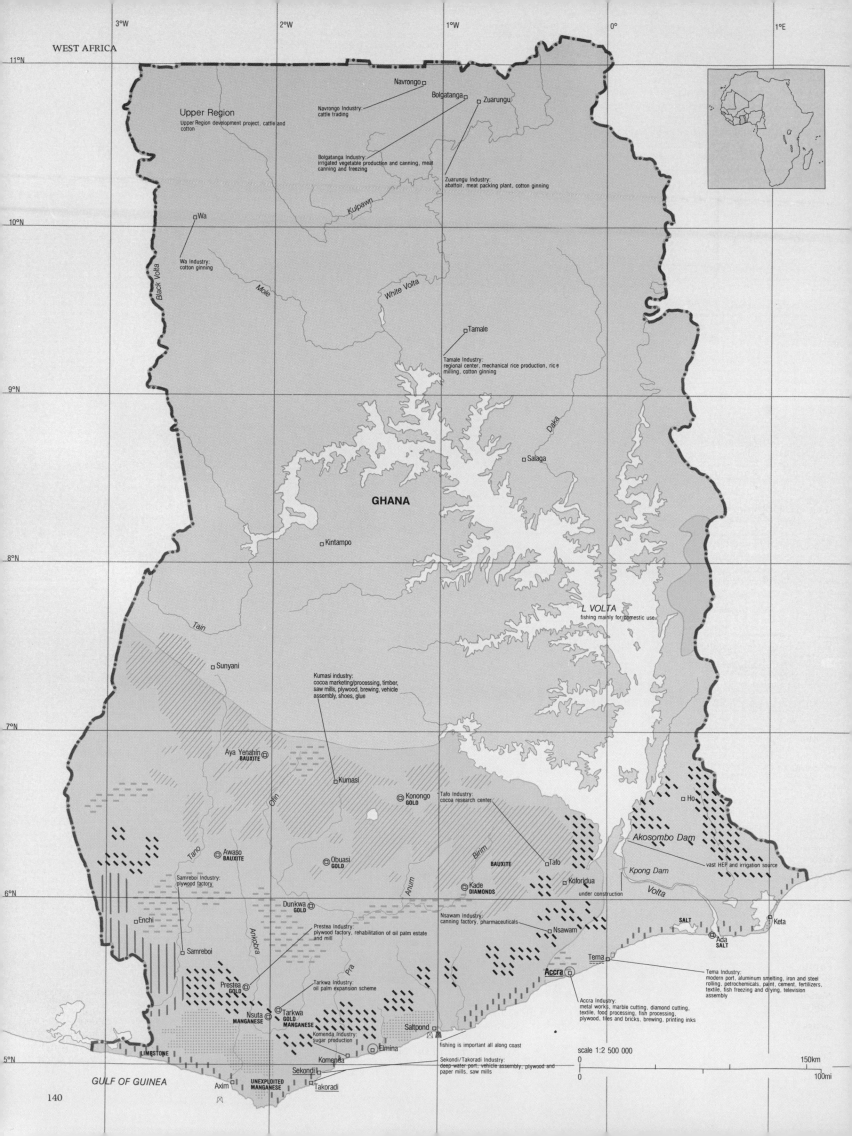

WEST AFRICA

3°W

11°N

Upper Region
Upper Region development project, cattle and
cotton

2°W

Navrongo
Navrongo Industry:
cattle trading

Bolgatanga
Zuarungu

1°W

Bolgatanga Industry:
irrigated vegetable production and canning, meat
canning and freezing

Zuarungu Industry:
abattoir, meat packing plant, cotton ginning

0°

1°E

□ Wa

10°N

Wa Industry:
cotton ginning

Black Volta

Mole

White Volta

Daka

9°N

□ Tamale

Tamale Industry:
regional center, mechanical rice production, rice
milling, cotton ginning

Kulpawn

□ Salaga

GHANA

8°N

□ Kintampo

L VOLTA
fishing mainly for domestic use

Tain

7°N

□ Sunyani

Kumasi industry:
cocoa marketing/processing, timber,
saw mills, plywood, brewing, vehicle
assembly, shoes, glue

Aya Yenahin
BAUXITE

□ Kumasi

Ofin

Konongo
GOLD

Tafo Industry:
cocoa research center

□ Ho

Taro

Awaso
BAUXITE

Obuasi
GOLD

Birim

BAUXITE

Tafo

Akosombo Dam
vast HEP and irrigation source

Samreboi Industry:
plywood factory

Kade
DIAMONDS

Koforidua
under construction

Kpong Dam

Volta

6°N

Enchi

Dunkwa
GOLD

Prestea Industry:
plywood factory, rehabilitation of oil palm estate
and mill

Ankobra

Nsawam Industry:
canning factory, pharmaceuticals

Nsawam

SALT

Keta

Ada
SALT

Samreboi

Pra

Prestea
GOLD

Tarkwa Industry:
oil palm expansion scheme

Tema

Tema Industry:
modern port, aluminum smelting, iron and steel
rolling, petrochemicals, paint, cement, fertilizers,
textile, fish freezing and drying, television
assembly

Nsuta
MANGANESE

Tarkwa
GOLD
MANGANESE

Komenda Industry:
sugar production

Saltpond

Accra

Accra industry:
metal works, marble cutting, diamond cutting,
textile, food processing, fish processing,
plywood, tiles and bricks, brewing, printing inks

LIMESTONE

Elmina

fishing is important all along coast

scale 1:2 500 000

0   150km

5°N

GULF OF GUINEA

Axim

UNEXPLOITED
MANGANESE

Komenda

Sekondi

Takoradi

Sekondi/Takoradi Industry:
deep-water port, vehicle assembly, plywood and
paper mills, saw mills

0   100mi

forest, often cleared for cultivation

subsistence agriculture (millet. maize. sorghum. rice) livestock in north. becoming more productive to south with intensive cultivation around lake

principal cash crops:

cocoa

oil palms

coffee

kola nuts

coconuts

fruit and vegetables

○ mineral resource site

⊠ oil field

▲ gas field

⊟ oil refinery

⊠ oil prospecting

Sekondi major port

Tema fishing port

○ tourist center

11°N

10°N

9°N

resources, until hampered by the 1980s world recession and droughts. It is the world's largest producer and exporter of cocoa, and a leading producer of coffee, cola, pineapples and bananas, as well as many other vegetable products. Once plentiful forests have been severely over-exploited. Since 1995 significant offshore oil and gas fields have been developed, and there are major mineral reserves on land. Côte d'Ivoire welcomes foreign investment, and tourism is growing.

The roots of independence were laid in 1944 by Félix Houphouët-Boigny, whose agrarian-based independence movement first clashed with the French and later cooperated with them, leading to peaceful independence in 1960. Houphouët-Boigny was elected president and established a one-party state under his Rassemblement Démocratique Africain (RDA). He ruled autocratically but moder-

ately, encouraging business and maintaining good relations with Europe and the USA. In 1990 he introduced some political reforms, culminating in the first contested elections. His overwhelming victory, and that of the RDA in legislative elections, were hotly disputed by growing opposition parties, leading to unrest and repression. He was also accused of supporting the rebel movement in Liberia.

On Houphouët-Boigny's death in 1993, the President of the National Assembly, Henri Konan Bédié, assumed the presidency. Under his rule a new electoral code was introduced which appeared to obstruct opposition parties. The 1995 elections were affected by violence, press repression and boycotts, and, apparently, by an abortive military coup. Some liberalization was reintroduced in 1996.

The influx since 1994 of some 400 000 Liberian refugees also affected the country; international aid appears to have been misused. There have been continuing border disputes with Liberia and Guinea, and health problems, including increasing incidence of the deadly Ebola fever.

Ghana

Extending from the Gulf of Guinea some 640 kilometers inland, Ghana ranges from a narrow coastal plain through a tropical forest belt to the northern savanna region. In the precolonial period, large parts of the country were often integrated under the aegis of centralized states – for instance the Gonja kingdom in the north or the Asante and Akwamu states in the south.

The first contacts with Western nations were made at the coast. British colonial rule grew out of trading contacts and treaty arrangements made with the Fante states there. In the 19th century Britain gradually extended its influence and control, buying out other European trading powers, suppressing the slave trade and allying itself with the Fante against the powerful Asante state of the southern interior. Britain annexed the territory south of the Pra river in 1874, the Northern Territories by 1900 and conquered Asante by 1902. The new colony arbitrarily brought together a host of very different peoples – although Akan languages are spoken widely through the south.

Little further unity was imposed on the colony during the period of British rule. Developments in all fields were extremely uneven. Virtually all exports, such as minerals, timber and agricultural products, were produced in the southern third of the colony. Northerners on the whole participated in the colony's economic development only by migrating south as laborers for the cocoa farms and mines. As elsewhere in Africa, the economy was based on the production and extraction of primary products, with little industrial development. Nevertheless, at independence Ghana enjoyed a small foreign debt and large foreign reserves.

In most areas – education, medicine, building and communications – development was concentrated in the south. Urbanization intensified, both around the ports and mining areas of the south, and also around traditional

centers like Kumasi. Virtually all secondary schools, hospitals and industry were in the southern third of the country.

Administratively, the government did little to unite the various regions. The original Gold Coast colony, British Togoland (a mandate after World War I), Asante and the Northern Territories were all administered separately. The colony was not united with Asante till 1946, and British Togoland was not added until a pre-independence plebiscite. The problems of regionalism inevitably surfaced in politics, given the administrative fragmentation and the uneven development. Both in the pre- and post-independence periods there have always been regional parties. Nkrumah's Convention People's Party (CPP) most closely approached national party status in the pre-independence period, but even then the opposition to the CPP was to some extent along regional lines.

Until the period following World War II African political activity was very much limited to the educated urban minority of the south. Such people made up the membership of the Congress of British West Africa, and the Youth Conference, and they demanded further participation in the existing colonial system. After the war, under the pressure of rapid social and political change, politics became a demand for independence rather than for reform. The major political force was the United Gold Coast Convention (UGCC), led by lawyers and still elitist in membership. In 1947 Kwame Nkrumah returned to the Gold Coast after 12 years in the USA and Britain, and became the UGCC's secretary. Under him the UGCC began to acquire mass support. But he came into conflict with the elitist leaders and in 1949 broke away to form the Convention People's Party. The CPP was a popular party in a way the UGCC had not been, with a younger, more impatient and less educated following. Nkrumah was arrested and imprisoned after a series of strikes, but the CPP won elections under a new democratic constitution. Nkrumah was released in 1951 to form a government, becoming prime minister in 1952. In 1956 British Togoland voted to join the Gold Coast, and in 1957 the newly named Ghana became the first British colony to gain independence, with Nkrumah as prime minister.

In 1960 he declared Ghana a republic, with himself as life president, and in 1964 it became a one-party state under the CPP. Nationalization and other socialist measures he introduced destabilized the economy, and inefficiency, combined with a fall in cocoa prices, led to severe shortages and virtual bankruptcy. The 1965 elections were canceled and the Preventive Detention Act was used to cope with opposition. In 1966, while visiting China, Nkrumah was deposed by a largely military coup, and the Russian and Chinese military advisers he had brought in were expelled.

Dr K. A. Busia's civilian government was elected in 1969 but was unable to arrest economic decline. In 1972 Colonel I. K. Acheampong took power. He announced a limited return to civilian rule in 1976, but when this was delayed he was deposed by Lieutenant General F. W. K. Akuffo, who allowed the formation of political parties and announced elections for June 1979. In that month, how-

Ghana

Official Name
Republic of Ghana

Area
238 537 sq km

Date of Independence
6 Mar 1957

Status and Name in Colonial Times
British colony: The Gold Coast

Population
18 338 000 (UN est 1997)

Rate of Change
2.7% (UN est 1995–2000)

Capital City
Accra

Population of Capital
965 000 (1988)

National Language(s)
English; Akan, Ewe

Gross National Product (US dollars)
430 per capita (1993)

Local Currency
1 new cedi = 100 pesewas

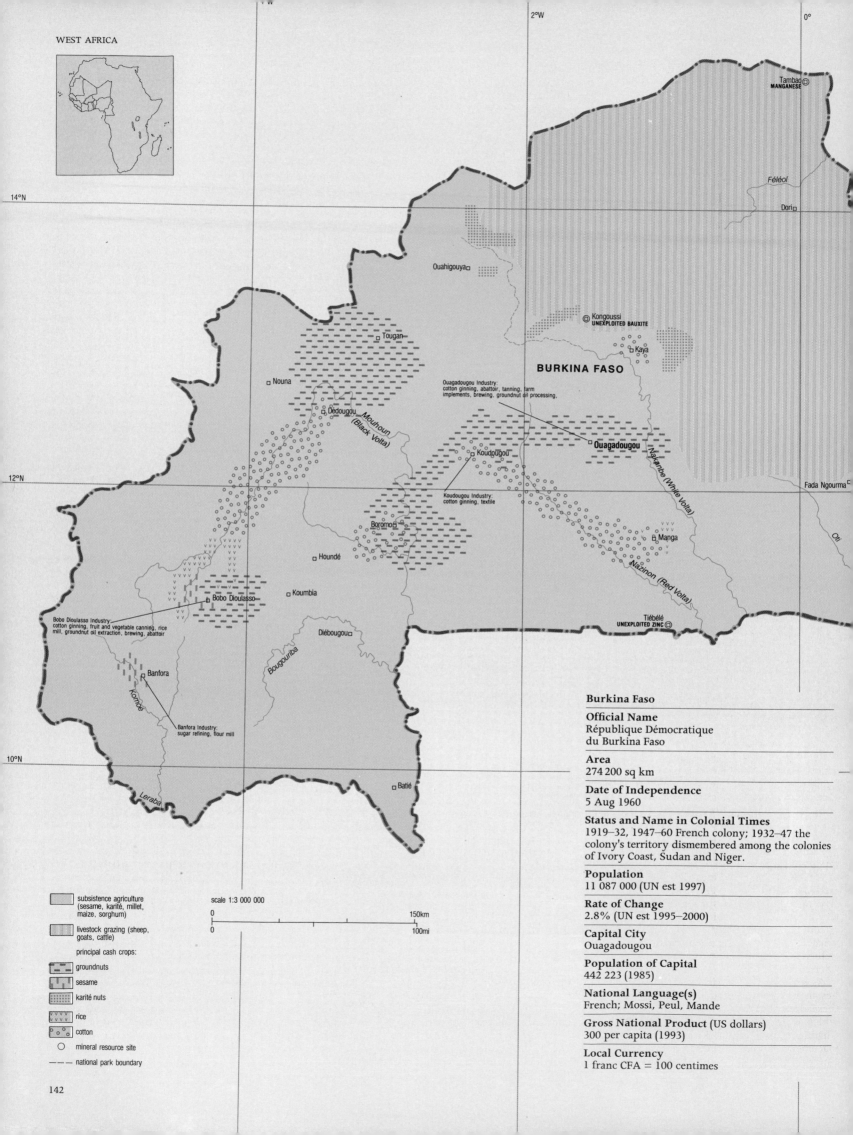

14°N

2°W

0°

Tambao
MANGANESE

Féléol

Dori

Ouahigouya

Kongoussi
UNEXPLOITED BAUXITE

Tougan

Kaya

BURKINA FASO

Nouna

Ouagadougou Industry:
cotton ginning, abattoir, tanning, farm
implements, brewing, groundnut oil processing,

Dédougou

Mouhoun
(Black Volta)

Koudougou

Ouagadougou

Nakambe (White Volta)

12°N

Fada Ngourma

Koudougou Industry:
cotton ginning, textile

Boromo

Manga

Houndé

Oti

Koumbia

Nazinon (Red Volta)

Bobo Dioulasso

Diébougou

Bougouriba

Bobo Dioulasso Industry:
cotton ginning, fruit and vegetable canning, rice
mill, groundnut oil extraction, brewing, abattoir

Tiébélé
UNEXPLOITED ZINC

Banfora

Comoé

Banfora Industry:
sugar refining, flour mill

10°N

Leraba

Batié

Burkina Faso

Official Name
République Démocratique
du Burkina Faso

Area
274 200 sq km

Date of Independence
5 Aug 1960

Status and Name in Colonial Times
1919–32, 1947–60 French colony; 1932–47 the
colony's territory dismembered among the colonies
of Ivory Coast, Sudan and Niger.

Population
11 087 000 (UN est 1997)

Rate of Change
2.8% (UN est 1995–2000)

Capital City
Ouagadougou

Population of Capital
442 223 (1985)

National Language(s)
French; Mossi, Peul, Mande

Gross National Product (US dollars)
300 per capita (1993)

Local Currency
1 franc CFA = 100 centimes

subsistence agriculture
(sesame, karité, millet,
maize, sorghum)

scale 1:3 000 000

livestock grazing (sheep,
goats, cattle)

0   150km
0   100mi

principal cash crops:

groundnuts

sesame

karité nuts

rice

cotton

○ mineral resource site

- - - national park boundary

ever, a coup was staged by junior officers under Flight-Lieutenant Jerry Rawlings. Acheampong, Akuffo and many others were publicly executed for corruption.

The elections took place in July, and the new civilian government was inaugurated in September. As the economy disintegrated further, and strikes and rioting, often along tribal lines, broke out, Rawlings again seized power in 1981. At the head of a National Defense Council he ruled by decree, introducing austerity measures to attract international aid and facing several coup attempts with heavy repression. During this time the Rawl-

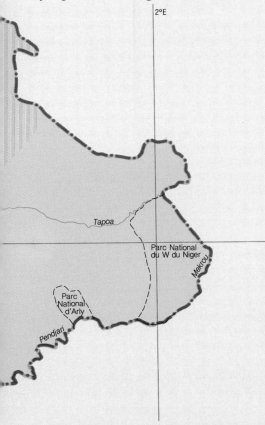

ings regime was also accused of involvement in attempted coups in neighboring Burkina Faso and Togo, resulting in serious tension. However, the economy, still largely agricultural despite an industrial and manufacturing sector more developed than most in the region – including the export of electricity from the Volta and other hydroelectric plants – began to show signs of recovery.

In 1991, under pressure from Western countries, Rawlings introduced a new constitution, allowing multiparty elections for the presidency and legislature. He resigned military rank and in 1992 was elected president as a civilian; an opposition boycott gave his National Democratic Party's coalition a massive majority in the subsequent parliamentary elections. Economic growth was severely affected at this time by a slump in the world price of cocoa, Ghana's principal export, by reduced government expenditure and by internal disorders.

As elsewhere in Africa many political parties in fact represented tribal divisions, and these were at the root of long-standing unrest which erupted at this time in the north of Ghana. Among ethnic killings and the displacement of some 150 000 people, a state of emergency was declared and troops stationed

to enforce a peace agreement. Further clashes broke out in 1995. Unrest also grew in the south over economic difficulties, especially an attempt to levy Value Added Tax on consumer goods, and Rawlings' administration was bitterly divided. A Commission on Human Rights and Administrative Justice was established to investigate abuses, and in 1996 its report caused the resignations of the Minister for Trade and Industry and a presidential aide.

Official involvement in further coups in Togo during 1993 and 1994 was denied, but there was little doubt that Ghanaian-based dissident organizations were involved. In 1995, however, border agreements were signed, and in 1996 the hostile atmosphere finally eased.

Economic restraint produced some improvements, and IMF and World Bank credits stimulated economic growth, but problems, including inflation and external debt, remained. Nonetheless Ghana was becoming relatively stable and democratic while many of its neighbors were in turmoil. In the 1996 elections Rawlings and the NDC were again returned by a strong majority, but against a substantial opposition vote; international observers declared the election generally fair. In 1997 Ghana's revival received implicit international endorsement in the appointment of Ghanaian Kofi Annan as United Nations Secretary-General

Burkina Faso

Burkina Faso, formerly Upper Volta, lies between 10° and 15° north, within the bend of the Niger river, and is over 500 kilometers from its main outlet to the sea: the port and former capital of Côte d'Ivoire, Abidjan.

Three ecological zones, the sahelian, Sudanic and Guinean, belts of increasing rainfall running from east to west, cross the country. The agricultural population, 90 per cent of the total, depends on the adequacy and timely arrival of the seasonal rains, which begin in April in the south and end in October.

Population densities vary greatly. The central region of the Mossi, the largest ethnic group, contains over half the total population (average density – 40 persons per square kilometer), and although only 6 per cent of the total land in the Mossi region is arable, certain overpopulated areas maintain over 190 persons per square kilometer. Burkina Faso has only two major cities, Ouagadougou and Bobo Dioulasso.

The Mossi kingdoms of Ouagadougou, Yatenga and Gourma dominate in the early history of the region. Having withstood the expansion of the empires of Mali and Songhay, they were until recently little influenced by Islam, and in this century were strongly proselytized by French Catholic missionaries. Both Islam and Christianity have made strong inroads, but the majority of the people follow traditional religions. The area was annexed by the French in the 1890s when they defeated competing British and German efforts. Most of the region was integrated into the French Sudan at the turn of the century.

French administration proved schizo-

phrenic, alternately composing and dismembering the territory until 1946. Development was hindered by isolation, poor transport and lack of natural resources. The greatest resource was surplus manpower. During World War I men were heavily conscripted as soldiers, laborers and plantation workers in Côte d'Ivoire. This recruitment, coupled with severe taxation, led to widespread revolt and migration to the then Gold Coast.

France instituted representative government in 1957, and full independence in 1960, with Maurice Yaméogo, a Mossi, as president. Re-elected in 1965, he was deposed in 1966 by Lieutenant-General Sangoulé Lamizana, who established joint military–civilian government in 1971. After a five-year drought caused unrest and shortages, he again seized power in 1974, introduced civilian government under his presidency in 1978, and in 1980 was ousted in the first of a rapid series of military coups which led, in 1984, to the radical regime of Captain Thomas Sankhara.

Sankhara renamed the country Burkina Faso, "Land of the Incorruptible People". Trade unions were suppressed and punitive tax laws imposed, and a brief war with Mali broke out. He and many others were murdered in a 1987 coup led by Captain Blaise Compaoré, who in 1988 executed members of his own government for alleged coup attempts. In 1990, however, he sanctioned a return to democratic rule, and in 1991 his ruling party renounced Marxism in favor of free enterprise. In the same year he was elected civilian president of a government still suffering from corruption and other economic problems. In 1996 there was apparently another coup attempt.

Agriculture, the mainstay of the economy, remains vulnerable, and the large mineral reserves discovered since independence cannot be properly exploited in such poor conditions, although gold production is increasingly significant. Ties with France have weakened, but remain important. Côte d'Ivoire is also a major trading partner, and employs large numbers of Burkina Faso laborers.

Togo

Togo shares a boundary with Ghana, and has had a long relationship with that neighbours peoples. Like Ghana, Togo stretches about 800 kilometers inland from the Gulf of Guinea through coastal, forest and savanna zones, but its coastline is only 52 kilometers long. At its height the Asante empire included parts of Togo. The Ewe people live on both sides of the modern border with Ghana and the natural links of trade and kinship continue.

Generally, in West Africa, European colonization occurred where earlier commercial interests had developed. In Togo, although the French government had supported the establishment of commercial posts, German diplomatic maneuvers and the expansion of trade into the interior culminated in German colonial rule after 1884. In common with other colonial powers, the Germans found it necessary to rely on local authorities in order to govern their territories. Where obvious chiefs existed they were recognized and used to

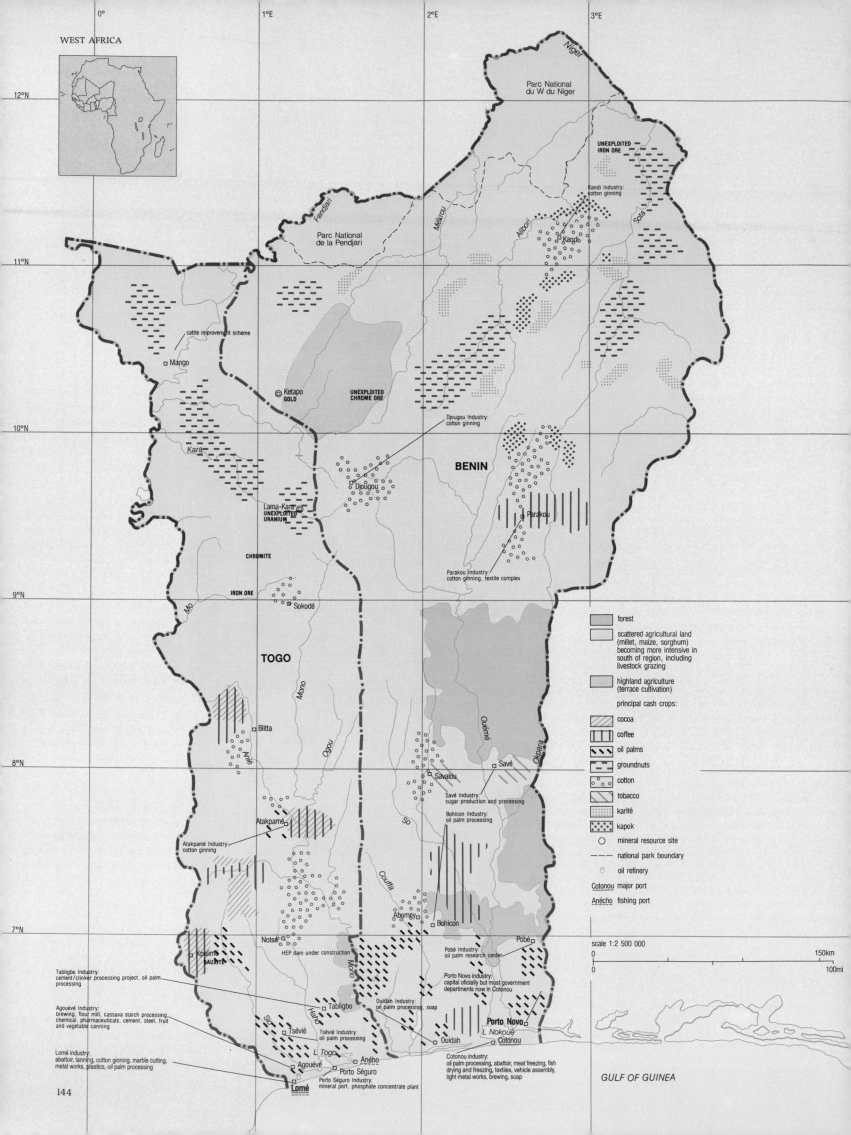

Togo

Official Name
République Togolaise
Togo Republic

Area
56 000 sq km

Date of Independence
27 Apr 1960

Status and Name in Colonial Times
1894–1918 German colony: Togoland
1919–60 joint mandate under League of Nations and UN: British and French Togoland (British part joined Ghana)

Population
4 316 000 (UN est 1997)

Rate of Change
2.7% (UN est 1995–2000)

Capital City
Lomé

Population of Capital
450 000 (1990)

National Language(s)
French; Ewe, Mina, Dagomba, Tim, Cabrais

Gross National Product (US dollars)
340 per capita (1993)

Local Currency
1 franc CFA = 100 centimes

Benin

Official name
République du Bénin

Area
112 622 sq km

Date of Independence
1 Aug 1960 (as Republic of Dahomey)

Status and Name in Colonial Times
French colony (part of French West Africa)

Population
5 720 000 (UN est 1997)

Rate of Change
2.8% (UN est 1995–2000)

Capital City
Porto Novo

Population of Capital
177 660 (1993)

National Language(s)
French; Fon, Mina, Yoruba, Dendi

Gross National Product (US dollars)
430 per capita (1993)

Local Currency
1 franc CFA = 100 centimes

administer government directives and collect taxes. In other parts of Togo, such as in Lomé district, political organization rarely extended beyond the village level. In such areas the Germans, having no inclination at the time to study social structure, simply created "chiefs", who operated as far as possible within the traditional context. The Germans began a study of Ewe law, hoping to issue a new legal code, but were forestalled by World War I.

The beginnings of an infrastructure were laid in the German period. Railroads were built along the coast and into the interior. German goods carried in this way were traded across to the Northern Territories of the Gold Coast, overshadowing British goods in many markets. Agricultural development and most land remained in African hands.

After World War I Togo was divided between the British and the French, under a League of Nations mandate. British Togoland was administered in a similar fashion to the rest of the Gold Coast. Most traditional chiefs recognized by the Germans were in the area now administered by Britain, and they fitted neatly into the pattern of indirect rule. The impact of the mandate was more significant in the French sector. The rest of French West Africa was highly centralized and ruled directly from Dakar. Togo, however, had its own High Commissioner and financial autonomy. The mandate ensured that forced labor and conscription were severely restricted and the French were not allowed to levy protective tariffs or keep out merchants of other nations. From the beginning of the mandate there was greater African participation in government, in an advisory capacity at first.

One result of the division of German Togoland was the rise of ethnic nationalism among the Ewe. During the war all Ewe had been under British rule and a single Presbyterian church had been created, which served as a focus for the community. The drawing of the border through Ewe territory naturally aroused discontent. In the 1930s attempts by the British and French to enforce border regulations led to riots. But despite Ewe pressure the colonial powers resisted unification. At independence British Togoland (although never tightly integrated with the Gold Coast) voted to join Ghana, splitting Ewe tribal territory and creating a lasting problem for both Togo and Ghana.

France was committed to increasing self-government in Togo, but at the same time hoped to keep it within the French sphere of influence. In 1958 French Togoland voted for self-government in a plebiscite, and in that year's free elections Sylvanus Olympio's Comité d'Unité Togolaise (CUT), the only political party not sponsored by France, swept to victory. Olympio, however, maintained economic links with France, and rejected a suggested union with Ghana. In 1960 Togo was granted full independence.

In 1963 the increasingly autocratic Olympio was murdered in a military coup. In 1967 his successor Nicholas Grunitzky was deposed by Lieutenant Colonel Gnassingbé Eyadéma, a member of the Kabiye tribe and reportedly Olympio's assassin. Despite a veneer of democratic forms, Eyadéma's rule was autocratic. Coup attempts were rife, as was government repression, especially

against Ewe-led opposition groups allegedly supported by Ghana. Togo became formally a one-party state in 1979, under Eyadéma's Rassemblement du Peuple Togolais (RPT). Civil unrest came to a head in the early 1990s, damaging the economy and losing foreign support. In 1991 international pressure and fear of civil war along tribal lines forced Eyadéma to relinquish much of his power to a transitional government and to legalize other parties. However, continuing violence, especially from the largely Kabiye army, enabled him to exact concessions. A new multiparty constitution was adopted in 1992. In 1993 Eyadéma was re-elected president, retaining much of his power, but at the head of a legislature dominated by a loose coalition between the RPT and opposition parties. The opposition has increasingly been excluded from government, but the prime minister's power has increased.

Relations with Togo's neighbors Ghana, on the west, and Benin, on the east, became more cordial in the 1990s. Since 1995 the economy has shown some improvement, but this has been overtaken by the increasing population, and, despite substantial cancellation, massive international debt.

Benin

Benin is physically small, economically poor and politically unstable. Squeezed between Togo and Nigeria, it has a coastline of only 125 kilometers and a hinterland stretching back 675 kilometers. Apart from the relatively fertile *terre de barre* near the coast, Benin has poor soils and there is little forest cover, the savanna reaching virtually to the Atlantic's edge.

As Dahomey, Benin became a French colony in 1894. It took its name from the kingdom which, from its capital at Abomey, 100 kilometers north of the coast, flourished by involvement in the slave trade in the late 18th and early 19th centuries. After 50 years of direct colonial rule, Dahomey was given elective representation and a territorial assembly in 1946. Universal suffrage was introduced in 1957 and increasing degrees of self-government led to independence in August 1960.

Both the population (largely concentrated in the south) and the government's exchequer are dependent for income on agriculture, which provides the main cash crops (palm produce and, increasingly, cotton). Low prices, lack of investment, inflation and a high birthrate have prevented a significant growth in real incomes since independence, although food production has increased to the point where Benin is practically self-sufficient in staple food crops. The small size of the domestic market has discouraged manufacturing industry, most of which has been limited to the processing of exportable commodities. The narrow range of such commodities and their low prices have kept down government revenue – over half of which comes from taxes on trade – and have contributed to a severe and chronic balance-of-payments problem, and the consequent growth of international debt.

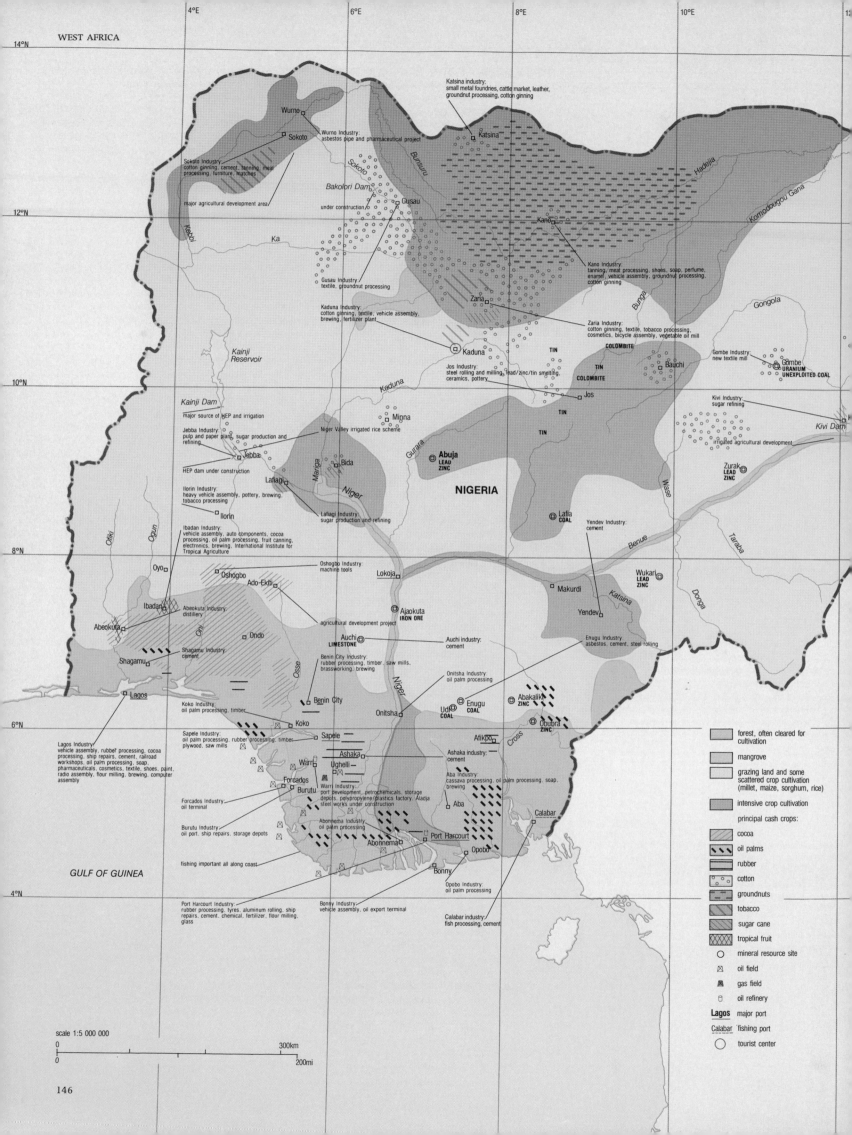

14°N

4°E

Katsina industry:
small metal foundries, cattle market, leather,
groundnut processing, cotton ginning

Wurno

Sokoto

Wurno Industry:
asbestos pipe and pharmaceutical project

Katsina

Sokoto Industry:
cotton ginning, cement, tanning, meat
processing, furniture, matches

Bursuru

major agricultural development area

Bakolori Dam
under construction

Gusau

Kano

12°N

Ka

Kano Industry:
tanning, meat processing, shoes, soap, perfume,
enamel, vehicle assembly, groundnut processing,
cotton ginning

Gusau Industry:
textile, groundnut processing

Zaria

Kaduna Industry:
cotton ginning, textile, vehicle assembly,
brewing, fertilizer plant

Bunga

Zaria Industry:
cotton ginning, textile, tobacco processing,
cosmetics, bicycle assembly, vegetable oil mill

Gongola

Kaduna

Kabbi

TIN

COLOMBITE

Gombe Industry:
new textile mill

Gombe
URANIUM
UNEXPLOITED COAL

10°N

Kainji
Reservoir

Jos Industry:
steel rolling and milling, lead/zinc/tin smelting,
ceramics, pottery

Kaduna

TIN
COLOMBITE

Bauchi

Komodougou Gana

Jos

Kainji Dam
major source of HEP and irrigation

Minna

Jebba Industry:
pulp and paper plant, sugar production and
refining

Niger Valley irrigated rice scheme

Kivi Industry:
sugar refining

Kivi Dam

Mariga

TIN

Zurak
LEAD
ZINC

irrigated agricultural development

Jebba

HEP dam under construction

Bida

Abuja
LEAD
ZINC

Lafiagi

Ilorin Industry:
heavy vehicle assembly, pottery, brewing,
tobacco processing

Niger

NIGERIA

Ilorin

Lafiagi Industry:
sugar production and refining

Gurara

Lafia
COAL

Yendev Industry:
cement

Wase

Benue

8°N

Oyo

 Oshogbo Industry:
machine tools

Lokoja

Makurdi

Wukari
LEAD
ZINC

Ado-Ekiti

Oshógbo

Ibadan Industry:
vehicle assembly, auto components, cocoa
processing, oil palm processing, fruit canning,
electronics, brewing, International Institute for
Tropical Agriculture

Lokoja

Katsina

Yendev

Donga

Oti

Ogun

Ibadan

Abeokuta Industry:
distillery

Ajaokuta
IRON ORE

Ondo

Enugu Industry:
asbestos, cement, steel rolling

Taraba

Abeokuta

Oni

Auchi
LIMESTONE

Auchi industry:
cement

Shagamu Industry:
cement

Shagamu

Benin City Industry:
rubber processing, timber, saw mills,
brassworking, brewing

Onitsha Industry:
oil palm processing

Abakaliki
ZINC

Osse

Niger

Koko Industry:
oil palm processing, timber

Lagos

Koko

Benin City

Udi
COAL

Enugu
COAL

Obubra
ZINC

Lagos Industry:
vehicle assembly, rubber processing, cocoa
processing, ship repairs, cement, railroad
workshops, oil palm processing, soap,
pharmaceuticals, cosmetics, textile, shoes, paint,
radio assembly, flour milling, brewing, computer
assembly

Sapele Industry:
oil palm processing, rubber processing, timber,
plywood, saw mills

Sapele

Afikpo

Cross

6°N

forest, often cleared for
cultivation

mangrove

Ashaka

Ashaka industry:
cement

Warri

Ughelli

Aba Industry:
cassava processing, oil palm processing, soap,
brewing

grazing land and some
scattered crop cultivation
(millet, maize, sorghum, rice)

intensive crop cultivation

Forcados

Burutu

Warri Industry:
port development, petrochemicals, storage
depots, polypropylene/plastics factory, Aladja
steel works under construction

Aba

principal cash crops:

Forcados Industry:
oil terminal

cocoa

Burutu Industry:
oil port, ship repairs, storage depots

Abonnema Industry:
oil palm processing

Calabar

oil palms

rubber

Abonnema

Port Harcourt

cotton

fishing important all along coast

Opobo

groundnuts

GULF OF GUINEA

Bonny

Opobo Industry:
oil palm processing

tobacco

4°N

sugar cane

Port Harcourt Industry:
rubber processing, tyres, aluminum rolling, ship
repairs, cement, chemical, fertilizer, flour milling,
glass

Bonny Industry:
vehicle assembly, oil export terminal

Calabar industry:
fish processing, cement

tropical fruit

○ mineral resource site

oil field

gas field

oil refinery

Lagos major port

Calabar fishing port

○ tourist center

scale 1:5 000 000

0 _____ 300km

0 _____ 200mi

Nigeria

Official Name
Federal Republic of Nigeria

Area
923 768 sq km

Date of Independence
1 Oct 1960

Status and Name in Colonial Times
1900–60 British colony: Nigeria (Northern and Southern) with many amalgamations including British-administered UN trusteeship territory of Northern Cameroons

Population
118 396 000 (UN est 1997)

Rate of Change
2.8% (UN est 1995–2000)

Capital City
Abuja

Population of Capital
378 671 (1992)

National Language(s)
English; Hausa, Fulani, Yoruba. Igbo

Gross National Product (US dollars)
300 per capita (1993)

Local Currency
1 naira = 100 kobo

Benin's problems arising from a lack of physical resources have, ironically, been compounded by its exceptional wealth of human resources, especially of skilled and educated manpower. This abundance, created by high rates of school attendance in the colonial period, became an embarrassment after the break-up in 1960 of the French West African Federation, of which Benin was a part and throughout which its educated elite was dispersed. The forcible repatriation of this elite led to the overstaffing of the domestic civil service. It led also to the creation of a sophisticated and demanding middle class which has resisted austerity programs (often insisted on as part of international debt reduction programs), pushed up import bills, and – not least – contributed to the curious blend of high-flown rhetoric and dismal performance that characterizes Beninois politics. Gorged with programs, analyses, promises and plots, Benin still has a high infant mortality rate and, for the average citizen, a life expectancy of around 48 years.

In the first twelve years since independence, the then Dahomey had ten heads of state and six coups d'état – more than any other African state in that period. This instability was constantly worsened by regional rivalries, reflected in the establishment of three regional parties (one in northern and two in southern and central Benin), sufficiently balanced, entrenched and exclusive to prevent the building of stable coalitions. The extreme parochialism of rural Benin was, before and after independence, aggravated by intense competition for office within the urban elite (including the officer corps of a very small army). The result was an apparently endless and unfathomable sequence of realignments, coups and conspiracies.

In the last of these, in 1972, Major Mathieu Ahmed Kérékou, a northerner, seized power, seeking to establish "scientific Marxism" and nationalizing significant sectors of the economy. In 1975 the country was given its present name, and a one-party state under the Benin People's Revolutionary Party (PRPB) was established. In 1977 a takeover attempt led by French mercenaries was repulsed. In 1979 new national assemblies were established, and in 1980 these elected Kérékou president. After this time the influence of the extreme left and the army was greatly reduced; in 1987 Kérékou resigned his rank to become a civilian president.

Nonetheless the climate of corruption and repressive political measures provoked an abortive coup in 1988. Benin's economic problems were worsened by a mounting burden of international debt, and in 1989, under pressure from France and other creditors, Kérékou formally abandoned his Marxist views and instituted a transition to democratic government.

In the 1991 presidential elections Kérékou was defeated, despite northern support, by prime minister Nicéphore Soglo. The legislative elections, however, resulted in a national assembly handicapped by a chaotic profusion of political parties and alliances. Civil unrest continued, exacerbated by austerity measures, as Soglo attempted to steer the economy onto a freer course, with a program to restructure and privatize the petroleum industry. He also faced problems due to the crises in Liberia and Togo, which in 1993 led to a vast influx of Togolese refugees.

Although Soglo espoused a new party, Renaissance du Benin (RB), he lost assembly support in the 1995 elections to Kérékou's supporters, and a coup attempt followed. In the somewhat inconclusive presidential elections held in March 1996, Kérékou, promising a halt to privatization and more welfare spending, was elected, despite allegations of fraud and corruption.

Nigeria

Named for the Niger river, whose lower portion the country encloses, Nigeria is Africa's most populous nation and one of its richest. It possesses vast reserves of petroleum and natural gas, significant deposits of coal, tin and colombite, and is a major producer of rubber, cocoa, peanuts, cotton, palm oil and kernels and timber.

With the longest north–south axis of any coastal West African nation, Nigeria is a land of great diversity and contrasts. The vigorous tropical monsoons which drench the southern states with 1250 to over 3500 millimeters of rain a year (with dry seasons in August and from mid-November to February) have produced coastal mangrove swamps and inland rain forest, the latter greatly modified by centuries of clearing and cultivation. While humidity is high in the southern states, temperatures generally stay between 20° and 30° day and night year round. Further north the coastal forests give way to more open plateaus, rainfall decreases, and the temperature range widens. The northern savannas receive under 1000 millimeters of rain a year during two shorter rainy seasons, with high temperatures averaging 30° to 40° and lows 15° to 25°. When the dry, dusty Harmattan wind blows out of the Sahara during the long dry season, frost is not unknown in parts of the north.

Diversity is also characteristic of Nigeria's people, whose spoken languages number over 200. When united, the different cultures are, in the words of one-time prime minister Abubakar Tafawa Balewa, "a source of great strength", but cultural rivalries have also fueled recent conflicts. Most important of the ethnic groupings are the Hausa, Fulani and Kanuri of the north, the Nupe and Tiv of the middle belt, and the Yoruba, Edo (Bini), Igbo (Ibo) and Ibibio of the south. Only about a fifth of the enormous population live in large towns, but many rural areas are also thickly settled, with densities of over 150 persons per square kilometer in several places. The main cities include Lagos (the former capital), Ibadan, Kano, Zaria, Ogbomosho and Onitsha; the capital is Abuja. Most northerners are Muslim, most southerners Christian, but traditional religions and syncretism are still common.

While Nigeria's boundaries are a product of British colonization at the end of the 19th century, they circumscribe much older political, economic and cultural units, The northern half of the country corresponds to the Sokoto caliphate, a vast Islamic empire founded by the reformer Usuman dan Fodio at the beginning

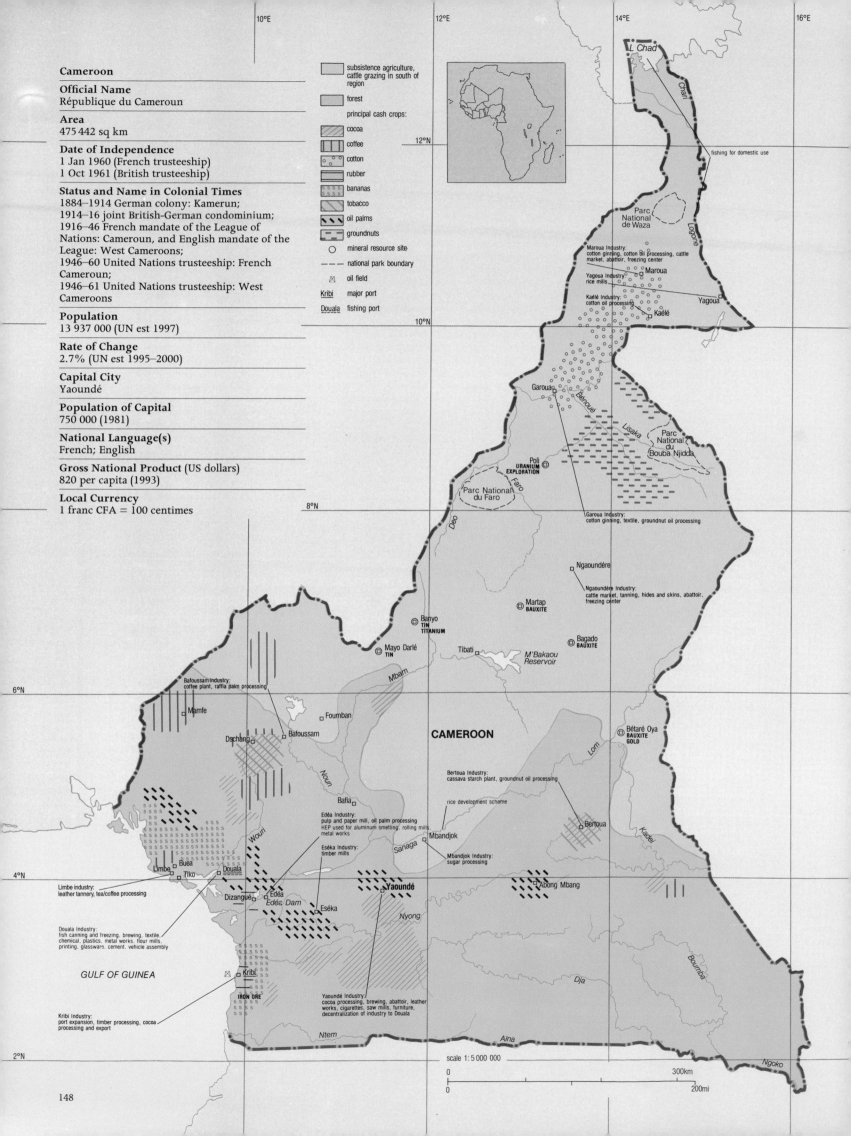

Cameroon

Official Name
République du Cameroun

Area
475 442 sq km

Date of Independence
1 Jan 1960 (French trusteeship)
1 Oct 1961 (British trusteeship)

Status and Name in Colonial Times
1884–1914 German colony: Kamerun;
1914–16 joint British-German condominium;
1916–46 French mandate of the League of
Nations: Cameroun, and English mandate of the
League: West Cameroons;
1946–60 United Nations trusteeship: French
Cameroun;
1946–61 United Nations trusteeship: West
Cameroons

Population
13 937 000 (UN est 1997)

Rate of Change
2.7% (UN est 1995–2000)

Capital City
Yaoundé

Population of Capital
750 000 (1981)

National Language(s)
French; English

Gross National Product (US dollars)
820 per capita (1993)

Local Currency
1 franc CFA = 100 centimes

subsistence agriculture,
cattle grazing in south of
region

forest

principal cash crops:

cocoa

coffee

cotton

rubber

bananas

tobacco

oil palms

groundnuts

○ mineral resource site

‑ ‑ ‑ national park boundary

⊠ oil field

Kribi major port

Douala fishing port

fishing for domestic use

L Chad

Chari

Logone

Parc
National
de Waza

Maroua Industry:
cotton ginning, cotton oil processing, cattle
market, abattoir, freezing center

Maroua

Yagoua Industry:
rice mills

Yagoua

Kaélé Industry:
cotton oil processing

Kaélé

Garoua

Benoué

Lisaka

Parc
National
du
Bouba Njidda

Poli
URANIUM
EXPLORATION

Faro

Parc National
du Faro

Garoua Industry:
cotton ginning, textile, groundnut oil processing

Déo

Ngaoundéré

Ngaoundéré Industry:
cattle market, tanning, hides and skins, abattoir,
freezing center

Martap
BAUXITE

Banyo
TIN
TITANIUM

Bagado
BAUXITE

Mayo Darlé
TIN

Tibati

M'Bakaou
Reservoir

Mbam

Bafoussam Industry:
coffee plant, raffia palm processing

Mamfe

Foumban

CAMEROON

Lom

Bétaré Oya
BAUXITE
GOLD

Dschang

Bafoussam

Noun

Bafia

Bertoua Industry:
cassava starch plant, groundnut oil processing

rice development scheme

Bertoua

Kadei

Edéa Industry:
pulp and paper mill, oil palm processing.
HEP used for aluminum smelting, rolling mills,
metal works

Eséka Industry:
timber mills

Wouri

Mbandjok

Sanaga

Mbandjok Industry:
sugar processing

Buea

Limbe
Tiko
Douala

Limbe industry:
leather tannery, tea/coffee processing

Edéa
Edéa Dam
Eséka

Dizangué

Yaoundé

Abong Mbang

Douala Industry:
fish canning and freezing, brewing, textile,
chemical, plastics, metal works, flour mills,
printing, glassware, cement, vehicle assembly

Nyong

GULF OF GUINEA

Kribi
IRON ORE

Yaoundé Industry:
cocoa processing, brewing, abattoir, leather
works, cigarettes, saw mills, furniture,
decentralization of industry to Douala

Kribi Industry:
port expansion, timber processing, cocoa
processing and export

Ntem

Aïna

Dja

Boumba

Ngoko

scale 1:5 000 000

0 ——— 300km

0 ——— 200mi

of the 19th century, and its smaller but much more ancient neighbor, the Kingdom of Bornu. Southwestern Nigeria contained many Yoruba kingdoms, founded ultimately from the holy city of Ife; of these the most important were Oyo, which flourished in the 18th century, and Ibadan, which flourished in the 19th. The Bendel state contains the ancient Benin empire, whose kings and craftsmen impressed a long succession of Western visitors. The Igbo, Ibibio and Ijo peoples of the southeast inhabited a multitude of small, generally egalitarian states in the precolonial era, but, like most other parts of the country, were closely linked by networks of trade routes and markets serving important internal and export trades.

These disparate peoples were brought under British control, beginning with the annexation of Lagos in 1861 and culminating with the declaration of separate protectorates over Southern Nigeria and Northern Nigeria in 1900. After subduing African resistance, the British combined the two protectorates into the Colony of Nigeria in 1914, largely to balance the administrative deficits in the north with the surpluses from the south. Despite amalgamation the two halves remained quite distinct culturally, economically and administratively.

The colonial economy until after 1945 was largely an expanded version of the precolonial; exports were dominated by cash crops produced by small farmers using traditional methods – palm products from the southeast, cocoa from the southwest, cotton and (from the 1890s) peanuts from the north. The construction of a network of motor roads and rail lines facilitated the movement of these products and stimulated increased production. The opening of new tin mines on the Jos plateau and coal mines near Enugu added minerals to the export list, but agricultural exports were still of paramount importance until after independence.

The profits from these expanding exports went largely to foreign trading companies and into supporting the colonial administration rather than to improving social services. It was not until after World War II that this policy altered significantly. Nevertheless, social change during the colonial period was extensive in the southern regions, with jobs in commerce, government service and transportation drawing many away from traditional agricultural employment. Larger cities developed in proximity to the roads, railroads and coastal ports. Much of the change in the south was facilitated by mission schools: a feature of some coastal towns in the 19th century, but now expanding rapidly in inland areas. The initiative for these schools as well as their financing and staffing came primarily from the African communties, with assistance and cooperation from foreign Protestant and Roman Catholic mission societies. Government subsidies (low until after 1945) and inspection helped improve quality.

In the northern region the rate of change was much slower because the colonial policy of indirect rule maintained conservative traditional leaders in power, causing less disruption of society. The influence of Western culture and education was also very much less in the north as a result of the government policy of excluding Christian missionaries from Islamic areas. By 1950 the north had only a fifth as many pupils in modern schools as the south, by 1960 only a tenth as many. While northern cities grew in this period, much of the expansion was due to the influx of southerners, especially Igbo.

Opposition to British rule goes back to the earliest days of imperialism, but coordinated national protest dates from the formation of the Nigerian Youth Movement in the 1930s. After World War II nationalist activity increased dramatically with the support of nascent trade unions, military veterans, urban dwellers and a growing number of educated leaders, of whom the American-educated Nnamdi Azikiwe, later the first president of Nigeria, was the most prominent. Though national in outlook, the independence movement was largely the work of southerners. Lack of education, conservatism and a regional outlook retarded northern participation. It is notable that the first prime minister of independent Nigeria, Balewa, who was a northerner, had first gained prominence as a critic of the diversity of Nigeria and of early self-government.

As a consequence of British colonial policies, Nigeria became independent as a federation of three unequally sized, self-governing regions, each dominated by a large ethnic group. The Northern Region alone comprised more than half of the federation's territory, and contained over half of its population. By 1965 political inexperience, corruption and personal, regional, political and ethnic rivalries had brought this uneasy federation to its knees. A coup d'état by junior military officers in January 1966 overthrew the civilian politicians, killing Prime Minister Balewa and the premiers of the Northern and Western Regions. Major General Aguiyi Ironsi attempted to reform and strengthen the federation, but hasty changes and a growing suspicion of domination by the Igbo of the Eastern Region led to his downfall in a new coup in July 1966. The youthful Colonel Yakubu Gowon, a Christian from a northern minority group, attempted to restore order and strengthen the increasingly fragile national unity, but appalling massacres of some 10 000–30 000 Igbo and other easterners in the north and a constitutional stalemate left the Eastern Region leaders with the conviction that secession was their only alternative. In May 1967 the region declared its independence as the Republic of Biafra under the leadership of Oxford-educated Colonel Odumegwu Ojukwu. At first Biafran forces made significant gains, but the outcome, prolonged by international involvement, was Biafran capitulation in January 1970.

The prospects for national recovery at this time seemed good. Oil revenues were strengthening the economy, even though agricultural production was stagnating. However, Gowon's delay in returning the country to civilian rule, and the continuing climate of corruption, led to his being deposed in 1975 in a bloodless coup by Brigadier Murtala Muhammad. The latter was promptly assassinated in an abortive coup in February 1976. His successor, Lieutenant General Olusegun Obasanjo, continued the transition process, introducing a new constitution in 1978 which divided Nigeria into 19 states along with a federal district centering on a new capital being built at Abuja in the heart of the country. In 1979 elections were held to the new National Assembly, comprising a Senate and House of Representatives; the government was headed by the new executive president Shehu Shagari, to whom the military handed over power.

Nigeria was by now a major world oil producer, and the new administration embarked on a program of economic development, with growth in manufacturing and mining. The oil price fall of the early 1980s, however, left Nigeria in debt and decline. Shagari's expulsion of foreign workers earned him reelection in 1983, but later that year a coup led by Major-General Muhammad Buhari restored military rule. In 1985, after instituting austerity measures to qualify for assistance from the IMF, he was similarly ousted by Major-General Ibrahim Babangida.

Despite a 1990 coup attempt, and growing problems with oil production in Ogoni tribal lands, Babangida was able to institute some reforms, and to allow a return to civilian rule in elections in 1992 and 1993. Unofficial results made it clear that the presidency was won by the Muslim businessman and tribal chief Moshood Kastumawo Olawale Abiola, but Babangida's government annulled the result, although he himself stepped down in favor of a transitional government which was almost immediately ousted by General Sani Abacha.

Abacha established draconian military rule, but promised an eventual return to civilian rule. This, however, he continually delayed, persecuting Abiola (who vanished, apparently imprisoned; his wife was murdered in 1996) and other opponents, including the internationally famous writer Wole Soyinka, who was forced into exile and in 1997 was charged with treason.

Meanwhile Ogoni opposition to oil exploitation grew, partly on ecological grounds, but also because they were denied a share of the oil revenues. Four moderate chieftains were murdered by extremists, a crime for which the Ogoni activist Ken Saro-Wiwa and 18 others were executed on slender evidence, and in the face of international criticism, in November 1995. This, and Abacha's refusal to set a reasonable date for civilian rule, led to Nigeria's suspension from the Commonwealth and the imposition of sanctions by the European Union.

Internal conflicts continued. Additionally, Nigerian troops within the joint West African peacekeeping forces operating in Liberia and Sierra Leone were found to be looting and even aggravating the conflicts, although under new command they imposed peace in Liberia; in 1998 they occupied Sierra Leone.

The economy, which, apart from a major oil workers' strike in 1994, had been slowly stabilizing and improving under international supervision, began to suffer once more. In 1997 oil production was again affected, this time by violence in the Ijaw tribal region and elsewhere, which resulted in paralyzing fuel shortages.

The sudden death of Abacha in June 1998 left a power vacuum, amid international concern that a struggle for the leadership could bring chaos and bloodshed to Nigeria. It is not clear if Abacha's successor will accelerate or obstruct the transition to democracy.

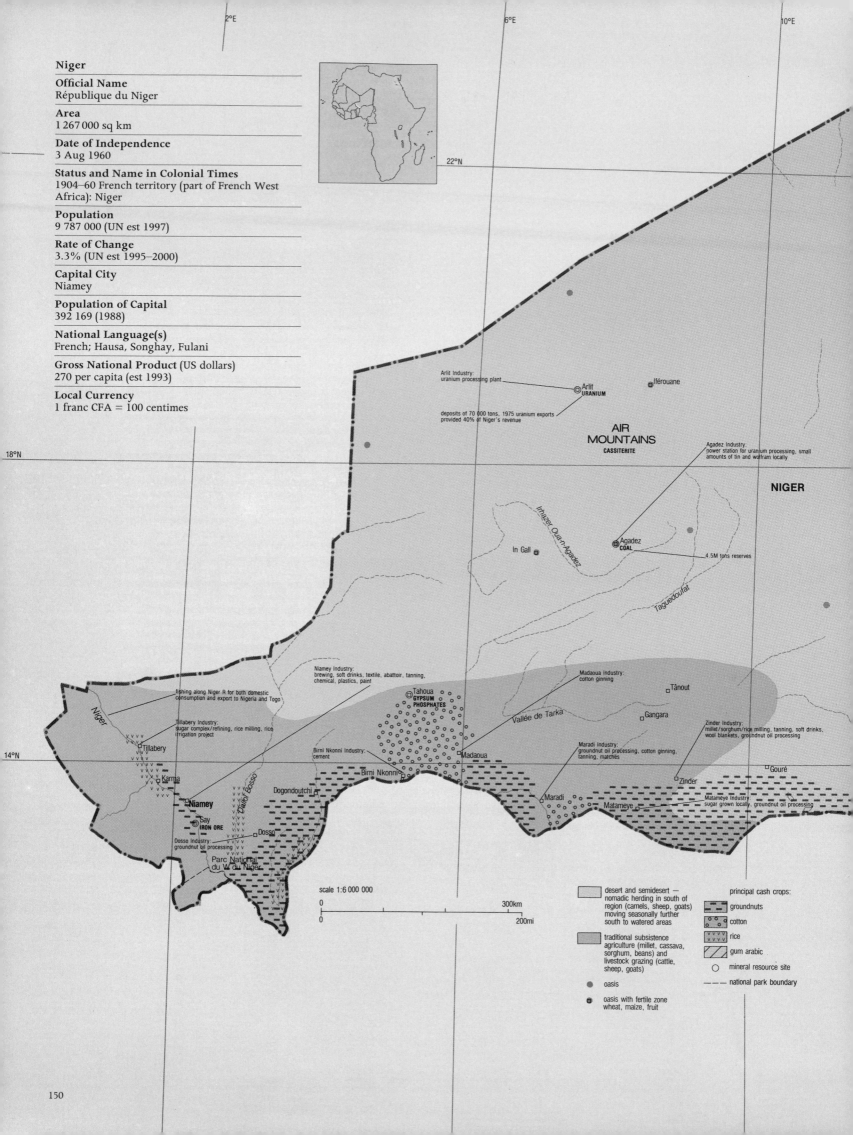

Niger

Official Name
République du Niger

Area
1 267 000 sq km

Date of Independence
3 Aug 1960

Status and Name in Colonial Times
1904–60 French territory (part of French West Africa): Niger

Population
9 787 000 (UN est 1997)

Rate of Change
3.3% (UN est 1995–2000)

Capital City
Niamey

Population of Capital
392 169 (1988)

National Language(s)
French; Hausa, Songhay, Fulani

Gross National Product (US dollars)
270 per capita (est 1993)

Local Currency
1 franc CFA = 100 centimes

2°E   6°E   10°E

22°N

Arlit Industry:
uranium processing plant

Arlit
URANIUM

Iférouane

deposits of 70 000 tons, 1975 uranium exports
provided 40% of Niger's revenue

AIR
MOUNTAINS
CASSITERITE

18°N

Agadez Industry:
power station for uranium processing, small
amounts of tin and wolfram locally

NIGER

Irhazer Ouan-Agadez

In Gall

Agadez
COAL

4.5M tons reserves

Taguedoufat

Niamey Industry:
brewing, soft drinks, textile, abattoir, tanning,
chemical, plastics, paint

Madaoua industry:
cotton ginning

Tànout

fishing along Niger R for both domestic
consumption and export to Nigeria and Togo

Tahoua
GYPSUM
PHOSPHATES

Vallée de Tarka

Gangara

Niger

Tillabery Industry:
sugar complex/refining, rice milling, rice
irrigation project

Zinder Industry:
millet/sorghum/rice milling, tanning, soft drinks,
wool blankets, groundnut oil processing

Tillabery

Birni Nkonni Industry:
cement

Madaoua

Maradi industry:
groundnut oil processing, cotton ginning,
tanning, matches

14°N

Karma

Birni Nkonni

Dogondoutchi

Dallol Bosso

Zinder

Gouré

Niamey

Maradi

Matameye

Matameye industry:
sugar grown locally, groundnut oil processing

Say
IRON ORE

Dosso

Dosso Industry:
groundnut oil processing

Parc National
du W du Niger

scale 1:6 000 000

0   300km

0   200mi

desert and semidesert —
nomadic herding in south of
region (camels, sheep, goats)
moving seasonally further
south to watered areas

principal cash crops:

groundnuts

cotton

rice

gum arabic

traditional subsistence
agriculture (millet, cassava,
sorghum, beans) and
livestock grazing (cattle,
sheep, goats)

mineral resource site

national park boundary

oasis

oasis with fertile zone
wheat, maize, fruit

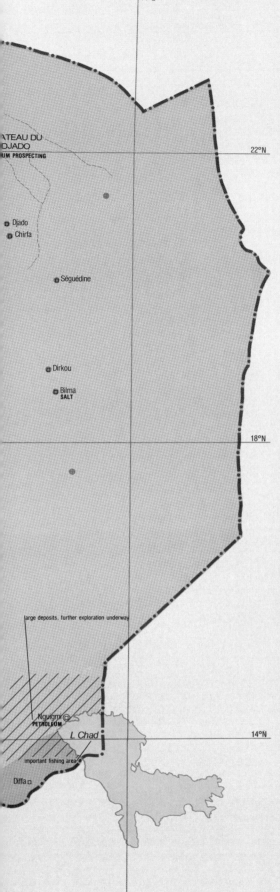

Cameroon

The most striking characteristic of the physical environment of Cameroon is its diversity. This is due in part to its latitudinal range, which extends between 2° and 13° north. Cameroon lies astride a volcanic belt which separates West and central Africa and is intermediate between the basins of the Niger and Congo rivers and Lake Chad. There is also considerable variation in altitude within the country, most dramatically manifested by Mount Cameroon (4070 meters) situated close to the shoreline of the Bight of Biafra (also known as the Bight of Bonny). In terms of the climate, vegetation and geography of Cameroon, five different environmental zones can be delineated. The most southerly is the Atlantic coastal forest plain, consisting mostly of dense forest and mangrove. This zone is characterized by a high rainfall (about 3800 millimeters per year) and extends between 72 and 128 kilometers inland. Bordering the coastal plain on the east is a region of plateaus (average elevation 640 meters) and dense tropical forests, extending from the Sanaga river to the Congo Basin. North of the Sanaga lies the Adamawa Plateau region. Elevations there range between 790 and 1500 meters and it can be seen as a transitional zone between northern and southern Cameroon. The fourth region is the extensive savanna and steppe of the Benoué and Chad plains in the north. During the rainy season (June through October) much of this region, particularly the area around Lake Chad, becomes a vast flood plain. The fifth region is the mountainous region of the west, including Mount Cameroon and the grassfields of the Bamenda Highlands and extending northwards to the Mandara Hills.

The geographical diversity of the nation is reflected in the human population. The environmental zones have tended to result in cultural areas that are based on different forms of adaptation. The coastal population has long been supported by fishing and coastal trade. The forest area is suitable for the cultivation of yams and cassava. The peoples of the Adamawa Plateau and the Benoué and Chad plains cultivate maize and other cereal crops and practice pastoralism. The attractive climate and fertile soil of the Bamenda Highlands have been responsible for the great density of population in that area, and a distinctive cultural pattern can be discerned throughout the many chieftaincies that exist there.

Human variation is reflected further in the great linguistic diversity of Cameroon. The southern peoples are mostly Bantu speaking, and linguists have suggested that the Bamenda Highlands may have been the point of origin of Bantu-speaking peoples. There are also several groups of pygmies in the forests of the south, and Sudanic and Afroasiatic languages are spoken in the north. Another aspect of the cultural diversity is in the realm of religion; the north is populated largely by Muslim peoples, such as the Fulani (Foulbe or Peul), while the south is predominantly Christian.

The beginnings of present-day Cameroon lie in the rivalry between European powers vying for control of the West African coast in the late 19th century. In July 1884 the German diplomat Nachtigal established the German Kamerun Protectorate, which lasted until 1916, when a combination of British and French forces brought German rule to an end. Although German rule was harsh, its accomplishments were impressive. These included setting up the vast and highly profitable set of plantations in the south which are now operated by the Cameroon Development Corporation.

Following World War I, four-fifths of the former Kamerun Protectorate became a French mandate. The rest (two non-contiguous areas in the west) became British Camcroons, a mandate administered as an adjunct to the colonial government of Nigeria. The French established a separate administration in French Cameroun and increased production of cocoa and palm. In 1946 the two mandates became United Nations Trusteeships, and before long emergent political groups embodied the people's aspirations for independence. After 1948 the Union des Populations du Cameroun (UPC) called for reunification of the two territories and the ending of French rule: support for them grew during the 1950s, leading to independence in 1960.

In 1961 a plebiscite was held in British Cameroons: Northern Cameroons voted to join Nigeria; Southern Cameroons became the western state of the newly reunified Cameroon Federal Republic. The governing party was the Union Camerounaise, led by Ahmadou Ahidjo, who became the first president. In 1966 his predominantly eastern party joined forces with the Kamerun National Democratic Party of the west to form the Union Nationale Camerounaise (UNC), later renamed the Rassemblement Démocratique du Peuple Camerounais (RDPC). In 1973 Ahidjo announced a Green Revolution that would make the country self-sufficient in agriculture, with surplus for export. Economic growth would be funded by exports of recently discovered petroleum.

Ahidjo handed over power to his prime minister, Paul Biya, in 1982; a year later he was accused of conspiracy against Biya, and in 1984 an attempted coup by the presidential guard was bloodily crushed. Biya's regime survived controversial elections in 1992, and remains repressive, with little press freedom. Biya's attempt in 1996 to replace elected mayors with appointees led to violent protests and some deaths, but he was re-elected president in October 1997 for a seven-year term.

Biya had inherited a border dispute with Nigeria, and in January 1994 Cameroon's Diamond and Djabane islands were briefly occupied by Nigerian troops. Conflict with Nigeria flared again in 1996, and continued despite a provisional truce. Biya also inherited an economy in crisis: oil revenues had been wasted on badly planned large-scale projects, and 1994 saw an internal financial crisis. Biya responded by speeding up the privatization of monopolies and state institutions. By 1995 the country's debt arrears had been cleared, and it joined the Commonwealth. However, high inflation, and a general strike in 1996, are symptoms of an economy that remains weak.

Mali

Official Name
République du Mali

Area
1 204 021 sq km

Date of Independence
22 Sept 1960

Status and Name in Colonial Times
French colony (part of French West Africa): French
Sudan; 1958–60 member state of the French
Community: Mali

Population
11 480 000 (UN est 1997)

Rate of Change
3.0% (UN est 1995–2000)

Capital City
Bamako

Population of Capital
658 275 (1987)

National Language(s)
French; Bambara, Fulani, Marka, Songhay,
Malinke, Tuareg

Gross National Product (US dollars)
270 per capita (1993)

Local Currency
1 franc CFA = 100 centimes

desert — nomadic herding
(sheep, goats, cattle) in
south with subsistence crops
(millet, maize)

scattered crop cultivation
(including millet, maize) with
livestock along fertile river
valleys

principal cash crops:

rice

cotton

groundnuts

gum arabic

○   mineral resource site

- - -   national park boundary

Kayes   major river port

scale 1:6 500 000

| 0 | 300km |
| 0 | 200mi |

MALI

Niger

Taoudenni
SALT

Tile
Val
PHOSP

Niger

Tombouctou

Goundam
Diré

Diré Industry:
export of dried fish, world's first commercial
solar energy power station

Hombori

Ballé

Nioro du Sahel

Dioura Industry:
rice mill

Dioura

L Debo

Bandiagara Industry:
millet/maize production project

Kayes Industry:
cattle market, abattoir, tanning, hides and skins

Doubabougou Industry:
sugar refining

irrigation water for Niono region

important fishing area

Mopti

Bandiagara

Sénégal

Kayes

Doubabougou

Niono

Diamou
LIMESTONE

Manantali Dam

Parc National
de la Boucle
du Baoulé

Mopti Industry:
rice research, rice mill, export of dried fish

Bafoulabé
MARBLE

Sansanding Dam
controls river irrigation

Niono Industry:
cotton ginning, cotton oil plant

Diamou Industry:
cement

Bafing

Bakoye

Djidian
IRON ORE

Ségou

Kita

Niger

Bamako Industry:
metal works, abattoir, meat canning, tanning,
textile, carpets, cigarettes, milk plant, radio
assembly, fruit and vegetable canning

Bani

Koulikoro

Ségou Industry:
cotton ginning, rice and millet milling, textile,
hides and skins, export of dried fish

Kéniéba
UNEXPLOITED
IRON ORE

Bamako

Selingué
Dam

major HEP and irrigation source

Koutiala

Bafing Makana
UNEXPLOITED
IRON ORE

Bougouni Industry:
government resettlement scheme based on cotton

Bougouni

Baoulé

Bagoé

Sikasso

Sikasso Industry:
cotton ginning, textile

Kalana
GOLD

152

Niger

Two-thirds of Niger is covered by the Sahara, the domain of the Tuareg. Even in the remaining southern and western third the very existence of agricultural societies reposes on a delicate balance, which an invasion of locusts, drought, unfavorable timing of the rain or too rapid demographic expansion can easily, and has often, upset.

The result is famine and all the problems, political and human, that go with it, most

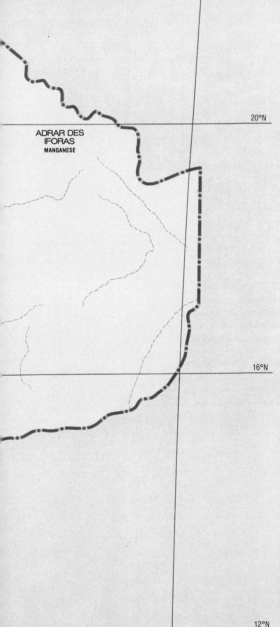

ADRAR DES
IFORAS
MANGANESE

4°E

20°N

16°N

12°N

recently in the 1970s and 1980s, even though the country is otherwise marginally self-sufficient in basic food crops. The economy is very poor, largely agricultural (predominantly stock-raising), except for the mining of uranium deposits in the north, which provides the main export. Uranium has proved vulnerable to world price fluctuations, as has another major export, the peanuts grown by the Hausa since French times.

Niger is composed of regions that constituted traditionally the outlying peripheral provinces of the more prominent central Sudanic empires and kingdoms – regions, that is, that served as refuge zones in times of upheaval. Indeed, after the defeat of the Songhay army in 1591, it was in the south (that is, among the Zerma/Songhay of present-day western Niger) that the Songhay emperors found a following ready to continue the resistance against the Moroccan occupiers. And it was to the Hausaland of modern Niger that those Hausa fled who refused to accept the new Fulani–Muslim regime established in central Hausaland (present-day Northern Nigeria) after 1804. Here, on the outer fringes of Hausaland, members of some of the dynasties deposed by the Fulani established the kingdoms of Maradi and Gobir/Tsibiri. They found a ready ally in the emerging and increasingly powerful state of Damagaram–Zinder, which owed its wealth to the trans-Saharan trade (still profitable in the 19th century). These kingdoms posed a continuous threat to the Sokoto Caliphate.

The French conquest from 1897 onwards was a by-product of "the march towards Chad" and the desire to operate a junction between the emerging colonial empires of North, West and Equatorial Africa. It was fiercely resisted by the Tuareg and other peoples. After an uneasy colonial history, the country was given full independence in 1960, under its first president Hamani Diori. After several coup and assassination attempts, he was finally toppled in 1974, like many neighboring leaders, in the famine and disorders resulting from the Sahel droughts.

His successor, Lieutenant-Colonel Seyni Kountché, pragmatically sought urgent aid from France and the international community, the more so as uranium revenue slumped. After initial unrest and coup attempts he increased civilian participation in government. After his death in 1987, his successor, Army Chief of Staff Ali Saibou, introduced a one-party state, but faced civil unrest and a growing Tuareg revolt, as many nomad refugees moved to Niger to escape the Sahel drought. Saibou was forced to make democratic concessions, handing over effective power to a transitional government. In the 1993 elections a coalition dominated the new Assembly, and one of its leaders, Mahamane Ousmane, was elected president.

The coalition split, and effective government was stalemated. This was used to justify the January 1996 military coup, supported by Saibou and led by Colonel Ibrahim Mainassara, who became president. Throughout 1996 his increasingly repressive rule attracted international criticism. Political unrest and strikes rapidly grew throughout 1997, as did regional banditry; and the Tuareg revolt, formerly close to a peaceful settlement, flared up once again.

Mali

Between forest in the south and desert in the north Mali bridges the sahel, which makes up much of its area. This scanty savanna is peopled by camel- or cattle-herding Tuareg and other nomads. In the arid northeast the shortness and uncertainty of the rains make famines a constant possibility. The Niger river provides almost the only guaranteed perennial water. Here, apart from riverine settlements, the sedentary population has tended to cluster in the defensible villages of the dramatic rocky outcrops around Hombori and the Bandiagara plateau, home of the Dogon. In the neck of Mali, above Tombouctou, are rich plains inhabited by a diversity of peoples: Songhay and Fulani farmers, Sorko and Bozo fishers and others. These regions have for centuries supplied the surplus agricultural products needed by trading centers like Tombouctou on the edge of the desert. In the extreme southwest Sudanic bush gives way to stretches of forest watered by a multitude of streams. Here live the related Malinke groups of Bambara, Dyola (the famous Mandinke traders) and Khassonke and, among others, the Sarakolle and Senufo.

Unlike some states named after ancient African kingdoms, Mali's present boundaries actually include the heartland of the old Mali empire, as well as its predecessor, Ghana, and the western core of its successor, Songhay. The centuries after the fall of Songhay to a Moroccan army in 1591 were a time of disorder and movement, but also of state-formation among non-Muslim people like the Bambara and Mossi. The 19th-century *jihad* movement led to the creation of a militant Islamic state centered on Masina and the Segu empire of al-Haj 'Umar, whose son Ahmadu was finally defeated by the French after a fierce resistance in 1892. Thus Mali's diverse peoples have had a long history of coexistence in states which, whether formally Muslim or pagan, have generally tended to combine elements of both Islam and traditional religion.

Colonial conquest produced a bitter but unsuccessful resistance from the Segu empire and later from the militant Islamic Hamalliyah movement. The Soudan Français was detached from Haut-Sénégal–Niger and formed into a distinct territory in 1920. The present boundaries were drawn up by 1947. Landlocked, with a single railroad to Dakar as its only outlet to the sea, Mali achieved a brief federation with Senegal, but two months after independence in 1960 Senegal seceded.

The Republic of Mali's first president, the Soviet-aligned autocrat Modibo Keita, was overthrown in 1968. His successor, Moussa Traoré, was confronted by the famine and economic problems resulting from the great Sahel drought, and by the armed rebellion of the nomadic Tuareg in the north. He was overthrown in 1991. Elections in 1992 returned the Alliance for Democracy in Mali (ADEMA) and its leader Alpha Oumar Konaré to office. Despite two coup attempts he was reelected in 1996. The Tuareg conflict was largely resolved, by strong suppression and Algerian mediation, and by 1996 it had mostly died out.

WEST CENTRAL AFRICA

The region we have chosen to call West Central Africa has no obvious geographic coherence, nor any superimposed cultural unity acquired during the colonial period. In the north the nations were part of French Equatorial Africa; the enormous nation of Congo (DRO), once Belgian Congo, borders former Portuguese Angola, and the enclave of Equatorial Guinea was once under Spanish rule. Geographically the variety is wide: arid semidesert in Chad, dense tropical rain forest in the Congo basin, grasslands in Angola. So from Sahara to sahel through forest to grasslands, bisected by the equator this region contains in itself all of Africa.

The peoples of the region are as diverse as the climate. From Arabic-speaking Muslims in northern Chad, we pass south to areas where languages of the Niger–Congo family, like Zande, are spoken. But over much of the region, from the equator south, Bantu languages are universally spoken, and it is probably from a heartland in the forests that Bantu expansion commenced.

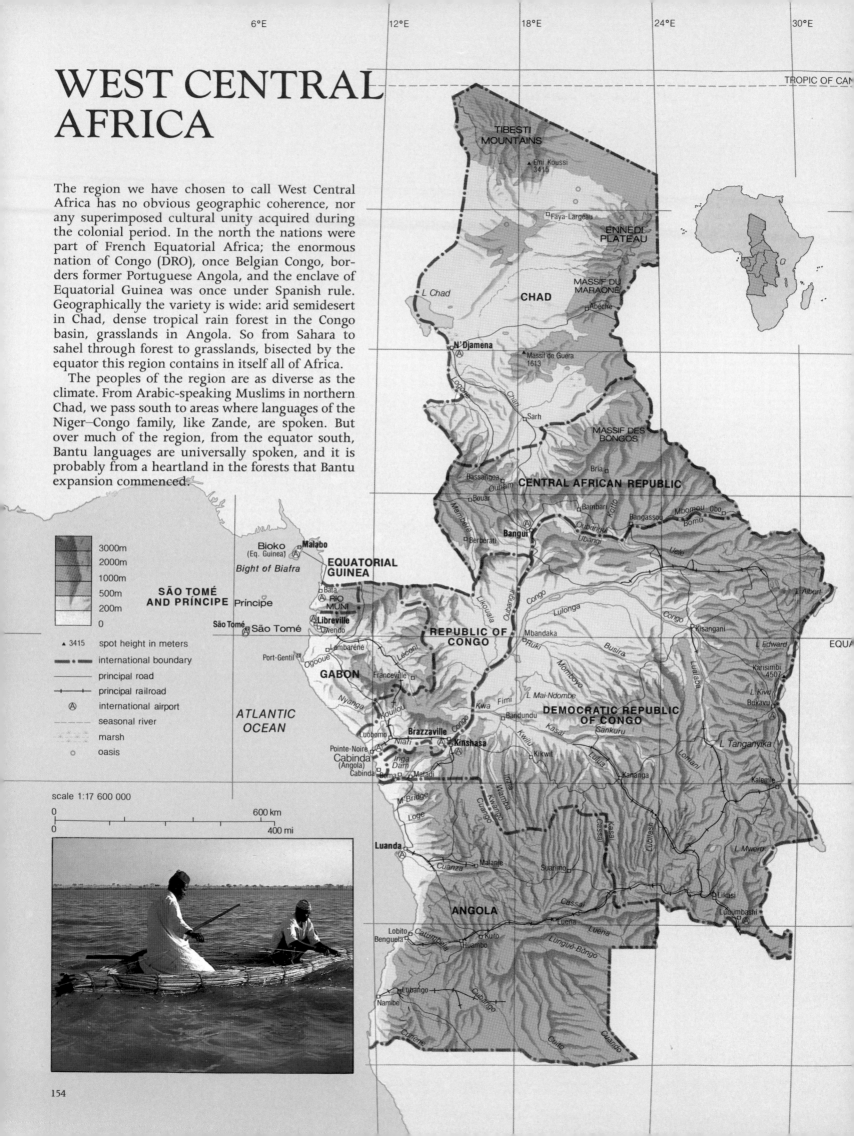

Map legend

- 3000m
- 2000m
- 1000m
- 500m
- 200m
- 0

▲ 3415 spot height in meters
•–•–• international boundary
—— principal road
——+——+ principal railroad
Ⓐ international airport
seasonal river
marsh
∘ oasis

scale 1:17 600 000

0 — 600 km
0 — 400 mi

Right Throughout West Central Africa hunting and fishing are important in the rural economy of the forest areas where cattle cannot be kept. Here, near Kisangani (Stanleyville) on the Congo river in northwest Congo (DRO), Wagenia fishermen use wicker fish traps to catch fish in the swirling rapids.

Below Scattered throughout the rain forests of the region are settlements of pygmies, hunters who preceded the majority population of Negroid agriculturalists. The pygmies now speak the language of their neighbors, with whom they exchange game and fish for grain and vegetables. Here, on the Central African Republic–Congo (DRO) border, a dance takes place in a forest clearing, in front of huts built of banana fronds.

Below right Minerals such as manganese and uranium are bringing radical change and wealth to finance modernization and further industrial development in West Central Africa. This manganese mine is at Moanda, near Franceville, in southeast Gabon.

Left Lake Chad, lying across the boundary of Nigeria and Chad, is the home of the Baduma, island dwellers who exist mainly by fishing. Papyrus boats are used for transportation on the lake.

Right Fulani (Fulbe) peoples are found across West Africa from the Atlantic coast to Cameroon and, as in this illustration, in southwest Chad. All speak a Nigritic language, although they vary greatly in physical appearance and in modes of livelihood.

Far right In southern Chad, near Léré, the main agricultural region of the country, villagers store their grain (mainly millet) in tall vermin-proof granaries

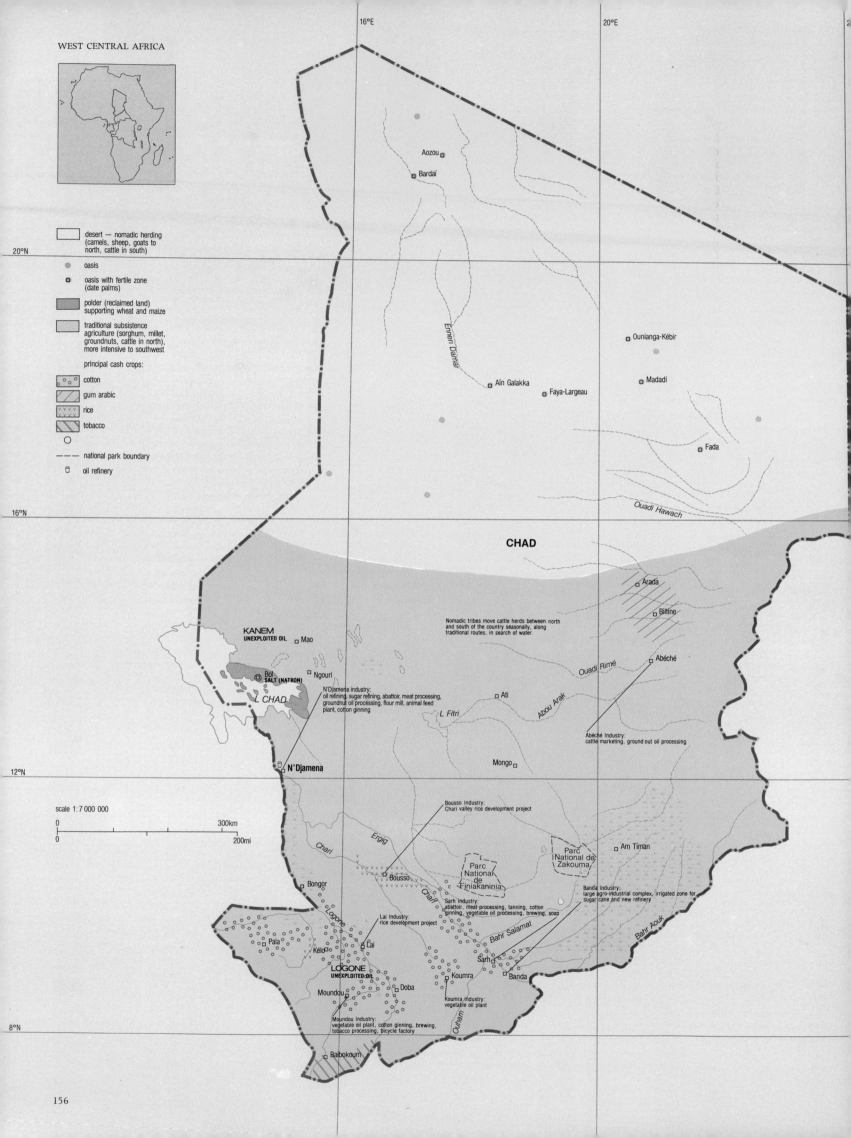

WEST CENTRAL AFRICA

20°N

16°N

12°N

8°N

16°E

20°E

desert — nomadic herding
(camels, sheep, goats to
north, cattle in south)

oasis

oasis with fertile zone
(date palms)

polder (reclaimed land)
supporting wheat and maize

traditional subsistence
agriculture (sorghum, millet,
groundnuts, cattle in north),
more intensive to southwest

principal cash crops:

cotton

gum arabic

rice

tobacco

national park boundary

oil refinery

Aozou

Bardaï

Enneri Damar

Ounianga-Kébir

Aïn Galakka

Faya-Largeau

Madadi

Fada

Ouadi Hawach

CHAD

Arada

Biltine

KANEM
UNEXPLOITED OIL

Mao

Nomadic tribes move cattle herds between north
and south of the country seasonally, along
traditional routes, in search of water.

Bol
SALT (NATRON)

Ngouri

Abéché

Ouadi Rimé

N'Djamena industry:
oil refining, sugar refining, abattoir, meat processing,
groundnut oil processing, flour mill, animal feed
plant, cotton ginning

L CHAD

Ati

L Fitri

Abou Arak

Abéché Industry:
cattle marketing, ground nut oil processing

N'Djamena

Mongo

Bousso Industry:
Chari valley rice development project

Ergig

Chari

Am Timan

Bongor

Bousso

Parc
National
de
Finiakaninia

Parc
National de
Zakouma

Chari

Banda Industry:
large agro-industrial complex, irrigated zone for
sugar cane and new refinery

Logone

Sarh Industry:
abattoir, meat-processing, tanning, cotton
ginning, vegetable oil processing, brewing, soap

Lai Industry:
rice development project

Bahr Salamat

Bahr Aouk

Pala

Kélo

Lai

LOGONE
UNEXPLOITED OIL

Koumra

Sarh

Banda

Moundou

Doba

Koumra Industry:
vegetable oil plant

Ouham

Moundou Industry:
vegetable oil plant, cotton ginning, brewing,
tobacco processing, bicycle factory

Baïbokoum

scale 1:7 000 000

0   300km

0   200mi

156

Chad

The Republic of Chad, previously the northernmost part of French Equatorial Africa, remains one of Africa's poorest and most isolated countries. Located near the geographical center of the continent, Chad is the fifth largest state, comprising roughly the eastern half of the Lake Chad drainage basin, yet its population is less than seven million. The climate ranges from full desert in the Tibesti mountains of the north to moist savanna in the Chari and Logone river valleys of the south.

Humankind has had a long and varied history in Chad, as the bones of *Chadanthropus* and the rock paintings of the northern mountains attest. Within the confines of the modern state are found speakers of three of Africa's four linguistic groupings. The Central-Sudanic-speaking Sara, the most numerous group, are politically the most important. Before the time of Christ the Sao of Chad were living in cities, and from the 9th century AD large states, whose economies were based on the trans-Saharan trade of slaves and other goods, have dominated the area. The earliest and most durable of these, Kanem-Bornu, was instrumental in the introduction and spread of Islam in this part of Africa at an early date. In the 14th century, Arabic-speaking people began moving into the Chad basin from the east and north, and the Bulala, Bagirmi and Wadai successfully challenged the dominance of Kanem-Bornu.

Chad

Official Name
République du Tchad

Area
1 284 000 sq km

Date of Independence
11 Apr 1960

Status and Name in Colonial Times
French territory (one of four territories of French Equatorial Africa): Chad

Population
6 702 000 (UN est 1997)

Rate of Change
2.7% (UN est 1995–2000)

Capital City
N'Djamena

Population of Capital
688 000 (1993)

National Language(s)
French; Arabic, Sara Madjingay, Tuburi, Mundang

Gross National Product (US dollars)
210 per capita (1993)

Local Currency
1 franc CFA = 100 centimes

During the 19th century several European expeditions visited the Chad area. Among them, Denham and Clapperton in 1822 were the first and Heinrich Barth in the 1850s was the most important. The present boundaries of Chad were established by the Franco-British Convention of 1898, despite subsequent arrangements between Germany and France that temporarily changed the borders prior to World War I. The military conquest of Chad by the French began on 22 April 1900 when French and African forces under Commandant Lamy defeated Rabih, the ruler of Bornu, on the site of the modern capital, N'Djamena. Parts of northern and eastern Chad resisted until the eve of World War I.

In the French colonial framework Chad was neglected and ignored. Its people were used as a reservoir of manpower to build the Congo–Ocean railroad, although Chad is still without its own rail system. Education was the worst in the French colonies. Despite the introduction of cotton as a cash crop in 1929, the Chadian economy has modernized only very slowly. The road network remains one of the poorest in Africa. In World War II, under the leadership of Félix Éboué, Chad rallied behind the Free French and became the base for French operations against the Axis in the Sahara.

In 1946 the Chadian Progressive Party (PPT) was formed by Gabriel Lisette, a West Indian. By 1956 it was the majority party, with Lisette as prime minister. During Lisette's absence, François Tombalbaye, a labor leader, emerged as a force within the party. Tombalbaye merged the major opposition party, based among the Muslims of the north, with his Sara-based PPT. Leading this coalition, Tombalbaye became Chad's first president in 1960.

As Tombalbaye's regime grew into a personal dictatorship, opposition groups began a guerrilla war in 1965, and in 1975 he was killed in a coup. Internal warfare continued unabated for two decades, and as one leader toppled another, foreign powers were drawn into the conflict – notably France and Libya, which several times occupied much of Chad on the basis of its claim to the mineral-rich Aozou Strip in the north (where it retained military control until 1994). In 1990 Hissen Habré, who had been president since 1982, was forced into exile in Sudan. Idriss Déby, leader of the Patriotic Salvation Movement (MPS), took over as president, promising to restore multiparty democracy.

The process of liberalization was a slow one, marked by accusations of human-rights abuses by the government-led Chadian National Army (ANT), and hampered by continued military incursions into the oil-rich Lake Chad region by the Libyan-backed Movement for Democracy and Development (MDD). There were also several coup attempts by dissident army factions and followers of Habré. In 1996 reconciliation was finally achieved between most of the warring factions. A multiparty constitution was adopted and Déby was elected president. The peace remains fragile, however, while the government faces the tough uphill task of bringing unity to Chad's many ethnic communities, and of finding ways of exploiting its acknowledged mineral wealth to bring prosperity to one of the poorest countries in the world.

Central African Republic

Placed in the center of the African continent north of the Oubangui river, the Central African Republic, formerly the French colony of Ubangi-Shari, sits astride the Chad–Congo watershed. The southern part of the country abuts the equatorial forest, but towards the north the climate becomes moist savanna. The eastern frontier follows the line of the Nile–Congo watershed, while in the west more arbitrary boundaries separate the country from Cameroon, Chad and the Congo.

Unlike the majority of African states, the boundaries of the Central African Republic correspond closely to the territory inhabited by the speakers of Ubangian languages. Not recent arrivals, the Ubangian speakers probably built the megaliths at Bouar during the last millennium BC. The large precolonial states of the Zande and Senoussi also show the importance of the region before the arrival of the white man.

Late in coming to the Oubangui basin, the first European, Georg Schweinfurth, reached the Zande states in 1870. During the rest of the 19th century and the first two decades of the 20th century the Oubangui became a bone of contention between rival European imperialisms. While the rights of the French had been recognized at the Berlin convention of 1894, the colony of Ubangi-Shari did not take its final form until after World War I.

Divided among 27 concessionary companies, which ruthlessly exploited the population either to gather rubber or other forms of forced labor, the colony suffered from a population decline. This trend, begun during the slave trade, was exacerbated by the concessions, a sleeping sickness epidemic and rebellions that persisted into the 1930s. Under these conditions economic and political development was at a standstill.

Following World War II, Barthélemy Boganda founded the Movement of Social Evolution in Black Africa (MESAN). He became the advocate of a confederation of all the colonies of French Equatorial Africa into a state he called the Central African Republic. After his death in 1959 his successor, David Dacko, was forced to settle for a reduced CAR, which he led to independence in 1960.

Dacko, who was not the leader that Boganda had been, was overthrown by Colonel Jean Bédel Bokassa in 1965. Bokassa gradually built a regime of personal rule that culminated in his declaring himself Emperor Bokassa I. The country's name was changed to the Central African Empire. Bokassa expropriated the profits from diamond production that might otherwise have provided funds for foreign exchange and development. Discontent grew in his Empire, finally erupting in January 1979, when soldiers gunned down students protesting against Bokassa's decree that they should wear uniforms they could not afford. In September 1979 a bloodless coup, carried out with French support, ousted Bokassa and returned David Dacko to power.

16°E   18°E   20°E

10°N

Bahr Ou

Bahr Aouk

Bangoran

Ndélé
DIAMONDS

Bamingui

8°N

Parc National du
Bamingui Bangoran

CENTRAL AFRICAN REPUBLIC

□ Batangafo

Bakassa

Pata

Bocaranga

□ Crampel

Bongou

Ouham

Fata

Bambari Industry:
cattle development; cotton oil plant

Bria ◉
DIAMONDS

Bossangoa □

□ Bouca

□ Bozoum

□ Dekoa

Korre

6°N

Ippy

Nana

□ Sibut

Bambari

Abba Industry:
tobacco processing

Mpoko

Bangui Industry:
timber, cotton ginning, textile, coffee processing,
abattoir, meat canning, animal food, brewing,
shoes, paint, radio assembly, bicycle assembly,
diamond cutting

Alindao Industry:
sesame processing, groundnut oil processing

Abba □

Berbérati Industry:
tobacco processing

Bossembélé □

Boali Industry:
cotton ginning, textile

Kémo

Ouaka

Alindao

□ Carnot

HEP source

Mbali

Boali Dam □ Boali
HEP source

Outangui

Berbérati □

Mambéré

Kadei

Mbaéré

Lobaye

□ Boda

Bangui

Mobaye-Mobayi
Dam

4°N

□ Gamboula

Mbaiki

Gamboula Industry:
tobacco processing

Komaso Industry:
cocoa development project

Lobaye

□ Komaso

Nola Industry:
saw mills

Nola ◉
DIAMONDS

Sangha

scale 1:4 000 000

0   300km

0   200mi

	forest
	subsistence agriculture (cassava, maize, millet, groundnuts, rice) more intensive production to southwest
	livestock grazing

principal cash crops:

	coffee
	cotton
	rubber
	tobacco
	fruit

○   mineral resource site

– – –   national park boundary

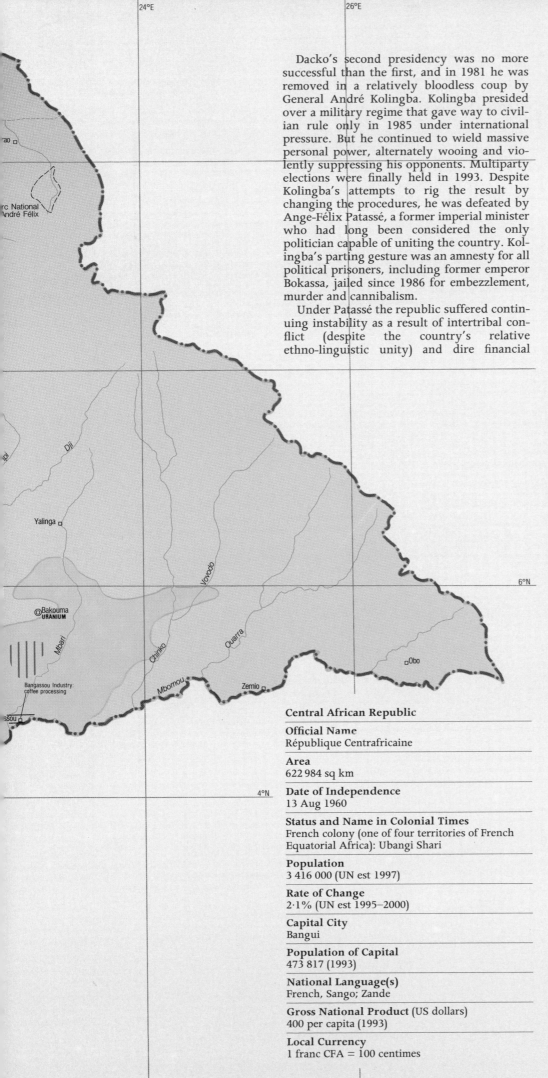

Dacko's second presidency was no more successful than the first, and in 1981 he was removed in a relatively bloodless coup by General André Kolingba. Kolingba presided over a military regime that gave way to civilian rule only in 1985 under international pressure. But he continued to wield massive personal power, alternately wooing and violently suppressing his opponents. Multiparty elections were finally held in 1993. Despite Kolingba's attempts to rig the result by changing the procedures, he was defeated by Ange-Félix Patassé, a former imperial minister who had long been considered the only politician capable of uniting the country. Kolingba's parting gesture was an amnesty for all political prisoners, including former emperor Bokassa, jailed since 1986 for embezzlement, murder and cannibalism.

Under Patassé the republic suffered continuing instability as a result of intertribal conflict (despite the country's relative ethno-linguistic unity) and dire financial problems. Virtually bankrupt, the government failed to pay its soldiers, teachers and civil servants, leading to a full-scale insurrection in 1996. A fragile calm was restored with the help of French, Chadian and Gabonese troops, but there were further rebellions in 1997 that led to fierce fighting in the capital Bangui.

One consequence of the unstable situation is that the Central African Republic remains poorly developed and unable to take advantage of its enormous resources (as yet untapped) of minerals, timber and potential hydroelectric power. The country now relies even more heavily than before on foreign financial aid, mainly from France, and on military assistance from French and African peacekeeping forces.

Gabon

Sitting astride the equator, Gabon receives heavy rainfall and warm temperatures, both of which favor the growth of tropical rain forest. Covering almost all of the country, the dense forest rests upon an impoverished clay subsoil and a thin surface layer of humus. Rivers and streams are abundant, and many of them are connected to Gabon's major waterway, the Ogooué. Navigable from its mouth at Cap Lopez to the first set of rapids over 160 kilometers inland, the Ogooué and its affluents drain the interior plateau down an escarpment to the coastal plain. Gabon has three major ports: Libreville (the capital) on the Gabon estuary; Owendo, also on the estuary; and Port Gentil near the mouth of the Ogooué. Gabon's population is increasingly centered in urban areas, leaving much of the interior plateau virtually uninhabited.

The first inhabitants of the region were the pygmies. They were followed by Bantu-speaking peoples, who moved into the region as early as 1000 AD. Europeans first sailed to the coast of Gabon in the 1470s and began trading contacts with Africans dwelling along the estuary. Slaves and ivory dominated Gabon's export trade with the West until the mid-19th century, when slave exports declined in favor of timber (ebony, dyewood) and rubber. During this time of commercial transition, European merchants, missionaries and officials established permanent footholds on the Gabon estuary shore near present-day Libreville. At the same time, a large ethnic group – the Fang – began a long-term migration from their homeland near Cameroon toward the dynamic commercial centers on the Gabon estuary and the Ogooué.

France obtained colonial title to the territory in the 1880s. The French government then parceled out the region to commercial companies, who administered and traded in their exclusive concessions. The policy was a commercial failure and was abandoned in the 1920s just as European companies began their first significant purchases of okoumé timber, an ideal wood for the manufacture of plywood. Gabon prospered thanks to okoumé, and its economic future was further assured by the discovery of oil near Port Gentil, and of manganese and uranium near Franceville around the year of independence, 1960.

Central African Republic

Official Name
République Centrafricaine

Area
622 984 sq km

Date of Independence
13 Aug 1960

Status and Name in Colonial Times
French colony (one of four territories of French Equatorial Africa): Ubangi Shari

Population
3 416 000 (UN est 1997)

Rate of Change
2·1% (UN est 1995–2000)

Capital City
Bangui

Population of Capital
473 817 (1993)

National Language(s)
French, Sango; Zande

Gross National Product (US dollars)
400 per capita (1993)

Local Currency
1 franc CFA = 100 centimes

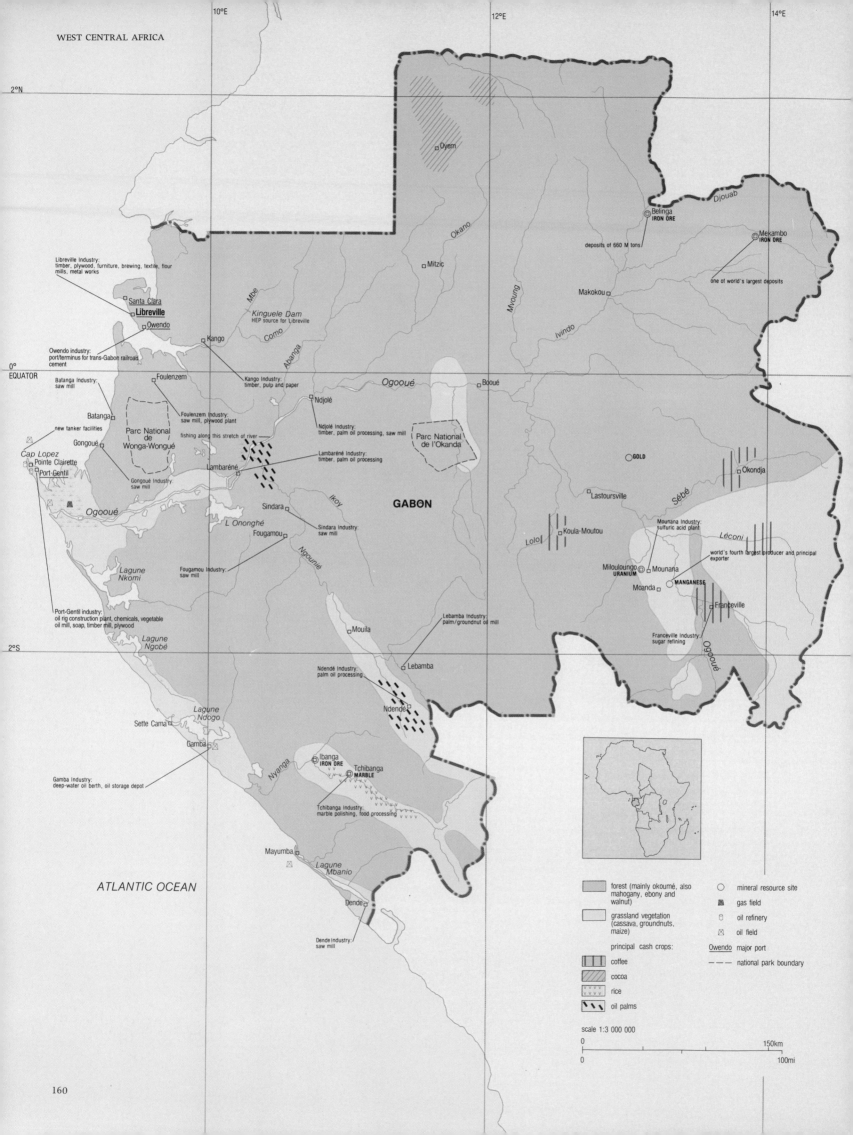

2°N

Oyem

Libreville Industry:
timber, plywood, furniture, brewing, textile, flour
mills, metal works

Djouab

Belinga
IRON ORE

Mekambo
IRON ORE

deposits of 660 M tons

one of world's largest deposits

Mitzic

Santa Clara
Libreville

Owendo

Kango

Kinguele Dam
HEP source for Libreville

Okano

Mvoung

Makokou

Ivindo

Mbe

Como

Abanga

Owendo industry:
port/terminus for trans-Gabon railroad,
cement

0°
EQUATOR

Batanga Industry:
saw mill

Foulenzem

Kango Industry:
timber, pulp and paper

Ogooué

Booué

Ndjolé

Batanga

new tanker facilities

Gongoué

Parc National
de
Wonga-Wongué

Foulenzem Industry:
saw mill, plywood plant

fishing along this stretch of river

Ndjolé Industry:
timber, palm oil processing, saw mill

Parc National
de l'Okanda

Cap Lopez
Pointe Clairette
Port-Gentil

Lambaréné

Lambaréné Industry:
timber, palm oil processing

GOLD

Okondja

Ogooué

Gongoué Industry:
saw mill

Sindara

GABON

Lastoursville

Sébé

Léconi

L Ononghé

Fougamou

Sindara Industry:
saw mill

Lolo

Koula-Moutou

Mounana Industry:
sulfuric acid plant

world's fourth largest producer and principal
exporter

Lagune
Nkomi

Fougamou Industry:
saw mill

Ngounié

Milouloungo
URANIUM

Mounana

Moanda MANGANESE

Franceville

Port-Gentil industry:
oil rig construction plant, chemicals, vegetable
oil mill, soap, timber mill, plywood

Mouila

Lebamba Industry:
palm/groundnut oil mill

Franceville Industry:
sugar refining

Ogooué

2°S

Lagune
Ngobé

Lebamba

Ndendé Industry:
palm oil processing

Lagune
Ndogo

Ndendé

Sette Cama

Gamba

Nyanga

Ibanga
IRON ORE

Tchibanga
MARBLE

Gamba Industry:
deep-water oil berth, oil storage depot

Tchibanga Industry:
marble polishing, food processing

Mayumba

Lagune
Mbanio

ATLANTIC OCEAN

Dende

Dende Industry:
saw mill

forest (mainly okoumé, also
mahogany, ebony and
walnut)

○ mineral resource site

grassland vegetation
(cassava, groundnuts,
maize)

gas field

oil refinery

oil field

principal cash crops:

Owendo major port

coffee

national park boundary

cocoa

rice

oil palms

scale 1:3 000 000

0   150km

0   100mi

Léon M'ba was elected the first president of Gabon in 1961. He survived an attempted coup in 1964 only because French paratroopers intervened to maintain him in power. French influence in Gabon has continued with M'ba's chosen successor, Omar Bongo, who carried on managing Gabon's economy to the satisfaction of the French (who still run it) and the Gabonese (who want to share in it).

In 1968 Gabon became a one-party state under Bongo's Gabonese Democratic Party (PDG). For some two decades the country remained stable both economically and politically, though it was reluctant to cooperate with its poorer African neighbors. However, a severe economic downturn in the late 1980s led to massive popular unrest and demands for a return to multiparty democracy. The constitution was amended accordingly, but legislative elections in 1990 were dogged by controversy amid opposition complaints of electoral fraud. The presidential elections of 1993, which returned Bongo to power, were similarly disorganized, leading to violent protests that effectively paralyzed the administration, and it was May 1996 before agreement could be reached between government and opposition parties.

Gabon is blessed with vast natural resources. However, overdependence on oil production has made it vulnerable to fluctuations in the international market – hence the economic problems of the early 1990s, which took several years to overcome. The economy is dominated by the mining sector, which is operated by foreign enterprises. Gabon has become a world leader in manganese production, thanks to the construction of the Trans-Gabon railroad, which reached Franceville in 1986; nearby reserves of uranium mostly supply the French atomic energy industry. The railroad has also revived an ailing timber industry, previously limited to fast-disappearing coastal forests. Financial problems have delayed an extension of the railroad to Mékambo, where the world's largest iron-ore deposits still await exploitation.

Gabon's economy requires a large, mostly imported, labor force. Agricultural production is inadequate despite costly market-gardening projects in the 1980s, and most food is imported. This array of Gabon's economic strengths and failings echoes patterns reaching back to the 19th century when foreign companies first arrived to export Gabon's natural wealth, but found that food and labor were in short supply.

Gabon

Official Name
République Gabonaise

Area
267 667 sq km

Date of Independence
17 Aug 1960

Status and Name in Colonial Times
French colony (one of the four territories of French Equatonal Africa) with the names French Congo (1890–1903), Gabon (within the French Congo 1903–10), Gabon (1910–60)

Population
1 138 000 (UN est 1997)

Rate of Change
2.7% (UN est 1995–2000)

Capital City
Libreville

Population of Capital
830 000 (1993)

National Language(s)
French

Gross National Product (US dollars)
4 960 per capita (1993)

Local Currency
1 franc CFA = 100 centimes

Equatorial Guinea

Equatorial Guinea consists of a mainland enclave called Río Muni (or Mbini) and five small islands: Bioko (formerly Fernando Póo), Annobón (or Pigalu), Corisco, Elobey Grande and Elobey Chico. Bioko, the largest of the five, was formed by three extinct volcanoes. It has fertile soil and high rainfall, conditions ideal for the cultivation of high-quality cocoa. The mainland, Río Muni, is covered by tropical rain forest through which the Mbini river (also known as the Benito or Woleu river) flows westward over the interior plateau and down an escarpment to the coastal plain. The Muni river on the southern border is actually an estuary fed by several rivers including the Utanboni. The only natural harbor is at the capital, Malabo (formerly Santa Isabel), on Bioko. Bata is the principal town on the mainland; its harbor was improved in the 1980s.

When Portuguese mariners first sailed to Bioko in 1472, they were met by the Bubi, the indigenous inhabitants who had crossed over from the mainland Río Muni area during the 13th century. On the mainland the Bubi were followed by several coastward waves of Bantu migrants, the last of whom were the Fang in the 19th century. The Portuguese ruled Bioko until 1778, when they surrendered the island and their rights to the mainland to Spain, but in 1827 Britain acquired from Spain the right to use the island as a forward base for her anti-slavery naval patrols. Britain resettled many captured slaves there, the descendants of whom are today called Fernandinos. This growing labor force was, however, insufficient to work the nascent cocoa industry on the island and laborers were recruited in Liberia and elsewhere in West Africa. They were frequently mistreated and forced to remain on the island.

Spain sent troops to occupy Río Muni in the 1920s and encountered stiff resistance from the Fang. Most Spaniards stayed on Bioko, acquired much of the land and developed the intensive cultivation of cocoa. After World War II a colonial policy of cultural and political assimilation failed to dampen the nationalistic feelings of the African population, which supported independence movements in the 1960s. These movements successfully won full independence from Spain on 12 October 1968. Francisco Macías Nguema was elected president in 1971; an absolute ruler, he proclaimed himself president for life, but was deposed in 1979 and executed. His nephew, Teodoro Obiang Nguema Mbasógo, replaced him and has been reelected several times, most recently in 1996.

In the 1970s the economy contracted rapidly. Spanish farmers and technicians left Bioko, and the cocoa crop fell eventually to one-tenth of its pre-independence level. Nigeria recalled approximately 45 000 agricultural workers from Bioko in 1975 and 1976 on reports of severe mistreatment and loss of life. Conditions on the plantations were little better than slavery. The once productive timber and coffee industries also shrank to low levels of production. Significant mineral deposits exist but have not been exploited. In the 1990s, however, petroleum and natural gas production has been developed, giving exports a much needed boost.

In the 1980s attempts were made to revive the ailing economy: the country joined the Customs and Economic Union of Central Africa in 1983 and adopted the CFA franc in 1985. In 1988 Spain canceled two-thirds of Equatorial Guinea's debt, but the burden of foreign debt remains huge; despite development aid from the IMF, Equatorial Guinea remains one of the poorest countries in Africa. Bilateral aid from Spain and France has been cut back in the 1990s in protest at human-rights abuses.

Equatorial Guinea under both Macías and Obiang Nguema has earned itself a reputation as a flagrant violator of human rights, with frequent political murders, imprisonment of opposition figures, torture, mass executions and religious persecution. A large minority of the country's population is in exile in Cameroon, Gabon and Spain, and there has been a succession of attempted coups.

From 1979 all political activity was banned, but in 1987 Obiang Nguema set up a single governing party, the Democratic Party of Equatorial Guinea (PDGE). Subsequent elections have been largely boycotted as unfair by opposition groups and rejected by international observers. The 1991 constitution, approved by a referendum but rejected by the opposition, introduced a multiparty system. Some provisions of the electoral law were highly contentious, such as a huge registration fee for political parties. Despite an amnesty for returning exiles, intimidation and arrests have continued.

São Tomé and Príncipe

The two islands of São Tomé and Príncipe are located in the Atlantic 440 and 200 kilometers respectively off the coast of northern Gabon. Part of a volcanic mountain chain extending from Mount Cameroon out into the Atlantic, the islands have fertile volcanic soil and mountainous relief. Both receive high rainfall and warm temperatures, conditions that favor the growth of dense tropical rain forests. The low-lying slopes and flatlands on the islands' perimeters are ideal for cocoa, coffee and copra production. The towns of São Tomé (São Tomé) and Santo António (Príncipe) are the main ports. The rocky islets of Pedras Tinhosas and Rolas are also part of the islands.

When Portuguese mariners first reached the

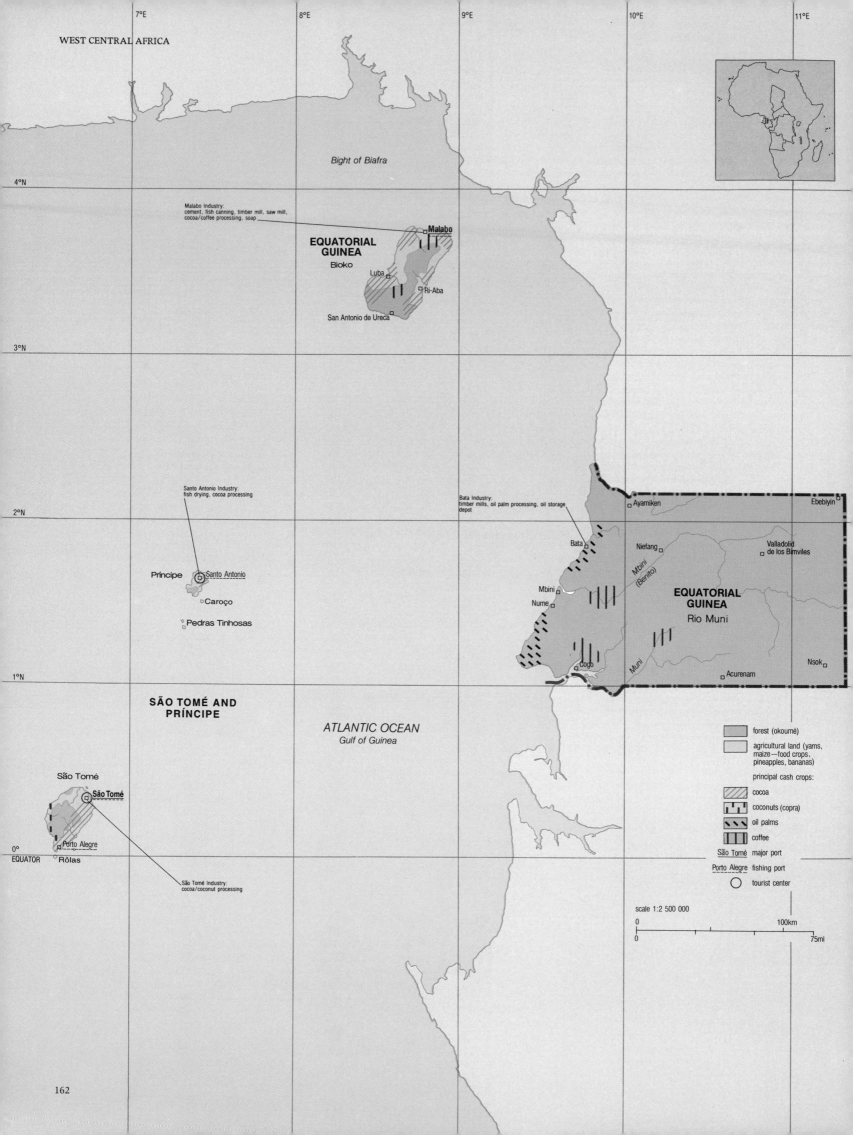

WEST CENTRAL AFRICA

7°E 8°E 9°E 10°E 11°E

4°N

Bight of Biafra

Malabo Industry:
cement, fish canning, timber mill, saw mill,
cocoa/coffee processing, soap

Malabo

EQUATORIAL
GUINEA

Bioko

Luba □

□ Ri-Aba

San Antonio de Ureca □

3°N

2°N

Santo Antonio Industry:
fish drying, cocoa processing

Bata Industry:
timber mills, oil palm processing, oil storage
depot

□ Ayamiken

Ebebiyin

Bata □

Niefang □

Valladolid
de los Bimviles □

Príncipe ⊙ Santo Antonio

EQUATORIAL
GUINEA

Rio Muni

○ Caroço

Mbini □
Nume □

*Mbini
(Benito)*

Pedras Tinhosas □

Cogo □

Muni

Acurenam □

Nsok □

1°N

SÃO TOMÉ AND
PRÍNCIPE

ATLANTIC OCEAN
Gulf of Guinea

forest (okoumé)

agricultural land (yams,
maize—food crops,
pineapples, bananas)

principal cash crops:

cocoa

coconuts (copra)

oil palms

coffee

São Tomé

São Tomé

São Tomé major port

Porto Alegre fishing port

○ tourist center

Porto Alegre
Rôlas

0°
EQUATOR

São Tomé Industry:
cocoa/coconut processing

scale 1:2 500 000

0   100km

0   75mi

Equatorial Guinea

Official Name
República de Guinea Ecuatorial

Area
28 051 sq km

Date of Independence
12 Oct 1968

Status and Name in Colonial Times
Spanish colony: Spanish Guinea (Territorios Españoles del Golfo de Guinea including Río Muni and Fernando Póo (1900–59)); 1959–68 two Spanish provinces: Equatorial Region of Spain

Population
420 000 (UN est 1997)

Rate of Change
2.4% (UN est 1995–2000)

Capital City
Malabo

Population of Capital
37 000 (1986)

National Language(s)
Spanish

Gross National Product (US dollars)
330 per capita (1991)

Local Currency
1 franc CFA = 100 centimes

São Tomé and Príncipe

Official Name
Republica Democratica de São Tomé e Príncipe/Democratic Republic of São Tomé and Príncipe

Area
964 sq km

Date of Independence
12 July 1975

Status and Name in Colonial Times
1522–1975 Portuguese colony: São Tomé and Príncipe (also called Cocoa Islands)

Population
117 000 (UN est 1997)

Rate of Change
2.0% (UN est 1995–2000)

Capital City
São Tomé

Population of Capital
43 420 (1991)

National Language(s)
Portuguese; Creole

Gross National Product (US dollars)
350 per capita (1993)

Local Currency
1 dobra = 100 centavos

islands in 1471, they found them uninhabited. The Portuguese monarch assumed administrative responsibility for the island colonies in 1522 after they had become major entrepôts in the African slave trade to the West Indies and the site of productive sugar plantations run by Portuguese criminals and outcasts. Intermarriage between Portuguese settlers and their slave laborers produced a mestizo population which survives to this day. The Angolares, survivors of a wrecked slave ship, still inhabit the southern area of São Tomé.

The islands enjoyed great prosperity during the 16th century, but fell into a slump during the 17th as Portuguese dominance of the slave trade waned. Growing slave exports from the mainland revived the islands' role as entrepôts in the 18th century, and the pattern continued well into the 19th century. After 1860 a boom in cocoa and coffee production on the islands created a new demand for labor, which was supplied at first by the purchase of slaves from the nearby mainland and from the 1870s by contract laborers (*libertos*) from Angola. The *libertos* were treated as slaves once they reached the islands, and in 1908 Britain officially boycotted São Tomé's cocoa in protest of the conditions which the workers suffered at the hands of the planters.

Labor abuses were curbed and the boycott lifted, but conditions soon reverted to their former state. In 1953 the Portuguese governor fired on striking plantation workers, killing nearly 1000 in what is remembered today as the "Batepa Massacre". In 1960 the forerunner of the Movement for the Liberation of São Tomé and Príncipe (MLSTP) was formed at a conference in Ghana, and from their base in Gabon the MLSTP pressed Portugal for independence. Following the fall of the Caetano dictatorship in 1974, Portugal met the MLSTP and arranged for the peaceful transition to independence on 12 July 1975. President Manuel Pinto da Costa, the country's first president, faced a colonial inheritance of widespread poverty, inadequate social facilities and a foundering economy thanks to the departure of the country's 3000 Portuguese planters after independence.

Once in power, the government immediately granted unrealistic wage and hours benefits to the plantation workers, a move that combined with the Portuguese exodus to reduce cocoa exports drastically. The government, aligning itself with the Eastern bloc, nationalized Portuguese plantations without compensation. In 1979 President da Costa banished his prime minister Miguel Trovoada (a well-known moderate) and consolidated his personal power with the help of troops from Angola and Cuba.

Drought in 1982 exacerbated the country's economic problems, while internal unrest fueled a series of coup attempts instigated by opposition groups in exile. These, however, forced the government to begin a reluctant process of political liberalization in order to attract Western aid as part of an economic recovery program. The eventual result was multiparty elections in January 1991 and victory for the opposition Party of Democratic Convergence (PCD). In March 1991 the exiled former prime minister Miguel Trovoada was elected president by a massive majority. However, austerity measures deemed neces-

sary to rebuild the economy led to internal unrest, culminating in an abortive coup in 1995. But Trovoada was reelected president in 1996, and continued his policy of economic reconstruction, with a government of national unity based on multiparty consensus. In the same year São Tomé and Príncipe became one of a commonwealth of five Portuguese-speaking nations committed to mutual cooperation and development. In 1994 Príncipe was granted autonomy with the establishment of a regional assembly and government.

Despite improvements due to IMF and World Bank aid, the economy remains overdependent on cocoa production and therefore vulnerable to market fluctuations.

Congo (RO)

In spite of its position, almost exactly straddling the equator, the Republic of the Congo presents some diversity of landscape and natural environment. This diversity is largely due to the influence of the cold Benguela Current along its coasts and of the anticyclone centered on the island of St Helena. In the north a true equatorial climate predominates, characterized by abundant rainfall (1550 to 2500 millimeters) and dense forest. The south, a savanna region, also has less rainfall (1350 millimeters) and has a long dry cool season from June through September. This geographical diversity determines the distribution of population in that in the southwest, between Brazzaville and the sea, 70 per cent of the total live on 25 per cent of the territory.

The history of the modern Congolese state begins in 1880, when the explorer Pierre Savorgnan de Brazza signed a treaty of friendship with the Makoko Iloo, king of the Teke, which bound the latter to France. The territory of the Congo did not make its appearance until 1886; in 1903 it was given the name Middle Congo (Moyen-Congo), though readjustments of the borders with Cameroon, Ubangi-Shari (Central African Republic) and Gabon continued until just after World War II.

In the Middle Congo, as in the rest of French Equatorial Africa, French colonialism showed itself more primitive than elsewhere in Africa. In 1899 the territory was handed over to 14 concessionary companies, who shared out between them over 220 000 square kilometers and embarked on systematic plundering of the country's natural resources. Despite reforms in 1911, the abuses continued: the construction of the Congo–Océan railroad, according to the grim formula, "cost a man a sleeper." By 1930 the population had been reduced to one-third of its precolonial level. Education was neglected until 1950.

African reaction at first took the form of messianic movements, particularly active in the southern areas. The church founded in 1921 by Simon Kimbangu in the Belgian Congo won many followers here. In 1926 André Matswa founded a French Equatorial Africa Association (Amicale des Originaires de l'Afrique Equatoriale Française), which opposed the colonial regime. The year 1939 saw the appearance of the *kakist* movement

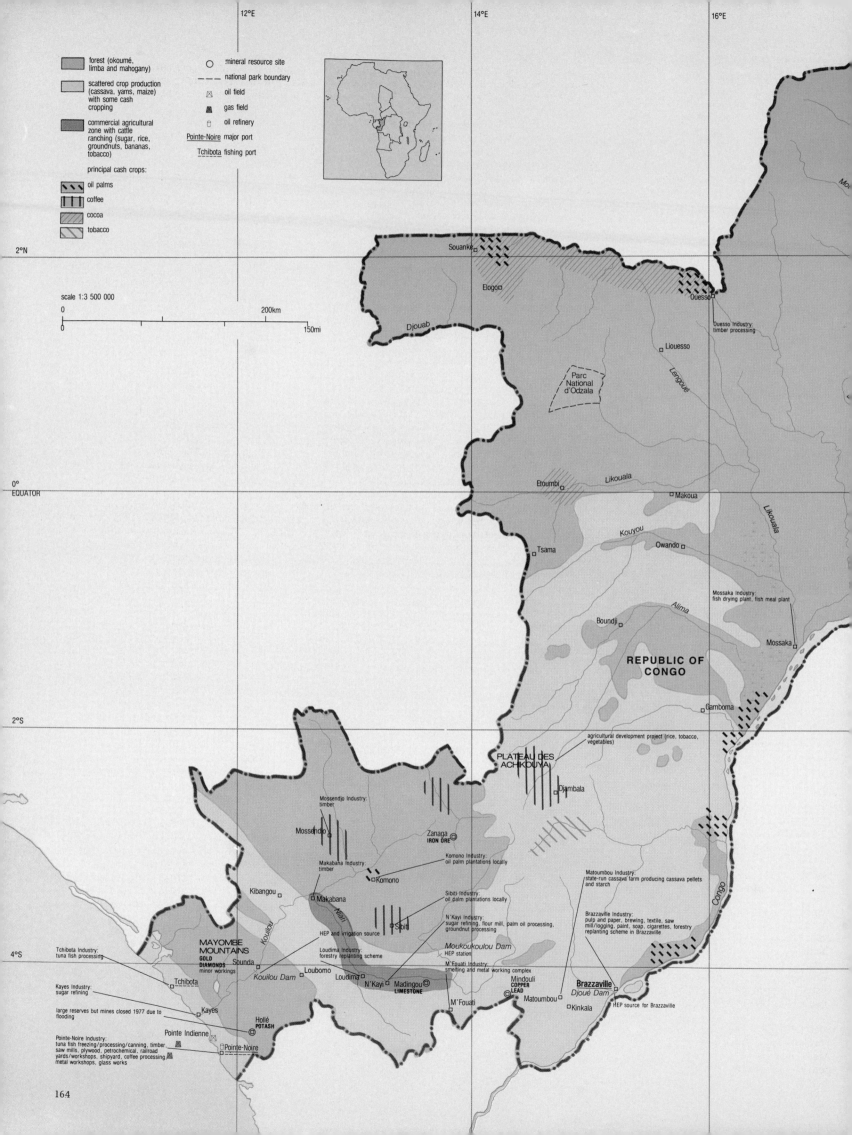

Legend

forest (okoumé, limba and mahogany)

scattered crop production (cassava, yams, maize) with some cash cropping

commercial agricultural zone with cattle ranching (sugar, rice, groundnuts, bananas, tobacco)

○ mineral resource site

- - - national park boundary

⊠ oil field

■ gas field

◻ oil refinery

Pointe-Noire major port

Tchibota fishing port

principal cash crops:

oil palms

coffee

cocoa

tobacco

scale 1:3 500 000

0   200km
0   150mi

2°N

12°E   14°E   16°E

Souanké

Elogo

Djouab

Ouesso

Ouesso Industry: timber processing

Liouesso

Lengoué

Parc National d'Odzala

0°
EQUATOR

Etoumbi

Likouala

Makoua

Kouyou

Likouala

Tsama

Owando

Alima

Mossaka Industry: fish drying plant, fish meal plant

Boundji

Mossaka

REPUBLIC OF CONGO

2°S

Gamboma

agricultural development project (rice, tobacco, vegetables)

PLATEAU DES ACHIKOUYA

Djambala

Mossendjo Industry: timber

Mossendjo

Zanaga
IRON ORE

Komono Industry: oil palm plantations locally

Makabana Industry: timber

Komono

Matoumbou Industry: state-run cassava farm producing cassava pellets and starch

Kibangou

Niari

Makabana

Sibiti Industry: oil palm plantations locally

Sibiti

N'Kayi Industry: sugar refining, flour mill, palm oil processing, groundnut processing

Brazzaville Industry: pulp and paper, brewing, textile, saw mill/logging, paint, soap, cigarettes, forestry replanting scheme in Brazzaville

Kouilou

HEP and irrigation source

Loudima Industry: forestry replanting scheme

Moukoukoulou Dam
HEP station

Congo

4°S

Tchibota Industry: tuna fish processing

MAYOMBE MOUNTAINS
GOLD DIAMONDS minor workings

Sounda

Loubomo

Loudima

N'Kayi

Madingou

M'Fouati Industry: smelting and metal working complex

Mindouli
COPPER LEAD

Brazzaville

Kayes Industry: sugar refining

Kouilou Dam

Djoué Dam

HEP source for Brazzaville

large reserves but mines closed 1977 due to flooding

Tchibota

Kayes

Matoumbou

Kinkala

Pointe-Noire Industry: tuna fish freezing/processing/canning, timber, saw mills, plywood, petrochemical, railroad yards/workshops, shipyard, coffee processing, metal workshops, glass works

Hollé
POTASH

Pointe Indienne

Pointe-Noire

M'Fouati

18°E

2°N

0°
EQUATOR

ondo

Congo (RO)

Official Name
République du Congo

Area
342 000 sq km

Date of Independence
15 Aug 1960

Status and Name in Colonial Times
French colony (one of the four territories of French
Equatorial Africa) with the names French Congo
(1882–86), Congo (1886–1903), Middle Congo
(1903–58); Republic of the Congo (1958–60)

Population
2 745 000 (UN est 1997)

Rate of Change
2.8% (UN est 1995–2000)

Capital City
Brazzaville

Population of Capital
938 000 (1995)

National Language(s)
French; Lingala, Monokutuba

Gross National Product (US dollars)
950 per capita (1993)

Local Currency
1 franc CFA = 100 centimes

inspired by Simon Pierre M'Padi, who claimed to be a successor of Kimbangu. The modern political parties made their appearance after the Brazzaville Conference (1944) which, while condemning the idea of self-government, stimulated a real liberalization of the colonial system. Three parties contended for votes, Jean-Félix Tchicaya's Congolese Progressive Party (PPC), Jacques Opangault's African Socialist Movement (MSA) and Abbé Fulbert Youlou's Democratic Union for the Defense of African Interests (UDDIA). Progress to independence was marked by persistent serious disturbances. After the proclamation of independence (15 August 1960) Abbé Youlou was elected head of state in 1961, but the new regime, moderate and corrupt, soon became very unpopular and was swept away by the popular revolution of the Glorious Three Days (13–15 August 1963). Alphonse Massamba-Débat took over as president.

Far from solving the problems which had appeared under the Youlou regime, this revolution plunged the Congo into a persistent crisis. Personal quarrels, ideological differences, ethnic antagonisms between northerners and southerners, the incoherence of the institutions, and finally the conflict between young and old, were all factors making for instability. The only permanent element was a constant appeal to communist ideology. As early as December 1963 Pascal Lissouba, prime minister in the new government, declared himself in favor of "scientific socialism". In 1964 this was written into the charter of the National Revolutionary Movement (MNR), the only party. In 1970 the Congolese Workers' Party (PCT) replaced the MNR and the country became the People's Republic of Congo. The 1973 constitution confirmed Marxism–Leninism as the basis of the regime. However, from 1963 onwards there were innumerable demotions, plots, political murders and executions. No one was exempt: the spokesman of the extreme Left, Ange Diwara, was murdered in 1973. Marien Ngouabi, head of state since 1968, was assassinated in his turn in 1977, after which several leading figures, including Massamba-Débat, were executed. Colonel Joachim Yhombi-Opango became president, but was replaced in 1979 by Colonel Denis Sassou-Nguesso.

The Congo has large reserves of mineral ores, petroleum and natural gas, and timber exports are also important. However, in the 1970s and 1980s the state-owned enterprises and huge civil service absorbed most of the Congo's earnings; despite petroleum revenues and French and Soviet aid, economic development was slow. Falling oil prices in the 1980s brought the country to crisis point: external debt grew rapidly, and the IMF imposed drastic cuts in spending and privatization as a condition of further aid. Instability and attempted coups continued.

In 1989 Sassou-Nguesso began a process of economic and political reform: political prisoners were released, and in 1990 an extraordinary Congress of the ruling PCT abandoned Marxism–Leninism and took the first steps towards a multiparty constitution. Opposition groups were well represented on a National Conference in 1991, and in 1992 the new constitution was approved in a referendum. In elections for the National Assembly the Pan-African Union for Social Democracy (UPADS) won the most seats, and Pascal Lissouba was elected president.

But the new democracy was short-lived. Shifting alliances, and controversial fresh elections in 1993, with former president Yhombi-Opango becoming prime minister, led to a rapid succession of administrations and worsening unrest. Armed militias were formed on ethnic and political bases, and conflict between these militias and government forces escalated. The government became increasingly repressive, and with the economy devastated the armed forces and state employees went largely unpaid. A new IMF structural adjustment program of austerity added to the unrest. Neither attempts to reconcile the opposing groups, to disarm the militias and to integrate them into the regular forces, nor international mediation, could stop the slide into chaos. In June 1997 Sassou-Nguesso launched his private militia in a full-scale civil war against Lissouba's government. In October Angola sent troops to support Sassou-Nguesso, and the withdrawal of French troops led to his immediate victory.

In January 1998 a National Transitional Council was set up to oversee the process of reconstruction, funded by UN emergency aid.

Congo (DRO)

The Democratic Republic of the Congo (previously Zaïre) is the third largest country on the African continent, encompassing an area four times the size of France. The country's topography is dominated by the Congo river, which rises in the southeast, flows north across the equator, then south again, to empty finally into the Atlantic Ocean some 4700 kilometers later. The Congo drainage basin is rimmed by high mountains in the east and by high plateaus in the north and south. The country's borders were largely set by the Treaty of Berlin in 1885, when western European nations carved up Africa into spheres of influence. These boundaries coincide with natural boundaries (rivers, lakes, divides between drainage basins) except for the southern border with Angola.

Congo (DRO) lies astride the equator between 5° north and 13° south. The climate within three or four degrees of the equator is characterized by constant high temperatures, high humidity and heavy rainfall (1800–2200 millimeters annual average). North and south of this zone the climate becomes tropical, with alternating wet and dry seasons. Depending on the distance from the equator, the dry seasons last from three to six months. They bring cool nights along with warm days; temperatures may drop to 2° or 3° on the high plateau. At the foot of the eastern mountains, which rise to an elevation of more than 5000 meters, the climate is quite temperate. Thanks to its climate, lakes, mountains and national parks, this area is the region most favored by tourists.

Slightly more than half of the country is covered by equatorial rain forest where the warm, humid soil produces tall trees and extremely dense vegetation. The forest, which includes the largest forest reserves in Africa, harbors a great wealth of flora and fauna. The plateau regions of Shaba in the south are savanna grasslands cut by forested river valleys. The lateritic soils of these regions are quickly leached and easily eroded, but with proper care they can produce a great variety of crops. The volcanic soils of the eastern Kivu province are even more fertile, but are losing their fertility.

The country's mainly rural population is concentrated in the east, between the forest and the mountains, and south of the forest that stretches from Matadi near the coast through the capital, Kinshasa, into East Kasai.

WEST CENTRAL AFRICA

Map legend:

equatorial rain forest

scattered crop cultivation (cassava, maize, rice, bananas) and grazing land (cattle, sheep, goats)

principal cash crops:

coffee

oil palms

rubber

cocoa

cotton

○ mineral resource site

--- national park boundary

⊠ oil field

▲ gas field

◘ oil refinery

Inongo major port

Matadi major fishing port

○ tourist center

Map labels:

Bomu

Ubangi

Libenge

Gemena

Bondo

GOLD

Uele

Aketi Industry: oil palm processing

Buta Industry: oil palm processing

Bumba Industry: oil palm processing

Aketi

Buta

HAUT ZAÏRE

Lisala

Bumba

Congo

Maringa

major timber-producing area

Bangwade industry: cocoa project

Lulonga

Basankusu

Lisala Industry: oil palm processing

Basoko

Bangwade

Yangambi

Congo

Kisangani

Mbandaka

Busira

Yangambi Industry: site of major international agricultural research station

Boyoma (Stanley)

Ruki

Boende

Lomela

Tshuapa

Kisangani Industry: vehicle assembly, food processing for surrounding agricultural region, cotton ginning, textile

Ubundu

Inongo

Parc National de la Salonga

DEMOCRATIC REPUBLIC OF CONGO

Kindu

L. Mai Ndombe

Mushie industry: timber plant

Fimi

Kwa

Lukenie

Mushie

Bandundu

Bandundu Industry: oil palm processing

Kasai

Sankuru

Lubefu

Kibombo

Boma Industry: food processing, chemical, growing port

Maluku Industry: iron and steel mill

Kwilu

Ilebo

Kananga Industry: palm oil and palm kernel processing

Banana industry: chemicals, metallurgy

Maluku

Kinshasa

Kwango

Kenge

Kinshasa Industry: vehicle assembly, brewing, shoes, biscuits, flour mill

Kikwit

Luebo

Kananga

Tshela

Seke-Banza

vast HEP complex, phase 1 completed

Mbanza-Ngungu

Kikwit Industry: oil palm processing

Kasai

Lulua

Lomami

Moanda Industry: oil storage depot

Inga Dam

Kimpese Industry: cement

Kimpese

Songololo

Wamba

Tshikapa

Mbuji-Mayi DIAMONDS

Moanda

Boma

Matadi

Kimvula

DIAMONDS

Banana

Matadi Industry: flour mill, food processing, chemical, plastics

Kwilu

Kwango

DIAMONDS

DIAMONDS

Lubilash

L. Upemba

Kamina

Kasai

Sandoa

Lubudi Industry: cement

Bukama

Luena COAL

Lubu...

Malonga

Likasi Industry: major sulfuric acid plant, copper smelting

HEP source

Delcommune Dam

MANGANESE

MANGANESE

Kolwezi Industry: copper smelting

COPPER

COPPER

Kolwezi

COPPER

The mines in this region yield mainly copper, but also the associated metals of radium, cadmium, silver, zinc, cobalt, lead and germanium.

Congo (DRO)

Official Name
Democratic Republic of the Congo

Area
2 345 409 sq km

Date of Independence
30 June 1960

Status and Name in Colonial Times
1884–1907 Congo Free State (Belgian)
1907–60 Belgian colony: Belgian Congo

Population
48 040 000 (UN est 1997)

Rate of Change
2.5% (UN est 1995–2000)

Capital City
Kinshasa

Population of Capital
4 055 313 (1994)

National Language(s)
French; Lingala; Swahili, Tshiluba, Kongo

Gross National Product (US dollars)
220 per capita (1991)

Local Currency
1 zaïre = 100 makuta

scale 1:7 500 000

0 — 400km
0 — 300mi

Although more than 250 languages are spoken, only four are dominant in addition to French, the official language. Lingala is spoken mainly in Kinshasa and in Equator province, Kikongo in the provinces of Lower Congo and Bandundu, Tshiluba in East and West Kasai provinces, and Swahili in Upper Congo, Kivu and Shaba.

Linguistic and archaeological evidence indicates that the ancestors of the Congolese began migrating into areas east and south of the rain forest some 1500 years ago. Originating from the Niger river basin, these early pioneers arrived with a knowledge of horticulture and metalworking techniques, which enabled them to supplant any possible predecessors. Since most Congolese today speak Bantu languages, it is thought that these pioneers were also Bantu speakers. In addition to Bantu languages some Sudanese and Nilotic languages are widely spoken in the north and northeast of the country.

Although most of these people remained politically decentralized until the colonial era, a number of kingdoms arose in the southern savanna region during the past 500 years. Located near the mouth of the Congo river, the Kongo kingdom dominated that area for several centuries. It established diplomatic relations with the Portuguese in the 16th century, but had fallen by the 18th century. The largest kingdoms at the time of the 19th-century European exploration were the Kuba, Lunda and Luba kingdoms, which all engaged in long-distance trade.

In the 1870s King Léopold of the Belgians became interested in central Africa and succeeded in gaining personal title to control the so-called Congo Free State at the Berlin Conference of 1884. He used the territory for commercial purposes but was forced to cede it to the Belgian government in 1908. Thus the Belgian Congo came into being. The Belgian colonial administration concentrated on exploiting the natural resources of the territory by granting huge concessions to private companies for mining copper, diamonds, manganese and iron, and for establishing plantations to produce palm oil, coffee, tea, cotton and other cash crops on territory which they simply appropriated. Troops were sent to quell any local resistance to Belgian rule. The Belgian government set up a paternalistic administration to maintain order, collect taxes and assure an adequate supply of labor for the private companies. Political unrest in the late 1950s forced Belgium to grant independence precipitately in 1960.

In the general elections that preceded independence, Patrice Lumumba was elected prime minister and Joseph Kasavubu became chief of state. When Katanga (later Shaba) and part of Kasai tried to secede in the months following independence, United Nations troops were called in to restore order. For some years the struggle for power among major politicians prevented any government from establishing firm control. While the problem of the secessions was resolved in 1963, other armed insurrections occurred throughout the 1960s. Lumumba was assassinated in 1961 and was afterwards adopted as a nationalist hero.

In 1965 General Joseph Mobutu seized power in a coup. In 1967, after bringing political and military stability to the country with the help of foreign mercenaries, Mobutu created a new political party – the Popular Revolutionary Movement (MPR) – as part of a new single-party constitution; he was elected president in 1970. In 1971, to help erase apparent ties to the colonial past, Mobutu changed the name of the country from Congo to Zaïre and renamed himself Mobutu Sese Seko. Zaïre continued to maintain close economic ties with Belgium and its Western allies, most notably Britain, France and the USA, who furnished most of its foreign aid and capital investment in return for exports of commodities. These allies gave military assistance to the regime in 1977 and 1978, after exiles from the southern Shaba province returned from Angola in an attempt to topple Mobutu's government.

For some 20 years Mobutu governed essentially by decree and personal patronage, presiding over a centralized regime that, for all its claims to African authenticity, bore a surprising resemblance to King Léopold's Congo Free State. There were repeated reports of human-rights violations: Mobutu responded positively to each of them by reshuffling his government, yet in practice the situation remained little changed.

In April 1990 Mobutu promised to introduce multiparty democracy, but soon retracted his promise, sparking off student demonstrations that were brutally suppressed: 100 or so students were massacred at Lubumbashi University alone, while others fled the country in terror. Western powers responded by threatening to withdraw foreign aid – and began to do so as it became clear that Mobutu had misappropriated large amounts of this aid for his personal gain. Faced with economic crisis, he conceded to demands both at home and abroad for democratic reforms, but by ingenious political tactics he managed to draw out the negotiations over several years, thwarting all efforts to bring about change.

Meanwhile the country plunged deeper into anarchy as disaster followed disaster. The Zaïrian currency collapsed, and looting and arson became commonplace as unpaid soldiers rebelled. In 1993 Shaba province, in response to the brutal suppression of local ethnic unrest, proclaimed itself autonomous under its former name of Katanga. Some eastern provinces considered following suit, although here the situation was further complicated by the arrival from neighboring Rwanda of a million or so Hutu refugees, some of whom threatened the Zaïrian Tutsis.

This in turn led to the development of armed rebel movements, allegedly supported by Tutsis in Rwanda and Burundi, which in 1996 united to form the Alliance of Democratic Forces for the Liberation of Congo-Zaïre (AFDL) under the leadership of Laurent-Désiré Kabila. What had begun as a regional movement soon escalated into a national rebellion with the aim of overthrowing the Mobutu regime. As AFDL forces swept through Zaïre, the ailing Mobutu refused to resign despite mounting international pressure. But in May 1997 he fled the country, the AFDL entered Kinshasa without meeting any resistance, and Kabila declared himself president of the renamed Democratic Republic of the Congo.

With the country in ruins, the Kabila regime faces an enormous task of reconstruc-

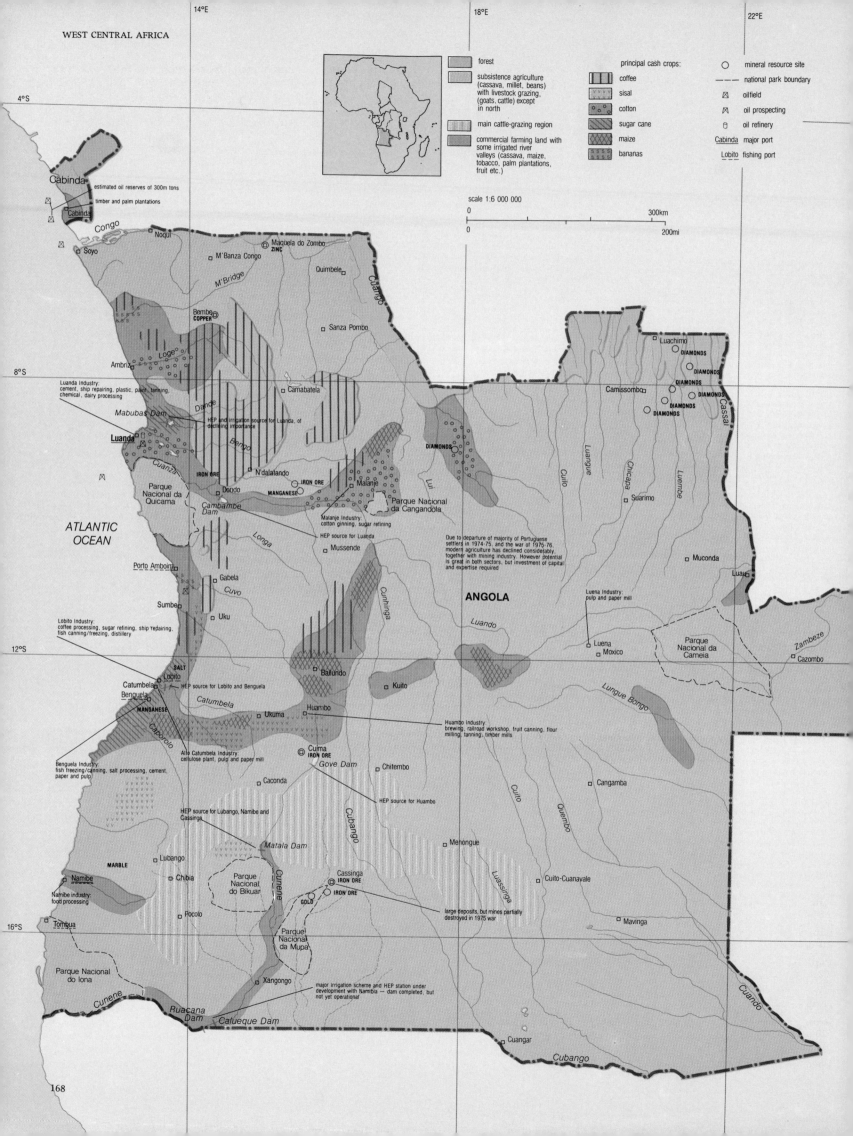

14°E   18°E   22°E

4°S

forest

subsistence agriculture
(cassava, millet, beans)
with livestock grazing,
(goats, cattle) except
in north

main cattle-grazing region

commercial farming land with
some irrigated river
valleys (cassava, maize,
tobacco, palm plantations,
fruit etc.)

principal cash crops:

coffee

sisal

cotton

sugar cane

maize

bananas

○ mineral resource site

---- national park boundary

oilfield

oil prospecting

oil refinery

Cabinda major port

Lobito fishing port

scale 1:6 000 000

0   300km

0   200mi

Cabinda

estimated oil reserves of 300m tons

timber and palm plantations

Cabinda

Congo

Noqui

Soyo

M'Banza Congo

Maquela do Zombo
ZINC

Quimbele

M'Bridge

Cuango

8°S

Sanza Pombo

Bembe
COPPER

Loge

Luachimo

DIAMONDS

Ambriz

DIAMONDS

Camabatela

DIAMONDS

Camissombo

DIAMONDS

DIAMONDS

Luanda Industry:
cement, ship repairing, plastic, paint, tanning,
chemical, dairy processing

DIAMONDS

Dande

Mabubas Dam

HEP and irrigation source for Luanda, of
declining importance

Luanda

Bengo

DIAMONDS

Cuilo

Chicapa

Suarimo

Luembe

N'dalatando

IRON ORE

Cuanza

IRON ORE

Malanje

Lui

Parque
Nacional da
Quicama

Dondo

MANGANESE

Parque Nacional
da Cangandola

Cambambe
Dam

Malanje Industry:
cotton ginning, sugar refining

Muconda

ATLANTIC
OCEAN

Longa

HEP source for Luanda

Luau

Mussende

Due to departure of majority of Portuguese
settlers in 1974-75, and the war of 1975-76,
modern agriculture has declined considerably,
together with mining industry. However potential
is great in both sectors, but investment of capital
and expertise required

ANGOLA

Porto Amboim

Cuvo

Gabela

Cunhinga

Luena Industry:
pulp and paper mill

Sumbe

Uku

Luando

Zambeze

Lobito Industry:
coffee processing, sugar refining, ship repairing,
fish canning/freezing, distillery

Luena

Moxico

12°S

Parque
Nacional da
Cameia

SALT

Lobito

HEP source for Lobito and Benguela

Balundo

Cazombo

Catumbela

Benguela

Kuito

Lungue Bongo

MANGANESE

Catumbela

Caporolo

Ukuma

Huambo

Huambo Industry:
brewing, railroad workshop, fruit canning, flour
milling, tanning, timber mills

Benguela Industry:
fish freezing/canning, salt processing, cement,
paper and pulp

Alto Catumbela Industry:
cellulose plant, pulp and paper mill

Cuima
IRON ORE

Gove Dam

Chitembo

Cuito

Cangamba

HEP source for Huambo

Caconda

Quembo

HEP source for Lubango, Namibe and
Cassinga

Matala Dam

Cubango

Menongue

Luassinga

MARBLE

Lubango

Namibe

Chibia

Parque
Nacional
do Bikuar

Cassinga
IRON ORE

Cuito-Cuanavale

Namibe industry:
food processing

Cunene

GOLD

IRON ORE

large deposits, but mines partially
destroyed in 1975 war

Mavinga

Pocolo

16°S

Tombua

Parque
Nacional
da Mupa

Parque Nacional
do Iona

Xangongo

Cunene

major irrigation scheme and HEP station under
development with Namibia — dam completed, but
not yet operational

Cuando

Ruacana
Dam

Calueque Dam

Cuangar

Cubango

tion. Yet Congo (DRO) is potentially one of the richest nations in Africa, thanks to its vast natural resources, particularly its minerals, especially copper, and hydroelectric potential. During the colonial period the Belgian administration concentrated on developing mining and agricultural production to create raw materials for the export market. By favoring the establishment of large plantations, and by forcing peasant farmers to plant a minimum acreage of food and cash crops each year, the administration was able to make the colony a net exporter of food during the 1950s.

Angola

The center of Angola consists of a plateau undulating between 1300 and 2000 meters, which is separated from the 1600-kilometer Atlantic shoreline by a sterile coastal plain ranging from 50 to 160 kilometers in width. In the north and east the plateau tilts down towards the Congo and Zambezi basins, and the river boundaries with the Democratic Republic of the Congo (formerly Zaïre) and Zambia. In the south the border with Namibia links the Cunene and Cubango rivers. The north has higher rainfall and a few pockets of

12°S

Angola

Official Name
República de Angola

Area
1 246 700 sq km

Date of Independence
11 Nov 1975

Status and Name in Colonial Times
Portuguese colony; 1972–75 overseas province: Angola

Population
11 570 000 (UN est 1997)

Rate of Change
2.8% (UN est 1995–2000)

Capital City
Luanda

Population of Capital
2 250 000 (1995)

National Language(s)
Portuguese; Umbundu, Kimbundu

Gross National Product (US dollars)
620 per capita (1991)

Local Currency
1 new kwanza = 100 lwei

dense tropical forest. Much of the south is acacia savanna. The average annual temperature at thè capital, Luanda, is 23°.

The farming populations of Angola began to evolve sophisticated forms of royal government in the later Middle Ages. The 15th-century kings built their power around agricultural ceremonies at rain shrines and in important iron-smelting and salt-mining districts. In the more southerly parts of the country cattle wealth was important. In the north the famous kingdom of Kongo had a local textile industry and national shell currency.

From 1493 Angola's agrarian economy was modified by an increasingly lucrative market for agricultural slave labor. In the next 400 years two million or more Angolans were bought or captured by Portuguese, French, British, Brazilian and other ocean merchants. Portugal established a small colony in Angola as a base for its operations and garrisoned it with half a dozen forts, a few hundred slave-soldiers and assorted convict settlers. Despite 19th-century efforts to suppress the traffic, captives continued to be sold at Angolan ports till about 1910.

Efforts to build a tropical colonial economy to replace slaving were at first unsuccessful. A coffee boom in the 1890s was short-lived but coffee returned in the mid-20th century to become Angola's major export crop. Production rose to over 200 000 tons by the 1970s and Angola was the world's fourth largest producer. The major coffee zones were Uige and Kwanza. The rise in coffee prices led to a rapid growth of the plantation sector and the partial elimination of the peasant sector.

Local government activity was primarily concerned with recruiting labor at below market cost and with raising African rural taxes to be funneled into development schemes for the benefit of Europeans. Government neglect was partially compensated for by mission health and education services: Baptists in the north, Methodists in the Kwanza regions, Congregationalists in the Benguela plateau and Spiritans in the south all provided some social services. Secondary schooling remained negligible till the 1960s and even then mainly white.

Before 1940 Angola was popularly considered fit only for convict settlement. After 1950 coffee prosperity brought in free colonists. The government sought to settle them as peasants but most became urban artisans, petty officials and above all retail traders. By 1970 the immigrant population probably surpassed 300 000, almost all of them of Portuguese or Cape Verdian origin.

The influx of settlers, the alienation of coffee land and the lack of educational opportunity in the 1950s led to severe African disaffection under the dictatorship of Salazar. By 1961 local despair was fueled by black political success in the rest of Africa, and mass rebellion led to a series of large-scale massacres. However, Portugal managed to hold on to Angola for a further 13 years of sporadic war.

In 1974 Portugal prepared to withdraw from Angola, and various regional and international powers intervened to serve their own interests. The discovery of offshore oil near the Cabinda enclave to the north attracted world business interests, while civil war developed between the country's three

nationalist parties, each of which was supported by a foreign invasion. The first was by Zaïre in support of the National Front for the Liberation of Angola (FNLA), a mainly northern party. The second was by South Africa, which supported and armed the Union for the Total Independence of Angola (UNITA), a party based in Huambo which dominated in the highlands. The third invasion was by airlifted Cubans in support of the Popular Movement for the Liberation of Angola (MPLA), a Soviet-backed Marxist party that, being based in Luanda, formed the *de facto* government. American mercenaries supported all three parties, while American business retained firm control of the oil wells, which provided sufficient revenue to postpone economic collapse.

Factionalism in the MPLA resulted in a coup attempt in 1977, after which it was purged and renamed the MPLA–PT (MPLA–Workers' Party). By now nearly all the white settlers had left, leaving an enormous skills shortage, while fighting and bombing had wrecked the infrastructure, cutting off the railroad link to Zambia and hampering the production and distribution of food. Massive unemployment in the towns had put paid to the high economic expectations associated with independence.

The FNLA surrendered to the MPLA–PT in 1984, but UNITA stepped up its guerrilla campaign as part of a South African counter-offensive against the South West Africa People's Organization (SWAPO), an MPLA-supported guerrilla movement fighting to free Namibia. With the approach of Namibian independence (granted in 1990) came the opportunity for peace negotiations between the Angolan factions – a process further assisted by the collapse of Soviet Communism, which led the MPLA–PT to abandon their Marxist views and promise multiparty elections by 1992.

The elections, held on schedule in September 1992, gave a narrow victory to the MPLA (which had resumed its original name) and to its leader José Eduardo dos Santos. But the results were sufficiently inconclusive to enable UNITA leader Jonas Savimbi to accuse the government of electoral fraud. Hostilities were quickly renewed and the country was again engulfed in war. For years all the efforts of the United Nations and other mediators, including the new South Africa, were to no avail. UNITA, now thought to be supported by dissident factions in Zaïre, made it virtually impossible even for the World Aid Program to bring food to some two million starving displaced people (about one-fifth of the population). In 1994, a growing separatist movement in the oil-rich Cabinda enclave added yet another dimension to the war, the nature of which had so far discouraged potential donors of foreign aid.

In 1995 dos Santos held out the prospect of a government of national unity in return for the incorporation of UNITA forces within the national army. April 1997 finally saw the inauguration of a government of national reconciliation. Although Savimbi's absence (he had been offered a vice-presidency) provided grounds for continuing unease, there was now a chance for a nation decimated by decades of war to begin the slow and painful process of reconstruction.

NORTHEAST AFRICA

Geographically this is a region of immense contrasts. Those countries that makeup what is often called the "Horn" of Africa – Djibouti, Somalia and parts of eastern Ethiopia – share the Islamic faith and a way of life as nomadic herders struggling to survive in a harsh and challenging environment. Culturally all these peoples have much in common, though they have lived as separated and often warring tribes.

Sudan, Eritrea and Ethiopia present great contrasts, within themselves and with the Horn. Like the sahel countries to its west, Sudan is a bridge between northern Islamic Arab Africa and black "pagan" Africa. Many of its southern inhabitants are now Christians. In the highlands of Ethiopia live peoples who are an exception to most generalizations about Africa. Their ancient church links them to Egypt, and through centuries of literacy the history of the kingdoms of the Ethiopian mountains has been preserved as in few other places in Africa.

Most borders in Africa are arbitrary, and nowhere more so than here. On all sides peoples' natural affinities are cut by artificial colonial boundaries, and this continues to be the source of great misery and suffering. The Somali-speaking peoples are found also in Ethiopia and northern Kenya, and their struggle to unite goes on. In southern Ethiopia and southern Sudan linguistic groups straddle the borders with Kenya and Uganda. The Nile flowing north through Sudan links that country with Egypt. Perhaps the Islamic faith is the strongest unifying force across all these very different nations.

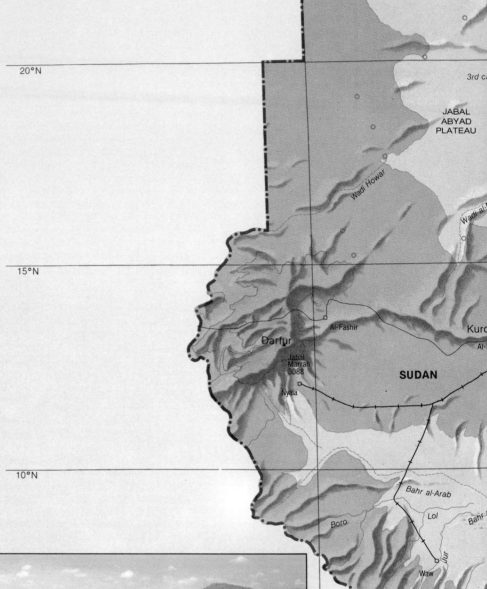

The Nile (seen here at the Tissisat Falls, on the Blue Nile, in Ethiopia) is the link between Mediterranean Africa and the deep interior, and the search for its source drew many Western explorers into Africa. Although cut by cataracts, it provides a highway where roads are still few or nonexistent, and despite the barrier of the Sudd swamps, the river is often the only route into the far south of Sudan.

Right In the Ethiopian highlands south of Asmara the village of Aruba, near Adigrat, is shown below carefully cultivated hillsides, which must be utilized to the full in mountainous country where every scrap of soil is valuable.

Below The Nuba inhabit the hills of southern Kordofan province in the north of Sudan, an area of the country that is otherwise entirely Arab and Islamic. Peoples of this group follow a traditional way of life based on crop-raising and herding. They practice an animistic form of religion that observes a series of agricultural rituals and sacrificial offerings to ancestral spirits. Here, men of a village prepare to take part in a funeral dance.

Below right Mogadishu, with a present population of 1 000 000, is an ancient Muslim city. It was visited by the North African traveler Ibn Battuta in the 14th century, when its influence was beginning to decline. In the colonial period it was the capital of Italian Somalia and its arthitecture retains a distinctly Italian flavor.

Far right The civil war that raged in Somalia in the late 1980s and early 1990s gave rise to a major humanitarian crisis. Refugees congregated in camps, such as this one at Bihen, and soon fell victim to hunger and insanitary conditions. Aid efforts after the war ended in 1991 were hampered by continuing political instability and factional fighting.

Below The Faron Mosque in Khartoum, capital of Sudan, lying at the junction of the White and Blue Niles. The city developed from an Egyptian garrison founded in the 1820s, and in 1885 became infamous in Europe as the scene of the death of General Gordon at the hands of the Mahdi's followers.

Below center The Dinka speakers of an Eastern Sudanic language, are transhumant herders in the southern Sudan. From dry-season river camps they move in the rains to permanent settlements where they grow food crops like millets. At their ceremonies, and in daily life, Dinka wear only body paint.

Below right A priest of the ancient Ethiopian Church, in liturgical dress, holds two of the processional crosses which are a special feature of that church's regalia. They show Greek influence, recalling the founding of the church by missionaries from Constantinople.

Center In many parts of northeast Africa cultivation is still by digging stick or hoe, but in some areas, as in this part of Ethiopia near Asmara, oxen are used to plow the stony soil. The chief cereal crops grown are wheat and barley

Sudan

Sudan, Africa's largest country, stretches southwards from Egypt for 2000 kilometers and westwards from the Red Sea for 1500 kilometers. Adjacent countries include Eritrea, Ethiopia, Kenya, Uganda, Congo (DRO), Central African Republic, Chad and Libya.

Lying mostly below 1000 meters, Sudan has relatively uniform relief, broken by volcanic uplands in the west, the south-central Nuba mountains, the edges of the East African highlands and the Red Sea hills. Over most of

Eritrea

Official Name
State of Eritrea

Area
121 320 sq km

Date of Independence
24 May 1993

Status and Name in Colonial Times
1890–1941 Italian colony; 1941–52 under British protection; 1952 federated with Ethiopia; 1962 incorporated into Ethiopia

Population
3 409 000 (UN est 1997)

Rate of change
3.6% (UN est 1995–2000)

Capital City
Asmara

Population of Capital
367 000 (1991)

National Language(s)
Arabic, Tigrinya

Gross National Product (US dollars)
not available

Local Currency
1 Ethiopian birr = 100 cents

Sudan

Official Name
Jamhuryat es-Sudan
Republic of the Sudan

Area
2 505 813 sq km

Date of Independence
1 Jan 1956

Status and Name in Colonial Times
1898–1955 Anglo-Egyptian Condominium: Sudan

Population
27 898 000 (UN est 1997)

Rate of Change
2.1% (UN est 1995–2000)

Capital City
Khartoum (El Khartum)

Population of Capital
476 218 (1983)

National Language(s)
Arabic; English

Gross National Product (US dollars)
450 per capita (1991)

Local Currency
1 Sudanese pound = 100 piastres = 1000 millièmes

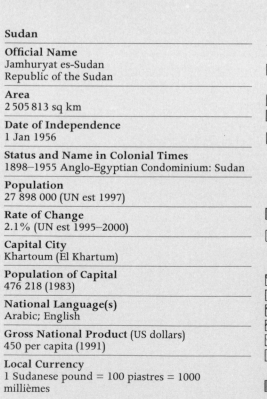

desert — nomadic herding (goats, sheep) and unproductive land

forest (eucalyptus, hardwood)

rainland (Sudan) (cotton, tobacco, coffee, groundnuts)

scattered grazing and crop cultivation

Sudan:	Ethiopia:
sorghum,	teff,
maize,	barley,
millet,	wheat,
groundnuts	maize,
	sorghum

cereal cultivation and cattle grazing

irrigated land — cereals, fruit, vegetables, tobacco

principal crops:
Sudan:
cotton
sesame
groundnuts
gum arabic
sugar
rice
Ethiopia:
coffee

cotton
sugar
tropical fruits

oasis
mineral resource site
oil refinery
oil pipeline
oilfield
oil prospecting

Sawakin major port
Mesewa major fishing port

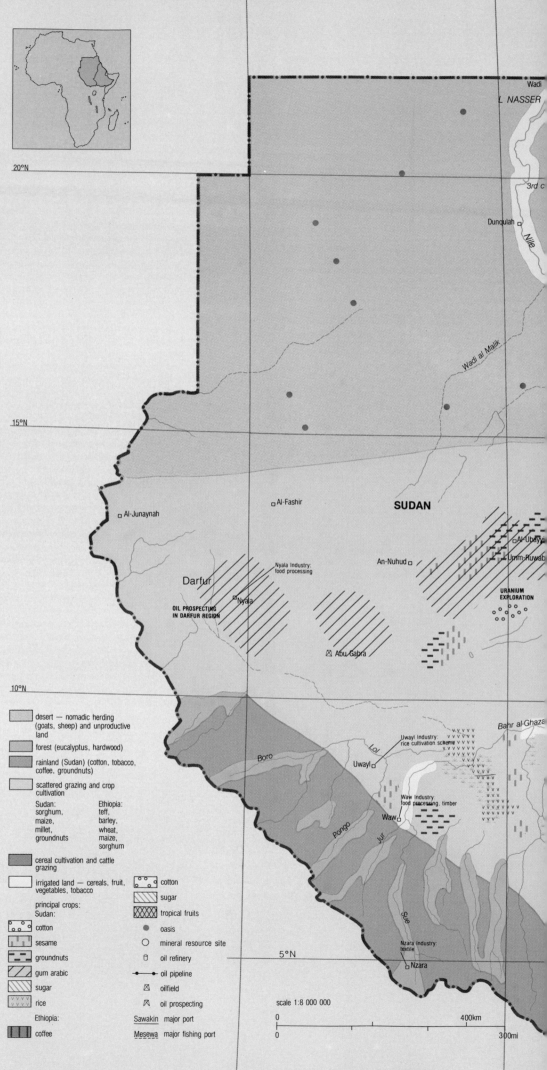

scale 1:8 000 000

0   400km

0   300mi

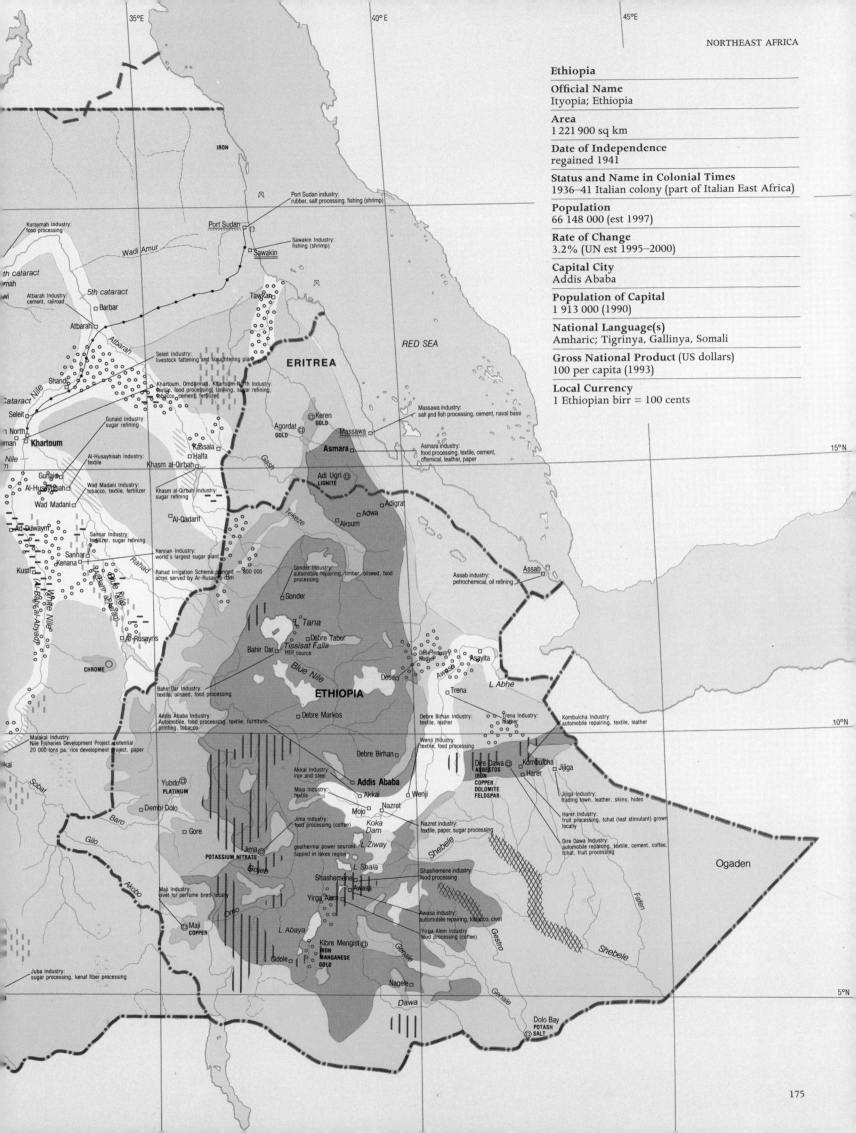

Ethiopia

Official Name
Ityopia; Ethiopia

Area
1 221 900 sq km

Date of Independence
regained 1941

Status and Name in Colonial Times
1936–41 Italian colony (part of Italian East Africa)

Population
66 148 000 (est 1997)

Rate of Change
3.2% (UN est 1995–2000)

Capital City
Addis Ababa

Population of Capital
1 913 000 (1990)

National Language(s)
Amharic; Tigrinya, Gallinya, Somali

Gross National Product (US dollars)
100 per capita (1993)

Local Currency
1 Ethiopian birr = 100 cents

IRON

Kuraymah Industry:
food processing

Wadi Amur

th cataract
mah
wi

Port Sudan industry:
rubber, salt processing, fishing (shrimp)

Port Sudan

Sawakin

Sawakin Industry:
fishing (shrimp)

RED SEA

5th cataract

Atbarah Industry:
cement, railroad

Barbar

Atbarah

Tawkar

Atbarah

Seleit Industry:
livestock fattening and slaughtering plant

ERITREA

Cataract
Seleit
Shandi

Khartoum, Omdurman, Khartoum North Industry:
textile, food processing, tanning, sugar refining,
tobacco, cement, fertilizer

Massawa industry:
salt and fish processing, cement, naval base

Keren
GOLD

Massawa

h North
man
Nile

Khartoum

Gunaid Industry:
sugar refining

Agordat
GOLD

Asmara industry:
food processing, textile, cement,
chemical, leather, paper

Kassala

Asmara

Al-Husayhisah Industry:
textile

Halfa

Adi Ugri
LIGNITE

Gunaid
Al-Husayhisah

Khasm al-Qirbah

Wad Madani Industry:
tobacco, textile, fertilizer

Adigrat

Gesh

Wad Madani

Al-Qadarif

Tekeze

Adwa

Aksum

Ad Duwaym

Sannar Industry:
fertilizer, sugar refining

Kennan Industry:
world's largest sugar plant

Khasm al-Qirbah Industry:
sugar refining

Gonder Industry:
automobile repairing, timber, oilseed, food
processing

Assab industry:
petrochemical, oil refining

Assab

Sannar
Kenana

Kusti

Rahad Irrigation Scheme planned — 300 000
acres served by Ar-Rusayris dam

Gonder

Al-Rusayris

L Tana

Debre Tabor

CHROME

Tissisat Falls
HEP source

Bahir Dar

Dese Industry:
leather

Asayita

CHROME

Blue Nile

Dese

Awash

L Abhe

Bahir Dar Industry:
textile, oilseed, food processing

ETHIOPIA

Trena

Malakal Industry:
Nile Fisheries Development Project: potential
20 000 tons pa, rice development project, paper

Addis Ababa Industry:
Automobile, food processing, textile, furniture,
printing, tobacco

Debre Markos

Debre Birhan Industry:
textile, leather

Trena Industry:
textile, leather

Kombulcha Industry:
automobile repairing, textile, leather

kal

Sobat

Wenji Industry:
textile, food processing

Dire Dawa
ASBESTOS
IRON
COPPER
DOLOMITE
FELDSPAR

Kombulcha

Jijiga

Yubdo
PLATINUM

Akkai Industry:
iron and steel

Debre Birhan

Harer

Jijiga Industry:
trading town, leather, skins, hides

Addis Ababa

Mojo Industry:
textile

Akkai

Wenji

Dembi Dolo

Nazret

Harer Industry:
fruit processing, tchat (leaf stimulant) grown
locally

Baro

Gore

Jima Industry:
food processing (coffee)

Mojo

Nazret industry:
textile, paper, sugar processing

Dire Dawa Industry:
automobile repairing, textile, cement, coffee,
tchat, fruit processing

Gilo

Koka
Dam

Shebele

Jima

geothermal power sources
tapped in lakes region

L Ziway

Akobo

POTASSIUM NITRATE

Gojeb

L Shala

Maji Industry:
civet for perfume bred locally

Shashemene

Awasa

Shashemene industry:
food processing

Ogaden

Omo

Yirga Alem

Awasa industry:
automobile repairing, tobacco, civet

Fafen

Maji
COPPER

L Abaya

Yirga Alem Industry:
food processing (coffee)

Gestro

Shebele

Gidole

Kibre Mengist
IRON
MANGANESE
GOLD

Genale

Juba Industry:
sugar processing, kenaf fiber processing

Nagele

Genale

Dawa

Dolo Bay
POTASH
SALT

the country a tropical continental climate prevails. In the south it merges into an equatorial rainy climate; in the north, into desert. Vegetation correlates generally with rainfall to produce a transition from desert, to semidesert and steppe scrub, to short- and tall-grass savannas, to flooded grasslands, forest savannas and mist forests. Draining north-wards, the Nile and its tributaries, such as the Sobat, Blue Nile and Atbarah, bring vital water from East Africa and Ethiopia. In the south the annual floods create a vast swamp, the Sudd.

Sudan is lightly populated. Half the people live in 14 per cent of the country: around the capital, the White and Blue Niles and in the south. Over 85 per cent live in rural areas, although urbanization is increasing. The rural populace consists mostly of village-dwelling farmers, but nomadic and seminomadic pastoralists occupy wide areas. The Khartoum conurbation dominates Sudanese economic, social, political and cultural life.

There are at least 56 separate ethnic groups, subdivided into 597 subgroups, and 115 languages. However, most northern peoples speak Arabic and accept an Arabic cultural heritage. Other northern ethnic groups include Nubians, Beja, Funj, Nuba and Fur. Dinka, Nuer, Shilluk and other Nilotic peoples straddle the Nile in the south. Heterogeneous peoples of Equatoria and western Bahr Al-Ghazal relate linguistically and culturally to larger groups in adjacent countries; most prominent are the Azande. Southerners speak local languages, but use Arabic as a lingua franca. Northern Sudan is predominantly Muslim and two-thirds of all Sudanese practice Islam. Most southerners adhere to traditional beliefs and practices; about 4 per cent, mainly southerners, are Christian.

Only along the Nile, where successive kingdoms contacted external civilizations, is a continuous Sudanese history known. Sequestered from the north by the Sudd, equatorial Sudanese lived in tribal isolation, which until the 20th century was only interrupted by explorers and slave raiders. Somewhat less remote, Darfur usually remained independent of outside control and did not maintain close relations with the Nile valley until the 20th century.

Pharaonic Egypt effectively controlled the riverine north (Cush) from 1530 BC until the Meroïtic kingdom (c. 750 BC–350 AD) achieved periods of independent central government. Three Christian kingdoms succeeded Meroë and survived Arab penetration until the establishment of the Islamic sultanate of the Funj in 1504. Thereafter, the loose federation of tribes ruled by the Funj dynasty dominated much of north-central Sudan. In 1821 Ottoman Egypt brought Sudan under Turco-Egyptian rule, which lasted until 1881 when the Sudanese revolted under Muhamad Ahmad, the Mahdi. The theocratic Mahdist state survived only until 1898 when it fell to Anglo-Egyptian conquerors.

British colonial rule was established under a nominal Anglo-Egyptian condominium. Gradually the entire country was subdued and southern and western appendages were incorporated. A coherent administration was established, a social infrastructure begun and an externally oriented commercial base laid. Sudanese nationalists, especially after World War II, pressed Britain for independence,

finally attained on 1 January 1956.

After a brief period of parliamentary rule (1956–58) the army established a military dictatorship (1958–64). Another period of ineffectual parliamentary rule (1964–69) was followed by renewed military domination. The continuing north–south conflict, centering around southern opposition to northern economic neglect and political hegemony, dominates Sudanese politics.

In 1971 southern rebels united under General Joseph Lagu, and won autonomy under the Addis Ababa Agreement in 1972. There followed a brief period of economic growth and a flurry of major development projects funded by IMF loans and foreign aid. However, with little central planning and widespread corruption, the results were disappointing. As President Nimeiri's support fell away he turned to the fundamentalist Muslim Brotherhood for help. In 1983 Sudan's laws were revised to meet the requirements of Islamic law, and Nimeiri divided the south into its original three provinces, effectively ending the Addis Ababa Agreement. Army mutineers joined with discontented southerners to form the Sudanese People's Liberation Army (SPLA). Attempts to crush the rebels exacerbated famine in the south, and there was growing discontent in the north. In 1985 Nimeiri was deposed in a bloodless military coup.

Three years later a second coup brought Lieutenant General Omar Hassan Ahmad al-Bashir and the Revolutionary Command Council (RCC) to power – and with them the Muslim Brotherhood. Bashir crushed dissent, restored Islamic law, and pressed the war in the south with renewed vigor. Economic decline was accelerated by Sudan's deteriorating relations with the international community. There were problems with Egypt, Ethiopia, Uganda, Chad and Libya over borders, refugees and dissident movements. Sudan backed Iraq in the 1991 Gulf War. In 1993 the IMF declared Sudan an "uncooperative state", and the USA listed it as a supporter of international terrorism.

As the situation in the south grew ever more desperate, the Khartoum government deliberately blocked relief efforts. A ceasefire in 1994 was rejected by the SPLA, and in 1995 Sudan was implicated in the attempted assassination of Egypt's President Husni Mubarak. 1996 saw the first elections since Bashir came to power, apparently giving him a clear victory. Relations with neighboring countries remained uneasy, despite an agreement securing the borders with Chad and the Central African Republic, while a peace treaty with the SPLA was ignored by one of its two factions. By 1998 a million and a half people had died, and as conflict escalated along the Ugandan border thousands faced famine.

Sudan's economy depends on trade and on agriculture, which employs around 80 per cent of the workforce. Subsistence farming is the norm in most areas, and livestock is ubiquitous. Traditional and mechanized farming of millet, peanuts and sesame coexists with the collection of gum arabic and nomadic herding of cattle, sheep, goats and camels. In recent years, agriculture has suffered from reduced rainfall, locusts, and flooding.

Industry is mainly confined to food production, though textiles, cement and petro-

leum refining are also important. An inadequate transport network has hindered economic development. The economy as a whole has suffered from conflict, instability, and very high inflation. It has also been crippled by heavy foreign debt (sometimes exceeding gross domestic product) and huge arrears. Poor relations with neighboring states and with the wider economic community have damaged prospects for trade.

Ethiopia

Northeast Africa's most populous country, Ethiopia, has long stood as a predominantly Christian society occupying protecting highlands. Its distinctive national identity, despite great cultural variation, may be attributed to a long history of political independence.

A massive complex of mountains and plateaus, dissected by a deep rift valley and surrounded by marginal lowlands, dominates the physical geography of what is now a completely landlocked country. The Rift Valley, bifurcating the highlands into western and eastern sectors, contains a chain of lakes. Although deeply entrenched rivers radiate from central heights in all directions, the principal drainage is to the Nile basin by the Sobat, Blue Nile and Tekeze rivers.

Climate and vegetation reflect the great variations in altitude. The hot lowlands include deserts and steppes around the foot of the highlands and reach up valleys and plateau slopes to 1500 meters. Above lies a cooler, moister subtropical belt extending up to 2400–2700 meters. This would, under natural conditions, be well forested, but instead contains pastures and fields. Above this is a still wetter temperate zone of high mountains, largely covered by grassland. Rainfall is concentrated into a main summer season, with some areas having minor rains in later winter.

Favored as an agricultural environment, the central highlands have the greatest population densities. About 90 per cent of Ethiopia's population is rural, comprising mostly farmers, who live in scattered family compounds and villages. The remainder reside in the capital Addis Ababa, and in highland commercial towns like Dire Dawa, Harer, and Gonder.

Ethnically Ethiopia is a composite of over 70 groups speaking nearly 100 languages. The dominating Amhara and the Tigre occupy the central and northern highlands respectively; Galla primarily inhabit the subtropical central and southern highlands; Somalis reside in the southeast; and there are scattered Bantu and Nilotic groups. Most Amhara and Tigre and some Galla are Ethiopian Orthodox Christians, but most Galla, Somalis and others who inhabit marginal reaches are Muslims. Many others practice traditional religions.

In some form Ethiopia has had a continuous national existence for 2000 years. Descendants of Arabian Semites established an empire at Aksum in the northeast in the 3rd century BC. Converted to Christianity, the Aksumite empire withstood Islamic expansions after the 9th century, but disintegrated before the 11th century. For almost a millennium incessant conflict between Christian and Muslim princes plunged Ethiopia into anarchical political fragmentation. The empire broke up into small kingdoms in the 1600s and the ensuing decentralization and civil war lasted until the mid-19th century.

Beginning in 1855, the related historical processes of political reunification, territorial expansion and resistance to Egyptian, Sudanese and European encroachments operated intermittently to reestablish the Ethiopian empire. Attempts were made after 1889 by Emperor Menelik II to modernize and regain lost provinces, culminating in the recognition of Ethiopian autonomy by regional and European powers. Emperor Haile Selassie's early reforms and modernization were interrupted by the Italian occupation of 1935–41. Then in 1952 the United Nations allowed the controversial federation of the formerly Italian Eritrea with Ethiopia. In 1960 Haile Selassie incorporated it into the empire. By the mid-1960s Eritrean resistance had transformed into a nationalist movement. Throughout the 1960s internal political opposition to Haile Selassie's rule grew, an abortive coup, student unrest and labor strikes weakening his political power by the end of the decade.

The emperor was overthrown by the army in 1974, and in 1975 the military abolished the empire and founded a socialist state, nationalizing industry, housing and land (which demotivated the peasant farmers). After seizing power, the ruling military council, the Derg, engaged in devastating power struggles out of which Lieutenant Colonel Mengistu Haile Mariam emerged paramount. The Derg found itself fighting with Somalia over Ogaden, with secessionists in Eritrea, and with rebels in Tigray; equally damaging was the failure of its land reforms during a disastrous cycle of drought and famine in the 1970s and 1980s. The collapse of the Soviet empire removed Mengistu's last prop.

In 1991 he was overthrown by a rebel coalition, the Ethiopian People's Revolutionary Democratic Front (EPRDF), which recognized Eritrea's independence in 1993. In 1995 a new federal constitution decentralized power into regions divided on ethnic lines. Elections were held in 1994 and 1995, but were largely boycotted by opposition parties. Meles Zenawi, the former president, became prime minister and head of government, working with a council of ministers reflecting Ethiopia's ethnic balance. In a move towards a free-market economy, state-owned businesses are being gradually privatized. However, the new government has made little or no progress in bringing members of the Mengistu regime accused of human-rights violations to trial.

Relations with the Sudan deteriorated after an attempt in 1995 to assassinate Egyptian President Mubarak in Addis Ababa, apparently with Sudanese connivance. At the same time Ethiopia claimed the use of Nile waters originating in its territory. In 1996, following an assassination attempt on the defense minister, reportedly by an extremist Islamic organization, Ethiopian aircraft attacked its bases in Somalia.

Ethiopia shows many of the characteristics of underdevelopment, such as a predominant subsistence sector, limited industry, immature infrastructure, little domestic capital and undiversified exports. Agriculture and livestock contribute half of gross domestic prod-

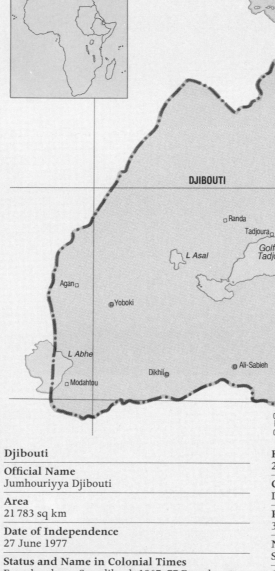

desert (pastoral nomadism - meats, hides, skins)

oasis – irrigation yielding vegetables, dates

oil refinery

Djibouti major port

Djibouti industry: international port, liquid oxygen, meat processing, market gardening, ship repairing

scale 1: 2 000 000

Djibouti

Official Name
Jumhouriyya Djibouti

Area
21 783 sq km

Date of Independence
27 June 1977

Status and Name in Colonial Times
French colony: Somaliland; 1967–77 French Territory of the Afars and Issas

Population
634 000 (UN est 1997)

Rate of Change
2.6% (UN est 1995–2000)

Capital City
Djibouti

Population of Capital
383 000 (1995)

National Language(s)
Somali, Afar, French; Arabic

Gross National Product (US dollars)
1000 per capita (1991)

Local Currency
1 Djibouti franc = 100 centimes

uct and support 90 per cent of the people. Agriculture is almost entirely rainfed and is primarily devoted to subsistence crops – wheat, barley, sorghum, millet, maize, ensete and teff. Coffee is by far the most valuable export crop, contributing some 60 per cent of export earnings, followed by oilseeds and pulses. The crop has frequently suffered from drought and civil war – and when cultivation has been possible, the results have often been disappointing. Peasant productivity has been hindered by simple technology, inadequate transport and limited credit. Ethiopia has large herds, especially cattle, but derives limited commercial benefit from them.

Manufacturing is little developed; processing of agricultural products, particularly cotton, is the main industrial activity, followed by light consumer goods. Most industry is located in the Addis Ababa region. Mineral deposits are either little known or little mined. Some hydroelectric power is generated. Relief handicaps transportation, leaving extensive areas inaccessible to railroads and all-weather, or even seasonal, roads – and the road system, like the water supply, suffered badly during the civil war. Major roads radi-

ate from Addis Ababa to the provincial centers, but mostly not to the borders. A railroad links Addis Ababa to Djibouti, which handles most foreign trade.

Eritrea

Eritrea extends some 1000 kilometers along the southwestern coastline of the Red Sea. It is bounded by Ethiopia to the south, Djibouti to the southeast, and the Sudan to the north.

Eritrea is dominated by the northern section of the Ethiopian plateau, typically 2000 meters high. To the west, lowlands clothed in acacia savanna and open woodland slope gradually towards the Sudan, while to the east the highlands fall away steeply towards an arid coastal plain; parts of the southeastern interior are below sea level and extremely hot. Rainfall is more plentiful in the west, where it falls mainly in summer. The eastern highlands and coastal plain receive far less rain, and it arrives in winter and spring.

The main local languages are Tigre and Tigrinya, both derived from the same Semitic language but mutually unintelligible. Tigrinya speakers (mostly Tigrays, who are Ethiopian Orthodox Christians) live as agriculturalists in the southern highlands and form about half of the country's population. Tigre speakers (mostly Muslim pastoralists) live in the north, and in the eastern and western lowlands. Other groups include Bilin speakers and Arabic-speaking Rashaida nomads in the north, Afar nomads, Saho pastoralists and Beja pastoralists in the western plain. About 15 per cent of the population live in towns – mainly in the capital Asmara.

Loosely attached to Ethiopia from the 12th century, Eritrea was occupied successively by the Ottoman Turks, Egypt and Italy. After brief resistance, Ethiopia recognized Italy's claims in 1889 and Eritrea became an Italian colony in 1890. In 1941 British forces drove the Italians out, and in 1952 the UN joined Eritrea with Ethiopia in a federation. In 1962 Ethiopia annexed it fully, and Eritrean secessionist groups began fighting for independence, which was eventually recognized in 1993 by the new Ethiopian administration.

Pending a new constitution, interim power rests with the president, elected by the 90 members of the National Assembly of the Eritrean People's Liberation Front (EPLF). Relations with Ethiopia are good, but in 1994 Eritrea severed diplomatic relations with Sudan following an attempted infiltration by Muslim fundamentalists. 1995 saw conflict with the Yemen over the Hanish islands, and 1996 brought a border dispute with Djibouti.

Eritrea is a poor country, largely dependent on subsistence farming, foreign aid, and remittances from its nationals working overseas. It has suffered civil war, drought, famine, and loss of infrastructure. However, offshore oil, fishing, and tourism offer opportunities for growth.

Djibouti

Bordering Ethiopia, Eritrea and Somalia, Djibouti is strategically situated at the southern entrance to the Red Sea. The physical core of the country consists of a triangular depression, part of the East African rift system, and is marked by a complex fragmented relief of volcanic plateaus, sunken plains and lakes. Djibouti is mostly desert. Temperatures are high, rainfall low and erratic, and lakes salty. Vegetation comprises seasonal grasses, thorn trees and scattered palms.

The human geography is dominated by the capital, Djibouti, with its port and rail linkage to Addis Ababa. The population is almost evenly divided between Somalis (Issas) and Afars, with a small number of Arabs and Europeans. Migrations of nomads swell or diminish the totals. The remainder live in Djibouti, or in small towns or oases. Most Djiboutis are Muslim.

French interest in this coast dates from 1859 and by 1896 the boundaries of French Somaliland were established. France's friendly relations with Ethiopia enabled the construction of the railroad from 1897 to 1917. The colony won increasing autonomy after 1957, achieving independence in 1977.

Djibouti is heavily dependent on foreign assistance (though less so than it was). Its economy is mainly based on trade through the port of Djibouti. Elsewhere the population largely subsists off animals, although small-scale agriculture exists in the oases.

The new nation's politics have been dominated by tensions between Issas and Afars. Ethnic balance has been maintained in the cabinet and between president and prime minister, but Issas have predominated in the administration. Hassan Gouled Aptidon (an Issa) was the sole candidate in the 1981 presidential elections, and his Rassemblement Populaire pour le Progrès (RPP) was declared the sole legal party before legislative elections in 1982. Aptidon was re-elected in 1987 and 1993. In 1991 three Afar movements united in the Front pour la Restauration de l'Unité et de la Democratie (FRUD) and launched an armed insurrection. In 1994 a peace settlement gave FRUD legal status; soon afterwards divisions appeared within it.

Somalia

Comprising a triangular wedge of dry, unproductive land, Somalia is located in the Horn of Africa, where it fronts the Indian Ocean and Gulf of Aden and borders Djibouti, Ethiopia and Kenya. Somalia's poverty, irredentism and strategic position dominate its geography.

In the north and northeast some terrain is mountainous, but most consists of a low, featureless plateau tilting gently southeastwards from Ethiopia. The prevailing climate features monsoon winds, hot temperatures and scarce, irregular rainfall. Droughts recur. Although low everywhere, in general rainfall increases southwards, where annual totals usually exceed 330 millimeters. Shrub bush and grass comprise the primary savanna cover, which is thicker in higher areas and in the south. A shortage of surface water presents difficulties everywhere, but towards the south the Shabeelle and Jubba rivers have a regular flow.

A low population density reflects a largely nomadic or seminomadic populace. Settled agricultural and urban components make up only a quarter of the total. With the exception of Hargeysa, all major towns are situated on the coast. The capital, Mogadishu, is by far the largest city. The Somalis, who constitute 98 per cent of the population, speak a Cushitic language, are relatively homogeneous in religion (Islam) and culture, but are often split by clan loyalties. Strongly nationalistic, Somalis have striven to incorporate their numerous kinsmen, cut off by artificial boundaries, into a single nation-state.

The Somalis first penetrated the northern coast about 1000 AD, and for the next 900 years they spasmodically pushed southwards to the Tana river, in the process driving out their Bantu and Galla predecessors. Despite some integration, the essential process was the establishment of a single cultural nation in continuous occupation of a vast territory extending westward to Ethiopia.

Imperialist European interests mingled competitively in the last quarter of the 19th century when France staked out its claim around Djibouti, Britain assumed control of the northern regions, and Italy established a colony in the southern regions. Italy attempted unsuccessfully to colonize and develop its territory agriculturally. Britain largely ignored its protectorate until 1941, when it took control of Italian Somaliland and extended administrative and public services. In 1949 the United Nations entrusted its ex-territory back to Italy for ten years in order to prepare it for independence.

In response to Somali nationalism and despite a weak economic base and separate colonial legacies, the Italian and British territories joined together on 1 July 1960 as the independent Somali Republic. Compounding the difficult transition to unification, the new government pressed on its neighbors the principle of self-determination for all Somalis. Eventually, widespread corruption, divisive politics and other problems provoked a bloodless military coup on 21 October 1969. The Supreme Revolutionary Council renamed the country the Somali Democratic Republic and appointed Major General Mohamed Siad Barre as head of a socialist state, underpinned by close ties with the Soviet Union.

Siad worked to suppress tribalism and aimed to unify all Somali peoples. The Ogaden region of Ethiopia was largely populated by Somalis, and in 1977 Siad invaded, intending to annex this territory. His forces were driven back, largely thanks to Soviet support for Ethiopia, and the fighting degenerated into civil war between clans. In 1991 Siad was deposed by a rebel confederation.

Drought and conflict wrecked Somalia's agricultural production, and in 1992 a UN peacekeeping force, led by the United States, landed in Somalia to restore order. They failed to disarm the contending clans, and in 1993 24 Pakistani peacekeepers were killed by troops of the Somali National Alliance (SNA) under the command of General Muhammad Farah Aydid. As a result, the UN force found itself a part of the conflict. After a series of phased withdrawals, the force was finally evacuated in 1995, but the fighting was far from over.

In the northwest, Mohamed Hagi Ibrahim Egal established a breakaway "Somaliland Republic" based on the old boundaries of British Somaliland. It achieved a measure of stability, though it had little support from the international community. Meanwhile Aydid's chief rival Muhammad Ali Mahdi, leader of the Somali Salvation Alliance (SSA), claimed, like Aydid, to be the true president.

Somalia has few resources: its economy and its small industrial base have been all but destroyed by years of civil war, and agriculture has suffered from repeated droughts and severe floods. Livestock normally yield some 40 per cent of Somalia's gross domestic product: crops, by contrast, yield only 10 per cent, with bananas forming the chief export crop. Until order is restored, however, there would seem to be little chance of recovery.

In 1996 Aydid was killed in battle, and his place was taken by his son Hussein Aydid. At the end of 1997, after a series of meetings, the factions signed the Cairo Declaration aimed at setting up a federal government. By then some 300 000 had died in the fighting. However, the meeting between Aydid and Ali Mahdi planned for February 1998 was postponed. Meanwhile heavy rains and severe flooding devastated the south, leaving thousands dead and some 200 000 homeless.

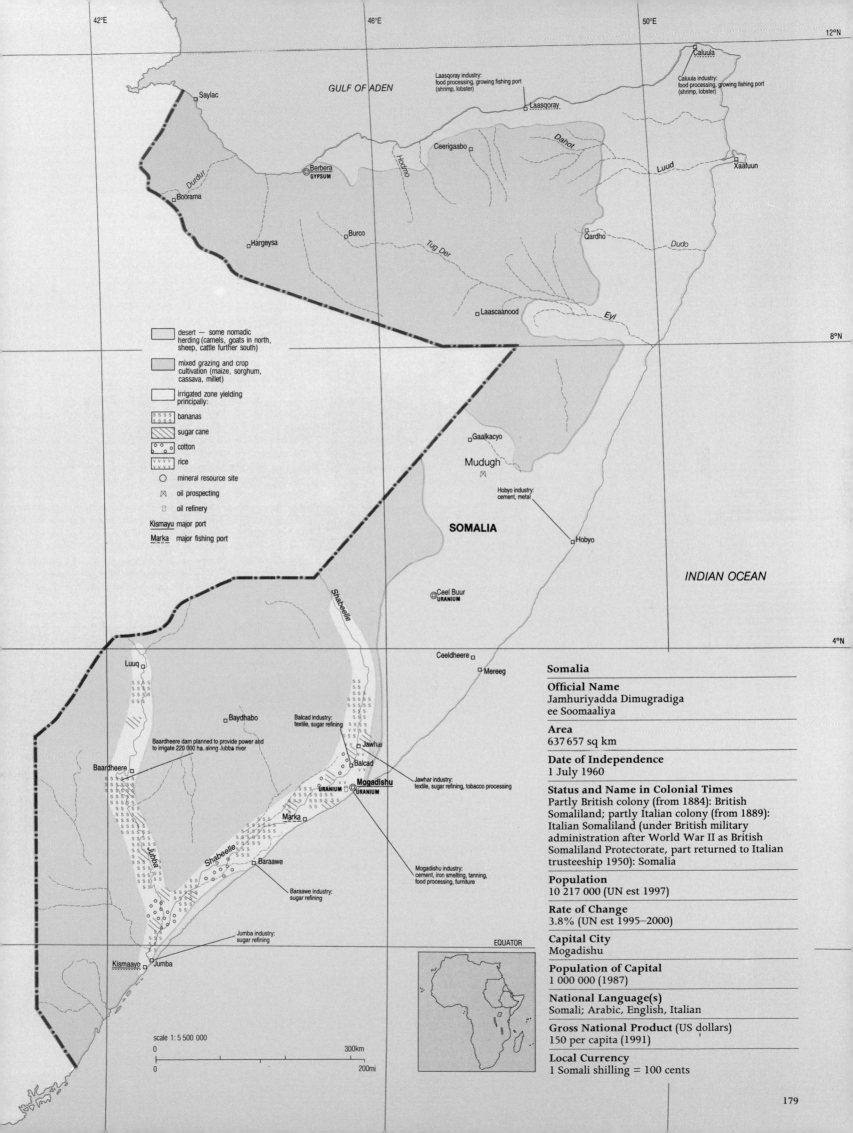

GULF OF ADEN

Saylac

Laasqoray industry:
food processing, growing fishing port
(shrimp, lobster)

Caluula

Caluula industry:
food processing, growing fishing port
(shrimp, lobster)

Laasqoray

Durdur

Berbera
GYPSUM

Boorama

Hoolmo

Ceerigaabo

Dahot

Luud

Xaafuun

Hargeysa

Burco

Tug Der

Qardho

Dudo

Laascaanood

Eyl

desert — some nomadic
herding (camels, goats in north,
sheep, cattle further south)

mixed grazing and crop
cultivation (maize, sorghum,
cassava, millet)

irrigated zone yielding
principally:

S S S S
S S S S   bananas

sugar cane

o o o o
o o o o   cotton

v v v v
v v v v   rice

O   mineral resource site

⋈   oil prospecting

⌂   oil refinery

Kismayu   major port

Marka   major fishing port

Gaalkacyo

Mudugh   ⋈

Hobyo industry:
cement, metal

SOMALIA

Hobyo

INDIAN OCEAN

Ceel Buur
URANIUM

Ceeldheere

Mereeg

Luuq

Shabeelle

Baydhabo

Balcad industry:
textile, sugar refining

Baardheere dam planned to provide power and
to irrigate 220 000 ha. along Jubba river

Baardheere

Jawhar

Balcad

Jawhar industry:
textile, sugar refining, tobacco processing

URANIUM

Mogadishu
URANIUM

Marka

Mogadishu industry:
cement, iron smelting, tanning,
food processing, furniture

Shabeelle

Baraawe

Jubba

Baraawe industry:
sugar refining

Jumba industry:
sugar refining

Kismaayo   Jumba

EQUATOR

scale 1:5 500 000

0   300km

0   200mi

Somalia

Official Name
Jamhuriyadda Dimugradiga
ee Soomaaliya

Area
637 657 sq km

Date of Independence
1 July 1960

Status and Name in Colonial Times
Partly British colony (from 1884): British
Somaliland; partly Italian colony (from 1889):
Italian Somaliland (under British military
administration after World War II as British
Somaliland Protectorate, part returned to Italian
trusteeship 1950): Somalia

Population
10 217 000 (UN est 1997)

Rate of Change
3.8% (UN est 1995–2000)

Capital City
Mogadishu

Population of Capital
1 000 000 (1987)

National Language(s)
Somali; Arabic, English, Italian

Gross National Product (US dollars)
150 per capita (1991)

Local Currency
1 Somali shilling = 100 cents

179

EAST AFRICA

Above left Zanzibar, an island off the East African coast, was the Western traveler's doorway into the interior and an important slave market throughout the 19th century. From the 1820s the Omani dynasty made it their capital, and from Zanzibar Islamic religion and culture and the Swahili language spread inland.

Above Tourists relaxing at a safari lodge at Tsavo East National Park in Kenya. These facilities are generally built, as here, overlooking watering-holes or other sites where animals are likely to gather. East African states have developed flourishing tourist industries based on wildlife viewing and photography, now that big-game hunting has been outlawed.

Left From the Persian Gulf and India the northeast monsoon takes craft to East Africa from November to January, and from April the southwest monsoon brings them north again. For many centuries small craft – dhows – have traded between the Gulf and the East African ports, and even smaller craft along the coast itself.

East Africa has been seen as a political and a geographical region throughout the colonial period. From the end of World War I to the granting of independence in the early 1960s Kenya, Uganda Tanganyika and Zanzibar were all under forms of British colonial rule. English and Swahili were taught and spoken to a greater or lesser degree throughout this region.

The two tiny but densely populated nations of Rwanda and Burundi might by some be considered to have closer links with West Central Africa. Under German rule (like Tanganyika) to the end of the Great War, they were then through Belgian trusteeship associated with the Congo, and through the use of the French language with the other Francophone nations. But their geographical ties with the British territories were strong, as were their links with the other interlacustrine kingdoms of southern Uganda and western Tanganyika, with their royal courts and almost feudal organization. Over most of the region societies were organized on a much smaller scale. Agriculturalists of the highlands and cattle keepers of the high grasslands alike settled disputes and celebrated rituals under the presidency of councils of elders, without any leader who could be called a chief.

Throughout much of Kenya, and down the Rift Valley into central Tanzania, are a number of ethnic groups which, although speaking totally different languages, share a number of distinctive cultural traits. The most notable are the initiation of both young men and girls through ceremonies including circumcision for males and a comparable physical operation on females. The circumcised males enter a named age group and formerly acted as warriors.

A last distinctive feature of East Africa has been the long-standing presence of Arabs along its coasts and offshore islands, and their influence in spreading Islamic faith and culture. The very recent settlement of merchants and craftsmen from the Indian subcontinent, and farmers and businessmen from Europe, has also left a distinctive mark on East Africa which is enduring into the period of independence.

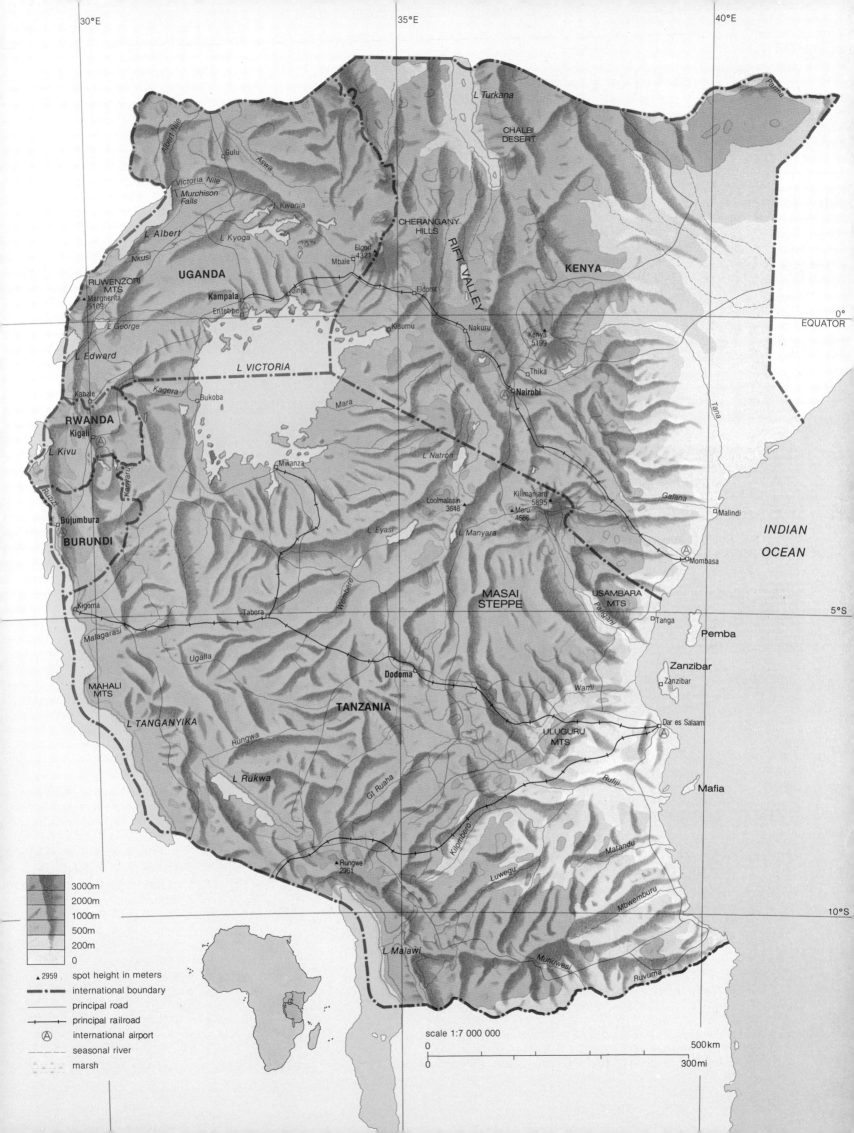

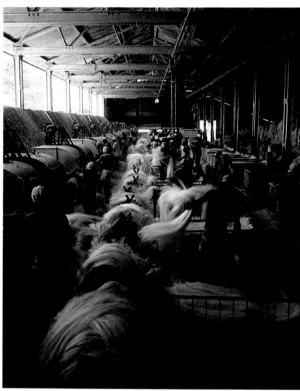

Top left In a number of archaeological sites along the East African coast there are evidences of trading connections between the coast and China via the so-called silk routes. At Kunduchi, 25 kilometers north of Dar es Salaam, this 18th-century pillar-tomb features embedded Chinese plates of the late Ming period.

Top right The cattle-keeping Maasai are famous as warriors of the East African grasslands. From the early period of European settlement some worked as herders on cattle ranches. Usually pictured in ocher cloth and pigtails, these men have added a raincoat and bowler.

Above Sisal has long been an important export crop in Kenya and especially in Tanzania. During the colonial period it was chiefly grown and processed on plantations owned by European firms, but African farmers grew hedgerow sisal, which was widely used by African women for baskets and mats.

Right Somali nomads have been moving south into Kenya for many years and the northeast corner of Kenya is inhabited almost exclusively by Somali. Their mode of life in Kenya is, as in Somalia, centered around the wells and water holes where their stock, often including camels, are watered.

Far left Tea has been a valuable cash crop in Kenya for many years but it was formerly grown only on large estates. In recent years African farmers in the higher altitudes of districts like Murang'a and Nyeri have been growing tea on smallholdings and sending it for processing in cooperatively owned tea factories.

Left One of the great tragedies in recent times was the inter-ethnic violence between Hutus and Tutsis that engulfed the states of Rwanda and Burundi in 1994-95. Here, refugees leave Ruhengeri camp, passing a pile of abandoned weapons.

Kenya

Kenya's origins as a modern nation lie in its existence as a colonial territory. There were no preexisting kingdoms uniting the very disparate African societies. The Sultan of Zanzibar exercised some control over the Arab-dominated cities along the coast, but this scarcely extended even to the Bantu-speaking Africans of the coastal interior.

The physical geography of Kenya has always been a dominating factor, with altitude more important than the equatorial latitude. Outside the narrow coastal strip there is a wide belt of thorn-tree savanna, game country, which in the north becomes semidesert. In the south the land rises gradually, and the mountains of central Kenya have their base at about 1600 meters. Here, around Lake Victoria to the west, and along the coastal strip rainfall is sufficient for fairly intensive agriculture, limited in the highlands by the altitude. Elsewhere subsistence pastoralism is all that is possible. Given this situation, communities have over the centuries competed for the fertile islands in an arid sea.

Kenya had been an area of migration long before the European incursion, and peoples of very diverse linguistic and ethnic origins met and mingled in the highlands and around the lakes. Later comers have displaced and to some extent assimilated previous populations. In the highlands these seem to have been Cushitic-speaking peoples, for later societies speaking both Bantu and Nilotic languages exhibit a number of markedly Cushitic traits (as cycling age sets). All these societies were organized politically on a small scale, with very localized authorities. But in the 19th century there were areas where religious leaders, or successful long-distance traders, or war leaders were beginning to extend their influence and build up a wider authority. The colonial intrusion cut short this process, and migration, as for instance of Somali tribes from the northeast, was also limited or halted.

British interest in Kenya proceeded out of an earlier involvement with Zanzibar and the coastal ports, her later involvement with Uganda and the necessity of limiting German territorial ambitions. The building of the Uganda railroad (completed to Kisumu 1904) and the related arrival of white settlers – farmers and businessmen – and of Indian artisans and traders laid the scene for the complicated interactions and competing ambitions that marked colonial Kenya. The areas most desirable to Africans were also those coveted by the newcomers. The Indian migrants were legally prevented from becoming landowners (outside very strict limits) but large areas of agricultural land were alienated for white farms and plantations, and the pastoral Maasai were forcibly moved to allow room for European-owned ranches.

The small-scale African societies were not equipped to offer massive resistance to the incomers, but the degree of force needed for "pacification," and the time it took, were considerable. Many of the agricultural peoples, especially the Kikuyu, already suffering from land shortage which losses to white farmers only intensified, took work as laborers and squatters on European farms. Many more, again largely from the agricultural peoples, attended the new schools opened by Christian missionaries, and obtained education which opened up some avenues of employment in the new society. Others, especially the pastoralists, were able to continue their traditional way of life with relatively little change.

White settlers and Indians soon demanded a share in the government, and by the 1920s some African groups were also making political claims. Among the Kikuyu and Luo, societies were formed which acted as a focus for an enlarged sense of ethnic identity. In 1929 the Kikuyu Central Association sent a representative to Britain to present their land claims to the Colonial Office. His name was Jomo Kenyatta and he remained there, on and off, for nearly 20 years.

Earlier, in 1923, the British government dashed the hopes of white settlers for internal self-government by declaring that "Kenya is an African territory" and that "the interests of the African natives must be paramount." It was largely the need to curb Indian claims that meant that European aspirations also had to be limited. Africans were not represented in the Legislative Assembly until 1944, when one African-nominated member was appointed.

This was too little, too late. Land and labor problems, rising population and rising expectations, serious land erosion, urban unemployment, the intransigence of white settler opinion and the "petty apartheid" they imposed combined to bring matters to a head. Jomo Kenyatta had returned in 1947 and became president of the Kenya African Union (KAU), but sections of the Kikuyu were not prepared to work slowly for constitutional change. Violence erupted in the early 1950s, and in 1952 the government declared a state of emergency which was not finally lifted till 1960. A few Europeans and Asians were killed, but the main victims were Kikuyu: thousands died in what became a civil war. Besides those killed by the security forces, thousands more were detained. The roots of the conflict seem to have lain in internal landholding rivalries, and in their determination to regain land alienated to whites. Kenyatta and other leaders of the KAU were tried and convicted for managing the movement, known as Mau Mau. But Kenyatta's involvement has been questioned, and after his release in 1961 he proved an intelligent and moderate leader.

Kenya achieved independence in 1963, and Kenyatta became prime minister. A year later, when a republic was declared, he became president, and was twice reelected, remaining in office until his death. However, towards the end of Kenyatta's presidency, elections were confined to candidates from the ruling Kenya African National Union (KANU) party. Two leading politicians were murdered, and others suffered suspicious deaths.

When Kenyatta died in 1978, his vice-president, Daniel arap Moi, was sworn in as president and later duly elected according to the constitution. In 1982 Kenya was officially declared a one-party state. Press censorship and political detentions followed, triggering a coup attempt in which hundreds died. Since then hundreds of members of opposition groups have been attacked, imprisoned, tortured and murdered. Under pressure from aid donors, Moi conducted, and won, multiparty elections in 1992; but there was little progress towards true democracy. Moi's promises of reform, and his finance minister's campaign against corruption, brought dividends in 1996: Kenya received around $836 million in loans to encourage stability before the 1997 election, and Moi arranged cooperation and assistance from China and Iran. The election itself was chaotic, with evidence of bribery and intimidation, making Moi's victory questionable. Constitutionally this should be his last term, but his sons are also actively involved in politics.

In 1998 Kenya suffered a series of disasters, with floods paralyzing much of the decaying road network, an epidemic of Rift Valley fever and a plague of locusts. There was also ethnic violence in the Rift Valley.

Relations with surrounding countries remain uncertain. In 1988 Kenya and Sudan accused one another of helping rebel factions, and in 1989 a dispute over wildlife poaching arose with Somalia. In January 1996 Kenya agreed joint action with Uganda and Tanzania on social and economic cooperation – but later in the year the Kenyan authorities alleged that the Ugandan government was supporting attempts to subvert Moi's administration.

After independence Kenya was initially stable, with its diversified agriculture and industry, and a valuable tourist industry. Drought, famine and political unrest have, however, led to serious economic problems, although Western investment continues.

L VICTORIA

Kenya

Official Name Djumhuri ya Kenya/Kenya

Area 582 600 sq km

Date of Independence 12 Dec 1963

Status and Name in Colonial Times
1895–1920 British colony and protectorate: East Africa Protectorate; 1920–63 crown colony and protectorate: Kenya

Population
28 414 000 (UN est 1997)

Rate of Change 2.2% (UN est 1995–2000)

Capital City Nairobi

Population of Capital
1 758 900 (1989)

National language(s) Swahili; English

National Product (US dollars)
270 per capita (est 1993)

Local Currency
1 Kenya shilling = 100 cents

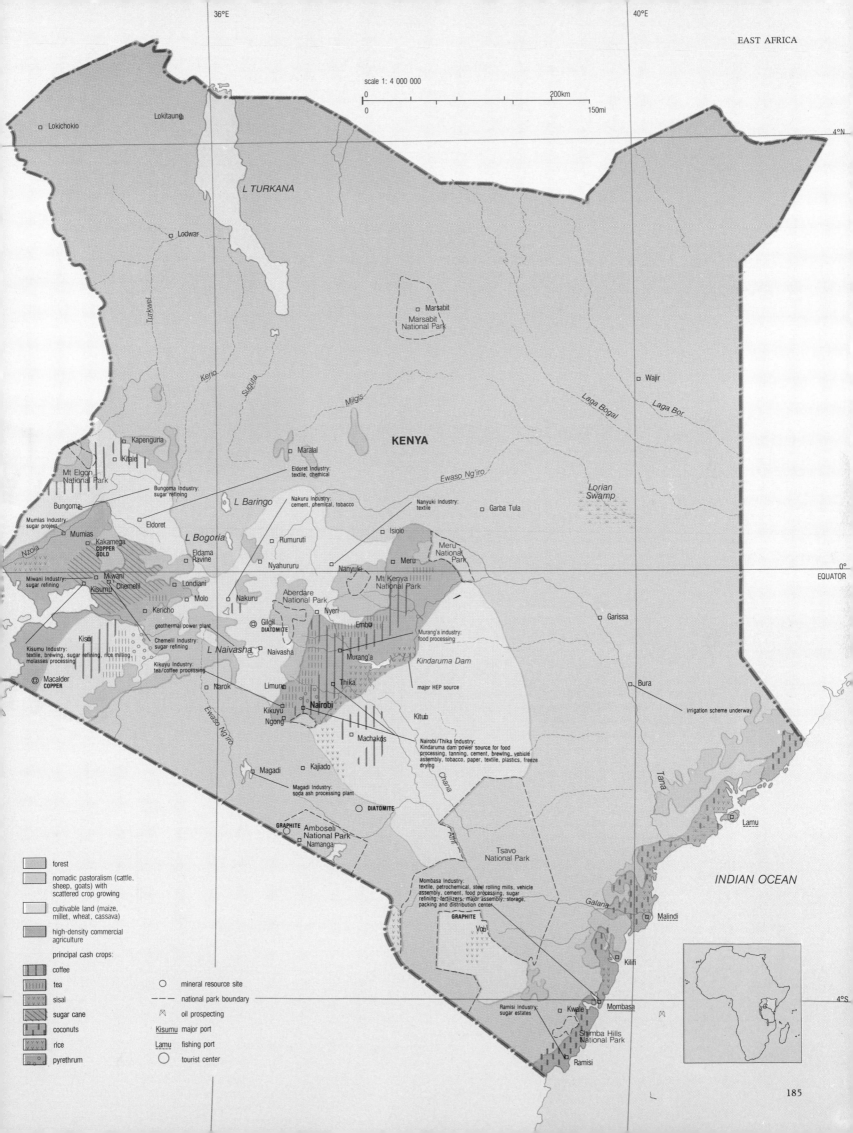

36°E

40°E

4°N

□ Lokichokio

Lokitaung □

L TURKANA

□ Lodwar

scale 1: 4 000 000

0   200km
0   150mi

□ Marsabit

Marsabit
National Park

□ Kapenguria
□ Kitale

□ Wajir

Mt Elgon
National Park

Eldoret Industry:
textile, chemical

KENYA

□ Maralal

Turkwel

Kerio

Sugura

Milgis

Ewaso Ng'iro

Bungoma Industry:
sugar refining

□ Bungoma

Nakuru Industry:
cement, chemical, tobacco

Nanyuki Industry:
textile

□ Garba Tula

Laga Bogal

Laga Bor

*Lorian
Swamp*

Mumias Industry:
sugar project

L Baringo

□ Mumias

Kakamega
**COPPER
GOLD**

L Bogoria

□ Rumuruti

□ Eldama
Ravine

□ Isiolo

□ Meru

Meru
National
Park

Nzoia

Miwani Industry:
sugar refining

□ Eldoret

□ Nyahururu

□ Nanyuki

EQUATOR   0°

□ Miwani
Kisumu □ Chemelii

□ Londiani

□ Molo

Mt Kenya
National Park

□ Garissa

Kisumu Industry:
textile, brewing, sugar refining, rice milling
molasses processing

geothermal power plant

Chemelil Industry:
sugar refining

□ Kericho

□ Kisii

Aberdare
National Park

□ Nakuru

□ Nyeri

□ Embu

Murang'a industry:
food processing

Kindaruma Dam

□ Macalder
COPPER

Kikuyu Industry:
tea/coffee processing

L Naivasha

□ Naivasha

□ Murang'a

major HEP source

□ Bura

irrigation scheme underway

□ Narok

□ Limuru

□ Thika

Nairobi

□ Kituii

Ewaso Ng'iro

□ Kikuyu
□ Ngong

□ Machakos

Nairobi/Thika Industry:
Kindaruma dam power source for food
processing, tanning, cement, brewing, vehicle
assembly, tobacco, paper, textile, plastics, freeze
drying

Tana

□ Magadi

□ Kajiado

Magadi Industry:
soda ash processing plant

○ **DIATOMITE**

Athi

Galana

INDIAN OCEAN

□ Gilgil
DIATOMITE

GRAPHITE
Amboseli
National Park
□ Namanga

Tsavo
National Park

□ Malindi

forest

nomadic pastoralism (cattle,
sheep, goats) with
scattered crop growing

cultivable land (maize,
millet, wheat, cassava)

high-density commercial
agriculture

principal cash crops:

coffee

tea

sisal

sugar cane

coconuts

rice

pyrethrum

○   mineral resource site

- - - national park boundary

⋈   oil prospecting

<u>Kisumu</u> major port

<u>Lamu</u>   fishing port

○   tourist center

Mombasa Industry:
textile, petrochemical, steel rolling mills, vehicle
assembly, cement, food processing, sugar
refining, fertilizers, major assembly, storage,
packing and distribution center

GRAPHITE
□ Voi

□ Kilifi

Ramisi Industry:
sugar estates

□ Kwale   <u>Mombasa</u>

□ Lamu

4°S

Shimba Hills
National Park
□ Ramisi

185

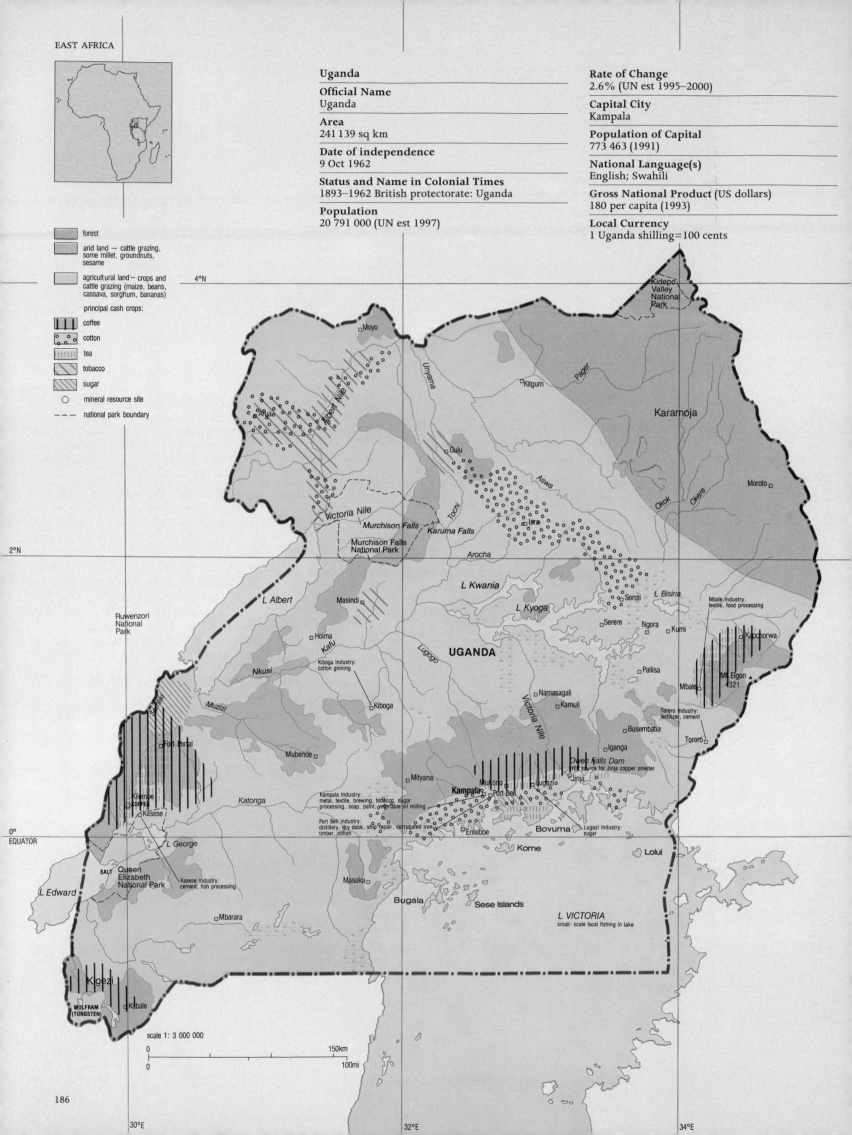

Uganda

Official Name
Uganda

Area
241 139 sq km

Date of independence
9 Oct 1962

Status and Name in Colonial Times
1893–1962 British protectorate: Uganda

Population
20 791 000 (UN est 1997)

Rate of Change
2.6% (UN est 1995–2000)

Capital City
Kampala

Population of Capital
773 463 (1991)

National Language(s)
English; Swahili

Gross National Product (US dollars)
180 per capita (1993)

Local Currency
1 Uganda shilling=100 cents

forest

arid land — cattle grazing,
some millet, groundnuts,
sesame

agricultural land— crops and
cattle grazing (maize, beans,
cassava, sorghum, bananas)

principal cash crops:

coffee

cotton

tea

tobacco

sugar

○ mineral resource site

- - - national park boundary

4°N

2°N

0°
EQUATOR

2°N

Kidepo
Valley
National
Park

Moyo

Kitgum

Pager

Karamoja

Apyao

Albert Nile

Unyama

Gulu

Moroto

Aswa

Okok

Okere

Victoria Nile

Murchison Falls

Karuma Falls

Tochi

Lira

Murchison Falls
National Park

Arocha

L Kwania

L Bisina

Soroti

L Kyoga

Mbale Industry:
textile, food processing

Ruwenzori
National
Park

L Albert

Masindi

Serere

Ngora

Kumi

Kapchorwa

Hoima

Kafu

Pallisa

Mt Elgon
4321

Nkusi

Kiboga Industry:
cotton ginning

UGANDA

Lugogo

Mbale

Semliki

Muzizi

Kiboga

Namasagali

Kamuli

Tororo Industry:
fertilizer, cement

Fort Portal

Mubende

Busembatia

Victoria Nile

Iganga

Tororo

Kilembe
COPPER

Kasese

Mityana

Mukono

Lugazi

Owen Falls Dam
HEP source for Jinja copper smelter

Jinja

Kampala

Port Bell

Kampala Industry:
metal, textile, brewing, tobacco, sugar
processing, soap, paint, vegetable oil milling

Katonga

Port Bell Industry:
distillery, dry dock, ship repair, corrugated iron
timber, cotton

Entebbe

Bovuma

Lugazi Industry:
sugar

L George

SALT

Queen
Elizabeth
National Park

Kasese Industry:
cement, fish processing

Kome

Loului

L Edward

Masaka

Bugala

Sese Islands

L VICTORIA
small-scale local fishing in lake

Mbarara

Kigezi

WOLFRAM
(TUNGSTEN)

Kabale

scale 1: 3 000 000

0   150km

0   100mi

186

30°E

32°E

34°E

Uganda

The territory of Uganda was defined during the 19th-century scramble for Africa. It contains a wide range of indigenous linguistic and political groupings. The eastern border largely consists of the mountainous western shoulder of the Kenyan Rift Valley and is dominated by the volcanic range of which Mount Elgon is the highest peak. To the southwest lies the Ruwenzori range and the mountains of Kigezi. Between these heights of over 3000 meters lies 84 per cent of Uganda's land, an extensive plateau with an elevation between 1000 and 1600 meters. This drains into Lake Kyoga and the vast Lake Victoria which forms the border with Tanzania to the south. Lakes Albert and Edward, forming the basin of the upper Nile, sketch in the line of the western frontier with Congo (DRO). Thus 17 per cent of Uganda's territory is lakes.

Uganda's equatorial climate varies little; temperature depends mainly on altitude. Rainfall patterns define ecology and agriculture. The savanna-like northeast of Karamoja, which, with some parts of southeast Ankole, gets less than 760 millimeters per year, relies on cattle husbandry and an annual sorghum crop. Some areas near Lake Victoria receive over 2000 millimeters and have a three-month dry season. But for most of central and west Uganda permanent cultivation of bananas and cash crops of coffee and tea are made possible by plentiful and regular rainfall. Only 7 per cent of Ugandans live in towns with a population of over 1000; more than half of these are in the capital, Kampala.

In the first millennium AD the region was a melting-pot for Nilotic-speaking cattle herders and Bantu-speaking agriculturalists from which the interlacustrine kingdoms emerged in the 14th and 15th centuries. Bunyoro was the first, acting as a stimulant for the creation of Buganda, Ankole and Toro: centralized kingdoms with elaborate kingship rituals that contrasted with the more diffuse political systems of Karamoja, Busoga, West Nile, Teso and Kigezi. By the 19th century Buganda had risen to preeminence.

Egyptian interests in the headwaters of the Nile drove the Buganda Kabaka to accept missionaries to his partially Islamized court in the 1870s. The rise of a Christian elite, threatening the delicate balance between king and chiefs, led to martyrdoms in 1885. The power struggle between the converts of the British Protestants and the French White Fathers finally involved the Imperial British East Africa Company in a costly war. A bankrupt company handed over to British administrators in 1893, leaving the numerically strong Buganda kingdom with its Christian chiefs the most powerful African polity in the Uganda Protectorate.

Ganda political and religious dominance was translated into economic power through extensive cotton plantations employing both tenants and migrant labor from Rwanda. The Kampala royalist riots of the 1940s indicated growing peasant discontent against landowners but, aside from concern over Indian and European control of markets, no common cause united Buganda with the rest of the

protectorate. When political parties were formed at the end of the 1950s, Buganda tried to secede, the king having suffered exile from 1953 to 1955 for his reaction to the proposed East African Federation. After the success of the nationalist leader Benedicto Kiwanuka, a Catholic Ganda commoner, and his Democratic Party, in the face of the official Buganda boycott of elections in 1961, Britain agreed to federal status for the kingdoms.

A coalition between the Uganda People's Congress led by Milton Obote and the chauvinist Kabaka Yekka Party of the king defeated the protectorate-wide Democratic Party before independence in October 1962. With the Kabaka as President of the Republic of Uganda, this uneasy alliance survived until February 1966. After a unanimous vote condemning the Obote government for gold-smuggling, the constitution was suspended. Troops stormed the Kabaka's palace and he was replaced as head of state by Milton Obote. The constitutional existence of the kingdoms was abolished in 1967 and the power of Buganda broken.

Centralization and modernization continued with the Common Man's Charter of 1969; opposition parties were banned, and state socialism gave government 60 per cent control of commercial enterprises and banking. By 1970 Obote had consolidated his position with a state security system and a one-party state giving more representation to his own region, the Nilotic-speaking north. In January 1971 his sacked chief of staff, Major General Idi Amin, seized power in his absence. Britain welcomed the coup, but it was soon followed by laws restricting civil rights. Ethnic killings began in early 1972 with the elimination of Obote's Langi and Acholi support in the army. Lugbara officers were murdered in February 1974, and between 50 000 and 300 000 Ugandan civilians were killed. Britain severed diplomatic relations in July 1976.

Systematic killing of educated Ugandans, and the expulsion of Asians in August 1972, left the economy bereft of technological and managerial expertise. Low capital inflow, a shortage of foreign exchange, transportation difficulties and declining imports soon followed. After 1973, production of cash crops fell by an average of 10 to 15 per cent per year, and exports of coffee, tea, cotton and sugar were greatly reduced. In 1976 the economy came close to total collapse when Kenya stopped petrol supplies until 52 million shillings' worth of debts were paid. Imports fell drastically and were restricted to countries offering credit. British aid ceased, though payments from the Lomé Convention's STABEX fund continued. Foreign exchange reserves were only 60 million dollars, despite aid from Libya and other Arab states.

In 1978, as a distraction, Amin invaded Tanzania, but he was defeated and driven into exile in April 1979. Leaders of the Ugandan National Liberation Front (UNLF) returned to form a National Consultative Council. The new government was torn by factionalism: only the continuing presence of a Tanzanian army force assured security. When Obote's Uganda People's Congress (UPC) party won controversial elections in December 1980, Yoweri Museveni, who

played a key role in Amin's overthrow, launched a guerrilla war. His support grew as Obote's Acholi and Langi army took the opportunity to settle old scores with the Ganda. When the army factions split, Obote was overthrown by General Tito Okello; soon afterwards he, too, was toppled by Museveni's National Resistance Army (NRA).

Museveni became president in January 1986. He restored the monarchies in 1993, but in the face of continuing instability he showed no desire to restore multiparty government. In 1994, 288 delegates were elected to a constituent assembly: it voted to continue the existing system for five years. At non-party elections in 1996 the President and his supporters won a clear mandate, and Uganda was readmitted to the Commonwealth.

Meanwhile conflict continued in and around Uganda. In 1995 thousands of corpses from the Rwandan war were swept downriver into Lake Victoria. After incursions by the 'Lord's Resistance Army', a rebel group based in Sudan, cross-border tension grew, but relations improved with Kenya and Tanzania: 1996 saw moves to revive the East African Economic Community. In the battle against AIDS Uganda's educated population has done better than its neighbors; yet despite natural advantages, economic support from the IMF and foreign governments, and improvements in its trading position, the country remains impoverished.

Rwanda

The territory of Rwanda represents the small expansion, under colonial rule, of an ancient precolonial kingdom. The Nile–Congo crest, running from north to south, provides an asymmetric backbone, which drops down to Lake Kivu in the west and to the central plateau of rugged hills in the east. The eastern border with Tanzania is a wide strip lying at an elevation of about 300 meters and marked by swampy lakes and the Kagera river basin. The northern border with Uganda is dominated by the Virunga volcanoes.

The central plateau has an average temperature of 19° but an impressive daily variation of 14°. Annual temperature variations are slight and there are two wet and two relatively dry seasons, June through September being dusty with only a rare shower. Offering the spectacle of endless hills, huts and banana groves, Rwanda has the highest population density in Africa, particularly in some northern provinces which have traditionally produced cash crops on the rich volcanic soils. There are well over half a million cattle, mostly in east-central Rwanda. Only along the Nile–Congo crest does the untouched forest survive to provide one of the few habitats for gorillas. Sorghum, maize, manioc, sweet potatoes, beans, coffee and tobacco are grown in gardens around, and in, banana plantations. Despite manuring and mixed crops, intermittent famines have occurred in the last century. Depopulation by death or emigration has not checked the erosion and exhaustion of most of the country's poor, thin soil.

The population comprised 14 per cent Tutsi, 85 per cent Hutu and 1 per cent Twa. The

Tutsi are descendants of Cushitic-speaking herdsmen who settled in the southeast from the 13th century onwards. A typical interlacustrine state, Rwanda developed a powerful kingship and army, but by the 19th century society showed signs of stratification into a cattle-owning and a peasant caste. German indirect rule left the polity little changed but the Belgians, from 1916, began reforms of chieftaincies, resulting in the abolition of feudal relations in the 1950s. However, access to political office remained a Tutsi prerogative.

The publication in 1957 of the Bahutu Manifesto spelled the end of Tutsi control. The creation of democratic machinery, nonexistent under the Belgian League of Nations mandate, was speeded up by United Nations pressure on the Trust Territory. Parti du Mouvement de l'Émancipation Hutu (PARMEHUTU) and Union Nationale Rwandaise (UNAR) were formed on social justice and nationalist platforms respectively. A dramatic peasant revolt in November 1959 ultimately pushed PARMEHUTU, under the leadership of Gregoire Kayibanda, to power on 28 January 1961. The king, *mwami* Kigeri Ndahindurwa, went into exile.

Since then Rwandan life has been dominated by ethnic conflict between Hutu and Tutsi. In 1963 thousands of Tutsi were slaughtered after raids by UNAR-backed rebels. In February 1973 Tutsi were expelled from institutes of higher education. In July 1973 the government was overthrown in a bloodless coup by the Hutu General Habyarimana, who himself survived an attempted coup in 1980 and twice extended his five-year presidency by means of referenda. In 1990, Tutsi-dominated rebels of the Front Patriotique Rwandais (FPR) invaded from Uganda; after a second invasion, in 1993, they won representation in a new government.

In April 1994 Habyarimana and President Ntaryarima of Burundi were both killed when their aircraft was shot down, possibly by Hutu extremists. The presidential guard and the Interahamwe militia immediately launched a systematic program of genocide. Perhaps half a million people, mostly Tutsi, were killed before the FPR could turn the tide; up to a million more died before the FPR declared itself victorious and set up an unstable transitional government in July 1994. In early August the new prime minister, Faustin Twagiramungu, declared the country bankrupt.

Hundreds of thousands of Rwandans had fled into former Zaïre; most returned, or were forced to return, in late 1996 and early 1997. In January 1998 120 000 people charged with ethnic murder were being held in desperately overcrowded prisons; less than 100 had been tried and sentenced. International efforts to bring the leaders of the genocide to justice move slowly, if at all, and extremist Hutu militias continue to threaten security.

The outlook for Rwanda seems bleak. It is a landlocked country with poor farmland. Its chief export crop, coffee, has fallen in value on world markets; the only other important crops are tea, tobacco, cotton and pyrethrum. Its other natural resources, cassiterite (tin ore) and wolframite (tungsten ore) are controlled by Belgian companies, and manufacturing industry is rudimentary. Rwanda depends on its neighbors for transportation and much of

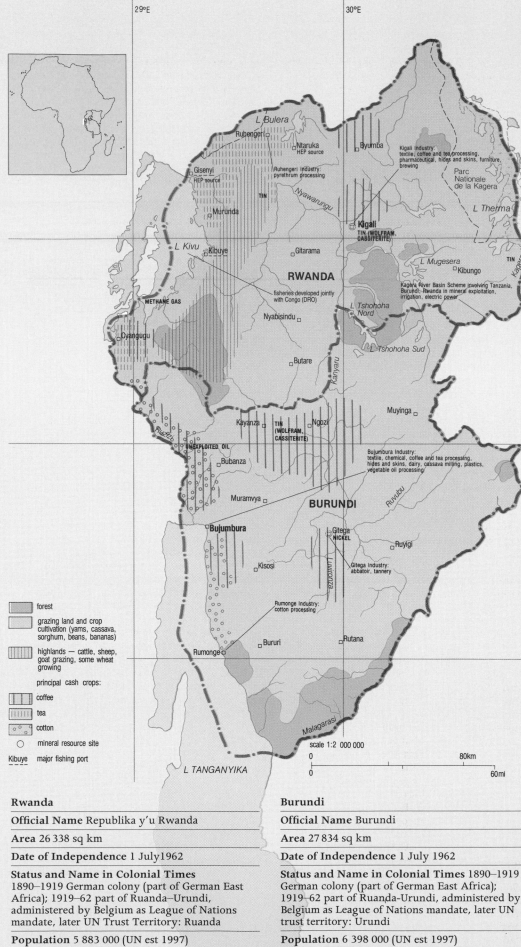

| forest |
| grazing land and crop cultivation (yams, cassava, sorghum, beans, bananas) |
| highlands — cattle, sheep, goat grazing, some wheat growing |

principal cash crops:
| coffee |
| tea |
| cotton |
○ mineral resource site
Kibuye major fishing port

scale 1:2 000 000

0 — 80km
0 — 60mi

Rwanda

Official Name Republika y'u Rwanda

Area 26 338 sq km

Date of Independence 1 July1962

Status and Name in Colonial Times
1890–1919 German colony (part of German East Africa); 1919–62 part of Ruanda–Urundi, administered by Belgium as League of Nations mandate, later UN Trust Territory: Ruanda

Population 5 883 000 (UN est 1997)

Rate of Change 7.5% (UN est 1995–2000)

Capital City Kigali

Population of Capital 234 500 (1993)

National Language(s) French, English, Rwanda

Gross National Product (US dollars)
210 per capita (1993)

Local Currency 1 franc rwandais = 100 centimes

Burundi

Official Name Burundi

Area 27 834 sq km

Date of Independence 1 July 1962

Status and Name in Colonial Times 1890–1919 German colony (part of German East Africa); 1919–62 part of Ruanda-Urundi, administered by Belgium as League of Nations mandate, later UN trust territory: Urundi

Population 6 398 000 (UN est 1997)

Rate of Change 2.8% (UN est 1995–2000)

Capital City Bujumbura (formerly Usumbura)

Population of Capital 300 000 (1996)

National Language(s) Rundi; French, Swahili

Gross National Product (US dollars):
180 per capita (1993)

Local Currency 1 Burundi franc = 100 centimes

its electricity is imported from Congo (DRO), though some is generated at the Mukungwa hydroelectric power installation. Rwanda receives more foreign aid per capita than any other country in Africa.

Burundi

Burundi's territory corresponds roughly with that of an ancient precolonial kingdom centered on the old capital of Gitega. Most of this tiny country is rolling plateau, 1500 to 2000 meters above sea level, where a rich volcanic soil supports the second highest population density in Africa (after Rwanda). A western backbone of mountains runs north into Rwanda and drops down into Lake Tanganyika, the northern tip of which provides the only natural exit for an otherwise landlocked transportation system. The average temperature on the southwestern lake shore is 23°, dropping to 20° at the 2000-meter-high crest of the Nile–Congo divide. Average rainfall throughout the country is 1200 millimeters.

Burundi was divided from neighboring states by both natural and political factors. Lake Tanganyika and the northern drainage river, the Ruzizi, running into Lake Kivu, provide a natural border with Congo (DRO). The irregular northern border follows the Kanyaru river and reflects the changing fortunes of the precolonial kingdoms of Gisaka and Rwanda, ancient enemies of Burundi. The long eastern border with Tanzania corresponds in the south with the edge of the plateau and in the north with the divisions of German colonial administration and the limits of Rundi political authority.

The population, similar to Rwanda, was made up of a Hutu majority (84 per cent), a Tutsi minority (15 per cent) and a few pygmoid Twa. Precolonial political authority was held by the Tutsi who provided the king and princes. Power struggles between Tutsi lineages allowed German military rule to be imposed in the 1890s. After World War I Burundi ceased to be politically linked with Tanganyika, and became a Belgian-administered Trusteeship Territory mandated by the League of Nations and loosely connected to the Congo. Belgium retained this mandate under the United Nations after World War II.

With the rapid Belgian decolonization, Union et Progrès National (UPRONA) came to power in 1961 under the leadership of Prince Louis Rwagasore. After his death, King Mwambutsa attempted to maintain parity in political office between Tutsi and Hutu. In 1966 Colonel Michel Micombero seized power and the monarchy was abolished. The government was ruled by a military junta representing a minority within the Tutsi, a leadership drawn from the southern Bururi province of Tutsi-Hima. The result, as in Rwanda, has been a history of growing murderous conflict between Tutsi and Hutu.

Systematic exclusion of Hutu from state positions sparked an abortive Hutu-led coup in April 1972; as a result some 200 000 Hutu were murdered and 120 000 fled to neighboring countries. In 1976 Micombero was ousted by Lieutenant Colonel Bagaza; he, in turn,

lost power to another Tutsi, Pierre Buyoya, in 1987. Hutu expectations were consistently disappointed, and their violent reaction in August 1988 led to another massacre of some 20 000 Hutus. Buyoya's response was conciliatory, and his regime arranged multiparty elections for June 1993. The surprise winners were the Front for Democracy in Burundi (FRODEBU), and as a result the Hutu leader Melchior Ndadaye became president, only to be killed in another Tutsi coup in October 1993. More ethnic violence followed, with 25 000–50 000 deaths. In January 1994 a Hutu, Cyprien Ntaryamira, was elected president, but he died that April, with President Habyarimana of Rwanda, when their airplane was shot down. Another Hutu, Sylvestre Ntibantunganya, succeeded him as president, but in July 1996 Buyoya initiated yet another coup, ousting Ntibantunganya and establishing a military dictatorship. Armed resistance to Buyoya's regime continues.

Like neighboring Rwanda, Burundi's economy is largely dependent on coffee (and, more recently, tea) production, and has suffered from variable rainfall and a declining market; since the conflict began, production has fallen even further. Even so, any cultivable land is urgently needed to grow food. This has led to overgrazing, deforestation and soil erosion, increasing the risks from landslides and flooding. Manufacturing industry (textiles, cement and insecticides) is rudimentary. Poor infrastructure – only 200 kilometers of some 6000 kilometers of roads are tarred – and civil strife have made Burundi one of the poorest countries in Africa.

In 1991 Burundi launched an economic reform agenda with support from the IMF and the World Bank. Its aim was to diversify agricultural exports, bring in foreign investors for industry, and modernize the government's budgetary practices. Again, the continuing conflict has made it all but impossible for a beleaguered and impoverished government to implement these measures. It has also largely destabilized the Economic Community of the Great Lakes Countries (CEPGL), which includes Burundi, Rwanda and Congo (DRO).

Tanzania

The United Republic of Tanzania goes back to 1964, when the newly independent territories of Tanganyika and Zanzibar formed one nation. Zanzibar, an island lying off the East African coast, has ancient links with both Arabia and the African mainland. Tanganyika took its name from the lake on its western border, which includes the lowest point on the African continent (some 358 meters below sea level). In the northeast Mount Kilimanjaro is the highest point (5895 meters) on the continent. Much of the mainland is a vast savanna plateau, 1000 to 1500 meters above sea level, with areas of higher altitude, higher rainfall and higher fertility on its borders. The plateau is cut by the eastern arm of the Great Rift Valley and falls gradually to the Indian Ocean coast. Rainfall over the plateau seldom exceeds 1000 millimeters a year and is often less, but except for periodic shortage of water

there are few natural obstacles to population movements.

Within Tanzania (which may be the original home of the human race) are spoken languages from all four language families of Africa. The hunting Sandawe speak a "click" (Khoisan) language. There are Cushitic-speaking groups like the Burungi, Nilotic-speaking pastoralists like the Maasai, but the majority for some centuries have been Bantu-speaking agriculturalists. Politically, organization ranged from centralized chiefdoms to small-scale, chiefless societies; so-called tribes were fluid groupings.

During the 19th century long-distance trade increased, involving both inland and coastal peoples. Ivory and slaves were the most valuable commodities. Traders from the coast carried with them the concept of *ustaarabu* (Arab culture and Islamic beliefs) and the Swahili language. Contacts with the outside world increased, especially after Sultan Seyyid Said moved his capital from Muscat to Zanzibar in 1840. French, American, German and British interests competed for trade, and from about 1860 Christian missionaries and Western explorers passed through Zanzibar to the mainland. Germany ultimately annexed the mainland area south of British East Africa (later Kenya). Agreements made in 1886 and 1890 ratified this division and Zanzibar came under a British protectorate.

German administration was resisted in several areas, and it was not until the end of the century that even minimal government was established. Railroads were built, German settlers encouraged and new cash crops introduced. Literate Swahili-speaking *akidas* from the coast, and later men educated at mission schools, were used as subordinate staff in government offices. Swahili became the language of government business. This had the indirect effect of encouraging the spread of Islam. Christian missions were also active. In 1905–07 the Maji Maji rebellion affected almost the whole of the center and south of the colony, one of the most serious challenges to a colonial power in all Africa.

During World War I civilians throughout the whole German colony suffered from the depredations of both sides. Unsettled conditions continued for a number of years. The mainland (except for Rwanda and Burundi in the extreme northwest) became a British mandate. British interests took over the more profitable German enterprises and Asian business interests also increased. The British saw Tanganyika as "primarily a black man's country"; extensive white settlement was not encouraged. Indirect rule, as in Nigeria, was the aim. Tanganyika was very large and very poor; development was slow and came unevenly, with cash crops such as coffee (in Kilimanjaro and Bukoba) and cotton (in Sukuma) bringing prosperity to some areas while other parts were scarcely touched.

In Zanzibar, little affected by the war, the British administration increasingly took power away from the Sultan and the Arab elite, but passed on little to the black African majority. Slavery was slowly abolished, being ended by 1911. The prosperity of both Pemba and Zanzibar was largely based on cloves, grown on Arab-owned plantations by African labor, with marketing and export largely in Asian hands.

African political associations emerged slowly: among the first was the Tanganyika African Association (TAA), a supra-tribal organization founded in the late 1920s. During World War II some 87 000 Africans were conscripted. As in 1914–18, German missionaries were interned, and church and educational work affected.

Change came faster after the war, and its main agent was the Tanganyika African National Union (TANU), founded in 1954. Julius Nyerere, a British-educated teacher, helped to make it an explicitly political association that soon gained mass support. TANU were clear winners in the 1958/59 elections, and after further elections in 1960 Nyerere was asked to form a government. After independence in December 1961 he resigned as prime minister to build up TANU's local strength. In 1962 the nation was declared a republic and he was elected president.

The years from 1954 to 1961 had their difficulties, but saw little of the violence so common elsewhere. The area was a United Nations' Trust Territory, with relatively few resources; it also had a tradition of supratribal organizations, and use of Swahili was widespread. There was no dominant ethnic group, and those who were most economically advanced lived far from the capital.

Zanzibar gained independence in 1963. Power passed to the Sultan and the Arabs, but a violent revolution in January 1964 killed or sent into exile one-fifth of the Arab population. Abeid Karume, leader of the Afro-Shirazi Party (ASP), seized power, and later in 1964 became First Vice-President of the new United Republic of Tanzania. Despite the 1977 amalgamation of the ASP and TANU as the Revolutionary Party of Tanzania (CCM), Zanzibar remained somewhat isolated from the rest of the continent.

During the 1970s relations with Kenya worsened, and in 1977 the border was closed. In October 1978 Idi Amin invaded from Uganda. Nyerere's counter-attack in January 1979 toppled Amin's regime, but the political and financial cost was high. His economic policies, based on egalitarianism and state self-reliance, proved less than successful. In November 1985 he retired, and Zanzibar's president, Ali Hassan Mwinyi, succeeded as president of the joint republic. Mwinyi's moves towards structural reform and denationalization brought new help from the IMF, and in May 1992 the constitution was changed to permit multiparty elections. However, when it emerged that Zanzibar had joined the Organization of the Islamic Conference, pressure from the mainland forced it to withdraw. The cultural gap between island and mainland continues to be a problem.

In April 1994, with the country at risk of famine after a long drought, some 250 000 Hutu refugees crossed the border from wartorn Rwanda in one day. Mwinyi closed the border and appealed for international help. In March 1995 he was forced to close the border again, against a second wave of refugees.

The first multiparty elections, in October 1995, were controversial and badly administered, but the CCM were clear winners and Benjamin Mkapa became president. He launched an attack on corruption and began moves towards a free-market economy. Meanwhile Tanzania still bore the burden of hundreds of thousands of refugees from Rwanda and Burundi. In December 1996 Mkapa sent them home, and soon had to forcibly expel them.

In 1996–97 Lake Victoria became infested with water hyacinth, its rapid growth aided by sewage and fertilizers. It has disrupted fishing and trade, threatening the economies of Kenya, Uganda and Tanzania.

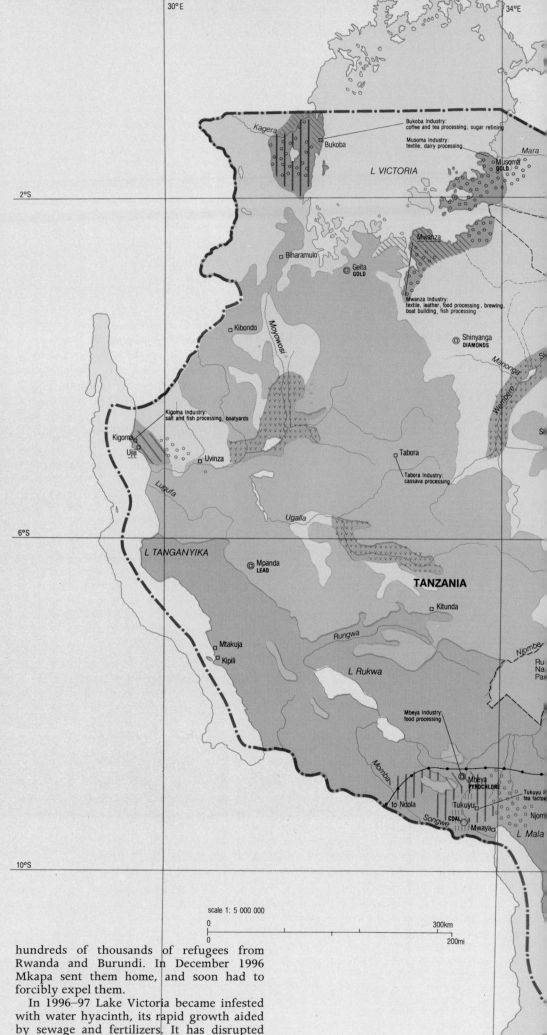

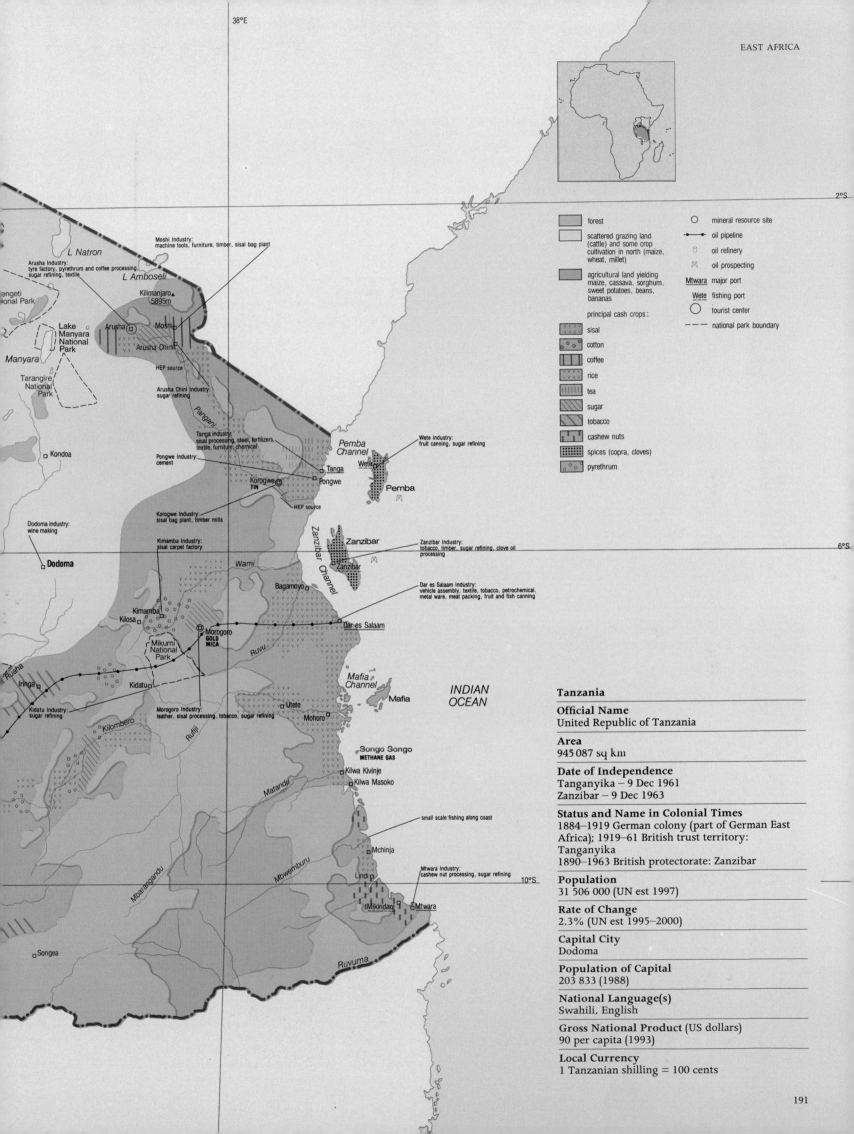

38°E

2°S

L Natron

Moshi Industry:
machine tools, furniture, timber, sisal bag plant

Arusha Industry:
tyre factory, pyrethrum and coffee processing,
sugar refining, textile

L Amboseli

Serengeti
National Park

Kilimanjaro▲
5895m

Lake
Manyara
National
Park

Arusha

Moshi

Manyara

Arusha Chini

Tarangire
National
Park

HEP source

Pangani

Arusha Chini Industry:
sugar refining

Kondoa

Tanga Industry:
sisal processing, steel, fertilizers,
textile, furniture, chemical

Pemba
Channel

Wete Industry:
fruit canning, sugar refining

Pongwe Industry:
cement

Tanga

Wete

Korogwe
TIN

Pongwe

Pemba

Dodoma industry:
wine making

Korogwe Industry:
sisal bag plant, timber mills

HEP source

Kimamba Industry:
sisal carpet factory

Zanzibar
Channel

Zanzibar

Zanzibar Industry:
tobacco, timber, sugar refining, clove oil
processing

Dodoma

Wami

Zanzibar

Bagamoyo

Kimamba

Kilosa

Dar es Salaam Industry:
vehicle assembly, textile, tobacco, petrochemical,
metal ware, meat packing, fruit and fish canning

Morogoro
GOLD
MICA

Dar es Salaam

Mikumi
National
Park

Ruvu

Ruaha

Iringa

Kidatu

Mafia
Channel

INDIAN
OCEAN

Mafia

Kidatu Industry:
sugar refining

Rufiji

Morogoro Industry:
leather, sisal processing, tobacco, sugar refining

Utete

Kilombero

Mohoro

Songo Songo
METHANE GAS

Matandu

Kilwa Kivinje

Kilwa Masoko

small scale fishing along coast

Mchinja

Mbwemburu

Mbarangandu

Lindi

Mtwara Industry:
cashew nut processing, sugar refining

Mikindani

Mtwara

10°S

Songea

Ruvuma

6°S

Legend

forest	
scattered grazing land (cattle) and some crop cultivation in north (maize, wheat, millet)	
agricultural land yielding maize, cassava, sorghum, sweet potatoes, beans, bananas	

principal cash crops:

- sisal
- cotton
- coffee
- rice
- tea
- sugar
- tobacco
- cashew nuts
- spices (copra, cloves)
- pyrethrum

○ mineral resource site
◆ oil pipeline
⌂ oil refinery
⊠ oil prospecting
<u>Mtwara</u> major port
<u>Wete</u> fishing port
○ tourist center
– – – national park boundary

Tanzania

Official Name
United Republic of Tanzania

Area
945 087 sq km

Date of Independence
Tanganyika – 9 Dec 1961
Zanzibar – 9 Dec 1963

Status and Name in Colonial Times
1884–1919 German colony (part of German East Africa); 1919–61 British trust territory: Tanganyika
1890–1963 British protectorate: Zanzibar

Population
31 506 000 (UN est 1997)

Rate of Change
2.3% (UN est 1995–2000)

Capital City
Dodoma

Population of Capital
203 833 (1988)

National Language(s)
Swahili, English

Gross National Product (US dollars)
90 per capita (1993)

Local Currency
1 Tanzanian shilling = 100 cents

SOUTHEAST CENTRAL AFRICA

Southeast Central Africa includes the three former British colonies which for a few years formed the Central African Federation, and the former Portuguese territory once often known as "Portuguese East." The Zambezi river system drains water from all four countries and economic development in the Zambezi valley, notably the Cabora Bassa dam, is of potential benefit to the region. The landlocked nations of the former CAF have historical economic links with Mozambique which were strengthened in the colonial period by their use of railroad and harbor facilities in the Portuguese colony.

Rivers and lakes are important features in all these countries. The forested highlands of Malawi are exceptional in the more general landscape of open woodland, with agricultural potential dictated by altitude and by rainfall. Cattle keeping has been of less importance and subsistence agriculture (with

hunting and fishing) was almost everywhere the mode of livelihood. All the African peoples of this region speak Bantu languages, and in many areas there were no sharp divisions between ethnicities. Identity was defined by residence and by loyalty to a chief or headman, and could be changed. Most people lived in small-scale communities, but Zimbabwe was once the site of the Monomotapa empire and later smaller states. The Lozi kingdom of southwest Zambia survived into the colonial period.

Mineral wealth has been important in all these nations. In Zambia the copper of the north led to early and rapid urbanization and industrialization. In all four countries large numbers of men earned their families' living as migrant laborers in the mines and towns of South Africa as well as in their own or neighboring territories.

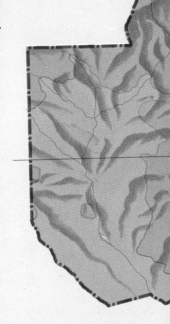

Left The Victoria Falls (named by David Livingstone) are on the Zambezi river between Zambia and Zimbabwe, south of the town of Livingstone.

Below Tea is an important cash crop grown on large estates in the highlands of Mozambique (as here at Gurue) and in Malawi.

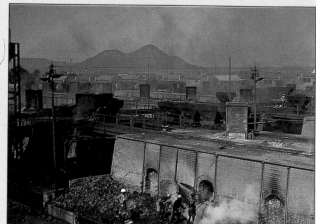

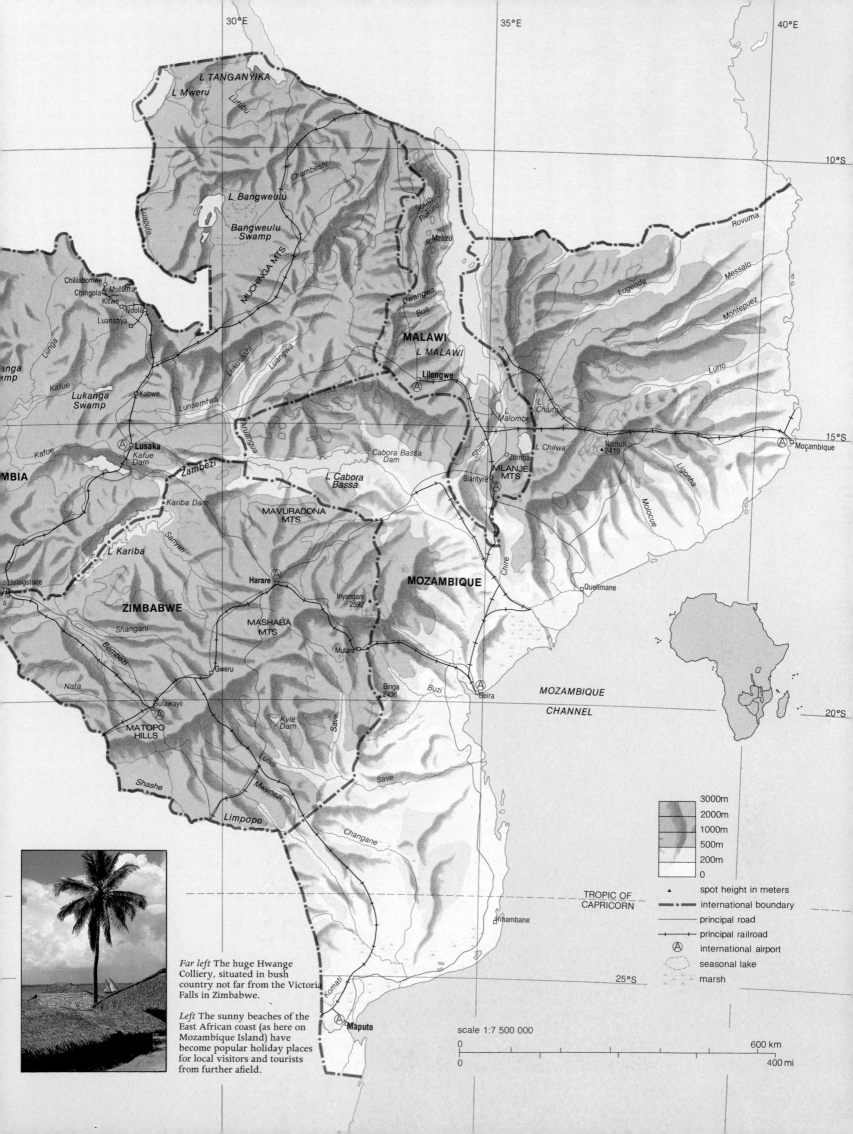

30°E 35°E 40°E

L TANGANYIKA
L Mweru
Lufubu
Luapula
10°S
L Bangweulu
Chambeshi
Bangweulu Swamp
Rovuma
Messalo
Chililabomwe □Mufulira
Chingola
Kitwe
Ndola
Luanshya
Lunga
South Rukuru
Mzuzu
Lugenda
Montepuez
Lukusashi
MUCHINGA MTS
Dwangwa
Bua
MALAWI
L MALAWI
Lurio
anga
mp
Kafue
Lukanga Swamp
□Kabwe
Lunsemfwa
Luangwa
Lilongwe Ⓐ
L Malombe
L Chiuta
15°S
Kafue
Ⓐ Lusaka
Kafue Dam
Zambezi
Luangwa
Cabora Bassa Dam
L Chilwa
Namuli ▲2419
Moçambique
MBIA
Kariba Dam
L Cabora Bassa
Shire
Zomba
MLANJE MTS
Blantyre Ⓐ
Ligonha
Molocue
MAVURADONA MTS
Sanyati
L Kariba
Livingstone
s
ZIMBABWE
Shangani
Harare Ⓐ
Inyangani ▲2592
MASHABA MTS
MOZAMBIQUE
Chire
Quelimane □
Bembezi
Mutare
Nata
Gweru □
Kyle Dam
Save
Binga ▲2436
Buzi
Ⓐ Beira
MOZAMBIQUE
CHANNEL
Bulawayo
Ⓐ
MATOPO HILLS
Lundi
Save
20°S
Shashe
Mwenezi
Limpopo
Changane

3000m
2000m
1000m
500m
200m
0

Komati
TROPIC OF CAPRICORN

▲ spot height in meters
■·■·■ international boundary
—— principal road
—+— principal railroad
Ⓐ international airport
seasonal lake
marsh

Inhambane □

25°S

Far left The huge Hwange Colliery, situated in bush country not far from the Victoria Falls in Zimbabwe.

Left The sunny beaches of the East African coast (as here on Mozambique Island) have become popular holiday places for local visitors and tourists from further afield.

Maputo Ⓐ

scale 1:7 500 000

0   600 km
0   400 mi

Zambia

The outlines of the nation-state known as Zambia only emerged with the advent of British colonial rule at the end of the 19th century. Prior to that, Zambia was a crossroads of tribal migrations and regional trade. These intertribal contacts produced a rich mixture of ethnic groups, and by the mid-1800s had stimulated the growth of several large kingdoms, notably the Lozi in the west and the Bemba in the north. Colonial rule severely restricted the earlier patterns of movement, but did not end them altogether. New migration patterns arose, as people were forced to seek employment in the mines and on farms in Zimbabwe, South Africa, Tanzania, Congo (DRO) and particularly within Zambia itself. Massive and continuing labor migration has given Zambia one of the largest percentages of urban population among African states.

Migration has never been impeded by Zambia's geographical characteristics. Most of the country is over 1000 meters in elevation, rising to about 1500 meters in the northeast. The country is primarily open woodland, giving way to a more arid landscape in the southwest. Rainfall occurs from late November to April, averaging about 1000 millimeters per year, but increasing in the northern sections of the country. The soils are sandy and light structured, but have supported very diverse agricultural systems as people have adapted their cropping methods to the soils and rainfall peculiar to their regions. Until the 1950s subsistence agriculture dominated, but government-sponsored agricultural programs have demonstrated that intensive production is possible, although the long dry season and low population density do not facilitate full utilization of existing arable land. Zambia's lakes and rivers provide abundant fish harvests, produced primarily by small-scale enterprise.

Colonial interest in Zambia was an adjunct of British involvement in Rhodesia, now Zimbabwe. African rulers became the extension of the colonial administration at the most local levels. Prior to World War I a railroad from the Rhodesian border, crossing at Victoria Falls, was extended through central Zambia to the copper-producing region of Shaba province, Congo (DRO). White settlers began to confiscate land along the railroad, and European farms were also established in the Eastern and Northern provinces. Many of these farms were only marginally productive prior to the mid-1930s, when demand for food from the copper industry stimulated serious agricultural output. Thereafter European desire for highly productive land increased and a number of Africans were forcibly resettled. Much of the best land still remains in the hands of European farmers or has been transferred to wealthy Zambians.

Although copper had been mined in precolonial times, a modern industry was not fully developed until stimulated by technological breakthroughs in the mid-1920s and increased world economic demand after the Depression. The copper mines were owned by American and British companies and only a small part of the revenue earned by them remained within the country. Thousands of Africans were drawn to the mines as temporary workers, but increasingly they formed the nucleus of today's large urban population.

The mining industry, with its large number of European workers, eventually led to their demands for a greater role within the government. After years of African opposition, the Europeans forced the creation in 1953 of the Federation of Rhodesia and Nyasaland, which to the African population epitomized the worst aspects of racial discrimination and colonial rule.

In early 1960 the United National Independence Party (UNIP) was formed, under the leadership of Kenneth Kaunda. Unlike earlier reformist parties, UNIP demanded an end to the Federation and the granting of immediate independence to the country under African rule. In 1963 the federation was dissolved, and in 1964 Britain held preliminary elections, won by UNIP. Later that year Nyasaland and Northern Rhodesia were granted independence as Malawi and Zambia respectively. Kaunda became the new republic's first president.

This peaceful transition left Zambia more stable than most African countries in the years after independence. Kaunda maintained a moderate and pragmatic regime, despite some outbreaks of internal unrest and border clashes with the rebel regime in Southern Rhodesia, against which Zambia supported guerrilla activity. Kaunda was able to play off rival political and ethnic factions against one another, making much of a Christian socialist political vision. In theory, this meant that his regime would progressively redistribute political and bureaucratic authority. In practice, however, the centralization of power increased, especially in the hands of UNIP. In 1972 UNIP declared the country a one-party state, increasing Kaunda's direct power.

Zambia remained dependent on its rail links through Rhodesia and South Africa to transport its copper exports. The cutting of trade links, culminating in the closure of the Rhodesian border in 1972, severely affected Zambia's economy, already damaged by falling copper prices and the effect of civil turmoil in neighboring countries. The establishment of a substitute rail link to Dar-es-Salaam in Tanzania in 1976 brought some improvement. However, a land nationalization program designed to boost agriculture proved largely ineffective. The economy continued to stagnate, and amid growing corruption UNIP tightened its grip on power.

In 1978 all political opposition was effectively banned, and Kaunda was reelected president in the face of increasing unpopularity. In 1980 he faced a coup attempt from within UNIP, and throughout the 1980s incurred further unpopularity by his failure to tackle economic decline and blatant corruption, while imposing harsh austerity measures. Rising food prices provoked civil unrest. In 1988, after another abortive coup, Kaunda was reelected as sole candidate for a sixth term, but in 1990, in response to rioting in the capital and yet another attempted coup, he agreed to democratic multiparty elections. The newly formed Movement for Multiparty Democracy (MMD) attracted powerful support. In elections under a reformed

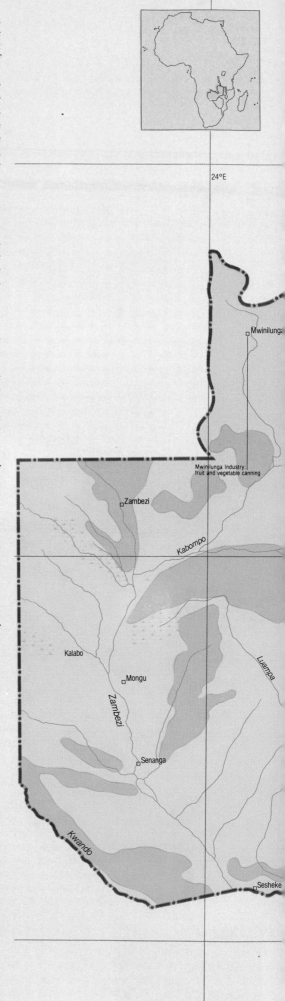

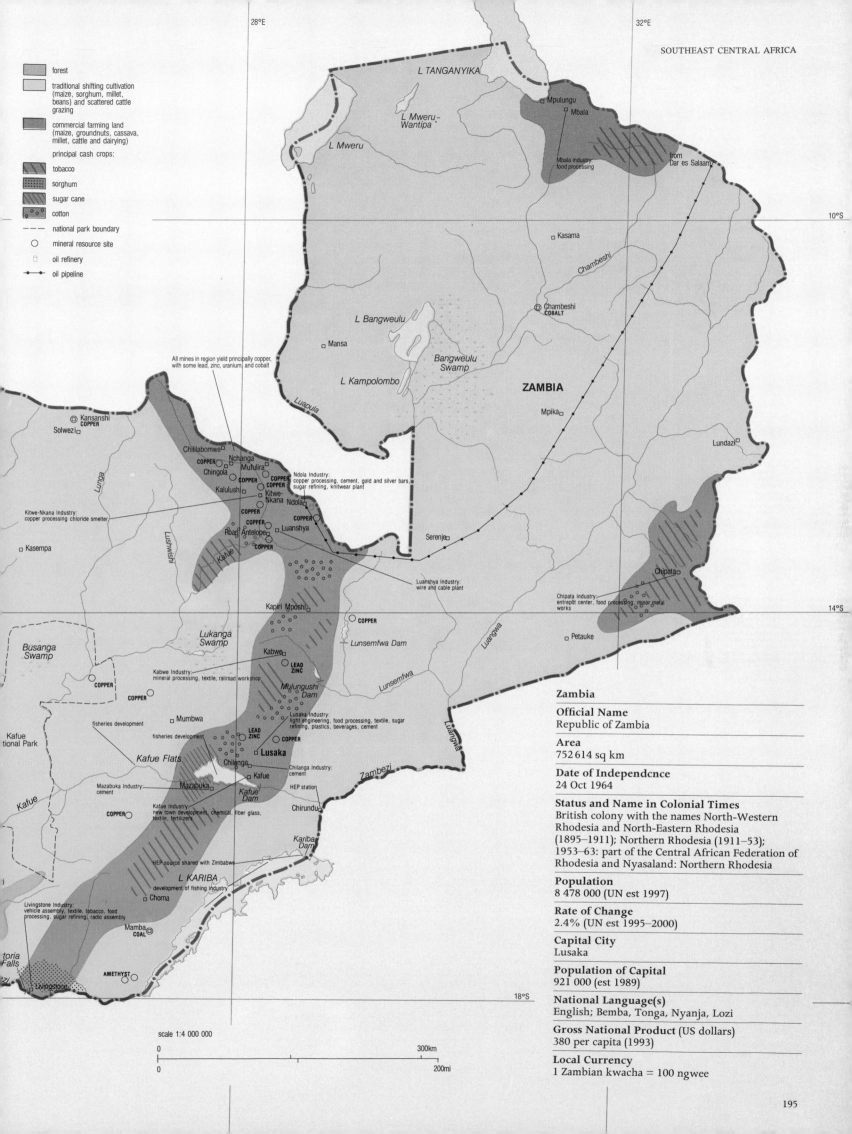

Legend

- forest
- traditional shifting cultivation (maize, sorghum, millet, beans) and scattered cattle grazing
- commercial farming land (maize, groundnuts, cassava, millet, cattle and dairying)

principal cash crops:
- tobacco
- sorghum
- sugar cane
- cotton

- – – national park boundary
- ○ mineral resource site
- oil refinery
- •—• oil pipeline

Map labels

L TANGANYIKA

L Mweru-Wantipa

Mpulungu
Mbala
Mbala industry: food processing
from Dar es Salaam

L Mweru

10°S

Kasama

Chambeshi

Chambeshi
COBALT

L Bangweulu

Bangweulu Swamp

Mansa

L Kampolombo

ZAMBIA

Mpika

Lundazi

All mines in region yield principally copper, with some lead, zinc, uranium, and cobalt

Kansanshi
COPPER
Solwezi

Luapula

Serenje

Mpika

Chililabombwe
COPPER
Nchanga
Chingola
Mufulira
COPPER
Kalulushi
Kitwe-Nkana
COPPER
Ndola
Ndola Industry: copper processing, cement, gold and silver bars, sugar refining, knitwear plant

Kitwe-Nkana Industry: copper processing chloride smelter

Kasempa

Lunga

Lushwishi

Kafue

Roan Antelope
COPPER
Luanshya
COPPER

Luanshya Industry: wire and cable plant

Chipata

Chipata Industry: entrepôt center, food processing, minor metal works

14°S

Kapiri Mposhi

COPPER

Luangwa

Petauke

Busanga Swamp

Lukanga Swamp

Lunsemfwa Dam

Kabwe
LEAD ZINC

Kabwe Industry: mineral processing, textile, railroad workshop

Lunsemfwa

COPPER

COPPER

Mumbwa

fisheries development

fisheries development

Mulungushi Dam

LEAD ZINC

COPPER

Lusaka Industry: light engineering, food processing, textile, sugar refining, plastics, beverages, cement

Kafue Flats

Lusaka

Kafue National Park

Chilanga
Kafue

Chilanga Industry: cement

Mazabuka Industry: cement

Mazabuka

Kafue Dam

HEP station

Kafue Industry: new town development, chemical, fiber glass, textile, fertilizers

Chirundu

COPPER

Zambezi

Kariba Dam

HEP source shared with Zimbabwe

L KARIBA

development of fishing industry

Choma

Livingstone Industry: vehicle assembly, textile, tobacco, food processing, sugar refining, radio assembly

Mamba
COAL

toria Falls

AMETHYST

Livingstone

18°S

28°E

32°E

scale 1:4 000 000

0 ____ 300km

0 ____ 200mi

Zambia

Official Name
Republic of Zambia

Area
752 614 sq km

Date of Independcnce
24 Oct 1964

Status and Name in Colonial Times
British colony with the names North-Western Rhodesia and North-Eastern Rhodesia (1895–1911); Northern Rhodesia (1911–53); 1953–63: part of the Central African Federation of Rhodesia and Nyasaland: Northern Rhodesia

Population
8 478 000 (UN est 1997)

Rate of Change
2.4% (UN est 1995–2000)

Capital City
Lusaka

Population of Capital
921 000 (est 1989)

National Language(s)
English; Bemba, Tonga, Nyanja, Lozi

Gross National Product (US dollars)
380 per capita (1993)

Local Currency
1 Zambian kwacha = 100 ngwee

constitution in October 1991 it won a large majority in the National Assembly, and its leader, Frederick Chiluba, ousted Kaunda as president by a huge margin.

Chiluba's government faced an enormous task in restoring the country, not least because of entrenched opposition by the previous government's appointees and supporters. Within only a few months it was also suffering from internal disputes. It lost its initial popularity, at first for its failure to tackle corruption, and then for its own involvement in it. The government followed economic policies laid down by the IMF and World Bank, including privatizing state-owned industries and raising food prices. Severe droughts in the early 1990s caused widespread food shortages.

In 1993 Chiluba declared a state of emergency, following the alleged discovery of a anti-government conspiracy by UNIP leaders, who were arrested. Scandals implicated MMD cabinet members in drug trafficking, and several were dismissed or resigned. Other financial allegations involved Chiluba himself. In 1994 Kaunda, living in retirement, announced his return to politics, and in 1995 regained the leadership of UNIP.

In 1996 Chiluba was reelected, amid fraud allegations, civil unrest and rumors of a thwarted coup. After another failed coup attempt in 1997 the government arrested Kaunda, now 73, on charges of involvement, but in 1998 were forced to release him after international protests.

Zimbabwe

Zimbabwe, formerly Rhodesia, is a colonial creation, but its borders make more sense than those of most African nations. Its territory roughly coincides with the distribution of Shona-speaking peoples, who comprise about 75 per cent of the total population. The largest non-Shona group is the Nguni-speaking Ndebele, in southwestern Zimbabwe. However, this region, too, is historically Shona territory.

Zimbabwe's main geographical handicap is lack of access to the sea; but its borders tend to follow natural features. The Zambezi river, which has historically divided culture regions, forms a logical boundary with Zambia on the north. The less formidable Limpopo river and its tributaries define the southern border. The Mozambique border runs down a string of ranges known collectively as the Eastern Highlands, a major watershed. The western, Botswana, border is the most arbitrary, but it runs through a sparsely populated region.

Zimbabwe lies entirely within the tropics, but its climate is ameliorated by its inland position and its altitude, mostly over 1000 meters. The central plateau extends from southwest to northeast. It and the Eastern Highlands are the most developed parts of the country, as well as the regions of greatest European settlement. Rainfall blows in from the east, drenching the Eastern Highlands and diminishing as the moist air moves west. Agriculture is most intensive in the well-watered highland areas, with most of the rest of the country given over to extensive

livestock production. The country's rich and diversified mineral deposits are, coincidentally, also concentrated in the highland regions, which thus contain the biggest towns, the richest farms, the most industry and the most highly developed infrastructure.

Archaeologists trace man's occupation of the region back 100 000 years, and it is rich in Stone Age remains, notably impressive rock paintings. The Iron Age began around the 2nd century AD, evidently introduced by the forebears of the Shona, who were – and are – primarily agriculturalists. By the 12th century the Shona were building in stone, initiating a unique African architectural tradition that left Great Zimbabwe (named by explorer Frederick Selous) and more than 400 other megalithic sites scattered around the country.

In the mid-15th century the Shona founded the Munhumutapa (or Monomotapa) empire in the north. The southwestern-based Changamire (or Rozvi) empire eclipsed Munhumutapa in the late 17th century, and dominated most of the area through the 18th century. After Changamire disintegrated in the early 19th century, more than 100 small, autonomous Shona states emerged. A wave of Nguni invasions, emanating from South Africa, deposited two intrusive state systems in Zimbabwe: Mzilikazi's Ndebele kingdom around present Bulawayo, and Soshangane's Gaza kingdom along the present Mozambique border, due east of the Ndebele. These new societies differed from the Shona in their greater emphasis on cattle keeping and in their more aggressive military orientations. Both states preyed upon the Shona for cattle and captives, but their territorial conquests were limited.

The Portuguese penetrated the region from the northeast in the 16th century, but were expelled by the Changamire in the late 17th century. European interest revived in the mid-19th century when hunters, traders, prospectors and missionaries began entering from South Africa. These new intruders dealt first with the Ndebele kingdom on the southern approaches. The British negotiated with the Ndebele in the 1880s, then conquered them militarily in the 1890s. Though the Shona were treated as nonentities in this process, many joined the Ndebele in a spectacular but futile anti-British revolt in 1896. Under a Royal Charter, Cecil Rhodes's British South Africa Company (BSAC) colonized the area from 1890 onwards. White political power grew steadily. In 1923 the British Colonial Office took over Rhodesia, and immediately gave the settlers almost total self-government. The local government effectively excluded Africans from political participation and institutionalized territorial segregation to ensure white supremacy.

African protest movements appeared only in the late 1950s, opposing the 1953 Federation of Rhodesia and Nyasaland. The National Democratic Party (NDP) grew in influence, and was subsequently banned. African opposition in the northern territories (now Zambia and Malawi) scuttled the Federation, forcing a reassessment of Rhodesia's own constitutional future. Britain refused to grant independence until adequate provisions were made for eventual majority rule. White opposition led the Rhodesian government unilaterally to declare independence (UDI) in 1965.

forest

land unsuitable for agriculture

traditional subsistence agriculture (maize, millet, groundnuts) and scattered grazing land (cattle)

intensive crop production — commercial farming land (maize, wheat, tobacco, cotton, tea, coffee)

major cattle-grazing area

principal cash crops:

tobacco

tea

sugar

cotton

coffee

citrus fruits

groundnuts

○ mineral resource site

ō oil refinery

○ tourist center

26°E

16°S

18°S

Victoria Falls National Park

Victoria Falls

Victoria Falls

Hwange
COAL

Hwange National Park

Zimbabwe

Official Name
Republic of Zimbabwe

Area
390 272 sq km

Date of Independence
18 Apr 1980

Status and Name in Colonial Times
1890–1923 British colony; 1923–53 self-governing colony of Southern Rhodesia; 1953–1965: part of the Central African Federation of Rhodesia and Nyasaland; 1965–79 illegal independence: Rhodesia; 1979–80 British colony: Zimbabwe Rhodesia

Population
11 682 000 (UN est 1997)

Rate of Change
2.0% (UN est 1995–2000)

Capital City
Harare

Population of Capital
1 184 169 (1992)

National Language(s)
English; Shona, Ndebele

Gross National Product (US dollars)
520 per capita (1993)

Local Currency
1 Zimbabwe dollar = 100 cents

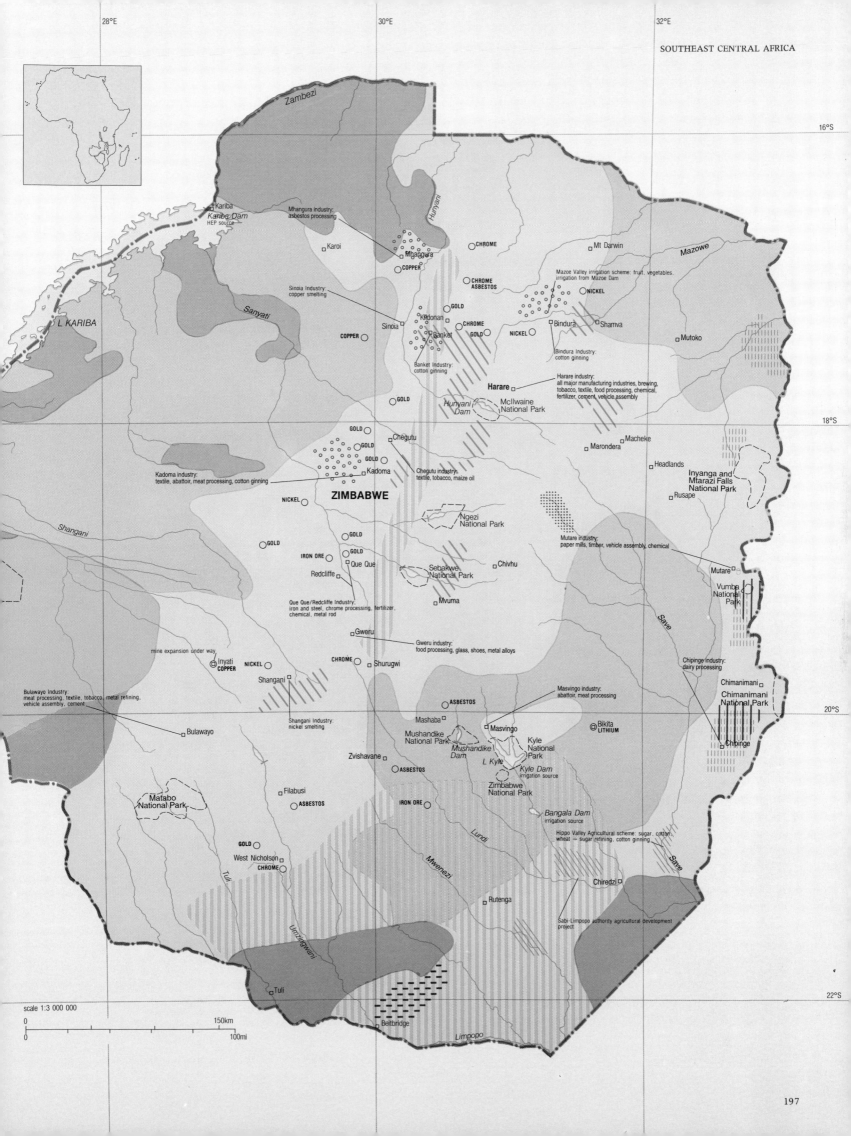

28°E

30°E

32°E

16°S

Zambezi

Kariba
Kariba Dam
HEP source

Mhangura industry:
asbestos processing

□ Karoi

□ CHROME

□ Mt Darwin

Mazowe

Mhangura
○ COPPER

□ CHROME
ASBESTOS

Mazoe Valley irrigation scheme: fruit, vegetables,
irrigation from Mazoe Dam

○ NICKEL

L KARIBA

Sanyati

Sinoia Industry:
copper smelting

○ GOLD

Hunyani

□ Shamva

Sinoia
Kadoma

□ CHROME
GOLD

○ NICKEL

□ Bindura

Mutoko

COPPER ○

Banket

Bindura Industry:
cotton ginning

Banket Industry:
cotton ginning

Harare industry:
all major manufacturing industries, brewing,
tobacco, textile, food processing, chemical,
fertilizer, cement, vehicle assembly

○ GOLD

Harare

Hunyani
Dam

McIlwaine
National Park

18°S

○ GOLD

□ Chegutu

□ Marondera

□ Macheke

Chegutu industry:
textile, tobacco, maize oil

□ Headlands

□ Rusape

Inyanga and
Mtarazi Falls
National Park

Kadoma industry:
textile, abattoir, meat processing, cotton ginning

○ GOLD
○ GOLD
Kadoma

○ NICKEL

ZIMBABWE

Ngezi
National Park

Shangani

○ GOLD

○ GOLD

Mutare industry:
paper mills, timber, vehicle assembly, chemical

□ Mutare

○ GOLD

IRON ORE ○

□ Chivhu

Sebakwe
National Park

Redcliffe

○ Que Que

□ Mvuma

Vumba
National
Park

Que Que/Redcliffe Industry:
iron and steel, chrome processing, fertilizer,
chemical, metal rod

Save

□ Gweru

Gweru industry:
food processing, glass, shoes, metal alloys

mine expansion under way

○ Inyati
COPPER

NICKEL ○

CHROME ○

□ Shurugwi

Chipinge industry:
dairy processing

Chimanimani

Bulawayo Industry:
meat processing, textile, tobacco, metal refining,
vehicle assembly, cement

Shangani

Masvingo industry:
abattoir, meat processing

Chimanimani
National Park

20°S

□ ASBESTOS

Mashaba □

□ Masvingo

○ Bikita
LITHIUM

□ Bulawayo

Shangani Industry:
nickel smelting

Mushandike
National Park

Mushandike
Dam

Kyle
National
Park

□ Chipinge

□ Zvishavane

○ ASBESTOS

L Kyle

Kyle Dam
irrigation source

Filabusi

Zimbabwe
National Park

○ ASBESTOS

IRON ORE ○

Matabo
National Park

Bangala Dam
irrigation source

Hippo Valley Agricultural scheme: sugar, cotton,
wheat — sugar refining, cotton ginning

Lundi

○ GOLD

West Nicholson □

CHROME □

Mwenezi

□ Chiredzi

Save

Tuli

□ Rutenga

Sabi-Limpopo authority agricultural development
project

Umzingwani

22°S

scale 1:3 000 000

0   150km

0   100mi

□ Tuli

Beitbridge

Limpopo

The UN responded by imposing economic sanctions. These disrupted Rhodesia's trade, but ultimately proved counterproductive in the face of Portuguese and South African noncooperation. Rhodesia diversified its comparatively developed economy, substituting more mixed agricultural products for tobacco and building up new secondary industries to supply formerly imported goods.

Meanwhile the exiled NDP had split in two: the Ndebele-based Zimbabwe African People's Union (ZAPU), led by Joshua Nkomo, and the Shona-based Zimbabwe African National Union (ZANU), led by Ndabaningi Sithole and later Robert Mugabe. Both launched guerrilla campaigns from their respective bases in Zambia and Mozambique. In 1977, after years of debilitating conflict, the Rhodesian regime agreed settlement terms with Britain and an African coalition headed by Bishop Abel Muzorewa but opposed by Mugabe. In 1980 the country became independent as Zimbabwe. A new constitution combined black majority rule with safeguards for the white minority. Among bitter disputes a ZANU–ZAPU coalition won the first elections; Canaan Banana became the first president, and Mugabe prime minister.

Nkomo was progressively driven from the government, leading to unrest in his power base Matabeleland, where dissent was savagely suppressed throughout the 1980s. Muzorewa was imprisoned on treason charges in 1984. Press censorship and other emergency powers used by the rebel regime were readopted. In 1987 the whites' guaranteed Assembly seats were abolished, ZANU and ZAPU merged to form ZANU–PF, and Mugabe became executive president with Nkomo as vice-president. Despite Mugabe's avowed desire for a one-party state, Zimbabwe has retained a multiparty system, at least in theory.

Agriculture was hit by severe droughts, and the economy was increasingly beset by corruption and mismanagement. A controversial seizure of white-owned lands in 1991 was left incomplete. Zimbabwe's economy remained precarious, although still relatively prosperous by African standards.

In 1995 Nkomo resigned on health grounds, Sithole was arrested – and later convicted – for plotting Mugabe's assassination, and food-price riots rocked the capital, Harare. In 1996 Mugabe was reelected in a poorly contested poll. He threatened to seize the remaining white-owned lands, but postponed this to secure international aid. New taxes and rising food prices led to widespread rioting and national strikes, bringing the country to the verge of anarchy. Mugabe was compelled to compromise; though universally unpopular, he maintained power largely by force.

Mozambique

Mozambique has a long Indian Ocean shoreline of over 2000 kilometers, but much of the country consists of a 300-kilometer-wide coastal strip lying below the continental escarpment. In the center Mozambique's territory extends inland along the Zambezi valley to reach Zimbabwe and Zambia. The southern tip of the Malawi rift valley system drives a wedge into Mozambican territory. The northern section of Mozambique, east of Lake Malawi, is over 500 kilometers broad and comprises some temperate upland above 800 meters on which hardwoods can grow. In the Zambezi basin and the south land is low-lying and sometimes swampy, with malarial mosquitoes and tsetse flies. Temperatures are high and rainfall is governed by the monsoons.

Mozambique's early history, from about the 3rd century AD, is dominated by the growth of tropical farming and stock raising in small scattered Iron Age communities. From the 10th century the country's economy developed growing outside links, first with the mining zones of the high plateau in the interior and secondly with the maritime trading nations in the Indian Ocean. From 1000 to 1500 the Shona miners of Zimbabwe sold their gold in Mozambique to Muslim seafarers from the Swahili cities of East Africa and also from India. Between 1500 and 1870 gold was bought by Portuguese merchants and settlers who penetrated the Zambezi valley. From 1870 the major growth of mining occurred in South Africa and large numbers of Mozambicans regularly went there as mine laborers. In exchange for recruitment rights to miners, British mining and other imperial interests agreed to use Portuguese rail and harbor services, especially those in Maputo and Beira. These facilities were built in the 1890s after Britain and Portugal had acrimoniously agreed to partition southeastern Africa between themselves.

After Portuguese sovereignty over Mozambique had been agreed to in Europe, large areas were rented out again by Portugal. Private enterprises with various terms of reference and varied patterns of international shareholder control were established. These companies only slightly modified the slave-like status of workers usual in 19th-century Mozambique. Before 1890 Mozambican slaves went mainly to Brazil, the Cape of Good Hope and the Indian Ocean islands. After 1890 forced labor was used widely for government projects as well as in private enterprise. African crops were taxed in kind, migrant labor suffered imposts and levies and the wives of migrant laborers were commonly compelled to plant crops of cotton or rice. One important tropical plantation crop which developed was sugar. Violent demonstrations of government force were met by equally violent bouts of organized resistance over the element of labor compulsion in the domestic economy. By the 1950s Mozambique had eliminated its land concession companies but not its migrant labor recruiters.

In the 1960s white immigrants came in increasing numbers, some of them little more skilled or educated than their depressed colonial subjects. Their presence heightened black aspirations for a more equitable return for labor and a restoration of lands transferred to European ownership. Nationalism grew and was encouraged by neighboring Tanzania's gaining independence. It was from bases in Tanzania and with its backing that in 1964 the movement Frente de Libertação de Moçambique (Frelimo) launched a guerrilla war in northern Mozambique. Portugal was able to contain the uprising for about seven years by fairly draconian policies, but by the early 1970s it had spread to central Mozambique. After the 1974 military coup in Portugal the new government negotiated a rapid transition to independence. Frelimo became a "Marxist–Leninist vanguard party" with restricted membership, and established a one-party state under the presidency of Samora Machel.

Frelimo immediately introduced economic restructuring along rigid Soviet and racial lines, nationalizing industry and collectivizing agriculture. The damage this caused was worsened by the exodus of virtually the entire white population, whose skills had to be rapidly replaced. Ethnic, regional and political opponents of Frelimo established a guerrilla movement known as Resistência Nacional Moçambicana (Renamo). In 1976 the Machel government made the country the main base for guerrilla operations against the rebel regime in what was then Rhodesia. The Rhodesian regime retaliated by incursions to attack guerrilla bases, and by sponsoring Renamo's campaign. For the next fifteen years the conflict between these two groups dominated and further impoverished the country.

Renamo, with Rhodesian arms and training, launched attacks against the country's vital economic arteries, the road and rail links from coastal ports. African National Congress (ANC) guerrillas also used Mozambique as a base for attacks against South Africa. When Rhodesia became independent as Zimbabwe in 1980, South Africa took over support for Renamo. Its attacks, especially on the important oil pipeline to Zimbabwe, led the Zimbabwean government to station troops in Mozambique, whose numbers increased throughout the 1980s.

In addition to the disruption caused by the war, in the 1980s the country suffered a devastating drought, which further ruined agricultural production. The result was famine in which more than a million died, and many times that number fled parts of the country.

In 1986 Machel died in an unexplained air crash in South Africa, and his place as president was taken by Joaquim Alberto Chissanó. He brought about some reduction of hostilities with South Africa, and sought an end to the war. In 1989 Frelimo renounced its Marxist allegiance. In 1990, as the Soviet and South African regimes which had largely brokered the conflict both faltered, peace negotiations were instituted with Renamo, mediated by the presidents of Kenya and Zimbabwe. To further these negotiations, Zimbabwean troops were withdrawn and in 1990 a new constitution ended the one-party state and restored democratic processes.

In 1991 Chissanó forestalled a coup attempt led by Machel's family, hardliners opposed to the negotiations and reforms. Despite sporadic unrest, a peace agreement was signed in 1992, and in 1994, amid chaos caused by the demobilization of Renamo troops, the country's first reasonably democratic elections were held. Chissanó secured the presidency, and Frelimo gained a majority in the new Assembly, both by definite margins, but Renamo attracted enough support to become an established opposition. Disputes continued as Frelimo sought to isolate Renamo by political maneuvering, and local elections scheduled for 1996 were delayed into 1997.

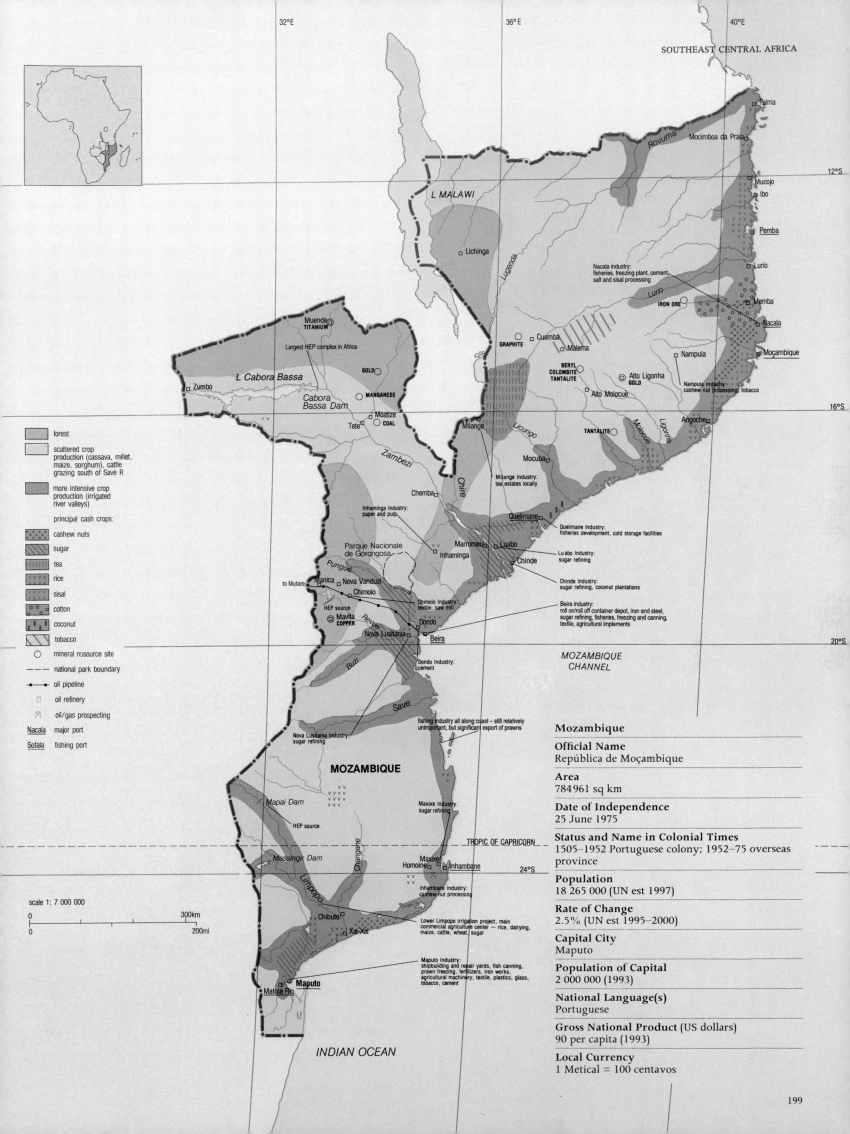

L MALAWI

Palma

Rovuma

Mocimboa da Praia

12°S

Mucojo

Ibo

Lichinga

Pemba

Nacala industry:
fisheries, freezing plant, cement,
salt and sisal processing

Lurio

Lurio

Memba

IRON ORE

Nacala

Cuamba

GRAPHITE

Malema

Moçambique

Nampula

BERYL
COLOMBITE
TANTALITE

Alto Ligonha
GOLD

Muenda
TITANIUM

Largest HEP complex in Africa

Alto Molocue

Nampula industry:
cashew nut processing, tobacco

L Cabora Bassa

GOLD

16°S

Zumbo

Cabora
Bassa Dam

MANGANESE

Moatize
COAL

Tete

Milange

TANTALITE

Angoche

Mocuba

Zambezi

Chire

Chemba

Milange industry:
tea estates locally

Quelimane

Quelimane Industry:
fisheries development, cold storage facilities

Inhaminga Industry:
paper and pulp

Parque Nacionale
de Gorongosa

Marromeu

Luabo

Inhaminga

Chinde

Luabo Industry:
sugar refining

Chinde Industry:
sugar refining, coconut plantations

Pungue

Manica

Nova Vanduzi

to Mutare

Chimoio

Chimoio Industry:
textile, saw mill

HEP source

Mavita
COPPER

Revue

Dondo

Nova Lusitania

Beira

Beira industry:
roll on/roll off container depot, iron and steel,
sugar refining, fisheries, freezing and canning,
textile, agricultural implements

20°S

MOZAMBIQUE
CHANNEL

Buzi

Dondo Industry:
cement

Save

fishing industry all along coast – still relatively
unimportant, but significant export of prawns

Nova Lusitania Industry:
sugar refining

MOZAMBIQUE

Mapai Dam

HEP source

Maxixe Industry:
sugar refining

TROPIC OF CAPRICORN

Massingir Dam

Maxixe
Homoine

Inhambane

24°S

Chicualacuala

Inhambane Industry:
cashew nut processing

Limpopo

Chibuto

Xai-Xai

Lower Limpopo irrigation project, main
commercial agriculture center – rice, dairying,
maize, cattle, wheat, sugar

Maputo Industry:
shipbuilding and repair yards, fish canning,
prawn freezing, fertilizers, iron works,
agricultural machinery, textile, plastics, glass,
tobacco, cement

Maputo

Matola Rio

INDIAN OCEAN

Legend

	forest
	scattered crop production (cassava, millet, maize, sorghum), cattle grazing south of Save R
	more intensive crop production (irrigated river valleys)

principal cash crops:

	cashew nuts
	sugar
	tea
	rice
	sisal
	cotton
	coconut
	tobacco

○ mineral resource site

--- national park boundary

•–•–• oil pipeline

oil refinery

oil/gas prospecting

Nacala major port

Sofala fishing port

scale 1: 7 000 000

0 _____ 300km

0 _____ 200mi

Mozambique

Official Name
República de Moçambique

Area
784961 sq km

Date of Independence
25 June 1975

Status and Name in Colonial Times
1505–1952 Portuguese colony; 1952–75 overseas province

Population
18 265 000 (UN est 1997)

Rate of Change
2.5% (UN est 1995–2000)

Capital City
Maputo

Population of Capital
2 000 000 (1993)

National Language(s)
Portuguese

Gross National Product (US dollars)
90 per capita (1993)

Local Currency
1 Metical = 100 centavos

199

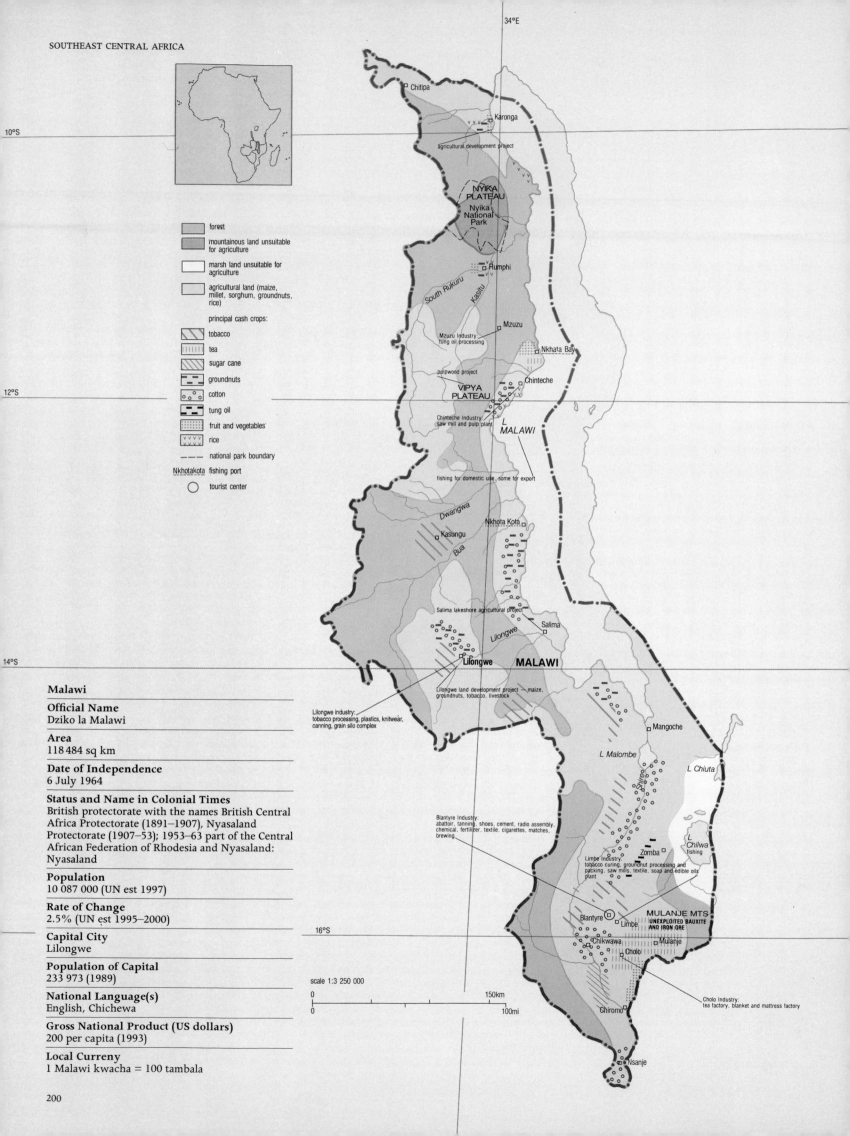

34°E

10°S

12°S

14°S

16°S

○ Chitipa

○ Karonga

agricultural development project

NYIKA
PLATEAU
Nyika National
Park

v v Rumphi

South Rukuru

Kasitu

Mzuzu Industry:
tung oil processing □ Mzuzu

□ Nkhata Bay

pulpwood project

○ Chinteche
VIPYA
PLATEAU

Chinteche industry:
saw mill and pulp plant

L
MALAWI

fishing for domestic use, some for export

Dwangwa

□ Nkhota Kota

Bua □ Kasungu

Salima lakeshore agricultural project

□ Salima

Lilongwe

○ Lilongwe MALAWI

Lilongwe land development project — maize,
groundnuts, tobacco, livestock

Lilongwe industry:
tobacco processing, plastics, knitwear,
canning, grain silo complex

□ Mangoche

L Malombe

L Chiuta

Blantyre industry:
abattoir, tanning, shoes, cement, radio assembly,
chemical, fertilizer, textile, cigarettes, matches,
brewing

□ Zomba L
Chilwa
fishing

Limbe industry:
tobacco curing, groundnut processing and
packing, saw mills, textile, soap and edible oils
plant

MULANJE MTS
UNEXPLOITED BAUXITE
AND IRON ORE

◎ Blantyre □ Limbe

○ Chikwawa □ Mulanje

Cholo

Cholo industry:
tea factory, blanket and mattress factory

○ Chiromo

○ Nsanje

Legend

	forest
	mountainous land unsuitable for agriculture
	marsh land unsuitable for agriculture
	agricultural land (maize, millet, sorghum, groundnuts, rice)

principal cash crops:

	tobacco
	tea
	sugar cane
	groundnuts
	cotton
	tung oil
	fruit and vegetables
	rice

- - - national park boundary

Nkhotakota fishing port

○ tourist center

Malawi

Official Name
Dziko la Malawi

Area
118 484 sq km

Date of Independence
6 July 1964

Status and Name in Colonial Times
British protectorate with the names British Central
Africa Protectorate (1891–1907), Nyasaland
Protectorate (1907–53); 1953–63 part of the Central
African Federation of Rhodesia and Nyasaland:
Nyasaland

Population
10 087 000 (UN est 1997)

Rate of Change
2.5% (UN est 1995–2000)

Capital City
Lilongwe

Population of Capital
233 973 (1989)

National Language(s)
English, Chichewa

Gross National Product (US dollars)
200 per capita (1993)

Local Curreny
1 Malawi kwacha = 100 tambala

scale 1:3 250 000

0 ———— 150km

0 ———— 100mi

The end of the conflict highlighted the country's appalling economic situation. The huge Cabora Bassa dam on the Zambezi, built in the 1970s and designed to supply two million kilowatts of electricity to South Africa, had brought few benefits to Mozambique. Agriculture, which had employed over 80 per cent of the workforce, had been stopped altogether in some areas by the war and the drought. Famine has slackened its grip, but the government has been plagued by civil unrest over rising food prices. Other production, underdeveloped during the colonial era, had been handicapped or killed off by post-independence restructuring.

Exports have been limited to shrimps and cash crops such as cotton, cashews and sugar, and are far outweighed by imports, which include almost all manufactured goods and some food staples. Consequently the country still labors under a vast foreign-debt burden, and remains one of the world's poorest. Nonetheless, as peace and some degree of freedom have been established, so in turn have some signs of regeneration appeared. There are significant resources of iron ore, tantalite and natural gas which offer hope for future development.

Malawi

Situated along the southern continuation of the rift valley system, Malawi is definitely a colonial creation. Its small size and irregular borders reflect late 19th-century big-power politics, rather than any geographical or economic rationale. Except for the narrow shore line around Lake Malawi and the Shire river valley, the country is part of the central African plateau. It has an average elevation of between 750 and 1200 meters, with high mountain ranges (1800 to 3000 meters) in both the north and the south. Rainfall occurs mainly between November and April, most areas receiving between 750 and 1000 millimeters annually; amounts of up to 2000 millimeters occur along the higher mountain ranges. Over half the land area is suitable for agriculture, which at present supports 90 per cent of the country's population. Fishing is a major source of income for people along the shores of lakes Malawi and Chilwa and the Shire river, and hydroelectric plants produce most of the country's electricity. The country is one of the most densely populated in Africa, although the distribution is uneven, with nearly 90 per cent of the total population contained within the southern and central regions. Most of the infrastructure is likewise located in these two regions.

The fertility of Malawi's soils has attracted people for hundreds of years. The Chewa-speaking people of the central area have over 350 years of documented history, with political units ranging in size from clans to kingdoms. During the 19th century the pace of change rapidly accelerated, as slave traders, African immigrants and finally European traders and missionaries entered Malawi. Many of the pre-19th-century societies were conquered or greatly disrupted by these events, and historians have tended to describe much of Malawi's subsequent history in terms of these changes. Despite the impact of new peoples and ideas, the strong cultural identity and solidarity (based upon an agricultural economy) of rural Malawians have provided the framework for later developments.

The British established a colony in 1891 in what was then called Nyasaland, and from the mid-1890s the colonial administration favored European settlers at the expense of native inhabitants, many of whom left their villages to work in South African plantations and mines. The message of Christian egalitarianism, mixed with widespread deprivation and the recruitment of porters from Malawi for use in World War I in East Africa, resulted in a brief and extremely violent revolt by Africans in 1915. Led by John Chilembwe, a mission-educated teacher, the revolt failed to win any substantial popular support, and was quickly suppressed.

Educated Malawians turned to more adaptive methods of accommodation with the authorities. Reformist associations provided the basis for the establishment of the Nyasaland African Congress in 1944. Congress was largely ineffective in its early years in attracting widespread support for its cause. However, the move by local whites and the British government towards the creation of the Federation of Rhodesia and Nyasaland in the early 1950s became a focus for effective political protest. At the same time, colonial development policy aroused opposition from rural native farmers, who disliked the restrictions upon their agricultural methods and the discriminatory crop-pricing arrangements which favored white farmers.

The African elite's political demands drew on this rural resentment to attract support for a nationalist movement. In 1958 this gained a leader with the return of the charismatic Dr Hastings Banda. Although born in the region, Banda had lived abroad for most of his life, gaining a medical degree in America and practicing in London. In 1959 the Malawi Congress Party (MCP) was formed under his leadership to fight for total independence. Under strong pressure from Malawians and Zambians, the Federation was dissolved in 1963. The following year Malawi was granted full independence, with Banda as president.

At independence, Malawi was one of the poorest countries in the world, with a per capita annual income of less than US $40. The question of internal economic and social development and its direction and leadership were central issues. Banda moved slowly, so as not to disrupt the economy or cut Malawi's ties with the white-ruled states to the south. However, several of the younger government ministers supported a strong stand against white-dominated southern Africa and called for a rapid Africanization of the Malawian bureaucracy. The political struggle quickly came to a head, and in 1964 several of Banda's opponents resigned from the government. In the south of the country Henry Chipembere led an armed revolt. By early 1965 this was firmly suppressed, and Banda, widely popular, set about consolidating his power base and position.

The country was declared a republic and a one-party state under the MCP, to which all citizens were required to belong. Opponents of Banda's policies were forced into exile. Strict cultural norms were established and deviation from them resulted in imprisonment or suppression. For example, in the 1970s thousands of Jehovah's Witnesses fled abroad to escape persecution as the rules of their church did not allow them to subscribe to the political party. Internationally Banda remained pragmatic, fostering relations with Malawi's major trading partners, the rebel white regime in Rhodesia, as it then was, and the Portuguese colonial regime in Mozambique. In 1967 he became the first African head of state to visit South Africa, with whom he signed a trade pact.

Banda progressively established a strong personality cult, and in 1971 he was declared president for life. Potential opponents were persecuted and sometimes murdered, even in exile. The country's first elections since independence were held in 1978, but on a one-party basis, as were those that followed. In the 1980s relations with Mozambique deteriorated among allegations that Banda was aiding the rebel Renamo movement; in the conflict a million or more Mozambicans fled to Malawi.

Banda's economic policies had some success, but not enough. Although largely self-sufficient in food, Malawi remains extremely poor even today. Agriculture remains dominant, with the major cash crops, tobacco, tea and sugar cane, providing the principal exports. These, just as much as subsistence farming, are highly vulnerable to the periodic droughts. Mining is minimal, although some reserves exist, and manufacturing, though increasing, is still small-scale; almost all machinery and basic manufactures are imported. Health and living standards even for the urban elite remain poor. Consequently Malawi remains heavily dependent on international aid, creating a large debt burden. As internal opposition to the regime intensified in the early 1990s, it was this burden which lent weight to international pressure for major reform.

In 1993 a UN-monitored referendum voted for multiparty rule, and Banda announced a revised constitution and elections within a year. In September 1993 his health deteriorated, requiring him to go abroad for brain surgery, and he temporarily relinquished power to a council. Under their rule the Malawi Young Pioneers (MYP), the MCP's powerful paramilitary wing, was disbanded and disarmed. Banda resumed power in December 1993, and in May 1994 the first multiparty elections were held. Banda was defeated by the United Democratic Front (UDF) candidate Bakili Muluzi.

Muluzi announced constitutional reforms, an anti-corruption drive, and set up a commission to investigate crimes under Banda's rule. In 1995 the ailing Banda and his closest associates were arrested on murder charges; they were acquitted, but were subsequently rearrested frequently on other charges. Banda apologized for suffering caused under his regime. At the same time opposition parties frequently accused Muluzi and his government of corruption and human-rights violations, and in 1996 his attempt to take over the powerful Press Corporation was declared illegal by the High Court. His government has become increasingly unpopular. In November 1997 Banda died in a South African hospital, at the age of 99, after contracting pneumonia.

SOUTHERN AFRICA

The enormous potential in almost every sphere of the southern African region is paradoxically a source of its major problems, since uneven development of this potential has exacerbated difficulties that the region shares with its northern neighbors. The industrial wealth of the Republic of South Africa – the zone's largest and richest country – contrasts dramatically with the struggling rural economies of Botswana and Lesotho. The Republic exercises a powerful economic hegemony over its neighbors, while its extensive mineral and industrial resources make it a key factor in global political strategies.

The balance of power and numbers among the southern African peoples is also unique. The original Khoisan inhabitants were expelled or exterminated by the migration of Bantu-speaking peoples from the northeast and white settlers from the south. Shock waves from the 19th-century *Mfecane* (scattering of the peoples) affected every Bantu group in southern Africa directly or indirectly, and a strong cultural similarity exists between most of these groups. White incursion, which began at the Cape in the 17th century, has played a major role in the political development of the region. A sizable and influential English-speaking white minority has long been established in the Republic, while Namibia is home to the descendants of 19th-century German settlers. Yet the recent history of South Africa has been shaped above all by the Boers or Afrikaners – descendants of Dutch settlers who evolved their own distinctive culture and language (Afrikaans). From the creation of the Republic in 1948 to the advent of majority rule in 1994, effective power was wielded by this group, most notoriously through the system of racial discrimination known as *apartheid*.

With proper management of human and agricultural resources most of the zone's populations could feed themselves, but the continued degradation of the African lands through overpopulation, overgrazing and soil erosion poses a serious threat to future political stability and economic progress.

Left The hilly terrain within Eastern Cape province near the southeastern coast of South Africa. From 1976–94 this area was part of the autonomous Xhosa territory of the Transkei. Rivers, descending abruptly from the central plateau, are too seasonal in flow to be of major economic importance, but reliable rainfall and an equable climate make the soil productive.

Above White-clad Xhosa youths take part in an initiation ceremony within their village. Traditional institutions still survive in the rural Eastern Cape province, and many Xhosa who work in the adjacent industrial centers of East London and Port Elizabeth try to maintain village behavioral sanctions even in the urban environment.

Above Groote Schuur, lying below the spectacular pinnacle of Devil's Peak, is the Cape Town residence of South Africa's premier. It stands on the site of the "great barn" in which Jan van Riebeeck stored grain from his first experimental farm in the Cape. Reconstructed after a disastrous fire, the house is in the Cape Dutch style of the early homesteads in the Cape.

Above right Cape Town occupies a spectacular site at the foot of Table Mountain (1,086 meters/3,563 feet). Much of the city's modern foreshore is reclaimed land, and its harbor was again expanded in the 1970s.

Right Growing only in the 80-kilometer-wide coastal strip of the Namib Desert and living for up to 2000 years, *Welwitschia bainesii* is a botanical curiosity. Its straplike leaves grow to a length of about 2 meters before being eroded away by sand and wind. It is adapted to live in an almost waterless environment.

Far left Herero women in western Botswana dress in the fashion introduced into the area last century by the Rhenish Missionary society.

Left Founded in 1886 after the discovery of gold in the nearby Witwatersrand, Johannesburg is the commercial capital of South Africa. Skyscrapers dominate the regular layout and straight streets of the city center.

Below left Western Cape province is renowned as a wine-growing area. A variety of wines including Colombard, Pinotage, and Chenin Blanc are produced in the Stellenbosch region and are enjoyed by an international market. Viticulture is a large-scale operation, as is evident from this winery in the Jonkershoekberg Valley.

Below A high percentage of the world's gem-quality diamonds comes from blue rock "pipes" located in or near long-extinct volcanoes in South Africa. Kimberley, in Northern Cape province, and Cullinan, east of Pretoria in Gauteng province, are the principal diamond-mining centers. As in gold mining, most of the underground workers are Africans. Here rock is drilled before being transported to the surface where it is crushed to release the diamonds.

South Africa

The topography of South Africa is dominated by a central plateau of varying elevations which stretches over the country. The interior plateau or high veld – roughly comprising Free State, Gauteng, Mpumalanga and Northern Province – is gently undulating grassland, broken occasionally by highland areas. Most of the country's mineral wealth is concentrated in this region. In the western half of the plateau, the elevation is around 900 meters. This area is dominated by a dry flatland known as the Karoo that merges with the Namib and Kalahari deserts. Southeast of the plateau and stretching from the Northern Province southwest to Eastern Cape province is a major mountain chain – the Drakensberg – which presents a major barrier to communication between the coastal and interior regions. In Western Cape province other mountain ranges rise to heights of 2250 meters. The interior plateau is in a wind belt, which brings in rain from the Indian Ocean. In the eastern plateau region, rainfall is heaviest during the summer months, while in the western Cape rainfall peaks during the winter. There are no navigable rivers in South Africa. Two major rivers, the Orange and its tributary the Vaal, flow from east to west. Hundreds of smaller rivers such as the Umzimvubu, Great Fish, Kei, Pongola, Umgeni and Tugela flow into the Indian Ocean. The Limpopo river forms much of the northern boundary of the country.

The peoples of South Africa represent many races, languages, religions, customs and life styles. As crudely defined by the former white government, there are four main groupings of people: Africans, Europeans, Coloreds and Asians. The largest grouping is the African, the majority of whom are Bantu-speakers. They comprise four major language groups. The largest, Nguni-speakers, includes Zulu, Xhosa, Ndebele and Swazi. The next largest are Tswana-speakers, who include Tswana, Pedi and Southern Sotho. The two other groups are the Venda and Shangaan-Tsonga. The ancestors of the present-day Africans may have begun settling in small groups south of the Limpopo river as early as the 3rd century AD. Most were cattle-keepers or agriculturalists. By the 15th century Bantu-speaking people were living as far south as the Fish river. Over the centuries, African societies have interacted with each other so much that it has become difficult to distinguish them with precision.

European settlement dates from the mid-17th century when, in 1652, the Dutch East India Company established a supply station at Table Bay for ships rounding the Cape of Good Hope. The Dutch settlers were augmented by French and German immigrants as well as slaves from Malaya and East and West Africa. From that early period the European settlers began intermixing with their slaves and the indigenous inhabitants, thereby creating a mixed-race group (the "Coloreds"), who have historically lived mainly in the western Cape.

In later decades, as some of the settlers took up cattle keeping, they began to move gradually eastward beyond official Dutch control in search of grazing land . In the process they came into contact and conflict first with Khoisan (or Khoikhoi) and then with Xhosa peoples, who resisted settler encroachment on their land.

In 1806 England wrested control of the Cape from Holland, thereby triggering a rivalry with the Dutch settlers or Boers. In 1820 the British settled a large group of English colonists in the eastern Cape. In the 1830s groups of Boers, reacting to the British abolition of slavery, deteriorating economic conditions, wars with Africans and resentment over British imperial control, moved off on the "Great Trek" into the South African interior and founded two republics, the Orange Free State and Transvaal. In order to prevent the Boers from laying claim to any coastline, the British annexed Natal in 1842.

In 1860 the British introduced Indians to Natal as indentured laborers on sugar plantations. At the turn of the century they were joined by a group of Indian merchants. Today about 70 per cent of Asians are Hindu and 20 per cent are Muslim. The majority live around the Durban area.

Just prior to the time the Boers were trekking into the interior, African societies were undergoing traumatic changes because of the widespread dispersal of African peoples in the wake of a revolutionary upheaval called the *Mfecane*. The *Mfecane* originated in Natal when a small clan, the Zulu, led by an imaginative military leader, Chaka, created a major kingdom based on raiding. Zulu expansionism ignited a chain reaction of violent conflict, population dispersion, migration and devastation which reshuffled African peoples throughout the whole of southern Africa. Despite the unsettled nature of the region, African societies resisted European expansion on a variety of fronts until the early 20th century.

The discovery of gold and diamonds in the last third of the 19th century dramatically transformed the political and economic character of southern Africa as the region's economy changed from one almost wholly based on agriculture to one predominantly industrial and urban. For Africans the period spelled the entrenchment of European rule; they were increasingly forced off their land to seek work in European areas as migrant laborers. For Europeans, the mineral discoveries provoked greater antagonism and conflict between the British and the Boer republics, resulting in two wars (1880–81, 1899–1902). The British won the latter one, the Anglo-Boer War, which signaled the end of Boer political independence.

In 1910 the four colonies of Natal, Cape of Good Hope, Orange Free State and Transvaal joined together in the Union of South Africa. Its European parliament was initially dominated by two political parties, the South African Party and the National Party, but in 1933, the two merged to form the United Party, which dominated political life until 1948, when the National Party (NP), representing extreme Afrikaner nationalism, won power. During this period, Africans for the most part were excluded from participating in the political life of the country and parliament passed numerous pieces of legislation that cemented the economic and politi-

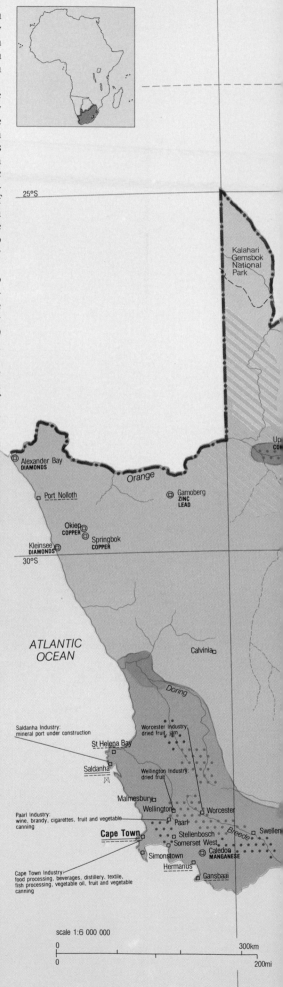

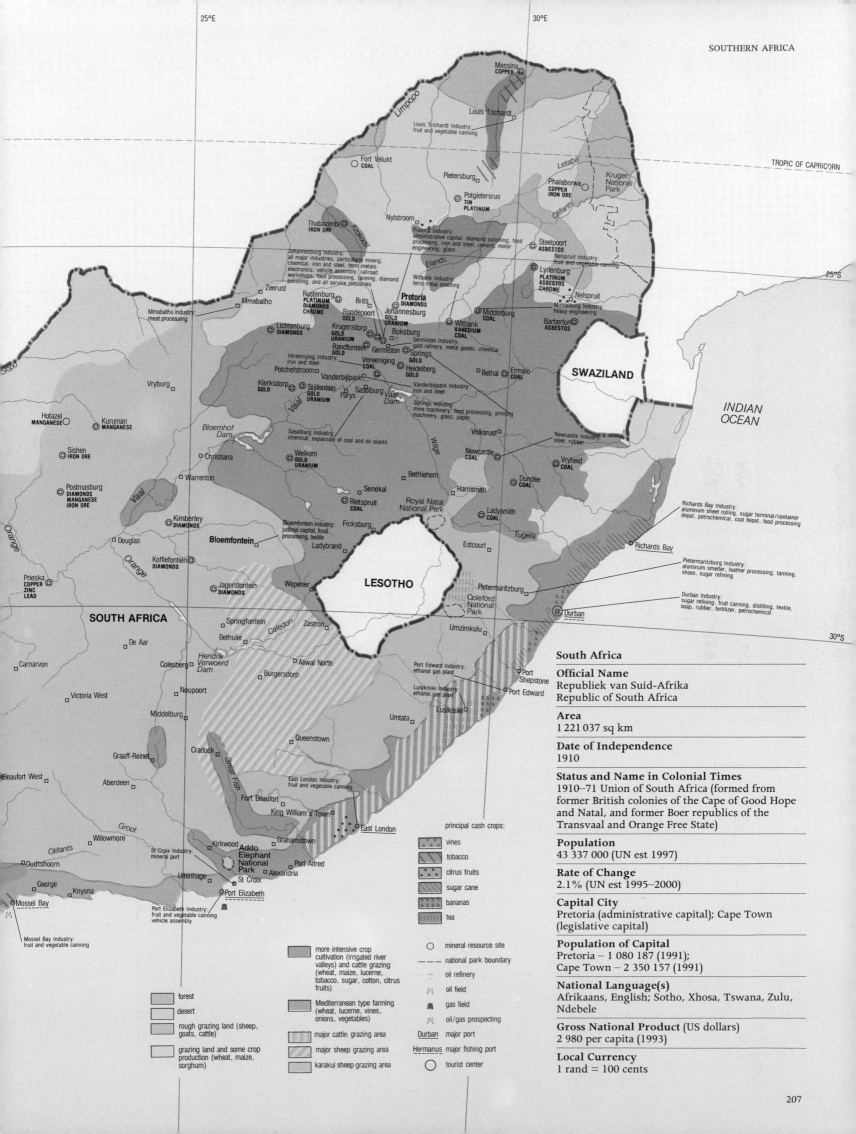

25°E 30°E

Messina
COPPER

Louis Trichardt

Louis Trichardt Industry:
fruit and vegetable canning

TROPIC OF CAPRICORN

Fort Velukt
COAL

Letaba

Kruger
National
Park

Pietersburg

Phalaborwa
COPPER
IRON ORE

Olifants

Potgietersrus
TIN
PLATINUM

Nylstroom

Thabazimbi
IRON ORE

Pretoria Industry:
administrative capital, diamond polishing, food
processing, iron and steel, cement, motor
engineering, glass

Steelpoort
ASBESTOS

25°S

Johannesburg Industry:
all major industries, particularly mining,
chemical, iron and steel, ferro metals,
electronics, vehicle assembly, railroad
workshops, food processing, tanning, diamond
polishing, and all service industries

Witbank Industry:
ferro metal smelting

Nelspruit Industry:
fruit and vegetable canning

Zeerust

Lydenburg
PLATINUM
ASBESTOS
CHROME

Nelspruit

Mmabatho industry:
meat processing

Mmabatho

Rustenburg
PLATINUM
DIAMONDS
CHROME

Brits

Pretoria
DIAMONDS

Middelburg Industry:
heavy engineering

Roodepoort

Johannesburg
GOLD
URANIUM

Middelburg
COAL

Barberton
ASBESTOS

SWAZILAND

Lichtenburg
DIAMONDS

Krugersdorp
GOLD
URANIUM

Boksburg

Witbank
VANEDIUM
COAL

Randfontein
GOLD

Germiston

Germiston Industry:
gold refinery, metal goods, chemical

Vereeniging Industry:
iron and steel

Vereeniging
COAL

Springs

Vryburg

Potchefstroom

Heidelberg
GOLD

Bethal

Ermelo
COAL

Klerksdorp
GOLD

Stilfontein
GOLD
URANIUM

Vanderbijlpark

Sasolburg

Parys

Vaal
Dam

Vanderbijlpark Industry:
iron and steel

Hotazel
MANGANESE

Kuruman
MANGANESE

Bloemhof
Dam

Springs Industry:
mine machinery, food processing, printing
machinery, glass, paper

Volksrust

Sishen
IRON ORE

Sasolburg Industry:
chemical, expansion of coal and oil plants

Welkom
GOLD
URANIUM

Christiana

Warrenton

Newcastle Industry:
steel, rubber

Postmasburg
DIAMONDS
MANGANESE
IRON ORE

Senekal

Bethlehem

Newcastle
COAL

Vryheid
COAL

Vaal

Kimberley
DIAMONDS

Rietspruit
COAL

Royal Natal
National Park

Harrismith

Dundee
COAL

Prieska
COPPER
ZINC
LEAD

Douglas

Ladysmith
COAL

Richards Bay Industry:
aluminum sheet rolling, sugar terminal/container
depot, petrochemical, coal depot, food processing

Orange

Koffiefontein
DIAMONDS

Bloemfontein industry:
judicial capital, food
processing, textile

Ficksburg

Estcourt

Tugela

Richards Bay

SOUTH AFRICA

Jagersfontein
DIAMONDS

Bloemfontein

Ladybrand

Wepener

LESOTHO

Pietermaritzburg

Coleford
National
Park

Pietermaritzburg Industry:
aluminum smelter, leather processing, tanning,
shoes, sugar refining

Springfontein

Caledon

Zastron

Umzimkulu

Durban

Durban Industry:
sugar refining, fruit canning, distilling, textile,
soap, rubber, fertilizer, petrochemical

De Aar

Bethulie

30°S

Carnarvon

Colesberg

Hendrik
Verwoerd
Dam

Aliwal North

Burgersdorp

Port Edward Industry:
ethanol gas plant

Port
Shepstone

Victoria West

Noupoort

Port Edward

Lusikisiki Industry:
ethanol gas plant

Middelburg

Umtata

Lusikisiki

Graaff-Reinet

Queenstown

Beaufort West

Aberdeen

Cradock

East London Industry:
fruit and vegetable canning

South Africa

Official Name
Republiek van Suid-Afrika
Republic of South Africa

Area
1 221 037 sq km

Date of Independence
1910

Fort Beaufort

King William's Town

Status and Name in Colonial Times
1910–71 Union of South Africa (formed from
former British colonies of the Cape of Good Hope
and Natal, and former Boer republics of the
Transvaal and Orange Free State)

East London

principal cash crops:

vines

Population
43 337 000 (UN est 1997)

Kirkwood

Addo
Elephant
National
Park

Grahamstown

tobacco

St Croix Industry:
mineral port

Port Alfred

citrus fruits

Rate of Change
2.1% (UN est 1995–2000)

Uitenhage

Alexandria

sugar cane

Capital City
Pretoria (administrative capital); Cape Town
(legislative capital)

George

Knysna

St Croix

bananas

Port Elizabeth

tea

Mossel Bay

Population of Capital
Pretoria – 1 080 187 (1991);
Cape Town – 2 350 157 (1991)

Port Elizabeth Industry:
fruit and vegetable canning,
vehicle assembly

National Language(s)
Afrikaans, English; Sotho, Xhosa, Tswana, Zulu,
Ndebele

Mossel Bay Industry:
fruit and vegetable canning

INDIAN
OCEAN

more intensive crop
cultivation (irrigated river
valleys) and cattle grazing
(wheat, maize, lucerne,
tobacco, sugar, cotton, citrus
fruits)

mineral resource site

national park boundary

Gross National Product (US dollars)
2 980 per capita (1993)

Local Currency
1 rand = 100 cents

forest

desert

rough grazing land (sheep,
goats, cattle)

Mediterranean type farming
(wheat, lucerne, vines,
onions, vegetables)

oil refinery

oil field

gas field

grazing land and some crop
production (wheat, maize,
sorghum)

major cattle grazing area

major sheep grazing area

karakul sheep grazing area

oil/gas prospecting

Durban major port

Hermanus major fishing port

tourist center

207

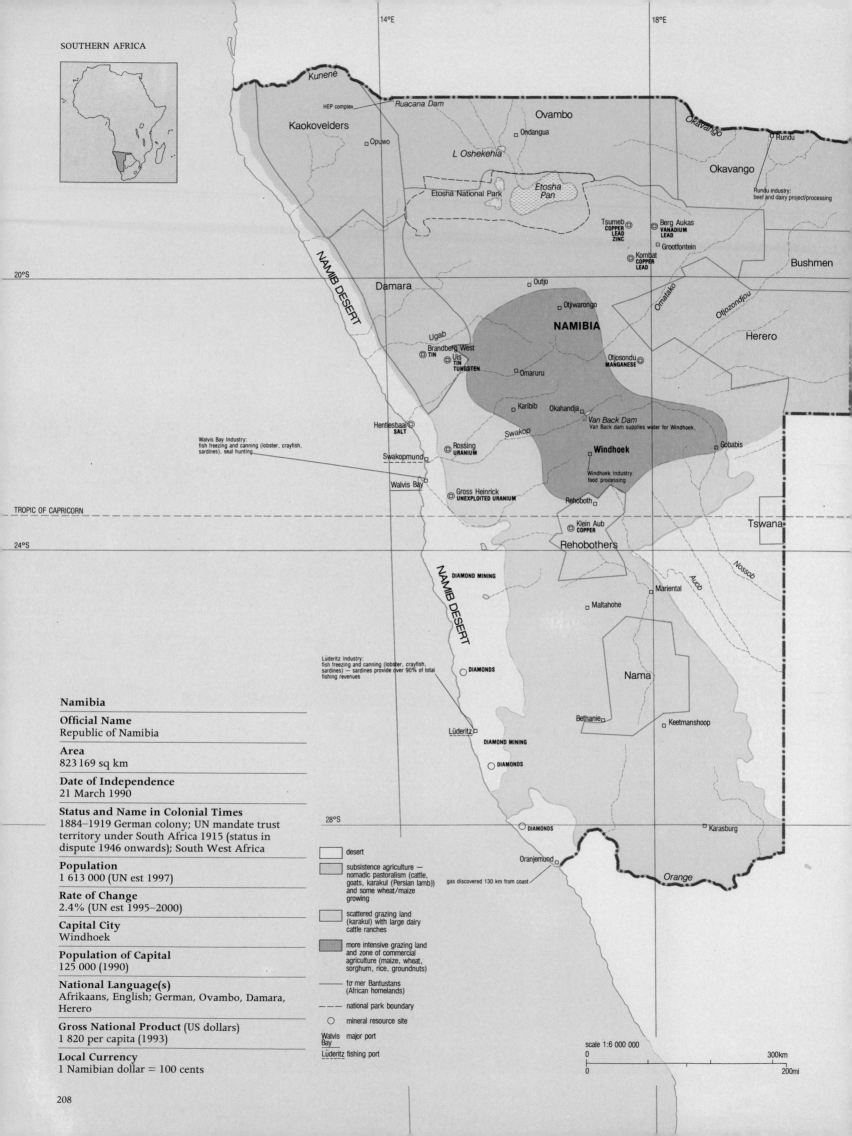

SOUTHERN AFRICA

14°E · · · 18°E

Kunene

HEP complex · Ruacana Dam

Kaokovelders

Opuwo

Ovambo

Ondangua

L Oshekehia

Okavango

Rundu

Okavango

Rundu industry:
beef and dairy project/processing

Etosha National Park

Etosha Pan

Bushmen

Tsumeb ◎ COPPER LEAD ZINC

◎ Berg Aukas VANADIUM LEAD

Grootfontein

◎ Kombat COPPER LEAD

20°S

Damara

Outjo

Otjiwarongo

NAMIBIA

Omatako

Otjozondjou

Herero

Ugab

Brandberg West ◎ TIN

◎ Uis TIN TUNGSTEN

Otjosondu ◎ MANGANESE

Omaruru

Karibib

Okahandja

Van Back Dam
Van Back dam supplies water for Windhoek,

Hentiesbaai ◎ SALT

◎ Rossing URANIUM

Swakop

Windhoek

Gobabis

Walvis Bay Industry:
fish freezing and canning (lobster, crayfish,
sardines), seal hunting

Swakopmund

Walvis Bay

◎ Gross Heinrick UNEXPLOITED URANIUM

Windhoek Industry:
food processing

TROPIC OF CAPRICORN

Rehoboth

◎ Klein Aub COPPER

Tswana

24°S

Rehobothers

NAMIB DESERT

DIAMOND MINING

Mariental

Auob

Nossob

Maltahohe

Lüderitz Industry:
fish freezing and canning (lobster, crayfish,
sardines) — sardines provide over 90% of total
fishing revenues

◎ DIAMONDS

Nama

Lüderitz

DIAMOND MINING

◎ DIAMONDS

Bethanie

Keetmanshoop

28°S

◎ DIAMONDS

Karasburg

Namibia

Official Name
Republic of Namibia

Area
823 169 sq km

Date of Independence
21 March 1990

Status and Name in Colonial Times
1884–1919 German colony; UN mandate trust
territory under South Africa 1915 (status in
dispute 1946 onwards); South West Africa

Population
1 613 000 (UN est 1997)

Rate of Change
2.4% (UN est 1995–2000)

Capital City
Windhoek

Population of Capital
125 000 (1990)

National Language(s)
Afrikaans, English; German, Ovambo, Damara,
Herero

Gross National Product (US dollars)
1 820 per capita (1993)

Local Currency
1 Namibian dollar = 100 cents

Oranjemund

gas discovered 130 km from coast

Orange

desert

subsistence agriculture —
nomadic pastoralism (cattle,
goats, karakul (Persian lamb))
and some wheat/maize
growing

scattered grazing land
(karakul) with large dairy
cattle ranches

more intensive grazing land
and zone of commercial
agriculture (maize, wheat,
sorghum, rice, groundnuts)

fσrmer Bantustans
(African homelands)

national park boundary

○ mineral resource site

Walvis Bay · major port

Lüderitz · fishing port

scale 1:6 000 000

0 ⊢————————⊣ 300km

0 ⊢————————⊣ 200mi

208

E Caprivians

cal dominance of the whites.

After assuming power, the NP – appealing primarily to the Afrikaners who constituted 60 per cent of the white population – built an overwhelming majority in the whites-only parliament. It was opposed by two minor parties, the New Republic Party and the Progressive Federal Party (PFP), appealing largely to English-speaking voters. In 1961, after a referendum, South Africa declared itself a republic and withdrew from the British Commonwealth.

The NP instituted a controversial "apartheid" policy that involved separating races into ethnic units and creating ten independent homelands – "Bantustans" – for African ethnic groups and one homeland for whites. In the Bantustans, Africans had nominal self-government, but those working in white areas had very few rights. In pursuit of this policy, the government granted "independence" to Transkei (1976), Bophuthatswana (1977) and Venda (1979). Asians and Coloreds had no homelands, so they were given separate representative councils with limited legislative powers. Most Africans, Coloreds and Asians rejected these policies.

With few mineral or industrial resources, the Bantustans were not economically viable, and effectively served as labor reservoirs for the white-dominated economy. Most Africans were compelled to become migrant workers in white areas, while subsistence agriculture eroded their land through overstocking and overgrazing. In pursuit of racial segregation the government forcibly relocated hundreds of thousands of people, mostly blacks, from one area to another within cities, or from urban areas to Bantustans – even so, over half of the black population remained on white farms or in the urban areas.

The first major African nationalist group, the African National Congress (ANC), was founded in 1912. After World War II, it was especially active in organizing major nonviolent protests against government policies. In 1959 the Pan Africanist Congress (PAC) broke away from the ANC and restricted its membership to blacks only. After the "Sharpeville massacre" of PAC demonstrators in 1960, the government declared the ANC, PAC and Communist Party illegal, forcing them underground and into exile; but their work continued despite the imprisonment of leaders such as Nelson Mandela and stringent security regulations.

Younger Africans began turning to other organizations, such as the South African Students' Organization and the Black People's Convention. These organizations, and many others, were banned after violent riots in the black township of Soweto (1976) and other black urban areas; and in 1977 the death in prison of a young black community leader, Steve Biko, aroused worldwide condemnation. The only significant black movement

allowed to operate legally was Inkatha, a cultural organization led by Chief Gatsha Buthelezi, head of the KwaZulu Bantustan.

In 1978 P. W. Botha became prime minister, and instituted a series of constitutional reforms intended to give a limited voice in government to Coloreds and Asians (but not to Africans). These were strongly opposed by the PFP and by NP members who broke away to form the Conservative Party in 1982. The adoption of a new constitution in 1984 also provoked serious riots in the black townships. A state of emergency was declared, and renewed after the 1987 elections. During the 1980s international pressure and economic sanctions intensified. Reforms continued, but so did repression. In 1989 ill-health forced Botha to resign; F. W. de Klerk became prime minister, and later in the year was elected president.

In 1990 de Klerk legalized the ANC and began to free political prisoners, including ANC leader Nelson Mandela. In 1991 he began to negotiate with black political groups, abandoning apartheid and working with the ANC to create a peaceful transition to majority rule and the re-incorporation of the Bantustans. After difficult negotiations with right-wing groups and with Inkatha, the first democratic elections were held in 1994, characterized by kilometer-long queues of people waiting patiently to vote for the first time in their lives. The ANC won a clear majority in the new parliament; but the new president, Nelson Mandela, at once set up a government of national unity. However, when a new, non-racial constitution came into force in 1996 the NP resigned from the government.

A Truth and Reconciliation Commission, chaired by Nobel Peace Prize winner Archbishop Desmond Tutu, was set up to examine human-rights abuses by all parties committed between 1960 and 1993. It had discretion to grant amnesty in return for full disclosure of a crime, and to arrange reparation for victims and their families.

The arrival of majority rule in South Africa signaled a fundamental change in its economy, which had been built on exploitation of the black population. At present, however, white people continue to enjoy the best incomes, health and living standards, while most blacks still live in poverty. In its efforts to improve these conditions, the new government must deal with massive unemployment, helped to some extent by the removal of economic sanctions and the promise of substantial foreign aid.

South Africa has the largest GDP in Africa, and its mineral wealth is still at the heart of its economic strength, accounting for more than half of all exports and some 7.5 per cent of GDP. Diamonds remain important, but gold and coal make the largest contribution. Energy is mostly produced from coal, supplemented by nuclear power and hydroelectric schemes, and there are recently discovered offshore oilfields some 140 kilometers southwest of the Cape. The South African Coal, Oil, and Gas Corporation, which produces oil from coal, was privatized by the new government. South Africa is also the world's largest producer of platinum and chromium. Other mining products include vanadium, nickel, copper, antimony, iron, asbestos, fluorspar,

manganese and limestone.

Manufacturing makes the largest single contribution to the economy, accounting for almost one-quarter of GDP in 1995. Key sectors include chemicals, petroleum and coal products, food products, the motor industry, iron and steel, metal products, machinery, paper and textiles. Most industries are concentrated in four areas – Witwatersrand, Port Elizabeth–Uitenhage, Durban–Pinetown, and the western Cape region – which account for the greater part of industrial output and employment.

Agriculture is another key economic sector, although its importance has diminished somewhat over the years. Land and water resources are generally poor except in areas such as the KwaZulu–Natal coast and western Cape river valleys. Only 15 per cent of the land is arable and rainfall is sporadic, so farmers rely heavily on irrigation; and in the former white farming areas, agriculture is highly mechanized and export-oriented. Farming contributed only about 4 per cent of GDP in 1995, but made a substantial contribution to exports with products including maize, fruit, sugar, wool and meat. Different crops are important in different regions: in the southwestern Cape wine and fruit are the major products, in KwaZulu–Natal sugar cane predominates, while on the high veld it is maize, wheat, citrus fruits, tobacco, and dairy and cattle ranching. A few timber plantations have been established in the east and southeast to help supply the mining, paper and building industries. Main fishing grounds lie of the southern and western coasts.

Namibia

Namibia, formerly known as South West Africa, has a long Atlantic coastline and its territorial neighbors are Angola, Botswana and South Africa. It also extends to Zambia along the 30- by 440-kilometer Caprivi Strip. The Namib Desert's shifting sand dunes and salt pans extend inland from the coast. The central plateau has elevations up to 2485 meters and on its eastern side is the Kalahari Desert. Wells, boreholes and over 10 000 dams supplement intermittent rivers.

Namibia's population density is among the world's lowest. The African peoples are broadly divided into about ten ethnic groups speaking Bantu and Khoisan languages. The northern part of Namibia is mainly inhabited by the Bantu-speaking Ovambo, by far the largest group, and by the Kavango and the Caprivian peoples. Other significant African peoples include the Damara, the Herero and the Nama. The Khoisan Bushmen live mostly in the Kalahari Desert area. The south has urban and rural areas and scattered African populations. Windhoek, the capital, contains almost half the small proportion of whites.

Namibia has a litigious history. The harsh environment and lack of obvious economic potential initially inhibited British and South African annexation. German missions established in the 1840s provided a continuing link before Bismarck formally acquired the area in 1884. The German colonial period was marked by unrest, most notably the 1904 Herero rebellion. When, following World War I, the League of Nations and Treaty of Versailles divested Germany of its colonial empire, South West Africa was made a Class C Mandate. On 2 December 1920 the Union of South Africa proceeded to administer the region.

Following World War II the prospect of decolonization prompted the South African Nationalist regime in 1949 unilaterally to extend its sovereignty to Namibia. Whites were represented in the Cape Town parliament. In 1966 the United Nations and the International Court of Justice called for South African withdrawal but by 1969 South Africa had extended its security, apartheid and Bantustan policies to Namibia.

The white National and Federal parties of Namibia were opposed by the clandestine South West Africa People's Organization (SWAPO), which stood for majority rule and operated from bases in Angola and Zambia. Guerrilla and industrial action increased after 1966. After the 1974 Portuguese coup, when Portugal withdrew from Angola and Mozambique, South Africa organized "tribal" elections, but a SWAPO boycott robbed them of credibility. For the next 15 years the country was involved in complex diplomatic negotiations as South Africa tried to secure withdrawal of Cuban troops from Angola in return for its own withdrawal from Namibia. This was finally achieved in 1989, after a brief outbreak of hostilities: some 280 SWAPO troops were killed while going to report to the United Nations Transition Assistance Group (UNTAG). In 1994 South Africa gave Namibia sovereignty over the disputed Walvis Bay area (now a free trade zone and Namibia's principal port), and agreed to revise the Orange River boundary to give Namibia water rights. Relations with Nelson Mandela's new government have been increasingly cordial.

In 1989 SWAPO won the first elections for an independent Namibian Constituent Assembly. In 1990 Namibia achieved full independence and the Assembly adopted a draft multiparty constitution. SWAPO were the clear winners in the 1992 regional and local elections and the 1994 parliamentary elections, when their leader Sam Nujoma was re-elected president, promising to submit any constitutional changes to a referendum. Opposition leader Misheke Muyongo called Namibia an "ethnic democracy", remarking that most of SWAPO's support came from the Ovambo ethnic group. A request for foreign aid was refused because earlier aid had been misused, and 1996 saw renewed allegations against SWAPO of detention and torture during the 1980s.

Namibia's economy has undergone a difficult transition. A new currency, the Namibian dollar, was created in 1993, and in 1994 President Mandela announced that South Africa – still Namibia's most important trading partner – would cancel the country's massive debt. South Africa has also cooperated in the fishery and canning operations at Luderitz and Walvis Bay, which have been badly affected by overfishing. Problems, however, remain, in particular with land ownership and with the mining companies, and as a result incomes are still very unevenly distributed. Mining accounted for over 10 per cent of GDP in 1995. Diamond mining makes up about one-third of this, and most diamonds are of gem quality, but De Beers Consolidated Mines still own by far the greater part of this output. Other mining products include uranium, lead, zinc, tin, silver and tungsten.

About half of the population depend on agriculture for their livelihood: this involves cattle, goat and sheep grazing, and subsistence millet and maize cultivation. Around Windhoek, farming activities include agriculture, livestock, sheep, Karakul (Persian lamb) and mohair goats. Ostrich feathers are a growing concern. Outside the fishing industry, processing and manufacturing have yet to be fully developed: current activities include brewing, meat processing and chemical production. Tourism is a growth industry.

There is a hydroelectric power station at Ruacana on the Angolan border; Namibia has good potential for further schemes, and for exploiting offshore deposits of natural gas.

Botswana

Botswana is a landlocked tableland surrounded by the territories of Zimbabwe, South Africa and Namibia. Roughly parallel to its southeastern border is a plateau about 1300 meters in elevation, which divides the country into two distinct sectors. The smaller, eastern sector covers part of the Limpopo river watershed; it contains the most fertile land and is home to 80 per cent of Botswana's people. The huge western sector is mostly too dry for dependable agriculture, but even its Kalahari Desert has sufficient vegetation to support large animal life. Rainfall throughout the country is sparse and erratic. Droughts are frequent, even in the east, making more efficient collection of surface water a top national priority.

About 98 per cent of Botswana nationals are ethnic Tswana – members of the western branch of Sotho-speaking Bantu peoples. Most other Botswanans are San-speaking Sarwa (Bushmen). Botswana's modern history began in the early 18th century when the first Tswana people, the Kwena, entered from the south. The Ngwato and Ngwaketse soon broke away from these original Kwena, and the Tawana later broke from the Ngwato. By the late 19th century these four groups and four other Tswana societies dominated the country.

During the early 19th century South Africa's *Mfecane* disturbances sent refugees and marauding Bantu bands through eastern Botswana, and the Ndebele settled in southwestern Zimbabwe, from where they continued to harass the Tswana. Meanwhile, Afrikaners occupied the Transvaal, making life harder for both local and neighboring Tswana communities. Afrikaner pressures pushed the Kgatla into Botswana in 1871.

By the 1880s these external pressures were clearly imperiling the security of Botswana's peoples, and international imperialist forces were closing in around the country. The leading Tswana rulers appealed to Britain for help against Afrikaner encroachments. A British military expedition arrived in 1884, and a year later the Bechuanaland Protectorate was declared over southern Botswana. Northern Botswana was soon added. The protectorate's southern border severed Botswana's Tswana from the bulk of the Tswana peoples, most of whom lived within a separately created British colony which was later incorporated into the present Cape Province of South Africa. Cecil Rhodes's land-hungry British South Africa Company threatened to absorb the Bechuanaland Protectorate into its domain in the 1890s, but another Tswana appeal to Britain forestalled this development.

When South Africa was unified in 1910, Britain provided for Botswana's eventual incorporation into the Union of South Africa. This provision lapsed when South Africa left the Commonwealth in 1961, and Botswana was then transformed into a more orthodox colony. Before this a High Commissioner based in South Africa was the fundamental law-making authority for Botswana, Lesotho and Swaziland, and Botswana's administrative capital was at Mafeking, outside its territory.

In 1961 executive and legislative councils were created, and major political changes followed swiftly. When self-government was granted in 1965, Seretse Khama became chief minister. Independence was attained a year later and Khama became president. Botswana's later history was a struggle for economic independence from South Africa. When Khama died in 1980, Dr Quett (later Sir Ketumile) Masire became president, and was re-elected in 1984, 1989 and 1994. In the late 1980s South Africa launched a series of raids against alleged ANC bases in Botswana, but Namibian independence in 1990 and the end of apartheid in South Africa eased regional tension. In 1994 full diplomatic relations with South Africa were restored. Internally, Botswana was shaken by a banking scandal in 1994 involving senior ministers, and by serious riots in 1995.

The country's communications lifeline is the Zimbabwe-owned railroad linking Mafeking and Bulawayo through eastern Botswana. A large part of the male labor force works in South Africa. Botswana has few significant resources and even these were little exploited until after independence. Livestock products dominated the colonial economy, but since independence substantial deposits of diamonds, nickel, copper and sulfur have been found, which the government is developing commercially. Mining, especially of diamonds, makes the largest contribution to GDP. Another post-independence development is the tourist industry, built around the country's still-abundant wildlife resources, particularly in northern regions. Following the recession of the early 1990s the government is seeking to diversify the economy, and to secure a better market share for its diamond production.

Lesotho

Lesotho is a mountainous country, and is the only nation in the world with all its land situated more than 1000 meters above sea level. Three-quarters of Lesotho is dominated by the rugged and lightly populated Maloti mountains. Its highest mountain, Thabana-Ntlenyana in the Drakensberg range, at 3481

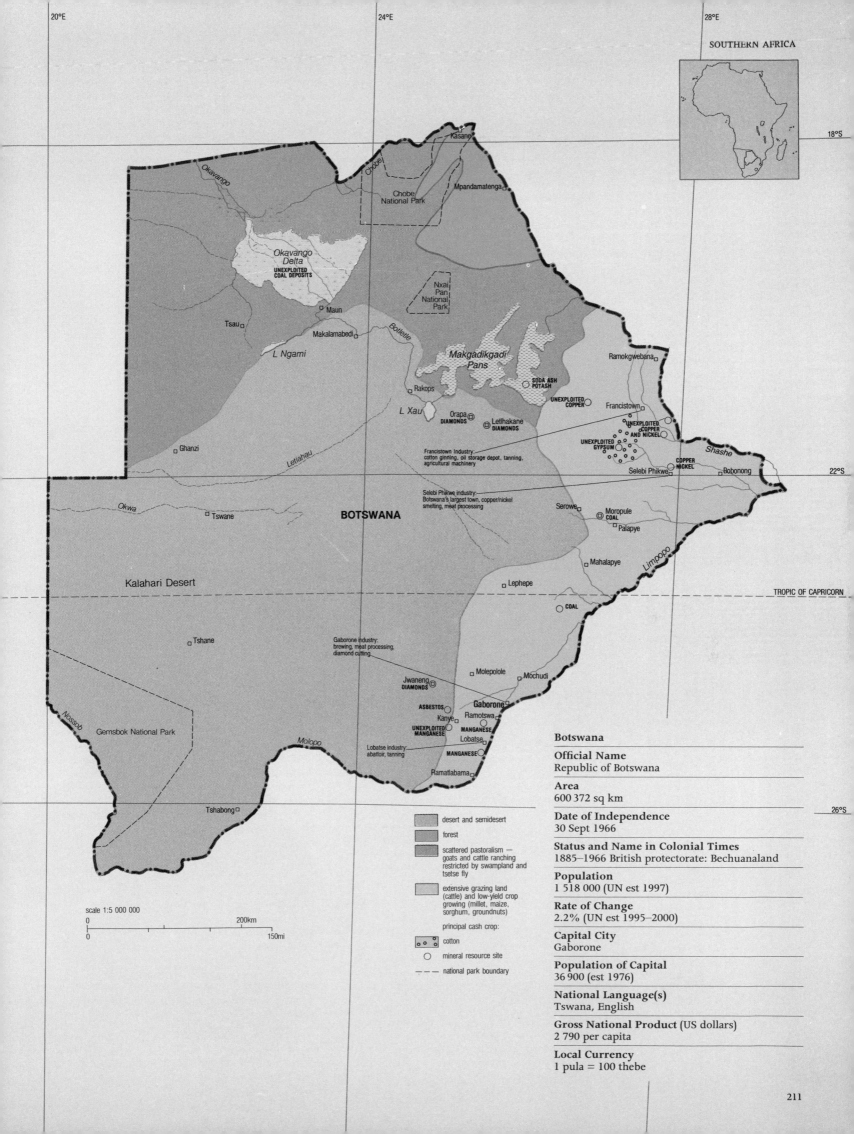

20°E 24°E 28°E

18°S

Okavango

Kasane

Chobe

Chobe
National Park

Mpandamatenga

Okavango
Delta
UNEXPLOITED
COAL DEPOSITS

Nxai
Pan
National
Park

Maun

Tsau

Makalamabedi

Bottetle

Ramokgwebana

L Ngami

Makgadikgadi
Pans

SODA ASH
POTASH

Rakops

UNEXPLOITED
COPPER

Francistown

L Xau

Orapa
DIAMONDS

Letlhakane
DIAMONDS

UNEXPLOITED
COPPER
AND NICKEL

Ghanzi

Letiahau

Francistown industry:
cotton ginning, oil storage depot, tanning,
agricultural machinery

UNEXPLOITED
GYPSUM

Shashe

COPPER
NICKEL

Selebi Phikwe

Bobonong

22°S

Okwa

Selebi Phikwe industry:
Botswana's largest town, copper/nickel
smelting, meat processing

Serowe

Moropule
COAL

Tswane

BOTSWANA

Palapye

Kalahari Desert

Mahalapye

Limpopo

Lephepe

TROPIC OF CAPRICORN

COAL

Tshane

Gaborone industry:
brewing, meat processing,
diamond cutting

Molepolole

Mochudi

Jwaneng
DIAMONDS

Nossob

ASBESTOS

Gaborone

Gemsbok National Park

Kanye

Ramotswa

UNEXPLOITED
MANGANESE

MANGANESE

Lobatse industry:
abattoir, tanning

Lobatse

Molopo

MANGANESE

Ramatlabama

Tshabong

26°S

legend:

| | desert and semidesert |
| | forest |
| | scattered pastoralism —
goats and cattle ranching
restricted by swampland and
tsetse fly |
| | extensive grazing land
(cattle) and low-yield crop
growing (millet, maize,
sorghum, groundnuts) |

principal cash crop:

cotton

○ mineral resource site

- - - national park boundary

scale 1:5 000 000

0   200km

0   150mi

Botswana

Official Name
Republic of Botswana

Area
600 372 sq km

Date of Independence
30 Sept 1966

Status and Name in Colonial Times
1885–1966 British protectorate: Bechuanaland

Population
1 518 000 (UN est 1997)

Rate of Change
2.2% (UN est 1995–2000)

Capital City
Gaborone

Population of Capital
36 900 (est 1976)

National Language(s)
Tswana, English

Gross National Product (US dollars)
2 790 per capita

Local Currency
1 pula = 100 thebe

meters, is the highest in southern Africa. The western quarter of the country consists of the so-called lowlands, which are actually high plains about 1500 to 1600 meters above sea level. Most of Lesotho's administrative head-quarters and towns, population and best agricultural lands are in the lowlands area. Lesotho is completely surrounded by South Africa, a fact that has heavily influenced its economic and political development.

The modern nation of Lesotho was created in the early 19th century largely through the creative leadership of Moshoeshoe I, who forged together remnants of Sotho-speaking groups which had been torn apart during the *Mfecane*, a series of inter-African wars which affected much of southern Africa between about 1820 and 1830. Using the mountains of Lesotho as defensive fortresses and exhibiting considerable military and diplomatic skills, Moshoeshoe was able to consolidate and expand the Sotho state.

The greatest threat in subsequent decades came from the Boers, who trekked into Sotho territory in the 1830s and created a rival state, the Orange Free State. Though the Sotho were initially able to contain the Boers, disputes over land led to wars in 1858 and 1865, which ended in the Orange Free State possessing large tracts of fertile land previously held by the Sotho. In order to stave off further Boer raids, Moshoeshoe successfully appealed in 1868 for British protection. Basutoland (as it was called) was initially administered by the Cape Colony, but after a Sotho rebellion in 1880–81, the British assumed responsibility for the territory.

Basutoland was administered as a High Commission Territory, but the British had limited objectives and spent little money on development. Thus, from the late 19th cen-tury, Basutoland's prosperous economy de-clined dramatically and thousands of Sotho men were forced annually to seek employment as migrant workers on South African mines and farms. As much as possible, the British allowed traditional chiefs and headmen to rule without interference. In 1903 a National Council was created as an advisory body, but since it was dominated by chiefs, it was later opposed by such nationalist organizations as the Progressive Association and Lekhotla la Bafo (Council of Commoners).

Modern Lesotho politics have been domi-nated by three parties: the Basutoland Congress Party (BCP) formed in 1952 and led by Ntsu Mokhehle, the Basutoland National Party (BNP), founded in 1958 by Chief Leabua Jonathan, and the monarchist Marema Tlou Party, established in 1957. In 1960 Britain granted a new democratic constitution. The BCP won the first election in 1960, but the BNP won the 1965 election.

In 1966 Britain granted Lesotho its inde-pendence as a constitutional monarchy under King Moshoeshoe II, and Chief Jonathan became the first prime minister. He swiftly clashed with the king, and when the BCP appeared likely to win the 1970 election, Jonathan declared a state of emergency and suspended the constitution, governing first by decree and then by an appointed assem-bly. Violent unrest and uprisings followed, blamed on South Africa; but it was not until 1983 that Jonathan was deposed in a coup led by Major-General Justin Lekhanya. The new

government improved relations with South Africa, expelling ANC activists.

In 1990, after a power struggle, the king was exiled to Britain, and replaced with his son Letsie III. The next year Lekhanya was deposed in a coup led by Colonel Elias Ramaema, who announced a return to civilian rule and suppressed subsequent counter-coups. Amid rising civil unrest and govern-ment repression the 1993 elections were won by the BCP under Mokhehle. Army unrest and mutinies continued into 1994, when King Letsie, widely supported by both civilians and military, dismissed Mokhehle's govern-ment. Botswana, South Africa and Zimbabwe brokered an agreement in which Letsie restored the government and Moshoeshoe was reinstated as king, Letsie becoming crown prince. After Moshoeshoe's death in a car crash the next year Letsie resumed the throne. From 1996 the government was riven by corruption scandals and police unrest, and in 1997 Mokhehle announced his retirement.

Lesotho is economically one of the world's least developed countries. Per capita GNP is about $650. The vast majority of the resident population is engaged in agriculture, but only one-eighth of the land is cultivable. Much of the land is severely eroded by overgrazing, and productivity is very low. Lesotho has some seven million cattle and over one and a half million sheep and goats – the basis for a thriving wool and mohair industry. Govern-ment attempts to develop small manufactur-ing industries have had some success, and tourism is growing. Diamonds are mined but on a small scale. The only significant natural resource is water, and a major construction scheme to export this to South Africa, while generating hydroelectric power, is nearing completion.

Only a small number of Lesotho citizens can find waged employment locally. Some 40 per cent of the workforce is still employed in South Africa's mines, and almost as many in its farming and industries. Their remittances are a major factor in the economy, but the absence of so many adult male migrant work-ers has had a detrimental effect on the family structure.

Swaziland

Swaziland is one of the smallest nations of Africa. It is bounded on the north, west and south by South Africa and on the east by Mozambique. It is divided into three zones geographically: the mountainous high veld in the west, which averages 1050 to 1200 meters in height; the rolling grasslands of the middle veld (450 to 600 meters); and the bush savanna of the low veld (150 to 300 meters), which covers the southern and eastern regions. Running the length of the low veld and separating Swaziland from Mozambique is the Lebombo range, a rolling plateau 450 to 825 meters in height. There are four main river systems, the Komati and the Umbeluzi in the north, the Great Usutu in the middle and the Ngwavuma in the south. Most industry and agriculture, as well as almost half of the country's population, are in the middle veld.

The precolonial history of Swaziland was dominated by the Dlamini clan. Led by its founder, Dlamini, this Nguni-speaking clan moved into southern Africa during the latter part of the 16th century, settling south and west of what is now Delagoa Bay, east of Swaziland. There they stayed for almost two centuries, when their leader, Ngwane III, brought them into what is now Swaziland. During the 19th century the Swazi nation, under the leadership of a series of outstanding military and political leaders, was a major force in the region, dominating and controlling an area much larger than present-day Swaziland. The Swazi derived their name from one of these leaders, Mswati II.

In the latter half of the 19th century the Swazi were able to retain their independence despite pressures from Boer and British settlers and the Zulu. However, one ruler, Mbandzeni (1874–89), acceded to European pressures for mineral and land concessions and gave away

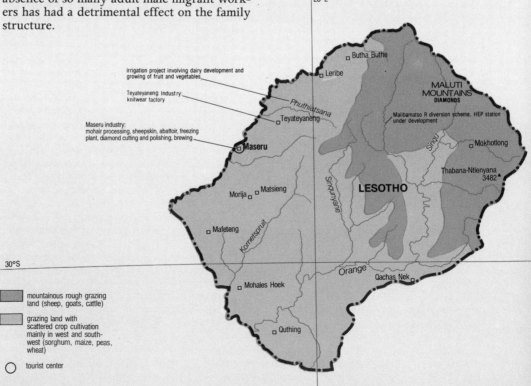

mountainous rough grazing land (sheep, goats, cattle)

grazing land with scattered crop cultivation mainly in west and south-west (sorghum, maize, peas, wheat)

tourist center

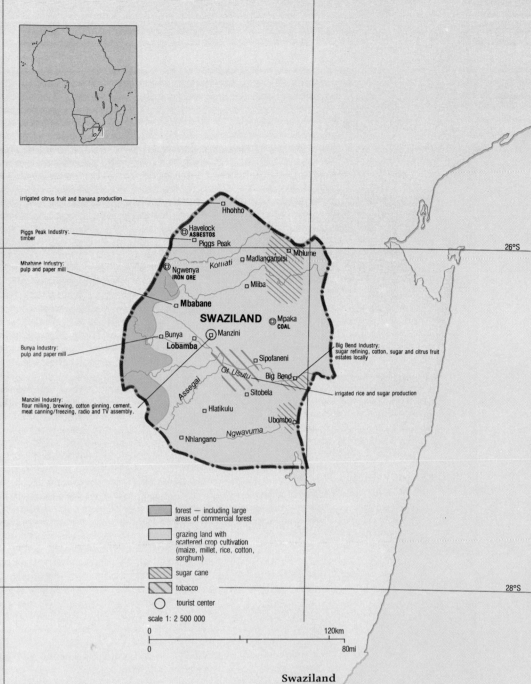

irrigated citrus fruit and banana production

Piggs Peak Industry:
timber

Mhahane Industry:
pulp and paper mill

Bunya Industry:
pulp and paper mill

Manzini Industry:
flour milling, brewing, cotton ginning, cement,
meat canning/freezing, radio and TV assembly,

Hhohho

Havelock
ASBESTOS
Piggs Peak

Mlume

Madlangampisi

Komati

Ngwenya
IRON ORE

Mliba

Mbabane

SWAZILAND

Mpaka
COAL

Bunya
Lobamba

Manzini

Big Bend Industry:
sugar refining, cotton, sugar and citrus fruit
estates locally

Sipofaneni

Gt Usutu

Big Bend

Assegai

Sitobela

irrigated rice and sugar production

Hlatikulu

Ubombo

Nhlangano

Ngwavuma

26°S

28°S

forest — including large
areas of commercial forest

grazing land with
scattered crop cultivation
(maize, millet, rice, cotton,
sorghum)

sugar cane

tobacco

tourist center

scale 1: 2 500 000

0   120km

0   80mi

Lesotho

Official Name
'Muso oa Lesotho; Kingdom of Lesotho

Area
30 355 sq km

Date of Independence
4 Oct 1966

Status and Name in Colonial Times
1868–1966 British High Commission Territory
(annexed to Cape Colony 1871–84): Basutoland

Population
2 131 000 (UN est 1997)

Rate of Change
2.4% (UN est 1995–2000)

Capital City
Maseru

Population of Capital
109 382 (1986)

National Language(s)
English, Sotho

Gross National Product (US dollars)
650 per capita (1993)

Local Currency
1 loti = 100 lisente

Swaziland

Official Name
Umbuso weSwatini; Kingdom of Swaziland

Area
17 363 sq km

Date of Independence
6 Sept 1968

Status and Name in Colonial Times
1894–1903 administered from the South African
Republic (later the Transvaal); 1906–68 British
High Commission Territory

Population
906 000 (UN est 1997)

Rate of Change
2.7% (UN est 1995–2000)

Capital City
Mbabane

Population of Capital
38 290 (1986)

National Language(s)
English, Swati

Gross National Product (US dollars)
1 060 per capita (1991)

Local Currency
1 lilangeni = 100 cents

large tracts of land. This was contrary to Swazi customary law. Later attempts to reclaim the land were rebuffed, but since independence the Swazi nation has been slowly buying back land. Nevertheless a significant minority of the land is still owned by Europeans, who have an influential role in the economy.

In 1903, after a brief period of administration by the Transvaal (1894–1903), Swaziland was brought under British rule. During the colonial period, the traditional system of rule was left virtually intact, leaving Swazi government in the hands of the royal family. In 1921 Sobhuza II became the reigning *nqwenyama* (lion), ruling with the advice of an inner council of advisers and the Swazi National Council, comprised of all adult Swazi males. Around 1960 a small group of younger, educated Swazi founded the Swaziland Progressive Party. Later it split into three factions, the most important being the Ngwane National Liberatory Congress (NNLC) led by Dr Ambrose Zwane. In 1964 Swazi royalists founded the Imbokodvo (grindstone) National Movement (INM) and allied themselves with the European Advisory Council, established in 1921 to advance the interests of the small European community. In pre-independence elections in 1964 for a legislative council, the INM swept all seats – but in 1973, five years after independence, Sobhuza restored the traditional form of government in which representatives are selected by *tinkhundla* (local councils). He retained a cabinet, but chose his own ministers, and the only recognized political party was now the INM.

Sobhuza's death in 1982 led to a prolonged power struggle, but in 1986 Prince Makhosetive finally succeeded to the throne as King Mswati III. He retained the country's pro-South Africa stance, opposing international sanctions and handing over anti-apartheid guerrillas to South Africa. The opposition Popular United Democratic Movement (PUDEMO) pressed for democratic reforms, and a lengthy drought in 1993 led to economic problems and discontent. In 1995 arson attacks on the House of Assembly and on ministers' houses accompanied widespread civil and industrial unrest, and in 1996 the king promised constitutional reform, including the repeal of laws banning political parties. Progress has been slow, however, and unrest has continued.

Being a landlocked nation, Swaziland is heavily dependent on South Africa, which receives about half its exports and provides around 90 per cent of its imports and most of its energy. Remittances from Swazi workers in South African mines are also an important source of income. Since independence Swaziland has been able to develop a prosperous and diversified economy, though more than 60 per cent of the population are still subsistence farmers and pastoralists. Cattle are highly valued as a source of wealth, but only a small percentage are bred for the market. The leading export crops are sugar and forestry products. Mining has declined in importance: coal is still an important export, but iron ore deposits are depleted, and safety concerns about asbestos have reduced its market. Manufacturing is mostly concerned with processing agricultural, livestock and forestry products.

AFRICA IN THE INDIAN OCEAN

These islands have one thing in common: their difference from anywhere else. They are neither "African" like Zanzibar nor "Asiatic" like Sri Lanka. A meeting point of different worlds, the islands form a world of their own. The breakup of the old continent of Gondwanaland many millions of years ago, volcanic eruptions, the slow accumulation of corals, above all, the great tropical ocean itself, have created this unique phenomenon. Isolated from the continental land masses for so long, the island world has evolved a rich diversity of flora and fauna.

Man's arrival on the islands had to wait for his ability to navigate across vast oceanic distances, a relatively recent human achievement. It is now almost certain that the first men in the island world landed in Madagascar about 2000 years ago and that they came from Indonesia, perhaps by way of India and Africa. Archaeological evidence shows the early settlers to have been in possession of fire and to have had the use of iron. If these proto-Malagasy knew of the existence of the other islands, there is no evidence of their having settled on any of them.

Next to arrive were Swahili-speaking Muslim sailors of mixed Arabic–Negro origins. They settled in the Comoros from about 1400 AD and from there spread in small numbers to the coast of Madagascar. Arab navigators had certainly sighted the other islands but they remained uninhabited until the arrival of Europeans in the 17th century.

Thus, in striking contrast to continental Africa, the peoples making up the present-day insular nations are all descended from immigrants. However, a categoric distinction must be made between, on the one hand, Madagascar and the Comoros which had been populated and had developed societies and cultures of their own before the coming of Europeans and, on the other hand, Réunion, Mauritius and Seychelles, which had no precolonial history and whose creole societies and cultures have been entirely created under European colonial rule.

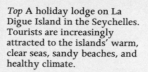

Top A holiday lodge on La Digue Island in the Seychelles. Tourists are increasingly attracted to the islands' warm, clear seas, sandy beaches, and healthy climate.

Above Rice growing in Madagascar on the flooded-field system is a reminder of the Asiatic origins of Malagasy culture. Grown extensively on the island's central plateau, wet

and dry rice occupies about half the total land under crops.

Lcft Sugar accounts for about 90 per cent of Mauritius's export trade. Descendants of imported Indian laborers own many of the smallholdings on which the crop is grown and hand-cutting of the sugarcane is still common.

Above right The lemurs are primitive primates virtually

confined to Madagascar. Several purely arboreal species, threatened by the destruction of their forest environment, are listed by the International Union for Conservation of Nature and Natural Resources in the Red Data Book.

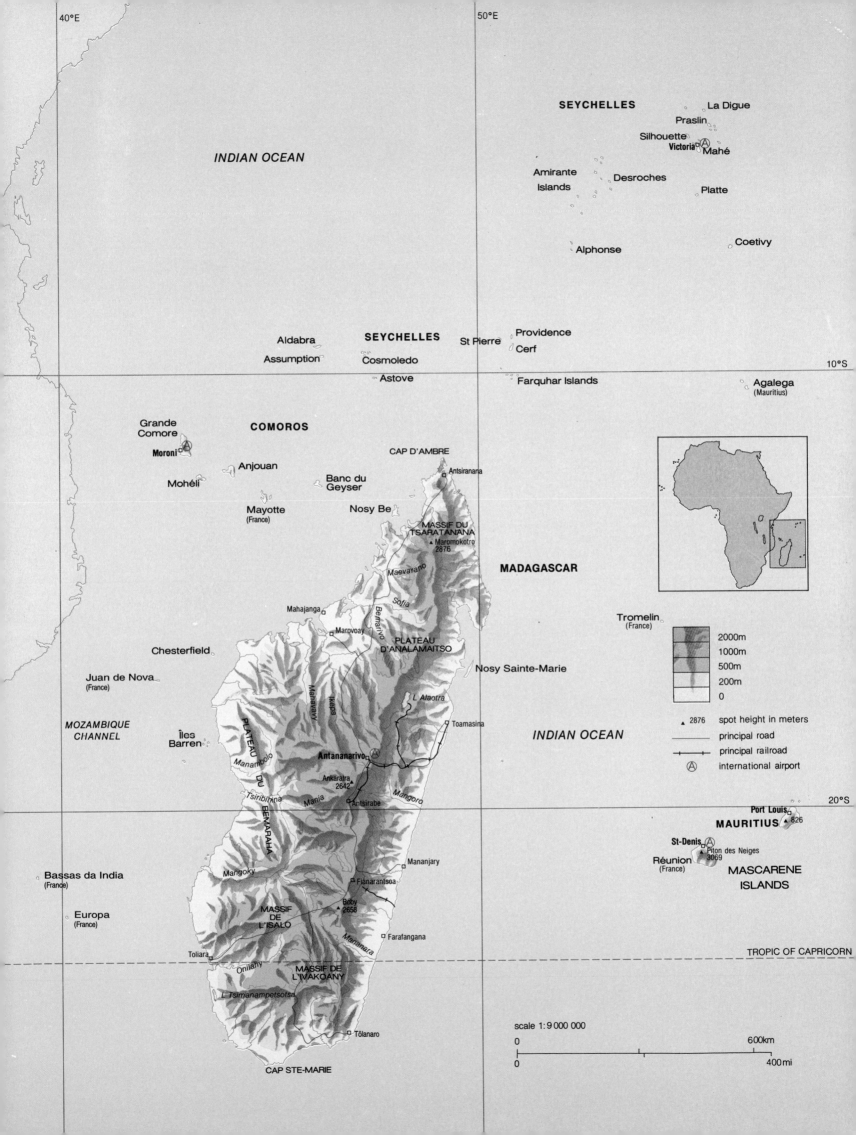

40°E 50°E

SEYCHELLES La Digue
Praslin
Silhouette
Victoria Ⓐ Mahé

Amirante Desroches
Islands Platte

Coetivy

Alphonse

INDIAN OCEAN

Aldabra SEYCHELLES St Pierre Providence
Assumption Cosmoledo Cerf 10°S

Astove Farquhar Islands Agalega
(Mauritius)

Grande COMOROS
Comore Ⓐ
Moroni

Anjouan CAP D'AMBRE
Mohéli Banc du Antsiranana
Geyser
Mayotte Nosy Be
(France) MASSIF DU
TSARATANANA
▲ Maromokotro
2876 MADAGASCAR

Maevarano

Sofia
Mahajanga
Marovoay Tromelin
PLATEAU (France)
D'ANALAMAITSO 2000m
Chesterfield 1000m
Nosy Sainte-Marie 500m
Juan de Nova 200m
(France) L Alaotra 0

MOZAMBIQUE Toamasina INDIAN OCEAN ▲ 2876 spot height in meters
CHANNEL Îles principal road
Barren Antananarivo Ⓐ principal railroad
Ankaratra Ⓐ international airport
2642
Mania Antsirabe Mangoro 20°S

Port Louis
▲ 826
MAURITIUS
Mananjary St-Denis Ⓐ
Mangoky Piton des Neiges
Fianarantsoa 3069
Réunion
Boby (France) MASCARENE
Bassas da India 2658 ISLANDS
(France)
Farafangana
Europa
(France) MASSIF
DE
L'ISALO Mananara

Toliara TROPIC OF CAPRICORN
Onilahy MASSIF DE
L'IVAKOANY
L Tsimanampetsotsa

Tôlanaro
scale 1:9 000 000

0 600km

CAP STE-MARIE 0 400mi

Madagascar

Official Name
Repoblikan'i Madagasikara

Area 594 180 sq km

Date of Independence 14 Oct 1958

Status and Name in Colonial Times
1896–1958 French colony: Madagascar

Population 15 845 000 (UN est 1997)

Rate of Change 3.1% (UN est 1995–2000)

Capital City Antananarivo (formerly Tananarive)

Population of Capital 1 052 835 (est 1993)

National Language(s)
Malgache (Malagasy); French

Gross National Product (US dollars)
220 per capita (est 1993)

Local Currency
1 Malagasy franc = 100 ariary

Madagascar

Madagascar, 1580 kilometers long and 580 kilometers broad, dwarfs the rest of the island world. A small continent in its own right, Madagascar basically comprises two coastal plains and a central plateau arranged in parallel north to south. Almost entirely within the tropics, Madagascar is warm and, except for the extreme southwest, wet most of the year round. The east coast is subject to the rain-bearing southeast trade wind and tropical cyclones, while the north and west of the island are affected by a local monsoon. The central plateau, relatively drier and much cooler, is the most densely populated and developed part of the country.

Forests once covered some 10 per cent of Madagascar, but deforestation by slash-and-burn cultivation, encouraged by government self-sufficiency drives, has left huge areas bare and eroded by the torrential rains to a brick-like, infertile laterite, threatening the ecology and unique animals such as the various species of lemur. On the plateau, marshes have been transformed into Asiatic-style flooded-field rice-growing areas. The savanna country supports large herds of cattle. The large rivers are little used for navigation, but fishing is extensive. On the west coast, estuaries provide natural harbors and the large continental shelf offers good fishing. In the north the splendid bay of Diégo-Suarez was developed as a French naval base. The east coast is straight but has one important man-made harbor: the port of Toamasina, the outlet for the plateau and linked by rail to Antananarivo, the capital and principal town.

The inhabitants of Madagascar, never very numerous, were Asiatic settlers who spread throughout the island and formed a number of kingdoms and clans, often at war with one another but retaining cultural and linguistic unity. Later arrivals, a few Arabs and numerous Negro slaves, were integrated, affecting

Réunion

Official Name
La Réunion

Area
2510 sq km

Date of Independence
not applicable

Status and Name in Colonial Times
1642–1946 French territory; 1946– French overseas *département*

Population
673 000 (UN est 1997)

Rate of Change
3.1% (UN est 1979)

Capital City
Saint-Denis

Population of Capital
207 158 (1995)

National Language(s)
French; Creole

Gross National Product (US dollars)
9 903 per capita (UN est 1994)

Local Currency
1 French franc = 100 centimes

Map labels:

MOZAMBIQUE CHANNEL

Antsiranana industry: dry docks, gold panning, salt, metal foundries

Port St-Louis industry: sugar production and refining

Andoany industry: rehabilitation of sugar estates/ refineries, distillery

Ambanja industry: chocolate factory

Bealanana industry: rice milling

Maroantsetra industry: timber

Mahajanga industry: textile, abattoir/freezing plant, tanning, cotton ginning, cement, sugar/rice milling, vegetable oil processing

Mitsinjo industry: sugar refining

Antananarivo industry: vehicle assembly, building materials, cable factory, rice milling, meat packing/canning, matches, timber, furniture

Toamasina industry: major commercial port, fertilizer, dairying, brewing, metal works, coffee/fruit processing, cement, timber mills

Anivorano industry: rehabilitation of sugar estates/refineries

Mangoro Valley 96 000 ha reafforestation scheme

Antsirabe industry: flour mill, cement, cotton ginning, tobacco/coffee processing

Morondava industry: sugar project/refining

Ambositra industry: paper mill

Fianarantsoa industry: rice milling, meat packing, vegetable oil processing, matches, timber

Toliara industry: cotton ginning, timber, food processing

Tôlanaro industry: sisal processing, mica works, vegetable oil processing

Parc National de la Montagne d'Ambre

Nosy Bé Antsiranana Ambilobe Iharana Ambanja Port St-Louis Andoany Bealanana BAUXITE Analalava Antalaha Maroantsetra Mahajanga BAUXITE Boriziny Mitsinjo Soalala IRON ORE L Kinkony Maevatanana Nosy Sainte-Marie Ambodifototra L Alaotra CHROMITE irrigated rice scheme Ambatondrazaka Toamasina Morafenobe BITUMEN Maintirano MADAGASCAR Nosy Barren UNEXPLOITED PHOSPHATES Tsiroanomandidy Anivorano Antananarivo Miarinarivo Moramanga NICKEL Arivonimamo Soavinandriana Vatomandry Ambatolampy Miandrivazo L Itasy GRAPHITE Antsirabe Morondava Ambositra IRON ORE Mananjary Fianarantsoa Mangoky Manakara Ankazoabo Parc National de l'Isalo Ihosy Farafangana BAUXITE MICA Betroka Toliara Vangaindrano Soalara COAL Betioky GRAPHITE UNEXPLOITED IRON ORE GRAPHITE MICA MICA MICA Manantenina BAUXITE Ambovombe Tôlanaro MICA

MOZAMBIQUE CHANNEL Mahalambo Ikopa Betsiboka Sofia INDIAN OCEAN Mangoro Canal des Pangalanes Mananara Onilahy

TROPIC OF CAPRICORN

Legend:
- forest
- scattered grazing land and crop cultivation — principally in river valleys (cassava, maize, rice, groundnuts)
- major cattle-grazing area
- modern estates and plantations (rice, sugar cane, fruit, vegetables, cotton)

principal cash crops:
- rice
- coffee
- cloves/vanilla
- tobacco
- oil palms
- sisal
- cotton
- cocoa

○ mineral resource site
--- national park boundary
⌂ oil refinery

Tôlanaro major port
Antalaha fishing port

scale 1:6 000 000
0 300km
0 200mi

but not fundamentally changing their predominantly self-sufficient agrarian society, a subsistence peasantry ruled by clan leaders. Nearly 80 per cent of Malagasys still live by subsistence farming.

Madagascar was united by the monarchy of the Hova, a people of the central plateau. Adrianapoinimerina (1785–1810) and his son Radama I (1810–28) completed the unification of the island and, playing on Franco-British rivalry, kept Madagascar independent. An enlightened monarch, Radama encouraged European customs and modernization. The Bible was translated into Malagasy and British Protestant missionaries provided the Malagasy language with a good written form. The reign of Radama marks the apogee of precolonial Madagascar. After his death xenophobia and isolationism alternated with periods when foreign influence was welcomed. France declared a protectorate over the island in 1885, and when this was recognized by Britain in 1890 France was left free to conquer Madagascar in 1895, depose the monarchy and impose colonial rule.

French colonialism restructured the economy through the enforced cultivation of cash crops, notably coffee, for export and the importation of French manufactured goods. The plantations diverted land and labor from food production and Madagascar had to import rice. French settlers did not come in large numbers, although Indians and some Chinese established themselves as retail traders. A few Malagasys were trained to fulfill secondary functions in administration and commerce. Roads, railroads and ports were built to handle trade. On the whole the Malagasys transferred their traditional loyalty for the elders to the new French rulers, but resentment lingered on, especially among those plateau peoples deprived of their domi-

nant positions. This resentment, spurred on by the disorganization of France during World War II, erupted into a widespread but badly organized anti-French uprising in 1947. French repression was swift and thorough; by 1948 over 11 000 Malagasys had been killed. In the 1950s, however, France favored the more moderately nationalist Social Democratic Party (PSD), drawn largely from the traditional underdog clans of the coastal regions. In 1960 the De Gaulle government, following an overwhelming "yes" in Madagascar for membership of the French Communauté, granted independence, with PSD leader Philibert Tsiranana as president.

French influence remained strong in every aspect of the new Malagasy Republic; France kept its large naval base at Diégo-Suarez and its air force base near Antananarivo. Economic problems and political unrest, however, led to a series of military coups which left power in the hands of a radical faction led by Captain Didier Ratsiraka, from the coastal peoples. He broke ties with France, closed the bases and withdrew from the franc zone, establishing the Democratic Republic of Madagascar in 1975–76 as a one-party state, and instituting a program of nationalization and economic centralization. Internationally Madagascar aligned itself with China and the Soviet bloc.

In the years that followed, autocratic rule and economic degeneration, combined with ethnic clashes, led to rising civil unrest which was met by harsh repression. In 1986 Ratsiraka moved swiftly back to a free-market economy and began to restore trade with Western nations. In 1991, faced by near-revolution at home and rising international pressure, he was compelled to restore democratic forms. Unrest continued, and in the first free presidential elections in 1993 he was defeated by one of the prominent opposition leaders, Albert Zafy.

The succession, however, was marred by political infighting, unrest led by Ratsiraka's supporters, and corruption scandals. Reforms demanded by the IMF and World Bank led to further problems. In 1996 Zafy resigned after being impeached for constitutional breaches, but both he and Ratsiraka contested the subsequent election. Ratsiraka was returned to the presidency by a very narrow margin. His government introduced far-reaching proposals for decentralization, to be decided on by referendum. In 1997 natural catastrophes – a cyclone which killed 30 000 people and an island-wide locust plague – devastated the already parlous economy and ecology.

Mauritius and Réunion

Mauritius and Réunion, frequently called "the twin sister islands," are about the same size, are not far apart, have the same volcanic origins, and are subject to more or less the same tropical climatic conditions. There are, however, important variations which have contributed to the different fortunes of the two islands. On the whole geography has been more generous to Mauritius. Réunion is

Mauritius

Official Name Republic of Mauritius

Area 1865 sq km

Date of Independence
12 Mar 1968

Status and Name in Colonial Times
1598–1710 Dutch colony; 1715–1810 French colony: Île de France; 1810–1968 British colony

Population
1 141 000 (UN est 1997)

Rate of Change 1.0% (UN est 1995–2000)

Capital City
Port Louis

Population of Capital
145 584 (1995)

National Language(s)
English; Creole, French, Urdu, Tamil, Chinese, Gujarati

Gross National Product (US dollars)
3 030 per capita (1993)

Local Currency
1 Mauritian rupee = 100 cents

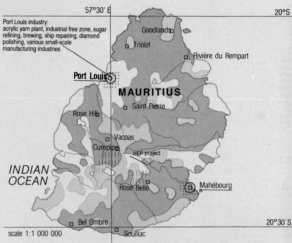

extremely mountainous and has a much smaller proportion of good level agricultural land. The fertile volcanic soils of Mauritius are not washed away by the torrential rains down the steep mountain slopes as in Réunion. Communication and transportation have always been much easier in and with Mauritius. The two good natural harbors and the necklace of coral reefs creating lagoons and splendid beaches around Mauritius contrast with Réunion's abrupt, rocky, forbidding coastline.

The French took possession of and settled in Réunion in 1642. The Dutch established a colony in Mauritius in 1638, but the few settlers were unable to conquer the natural environment. They abandoned the island in 1710. In 1715 the French from Réunion moved in and by importing slaves from Madagascar and Africa were able to cut down the forests and make a permanent settlement. The French East India Company initially used Réunion and Mauritius as supply bases on the long route to India, but the islands soon became plantation colonies in their own right. Mauritius, in particular, acquired great significance as a trade entrepôt, and as a base from which British shipping might be harassed during the long Franco-British duel for the control of the Indian Ocean. This culminated in the British conquest of the islands in 1809–10. Réunion was returned to France

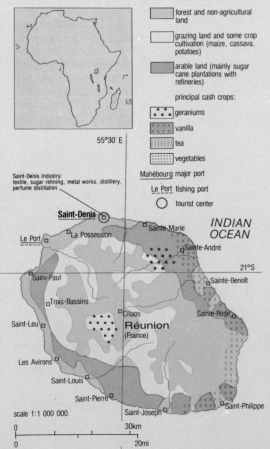

after the Napoleonic wars, but Mauritius, which then included the Seychelles, became a British Crown Colony. Under British rule the sugar plantations were extended, with large numbers of Indian indentured laborers replacing the Africans in the sugar fields after the abolition of slavery. The ethnic composition of the population was thus permanently altered. A colonial partnership was established between the few British civil servants and the well-established French creole sugar planters which lasted to the end of World War II.

From 1947 Mauritius was led through gradual stages of self-government, and, in spite of some ethnic violence, into independence in 1968 with a governmental system modeled on Westminster. A series of coalitions has held power. Initially the Mauritius Labour Party led by Sir Seewooagur Ramgoolam was dominant. However, its partial collaboration in the 1965 takeover by Britain of the Chagos islands, left the administration open to attack. In 1982 an alliance led by the radical Third World Mauritius Militant Movement (MMM) won all 60 seats — to be unseated just a year later. The December 1995 elections returned an equally dominant but rather uneasy coalition between the MMM and MLP. Today Mauritius has universal suffrage with the vote at 18, a free and very vocal press, a very high rate of literacy, almost 100% access to health services, water and sanitation, and a relatively high GNP per capita. In recent years textile manufacture has overtaken sugar as the dominant export industry, and tourism also makes a substantial contribution to GNP. Together with extensive government employment, a successful demographic policy, and attempts to make Mauritius a center for international finance, these industries have reversed a serious unemployment problem. The island's associations with the Commonwealth, and the European Common Market, and strong links with France and India, reflect its ethnic composition.

Sugar continues to dominate Réunion, but less favorable natural conditions and the inability to import cheap Indian labor on the same scale as Mauritius have kept production well behind the sister island. Relative neglect from Paris, culminating in the near collapse of the economy during World War II, led to the island becoming a department of France in 1946. Massive transfers of capital and the extension of French laws to Réunion transformed the infrastructure of the economy, and the social and educational conditions, but failed to pull Réunion out of underdevelopment. The apparent prosperity of Réunion is artificial, being based on aid and the salaries of civil servants. The island produces only a small fraction of what it consumes. Without large-scale emigration to France its unemployment problem would be catastrophic. The hub of the French military, political and cultural presence in the region, Réunion is deeply dependent on the mother country, a situation exploited by the communist opposition parties. For instance, an attempt to close down the television station run by Dr Camille Sudre, the moving spirit behind the radical Free-DOM party, led to rioting, and some 11 deaths, in 1991.

Comoros

The four principal islands of the Comoros archipelago – Grande Comore, Anjouan, Mayotte and Mohéli – lie about 300 kilometers west of the northern tip of Madagascar. They are volcanic in origin, but there are also numerous coral islets. The climate is generally warm, with a six-month rainy season, and the land generally supports abundant tropical vegetation. Traditional pursuits are the cultivation of rice, maize and tropical fruits, fishing and inter-island trade.

Precolonial Comoros was not a nation. Its original Swahili-speaking Muslim settlers founded sultanates almost continuously at war with one another. A rigid distinction was maintained between the ruling "Arabic" landowners and the serf-like Negroid peasants. In 1841 France, expanding its rule into Madagascar, obtained Mayotte by a treaty with the local sultan. Large numbers of Christianized Malagasys settled on Mayotte under French rule, thus differentiating it ethnically from the rest of the Muslim archipelago. From Mayotte France gradually extended its rule over the other islands through treaties of protectorate with the ruling sultans. Cash crops of spices and essential oils were introduced, but the French made no great effort to transform the traditional societies of the islands. From 1919 to 1946 the Comoros were administered as part of the colony of Madagascar but French rule remained distant and indirect.

The Comoros became a French Overseas Territory in 1946, and decided in 1958 to retain that status. In 1961 they were given internal self-government, and in a 1974 referendum the majority for independence was overwhelming – except on Mayotte, which sought French *département* status. When in 1975 the Comoros government declared independence, France granted Mayotte the status of *collectivité territoriale* and recognized the independence of the other islands. Mayotte remains a French dependency.

The first president of the Comoros, Ahmed Abdallah, was almost immediately overthrown by a left-wing coup headed by Ali 'Soilih. He assumed dictatorial powers, but created economic chaos, and in 1978 was killed in a coup on behalf of Abdallah, led by French mercenaries under Bob Denard. Denard became a prime mover in the tragic chaos to come, leading coups at the behest of various political figures. Throughout the 1980s Abdallah too became autocratic and corrupt, and he was assassinated in a 1989 coup led by Denard. French troops removed Denard's men, and Said Mohammed Djohar assumed the presidency.

Comoros

Official Name
République Féderale Islamique des Comoros

Area
1862 sq km (2236 sq km including Mayotte)

Date of Independence
6 July 1975 (unilateral declaration of independence); 1 Jan 1976 French recognition of independence (exc. Mayotte)

Status and Name in Colonial Times
French colony (subject to governor-general of Madagascar 1919–46): Les Comores

Population
652 000 (est 1997 excluding Mayotte); Mayotte (Maboré) 121 700 (est 1996)

Rate of Change
3.0% (UN est 1995–2000)

Capital City
Moroni (on Grand Comore)

Population of Capital
22 000 (1997)

National Language(s)
Swahili; Arabic, French

Gross National Product (US dollars)
500 per capita (1991)

Local Currency
1 Comorian franc = 100 centimes

Seychelles

Official Name
Republic of Seychelles

Area
308 sq km

Date of Independence
June 1976

Status and Name in Colonial Times
1756–94 French colony: Séchelles; 1794–1965
British colony (a dependency of Mauritius
1814–1903): Seychelles; 1965–76 part of British
Indian Ocean Territory

Population
74 000 (UN est 1997)

Rate of Change
1.0% (UN est 1995–2000)

Capital City
Victoria (on Mahé)

Population of Capital
24 000 (1987)

National Language(s)
English, French

Gross National Product (US dollars)
5 110 per capita (1991)

Local Currency
1 Seychelle rupee = 100 cents

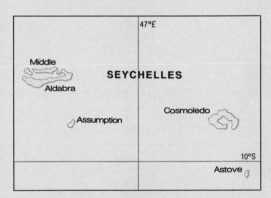

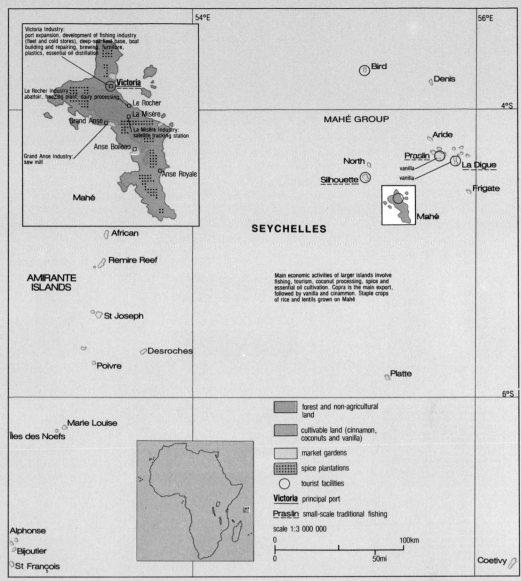

His increasingly dictatorial regime was dogged by coup attempts and corruption, often involving his relatives, and by Mohéli's demands for autonomy. Strikes, and major scandals such as the national airline's sale to a confidence trickster backed by cabinet members, paralyzed his government. In 1995 he was ousted in another coup led by Denard. Denard was again removed by French troops, but Djohar, absent for medical treatment, was deposed by Mohammed El Yachroutu. The two established rival governments, neither commanding conclusive support, and after OAU intervention Mohammed Taki Abdulka-rim was elected president in 1996. Taki soon assumed absolute powers, but faced a wave of strikes and unrest. In 1997 Anjouan, like Mohéli, sought autonomy and a return to French rule, and fought off government troops sent to suppress the rebellion.

Seychelles

The 92 islands and islets making up the Seychelles archipelago, spread out over 700 000 square kilometers of the Indian Ocean, fall into two distinct categories: the larger mountainous islands of very ancient granite formation and the small, low-lying, much younger coral islands. Mahé, the principal island, lies at the center of the archipelago, 900 kilometers northeast of Madagascar. Unlike the volcanic rocks of Mauritius the granite base of the Seychelles main islands does not weather into good soils. Rain, heavier and more frequent than in Mauritius, washes the poor soils of the Seychelles down mountainsides as steep as those of Réunion, leaving a hard laterite as infertile as Madagascar's. With a more equatorial than tropical climate, tempered by the oceanic location and by altitude, the Seychelles, in contrast to Mauritius and Réunion, are fortunate to be outside the cyclone zone. This, together with the coral formations, magnificent beaches and great variety of the numerous islands, has given the Seychelles an even better natural environment than Mauritius for the tourist industry which has burgeoned there, thanks to the major airport which Britain built to give the islands some economic viability after independence. The capital, Victoria on Mahé, stands on a fine natural harbor.

Although formally annexed by France in 1744, the Seychelles were not settled until the 1770s. Slaves from Mauritius were introduced to work the spice plantations. A dependency of Mauritius from 1810, the Seychelles were ceded with Mauritius to Britain at the end of the Napoleonic wars. Anti-slave-trade activities by the British navy brought liberated African slaves to the Seychelles, increasing the labor force for the copra plantations. The new British administration did not displace the "creole" French society, language and culture of the islands, or the majority religion, Roman Catholicism. In 1903 Seychelles became a separate colony. Fishing and agriculture continued as the most important activities, with copra and other coconut products dominating exports.

Britain gave the Seychelles a constitution in 1970, but internal political disputes delayed independence until 1976, when the Seychelles became a republic under a coalition government headed by President James Mancham and Prime Minister Albert René. In 1977 René ousted Mancham in a coup, and established a one-party state under his autocratic control. Throughout the 1970s and 1980s his exiled opponents, including Mancham, staged several coup attempts, often with foreign mercenaries; many such opponents disappeared or were assassinated.

In 1993, under pressure from major aid donors Britain and France, René held multiparty elections and was re-elected. He began a program of economic liberalization and privatization, attempting to establish an international financial center. His attempt in 1996 to make the Seychelles a zone of immunity from extradition or asset seizure was severely criticized internationally as an open door to organized crime.

Flags-Symbols of Nationhood

The flags of the independent African states are a colorful and symbolic assemblage. A few – Ethiopia, Liberia and Tunisia among them – have been in use since the 19th century. The majority, however, were designed in the late 1950s or 1960s to celebrate their countries' attainment of independence. Contemporary symbolism tends therefore to dominate historical association, though certain of the former French territories (Cameroon, Senegal, Mali, Côte d'Ivoire) have adopted variations on the tricolor theme.

The pan-African colors of green, red and yellow are widely favored. Green generally represents the actual or hoped-for fertility of the land; red the struggle for independence; yellow mineral wealth or the sun as a general symbol of beneficence. A black stripe or star sometimes appears to symbolize the African people.

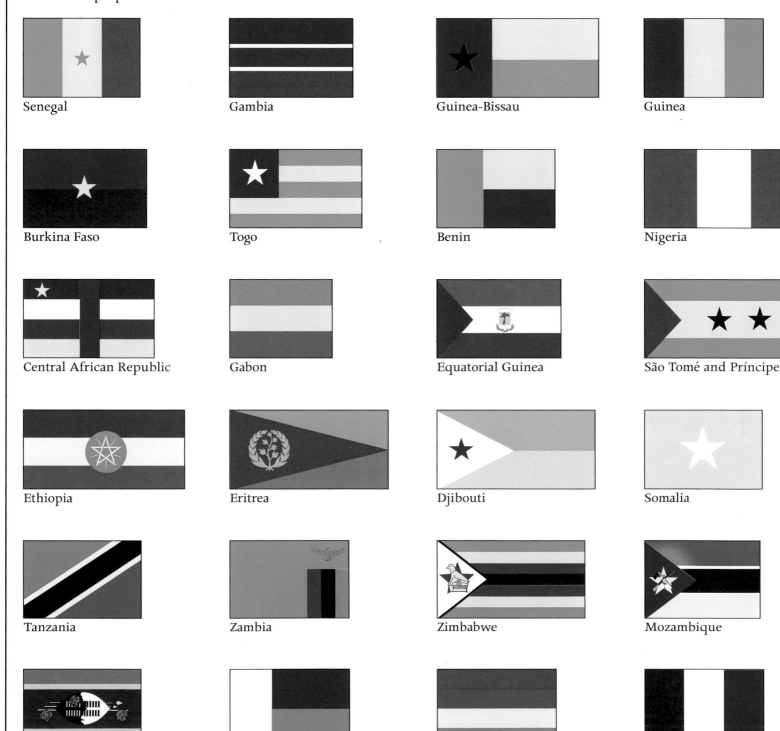

Senegal	Gambia	Guinea-Bissau	Guinea
Burkina Faso	Togo	Benin	Nigeria
Central African Republic	Gabon	Equatorial Guinea	São Tomé and Príncipe
Ethiopia	Eritrea	Djibouti	Somalia
Tanzania	Zambia	Zimbabwe	Mozambique
Swaziland	Madagascar	Mauritius	Réunion

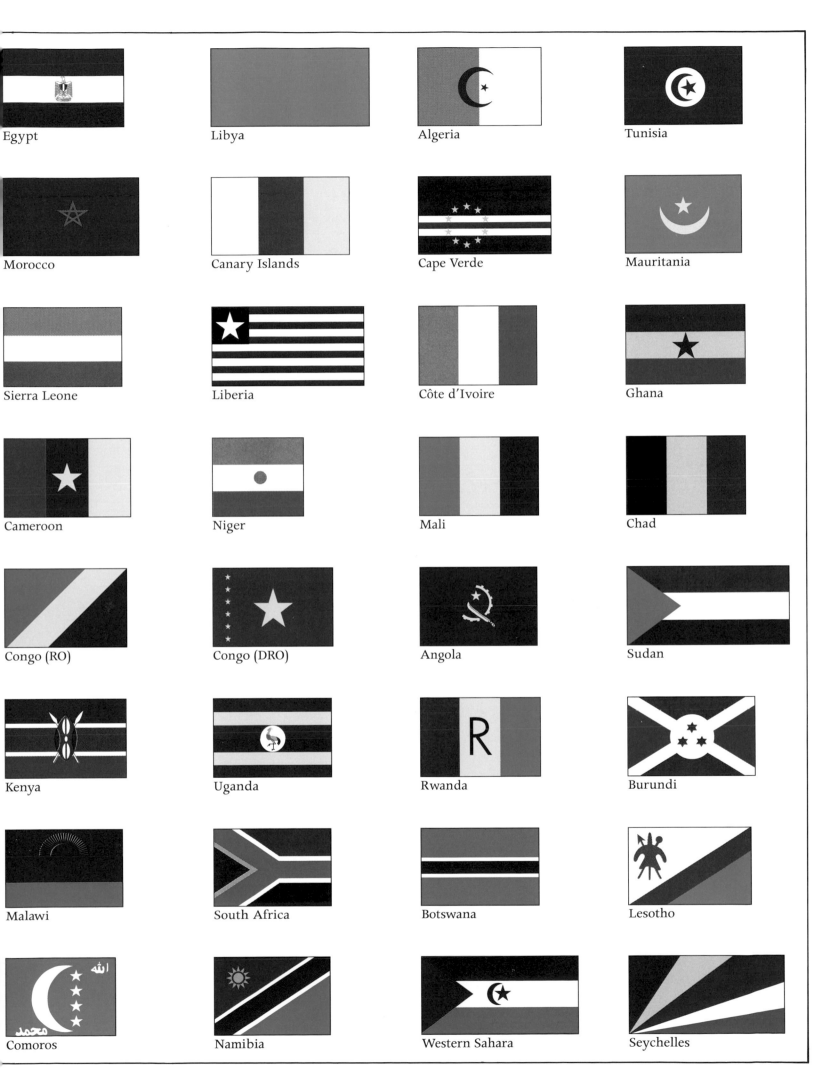

Egypt

Libya

Algeria

Tunisia

Morocco

Canary Islands

Cape Verde

Mauritania

Sierra Leone

Liberia

Côte d'Ivoire

Ghana

Cameroon

Niger

Mali

Chad

Congo (RO)

Congo (DRO)

Angola

Sudan

Kenya

Uganda

Rwanda

Burundi

Malawi

South Africa

Botswana

Lesotho

Comoros

Namibia

Western Sahara

Seychelles

AFRICA IN THE WORLD

Many African nations have attained independence in the last two decades and thus have become members of various international bodies. There are now 49 members of the United Nations, which could include only four African nations – Egypt, Ethiopia, Libya and South Africa – when it was founded in 1945. Since apartheid was dismantled in South Africa, its relations with other African states have improved considerably.

Organization of African Unity (OAU)
This is a grouping set up by African states themselves and includes all member-states of the United Nations. It was founded at the Conference of Addis Ababa in 1963, with the stated aim of pro-

moting "unity and international cooperation among African States and of eradicating "all forms of colonialism in Africa." Its full assembly meets once a year in the capital of the member-state that provides that year's chairman, who is usually the head of state of the host country.

League of Arab States
Several African nations also belong to the League of Arab States (Arab League), "a voluntary organization of sovereign Arab states," founded in 1945. In addition to the North African nations of Egypt, Libya, Tunisia, Algeria and Morocco, three other states, Sudan, Somalia and Mauritania, belong to the Arab League and so form an important bridge

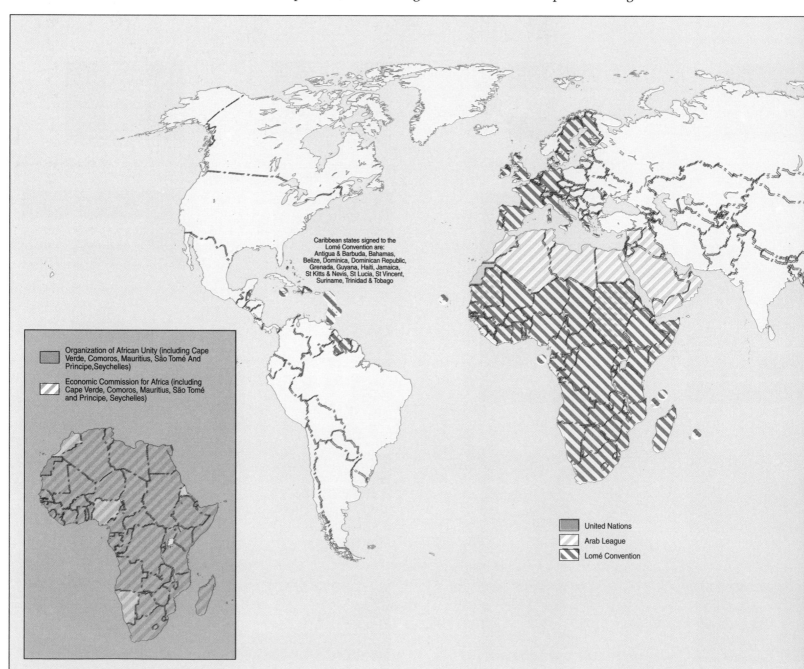

Caribbean states signed to the Lomé Convention are: Antigua & Barbuda, Bahamas, Belize, Dominica, Dominican Republic, Grenada, Guyana, Haiti, Jamaica, St Kitts & Nevis, St Lucia, St Vincent, Suriname, Trinidad & Tobago

Organization of African Unity (including Cape Verde, Comoros, Mauritius, São Tomé And Principe, Seychelles)

Economic Commission for Africa (including Cape Verde, Comoros, Mauritius, São Tomé and Principe, Seychelles)

United Nations
Arab League
Lomé Convention

President Kaunda of Zambia (left) conversing with Prime Minister Mugabe of Zimbabwe at the 1980 meeting of the Organization of African Unity in Freetown, Sierra Leone.

Pacific states signed to the Lomé Convention are: Fiji, Kiribati, Papua New Guinea, Solomon Islands, Tonga, Tuvalu, Vanuatu, and Western Samoa

between black Africa and Arab Africa. In March 1977 an Afro–Arab summit was held in Cairo, comprising member countries of both the Arab League and the OAU. One result of this summit has been a decision by the oil-rich Arab states to give increased aid to the nations of black Africa.

Economic Commission for Africa (ECA)

All the sovereign African nations belong also to the Economic Commission for Africa, which has its headquarters in Addis Ababa. This includes the Republic of South Africa, which was suspended in 1963 but has now been reinstated. France, Britain and Namibia are associate members of the ECA.

Lomé Convention

The Lomé Convention is a newer grouping which has had important economic implications for Africa. It involves almost 70 nations of Africa, the Caribbean and the Pacific (known as ACP countries) and the member nations of the European Union (EU). The Convention was signed at Lomé, Togo, in February 1975 and came into force in April 1976, replacing the Yaoundé Convention, which had been in force between 19 African and six EEC countries. It is due to be renewed in the year 2000.

All the independent nations of sub-Saharan Africa are now members or potential members of the Lomé Convention. In its more limited role the Lomé Convention regards all countries of the ACP as a single customs area, with provision made for products manufactured or processed in part in one ACP country to pass through processes in another

without tax complications. Its aims thus include trade cooperation, as well as export stabilization and financial and technical cooperation. But in its extended role the Lomé Convention is concerned with the development of ACP countries within a global context. Industrial cooperation leading to industrial development is to be furthered by offering mutual access to technology and the adaptation of technology to local needs and conditions.

The Lomé Convention has had only mixed success; the problems that faced the majority of African states in the 1960 have not improved, and are exacerbated by continuing wars in several states. Negotiations began in mid-1998 to discuss more appropriate strategies to take the agreement into the 21st century.

United Nations Agencies

African nations also participate in and benefit from the activities of the various United Nations agencies. There are regional offices in various locations: the Food and Agricultural Organization (FAO) has its regional office in Accra, the World Health Organization (WHO) in Brazzaville, and the International Labor Organization (ILO) in Addis Ababa. The more recently formed United Nations Environment Protection Agency (UNEP) is in Nairobi. The United Nations Educational, Scientific and Cultural Organization (UNESCO) is divided into two sections – Education, and Science and Technology. For sub-Saharan Africa the regional offices are in Dakar and Nairobi. Both UNESCO offices for the Arab states are in Cairo.　　　J.M.

LIST OF CONTRIBUTORS

L.A.   'Ladipo Adamolekun is Dean of the Faculty of Administration at the University of Ife, Ile-Ife, Nigeria.

D.B.   David Birmingham is Professor of History at the University of Kent, Canterbury.

M.B.   Mark Bray is a lecturer in education at the Centre of African Studies, University of Edinburgh.

R.C.B.   R. C. Bridges is senior lecturer in history at the University of Aberdeen.

C.C.   Christopher Chamberlin, who completed a Ph.D. in African history at the University of California, Los Angeles, now works on the research staff of a United States Senator.

P.C.   Peter Clarke has taught African history at the University of Ibadan, Nigeria, and sociology of religion at King's College, London.

R.C.   Richard Curley is an associate professor of anthropology at the University of California, Davis.

S.D.   Susan Denyer has lived in East and West Africa, and published on art and architecture in Africa.

W.E.   William Eaton is a research analyst in the Library of Congress, Washington, D.C.

R.E.   Robert Edgar is a professor of history in the African Studies Program at Howard University, Washington, D.C.

C.E.   Christopher Ehret is a professor of history at UCLA.

F.F.   Finn Fuglestad is on the staff of the Historisk Institutt, University of Trondheim, Norway.

C.F.   Christopher Fyfe is Reader in History at the University of Edinburgh's Centre of African Studies.

T.G.   Thomas F. Glick is a professor of geography at Boston University, Massachusetts.

G.A.H.   Gerry A. Hale is a professor of geography at UCLA.

E.H.   Elizabeth Hodgkin, who has taught in Sudan and done fieldwork in Mali, is now at the Centre for West African Studies, University of Birmingham.

J.H.   Jean Houbert, a Mauritian by birth, is a lecturer in the Department of Politics at the University of Aberdeen.

E.J.   Emrys Jones is Professor of Geography at the London School of Economics and Political Science.

G.K.   Gerhard Kubik is a cultural scientist specializing in African and Afro-American studies and a lecturer at the University of Vienna.

I.L.   Ian Linden was recently a professor of history at the University of Hamburg and is now a freelance writer living in England.

M.L.   Mark Lipschutz, who completed a Ph.D. in African history at UCLA, now works in educational administration there.

J.M.M.   Joseph M. McCarthy is a professor of education at Suffolk University, Boston, Massachusetts.

E.M'B.   Elikia M'Bokolo is on the staff of the École des Hautes Études en Sciences Sociales, Paris.

J.M.   Jocelyn Murray is house editor at the International African Institute, London.

D.N.   David Northrup is a professor of history at Boston College, Boston, Massachusetts.

J.O'S.   John O'Sullivan is a professor of history at Tuskegee Institute, Tuskegee, Alabama.

O.P.   Oliver Pollak is a professor of history at the University of Nebraska, Omaha.

K.R.   Kent Rasmussen completed a Ph.D. in African history at UCLA and writes on central and southern Africa.

W.R.   William Rau completed a Ph.D. in African history at UCLA and later worked as an adult education organizer in Zambia.

C.D.R.   C. Duncan Rice is Professor of History and Dean of Hamilton College, Clinton, New York.

D.E.S.   Douglas E. Saxon has completed fieldwork and is writing up his research for the degree of Ph.D. at UCLA.

M.S.   Martin Staniland is a professor at the Center for International Studies, University of Pittsburgh, Pennsylvania.

J.C.S.   J. C. Stone is senior lecturer in geography and secretary of the African Studies Group at the University of Aberdeen.

I.S.   Inez Sutton is a lecturer in history at the University of Ghana, Legon.

J.E.G.S. J. E. G. Sutton is Professor of Archaeology at the University of Ghana, Legon.

J.B.W.   Jerome B. Weiner is a professor of history at Old Dominion University, Norfolk, Virginia.

A.W.   Ann Williams is a lecturer in history at the University of Aberdeen.

S.Y.   Stanley Yoder is completing a Ph.D. degree at UCLA after periods of fieldwork in Zaïre.

LIST OF ILLUSTRATIONS

BIBLIOGRAPHY

For the most up-to-date information see the current edition of the two yearbooks on Africa published annually by Europa Publications Ltd., London: *Africa South of the Sahara* and *The Middle East and North Africa*. Colin Legum (ed.), *Africa Contemporary Record: Annual Survey and Documents* (London) provides an annual review of current issues affecting Africa.

For a general historical background to the continent, see the Cambridge History of Africa (J. D. Fage and R. Oliver, gen. eds.) and the UNESCO General History of Africa, both published in eight volumes. The Cambridge volumes with editors are:
Vol. 1 (J. Desmond Clark, ed.), *From the earliest times to c. 500 BC* (1982)
Vol. 2 (J. D. Fage, ed.), *From c. 500 BC–AD 1050* (1979)
Vol. 3 (R. Oliver, ed.), *From c. 1050–c.1600* (1977)
Vol. 4 (R. Gray, ed.), *From c. 1600–c. 1790* (1975)
Vol. 5 (J. E. Flint, ed.) *From c. 1790–c. 1870* (1977)
Vol. 6 (R. Oliver & G. N. Sanders, eds.), *From c. 1870–c. 1905* (1985)
Vol. 7 (A. D. Roberts, ed.), *From c. 1905–c. 1940* (1986)
Vol. 8 (Michael Crowder, ed.), *From c. 1940–1975* (1984)
The eight U N E S C O volumes were published between 1981 and 1993 by Heinemann International. Among several useful one-volume general histories are:
B. Davidson, *Africa: history of a continent.* London 1966.
J. D. Fage, *A History of Africa.* London 1978.
John Iliffe, *Africans. The history of a continent.* Cambridge 1995.
Elizabeth Isichei, *A History of African societies to 1870.* Cambridge 1997.

For a cartographical approach see J. D. Fage, *An Atlas of Africa History*, 2nd. ed. (London 1978) and C. McEvedy, *The Penguin Atlas of African History* (Harmondsworth 1980). R. V. Tooley, *Collectors' Guide to maps of the African continent and southern Africa* (London 1969) contains numerous plates illustrating the progress of cartographic knowledge of Africa. R. I. Rotberg (ed.), *Africa and its explorers. Motives, methods and impact* (2nd. ed., Harvard, MA 1974), and the diaries of the explorers themselves, many of which have been republished in abridged or selected versions, trace the advance of European knowledge of the continent.

The listing below contains details of the national bibliographies published by Clio Press of Oxford in their World Bibliographical Series. Another useful series of bibliographies is African Historical Dictionaries, published by the Scarecrow Press of Metuchen NJ and London.

For on-going bibliographical information, see the quarterly: David Hall (compiler), *International African Bibliography* (Hans Zell Publishers, East Grimstead), begun in 1971, which is comprehensively indexed.

Part One: The Physical Background

The Geography of Africa
J. I. Clarke (ed.), *An Advanced geography of Africa.* Amersham 1975.
A. T. Grove, *Africa* (3rd. ed.). Oxford 1978.
J. L. Newman, *The Peopling of Africa: a geographical interpretation.* New Haven 1995.
A. M. O' Connor, *The Geography of Tropical African development* (2nd. ed.). Oxford 1978.
P. Richards (ed.), *African environment: problems and perspectives.* London 1975.

Part Two: The Cultural Background

Languages and Peoples
J. H. Greenberg, *The Languages of Africa.* The Hague 1970.
G. P. Murdock, *Africa: its peoples and their culture history.* New York 1959.
Ngugi wa Thiong' o, *Moving the Centre: the struggle for cultural freedom.* London 1993.

Religions
T. D. Blakely, W. E. A. van Beck & D. L. Thompson (eds.), *Religion in Africa.* London 1994.
A. Hastings, *A History of African Christianity 1950–1975.* Cambridge 1979.
—— *The Church in Africa, 1450–1950.* Oxford 1996.
I. M. Lewis (ed.), *Islam in Tropical Africa*, rev. ed. London 1980.
J. S. Mbiti, *Concepts of God in Africa.* London 1970.
J. Spencer Trimingham, *The Influence of Islam upon Africa.* London and NY 1968.

Early Man in Africa
J. D. Clark, *The Prehistory of Africa.* London 1970
S. Cole, *Leakey's luck.* London 1975.
G. L. Isaac & E. R. McCown (eds.), *Human origins: Louis Leakey and the East African evidence.* Berkeley CA 1976.
R. Oliver & B. M. Fagan, *Africa in the Iron Age.* Cambridge 1975.
D. W. Phillipson, *The Later prehistory of Eastern and Southern Africa.* London 1977.
T. Shaw, *Nigeria: its archeology and early history.* London 1978.

Kingdoms and Empires
P. Garlake, *The Kingdoms of Africa.* Oxford 1978.
R. Gray & D. Birmingham (eds.), *Pre-colonial African trade.* London 1970.
M. Shinnie, *Ancient African kingdoms.* New York 1966.
J. Vansina, *Kingdoms of the savanna.* Madison WI 1966.

Europe in Africa
D. Birmingham, *The Decolonization of Africa.* London 1995.
J. Duffy, *Portuguese Africa.* Cambridge MA 1961.
L. H. Gann & P. Duignan (gen. eds.), *Colonialism in Africa.* Vol. 1, *The history and politics of colonialism 1870–1914.* Cambridge 1969.; vol. 2: *The history and politics of colonialism, 1914–1960,* 1970; vol. 3, *Profiles of change: African society and colonial rule,* 1971.
J. D. Hargreaves, *Prelude to the partition of West Africa.* London 1963.
—— *West Africa: the former French states.* Englewood Cliffs NJ 1967.
J. Iliffe, *Tanganyika under German rule, 1905–1912.* Cambridge 1969.
J. Ravenhill, *Collective clientelism: the Lomé Convention and North–South relations.* NY 1985.

The African Diaspora
R. Bastide, *African civilisations in the New World.* NY 1972
P. Curtin, *The Atlantic Slave Trade. A Census.* Madison WI 1969.
M. Kilson & R. Rotberg (eds.), *The African diaspora. Interpretative essays.* Cambridge MA 1976.
P. Manning, *Slavery and African life: occidental, oriental and African slave trades.* Cambridge 1990.
D. Northrup (ed.), *The Atlantic slave trade.* Lexington MA 1994.
Ibrahim K. Sandiata, *From Slavery to neoslavery: the Bight of Benin and Fernando Po in the era of abolition, 1827–1930.* Madison WI 1996.

The Growth of Cities
J. Gugler & W. B. Flanagan, *Urbanisation and social change in West Africa.* Cambridge 1978.
K. Little, *Urbanisation as a social process.* London 1974.

Vernacular Architecture
K. B. Anderson, *African traditional architecture.* Oxford 1978.
S. Denyer, *African traditional architecture.* London 1978.
R. Gardi, *Indigenous African architecture.* NY 1973
P. Oliver, *Shelter in Africa.* London 1971.
L. Prussin, *Architecture in Northern Ghana.* Berkeley & Los Angeles 1969.

African Arts
U. Beier, *Contemporary art in Africa.* London 1971.
L. Holy, *Art of Africa: masks and figures from Eastern and Southern Africa.* London 1967.
M. Trowell, *African design.* London 1960.
F. Willett, *African art.* London 1971.

Music and Dance
John Blacking (ed.), *The Anthropology of the body* (ASA Monograph 15). London 1977.
—— *Theory of African music. Nine essays.* Urbana IL 1980.
Reginald Byron (ed.), *Music, culture and experience: selected papers of John Blacking.* Chicago 1995.
John Gray, *African music: a bibliographical guide to the traditional, popular, art and liturgical musics of sub-Saharan Africa.* Westport CT 1991.
A. M. Jones, *Studies in African music*, 2 vols. London 1959.
—— *Africa and Indonesia: the evidence of the xylophone and other musical and cultural factors*, 2nd. ed. Leiden 1971.
J. H. Kwabena Nketia, *The Music of Africa.* London 1975.

Education, Literacy and Literature
G. N. Brown & M. Hiskett (eds.), *Conflict and harmony in education in tropical Africa.* London 1975.
P. H. Coombs, R. C. Prosser & M. Ahmed, *New Paths to learning.* NY 1973.
L. Ibnlfassi & N. Hitchcott (eds.), *African Francophone writing.* Oxford 1996.
L. Mallasis, *The Rural world. Education and development.* London 1976.
A. A. Mazrui, *Political values and the educated class in Africa.* London 1978.
Oyekan Owomoyela (ed.), *A History of Twentieth century African literatures.* Lincoln NB 1993.
J. Simmons, *The Education dilemma: policy issues for developing countries in the 1980s.* NY 1980.
J. Wilkinson (ed.), *Talking with African writers.* London 1992.

Part Three: the Nations of Africa

North Africa
S. Amin, *The Maghreb in the modern world: Algeria, Tunisia, Morocco.* Harmondsworth 1970.
D. Gordon, *North Africa's French legacy, 1954 – 1963.* London 1963.

Egypt
J. Berque, *Egypt: imperialism and revolution.* London 1972.
P. M. Hold (ed.), *Political and social change in modern Egypt.* London 1968.
Ragai N. Makar (compiler), *Egypt* (World Bibliographic Series, 86). Oxford: Clio Press 1988.

Libya
Ali Abdullatif Ahmida, *The Making of modern Libya: state formation, colonisation and resistance, 1830–1932.* Albany NY 1994.
J. A. Allan, K. S. McLachlan & E. Penrose (eds.), *Libya: agriculture and economic development*, 2nd. ed. London 1978.
Mary-Jane Deeb, *Libya's foreign policy in North Africa.* Oxford 1991.
R. I. Lawless (compiler), *Libya* (World Bibliographical Seres, 79). Oxford: Clio Press 1987.
D. Vandewalle (ed.), *Qadhafi's Libya, 1969–1994.* London 1995.

Algeria
M. Brett & E. Fentress, *The Berbers.* Oxford 1996.
F. Fanon, *Les Damnés de la terre.* Paris 1961. (Eng. trans., *The Wretched of the earth.* London 1965.)
S. El Machet, *Les États-Unis et l'Algérie: de la méconnaissance à la reconnaissance.* Paris 1996.
R. I. Lawless (compiler), *Algeria* (World Bibliographical Series, 19), rev. ed. Oxford: Clio Press 1995.

Tunisia
H. Bourguiba, *La Tunisie et la France.* Paris 1954.
S. El Machet, *Les États-Unis et la Tunisie: de l' ambiguité à la entente.* Paris 1996.
R. I. Lawless, A. M. Findlay & Anne M. Findlay (compilers), *Tunisia* (World Bibliographical Series, 33.) Oxford: Clio Press, 1982.

M. Nerfin, *Entretiens avec Ahmed Ben Salah*. Paris 1974.

Morocco
R. Bidwell, *Morocco under colonial rule*. London 1973.
J. B. Bookin-Weiner & M. El Mansour (eds.), *The Atlantic connection: 200 years of Moroccan-American relations 1786–1986*. Rabat, Morocco 1990.
A. M. Findlay & Anne M. Findlay (compilers), *Morocco* (World Bibliographical Series, 47), rev. ed. Oxford: Clio Press 1995.
J. P. Halstead, *Rebirth of a nation: the origins and rise of Moroccan nationalism, 1912–1944*. Cambridge Ma 1967.
S. El Machat, *Les États-Unis et la Maroc: le choix stratégique, 1945–1959*. Paris 1996.

Canary Islands
J. Mercer, "The Canary Islands in Western Mediterranean politics." African Affairs 78 1979), pp. 159–176.
R. Pélissier, *Los Territorios Españoles de Africa*. Madrid 1964.

Western Sahara
M. de Froberville, *Sahara occidental–la confiance perdue*. Paris 1996.
T. Hodges, *Western Sahara: the roots of a desert war*. Westport CT 1983.
J. Mercer, *Spanish Sahara*. London 1975.
A. G. Pazzanita (compiler), *Western Sahara* (World Bibliographical Series, 190). Oxford: Clio Press 1996.

West Africa
J. F. A. Ajayi & M. Crowder (eds.), *History of West Africa*, 2 vols. London 1971, 1974.
J. D. Hargreaves, *Prelude to the partition of West Africa*. London 1963.

Cape Verde
Elisa Silve Andrade, *Les îsles du Cap-Vert: de la "découvert" à l' indépendance nationale (1460–1975)*. Paris 1996.
C. S. Shaw (compiler), *Cape Verde* (World Bibliographical Series, 123). Oxford: Clio Press 1991.

Mauritania
S. Calderini *et al.* (compilers), *Mauritania* (World Bibliographical Series, 141). Oxford: Clio Press 1992.
J. L. A. Webb Jr., *Desert Frontier: ecological and economic change along the Western Sahel, 1600–1850*. Madison WI 1995.

Senegal
M. Crowder, *Senegal: a study in French assimilation policy*, 2nd ed. London 1996.
R. M. Dilley & J. S. Eades (compilers), *Senegal* (World Bibliographical Series, 166). Oxford: Clio Press 1994.
S. Diop, *The Oral history and literature of the Wolof people of Waalo, northern Senegal*. Lewistown 1995.
A. Ly, *La Compaganie du Sénégal*, new edition. Paris 1993.
I. L. Markovitz, *Léopold Sédar Senghor and the politics of Negritude*. NY 1969.

Gambia
B. Berglund, *Gambia*. Uppsala 1975.
H. A. Gailey, *A History of the Gambia*. London 1964.
D. P. Gamble (compiler), *The Gambia* (World Bibliographical Series, 91). Oxford: Clio Press 1988.

Guinea-Bissau
J. Barreto, *Historia da Guiné, 1418–1918*. Lisbon 1938.
R. Galli (compiler), *Guinea-Bissau* (World Bibliographical Series, 121). Oxford: Clio Press 1990.
R. Galli & J. Jones, *Guinea-Bissau: politics, economics and society*. NY & London 1987.
I. K. Sundiata, *From Slavery to neoslavery: the Bight of Biafra and Fernando Po in the era of abolition, 1827–1930*. Madison WI 1996.

Guinea
L. Adamolekun, *Sékou Touré's Guinea: an experiment in nation-building*. London 1976.
M. Binns (compiler), *Guinea* (World Bibliographical Series, 191). Oxford: Clio Press 1996.
S. Soriba, *La Guinée sans la France*. Paris 1977.
J. Suret-Canale, *La République de Guinée*. Paris 1970.

Sierra Leone
M. Binns & T. Binns (compilers), *Sierra Leone* (World

Bibliographical Series, 148). Oxford: Clio Press 1992.
C. A. Fyfe, *A History of Sierra Leone*. London 1962.
P. Richards, *Fighting for the rain forest: war, youth and resources in Sierra Leone*. London 1996.

Liberia
D. E. Dunn, *A History of the Episcopal Church in Liberia, 1821–1980*. Metuchen NJ 1992.
—— (compiler), *Liberia* (World Bibliographical Series, 157). Oxford: Clio Press 1995.
P. Gifford, *Christianity and politics in Doe's Liberia*. Cambridge 1993.
A. Konneh, *Religion, commerce and the integration of the Mandingo in Liberia*. Lanham NY & London 1996.
J. G. Liebenow, *Liberia: the evolution of privilege*. Ithaca NY & London 1969.

Côte d' Ivoire
M. Daniels (compiler), *Côte d' Ivoire* (World Bibliographical Series, 131). Oxford: Clio Press 1996.
M. Rémy, *The Ivory Coast today*. Paris 1976.
D. A. Shank, *Prophet Harris, the 'Black Elijah' of West Africa*. Leiden 1994.
A. R. Zolberg, *One-Party Government in the Ivory Coast*, 2nd ed. Princeton NJ 1969.

Ghana
A. A. Boahen, *Ghana: evolution and change in the nineteenth and twentieth centuries*. London 1975.
F. Danqah, *Cocoa diseases and politics in Ghana, 1909–1966*. New York 1995.
R. A. Myers (compiler), *Ghana* (World Bibliographical Series, 124). Oxford: Clio Press 1991.
I. Wilks (ed.), *Forests of gold: essays on the Akan and the Kingdom of Asante*. Athens OH 1993.

Burkina Faso
S. Anderson (ed. and trans.) *Thomas Sankara speaks. The Burkina Faso revolution 1983–87*. NY & London 1988.
D. D. Cordell, J. W. Gregory & V. Piché, *Hoe and wage: a social history of a circular migrating system in West Africa*. Boulder CO 1996.
S. Decalo (compiler), *Burkina Faso* (World Bibliographical Series, 169). Oxford: Clio Press 1994.

Togo
R. Cornevin, *Histoire du Togo*, 3rd.ed. Paris 1969.
S. Decalo (compiler), *Togo* (World Bibliographical Series, 178). Oxford: Clio Press 1995.
L. de Haan, *La région des savanes au Togo: l' État, les paysans et l' intégration régionale (1885–1985)*. Paris 1993.

Benin
R. Cornevin, *Histoire du Dahomey*. Paris 1962.
J. S. Eades & C. Allen (compilers), *Benin* (World Bibliographical Series, 192). Oxford: Clio Press 1996.
M. J. Herskovitz, *Dahomey: an ancient West African kingdom*, 2 vols. New ed., Evanston IL 1967.

Nigeria
E. A. Ayandele, *The Ijebu of Yorubaland, 1850–1950: politics, economy and society*. Ibadan 1996.
Toyin Falola, *Development planning and decolonization in Nigeria*. Gainseville FL 1996.
M. Crowder, *The Story of Nigeria*, 4the ed. London 1978.
D. K. Fieldhouse, *Merchant capital and economic decolonization: the United Africa Company, 1929–1987*. Oxford 1994.
R. A. Myers (compiler), *Nigeria* (World Bibliographical Series, 100). Oxford: Clio Press 1989.

Cameroon
M. W. Delancy & P. J. Schraeder (compilers) *Cameroon* (World Bibliographical Series, 63). Oxford: Clio Press 1986.
V. J. Ngoh, *Cameroon 1884–1985: a hundred years of history*. Yaoundé 1988.

Niger
F. Lancrenon & P. Donaint, *Le Niger*. Paris 1972.
J. Nicolaisen, *Ecology and culture of the Pastoral Tuareg*. Copenhagen 1963.
L. F. Zamponi (compiler), *Niger* (World Bibliographical Series, 164). Oxford: Clio Press 1998.

Mali
R. A. Myers *et al.* (compilers), *Mali* (World Bibliographical Series, 207). Oxford: Clio Press 1998.

K. G. Prasse, *The Tuareg: the Blue People*. Copenhagen 1995.

West Central Africa
J. Suret-Canale, *Afrique noire occidentale et centrale: l' ère colonial 1900–1945*, 3 vols. 2nd. ed, Paris 1968.
—— *French colonialism in tropical Africa, 1900–1945*. London 1971.

Chad
G. Joffé & V. Day-Viaud (compilers), *Chad* (World Bibliographical Series, 177). Oxford: Clio Press 1995.
S. C. Nolutshungu, *Limits of anarchy: intervention and state formation in Chad*. Charlottesville 1996.

Central African Republic
P. Kalck (compiler), *Central African Republic* (World Bibliographical Series, 152). Oxford: Clio Press 1993.
T. O' Toole, *The Central African Republic: the continent's hidden heart*. Boulder CO 1986.

Gabon
D. Gardinier (compiler), *Gabon* (World Bibliographical Series, 149). Oxford: Clio Press 1992.
K. D. Patterson, *The Northern Gabon Coast to 1875*. Oxford 1975.

Equatorial Guinea
W. G. Clarence-Smith (ed.), *Cocoa pioneer fronts since 1800: the role of smallholders, planters and merchants*. Basingstoke 1996.
R. Fegley (compiler), *Equatorial Guinea* (World Bibliographical Series, 136). Oxford: Clio Press 1991.

São Tomé and Princípé
C. S. Shaw (compiler), *São Tomé and Princípé* (World Bibliographical Series, 172). Oxford: Clio Press 1994.

Congo, Democratic Republic of the [former Zäire]
M.-L. Martin, *Prophetic Christianity in the Congo. The Church of Jesus Christ on the Earth through the Prophet Simon Kimbangu*. Johannesburg [1968].
R. Slade, *King Leopold's Congo*. London 1962.
J. Vansina, *Living with Africa*. Madison WI 1994.
D. B. Williams et al. (compilers), *Zaïre* (World Bibliographical Series, 176). Oxford: Clio Press 1995.

Congo, Peoples' Republic of the
R. Fegley (compiler), *Congo* (World Bibliographical Series, 162). Oxford: Clio Press 1993.
S. Nelson, *Colonialism in the Congo Basin, 1880–1940*. Athens OH 1994.
M. Soret, *Histoire du Congo Brazzaville*. Paris 1978.
J. Vansina, *The Tio Kingdom of the Middle Congo, 1880–1892*. London 1979.

Angola
D. Birmingham, *Frontline nationalism in Angola and Mozambique*. London 1992.
R. Black (compiler), *Angola* (World Bibliographical Series, 151). Oxford: Clio Press 1992.
W. G. Clarence-Smith, *Slaves, peasants and capitalists in Southern Angola*. Cambridge 1979.

Northeast Africa
K. Fukui & J. Markakis (eds.), *Ethnicity and conflict in the Horn of Africa*. London 1994.
P. Woodward & M. Forsyth (eds.), *Conflict and peace in the Horn of Africa: federalism and alternatives*. Aldershot & Brookfield VT 1994.

Sudan
M. W. Daly (compiler), *Sudan* (World Bibliographical Series, 40, rev. ed.).Oxford: Clio Press 1992.
J. Garang (ed. by Mansour Khalid), *The Call for Democracy in Sudan*. London & NY 1992.
Deng D. Akol Ruay, *The Politics of the two Sudans: the South and the North, 1821–1969*. Uppsala 1994.
P. Woodward, *Sudan, 1898–1989: the unstable state*. London 1990.

Eritrea
R. Fegley (compiler), *Eritrea* (World Bibliographical Series, 181). Oxford: Clio Press 1995.
R. Iyob, *The Eritrean struggle for independence: domination, resistance, nationalism, 1941–1993*. Cambridge 1995.
A. Wilson, *The Challenge road: women and the Eritrean revolution*. London 1991.

Ethiopia
H. G. Marcus, *A History of Ethiopia*. Berkeley & London 1994.
J. Markakis, *Ethiopia: anatomy of a traditional policy*. Oxford 1974.
S. Monro-Hay & R. Pankhurst (compilers), *Ethiopia* (World Bibliographical Series, 179). Oxford: Clio Press 1995.
T. Tibebu, *The Making of modern Ethiopia*. Lawrenceville NJ 1995.

Djibouti
P. J. Schraeder (compiler), *Djibouti* (World Bibliographical Series, 118). Oxford: Clio Press 1991.
V. Thompson & R. Adloff, *Djibouti and the Horn of Africa*. Stanford CA 1968.

Somalia
F. Couchard, *La Fantasme de séduction dans la culture musulmane: mythes et représentations sociales*. Paris 1994.
M. W. DeLancey *et al.* (compilers), *Somalia* (World Bibliographical Series, 92). Oxford: Clio Press 1988.
I. M. Lewis, *A modern history of Somalia: nation and state in the Horn of Africa*, rev. ed. London 1988.

East Africa
E. A. Alpers, *Ivory and slaves in East Central Africa*. London 1975.
H. B. Hansen & M. Twaddle (eds.), *Religion and politics in East Africa: the period since independence*. London 1995.
B. A. Ogot & J. A. Kieran (eds.), *Zamani: a survey of East African history*, rev. ed. Nairobi 1974.
R. Oliver, *The Missionary factor in East Africa*, rev. ed. London 1965.
R. Oliver *et al.* (eds.), *A History of East Africa*, 3 vols. Oxford 1963–1975.

Kenya
T. Askwith (ed. J. Lewis), *From Mau Mau to Harambee: memoirs and memoranda of colonial Kenya*. Cambridge 1995.
B. Berman & J. Lonsdale, *Unhappy valley: conflict in Kenya and Africa*. London 1992.
D. Coger (compiler), *Kenya* (World Bibliographical Series, 25, rev. ed.). Oxford: Clio Press 1996.
E. Huxley, *White Man's Country: Lord Delemere and the making of Kenya*, 2 vols. 2nd ed., London 1953.
Jomo Kenyatta, *Facing Mount Kenya*, new ed. London 1979.
J. Murray-Brown, *Kenyatta*. London 1972.
B. A. Ogot (ed.), *Politics and nationalism in colonial Kenya*. Nairobi 1972.
C. Reed, *Pastors, partners and paternalists: African church leaders and Western missionaries in the Anglican Church in Kenya, 1850–1900*. Leiden 1997.

Uganda
H. B. Hansen & M. Twaddle (eds.), *From Chaos to order: the politics of constitution-making in Uganda*. London 1995.
Balam Nyeko (compiler), *Uganda* (World Bibliographical Series, 11, rev. ed.) Oxford: Clio Press 1996.
P. G. Okoth (ed.), *Uganda: a century of existence*. Kampala 1995.
J. V. Taylor, *The Growth of the church in Buganda*. London 1958.
C. Wrigley, *Kingship and state: the Buganda dynasty*. Cambridge 1996.

Rwanda
R.Fegley (compiler), *Rwanda* (World Bibliographical Series, 154). Oxford: Clio Press 1993.
I. Linden, *Church and revolution in Rwanda*. Manchester 1977.
J. J. Maquet, *Le Système des relations sociales dans le Rwanda ancien* (Eng. trans., *The Premise of inequality in Rwanda*). Oxford 1961.
G. Prunier, *The Rwanda crisis: history of a genocide*. New York 1995.

Burundi
J.-P. Chrétien, *Burundi: l' histoire retrouvée: 25 ans d' historien en Afrique*. Paris 1993.
M. Daniels (compiler), *Burundi* (World Bibliographical Series, 145). Oxford: Clio Press 1992.
R. Lemarchand, *Burundi: ethnocide as discourse and practice*. Washington & Cambridge 1996 (1st ed. 1994).

Tanzania
C. Darch (compiler), *Tanzania* (World Bibliographical Series, 54, rev. ed.).Oxford: Clio Press 1996.
J. Iliffe, *A modern history of Tanganyika*. Cambridge 1979.
I. N. Kimambo, *Three decades of production of historical knowledge at Dar es Salaam*. Dar es Salaam 1993/1994.
M. Lofchie, *Zanzibar: background to revolution*. London 1965.
A. Roberts (ed.), *Tanzania before 1900*. Nairobi 1968.
A. Sheriff & E. Ferguson (eds.), *Zanzibar under colonial rule*. Athens OH 1991.

Southeast Central Africa
R. Gray, *The two nations: aspects of the development of race relations in the Rhodesias and Nyasaland*. London 1960.
R. Palmer & N. Parsons (eds.), *The roots of rural poverty in central and southern Africa*. Berkeley CA 1977.

Zambia
A. M. Bliss & J. A. Rigg (compilers), *Zambia* (World Bibliographical Series, 51). Oxford: Clio Press 1984.
J. O. Ihonvbere, *Economic crisis, civil society and democratization: the case of Zambia*.Trenton NJ 1996.
N. Musiker (compiler), *Kaunda's Zambia, 1964–1991: a selected and annotated bibliography*. Johannesburg 1993.
J. M. Mwanakatwe, *End of Kaunda era*. Lusaka 1994.

Zimbabwe
N. Bhebe & T. O. Ranger (eds.), *Society in Zimbabwe's liberation war*. London 1995.
D. Potts (compiler), *Zimbabwe* (World Bibliographical Series, 78, rev. ed.). Oxford: Clio Press 1993.
T, O. Ranger, *Are we not also men? The Samkange family and African politics in Zimbabwe 1920–64*. London 1995.
L. Vambe, *From Rhodesia to Zimbabwe*. London 1976.

Mozambique
C. Darch (compiler), *Mozambique* (World Bibliographical Series, 78). Oxford: Clio Press 1987.
D. Hoile, *Mozambique, resistance and freedom: a case for reassessment*. London 1994.
A. Isaacman, *Cotton is the mother of poverty: peasants, work and rural struggle in colonial Mozambique, 1938–1961*. London 1996.
E. Mondlane, *The struggle for Mozambique*. Harmondsworth 1969.
M. Newitt, *A history of Mozambique*. London & Bloomington IN 1995.

Malawi
T. Cullen, *Malawi: a turning point*. Edinburgh 1994.
S. Decalo (compiler), *Malawi* (World Bibliographical Series, 8, rev. ed.). Oxford: Clio Press 1995.
B. Pachai, *Malawi: the history of the nation*. London 1973.
G. Shepperson & T. Price, *Independent African. John Chilembwe and the origins, setting and significance of the Nyasaland Native Rising of 1915*. Edinburgh 1958.
T. J. Thompson, *Christianity in northern Malawi. Donald Fraser's missionary methods and Ngoni culture*. Leiden 1995.

Southern Africa
P. du Toit, *State building and democracy in southern Africa: Botswana, Zimbabwe and South Africa*. Washington DC 1995.
M. Wilson & L. M. Thompson, *Oxford History of South Africa*. Vol. I, to 1870; Vol. II, 1870 to 1966. Oxford 1969 and 1971.

South Africa
W. Beinart, *Twentieth-century South Africa*. Oxford 1994.
G. V. Davis (compiler), *South Africa* (World Bibliographical Series, 7, rev. ed.). Oxford: Clio Press 1994.
A. Lester, *From colonization to democracy: a new historical geography of South Africa*. London and New York 1996.
R. Ross, *Beyond the pale. Essays on the history of colonial South Africa*. Hanover NH 1993.
E. Schoeman *et al.* (compilers), *Mandela's five years of freedom. South African politics, economics and social issues 1990–1995: a select and annotated bibliography*. Johannesburg 1996.
N. Worden, *The making of modern South Africa: conquest, segregation and apartheid*. Oxford 1994.

Namibia
H. Bley, *Namibia under German rule*. Hamburg & Windhoek 1996.
L. Cliffe *et al.*, *The transition to independence in Namibia*. Boulder CO & London 1994.
Ruth First, *South West Africa*. Harmondsworth 1963.
C. Leys & J.S. Saul (eds.), *Namibia's liberation struggle: the two-edged sword*. London & Athens OH 1995.
S. Schoeman & E. Schoeman (compilers), *Namibia* (World Bibliographical Series, 53, rev. ed.). Oxford: Clio Press 1997.

Botswana
C. Harvey & S. R. Lewis Jr., *Policy choice and development performance in Botswana*. Basingstoke & London 1990.
P. Landau, *The realm of the Word. Language, gender and Christianity in a South African kingdom*. London 1995.
A. Sillery, *Botswana: a short political history*. London 1974.
J. A. Wiseman (compiler), *Botswana* (World Bibliographical Series, 150). Oxford: Clio Press 1992.

Lesotho
E. Eldredge, *A South African kingdom: the pursuit of security in nineteenth century Lesotho*. Cambridge 1996.
D. Johnston (compiler), *Lesotho* (World Bibliographical SEries, 3, rev. ed.). Oxford: Clio Press 1996.
L. B. Machobane, *Government and change in Lesotho, 1800–1966: a study of political institutions*. London 1990.
L. M. Thompson, *Survival in two worlds: Moshoeshoe of Lesotho, 1786–1870*. London 1975.

Swaziland
H. Kuper, *The Swazi, a South African kingdom*. London & New York 1963.
—— *Sobhuza II, Ngwenyama and King of Swaziland*. London 1978.
J. S. M. , *A History of Swaziland*. [London &] Cape Town 1972; 2nd ed., 1988.
B. Nyeko (compiler), *Swaziland* (World Bibliographical Series, 24, rev. ed.). Oxford: Clio Press 1994.
N. Simelane (ed.), *Social transformation: the Swaziland case*. Dakar, Senegal: CODESRIA 1995.

Africa in the Indian Ocean
J. J. Gotthold with the assistance of D. W. Gotthold (compilers), *Indian Ocean* (World Bibliographical Series, 85). Oxford: Clio Press 1988.

Comoros (which remains a French Overseas Territory, and includes Mayotte)
M. Newitt, *The Comoros Islands: struggle against dependency in the Indian Ocean*. Aldershot 1985.

Madagascar
H. Bradt (compiler), *Madagascar* (World Bibliographical Series, 165). Oxford: Clio Press 1993.
M. Brown, *A History of Madagascar*. Ipswich 1995.
M. Covell, *Madagascar: politics, economics and society*. London 1987.
H. Deschamps, *Madagascar*. Paris 1976.
B. Hübsch, *Madagascar et le Christianisme*. Fianarantsoa 1993.

Mauritius & Réunion
P. R. Bennett(compiler), *Mauritius* (World Bibliographical Series, 140). Oxford: Clio Press 1992.
M. Debré, *Une politique pour la Réunion*. Paris 1974.
H. Mathur, *Parliament in Mauritius*. Stanley, Rose-Hill 1991.
M. Robert, *La Réunion*. Paris 1976.
A. Toussaint, *Histoire des îles Mascareignes*. Paris 1972.
——*A History of Mauritius*. London 1977.

Seychelles
G. Bennett *et al.* (compilers), *Seychelles* (World Bibliographical Series, 153). Oxford: Clio Press 1993.
M. Franda, *The Seychelles: unquiet islands*. Boulder CO 1982.
J. Hatchard, "Re-establishing a multi-party state: some constitutional lessons from the Seychelles." *Journal of Modern African Studies* 31 (4), 1993, 601–612.

GAZETTEER

Aaiun (*Western Sahara*), 27°09′N 13°12′W, 110, 125
Aba (*Nigeria*), 5°06′N 7°21′E, 146
Abakaliki (*Nigeria*), 6°17′N 8°04′E, 146
Abanga (*r*), (*Gabon*), 160
Abay see Nile
Abaya (*l*), (*Ethiopia*), 6°20′N 37°55′E, 11, 171, 175
Abba (*Central African Republic*), 5°20′N 15°11′E, 158
Abéché (*Chad*), 13°49′N 20°49′E, 154, 156
Abengourou (*Côte d'Ivoire*), 6°44′N 3°29′W, 138
Abeokuta (*Nigeria*), 7°10′N 3°26′E, 127, 146
Aberdeen (*South Africa*), 32°29′S 24°03′E, 207
Abhe (*l*), (*Djibouti/Ethiopia*), 11°06′N 41°50′E, 171, 175, 177
Abid, Oued el (*r*), (*Morocco*), 122
Abidjan (*Côte d'Ivoire*), 5°19′N 4°02′W, 22, 74, 127, 138
Aboisso (*Côte d'Ivoire*), 5°28′N 3°12′W, 138
Abomey (*Benin*), 7°11′N 1°59′E, 144
Abong Mbang (*Cameroon*), 3°59′N 13°10′E, 148
Abonnema (*Nigeria*), 4°43′N 6°47′E, 146
Abou Arak (*r*), (*Chad*), 156
Abu (*Guinea-Bissau*), 11°26′N 15°58′W, 132
Abu Gabra (*Sudan*), 11°02′N 26°50′E, 174
Abuja (*Nigeria*), 9°12′N 7°11′E, 11, 22, 74, 127, 146
Abu Tartur (*Egypt*), 25°12′N 30°10′E, 116
Abuye Meda (*mt*), (*Ethiopia*), 10°28′N 39°44′E, 171
Accra (*Ghana*), 5°33′N 0°13′W, 11, 22, 74, 127, 140
Acurenam (*Equatorial Guinea*), 1°04′N 10°46′E, 162
Ada (*Ghana*), 5°47′N 0°24′E, 140
Ad-Dab'ah (*Egypt*), 31°02′N 28°26′E. 116
Addis Ababa (*Ethiopia*), 9°00′N 38°50′E, 11, 22, 74, 171, 175
Ad-Duwaym (*Sudan*), 14°00′N 32°19′E, 171, 175
Adigrat (*Ethiopia*), 14°18′N, 39°31′E, 175
Adi Ugri (*Eritrea*), 14°55′N 38°53′E, 175
Ado-Ekiti (*Nigeria*), 7°38′N 5°12′E, 146
Adrar (*Algeria*), 27°51′N 0°39′W, 110, 118
Adwa (*Ethiopia*), 14°10′N 38°55′E. 175
Afikpo (*Nigeria*), 5°53′N 7°56′E, 146
African (*isl*), (*Seychelles*), 5°00′S 53°16′E, 219
Agadez (*Niger*), 17°00′N 7°56′E, 127, 150
Agadir (*Morocco*), 30°30′N 9°40′W, 122
Agalega (*isl*), (*Mauritius*), 12°24′S 56°24′E, 215
Agan (*Djibouti*), 11°32′N 42°01′E, 177
Agordat (*Eritrea*), 15°35′N 37°54′E, 175
Agboville (*Côte d'Ivoire*), 5°56′N 4°13′W, 138
Agouévé (*Togo*), 6°20′N 1°18′E, 144
Agsumal, Sebjet (*l*), (*Western Sahara*), 24°21′N 12°52′W, 125
Aguenit (*Western Sahara*), 22°12′N 13°08′W, 125
Alhel, Oued el- (*r*), (*Mauritania*), 131
Aïna (*r*), (*Cameroon/Gabon*), 148
Aïn Beïda (*Algeria*), 35°44′N 7°22′E. 118
Aïn Galakka (*Chad*), 18°04′N 18°24′E, 156
Aïn Sefra (*Algeria*), 32°45′N 0°35′W, 110, 118
Aïn Sukhna (*Egypt*), 29°35′N 32°21′E, 116
Ait Amar (*Morocco*), 33°00′N 6°34′W, 122
Ajaokuta (*Nigeria*), 7°26′N 6°43′E, 146
Ajdabiya (*Libya*), 30°48′N 20°15′E, 111, 119
Aketi (*Democratic Republic of the Congo*), 2°42′N 23°51′E, 166
Akjoujt (*Mauritania*), 19°44′N 14°20′W, 43, 131
Akkai (*Ethiopia*), 8°55′N 38°52′E, 174
Akobo (*r*), (*Ethiopia/Sudan*), 171, 175
Akosombo Dam (*Ghana*), 6°16′N 0°10′E, 127, 140
Aksum (*Ethiopia*), 14°08′N 38°48′E, 43, 48, 175
Al 'Adam (*Libya*), 31°52′N 23°59′E, 119
Al-Amiriyah (*Egypt*) 31°01′N 29°48′E, 116
Alaotra (*l*), (*Madagascar*), 17°30′S 48°30′E, 215, 216
Al-Bahr al-Abyad *see* Nile
Al-Bahr al-Azraq *see* Nile
Albert (*l*), (*Democratic Republic of the Congo/Uganda*), 1°40′N 31°00′E, 11, 154, 167, 181, 186
Albert Nile *see* Nile
Al Bir Lahlou (*Western Sahara*), 26°23′N 9°40′W, 125
Aldabra (*isl*), (*Seychelles*), 9°25′S, 46°20′E, 215, 219
Aleg (*Mauritania*), 17°02′N 13°58′W, 131
Alegranza (*isl*), (*Canary Islands*), 29°23′N 13°30′W, 124
Alexander Bay (*South Africa*), 28°40′S 16°30′E, 206
Alexandria (*Egypt*), 31°13′N 29°55′E, 22, 74, 111, 116
Alexandria (*South Africa*), 33°39′S 26°25′E, 207
Al Farciya (*Western Sahara*), 27°06′N 9°50′W, 125
Al-Fashir (*Sudan*), 13°38′N 25°21′E, 170, 174
Al-Fayyum (*Egypt*), 29°19′N 30°50′E, 22, 74, 111, 116
Algiers (*Algeria*), 36°50′N 3°00′E, 11, 22, 58, 74, 110, 118
Al Haggounia (*Western Sahara*), 27°30′N 12°27′W, 125
Al-Hoceima (*Morocco*), 35°14′N 3°56′W, 123
Al-Husayhisah (*Sudan*), 14°44′N 33°48′E, 174
Alibori (*r*), (*Benin*), 144
Alima (*r*), (*Republic of the Congo*), 164
Alindao (*Central African Republic*), 5°01′N 21°11′E, 158
Ali-Sabieh (*Djibouti*), 11°10′N 42°33′E, 177
Al-Isma'iliyah (*Egypt*), 30°35′N 32°16′E, 116
Aliwal North (*South Africa*), 30°42′S 26°43′E, 207
Al-Jawf (*Libya*), 24°09′N 23°19′E, 111, 119
Al Jufrah Oasis (*Libya*), 29°09′N 15°47′E, 119
Al-Junaynah (*Sudan*), 13°27′N 22°30′E, 174
Al Kufrah Oasis (*Libya*), 24°16′N 22°56′E, 119
Allaqi, Wadi al- (*r*), (*Egypt*), 116
Al Mahallah al-Kubra (*Egypt*), 30°59′N 31°10′E, 116
Al-Mansurah (*Egypt*), 31°03′N 31°23′E, 116
Al-Marj (*Libya*), 32°30′N 20°50′E, 111, 119
Al-Minya (*Egypt*), 28°06′N 30°45′E, 116
Alphonse (*isl*), (*Seychelles*), 7°05′E 42°50′E, 215, 219
Al-Qadarif (*Sudan*), 14°01′N 35°32′E, 171, 175
Al Qantarah (*Egypt*), 31°00′N 32°24′E, 116
Al-Qatrun (*Libya*), 24°55′N 14°38′E, 119
Alrar (*Algeria*), 28°40′N 9°43′E, 119
Alto Ligonha (*Mozambique*), 15°30′S 38°20′E, 199
Alto Molocué (*Mozambique*), 15°37′S 37°36′E, 199
Al-Ubayyid (*Sudan*), 13°11′N 30°10′E, 170, 174
Ambanja (*Madagascar*), 13°40′S 48°27′E, 216
Ambatolampy (*Madagascar*) 19°21′S 47°27′E, 216
Ambatondrazaka (*Madagascar*), 17°42′S 48°44′E, 216
Ambilobe (*Madagascar*), 13°10′S 49°03′E, 216
Ambodifototra (*Madagascar*), 16°59′S 49°51′E, 216
Ambositra (*Madagascar*), 20°31′S 47°15′E, 216
Ambovombe (*Madagascar*), 25°10′S 46°06′E, 216
Ambriz (*Angola*) 2°50′S 13°09′E, 168
Amirante Islands (*Seychelles*), 215, 219
Am Timan (*Chad*), 11°02′N 20°17′E, 156
Amur, Wadi (*r*), (*Sudan*), 175
Analalava (*Madagascar*), 14°38′S 47°46′E, 216
Andoany (*Madagascar*), 13°24′S 48°17′E, 216
Aného (*Togo*), 6°14′N 1°36′E, 144
Angoche (*Mozambique*), 16°10′S 39°58′E, 199
Anié (*r*), (*Togo*), 144
Anivorano (*Madagascar*), 18°54′S 49°07′E, 216
Anjouan (Nzwani) (*isl*), (*Comoros*), 12°15′S 44°25′E, 216, 218
Ankazoabo (*Madagascar*), 22°18′S 44°30′E, 216
Ankobra (*r*), (*Ghana*), 140
Annaba (*Algeria*), 36°55′N 7°47′E, 22, 74, 110, 119
An-Nuhud (*Sudan*), 12°42′N 28°26′E, 174
Anse Royale (*Seychelles*), 4°44′S 55°31′E, 219
Antalaha (*Madagascar*), 14°53′S 50°16′E, 216
Antananarivo (*Madagascar*), 18°52′S 47°30′E, 11, 22, 74, 215, 216
Antsiranana (*Madagascar*), 12°19′S 49°17′E, 215, 216
Antsirabe (*Madagascar*), 19°51′S 47°01′E′, 215, 216
Anum (*r*), (*Ghana*), 140
Aozou (*Chad*), 21°45′N 17°28′E, 156
Arabah, Wadi (*r*), (*Egypt*), 116
Arada (*Chad*), 15°00′N 20°38′E, 156
Argoub (*Western Sahara*), 23°37′N 15°50′W, 125
Aridal, Sebjet (*l*), (*Western Sahara*), 26°12′N 14°05′W, 125
Aride (*isl*), (*Seychelles*), 4°13′S 55°40′E, 219
Arivonimamo (*Madagascar*), 19°00′S 47°11′E, 216
Arkanu, Jabal (*mt*), (*Libya*), 22°13′N 24°41′E, 111
Arlit (*Niger*), 19°16′N 7°19′E, 150
Arocha (*r*), (*Uganda*), 186
Arrecife (*Canary Islands*), 28°57′N 13°33′W, 124
Ar-Rusayris (*Sudan*), 11°51′N 34°23′E, 175
Ar-Rusayris Dam (*Sudan*), 11°50′N 34°24′E, 171
Arua (*Uganda*), 3°01′N 30°55′E, 186
Arusha (*Tanzania*), 3°22′S 36°41′E, 191
Arusha Chini (*Tanzania*), 3°35′S 37°20′E, 191
Aruwimi (*r*), (*Democratic Republic of the Congo*), 166
Arzew (*Algeria*), 35°50′N 0°23′W, 118
'Asal (*l*), (*Djibouti*), 11°41′N 42°23′E, 177
Asayita (*Ethiopia*), 31°33′N 41°30′E, 175
Ashaka (*Nigeria*), 5°45′N 6°21′E, 146
Askarene (*Algeria*), 28°46′N 8°59′E, 119
Asmara (*Eritrea*), 35°20′N 38°58′E, 11, 22, 74, 171, 175
Assab (*Eritrea*), 13°00′N 42°45′E, 175
Assaq, Uad (*r*), (*Western Sahara*), 125
Assegai (*r*), (*Swaziland*), 213
Assekaifaf (*Algeria*), 27°22′N 8°41′E, 119
Assumption (*isl*), (*Seychelles*), 9°45′S 46°30′E, 215, 219
Astove (*isl*), (*Seychelles*), 30°05′S 47°40′E, 215, 219
Aswa (*r*), (*Uganda*), 181, 186
Aswan (*Egypt*), 24°05′N 32°56′ E, 111, 116
Aswan High Dam (*Egypt*), 23°54′N 32°52′E, 111, 116
Asyut (*Egypt*), 27°14′N 33°07′E, 22, 74, 111, 116
Asyuti, Wadi al- (*r*), (*Egypt*), 116
Atakpamé (*Togo*), 7°32′N 1°08′E, 144
Atar (*Mauritania*), 20°32′N 13°00′W, 131
Atbarah (*Sudan*), 17°42′N 34°00′E, 171, 175
Atbarah (*r*), (*Sudan*), 171, 175
Athi (*r*), (*Kenya*), 185
Ati (*Chad*), 13°11′N 18°20′E, 156
At-Taj (*Libya*), 24°13′N 23°18′E, 119
Atui, Uad (*r*), (*Western Sahara*), 125
Auchi (*Nigeria*), 6°58′N 6°15′E, 146
Auleitis, Uad (*r*), (*Western Sahara*), 125
Auob (*r*), (*Namibia*), 208
Ausert (*Western Sahara*), 22°38′N 14°18′W, 125
Awasa (*Ethiopia*), 7°02′N 38°28′E, 175
Awash (*r*), (*Ethiopia*), 171, 175
Awaso (*Ghana*), 6°14′N 2°16′W, 140
Awbari (*Libya*), 26°35′N 12°47′E, 119
Awjilah (*Libya*), 29°05′N 21°12′E, 119
Axim (*Ghana*), 4°52′N 2°14′W, 140
Aya Yenahin (*Ghana*), 6°43′N 2°03′W, 140
Ayé-Koyé (*Guinea*), 11°08′N 14°06′W, 134
Ayoûn el Atroûs (*Mauritania*), 17°02′N 9°41′W, 131
Azegour (*Morocco*), 31°14′N 8°14′W, 122
Azrou (*Morocco*), 33°27′N 5°14′W, 122
Azzel Matti, Sebkha (*l*), (*Algeria*), 26°00′N 0°50′E, 118
Az-Zawiyah (*Libya*), 32°45′N 12°14′E, 119

Baardheere (*Somalia*), 2°21′N 42°20′E, 179
Bafata (*Guinea-Bissau*), 12°10′N 14°40′W, 133
Bafia (*Cameroon*), 4°44′N 11°16′E, 148
Bafing (*r*), (*Guinea/Mali*), 126, 134, 152
Bafing Makana (*Mali*), 12°33′N 10°15′W, 152
Bafoulabé (*Mali*), 13°48′N 10°50′W, 152
Bafoussam (*Cameroon*), 5°29′N 10°24′E, 148
Bagado (*Cameroon*), 6°26′N 13°43′E, 148
Bagamoyo (*Tanzania*), 6°26′S 38°55′E, 191
Bagbe (*r*), (*Sierra Leone*), 136
Bagoé (*r*), (*Mali*), 152
Bagzane (*mt*), (*Niger*), 17°45′N 8°30′E, 127
Bahariya Oasis (*Egypt*), 28°20′N 28°50′E, 111, 116
Bahir Dar (*Ethiopia*), 11°33′N 37°25′E, 175
Bahr Aouk (*r*), (*Central African Republic/Chad*), 156, 158
Bahr al-Arab (*r*), (*Sudan*), 170
Bahr al-Ghazal (*r*), (*Sudan*), 170, 174
Bahr Oulou (*r*), (*Central African Republic*), 158
Bahr Salamat (*r*), (*Chad*), 156
Baibokoum (*Chad*), 7°46′N 15°43′E, 156
Bailundo (*Angola*), 12°11′S 15°52′E, 168
Bakassa (*r*), (*Central African Republic*), 158
Bakel (*Senegal*), 14°54′N 12°27′W, 133
Bakolori Dam (*Nigeria*), 12°18′N 6°19′E, 146
Bakouma (*Central African Republic*), 5°42′N 22°50′E, 159
Bakoye (*r*), (*Mali*), 152
Balcad (*Somalia*), 2°20′N 45°22′E, 179
Ballé (*Mali*), 15°20′ N 8 35′W, 152
Bamako (*Mali*), 12°40′N 7°59′W, 11, 22, 74, 126, 152
Bambao (*Comoros*), 12°14′S 44°30′E, 218
Bambari (*Central African Republic*), 5°45′N 20°40′ E, 154, 158
Bambey (*Senegal*), 14°40′N 16°28′W, 132
Bamingui (*r*), (*Central African Republic*), 158
Banana (*Democratic Republic of the Congo*), 5°58′S 12°27′E, 166
Banankoro (*Guinea*), 9°09′N 9°38′W, 134
Banda (*Chad*), 8°56′N 17°34′E, 156
Bandama (*r*), (*Côte d'Ivoire*), 127, 138
Bandama Blanc (*r*), (*Côte d'Ivoire*), 138
Bandama Rouge (*r*), (*Côte d'Ivoire*), 138
Bandélé (*Comoros*), 12°52′S 45°25′E, 218
Bandiagara (*Mali*), 14°21′N 3°37′W, 152
Bandundu (*Democratic Republic of the Congo*), 3°20′S 17°24′E, 154, 166
Banfora (*Burkina Faso*), 10°38′N 4°46′W, 142
Bangala Dam (*Zimbabwe*), 20°55′S 31°35′E, 197
Bangassou (*Central African Republic*), 4°50′N 23°07′E, 154, 159
Banghazi (*Libya*), 32°07′N 20°04′E, 22, 74, 111, 119
Bangolo (*Côte d'Ivoire*), 7°01′N 7°29W, 138
Bangoran (*r*), (*Central African Republic*), 158
Bangui (*Central African Republic*), 4°23′N 18°37′E, 11, 22, 74, 154, 158
Bangwade (*Democratic Republic of the Congo*), 0°58′N 25°11′E, 166
Bangweulu (*l*), (*Zambia*), 11°15′S 29°45′E, 11, 193, 195
Bangweulu Swamp (*Zambia*), 11°15′S 29°50′E, 193, 195
Bani (*r*), (*Mali*), 11, 127, 152
Bani Suwayf (*Egypt*), 29°05′N 31°05′E, 116
Banjul (*Gambia*), 13°28′N 16°39′W, 11, 126, 132
Banket (*Zimbabwe*), 17°22′S 30°29′ E, 197
Banyo (*Cameroon*), 6°45′N 11°′49′ E, 148
Baoulé (*r*), (*Mali*), 152
Baraawe (*Somalia*), 1°02′N 44°02′E, 179
Barbar (*Sudan*), 18°01′N 33°59′E, 171, 175
Barberton (*South Africa*), 25°48′S 31°03′E, 207
Bardaï (*Chad*), 21°21′N 16°56′E, 156
Baringo (*l*), (*Kenya*), 1°32′N 36°05′E, 185
Baris (*Egypt*), 24°40′N 30°36′E, 116
Barjuj, Wadi (*r*), (*Libya*), 119
Barlavento Islands (*Cape Verde*), 16°45′N 24°40′W, 130
Baro (*r*), (*Ethiopia*), 171, 175
Barren, Nosy (*isl*), (*Madagascar*), 18°24′S 43°50′E, 215, 216
Basankusu (*Democratic Republic of the Congo*), 1°12′N 19°50′ E, 166
Basoko (*Democratic Republic of the Congo*), 1°14′N 23°36′E, 166
Bassas da India (*isl*), (*France*), 21°30′S 39°50′ E, 215
Basse Santa Su (*Gambia*), 13°19′N 14°13′W, 133
Bata (*Equatorial Guinea*), 1°51′N 9°49′E, 154, 162
Batanga (*Gabon*), 0°28′S 9°11′E, 160
Batangafo (*Central African Republic*), 7°18′N 18°18′E, 158
Batié (*Burkina Faso*), 9°53′N 2°55′W, 142
Batna (*Algeria*), 35°34′N 6°10′E, 118
Batu (*mt*), (*Ethiopia*), 6°55′N 39°49′E, 171
Bauchi (*Nigeria*), 10°19′N 9°50′E, 146
Bawiti (*Egypt*), 28°21′N 28°51′E, 116
Baydhabo (*Somalia*), 3°08′N 43°34′E, 22, 74, 171, 179
Be, Nosy (*isl*), (*Madagascar*), 13°20′S 48°15′E, 215, 216
Bealanana (*Madagascar*), 14°33′S 48°44′E, 216
Beaufort West (*South Africa*), 33°18′S 22°36′E, 207
Béchar (*Algeria*), 31°35′N 2°17′W, 110, 118
Beda (*Libya*), 28°30′N 18°54′E, 119
Beht (*r*), (*Morocco*), 122
Beida (*Libya*), 32°49′N 21°45′E, 111, 119
Beila (*Mauritania*), 18°09′N 15°56′W, 131
Beira (Sofala), (*Mozambique*), 19°49′S 34°52′E, 22, 48, 58, 74, 193, 199
Beitbridge (*Zimbabwe*), 22°13′S 30°00′E, 197
Béja (*Tunisia*), 36°43′N 9°13′E, 121
Bejaia (*Algeria*), 36°49′N 5°03′E, 110, 118
Belhedan (*Libya*), 28°00′N 19°12′E 119
Belinga (*Gabon*), 1°09′N 13°12′E, 160
Bel Ombre (*Mauritius*), 20°30′S 57°23′E, 217
Bemarivo (*r*), (*Madagascar*), 215, 216
Bembe (*Angola*), 7°03′S 14°25′E, 168
Bembezi (*r*), (*Zimbabwe*), 193, 197
Bendaja (*Liberia*), 7°16′N 11°13′W, 136
Bengo (*r*), (*Angola*), 168
Benguela (*Angola*), 12°34′S 13°24′E, 154, 168
Benguerir (*Morocco*), 32°19′N 7°59′W, 122
Béni Abbès (*Algeria*), 30°11′N 2°14′W, 110, 118
Beni-Mellal (*Morocco*), 32°22′N 6°29′W, 122
Benin City (*Nigeria*), 6°19′N 5°41′E, 127, 146
Beni-Saf (*Algeria*), 35°28′N 1°22′W, 118
Benoni (*South Africa*), 26°12′S 28°18′E, 203
Bénoué (*r*), (*Cameroon*), 11, 126, 148
Benty (*Guinea*), 9°10′N 13°14′W, 134
Benue (*r*), (*Nigeria*), 126, 146
Berbera (*Somalia*), 10°28′N 45°02′E, 171, 179
Berbérati (*Central African Republic*), 4°19′N 15°5l′E, 154, 158
Berg Aukas (*Namibia*), 19°20′S 18°10′E, 208
Bertoua (*Cameroon*), 4°35′N 13°41′E, 148
Betancuria (*Canary Islands*), 28°24′N 14°05′W, 124
Bétaré Oya (*Cameroon*), 5°36′N 14°05′E, 148
Betclhe (*Guinea-Bissau*), 11°35′N 16°20′W, 132
Bethal (*South Africa*), 26°27′S 29°28′E, 207
Bethanie (*Namibia*), 26°32′S 17°11′E, 208
Bethlehem (*South Africa*), 28°15′S 28°15′E, 207
Bethulie (*South Africa*), 30°32′S 25°59′E, 207
Betioky (*Madagascar*), 23°42′S 44°22′E, 216
Betroka (*Madagascar*), 23°15′S 46°07′E, 216
Betsiboka (*r*), (*Madagascar*), 216
Bette, Picco (*mt*), (*Libya*), 22°00′N 19°12′E, 111
Beyla (*Guinea*), 8°41′N 8°37′W, 135
Biankouma (*Côte d'Ivoire*), 7°44′N 7°37′W, 138
Bida (*Nigeria*), 9°06′N 5°59′E, 146
Big Bend (*Swaziland*), 26°48′S 31°56′E, 212
Bignona (*Senegal*), 12°49′N 16°14′W, 132
Biharamulo (*Tanzania*), 2°37′S 31°20′E, 190
Bijagós, Arquipélago dos (*isls*), (*Guinea-Bissau*), 11°20′N 16°00′W, 132
Bijoutier (*isl*), (*Seychelles*), 7°05′S 52°45′E, 219
Bikita (*Zimbabwe*), 20°06′S 31°41′E′, 197
Bilma (*Niger*), 18°46′N 12°59′E, 151
Biltine (*Chad*), 14°30′N 20°53′E, 156
Bindura (*Zimbabwe*), 17°20′S 31°21′E, 197
Binga (*mt*), (*Mozambique*), 19°47′S 33°03′E, 193
Bioko (*isl*), (*Equatorial Guinea*), 3°30′N 8°40′E, 11, 154, 162
Bir Abu Gharadiq (*Egypt*), 30°08′N 28°08′E, 116
Bir Anzarane (*Western Sahara*), 23°56′N 14°33′W, 125
Birao (*Central African Republic*), 10°17′N 22°47′E, 159
Bir Aouine (*Tunisia*), 32°22′N 9°02′E, 121
Bird (*isl*), (*Seychelles*), 3°41′S 55°13′E. 219
Birim (*r*), (*Ghana*), 140
Birkat Oarun (*l*), (*Egypt*), 29°25′N 30°45′E, 116
Bir Mogrein (*Mauritania*), 25°10′N 11°35′E, 131
Birni Nkonni (*Niger*), 13°49′N 5°19′E, 127, 150
Bisina (*l*), (*Uganda*), 1°46′N 34°00′E, 186
Bissau (*Guinea-Bissau*), 11°52′N 15°39′W, 11, 126, 132
Bissora (*Guinea-Bissau*), 12°14′N 15°31′W, 132
Biu (*Nigeria*), 10°35′N 12°13′E, 146
Bizerte (*Tunisia*), 37°18′N 9°52′E, 111, 121
Black Volta *see* Volta
Blantyre (*Malawi*), 15°47′S 35°00′E, 22, 74, 193, 200
Bleida (*Morocco*), 30°25′N 6°45′W, 122
Blida (*Algeria*), 36°30′N 2°50′E, 110, 118
Blitta (*Togo*), 8°19′N 0°59′E, 144
Bloemfontein (*South Africa*), 29°12′S 26°07′E, 11, 22, 74, 203, 207
Bloemhof Dam (*South Africa*), 27°18′S 25°32′E, 203, 207
Blue Nile *see* Nile
Bo (*Sierra Leone*), 7°58′N 11°45′W, 136
Boali (*Central African Republic*), 4°48′N 18°07′E, 158
Boali Dam (*Central African Republic*), 4°48′N 18°07′E, 158
Boa Vista (*isl*), (*Cape Verde*), 16°10′N 22°50′W, 126, 130
Bobo Dioulasso (*Burkina Faso*), 11°12′N 4°18′W, 22, 74, 127, 142
Bobonong (*Botswana*), 21°58′S 28°26′E, 211
Boby (*mt*), (*Madagascar*), 22°10′S 46°51′E, 215
Bocanda (*Côte d'Ivoire*), 7°05′N 4°31′W, 138
Bocaranga (*Central African Republic*), 6°59′N 15°39′E, 158
Boda (*Central African Republic*), 4°19′N 17°28′E, 158
Boende (*Democratic Republic of the Congo*), 0°15′S 20°51′E, 166
Boffa (*Guinea*), 10°10′N 14°02′W, 134
Bogal, Laga (*r*), (*Kenya*), 185
Bogoria (*l*), (*Kenya*), 0°16′N 36°05′E, 185
Bohicon (*Benin*), 7°12′N 2°04′E, 144
Boké (*Guinea*), 10°56′N 14°18′W, 134
Boksburg(*South Africa*), 26°12′S 28°14′E, 207
Bol (*Chad*), 13°27′N 14°40′E, 156
Bolama (*Guinea-Bissau*), 11°35′N 15°28′W, 132
Bolgatanga (*Ghana*), 10°46′N 0°52′W, 140
Bolobo (*Democratic Republic of the Congo*), 2°10′S 16°17′E, 166
Boma (*Democratic Republic of the Congo*), 5°50′S 13°03′E, 154, 166
Bomi Hills (*Liberia*), 7°00′N 10°55′W, 136
Bomu (*r*), (*Democratic Republic of the Congo*), 154, 166
Bondo (*Democratic Republic of the Congo*), 3°47′N 23°50′E, 166
Bongor (*Chad*), 10°18′N 15°20′E, 156
Bongou (*r*), (*Central African Republic*), 158
Bonny (*Nigeria*), 4°27′N 7°10′E, 146
Bonthe (*Sierra Leone*), 7°32′N 12°30′W, 136
Boorama (*Somalia*), 9°56′N 43°13′E, 179
Booué (*Gabon*), 0°03′S 11°58′E, 160
Bopolu (*Liberia*), 7°03′N 10°32′W, 136
Bor, Laga (*r*), (*Kenya*), 1°25′N 33°59′E, 185
Bordj Messouda (*Algeria*), 30°10′N 9°19′E, 119
Boriziny (*Madagascar*), 15°31′S 47°40′E, 216
Boro (*r*), (*Sudan*), 170, 174
Boromo (*Burkina Faso*), 11°45′N 2°56′W, 142
Bossangoa (*Central African Republic*), 6°29′N 17°27′E, 158
Bossembélé (*Central African Republic*), 5°16′N 17°39′E, 158
Botletle (*r*), (*Botswana*), 211
Botro (*Côte d'Ivoire*), 7°51′N 5°19′W, 138
Bouaflé (*Côte d'Ivoire*), 6°59′N 5°45′W, 138
Bouaké (*Côte d'Ivoire*), 7°41′N 5°02′W, 22, 74, 126, 138
Bouar (*Central African Republic*), 5°58′N 15°35′E, 154
Bou Arfa (*Morocco*), 32°30′N 1°59′W, 123
Bou Azzer (*Morocco*), 30°35′N 6°45′W, 122
Bou Beker (*Morocco*), 34°30′N 1°48′W, 123
Bouca (*Central African Republic*), 6°30′N 18°17′E, 158
Bougouni (*Mali*), 11°25′N 7°29′W, 152
Bougouriba (*r*), (*Burkina Faso*), 142
Boujdour (*Western Sahara*), 26°08′N 14°30′W, 125
Bouka (r), (*Guinea*), 134
Bou Khadra (*Algeria*), 35°50′N 7°51′E, 119
Boukra (*Western Sahara*), 26°21′N 12°57′W, 125
Boulanouar (*Mauritania*), 21°17′N 16°29′W, 131
Boumba (*r*), (*Cameroon*), 12°25′N 2°51′E, 148

Niari (r), (Republic of the Congo), 154, 164
Niefang (Equatorial Guinea), 1°50′N 10°14′E, 162
Niger (r), (Benin/Guinea/Mali/Niger/Nigeria), 11, 126, 127, 134, 135, 144, 146, 150
Nile (r), (Egypt/Sudan), 11, 111, 116, 171, 174, 175
1st cataract (Egypt), 116
3rd cataract (Sudan), 170, 174
4th cataract (Sudan), 171, 175
5th cataract (Sudan), 171, 175
6th cataract (Sudan), 171, 175
Nile, Albert (r), (Uganda), 181, 186
Nile, Blue (Abay, Al-Bahr al-Azraq) (r), 11, 171, 175
Nile, Victoria (r), (Uganda), 186
Nile, White (Al-Bahr al-Abyad, Al-Bahr al-Jabal) (r), (Sudan), 11, 171, 175
Nile Dam, White (Sudan), 14°18′N 32°30′E, 171, 175
Nimba (mt), (Guinea), 7°39′N 8°30′W, 126, 135
Niono (Mali), 14°15′N 6°00′W, 152
Nioro du Sahel (Mali), 15°12′N 9°35′W, 152
Njombe (Tanzania), 9°20′S 34°47′E, 190
Njombe (r), (Tanzania), 191
N'Kayi (Republic of the Congo), 4°07′S 13°17′E, 164
Nkhata Bay (Malawi), 11°37′S 34°20′E, 200
Nkhota Kota (Malawi), 12°55′S 34°19′E, 200
Nkomi, Lagune (l), (Gabon), 1°35′S 9°17′E, 160
Nkusi (r), (Uganda), 181, 186
Noefs, Îles des (isls), (Seychelles), 6°13′S 53°03′E, 219
Nokoué (l), (Benin), 6°25′N 2°30′E, 144
Noqui (Angola), 5°54′S 13°30′E, 168
North (isl), (Seychelles), 4°23′S 55°15′E, 219
Nossob (r), (Botswana/Namibia), 203, 208, 211
Notsé (Togo), 6°59′N 1°17′E, 144
Nouadhibou (Mauritania), 20°54′N 17°01′W, 131
Nouakchott (Mauritania), 18°07′N 15°58′W, 11, 22, 74, 126, 131
Noun (r), (Cameroon), 148
Nouna (Burkina Faso), 12°44′N 3°54′W, 142
Noupoort (South Africa), 31°11′S 24°57′E, 207
Nouss (Algeria), 29°43′N 7°45′E, 118
Nova Sintra (Cape Verde), 14°51′N 24°42′W, 130
Nsanje (Malawi), 16°55′S 35°12′E, 200
Nsawam (Ghana), 5°47′N 0°19′W, 140
Nsok (Equatorial Guinea), 1°08′N 11°16′E, 162
Nsuta (Ghana), 5°16′N 1°59′W, 140
Ntaruka (Rwanda), 1°45′S 29°37′E, 188
Ntem (r), (Cameroon), 148
Nume (Equatorial Guinea), 1°31′N 9°35′E, 162
Nyabisindu (Rwanda), 2°20′S 29°43′E, 188
Nyahururu (Kenya), 0°04′N 36°22′E, 185
Nyala (Sudan), 12°01′N 24°50′E, 174
Nyanga (r), (Gabon), 154, 160
Nyawarungu (r), (Rwanda), 188
Nyeri (Kenya), 0°25′S 36°56′E, 185
Nylstroom (South Africa), 24°42′S, 28°20′E, 207
Nyong (r), (Cameroon), 127, 148
Nzara (Sudan), 4°40′N 28°13′E, 174
Nzérékoré (Guinea), 7°49′N 8°48′W, 135
Nzi (r), (Côte d'Ivoire), 138
Nzo (r), (Côte d'Ivoire), 138
Nzoia (r), (Kenya), 185

Obo (Central African Republic), 5°18′N 26°28′E, 154, 159
Obock (Djibouti), 11°59′N 43°20′E, 177
Obuasi (Ghana), 6°15′N 1°38′W, 140
Obubra (Nigeria), 6°05′N 8°20′E, 146
Oda, Jabal (mt), (Sudan), 20°21′N 36°39′E, 171
Odienne (Côte d'Ivoire), 9°36′N 7°32′W, 138
Ofiki (r), (Nigeria), 146
Ofin (r), (Ghana), 140
Ogbomosho (Nigeria), 8°05′N 4°11′E, 22, 74, 127
Ogooué (r), (Gabon), 11, 154, 160
Ogou (r), (Togo), 144
Ogun (r), (Nigeria), 146
Ohanet (Algeria), 28°40′N 8°50′E, 118
Okahandja (Namibia), 21°59′S 16°58′E, 208
Okano (r), (Gabon), 160
Okavango (r), (Angola/Botswana/Namibia), 203, 208, 211
Okavango Delta (Botswana), 19°00′S 23°00′E, 11, 203, 211
Okere (r), (Uganda), 186
Okiep (South Africa), 29°38′S 17°54′E, 206
Okok (r), (Uganda), 186
Okondja (Gabon), 0°41′S 13°47′E, 160
Okpara (r), (Benin), 144
Okwa (r), (Botswana), 211
Olduvai (Tanzania), 2°44′S 35°19′E, 43
Olifants (r), (South Africa), 207
Oliva (Canary Islands), 28°33′N 13°57′W, 124
Omaruru (Namibia), 21°28′S 15°56′E, 208
Omatako (r), (Namibia), 208
Omdurman (Sudan), 15°37′N 32°29′E, 22, 74, 171, 175
Omo (r), (Ethiopia), 171, 175
Ondangua (Namibia), 17°52′S 15°59′E, 208
Ondo (Nigeria), 7°05′N 4°55′E, 146
Oni (r), (Nigeria), 146
Onilahy (r), (Madagascar), 215, 216
Onitsha (Nigeria), 6°10′N 6°47′E, 127, 146
Ononghé (l), (Gabon), 1°00′S 10°10′E, 160
Opobo (Nigeria), 4°35′N 7°34′E, 146
Opuwo (Namibia), 18°03′S 13°54′E, 208
Ora (Libya), 28°36′N 19°32′E, 119
Oran (Algeria), 35°45′N 0°38′W, 22, 74, 110, 118
Orange (r), (Lesotho/Namibia/South Africa), 11, 203, 206, 207, 208, 212
Oranjemund (Namibia), 28°33′S 16°25′E, 208
Orapa (Botswana), 21°18′S 25°30′E, 211
Oshekehia (l), (Namibia), 18°08′S 15°45′E, 208
Oshogbo (Nigeria), 7°50′N 4°35′E, 22, 74, 127, 146
Osse (r), (Nigeria), 146
Oti (r), (Burkina Faso), 142
Otjiwarongo (Namibia), 20°29′S 16°36′E, 208
Otjozondjou (r), (Namibia), 208
Otjosondu (Namibia), 21°19′S 17°51′E, 208
Ouadane (Mauritania), 20°55′N 11°34′W, 131
Ouadda (Central African Republic), 8°09′N 22°20′E, 158
Ouagadougou (Burkina Faso), 12°20′N 1°40′W, 11, 22, 74, 127, 142
Ouahigouya (Burkina Faso), 13°31′N 2°20′W, 142
Ouaka (r), (Central African Republic), 158
Oualâta (Mauritania), 17°18′N 7°02′W, 131
Ouan Taredert (Algeria), 27°38′N 9°28′E, 119
Ouargla (Algeria), 32°00′N 5°16′E, 118
Ouarra (r), (Central African Republic), 159
Ouarzazate (Morocco), 30°57′N 6°50′W, 122
Ouassou (Guinea), 10°02′N 13°39′W, 134
Oubangui (r), (Central African Republic/Republic of the Congo), 154, 158, 165
Oudtshoorn (South Africa), 33°35′S 22°12′E, 207
Oued Zem (Morocco), 32°52′N 6°35′W, 122
Ouémé (r), (Benin), 127, 144
Ouenza (Algeria), 35°57′N 8°04′E, 119
Ouesso (Republic of the Congo), 1°38′N 16°03′E, 164
Ouezzane (Morocco), 34°52′N 5°35′W, 122
Ouham (r), (Central African Republic/Chad), 154, 156, 158
Ouidah (Benin), 6°23′N 2°08′E, 144
Oujda (Morocco), 34°41′N 1°45′W, 22, 74, 110, 123
Oum er Rbia, Oued (r), (Morocco), 110, 122
Ounianga-Kébir (Chad), 19°05′N 20°29′E, 156
Outjo (Namibia), 20°08′S 16°08′E, 208
Owando (Republic of the Congo), 0°27′S 15°44′E, 164
Owendo (Gabon), 0°21′N 9°29′E, 160
Owen Falls Dam (Uganda), 0°29′N 33°11′E, 186
Oyem (Gabon), 1°34′N 11°37′E, 160
Oyo (Nigeria), 7°50′N 3°55′E, 48, 127, 146

Paarl (South Africa), 33°45′S 18°58′E, 203, 206
Pager (r), (Uganda), 186
Pala (Chad), 9°23′N 15°01′E, 156
Palapye (Botswana), 22°37′S 27°06′E, 211
Pallisa (Uganda), 1°11′N 33°43′E, 186
Palma (Mozambique) 10°48′S 40°29′E, 199
Pangani (r), (Tanzania), 181, 191
Pangalanes, Canal des (Madagascar), 216
Panguma (Sierra Leone), 8°18′N 11°03′W, 136
Parakou (Benin), 9°28′N 2°35′E, 126, 144
Parma (r), (Kenya), 181
Parys (South Africa), 26°55′S 27°28′E, 207
Pata (r), (Central African Republic), 158
Pedras Tinhosas (isl), (São Tomé & Príncipe), 1°20′N 7°21′E, 162
Pemba (Mozambique), 13°00′S 40°30′E, 199
Pemba (isl), (Tanzania), 5°00′S 39°25′E, 181, 191
Pendembu (Sierra Leone), 8°09′N 10°42′W, 136
Pendjari (r), (Benin/Burkina Faso), 143, 144
Pepel (Sierra Leone), 8°39′N 13°04′W, 136
Petauke (Zambia), 14°16′S 31°21′E, 195
Phalaborwa (South Africa), 23°55′S 31°13′E, 207
Phuthiatsana (r), (Lesotho), 212
Pietermaritzburg (South Africa), 29°36′S 30°24′E, 203, 207
Pietersburg (South Africa), 23°54′S 29°23′E, 22, 74, 203, 207
Piggs Peak (Swaziland), 25°54′S 31°13′E, 213
Pipi (r), (Central African Republic), 159
Piton des Neiges (mt), (Réunion), 21°05′S 55°28′E, 215
Platte (isl), (Seychelles), 5°52′S 55°23′E, 215, 219
Pobé (Benin), 6°55′N 2°36′E, 144
Pocolo (Angola), 15°43′S 13°49′E, 168
Pointe Clairette (Gabon), 0°37′S 8°45′E, 160
Pointe Indienne (Republic of the Congo), 4°30′S 11°55′E, 164
Pointe-Noire (Republic of the Congo), 4°46′S 11°53′E, 22, 74, 154, 164
Poivre (isl), (Seychelles), 5°50′S 53°20′E, 219
Poli (Cameroon), 8°31′N 13°10′E, 148
Pongo (r), (Sudan), 174
Pongwe (Tanzania), 5°10′S 39°00′E, 191
Port Alfred (South Africa), 33°36′S 26°54′E, 207
Port Brega (Libya), 30°23′N 19°37′E, 119
Port Edward (South Africa), 31°03′S 30°14′E, 207
Port Elizabeth (South Africa), 33°58′S 25°36′E, 22, 74, 203, 207
Port-Gentil (Gabon), 0°40′S 8°50′E, 154, 160
Port Harcourt (Nigeria), 4°43′N 7°05′E, 22, 74, 127, 146
Port Loko (Sierra Leone), 8°50′N 12°50′W, 136
Port Louis (Mauritius), 20°10′S 57°30′E, 215, 217
Port Nolloth (South Africa), 29°17′S 16°51′E, 206
Porto Alegre (São Tomé & Príncipe), 0°02′N 6°32′E, 162
Porto Amboim (Angola), 10°47′S 13°43′E, 168
Porto Novo (Benin), 6°30′N 2°47′E, 11, 127, 144
Porto Novo (Cape Verde), 17°04′N 25°06′W, 130
Porto Séguro (Togo), 6°15′N 1°35′E, 144
Port Said (Egypt), 31°17′N 32°18′E, 22, 74, 111, 116
Port St-Louis (Madagascar), 13°00′S 48°56′E, 216
Port Shepstone (South Africa), 30°44′S 30°28′E, 207
Port Sudan (Sudan), 19°37′N 37°14′E, 22, 74, 171, 175
Postmasburg (South Africa), 28°20′S 23°05′E, 207
Potchefstroom (South Africa), 26°42′S 27°06′E, 207
Potgietersrus (South Africa), 24°15′S 28°55′E, 207
Pra (r), (Ghana), 140
Praia (Cape Verde), 14°55′N 23°30′W, 126, 130
Praslin (isl), (Seychelles), 4°18′S 55°45′E, 215, 219
Prestea (Ghana), 5°26′N 2°07′W, 140
Prieska (South Africa), 29°40′S 22°45′E, 207
Pretoria (South Africa), 25°45′S 28°12′E, 11, 22, 74, 203, 207
Príncipe (isl), (São Tomé & Príncipe), 1°37′N 7°27′E, 11, 154, 162
Providence (isl), (Seychelles) 9°14′S 51°02′E, 215
Puerto de la Cruz (Canary Islands), 28°24′N 16°33′W, 124
Puerto del Rosario (Canary Islands), 28°29′N 13°52′W, 124
Pujehun (Sierra Leone), 7°23′N 11°44′W, 136
Pungue (r), (Mozambique), 199
Punia (Democratic Republic of the Congo), 1°28′S 26°25′E, 166

Qachas Nek (Lesotho), 30°08′S 28°41′E, 212
Qardho (Somalia), 9°30′N 49°06′E, 179
Qaryat az Zuwaytinah (Libya), 30°58′N 20°07′E, 119
Qasr Farafra (Egypt), 27°03′N 28°00′E, 116
Qina (Egypt), 26°10′N 32°43′E, 116
Qina, Wadi (r), (Egypt), 116
Queenstown (South Africa), 31°54′S 26°53′E, 203, 207
Quelimane (Mozambique), 17°53′S 36°51′E, 193, 199
Quembo (r), (Angola), 168
Que Que (Zimbabwe), 18°55′S 29°49′E, 197
Quesir (Egypt), 26°18′N 34°31′E, 116
Quimbele (Angola), 6°30′S 16°25′E, 168
Quthing (Lesotho), 30°25′S 27°43′E, 212

Rabat (Morocco), 34°02′N 6°51′W, 11, 22, 74, 110, 122
Raguba (Libya), 29°04′N 19°08′E, 119
Rakops (Botswana), 21°00′S 24°32′E, 211
Ramatlabama (Botswana), 25°41′S 25°28′E, 211
Ramisi (Kenya), 5°31′S, 39°27′E, 185
Ramokgwebana (Botswana), 20°38′S 27°40′E, 211
Ramotswa (Botswana), 24°56′S 25°50′E, 211
Randa (Djibouti), 11°52′N 42°39′E, 177
Randfontein (South Africa), 26°10′S 27°43′E, 207
Ras Dashen (mt), (Ethiopia), 13°15′N 38°27′E, 11, 171
Ras Gharib (Egypt), 28°22′N 33°04′E, 116
Ras Kebdena (Morocco), 35°01′N 2°25′W, 123
Ras Muhammad (Egypt), 27°41′N 34°15′E, 116
Raso (isl), (Cape Verde), 16°39′N 24°38′W, 130
Ra's al-Unuf (Libya) 31°53′N 18°30′E, 119
Razzaq (Egypt), 30°37′N 28°54′E, 116
Redcliffe (Zimbabwe), 19°00′S 29°49′E, 197
Rehoboth (Namibia), 23°18′S 17°03′E, 208
Remire Reef (isl), (Seychelles) 5°05′S, 53°25′E, 219
Réunion (isl), (France), 21°06′S 55°36′E, 215, 217
Revue (r), (Mozambique), 199
Rharsa, Chott el (l), (Tunisia), 34°10′N 7°50′E, 121
Rhourd (Algeria), 29°23′N 7°10′E, 118
Rhourd el Baguel (Algeria), 31°14′N 6°42′E, 118
Ri-Aba (Equatorial Guinea), 3°30′N 8°50′E, 162
Ribeira Grande (Cape Verde), 17°12′N 25°08′W, 130
Richards Bay (South Africa), 28°47′S 32°06′ E, 207
Richard Toll (Senegal), 16°25′N 15°42′W, 132
Riet (r), (South Africa), 203
Rietspruit (South Africa), 28°26′S 27°18′E, 207
Rimé, Ouadi (r), (Chad), 156
River Cess (Liberia), 5°28′N 9°32′W, 136
Riversdale (South Africa), 34°05′S 21°15′E, 206
Rivière du Rempart (Mauritius), 20°06′S 57°41′E, 217
R'Kiz (l), (Mauritania), 16°46′N 15°55′W, 131
Roan Antelope (Zambia), 13°13′S 28°05′E, 195
Robertsport (Liberia), 6°45′N 11°22′W, 136
Rokel (r), (Sierra Leone), 136
Rôlas (isl), (São Tomé & Príncipe), 0°01′S 6°31′E, 162
Roodepoort (South Africa), 26°10′S 27°53′E, 207
Rose Belle (Mauritius), 20°24′S 57°36′E, 217
Rose Hill (Mauritius), 20°14′S 57°27′E, 217
Ross-Béthio (Senegal), 16°16′N 16°08′W, 132
Rossing (Namibia), 22°31′S 14°52′E, 208
Rosso (Mauritania), 16°29′N 15°53′W, 131
Rovuma (r), (Mozambique), 193, 199
Ruacana Dam (Angola/Namibia), 17°22′S 14°12′E, 168, 208
Rufiji (r), (Tanzania), 181, 191
Rufisque (Senegal), 14°43′N 17°16′W, 132
Ruhengeri (Rwanda), 1°30′S 29°39′E, 188
Ruhuhu (r), (Tanzania), 190
Ruki (r), (Democratic Republic of the Congo), 154, 166
Rukwa (l), (Tanzania), 8°00′S 32°25′E, 11, 181, 190
Rumonge (Burundi), 3°59′S 29°26′E, 188
Rumphi (Malawi), 10°59′S 33°50′E, 200
Rumuruti (Kenya), 0°16′N 36°32′E, 185
Rundu (Namibia), 17°52′S 19°49′E, 208
Rungwa (r), (Tanzania), 181, 190
Rungwe (mt), (Tanzania), 9°10′S 33°40′E, 181
Rusape (Zimbabwe), 18°31′S 32°15′E, 197
Rustenburg (South Africa), 25°40′S 27°15′E, 207
Rutana (Burundi), 3°56′S 30°00′E, 188
Rutenga (Zimbabwe), 21°08′S 30°45′E, 197
Ruvu (r), (Tanzania), 191
Ruvubu (r), (Burundi), 188
Ruvuma (r), (Tanzania), 181, 191
Ruyigi (Burundi), 3°26′S 30°14′E, 188
Ruzizi (r), (Burundi/Rwanda), 181, 188

Sabha (Libya), 27°31′N 14°41′E, 111, 119
Safi (Morocco), 32°20′N 9°17′W, 122
Saguia el Hamra (r), (Western Sahara), 125
Sahel Canal (Mali), 152
Saint Croix (South Africa), 33°48′S 25°46′E, 207
Saint-Denis (Réunion), 20°52′S 55°27′E, 215, 217
Sainte-André (Réunion), 20°57′S 55°39′E, 217
Sainte-Benoît (Réunion), 21°02′S 55°43′E, 217
Sainte-Marie (Réunion), 20°53′S 55°33′E, 217
Sainte-Marie, Nosy (isl), (Madagascar), 17°00′S 49°43′E, 215, 216
Sainte-Rose (Réunion) 21°07′S 55°47′E, 217
Saint François (isl), (Seychelles), 7°10′S 52°40′E, 219
Saint Helena Bay (South Africa), 32°44′S 18°21′E, 206
Saint John (r), (Liberia), 136
Saint-Joseph (Réunion), 21°22′S 55°37′E, 217
Saint Joseph (isl), (Seychelles), 5°46′S 53°43′E, 219
Saint-Leu (Réunion), 21°09′S 55°17′E, 217
Saint-Louis (Réunion), 21°17′S 55°25′E, 217
Saint Louis (Senegal), 15°52′N 16°30′W, 126, 132
Saint-Paul (Réunion), 21°00′S 55°16′E, 217
Saint Paul (r), (Liberia), 126, 136
Saint-Philippe (Réunion), 21°21′S 55°46′E, 217
Saint Pierre (Mauritius), 20°13′S 57°32′E, 217
Saint-Pierre (Réunion), 21°19′S 55°29′E, 217
Saint Pierre (isl), (Seychelles), 9°35′S 50°27′E, 215
Sal (Cape Verde), 16°45′N 22°55′W, 126, 130
Salaga (Ghana), 8°34′N 0°28′W, 140
Saldanha (South Africa), 33°00′S 17°56′E, 206
Salé (Morocco), 34°04′N 6°50′W, 22, 74, 122
Salima (Malawi), 13°45′S 34°29′E, 200
Salisbury see Harare
Saloum (r), (Senegal), 132
Sal-Rei (Cape Verde), 16°11′N 22°55′W, 130
Saltpond (Ghana), 5°13′N 1°01′W, 140
Samreboi (Ghana), 5°31′N 2°34′W, 140
Sanaga (r), (Cameroon), 11, 127, 148
San Antonio de Ureca (Equatorial Guinea), 3°16′N 8°39′E, 162
Sandoa (Democratic Republic of the Congo), 9°41′S 22°56′E, 166
Sandougou (r), (Senegal), 133
Sangha (r), (Central African Republic/Republic of the Congo), 158, 164
Sankarani (r), (Guinea), 135
Sankuru (r), (Democratic Republic of the Congo), 154, 166
Sannar (Sudan), 13°33′N 33°38′E, 175
Sanniquellie (Liberia), 7°24′N 8°45′W, 136
Sanouya (Guinea), 10°05′N 11°12′W, 134
San Pedro (Côte d'Ivoire), 4°45′N 6°37′W, 138
Sansanding Dam (Mali), 13°44′N 6°00′W, 152
San Sebastian (Canary Islands), 28°07′N 17°06′W, 124
Santa Clara (Gabon), 0°33′N 9°17′E, 160
Santa Cruz de la Palma (Canary Islands), 28°41′N 17°46′W, 124
Santa Cruz de Tenerife (Canary Islands), 28°28′N 16°15′W, 110, 124
Santa Luzia (isl), (Cape Verde), 16°46′N 24°45′W, 130
Santa Maria (Cape Verde), 16°38′N 22°56′W, 130
Santo Antão (isl), (Cape Verde), 17°05′N 25°14′W, 126, 130
Santo Antonio (Cape Verde), 15°19′N 24°07′W, 130
Santo Antonio (São Tomé & Príncipe), 1°37′N 7°27′E, 162
Sanyati (r), (Zimbabwe), 193, 197
Sanza Pombo (Angola), 7°20′S 16°00′E, 168
São Filipe (Cape Verde), 14°52′N 24°29′W, 130
São Nicolau (isl), (Cape Verde), 16°32′N 24°20′W, 126, 130
São Tiago (isl), (Cape Verde), 15°07′N 23°40′W, 126, 130
São Tomé (São Tomé & Príncipe), 0°19′N 6°43′E, 11, 154, 162
São Tomé (isl), (São Tomé & Príncipe), 0°15′N 6°40′E, 11, 154, 162
São Vicente (isl), (Cape Verde), 16°50′N 25°00′W, 126, 130
Sapele (Nigeria), 5°55′N 5°46′E, 146
Sarh (Chad), 9°08′N 18°22′E, 154, 156
Sarir (Libya), 27°36′N 22°32′E, 119
Sasolburg (South Africa), 26°50′S 27°51′E, 207
Sassandra (Côte d'Ivoire), 4°58′N 6°08′W, 138
Sassandra (r), (Côte d'Ivoire), 11, 127, 138
Savalou (Benin), 7°59′N 2°03′E, 144
Savé (Benin), 8°04′N 2°27′E, 144
Save (r), (Mozambique/Zimbabwe), 193, 197, 199
Sawakin (Sudan), 19°07′N 37°20′E, 175
Sawhaj (Egypt), 26°33′N 31°42′E, 116
Say (Niger), 13°08′N 2°20′E, 150
Saylac (Somalia), 11°21′N 43°30′E, 179
Sébé (r), (Gabon), 160
Sebou, Oued (r), (Morocco), 110, 122
Secos Islets (Cape Verde), 14°58′N 24°40′W, 130
Sefadu (Sierra Leone), 8°39′N 10°59′W, 136
Sefrou (Morocco), 33°50′N 4°50′W, 122
Ségou (Mali), 13°28′N 6°18′W, 48, 127, 152
Séguédine (Niger), 20°12′N 12°59′E, 151
Séguéla (Côte d'Ivoire), 7°58′N 6°44′W, 138
Seke-Banza (Democratic Republic of the Congo), 5°20′S 13°16′E, 166
Sekhira (Tunisia), 34°17′N 10°06′E, 121
Sekondi (Ghana), 4°59′N 1°43′W, 140
Selebi Phikwe (Botswana), 22°00′S 27°51′E, 211
Seleit (Sudan), 16°13′N 32°15′E, 174
Selibaby (Mauritania), 15°14′N 12°11′W, 131
Selingué Dam (Mali), 12°31′N 7°50′W, 152
Semliki (r), (Uganda), 186
Senanga (Zambia), 16°08′S 23°16′E, 194
Sénégal (r), (Mali/Mauritania/Senegal), 11, 126, 131, 152
Senekal (South Africa), 28°19′S 27°38′E, 207
Serenje (Zambia), 13°12′S 30°15′E, 195
Serere (Uganda), 1°31′N 33°27′E, 186
Serowe (Botswana), 22°25′S 26°44′E, 203, 211
Sese Islands (Uganda), 0°20′S 32°20′E, 186
Sesheke (Zambia), 17°29′S, 24°18′E, 194
Sétif (Algeria), 36°11′N 5°24′E, 110, 118
Settat (Morocco), 33°04′N 7°37′W, 122
Sette Cama (Gabon), 2°32′S 9°46′E, 160
Sewa (r), (Sierra Leone), 136
Sfax (Tunisia), 34°45′N 10°43′E, 22, 74, 111, 121
Shabeelle (r), (Somalia), 171, 179
Shabunda (Democratic Republic of the Congo), 2°42′S 27°20′E, 167
Shagamu (Nigeria), 6°50′N 3°43′E, 146
Shala (l), (Ethiopia), 7°25′N 38°30′E, 171, 175
Shamva (Zimbabwe), 17°20′S 31°38′E, 197
Shandi (Sudan), 16°42′N 33°26′E, 175
Shangani (Zimbabwe), 19°41′S 29°20′E, 197
Shangani (r), (Zimbabwe), 193, 197
Shashemene (Ethiopia), 7°13′N 38°33′E, 175
Shashe (r), (Botswana/Zimbabwe), 193, 211
Shebele (r), (Ethiopia), 11, 171, 175
Sherbro (isl), (Sierra Leone), 7°45′N 12°55′W, 136
Shiker (Morocco), 34°17′N 4°06′W, 123
Shinyanga (Tanzania), 3°46′S 33°20′E, 190
Shire (r), (Malawi), 11, 193, 200
Shurugwi (Zimbabwe), 19°40′S 30°00′E, 197
Sibiti (Republic of the Congo), 3°40′S 13°24′E, 164
Sibiti (r), (Tanzania), 190
Sibut (Central African Republic), 5°46′N 19°06′E, 158
Sidi Barrani (Egypt), 31°38′N 25°58′E, 111
Sidi bel Abbes (Algeria), 35°15′N 0°39′W, 118
Sidi el Hani, Sebkra De (l), (Tunisia). 35°30′N 10°27′E, 121
Sidi Hajjaj (Morocco), 32°50′N 7°35′W, 122
Sidi Ifni (Morocco), 29°24′N 10°07′W, 122
Sidi Kacem (Morocco), 34°15′N 5°49′W, 122
Sidi Sa'ad (Tunisia), 35°22′N 9°45′E, 121
Siguiri (Guinea), 11°28′N 9°07′W, 134
Sikasso (Mali), 11°18′N 5°38′W, 152
Silhouette (isl), (Seychelles), 4°29′S 55°12′E, 215, 219
Sima (Comoros), 12°11′S 44°18′E, 218
Simonstown (South Africa), 34°14′S 18°26′E, 206
Sindara (Gabon), 1°07′S 10°31′E, 160
Singida (Tanzania), 4°45′S 34°45′E, 190
Singu (r), (Lesotho), 212
Singunyane (r), (Lesotho), 212
Sinoia (Zimbabwe), 17°21′S 30°13′E, 197
Sio (r), (Togo), 144
Sipofaneni (Swaziland), 26°41′S 31°41′E, 213
Sirte (Libya), 31°32′N 16°56′E, 119
Sishen (South Africa), 27°55′S 22°59′E, 207
Sitobela (Swaziland), 26°53′S 31°36′E, 213
Sitrah (Egypt), 28°42′N 26°54′E, 116
Siwa (Egypt), 29°11′N 25°31′E, 116
Siwa Oasis (Egypt), 29°12′N 25°31′E, 111, 116

INDEX